# the developing child

## child
### fourth edition

## Helen Bee
*University of Washington*

**HARPER & ROW, PUBLISHERS, New York**
Cambridge, Philadelphia, San Francisco,
London, Mexico City, São Paulo, Singapore, Sydney

*1817*

To C.

Sponsoring Editor: Susan Mackey
Project Editor: Ronni Strell
Text Design: Robert Sugar
Cover Design: Robert Sugar
Cover Photo: George Ancona
Text Art: J&R Art Services, Inc.
Photo Research: Mira Schachne
Production: Willie Lane
Compositor: ComCom Division of Haddon Craftsmen, Inc.
Printer and Binder: The Murray Printing Company

**The Developing Child,** Fourth Edition

Library of Congress Cataloging in Publication Data

Bee, Helen L., 1939–
   The developing child.

   Includes bibliographies.
   1. Child psychology.   2. Child development.   I. Title.
BF721.B336 1985        155.4        84–12823
ISBN 0–06–040577–5

ISBN 0–06–350131–7
HARPER INTERNATIONAL EDITION

   86 87 9 8 7 6 5 4 3

# acknowledgments

We gratefully acknowledge the use of the following materials:

Cover photo: © George Ancona, 1982, International Stock Photo.

Chapter 1: 1.1, © Elizabeth Crews; 1.3, Weisbrot, Stock, Boston; 1.4, Bennett Hall; 1.5, Sydlow, Monkmeyer; 1.6, Johnson, Jeroboam; 1.8, Karp, Omni; 1.9, © Sobol, Stock, Boston; 1.11, © Elizabeth Crews.

Part I opener: Melissa Dunlop.

Chapter 2: 2.1, © Arms, Jeroboam; 2.3a, Klutinis, Jeroboam; 2.3b, Strickler, Monkmeyer; 2.7, Johnson, Jeroboam; 2.11, © Dietz, 1981, Stock, Boston.

Chapter 3: 3.2, © Joel Gordon, 1983; 3.3, © Elizabeth Crews; 3.4, H. F. R. Prechtl "The neurological examination of the full-term newborn infant," Clinics in Developmental Medicine, #63/2nd ed. Spastics International Medical Publications, 1977 Heinemann, London; 3.5, © SUVA/DPI; 3.6, © Arms, 1983, Jeroboam; 3.7, Johnston, L. *Hi Mom! Hi Dad* 101 cartoons for new parents. Meadowbrook Press, p. 18; 3.8, Suzanne Szasz.

Part II opener: Elissa Mara Strell.

Chapter 4: 4.1, © Elizabeth Crews; 4.2, © Marjorie Pickens, 1979; 4.9, Bob East/Photo Trends; 4.10, J. M. Tanner/Institute of Child Health, London; 4.11, Jim Engle; 4.12, © Elizabeth Crews.

Chapter 5: 5.4, William Vandivert, courtesy *Scientific American,* April, 1960; 5.5, Zimbel/Monkmeyer; 5.8, Jean-Claude Lejeune/Stock, Boston.

Part III opener: Joshua Jason Andra.

Chapter 6: 6.3, Shelton, Monkmeyer; 6.5, Jean-Claude Lejeune/Stock, Boston.

Chapter 7: 7.1, Merrim, Monkmeyer; 7.2, © Elizabeth Crews; 7.4, © The Society for Research in Child Development, Inc.

Chapter 8: 8.1, *Psychology Today* Magazine © 1979 American Psychological Association; 8.2, Johnston, L. *Do they ever grow up?* Meadowbrook Press, 1978, p. 8.

Part IV opener: Melissa Dunlop.

Chapter 9: 9.1, © Elizabeth Crews; 9.2, John Garrett/Woodfin Camp; 9.3, Lois Inman Engle © 1980; 9.4, © Siteman, 1983, Taurus; 9.5, Suzanne Szasz.

Chapter 10: 10.1, © Elizabeth Crews; 10.4, © Tana Hoban/DPI; 10.9, Frank Siteman/Stock, Boston.

Chapter 11: 11.1, © O'Neil, Stock, Boston; 11.2, © R. Duane Cooke/DPI; 11.3, © Elizabeth Crews; 11.5, Chester Higgins/Photo Researchers; 11.8, Lois Inman Engle © 1980; 11.9, Conklin, Monkmeyer; 11.10, Marion Faller/Monkmeyer.

Chapter 12: 12.1a, © Elizabeth Crews; 12.1b, Collidge, Taurus; 12.3, © Elizabeth Crews; misc. text from Selman, R. L., *The growth of interpersonal understanding.* New York: Academic Press, 1980.

Part V opener: Melissa Dunlop.

Chapter 13: 13.1, © Marjorie Pickens, 1983; 13.2, Conklin, Monkmeyer; 13.3, © Holland, Stock, Boston; 13.4, Park, Monkmeyer; 13.7, © Marjorie Pickens, 1984.

Chapter 14: 14.1, L. Roger Turner/Wisconsin State Journal; 14.2, Stephen Potter/Stock, Boston; 14.3, Irene Bayer/Monkmeyer; 14.4, Raimondo Borea.

Chapter 15: 15.2, Jean Shapiro; 15.3, Karp, Omni; 15.5 Forsyth, Monkmeyer; 15.6, Forsyth, Monkmeyer; 15.8, Mahon, Monkmeyer; 15.10, Bruce Roberts/Photo Researchers

# contents

## part one:
## the beginnings of life

part two:
the physical child

## CHAPTER 4  Physical Growth and Development                    **115**

## CHAPTER 5  Perceptual Development                             **153**

part three:
the thinking child

## CHAPTER 6  Cognitive Development I: Cognitive Power           **189**

**CHAPTER 7   Cognitive Development II: Cognitive Structure**    **224**

**CHAPTER 8   The Development of Language in Children**    **270**

part four:
the social child

**CHAPTER 9   Personality Development: Alternative Views**    **309**

part five:
the whole child

# preface

## GOALS OF THE FOURTH EDITION

As has been true from the first edition of this book, I have had several goals in writing this text. First of all, I have aimed for relative brevity. When I teach this class, I do not want an encyclopedic book. I want one that will give the basic concepts, orient the students to the issues, and still allow me a lot of room to explore issues in class.

A second goal has been to write a book that is as relevant and useful to faculty and students in education or nursing or home economics as it is to a psychologist. Courses in human development are taught in many departments, to students with many different needs and interests. Of course, it is impossible to meet all those needs in one book; but by including applied material that relates to school settings, to physical disabilities or disorders of development, and to family functioning, I have made an effort to link up the core information to the practical issues of related fields.

A third goal has been to find that often-elusive balance between theory and research on the one hand and practical application on the other. I am convinced that both are important. I find the theoretical arguments and the research fascinating, but—perhaps especially for beginning students—the ideas and findings need to be linked up to everyday issues. The strong theoretical flavor that has been characteristic of this book from the first edition remains in this fourth edition. Applications, through boxes and in the text itself, also remain prominent.

## ORGANIZATION

This fourth edition remains organized by topics rather than by age, although I have (as in every earlier edition) included a synthesis chapter at the end in which the several topical threads are brought together.

There have been some changes, however, in the sequence of chapters to accommodate changes in my own thinking and in the way the field seems to me to be organized these days. The major changes are in the sections entitled "The Thinking Child" and "The Social Child."

After three editions in which I discussed language before cognition, in this edition I have switched the order. So much of the current research and theory in language development seems to me to be linked to issues of cognitive development—such as questions about early semantic development or about the child's role in creating syntax—that it seemed much clearer to talk about language after introducing Piaget and other theories of cognitive development. Then, in order to have the discussion of cognitive structure and the discussion of language follow each other directly, I have reversed the order of the IQ and cognitive structure chapters. Thus, the sequence in this section moves from a discussion of cognitive power (IQ) to a discussion of cognitive structure to a discussion of language.

Similarly, in the section on the social child, I have placed the discussion of the child's emerging self-concept before the discussion of social relationships, reflecting a kind of decentering process from self to others.

I realize that these changes of organization will pose some small difficulties for faculty who have used earlier editions and have organized their lectures around the old system. But the changes reflect alterations in my own thinking and teaching, based on the new perspectives evident in the field. I think you will find that this order flows very well.

## OTHER CHANGES AND UPDATING

A look at the contents will tell you rather quickly that this is a substantial revision of the third edition in other ways as well. In particular, there are two new chapters, and two old chapters have been deleted or greatly altered.

### New Combined Chapter on Language

I have combined the two chapters on language into a single chapter in order to make room for expanded coverage of other topics. I think you will find that this new, single chapter still covers the waterfront well.

### New Chapter on Social Cognition

The material on moral development, which previously comprised an entire chapter, has now been considerably shortened and embedded in a much broader discussion of social cognition. This chapter (Chapter 12) now provides a link between the material on cognition and that on social development.

### New Chapter on the Ecology of Development

The largest addition to the book is an entirely new chapter covering the impact of families, schools, and culture on the child's development. Some of this material had been included in previous editions but scattered through the chapters. Now I have pulled this together and added a great deal of new information as well. Included here is an extended discussion of family disciplinary techniques and their effects, an exploration of influences *on* the family (such as stress, social support, and poverty) and their subsequent impact on the child, and an examination of the impact of schooling and television as examples of larger cultural forces. Explicit discussion of family influences had been missing in previous editions. The addition of this chapter greatly strengthens the book.

### Expanded and Updated Coverage

Of course, the entire book has been revised and updated. (It always amuses me when people say, "Oh, it's only a *revision* you're working on," as if that meant one was not working very hard!) Probably 60 percent of this book, if not more, consists of new material or new research examples or new organization of old material. In addition to the major changes in organization and chapter content, which I have just described, there are a great many individual topics that have been expanded or substantially updated. Some examples:

> The chapter on cognitive development now includes a greatly expanded section on information-processing approaches. Research on information processing is also included in the section on retardation in Chapter 14.

> Material on early bonding has been updated in light of recent research, which shows fewer long-term effects of early parent-infant contact than had at first been supposed.

Coverage of perceptual development has been expanded to include more information on hearing and other senses.

The discussion of physical development has been reorganized, and expanded material on hormonal processes in adolescence has been included.

In addition to the material on information processing in the chapter on cognitive structure, I have also included a great deal more discussion of "neo"-Piagetian research—work that modifies or amplifies or calls into question the ideas first proposed by Piaget.

Coverage of the role of fathers has been strengthened throughout the book and now appears consistently in the text itself instead of being relegated to a series of boxes (as if to imply that the father was tangential), as it was in previous editions.

Material on children's friendships—a topic on which there is a great deal of new research—has been considerably expanded.

The final "synthesis" chapter includes a much stronger "family systems" emphasis, with discussion of the impact of the child on the family as well as the reverse. I have also speculated on the effect on the child of some of the developmental changes occurring in the parents.

All in all, I think you will find that the strengths of the first three editions have been retained. The writing style is still personal, the descriptions of theory and research clear, the organization flowing smoothly from one point to the next. But I also think you will find that this new edition more closely reflects the current thinking of the field. I found the job of reorganizing the material extremely challenging. In several areas—perhaps most notably cognitive development—we seem to be in the midst of a sort of "paradigm shift," which makes organization of the material difficult. In other areas, such as family ecology, we are only at the edge of an explosion of new research. There is still plenty of room for each of you to expand this material into areas that are of special interest to you.

## SUPPLEMENTS

### Instructor's Manual (IM)

The *IM,* which I prepared, continues to include both multiple-choice and essay questions, as well as suggestions for lecture topics, new material, or helpful sources for the instructor. I have omitted a list of films from this edition of the *IM* for the simple reason that I almost never use films in my own classes and thus do not know enough about the quality of the available films to make good recommendations.

### Study Guide

The *Study Guide* has been thoroughly revised and rewritten to correspond with the fourth edition. A dual format allows for either traditional or programmed personalized system of instruction (PSI) review. Each chapter includes chapter objectives, key terms and concepts, a multiple-choice self-quiz, open-ended study questions, and an end-of-chapter programmed review unit.

## ACKNOWLEDGMENTS

As in earlier editions, my work on this edition has been greatly aided by the comments of excellent reviewers. Sharon Antonelli, San Jose City College; Maria Taranta,

Nassau Community College; Robert Orr, University of Windsor; Phil O'Neil, Oregon State University; Jane Stormer, Cuyahoga Community College; and Charles Halverson, University of Georgia all reviewed the third edition and suggested needed changes and areas requiring updating. They also helped me think through the changes in chapter sequence and content.

An equally fine crew of reviewers then read the first draft of the manuscript. I am grateful for their supportive comments as well as their helpfully picky ones. They are Robert Orr, University of Windsor; Lynn Ourth, University of Tennessee; Carol Neuhauser, William R. Harper Community College; Sharon Antonelli, San Jose City College; and James Booth, Community College of Philadelphia.

Finally, I need to say a word about friends. This edition has been written at a time of major transition in my life—a time when I have come to appreciate my friends as never before. During this same time I have been teaching courses in adult development as well as child development. My reading of the adult literature has increased my awareness of the importance of all those supportive encounters—even the brief ones—in helping each of us to grow inwardly. This list cannot be complete, but each of these people has been significant to me during the writing of this book: Sandra Mitchell, constant colleague and friend, is always there with penetrating insight as well as humor; Kathryn Barnard, a sister of the mind, has tolerated my various waywardnesses and never faltered in her support; Larry Stettner, Frank Vellutino, and Shep White have each said the right words at the right moment, helping me to see old things in new ways. I thank them all.

Helen Bee

# 1.
# basic processes and theories

1

It is hard to pick up a magazine or newspaper these days that does not have some article about *parenting* (not my favorite word!) or childbirth or some aspect of children's development. The fascinations and delights of children's development are becoming widely recognized, and the task of rearing children is now seen as a complex and difficult one rather than a natural process. As a developmental psychologist, I am both pleased and concerned by this outpouring of popular information about children and their growth. I am pleased because I think this *is* important and fascinating; and the more that people know, the better off we all are. But I am also concerned because much of what is said is oversimplified or misleading or sensationalized. In fact, one of my purposes in this book is to give you enough information so that you can tell the good stuff from the bad stuff when you read articles in magazines and newspapers.

To give you some sense of how much you do know already about child development, see what you can do with the "test" in Table 1.1. (The correct answers are upside down at the bottom of the table.) Obviously, these questions cannot cover all the knowledge in this book, but if you can answer all 10 correctly, you may not need a course in child development. If you've missed some, and most of you will, you will certainly have some new areas to explore in reading this book.

I use the word *explore* intentionally. For me, the study of human development is an adventure, like climbing up a mountain trail, turning a corner, and coming upon some breathtaking view. You may have been on that mountain before and think you know it well, but suddenly you see it differently. Or you take a different trail over familiar territory and find the change in perspective has changed the view as well. There is a great deal that we already know about children's development, but I find myself constantly seeing things from new perspectives, taking new trails, asking questions in a different way, discovering new facets. For me the process has that same sense of in-

TABLE 1.1

**How much do you already know about child development?**

1. Which of the following aspects of a day-care center makes the most difference in a child's development?
   a. How many children there are per teacher
   b. How many children are in each class or group
   c. Whether the teachers have college degrees
   d. Whether children of different ages are in each class

2. Which sex is better at tasks that require the ability to visualize spatial relationships?
   a. Boys
   b. Girls
   c. Boys, but only after adolescence
   d. Girls, but only before adolescence

TABLE 1.1   *(Continued)*

3. How early should a mother be able to hold her newborn to maximize attachment of the mother to the child?
   a. Right away
   b. 6 hours
   c. 10 hours
   d. Any time in the first 24 hours

4. What is the youngest age at which most children know that you don't switch from being a boy to a girl (or vice versa) by putting on different clothes?
   a. 1 year
   b. 3 years
   c. 5 years
   d. 7 years

5. What is the earliest age an infant can see and hear most things near her?
   a. Immediately after birth
   b. 1 month
   c. 2 months
   d. 3 months

6. At adolescence, which group of boys is most likely to be popular and be leaders among the boys?
   a. Those who are extremely early in physical development
   b. Those who develop early, but not extremely early
   c. Average developers
   d. Late developers

7. Which of the following sentences spoken by a child is the most advanced developmentally?
   a. "See Dad."
   b. "Allgone cookie."
   c. "Sarah shoes."
   d. "Want more."

8. Which of the following tasks could an adolescent do that younger children would not be likely to accomplish?
   a. Classify a new insect according to genus and species
   b. Figure out all possible combinations of cards that will give a "21" in blackjack
   c. Arrange a set of pictures in one pattern, then another, and then reproduce the first
   d. Organize a group of blocks into sets that share color and shape

9. Which of the following types of discipline is most likely to lead to honesty or generosity in the child?
   a. Physical punishment
   b. Withdrawal of love
   c. Isolation
   d. Persuasion by reason

10. At what age do we first see a consistent IQ difference between poor and middle-class children?
    a. 6 months
    b. 18 months
    c. 36 months
    d. 60 months

1. (b), 2. (c), 3. (a), 4. (c), 5. (a), 6. (b), 7. (c), 8. (b), 9. (d), 10. (c).

ner excitement and satisfaction as does the hike up a new trail on a beautiful autumn day. I hope in this book to be able to convey some of that excitement to you.

Let me see if I can give you some flavor of the adventure and some sense of the key questions and issues by taking a brief journey into the territory of research.

## A JOURNEY INTO RESEARCH: THE EFFECTS OF DAY CARE

The great majority of you reading this book will face (or have already faced) the problem of deciding who shall care for your young children. Should one parent stay home full time? Is this *necessary* for the best development of the child? Or will the child do fine if she spends parts of her early years cared for by a baby-sitter or in a day-care center? Actually, of course, many parents don't really have such a choice: they cannot afford to have one parent stay home with the children. For such parents, the question is not *whether* the child will be cared for part of the time by someone else but *when* such care will begin and *what kind* of care is best for their child.

**Figure 1.1** A growing number of mothers with infants and toddlers are now working part or full time. These mothers (and fathers) must make difficult decisions about what sort of day care to seek for their children. Does it matter whether the child is in a large center, or is day care better in someone's home? And what will the effects be on the child? Will the child be less attached to the parents after spending all day, five days a week, with other people? Research is beginning to give us answers to these important questions.

These questions are critical for parents. They are also relevant for those of us who are trying to understand and explain the way children develop. What is the effect of "multiple mothering"? How is the child's attachment to his parents affected by such major variations in early experience? Does extra contact with other children early in life make youngsters more sociable, more skillful with their peers?

As recently as 15 years ago (1970 or so), the popular press (women's magazines, child-care books like Dr. Spock's, and the like) painted a pretty bleak picture of the prospects of the child in day care (Etaugh, 1980). Being reared by a loving mother at home was assumed to be essential for children's emotional development. Furthermore, day care was thought to undermine the family unit. (Former President Nixon, in fact, vetoed a bill in 1971 that would have provided for some government funding of day care on the grounds that such care would be damaging to the child and threaten the stability of the nuclear family.)

But government support or not, more and more mothers of young children were going back to work, and they needed care for their children. Serious research on these questions really began in the early 1970s and has been flourishing ever since. The questions are not easy to answer. But let's take a look at some of the conclusions that have emerged from the past 15 years of effort.

## Effects on Children's Intellectual and Emotional Development

Researchers have mainly been interested in the impact of day care on three aspects of children's development: their intellectual skill, their attachment to their mother, and their relationships with other children.

*The Effects on Intellectual Development*   One might argue that for many children a day-care environment would be *more* intellectually stimulating than a home—a wider variety of children, perhaps more books, more different toys, more activities. Following this line of reasoning, a number of researchers have proposed that infant day care could be a helpful way of improving the intellectual prognosis for children from very poor or unstimulating families. In fact, that seems to be true: children from poor families who have spent their early years in specially enriched day-care centers typically have higher IQs and better language development than children from similar families who were reared at home.

For example, The Carolina Abecedarian Project (Ramey, 1981), at the University of North Carolina, provided special day care to a group of 27 children from poverty-level families, from about 2 months of age until they were 3 years old. Another group of children, from the same kind of families, were home-reared. In Figure 1.2 you can see the IQ scores of the children in these two groups at various points in their early years. (An IQ score of 100 is defined as average.) It's clear in the figure that beginning at 18 months of age, the children in special day care achieved higher scores. Other researchers, in similar studies, have found parallel results. It seems clear that for "high-risk" children (those from families in which lower IQ scores are typical), really good day care can offer real benefits. Whether more ordinary, run-of-the-mill neighborhood day care has the same effects is less clear, although there are at least a few hints from a very large study in New York City that it does (Golden et al., 1978).

In contrast, children from middle-class families rarely show any positive intellectual effect from being in day care. But neither do they show any deficit. In sum, day care appears to have no negative effect on children's intellectual development and *may* have positive effects under special conditions.

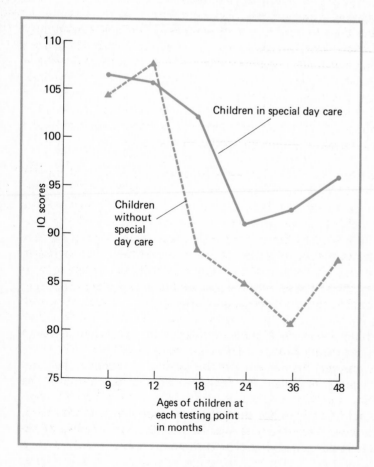

**Figure 1.2** IQ-test scores of children who were either in a special day-care program from the first months of life or were reared at home by their mothers. Both groups of children were from poor families. As you can see, the special day-care group (the experimental group) maintained higher IQ scores than the home-reared (control) group throughout early childhood. (*Source:* Ramey, 1981, p. 72.)

*The Effects on Children's Attachments*  The arguments about the possible effects of day care on children's emotional bonds (their attachments) with their caregivers have been much more heated. As you'll see in Chapter 11, children develop their first strong single attachment (usually to the mother) between about 6 and 12 months of age. Since many important theorists—including Sigmund Freud and Erik Erikson—believe that the security of this first attachment is critical for the child's emotional and personal growth, anything that might interfere with the formation of this attachment should be avoided. It seems logical that the repeated separations of mother and child that are part of day care could seriously interfere with a baby's attachment to his mother.

Because of such theoretical arguments, researchers in this area have looked hard for any signs of weakness or lack of security in the day-care child's attachment. Ordinarily, they have not found such signs. In general, the evidence tells me that infants and toddlers in day care are as strongly attached to their mothers as are children raised at home by mom. They are also typically more strongly attached to their mothers than to their day-care workers, regardless of how early they began in day care (Rutter, 1982). There are one or two exceptions to this general statement—studies that show that day-care children are more anxious in their attachments to their mothers than are children reared at home (e.g., Blehar, 1974). Obviously, we need to know more about the special conditions that might lead to such anxiety. But the typical findings offer considerable comfort to a parent faced with the necessity of placing an infant or toddler in day care.

*Effects on Children's Relationships with Peers*  The one real hint of a potential problem from day-care experience comes from quite recent studies that have followed day-care–reared children into preschool or elementary school. Some (but not all) of these studies indicate that day-care children may later be more aggressive, more argumentative, and less compliant with both other children and teachers. For example, the children who had been in the Carolina Abecedarian program (who began in day care in early infancy) were more aggressive and hostile toward other children in kindergarten than were the comparison group children in the same study (McKinney & Edgerton, 1983). At the same time, the children who had had the special day-care program were also seen by the teachers as more curious and more intelligent.

Not all observers would consider this pattern a sign of a problem. One might equally well describe day-care children as assertive or as low in docility, and these might be seen as pluses rather than minuses. We also do not know whether this difference (however it is described) persists into later elementary school. But the fact that such a difference exists is important and obviously deserves further study. It suggests that there may be a price to be paid—both in the family and in school—for the child's early day-care experience.

## Some Unanswered Questions

Despite the burgeoning research and the emerging answers, there is a string of important practical and theoretical questions to which we have either no answers or only the most tentative answers. Let me suggest just a few of these:

*Does It Matter When Day Care Starts?*   If the key attachment to the parents is formed between 6 and 12 months, then perhaps that would be a particularly *bad* time for a child to go through the process of separation that is involved with starting day care. Curiously, there is almost no research to help us answer this question. Children who start in day care in early infancy (3 to 6 months, for example) seem to do okay (Kagan, Kearsley, & Zelazo, 1978), as do children who start later in toddlerhood. But no researcher I know of has looked specifically at the 6- to 12-month period. If I were advising parents (which I sometimes do!), I'd suggest timing the beginning of day care either before about 4 months or after about 12 to 14 months—but I don't have much more than a hunch to back up that advice.

*Does It Matter What Kind of Day Care?*   Most parents of infants, if given a choice, will select what is usually called *family day care*—an arrangement in which the infant is cared for in someone's home, usually with one or two other children and one caregiver. In fact, 83 percent of children being cared for away from home are in unlicensed family day care of some kind (Ruopp & Travers, 1982). Such arrangements may be less expensive and may seem much more homelike than a day-care center. Is this a good choice? Again there is little directly useful research information to help a parent decide. What little information there is (e.g., Golden et al., 1978) indicates that center care is a bit better for fostering cognitive development and that the two types of care are about the same in nurturing emotional development. Obviously, the qualities of the particular caregiver in family day care will make an enormous difference.

*What Characteristics of Day-Care Homes or Centers Make a Difference?*   I have been talking about "day care" as if it were a single entity. But it is not. Care varies *widely*, from stimulating, high-quality care with many well-trained adults and attractive surroundings to centers in which there are hundreds of children, cared for by a few people, with little for the child to do. There is far less research on the effects of such variations than I would like, but recent work points to a number of dimensions that seem to matter:

**Figure 1.3** Research on day care across the United States shows that the number of children cared for in a single group is more significant for the child's progress than the ratio of caregivers to children. Larger groups like this one seem to be worse than smaller groups.

The child-teacher ratio. The results of the National Day Care Study (Smith & Spence, 1981; Ruopp & Travers, 1982) show that within a range of 5:1 to 10:1, it doesn't seem to matter much how many children are cared for by each adult. But ratios of 15:1 or higher seem to be less optimal. Children in centers with very few adults per child show more wandering, unoccupied behavior and fewer positive interactions with adults (Vandell & Powers, 1983).

The number of children in each group. Regardless of the child-teacher ratio, the smaller the number of children cared for together—in one room or in one home—the better off the child appears to be (Smith & Spence, 1981). So, for example, a single large group of 30 children, cared for by 5 adults (a 5:1 ratio), would not be as optimal as three smaller groups of 10, each cared for by 1 adult (a 10:1 ratio).

The amount of personal contact the child has with the caregiver. The more the child has a one-on-one relationship with a single caregiver who spends time with that child, the more attached the child seems to be to the caregiver and the more the child explores (Anderson et al., 1981).

**9**

The physical qualities of the day-care home or center. The cleaner, more organized, and more colorful the environment and the better adapted it is to children's play, the more the children show creative play and exploration (Anderson et al., 1981).

The caregiver's knowledge of child development. Total years of experience or years of education seem to matter less than whether the caregiver has had specific training in child development—a finding that warms the hearts of developmental psychologists (Smith & Spence, 1981).

None of these points is supported by a whole lot of research, but they at least suggest some guidelines for parents.

*Do All Children Respond the Same to Day Care?*  The obvious answer is "no." All children do not respond the same way to *any* experience. But we know *nothing* about the ways in which children's own individual qualities might affect their adjustment to day care. Psychologists (e.g., Rutter, 1979) have recently been using the words *resilient* and *vulnerable* to describe groups of children who seem—for largely unknown reasons—to adjust easily or with difficulty to many kinds of experiences in the early years. A fascinating subject—one to which I'll return at several points in the book.

*What Is the Effect of the Child's Day Care on the Parents?*  This question is one of the really crucial ones and is almost never studied. Are parents less attached to their babies if the baby has been in day care since early infancy? If day care continues for several years, does the parent get less interested or involved over time? There are some hints that this may happen (Belsky & Steinberg, 1978), but they are only the barest of hints. We know even less about the impact of the child's participation in day care on the parents' marital relationship or on other aspects of the parents' lives. If we are to understand the full family *system* in which the child develops, *and which the child influences*, we badly need more research on questions of this kind.

This research "journey," like all such trips into the unknown, is a continuous process. To use a different analogy, it's a little like playing with the child's toy in which there is a tiny box inside a slightly bigger box, inside a bigger box, and so on. We start with the biggest box and figure out how to open it, only to discover there is another one inside. Similarly, each "answer" we come up with only raises more questions. I find this process exhilarating, both in my own research and when I read about other people's studies. Some of you may find the process frustrating, since there are so few absolutely firm answers. But I hope that most of you can share in the exhilaration.

If we are to get past the biggest box and you are to understand anything about the process of development, there are several basic questions I must try to answer. Fundamentally, there are two tasks: to *describe* development (*what* happens), such as questions about the characteristics or intellectual skills of children in day care, and to *explain* development (*why* it happens that way). For example, why would children in day care show somewhat heightened levels of assertive behavior?

## DESCRIBING DEVELOPMENT

Reporters are taught to ask five basic questions about any story: who, what, when, where, and why. The first four of these all touch on some aspect of the task of description. The final one (which many scientists would rephrase as "how") touches on the task of explanation.

### Who?

The "who" in this case is primarily children. We are talking here about *child* development, so I will nearly always be describing studies of children or adolescents and only rarely studies of adults. Still, the child develops in the context of a family, a neighborhood, a school, a culture. I will need to talk about these other people and institutions in the child's life as well.

　More narrowly, I have to ask who participated in any given study. Did the researchers talk only to middle-class parents or observe only boys in some special setting? In other words, who was studied or observed, and can we generalize from this group to all other children or all other families?

### What?

In many ways, "what" is the most basic question, the one most psychologists spend their time answering. Our most fundamental task is to describe behavior or development. What does a newborn baby do? What is an older child's reaction to a stranger? What does a 7-year-old do when confronted with a difficult intellectual task? What is the effect of a poor diet on the child's development? What are the effects of poverty? In what ways do boys respond differently from girls? In nearly every chapter of this book, I will begin by trying to describe what we know about some aspect of development.

### When?

The "when" question is perhaps more relevant for developmental psychologists than for others. The central question here is whether there are times in an individual's development when a particular type of experience will have a distinctly different or more powerful effect than at any other time. For example, baby ducks will become *imprinted* on (become attached to and follow) any duck or any other quacking, moving object that happens to be around them about 15 hours after they hatch. If nothing is moving or quacking at that critical point, they don't follow anything (Hess, 1972). So the period just around 15 hours after birth is a **critical period** for the duck's development of a proper following response.

Examples of critical periods of this same very precise type are hard to find in human development (Colombo, 1982), although some events in prenatal development fit this definition, such as the timing of a mother's contracting German measles while pregnant. If the German measles virus enters the mother's system during a narrow range of days in the first three months of pregnancy, some damage or deformity occurs in the fetus. The same virus at a later time has no effect.

A similar, but somewhat looser, concept of a **sensitive period** is used more frequently by developmental psychologists. As an example, the period from 6 to 12 months may be a sensitive period for the formation of a core attachment to the parents. Other periods may be especially significant for intellectual development or language. The experiences the child has during such sensitive periods may then shape the future course of her development in a manner that will be hard to change later.

The importance (or even the existence) of such critical or sensitive periods is still very much in dispute among developmental psychologists. It is a question you will be meeting, in one form or another, throughout the book.

## Where?

Until perhaps 10 years ago, I would have left the word *where* out of my list. A reporter certainly needs to describe where something happened. But as a rule, psychologists have paid relatively little attention to location or context. Recently, however, Urie Bronfenbrenner (1977, 1979) has taken us to task on this point, joined by quite a chorus of other voices, such as Arnold Sameroff (1982), Frank Pedersen (1981), and Michael Lewis (Lewis, Feiring, & Weinraub, 1981).

Bronfenbrenner makes two key points, the first of which has to do with the way psychologists do business. A great deal of what we "know" about development is based on studies in artificial situations. We arrange some special set of circumstances, put children into that setting, and see what they do. If we want to know about fear of strangers among 10-month-old children, we may systematically expose children to a particular stranger, who acts in the same way toward each child. This *does* tell us something about the way babies react to strangers. But we also need to observe the same babies or other babies of the same age in their natural, complex environments to make sure that what we think we learned from the controlled situation still holds in the "real" world. Too often this second step is missing in our research.

Bronfenbrenner's second point is that if we are to describe development properly, we need to describe the total setting or *system* in which it occurs. Each child grows up in a complex family system, with a distinct cast of characters: brothers and sisters, one or both parents, grandparents, baby-sitters, pets, schoolteachers, and all the "character actors" and "bit players." My own children, for example, spent six years of their early lives living on an island, going to a small school. They also had four sets of grandparents (a situation that would take me three pages to explain!) and large numbers of step uncles, step cousins, and step-step grandmothers. To call these elements "the environment" or "sources of stimulation" is to grossly oversimplify the process. All are parts of a complex matrix within which the child grows. To describe or to understand development, we must describe and understand those matrices. More important, we need to discover whether the patterns of development themselves are different for children growing up in different contexts, different systems. The question I asked earlier, about the impact of the child's day-care experience on the family, is another example of a "systems" approach.

I will be talking about these issues very specifically in Chapter 13 ("The Ecology of Development"), but we need to keep this perspective steadily in mind.

## EXPLAINING DEVELOPMENT: ANSWERING THE "WHY" QUESTION

If the task of describing development is difficult (and it is!), the task of explaining it is far tougher. But we attempt it because most scientists agree that merely to describe is not enough. For example, only if we understand the *reasons* for a particular pattern can we predict new patterns or intervene effectively to change an unwanted outcome.

Answering the "why" question takes us immediately into the realm of theory. (Any scientific theory, after all, is a set of propositions designed to explain and predict some phenomena.) A great many of the theoretical arguments within the field of developmental psychology have centered on the issue of *internal* versus *external* influences on development. That is, does the child develop the way he does because of some inner, biological pattern built into the organism? Or is the child shaped by the experiences he has had (such as day care)? This dispute is sometimes referred to as the **nature/nurture controversy** or in terms of **heredity versus environment.**

This either/or, black or white argument has led to research that has added greatly to our understanding of the developmental process. But in the real world, *nothing* is entirely internally or entirely externally determined. There is always some interaction between the two. Our task is normally to discover the particular contributions of "heredity" and "environment" or "biology" and "experience" to each aspect of development. But for the sake of clarity, let me start by using this old category system.

### Internal Influences

*Individual Inheritance: Heredity*    The most obvious internal influence is a child's unique **heredity.** Each of you inherited from your parents a specific set of characteristics or tendencies. (I'll describe the process by which this occurs in Chapter 2.) For example, I inherited blue eyes, tallness, and a tendency to prematurely white hair.

Beyond such physical characteristics, the direct effects of heredity are much harder to pin down. Some aspects of an individual's skill in handling intellectual tasks (as measured by an IQ test) seem to be inherited, although just how large the genetic influence may be in this area is still being actively debated. In fact, the debate about hereditary influences on IQ or personality has been so extended that many of us (including me) wearied of the argument and set the issue aside. But in the past decade or so, possible hereditary influence on a wide range of behaviors has reemerged as an important possibility.

For example, think about shyness. Are you shy or outgoing? Have you always been like that? It turns out that temperament patterns, such as a tendency to be slow- or fast-paced or to be outgoing or shy, may be partly inherited (Buss & Plomin, 1975; Goldsmith & Gottesman, 1981). It is even possible that individual differences in "vulnera-

**Figure 1.4** These children obviously have different heredities. They are all about the same age but differ greatly in height; one has poor eyesight, while the others do not. But they also share basic maturational patterns. They all crawled before they walked; they will all go through adolescent changes in the same order. So hereditary "information" affects the ways we are the same as well as the ways we differ.

bility" or "resilience" may have genetic roots. I confess that I began with a bias against such hereditary explanations, but the recent evidence has forced me to reopen the door in my closed mind.

*Maturation*    A special subcategory of hereditary influence is **maturation,** genetically programmed *sequential patterns of change* in such physical characteristics as body size and shape, hormone patterns, or coordination. You can probably remember your own physical changes during adolescence. The timing of the pubertal changes differs from one child to the next (I remember being the tallest child in the school at age 11), but the basic sequence is the same for us all. These sequences, which begin at conception and continue until death, are shared by all members of our species. The "instructions" for these sequences are part of the specific hereditary information that is passed on at the moment of conception. So we inherit both instructions that make us all similar to each other and unique combinations of genetic instructions that make each of us different.

In its pure form, maturationally determined development occurs regardless of practice or training. You don't have to practice growing pubic hair; you don't have to be taught how to walk. But these changes do not occur in a vacuum. Even these powerful, "automatic" maturational patterns can be disturbed by environmental conditions, such as deprivation or accidents.

A child who does not get enough to eat may walk later than one who has a good diet. Even the physical changes at adolescence can be altered in extreme circumstances, particularly by malnutrition. Severely undernourished girls do not menstruate, for example.

I need to touch on one other possible point of confusion about the term maturation. Maturation is often used as a synonym for growth, but the terms do not mean exactly the same thing. Growth refers to some kind of step-by-step change in quantity, as in size. We speak of the growth of the child's vocabulary or the growth of his body. Such changes in quantity *may* be the result of maturation, but not necessarily. A child's body might change in size because her diet has changed, which is an external effect, or because her muscles and bones have grown, which is probably a maturational effect. Put another way, "growth" is a *description* of change, while the concept of maturation is one *explanation* of that change.

## External Influences

It doesn't take a great genius to figure out that the environment in which a child grows makes a difference. The task for developmental psychologists has been to try to specify much more precisely what it is (or is not) about particular life circumstances or experiences that affects the child. The critical elements seem to be somewhat different for different aspects of development (such as language or personality)—differences that I'll describe in later chapters. But there are several consistent threads that I can identify for you at this point.

*Diet*   A mother's diet during her pregnancy and the child's diet after birth have a widespread impact on the entire developing system. In this case, there seems to be a kind of "threshold" effect. There are many diets that are adequate to support normal growth, but if the child's diet falls below the "adequate" threshold—because the family is too poor to provide a decent diet, or because the child eats only junk food—we see the effects as slower or more stunted physical growth, less active interactions with peers, and poorer intellectual performance (Ricciuti, 1981).

*Poverty Versus Affluence*   Another major environmental dimension that has been widely studied is the general economic situation of the family in which the child is reared. No one I know seriously suggests that the amount of money a family has is the critical variable. But poverty is often accompanied by a whole cluster of conditions, including greater crowding, fewer toys or books or other stimulating materials for the child, perhaps more haphazard child-care arrangements, perhaps more noise and confusion. A wide range of research (summarized nicely by Wachs & Gruen, 1982) shows that children whose environments are more physically and cognitively stimulating and more predictable and stable are likely to show more rapid or more optimal intellectual, physical, and emotional development.

*Affection and Nurturance*   The amount of affectionate contact parents (and others in the child's world) have with the child is equally important. This may be expressed in cuddling or touching, but equally important, it is expressed through attention to the child's needs, time spent with the child, attunement to the child's needs and feelings. As Byron Egeland and Alan Sroufe (1981b) have put it so well, the parent must be "psychologically available" to the child to foster optimum emotional and social development.

*Contingent Stimulation*   The final thread I want to identify at this point has the rather technical-sounding label of *contingent stimulation.* Evidence is mounting that a key ingredient for almost all facets of the child's development is the extent to which parents (and others) react appropriately to the child's signals. Does the parent of the young infant engage in those wonderful interchanges (which John Watson, 1972, calls "the game") in which the baby and parent take turns—like blowing on the baby's belly every time he makes a gurgling sound or playing peekaboo? Is the baby or the toddler picked up when she cries?

**Figure 1.5** Children reared in poverty environments like this one not only have fewer toys and possibly less-consistent or less-stimulating environments, they may also live in an entirely different family system, with different relationships between parents, different sources of family strain. If we are to understand the impact of the environment on the child, we have to study the entire system and not just its parts.

If the 5-year-old tells his mother about his day at kindergarten, does she listen and then respond appropriately? When adults make their behavior toward the child at least partially *contingent on* what the child says or does, this encourages faster language development, more optimum cognitive development, a more secure attachment of the child to the parent, and a better self-concept (Blehar, Lieberman, & Ainsworth, 1977; Wachs & Gruen, 1982).

## Processing the Experience

So far I have talked about the environment as if somehow it "happens" to the child. But if we are to understand development, we have to understand the mechanism(s) by which the child's experiences influence her behavior. Two very different sets of principles or mechanisms have been proposed: learning and adaptation.

**Figure 1.6** Nurturance, love, and affection all really do matter to children. Research shows that this is one aspect of the environment that affects all aspects of the child's development, particularly emotional and social development.

## Learning

Some of you may have encountered the basic principles of learning in earlier courses in psychology. But let me review the concepts here. There are three basic types of learning, all of which describe important ways in which the child (or adult) is influenced by her experiences.

*Classical Conditioning*    This type of learning involves the acquisition of new signals for existing responses. If you touch a baby on the cheek, he will turn toward the touch and begin to suck. In the technical terminology of **classical conditioning**, the touch on the cheek is the **unconditioned stimulus**; the turning and sucking are **unconditioned responses**. The baby already knows how to do all that; in fact, these are automatic reflexes. But suppose that the sound of the mother's footsteps and the feeling of being picked up always come just before the baby is touched on the cheek. Now what happens? The sound and the feelings eventually "trigger" the responses of turning and sucking. They have become **conditioned stimuli**. The steps in the process are described in Figure 1.7

This might seem a relatively minor sort of learning, but it is particularly important in the child's developing emotional responses. Things or people that are present when you feel good come to be associated

| | Step 1 | | Step 2 | | Step 3 | |
|---|---|---|---|---|---|---|
| Stimulus | Response | Stimulus | Response | Stimulus | Response |
| Touch on the cheek (Unconditioned Stimulus: UCS) | → Head turn (Unconditioned response: UCR) | Touch on the cheek UCS) \| Mother's voice (Conditioned stimulus: CS) | → Head turn (UCR) | Voice (CS) | → Head turn (CR) |

**Figure 1.7** The three steps in the development of a classically conditioned response. In the first step, the unconditioned stimulus automatically triggers the unconditioned response. In step 2, some additional stimulus occurs at the same time as the unconditioned stimulus. In the final step, the new stimulus—called the conditioned stimulus—is also able to trigger the original response.

with "feeling good." Those that are associated with uncomfortable feelings may later trigger fear or anxiety or embarrassment. Since a child's mother (or father) is present so often when nice things happen—when the child feels warm, comfortable, and cuddled—"mother" or "father" usually comes to be a conditioned stimulus for pleasant feelings. A tormenting older sibling, however, may come to be a conditioned stimulus for angry feelings, even after the sibling has long since stopped tormenting the child.

Sometimes it can take only one instance to create an emotionally conditioned response. I remember an occasion at least 15 years ago when I was invited to give a talk to a group of psychologists in a town near Seattle. It turned out to be one of the worst talks I have ever given. I was not nearly as well prepared as I had thought I was, and as a result, the talk was disorganized and even unclear. I was embarrassed. Ever since then, every time I even drive by that particular town on the freeway, I feel embarrassed. The sight of the place has become a conditioned stimulus for my discomfort. The feeling has weakened over the years, but it is still there.

The important point here is that from the earliest months of life, children learn new cues through classical conditioning, particularly cues for emotional responses.

*Operant Conditioning*   This type of learning, also called *instrumental conditioning*, involves the use of rewards and punishments to change a person's behavior. The basic principles are these:

First, any behavior that is reinforced will be more likely to occur again in the same or similar situation. There are two types of reinforcements. **Positive reinforcements** are pleasant consequences, such as praise, a smile, food, a hug, or attention. Experiencing any one of these increases the chances that the child will try to repeat whatever behavior it was that preceded (seemed to trigger) the pleasant event.

A second major type of reinforcement is a **negative reinforcement**. This term has been used in a variety of ways over the years, so there is some confusion about its meaning (Maccoby, 1980). The definition I am giving you here, however, is the most widely used. Negative reinforcement occurs when something *unpleasant* is stopped. An example will make this clearer. Suppose your child is whining and whining at you to be picked up. At first you ignore him, but finally you do pick him up. What happens? He stops whining. So your picking-up behavior has been *negatively reinforced* by the cessation of the child's whining, and you will be *more* likely to pick him up next time he whines. At the same time, his whining has been *positively reinforced* by your attention and picking up, so he will be more likely to whine on other occasions.

Both positive and negative reinforcements strengthen behavior. **Punishments**, in contrast, are intended to weaken some undesired behavior. Sometimes punishments involve eliminating nice things (like "grounding" a child or taking away TV privileges or sending her to her room—things I'm sure you remember from your own childhood); often they involve administering unpleasant consequences, such as a scolding or spanking.

This use of the word *punishment* fits with the common understanding of the term and shouldn't be too confusing. What *is* confusing is the fact that punishments don't always do what they are intended to do. For example, your child may have thrown his milk glass at you to get your attention, so spanking him may be a positive reinforcement instead of a punishment, as you had thought. Punishment—as you'll see more fully in Chapter 13—is definitely a two-edged sword.

A second basic "law" of learning is that if you reinforce someone part of the time, but not all the time, for a particular behavior—a procedure called **partial reinforcement**—not only is his behavior strengthened, but it is also harder to get rid of. If you only smile at your daughter every fifth or sixth time she brings a picture to show you (and if she finds your smile reinforcing), she'll keep on bringing pictures for a very long stretch, even after you quit smiling altogether. In the technical words of learning theory, the partially reinforced response is highly "resistant to **extinction**."

Reinforcements are not all external to the child. There are also internal reinforcements, called **intrinsic reinforcements** or intrinsic rewards, such as the pleasure a child feels when she finally figures out how to draw a star or the sense of satisfaction you may experience after strenuous exercise. Pride, discovery, that "aha!" experience are all powerful intrinsic reinforcements.

Interestingly, there is now some evidence that the intrinsically reinforcing quality of some experience may be *reduced* by external, positive reinforcers. If you watch to see what toys children choose to play with spontaneously and then give them "good work" certificates or praise for playing with those toys, children will continue playing with the toys as long as the reward lasts but later are *less* likely to choose those toys in spontaneous play (Danner & Lonky, 1981; Lepper, 1980). So although rewards (positive reinforcements) "work," there are some hidden costs, too.

Despite this caution, though, these basic principles of operant conditioning have direct relevance for day-to-day child-rearing practices. Some of the applications are discussed in Box 1.1.

*Observational Learning*   Reinforcements clearly do affect behavior. But many theorists (most notably Albert Bandura, 1977) think that reinforcement is not always necessary for learning to occur. Learning may also occur merely as a result of watching someone else perform some action. Learning of this type, called **observational learning**, or **modeling,** is involved in a wide range of behaviors. Children learn ways of hitting from watching other people in real life and on TV. They learn generous behavior by watching others donate money or goods. They learn attitudes by copying the words and actions of their parents. They learn physical skills such as bike riding or skiing partly from watching other people demonstrate them.

Traditionally, all three types of learning—classical and operant conditioning and observational learning—have been thought of as essentially automatic processes. The child has been viewed as a passive recipient of these environmental influences: the environment is writing on a blank slate, following these "rules" of learning. But increasingly, researchers and theorists are coming to understand that the child is actively involved in the learning process (something nearly any parent or teacher could have told us!). The concept of intrinsic motivation obviously puts the child back into the picture. Observational learning also requires the child's involvement, in the sense that she can only learn from what she sees, and she is in control of what she looks at. Her understanding of what she has observed also affects what she learns, so her learning will change as her cognitive development proceeds.

This begins to get at another way of looking at the child's interaction with the environment, though—one that places the child's own processing at the very center of the system. Jean Piaget, an enormously influential Swiss psychologist (1975; Piaget & Inhelder, 1969), who died only recently after a long and fruitful career, used the word *adaptation* to describe the way the child responds to and *uses* the environment to make developmental progress.

BOX 1.1

# SOME APPLICATIONS OF LEARNING PRINCIPLES TO CHILD REARING

All parents, whether they are aware of it or not, reinforce some behaviors in their children by praising them or by giving them attention or treats. And all parents do their best to discourage unpleasant behavior through punishment. Often, however, parents (myself included) think we are rewarding behaviors we like and ignoring those we don't like, and yet the results don't seem to meet our expectations. When this happens, it may be because more than one learning principle is operating at once, and as parents, we have misapplied these principles.

For example, suppose your have a favorite armchair in your living room that is being systematically ruined by the dirt and pressure of little feet climbing up the back of the chair. You want the children to *stop* climbing up the chair. So you scold them. After a while you may even stoop to nagging. If you are really conscientious and knowledgeable, you may carefully try to time your scolding so that it operates as a negative reinforcer, by stopping your scolding when they stop climbing. But nothing works. They keep on leaving those muddy footprints on your favorite chair. Why? It could be because the children *enjoy* climbing up the chair. So the climbing is intrinsically reinforcing to the children, and that effect is clearly stronger than your negative reinforcement or punishment. One way to deal with this might be to provide something *else* for them to climb on.

A second example of the complications of applying learning principles to everyday dealings with children is what happens when you inadvertently create a partial reinforcement schedule. Suppose your 3-year-old son repeatedly demands your attention while you are fixing dinner (a common state of affairs, as any parent of a 3-year-old can tell you). Because you don't want to reinforce this behavior, you ignore him the first six or eight times he says "Mommy" or tugs at your clothes. But after the ninth or tenth repetition, with his voice getting louder and whinier each time, you can't stand it any longer and finally say something like "All right! What do you want?" Since you have ignored most of his demands, you might well be convinced that you have not been reinforcing his demanding behavior. But what you have actually done is to create a partial reinforcement schedule; you have rewarded only every tenth demand or whine. And we know that this pattern of reinforcement helps to create behavior that is *very* hard to extinguish. So your son may continue to be demanding and whining for a very long time, even if you succeed in ignoring it completely.

Because many parents have difficulty with situations just like this and with seeing exactly what it is they are reinforcing, many family therapists have begun to ask families to keep detailed records of their child's behavior and their responses to it. Gerald Patterson, in his book *Families* (1975), lays out a plan for families to follow in doing this. He has used such strategies with good success as a first step in treating families with highly aggressive or noncompliant children, and you may find it helpful as well. When you see, through your own records and observations, just what it is you are doing to reinforce whining or noncompliance or destructive behavior (or whatever), it is much easier to change your patterns of response.

**Figure 1.8** Children learn a vast array of specific skills and behaviors from watching other people perform them. Parents, of course, are the models that young children most often copy.

### Adaptation

Piaget assumed that it is the nature of the human organism to adapt to its environment. This is an active process, not a passive one. In contrast to the assumptions underlying most descriptions of learning processes, Piaget did not think that the environment *shapes* the child. Rather, the child actively seeks to understand the world around him. In the process, he examines, manipulates, and explores the objects and people in his world.

But like the learning approach, the process of **adaptation** can be broken down into subprocesses, which Piaget calls "functional invariants"—namely, **assimilation**, **accommodation**, and **equilibration**.

*Assimilation*   Each time we encounter a particular object, a particular person, a particular experience, we "assimilate" it in some way. We notice it, "recognize" it, take it in, hook it up with earlier experiences or categories. You are assimilating as you read this paragraph. You assimilate when you see the crocuses coming up in your garden and recognize them as crocuses—or tulips. (We do not always assimilate accurately.) Probably you also assimilate those same crocuses to your mental category of "spring." If you are trying to learn how to bake bread and you watch a friend kneading dough, you will assimilate parts of what he is doing—those parts that you notice and understand.

*Accommodation* The complementary process is accommodation, which involves changing (or creating new) concepts, strategies, or actions as a result of the new information you have taken in by assimilation. In other words, Piaget is saying that we do not simply passively absorb information and store it "as is" in our memory. We reorganize our thoughts, improve our skills, change our strategies. This is an *active* process, not a passive one. For example, your "dough-kneading strategy" will have altered and probably become more efficient because of the new information you assimilated while watching your friend. Incidentally, just to add one more bit of terminology, Piaget uses the word **schemes** for those categories, concepts, and action patterns to which we assimilate experiences and that are in turn changed through accommodation.

*Equilibration* This third part of the adaptation process is more difficult to describe briefly, and I will save most of my discussion of this until Chapter 7. For the moment it is enough to say that the concept

**Figure 1.9** When you recognize someone or see someone and immediately think "He looks just like Uncle Joe," you are *assimilating*—you are taking in that piece of information and incorporating it into an existing category.

of equilibration rests on the assumption that there is a fundamental motive in each of us to stay "in balance." The child is always striving to achieve an overall understanding, an overall mental structure, that fits the experience she has had. In order to do this, she has to keep the assimilations and accommodations in some sort of balance. Equilibration is, fundamentally, the self-regulatory process required to stay in balance with or to make sense out of the world around us.

An example from your own learning in this course may help to make this clearer. You start reading this book with some ideas about children already in mind. You assimilate new information as you read and change your existing ideas as a result (accommodation). But at the early stages you are still just adding things to and slightly changing your original, preconceived ideas. Eventually, though, you may find that a whole new way of thinking—a whole new set of mental "schemes"—may be needed, so an equilibration process occurs as well.

You will often find the learning and adaptation models of the child/environment interaction presented as if only one of them could be correct. Certainly it is true that they rest on very different assumptions about the fundamental nature of human behavior and motivation. But my own view is that there is strength to be found in each approach, and I will use both in trying to understand why the child develops as he does.

### Combining the Pieces: Interactions and Transactions

As I pointed out earlier, most psychologists today assume that development is neither wholly internally nor wholly externally determined. It is both. The basic task, therefore, is to describe the particular mixture of forces that affects each aspect of development and to understand how that mixture has the effect it does.

One possible kind of mixture would be an additive one. For example, a child's diet might add to the effects of his heredity: good intellectual heredity plus good diet would produce the brightest children. Either good diet and bad heredity or good heredity and bad diet would result in people of medium brightness, and poor diet and poor heredity would result in the least-gifted individuals.

There may be some additive combinations like this, but most often what we see instead is an *interaction* between several influences. A particularly elegant example of an interaction effect is the model in Figure 1.10, which has been suggested by Frances Horowitz (1982). She is arguing that some aspect of the vulnerability of the organism (either inherited or because of prenatal trauma, for example) *interacts with* the enrichment or facilitative quality of the environment. An "invulnerable" or "resilient" child will do quite well even in relatively unstimulating environments. And really facilitative environments will support nearly optimum development of even the most vulnerable children.

But vulnerable children in inadequate environments are markedly worse off than any other group.

There is a growing body of research evidence that fits this general pattern. One intriguing recent example is a study by Philip Zeskind and Craig Ramey (1981) of a small group of 10 infants who were extremely thin at birth—usually a sign of malnutrition prenatally. Half of these babies happened to be in the Carolina Abecedarian special day-care program beginning when they were 3 months old. The other 5 malnourished babies received nutritional supplements but were reared at home, in much less stimulating circumstances. Other children in the day-care center had been of normal weight at birth, as were other home-reared children included in the study. Table 1.2 gives the

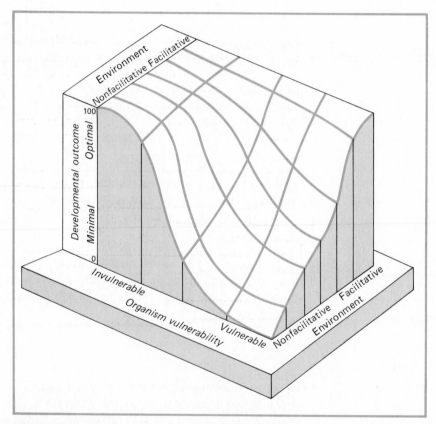

**Figure 1.10** Horowitz's model of the interaction between the vulnerability of the child and the quality of the environment. The height of the surface is the goodness of the developmental outcome (like later IQ or language skill or skillful social relationships). The higher the surface, the better the outcome. You can see that Horowitz is proposing that the combination of a vulnerable infant and a nonfacilitative environment will result in by far the worst outcomes. (*Source:* Horowitz, 1982, p. 28, Figure 2.1.)

TABLE 1.2

**IQ scores of 3-year-old children**

| EXPERIENCE AFTER BIRTH | PRENATAL NUTRITIONAL STATUS | |
| --- | --- | --- |
| | *Malnourished* | *Well-Nourished* |
| Enriched day care | 96.4 | 98.1 |
| Home-reared | 70.6 | 84.7 |

*SOURCE:* Zeskind & Ramey, 1981, p. 215.

IQ scores of these four groups of children when they were 3 years old. As you can see, the results match Horowitz's model very well. Malnourished ("vulnerable") infants did well in the stimulating environment of the day-care center but extremely poorly in a less-supportive environment. Less-vulnerable infants did better in the stimulating environment of the day-care center than at home, but the difference is not nearly so large, just as Horowitz predicts. (Although it is worth noting that the less-vulnerable children, when reared in unstimulating environments, certainly did not develop optimally either.)

It is extremely important to be aware of such interactive effects in development. But in fact, the process is even more complicated than this, since the child also has an impact on the environment around him. A cranky or difficult baby calls forth different behaviors from her parents than does an easygoing child; a child who complies right away with requests or demands develops a very different relationship with his parents than a child who is more defiant. The parents bring their own tendencies to these encounters and provide environments that vary in warmth, responsiveness, and cognitive stimulation. But the child is a dynamic partner in the developing patterns. It is this *transaction* between the parent and the child, between the child's qualities and the environment, that developmental psychologists have recently begun to focus on. Studying the developmental process in this way obviously makes our answers to the "why" questions much more complex. But I think we are also inching closer to the real processes involved.

## THEORIES OF DEVELOPMENT

I cannot leave this discussion of explanations without introducing you to the major theories of development. Any theory is an attempt at an explanation, one that not only accounts for things that we have already observed but also tells us what *ought* to be true. A really good theory helps make order out of tangled bits of information and directs further research by focusing our attention on different aspects of the total problem or by suggesting new solutions.

Within developmental psychology there are four major theoretical approaches, each of which represents a different mix of the concepts I have already discussed. I'll be describing each in detail in later chapters, but a brief sketch here will help orient you to the world of developmental theory.

### Biological Theories

Theorists in the biological group place the greatest emphasis on internal influences on development, particularly genetic programming. This does not mean that biological theorists think that behavior is uninfluenced by experience. No one takes such an extreme position. But genetic programming is seen by many psychologists as a powerful framework, affecting both shared and individual patterns of development.

Included in this group of theorists is Arnold Gesell (1925), who originated the concept of maturation. His emphasis was on the role of internal "programming" in shaping the shared patterns of growth we can see in so many aspects of development. A second group of theorists has used genetic mechanisms to explain *differences* among children in speed or pattern of development. Theorists such as Alexander Thomas and Stella Chess (1977) or Arnold Buss and Robert Plomin (1975), who emphasize the importance of inherited temperament patterns, fall in this group. So do theorists like Arthur Jensen (1979), who argues for the central role of heredity in explaining individual differences in intelligence. Lately, there has been a real revival of interest in biological theories of development, as you will see throughout the book.

### Learning Theories

The central notion in any learning theory of development is that the child is shaped by the environment through the basic process of learning I described earlier. Biological factors such as different inherited tendencies and maturational patterns are granted, but it is the reinforcements the child encounters along the way that are regarded as the real determinants of the particular behaviors we will see in any given child.

Included among theorists in this category are those like Donald Baer (1966) and Gerald Patterson (1980), who emphasize operant conditioning as the key process, and those like Albert Bandura (1977), who see observational learning as central. All these theorists, however, share the assumption that the primary "cause" of development and of differences among children lies in the external environment and in the particular models and reinforcements the child encounters.

### Cognitive-Developmental Theories

A third major group of theorists have followed Piaget's lead and focused on the adaptational process rather than on learning. Again, Piaget and his followers have not rejected biology. But they see the child's *action* with the world around him as the key element. This theoretical approach is usually referred to as **cognitive-developmental** theory because Piaget's original interest was in the development of thinking. But many of the same ideas, the same assumptions about the underlying processes of development, have recently been applied to emotional and social development as well.

### Psychoanalytic Theories

The psychoanalyic approach stands in sharp contrast to learning and biological theories. Like cognitive-developmental theorists, psychoanalytic theorists, such as Sigmund Freud (1905, 1920) and Erik Erikson (1950; 1959; 1980), assume that internal processes are as important as external experiences in shaping behavior. But the internal process that Freud emphasized was rooted in fundamental biological *instincts*. Freud argued that each individual is focused on gratification of a set of instincts (primarily sexual and aggressive). The specific form of gratification sought and the strategies the child or adult uses to obtain it change with age, but the inner push to obtain gratification remains constant over the entire life span.

### The Theories Compared

Such brief descriptions of these theories cannot begin to give either the specifics or the flavor of each approach. But it is at least clear that each group of theorists has focused on somewhat different aspects of development and has made different assumptions about the relative importance of internal versus external influences. I should emphasize, though, that the contrasts between these alternative approaches are not nearly as sharp as they used to be. Many developmental psychologists are beginning to blend one or more of these theories. In other words, I do not think that we must choose one of these theories as "right" and reject all the others. Each has great strengths to offer, and combinations of them are both possible and fruitful.

## FINDING THE ANSWERS: RESEARCH ON DEVELOPMENT

I have already asked a great many questions in this chapter and will ask hundreds more before I'm through. Before I go further, I need to say at least a few words about how psychologists answer questions

**Figure 1.11** The four theoretical approaches would offer quite different explanations of this child's angry or aggressive outburst. Biological theorists may argue that this child is genetically temperamentally "difficult" and simply shows more of this kind of behavior. Learning theorists would say that this child has been reinforced for such behavior in the past. Psychoanalytic theorists would emphasize the child's inborn aggressive instincts, while cognitive-developmental theorists—who have had little to say about such social behaviors—might describe it in terms of previous assimilations or of explorations of the environment.

about development: How do we go about the task of describing or explaining the changes that we see in children?

## Ways to Describe Behavior

The most basic need for any research on development is to be able to describe children's actual behavior accurately. How does a 2-year-old react to the presence of a strange adult? How does this reaction differ from the reaction of a 4-year-old to the same stranger? How do teenagers behave in groups? What are the physical skills of an 8-year-old or the vocabulary of a 10-year-old?

*Observation*   One very basic way to answer questions like these is simply to watch people, although as you might guess, it is more complicated than that! Before you begin observing, you have to make a whole series of decisions. First of all, should you try to watch *all* the behavior you see, or should you focus your attention only on specific aspects of the behavior of children or adults? You can try to record the entire context and each action by a child (*very* hard work, by the way, as you'll see if you try the project for this chapter), or you can count smiles or aggressive behaviors or the number of children in play groups or whatever specific behavior may interest you. Obviously, there are benefits and drawbacks to each choice.

A second decision is whether you are going to observe in a natural setting or whether you are going to set up special conditions or a controlled setting in which to observe. Again, there are benefits and drawbacks to each choice. After years in which most observation was done in artificial settings (which gives you good control), there is presently a strong push to move back to natural settings, where we can gain a better understanding of the complex dynamics of real-life interactions.

*Questionnaires and Interviews*   Because observation is a very time-consuming procedure, researchers sometimes try a shortcut: They ask people about themselves, using written questions or **interviews**. Questionnaires are not often used with young children, but interviews with both children and parents are quite common.

## Ways to Describe Changes with Age

A special problem facing developmental psychologists is to describe changes over age. Two basic research designs have been devised to solve this problem: **cross-sectional** and **longitudinal** research.

*Cross-Sectional Research*   If we want to know whether 4-year-olds can learn the same kind of concepts in the same way as 8-year-olds or to answer any one of hundreds of equivalent descriptive questions about development, the simplest and least time-consuming strategy is to study *separate groups* that differ in age. Such comparisons of age groups are called cross-sectional studies. This can be a very useful strategy: It is quick, and it shows age differences quite well. But this design also has distinct limitations, especially when we want to trace *sequences* of development, or when we want to study the consistency of behavior over time.

*Longitudinal Research*   To answer questions about sequence or consistency, we have to study the *same* group of individuals over time, which is called a longitudinal design. Short-term longitudinal studies, in which groups of children are studied for a period of several years, have become fairly common in recent years. There are also some famous long-term longitudinal studies—such as the Fels study in Ohio (Kagan & Moss, 1962), the Kauai study in Hawaii (Werner, Bierman, & French, 1971), and the Berkeley Growth Study in California (Macfarlane, Allan, & Honzik, 1954; Block, 1971)—in which groups of children have been followed from infancy through adolescence or even into adulthood. These sets of observations have proved to be a rich vein of information about development.

## Ways to Describe Relationships among Variables

Another central task for developmental psychologists is to describe the *relationships* among variables: What sorts of behaviors go together? What are the features of the environment that are associated with rapid or slow development or with one pattern of development or another? The most common way to describe relationships of this kind is with a statistic called a **correlation**. I will mention this statistic repeatedly throughout the book, so you should know a bit about how to interpret it.

A correlation is simply a number, which can range from −1.00 to +1.00, that describes the strength of a relationship between two variables. A correlation of .00 indicates that there is no relationship between those variables. You might expect, for example, to find a zero or near-zero correlation between the length of big toes and IQ. People with toes of all sizes have high IQs, and those with toes of all sizes have low IQs, too. The closer a correlation comes to 1.00, the stronger the relationship being described. The length of big toes is probably highly correlated with shoe size, for example. Height and weight are also strongly positively correlated, as are the hours of weekly exercise you engage in and your aerobic capacity.

A negative correlation describes a relationship in which a lot of one thing is associated with low amounts of something else. There is a negative correlation between the amount you eat when you are on a diet and the number of pounds you lose; there is a negative correlation between the amount of disorder and chaos in a family and the child's later IQ (more chaos goes with lower IQ).

Perfect correlations (−1.00 or +1.00) do not happen in the real world, but correlations of .80 or .70 do occur and correlations in the range of .50 are common in psychological research. Remember that you can judge the strength of the relationship between two things by the size of the correlation. But keep one more thing in mind: *correlations describe; they do not explain*. They tell us that two things happen together but not *why* they go together. Knowing that families with high levels of noise and confusion are more likely to have children with lower IQs does *not* tell us that quiet and orderliness *cause* better intellectual development. They may, but other explanations are possible. Correlations are tempting; it is easy to move from description to explanation without realizing what you are doing. While this statistic is useful, then, we must be cautious in our interpretations.

## Ways to Explain Development: Experiments and Quasi Experiments

When psychologists want to move beyond description to explanation, we normally shift from observation of naturally occurring events and introduce some intentional variations or control the situation systematically. That is, we do **experiments**.

Ordinarily, in an experiment there are at least two groups, to which subjects are assigned randomly. One group (usually called the **experimental group**) is provided with some special experience, such as giving some mothers extended contact with their newborns or assigning some children to special day care, as Ramey (1981) did. A second group (usually called the **control group**) goes through the same experiences, except without the key added ingredient, such as a group of mothers with normal hospital treatment (no extended contact) or a group of children without special day care. If, after the treatment, the two groups differ in some key way (such as the amount of affectionate touching of the newborn in the first example or the amount of aggression shown by the children in the second), the experimenter can be fairly sure that the difference has been caused by the particular experience provided.

One of the critical elements of an experiment is that subjects are assigned randomly to the different groups. For example, suppose we want to know if watching aggressive films makes children more aggressive. If we put all the children who already showed high rates of aggression in the experimental group and showed them an aggressive cartoon and put previously low-aggression children in a control group that watched a nature film, we couldn't be sure whether any later differences in behavior were because of what the children saw or because of their initial level of aggressiveness. Part of the solution to this problem is to assign children at random to each group. We would still want to be sure that there were equal numbers of boys and girls in each group and that the groups were alike in other important ways (family composition, recent divorces, children's IQs, etc.), but random assignment is a critical first step.

*Problems with Experiments in Studying Development* It is this very requirement of random assignment of subjects that makes it impossible to use true experiments in studying many questions about development: *We cannot assign subjects randomly to age groups*. Neither can we assign them randomly to sex or social class or educational groups—all groups that we need to study and compare if we are to explain development fully. To put the problem another way, unlike psychologists studying other aspects of behavior, developmental psychologists *cannot* systematically manipulate many of the variables we are most interested in, such as age or broad environmental features.

To get around this problem, we can use any one of a series of strategies that are sometimes called *quasi experiments*, in which we are comparing groups, but without assigning them randomly. Cross-sectional comparisons (comparing different age groups) are quasi experiments. So are studies in which we select naturally occurring groups that differ in some dimension of interest, such as children with prenatal malnutrition versus those without it (as Zeskind and Ramey, 1981, did) or children whose parents choose to place them in day care versus children whose parents rear them at home.

Such comparisons have built-in problems, since groups that differ in one way are likely to be different in other ways as well. For example, parents who place their children in day care, compared to those who rear them at home, are also likely to be poorer, may more often be single-parent families, may have different values or even different religious backgrounds. If the children differ, is it because they have been reared in different places or because of these other differences in their families? We can sometimes make such comparisons a bit clearer if we match the two groups on other variables (like income or marital status), but quasi experiments, by their very nature, will always be more complicated to interpret and understand than completely controlled experiments.

All of these strategies are common in developmental research. Explaining developmental sequences is a complex and difficult task, and researchers have become increasingly inventive in devising ways of sorting out the alternative possibilities.

I do not expect you to become experts in analyzing research strategies. But I do hope that you will develop some skill in judging the quality of research. Table 1.3 gives you a checklist you might use as a starting point in making a judgment about research.

This checklist should be particularly helpful when you come across reports of research in magazines and newspapers. Be critical of readers' surveys or even of casual statements like "Research shows that pregnant women who drink coffee have smaller babies." Ask yourself what kind of research would have to be done to support that particular point or whether the evidence given really is good enough. Remember, not everything you read is true!

TABLE 1.3
## A checklist of things to look for in evaluating research

| | |
|---|---|
| Clarity | Can you understand what was done and what was found? |
| Importance of findings | Does the study have some obvious practical relevance? Does it help to untangle a theoretical puzzle? Does it advance our understanding of some problem? |
| Promotion of new ideas | Good research should lead to new ideas, new theoretical insights, and new questions as well as answer old questions. Does this study do that? |
| Consistency | Are the findings from this study consistent with the results of other research? Are they consistent with your own experience? This may be hard for you to judge, since you don't know all the other research on a given question, but it is important to keep it in mind if you can. Don't throw out inconsistent results, but look carefully at any study that doesn't fit with other evidence. |
| Replicability | If the same research were done again, would the same result occur? Exact replications aren't often done in social science research, but they probably ought to be done more often. |
| Choice of subjects | Were all the children or families studied middle-class? Or all from poverty environments? Did all the subjects volunteer? Can we generalize the results to other groups? |
| Appropriateness of method | Was the method chosen for the study consistent with the questions being asked? For example, is the researcher using a cross-sectional design to study consistency of behavior? If so, it's the wrong design for that question. |

## SUMMARY

1. The study of human development can be seen as a kind of adventure, even a detective story, in which clues are followed from one study to the next, leading toward greater understanding.

2. One example of this has been the search for understanding of the effects of day care on children. Most research shows that day care has either positive or no effects on intelligence and little impact on children's attachments to parents but may increase the rate of aggressiveness later in childhood. Many questions remain, however.

3. In understanding development, there are two major tasks: describing developmental sequences and processes and explaining the patterns we see.

4. Descriptions of development must involve not only what happens but to whom, when, and in what context (where).

5. Explanations of development have centered around specifications of internal and external influences. Major internal influences are genetically programmed, shared, sequential patterns of growth (maturation) and unique individual genetic inheritances.

6. Some of the key aspects of the environment that appear to be significant are the child's diet, the level of stimulation and richness of the home, the nurturance and support offered to the child, and the degree to which the adults' responses to the baby or child, such as smiling back when the child smiles, are contingent on the child's behavior.

7. Two quite different descriptions have been given of the way the child "processes" the information from the environment: learning and adaptation.

8. Three major types of learning occur: classical conditioning, operant conditioning, and observational learning. Adaptation, a process described by Piaget, includes the elements of assimilation, accommodation, and equilibration.

9. Both internal and external influences are involved in virtually every facet of development, and the two interact in complex ways. Since the child also influences the environment she experiences, we must think of complex transactions between the child and the world around her, which change as the child develops.

10. Four major theories of development have been proposed, each emphasizing different aspects of these explanatory principles: biological theory, learning theory, cognitive-developmental theory, and psychoanalytic theory. The four differ in the questions they ask and the assumptions they make about the relative importance of internal and external influences on behavior.

11. Doing research to describe and explain development requires accurate and detailed observation of children's behavior in various settings. It also requires us to describe changes with age.

12. Both cross-sectional and longitudinal studies, each of which has certain benefits and disadvantages, can be used to study age changes.

13. A correlation is a statistic designed to describe the degree or strength of relationship between two variables and is very frequently used in developmental research. It can range from +1.00 to −1.00.

14. To explain development ordinarily requires an experiment or a quasi experiment. In an experiment, the researcher controls (manipulates) one or more relevant variables and assigns subjects randomly to different treatment and control groups. Quasi experiments, in which subjects are not randomly assigned, are needed in developmental research because subjects cannot be randomly assigned to age groups.

**Accommodation**  That part of the adaptation process by which a person adapts existing structures—ideas, actions, or strategies—to fit new experiences.

**Adaptation**  The basic process of biological existence according to Piaget, which characterizes intellectual as well as physical functioning. Both assimilation and accommodation are adaptive processes.

**Assimilation**  That part of the adaptation process that involves the taking in of new experiences, new information into existing categories or strategies or actions.

**Classical conditioning**  One of three major types of learning. An automatic, unconditioned response such as an emotional feeling or a reflex comes to be triggered by a new cue, called the conditioned stimulus (CS), after the CS has been paired several times with the original unconditioned stimulus.

**Cognitive-developmental theory**  A major theoretical approach associated primarily with the work of Piaget and his followers; through the adaptational processes of assimilation and accommodation, the child slowly comes to understand his world. The child's own activity is the key to development.

**Conditioned stimulus**  In classical conditioning, this is the stimulus that, after being paired a number of times with an unconditioned stimulus, comes to trigger the unconditioned response.

**Control group**  The group of subjects in an experiment that does *not* receive any special treatment.

**Correlation**  A statistic used to describe the degree or strength of a relationship between two variables. It can range from $+1.00$ to $-1.00$. The closer it is to $1.00$, the stronger the relationship being described.

**Critical period**  A period of time during development when the organism is especially responsive to and learns from a specific type of stimulation. The same stimulation at other points in development has little or no effect.

**Cross-sectional study**  A study in which different groups of individuals of different ages are all studied at the same time.

**Equilibration**  The third part of the adaptation process, as proposed by Piaget, involving the balance between assimilation and accommodation.

**Experiment**  A research strategy in which the experimenter controls or manipulates a key variable of interest and assigns subjects randomly to groups.

**Experimental group**  The group (or groups) of subjects in an experiment that is given some special treatment intended to produce a specific consequence.

**Extinction**  A term used in learning theory to describe the weakening or disappearance of a response in a person's behavioral repertoire.

**Heredity**  The unique set of genetic "instructions" for physical and possibly emotional and intellectual skills that makes each individual different from every other.

**Heredity versus environment**  A classic "argument" within psychology, in which two major sources of potential influence on behavior are contrasted.

**Interviews**  A broad category of research strategy in which people are asked about themselves, their behavior, their feelings.

**Intrinsic reinforcements**  The inner sources of pleasure, pride, or satisfaction that serve to strengthen the likelihood of whatever behavior triggered the feeling.

**Longitudinal study**  A study in which the same subjects are observed or assessed repeatedly over a period of months or years.

**Maturation**  The sequential unfolding of physical characteristics, governed by "instructions" contained in the genetic code and shared by all members of the species.

**Modeling**  A term used by Bandura and others to describe observational learning.

**Nature/nurture controversy**  Another common description of the classic "argument" between the advocates of internal and external influences on development.

**Negative reinforcement**  The strengthening

of a behavior by the removal or cessation of an unpleasant stimulus.

**Observational learning**   Learning of motor skills, attitudes, or other behaviors through observing someone else perform them.

**Partial reinforcement**   Reinforcement of behavior on some schedule less frequent than every occasion.

**Positive reinforcement**   Strengthening of a behavior by the presentation of some pleasurable or positive stimulus.

**Punishment**   Unpleasant consequences, administered after some undesired behavior by a child or adult, with the intent of extinguishing the behavior.

**Scheme**   Piaget's word for the basic actions, ideas, and strategies to which new experience is assimilated and that are then modified (accommodated) as a result of the new experience.

**Sensitive period**   Similar to a critical period, except broader and less specific. A time in development when a particular type of stimulation is especially important or effective.

**Unconditioned response**   In classical conditioning this is the basic unlearned response that is triggered by the unconditioned stimulus.

**Unconditioned stimulus**   In classical conditioning this is the cue or signal that automatically triggers (without learning) the unconditioned response.

### SUGGESTED READINGS

Achenbach, T. M. *Research in developmental psychology: Concepts, strategies, methods.* New York: Free Press, 1978.

This is a difficult book but an excellent source for more detailed information about developmental research. The author also includes information about topics such as the ethics of research.

Crain, W. C. *Theories of development.* Englewood Cliffs, N.J.: Prentice-Hall, 1980.

A good introduction to the major theoretical approaches outlined in this chapter as well as to many specific theories you will encounter throughout the book.

PROJECT 1.1

# Observation of a Child

I have several purposes in suggesting this project. First, many of you will have had relatively little contact with young children and need to spend some time simply observing a child to make other sections of the book more meaningful. Second, I think it is important for you to begin to get some sense of the difficulties involved in observing and studying children. So I am suggesting here, as a preliminary step, that you keep a straightforward, observational record, noting down each thing that the child does or says. You will find, I think, that the task is less straightforward than it seems, but this type of observation is the best place I know to begin.

Step 1   Locate a child between 18 months and 6 years of age; age 2, 3, or 4 would be best.

Step 2 Obtain permission from the child's parents for observation. Tell them that it is for a course assignment, that you will not be testing the child in any way but merely want to observe a normal child in her normal situation.

Step 3 Arrange a time when you can observe the child in his "natural habitat" for about one hour. If the child is in nursery school, it's all right to observe him there if you get permission from the teachers. If not, the observation should be done in the home or in some situation familiar to the child. You must not baby-sit during the observation. You must be free to be in the background and cannot be responsible for the child during the observation.

Step 4 When the time for the observation arrives, place yourself in as unobtrusive a place as possible. Take a small stool with you if you can so that you can move around as the child moves. If you are in the child's home, she will probably ask what you are doing. Say that you are doing something for school and will be writing things down for a while. Don't invite any kind of contact with the child; don't meet her eyes; don't smile; and don't talk except when the child talks to you directly, in which case you should say that you are busy and will play a little later.

Step 5 For one hour, write down everything the child does insofar as possible. Write down the child's speech word for word. If the child is talking to someone else, write down the other person's replies, too, if you can. Describe the child's movements. Throughout, keep your description as free of evaluation and words of intent as you can. Do not write "Michael went into the kitchen to get a cookie." You don't know why he went. What you saw was that he stopped what he had been doing, got up, and walked into the kitchen. There you saw him getting a cookie. Describe the behavior that way rather than making assumptions about what is happening in the child's head. Avoid words like *try, angrily, pleaded, wanted,* and the like. Describe only what you see and hear.

Step 6 When you have completed the observation, reread what you wrote and consider the following questions: Did you manage to keep all description of intent out of your record? Were you able to remain objective? Were you able to write down all that the child did? If not, what sort of things were left out? What kind of information about this child could be extracted from your record? Could anyone get a measure of the child's level of activity or count the number of times the child asked for attention? What changes in this method of observation would you have to introduce to obtain other sorts of information? What do you think was the effect on the child of your presence?

# part one
## *the beginnings of life*

# 2.

# *prenatal development*

Last Christmas, while my large extended family was gathered for our traditional celebration, my four-months-pregnant sister-in-law Nancy complained of a headache. Having heard warnings about the possible ill effects of various kinds of drugs on the developing infant, she was very reluctant to take any aspirin. We tried all the usual home remedies (shoulder rubs, warm baths, herb tea), but the headache persisted. Finally she took a nonaspirin pain medicine, which did the trick.

This incident brought home to me how very far we have come in this country in increasing women's awareness of the potential hazards associated with drugs or other outside agents during pregnancy. I was impressed by Nancy's determination to avoid doing anything harmful, but I was also struck by how long the list of "don'ts" had become and how hard it is for a conscientious woman to be sure what is okay and what is not. I certainly did not have all the answers for her. Still, our knowledge has increased greatly in the past decades.

In this chapter I want to explore what physiologists, psychologists, and biologists have discovered about the basic processes of development from conception to birth. What does normal prenatal development look like? What are the forces that shape that development? Equally important, we need to look at the factors that can influence or alter those normal patterns. How much can the mother's health practices, such as drugs or diet or exercise, help or hinder the process? Do other charac-

**Figure 2.1** The period of pregnancy is normally one of excited anticipation for both the mother and the father.

teristics of the mother, such as her age or her level of anxiety or her general health, make a difference? These questions have great practical importance for those of you who expect to bear (or father) children in the future. But they are also important basic issues as we begin the study of the developing child.

## CONCEPTION

The first step in the development of a human being is that moment of conception when a single sperm cell from the male pierces the wall of the ovum of the female. That sounds so simple when it is put into one sentence; but since the sperm and the ovum both have to be in the right place at the same time, it is far more complicated than it sounds.

Ordinarily, a woman produces one **ovum** (egg) per month from one of her two ovaries. This occurs roughly midway between two menstrual periods. If it is not fertilized, the ovum travels from the ovary down the **fallopian tube** toward the **uterus**, where it gradually disintegrates and is expelled as part of the next menstruation.

When a woman has intercourse, millions of sperm are deposited in her vagina. They travel through the cervix and the uterus, and several thousand of them survive to make their way up the fallopian tubes. If the timing is right and there is an ovum in the fallopian tube or about to be released by the ovary, then one of the sperm may manage to penetrate the ovum, and a child will be conceived.

Once conception has occurred, the ovum continues on its journey down the fallopian tube, where, instead of disintegrating, it implants itself in the wall of the uterus and begins the long developmental process. Figure 2.2 shows part of this sequence of events in schematic form.

This description may leave you with the impression that virtually all fertilized ova eventually progress through the full sequence of prenatal development. In fact, that is far from true. Perhaps as many as 50 percent of all fertilized ova are spontaneously aborted during the first weeks (more often if it is a male conceptus than a female), usually without the mother even knowing she was pregnant at all. Of those that survive the first three to four weeks of development, perhaps another 10 to 25 percent are subsequently spontaneously aborted—an event usually called a *miscarriage* in everyday language (Tanner, 1978; Smith & Stenchever, 1978). So considerably fewer than half of all fertilized ova eventually result in living children.

## THE BASIC GENETICS OF CONCEPTION

As most of you no doubt know from biology courses, the nucleus of each cell of our bodies contains a set of 46 **chromosomes**, arranged in 23 pairs. These chromosomes include all the genetic information for that

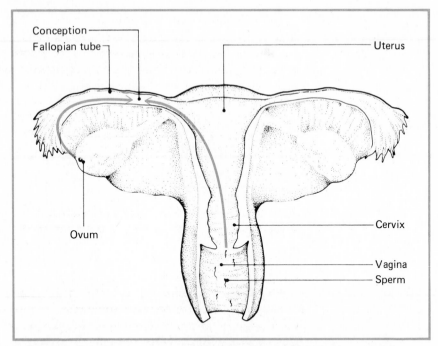

**Figure 2.2** Schematic diagram of the female reproductive system showing how conception occurs. The ovum has traveled from the ovary partway down the fallopian tube, where it is met by one or more sperm, which have traveled from the vagina, through the cervix and the uterus.

individual. They control the development of unique physical characteristics; shared growth patterns; and possibly temperament, intelligence, and other individual qualities.

Whenever a new cell is needed for growth or tissue replacement, an existing cell divides, in a process called **mitosis.** Just before the division, the chromosomes are duplicated, so that when the division is complete, both the old cell and the new cell have the full set of 23 pairs of chromosomes.

## Germ Cells

The process differs only in the case of **germ cells**, which is the technical term for the sperm and the ovum. In the early stages of development, germ cells divide by mitosis, just as other cells do. But the final step, called **meiosis,** is different. In meiosis, the chromosomes do *not* double themselves when cell division occurs. Instead, both the old cell and the new cell receive one chromosome from each of the 23 pairs. Germ cells (sperm and ova), then, each have only 23 chromosomes (half of each pair) instead of 46.

A second characteristic of meiosis is a process called **crossing**

**over**. At one point in the cell division sequence, the two chromosomes that make up each pair line up directly opposite each other, and some portions of each chromosome may be exchanged from one member of the pair to the other. One of the effects of crossing over is to increase immensely the number of possible combinations of "instructions" in each set of 23 chromosomes in sperm and ova.

When a child is conceived, the 23 chromosomes in the ova and the 23 in the sperm combine to form the 23 *pairs* that will be part of each cell in the newly developing body.

## Males and Females

Just as there are two kinds of cells, there are also two kinds of chromosomes. In 22 of the pairs, called **autosomes**, the members of the pair look alike and contain information relating to the same set of characteristics. But one pair, called the *sex chromosomes*, is unique. It determines the sex of the child.

In the normal female each of the chromosomes in this pair is large and under a microscope bears some resemblance to an *X*. In the male there is only one X chromosome and one smaller chromosome that looks a bit like a *Y*. Thus, the female pattern is described as XX and the male pattern as XY.

Given what I have just said about the special chromosomal characteristics of germ cells, you can see how the sex of the child is determined by the X or Y chromosome from the sperm. Since the mother has *only* X chromosomes on this pair, every ovum carries an X. But the father has both X and Y chromosomes. When the father's germ cells divide, half the sperm will carry an X, half a Y. If the sperm that fertilizes the ovum carries an X, then the child inherits an XX pattern and will be a girl. If the fertilizing sperm carries a Y, then the combination is XY, and the infant will be a boy.

It thus appears (contrary to historical belief) that it is the father, not the mother, who determines the sex of the child. But even that is too simple a statement for this splendidly complicated process. It turns out that the mother really does have an effect, since the relative acidity or alkalinity of the mucus in the vagina (which varies from one woman to the next and in all women over the course of their monthly cycle) affects the survival rate of X-carrying or Y-carrying sperm. So the woman's chemical balance can sharply alter the probability of conceiving a child of a particular gender, even though it is still true that the X or Y in the sperm is the final determining factor.

## Twins and Siblings

At this stage, many people begin to wonder why all the children in a given family don't turn out to be exactly alike. If each of you receives

23 chromosomes from your mother and 23 from your father, why don't you look and act just like your brothers and sisters?

The answer should be clear from what I've already said about meiosis and crossing over. Not only does each germ cell have a different combination of 23 chromosomes, but because of crossing over, the chromosomes themselves may contain different sets of information.

The exception to this rule is the case of identical twins, who come from the *same* fertilized ovum. In such cases the ovum divides into two distinct identities *after* it has been fertilized by the sperm. Each of the two developing organisms then has the same genetic material in the same combination, and the two children should turn out to be alike in all those areas affected by heredity.

Fraternal twins, in contrast, develop out of separately fertilized ova. This can happen if the woman ovulates more than once in a given month (fairly common in women taking fertility drugs). Because two separate combinations of chromosomes are involved, fraternal twins don't even need to be of the same sex (as you can see in Figure 2.3), while identical twins are always same-sex pairs.

## Genes

The 23 pairs of chromosomes are themselves made up of thousands of *genes*, which are even tinier particles. If we go down to a still finer level, we find that the genes are, in turn, composed of molecules of a chemical called **deoxyribonucleic acid** (DNA for short). According to a theory originally proposed by James Watson and Francis Crick (1958), DNA is in the shape of a double helix, a kind of twisted ladder or spiral staircase. The remarkable feature of this ladder is that the rungs are made up in such a way that the whole thing can "unzip" and then each half can reproduce the missing part. It is this characteristic of DNA that makes it possible for the full set of genetic "instructions" contained in the fertilized ovum to be doubled and then reproduced in each new cell.

*Dominant and Recessive Genes*   One of the intriguing questions about the genetic mechanisms is what happens when the instructions from the father's genes and those from the mother's genes are not the same. If the father transmits a gene signaling blue eyes and the mother transmits a gene signaling brown eyes, what color eyes does the baby end up with?

The basic rules for combining genetic information were worked out many years ago by an Augustinian monk, Gregor Mendel (the rules are usually called "Mendelian laws"). For our purposes, the crucial bit of information is that some genes are **dominant** and others **recessive**. A dominant gene is one that always "wins" in the case of conflicting instructions. A gene for brown eyes, for example, is dominant; if you

**Figure 2.3** Identical twins, like the ones on the left, come from the same fertilized ovum and have exactly the same heredity. They look alike and frequently act alike, too. Fraternal twins, like the ones below, are no more like each other than any other pair of brothers or sisters.

receive a brown-eye gene from either parent, you will have brown eyes, no matter what the other gene may signal.

A recessive gene, on the other hand, "loses" in any contest with a dominant gene. The gene for blue eyes is recessive. The only way such a gene is normally expressed is if a child receives the *same* recessive gene from *both* parents. Thus, if you receive a blue-eye gene from both parents, you will have blue eyes.

This set of rules is important not only for such physical characteristics as eye or hair colors, but—as we'll see in more detail later in the chapter—also for inherited diseases, many of which are transmitted through recessive genes.

## DEVELOPMENT FROM CONCEPTION TO BIRTH

The period of gestation for the human infant is 280 days (40 weeks), counting from the first day of the last menstrual period until birth. Three subperiods are usually distinguished: the period of the ovum, the **embryo, and the fetus**

### The Period of the Ovum

Sometime during the first 24 to 36 hours after conception, mitosis begins. The single cell splits in two. During the splitting, the DNA making up the genes "unzips" so that each of the new cells contains a duplicate set of the full 23 pairs of chromosomes. Mitosis continues, and within two to three days, there are several dozen cells, with the whole mass about the size of a pinhead.

You can see the steps in this process in Figure 2.4. In the early stages of cell division, there is an undifferentiated mass of cells. But within about four or five days, several different types of cells develop. Fluid appears in the ball of cells, which separates the mass into two parts. The outer cells will form the **placenta**, and the inner mass forms the embryo. As it comes into contact with the wall of the uterus, the outer shell of cells breaks down at the point of contact, and small tendrils develop, which attach the cell mass (called a **blastocyst** at this stage) to the uterine wall. At the time of implantation, about one week after conception, there are perhaps 150 cells in the total mass (Tanner, 1978).

### The Period of the Embryo

The second major phase of prenatal development lasts from implantation until about eight weeks after conception. During this period, rapid cell division and differentiation take place. A series of membranes develops around the embryo, with a liquid substance (the amniotic fluid) filling the cavity. The embryo floats in this liquid and is attached to the enveloping sac by the umbilical cord.

The umbilical cord, in turn, is attached to the placenta, a remarkable organ developed during gestation that lies next to and is attached to the uterus. The placenta serves essentially as liver, lungs, and kid-

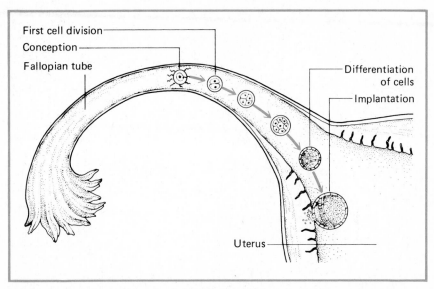

**Figure 2.4** The normal progression of development from conception to implantation, which covers approximately the first 10 days of gestation. (*Source:* Smith, 1978, p. 43.)

neys for the embryo and fetus. It provides nutrition and oxygen and filters out many of the disease organisms and other substances that may be in the mother's blood.

The mother's bloodstream opens into the placenta but does not pass directly to the embryo's separate circulatory system. Instead, the blood first passes through several membranes in the placenta. Useful substances such as proteins, sugars, and vitamins are ordinarily small enough to pass through these filters, while many (but not all) harmful substances such as viruses are too large and are filtered out, as are most of the mother's own hormones. Most drugs and anesthetics, however, do pass through the placental barrier (Smith, 1978), as do some disease organisms—as we'll see in more detail shortly. All of these separate organs are shown in Figure 2.5.

Growth during the embryonic period is extremely swift. By eight weeks of gestation, the embryo, now about 1½ inches in length, has eyes, the beginnings of ears, a mouth that opens and closes, a nose, hands and feet (though the fingers and toes are still webbed together), arms with elbows and legs with knees, a primitive circulatory system, including a heart that beats, some kidney and liver function, and a spinal cord.

## The Fetal Period

From about eight weeks of gestation until birth, the developing organism is referred to as the fetus. As you can see from the above list of

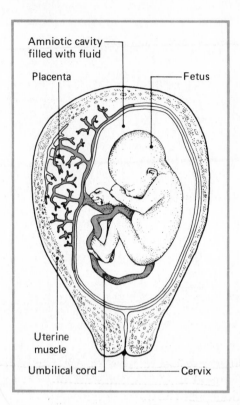

Amniotic cavity
filled with fluid

Placenta

Fetus

Uterine
muscle

Umbilical cord

Cervix

**Figure 2.5** The organization of body structures during the fetal period. Note especially the placenta and the umbilical cord, and the fact that the fetus "floats" in the amniotic fluid.

characteristics of the embryo at eight weeks of gestation, virtually all major organs, parts of the body, muscles, and nerves are present in at least rudimentary form very early. The remaining seven months involve primarily a process of refining what has already begun. It's a bit like the process of building a house. You first put up the floor and then the framework for the walls and roof. The plumber and the electrician do their work early, too, while the framework is still open. This skeleton of the house has the full shape of the final house; you can see where the windows and doors will go, what the shape of the rooms will be, how the roof will look. This stage is reached quickly, but after that there is a very long process of filling in around the skeleton already established. So it is with the embryo and the fetus. At the end of the embryonic period, the main parts are all there, at least in some basic form; the next seven months are for the finishing process. Table 2.1 lists some of the milestones of fetal development.

Analogies, such as thinking of fetal development as being like finishing a house, can be very useful, but I want to be careful about pushing this particular one too far. When you build a house, the full, final size is present as soon as the framing is completed; and when the electrician is finished, all the wiring for the final house is in place. Neither of these things is true for the embryo/fetus.

**TABLE 2.1**

**Major milestones of fetal development**

| Gestational Age | Major New Developments |
| --- | --- |
| 12 weeks | Sex of child can be determined; muscles are developed more extensively; eyelids and lips are present; feet have toes and hands have fingers. |
| 16 weeks | First fetal movement is usually felt by the mother at about this time; bones begin to develop; fairly complete ear is formed. |
| 20 weeks | Hair growth begins; child is very human-looking at this age, and thumbsucking may be seen. |
| 24 weeks | Eyes are completely formed (but closed); fingernails, sweat glands, and taste buds are all formed; some fat deposit beneath skin occurs. The infant is capable of breathing if born prematurely at this stage, but survival rate is low for infants this small. |
| 28 weeks | Nervous system, blood, and breathing systems are all well enough developed to support life; prematures born at this stage have poor sleep/wake cycles and irregular breathing, however. |
| 29–40 weeks | Nervous system develops further; weight is added; general "finishing" of body systems takes place. |

The nervous system is only barely sketched in at eight weeks of gestation. Only a small part of the brain and only the suggestion of a spinal cord have developed. The major development of the brain and nervous system does not occur until the last 3 months of gestation and the first 6 to 12 months after the baby is born.

Similarly, the major growth in size occurs later in the fetal period, with the gain in length occurring earlier than the major gain in weight. As you can see from Figure 2.6, the fetus has gained about half of her birth length by about 20 weeks of gestation but does not reach half her birth weight until nearly 3 months later, at about 32 weeks.

## PRENATAL SEXUAL DIFFERENTIATION

I've already said that the sex of the child is determined at the moment of conception by the XX or XY combination of chromosomes. You'd think that was the end of the story, but interestingly enough, it is not. The basic genetic patterning does not *guarantee* the later sexual development of the infant. It turns out that the process of gender differentiation prenatally is extremely complex, involving the action of a series of hormones (Hines, 1982). But if I can simplify it a bit, it seems that for the development of a male child, both the genetic programming (XY) *and* a particular pattern of hormone action are required for normal gender development. For the girl the genetic programming (XX) alone is sufficient. But for the male, sometime between the fourth and eighth week after conception, the male hormone *testosterone* is se-

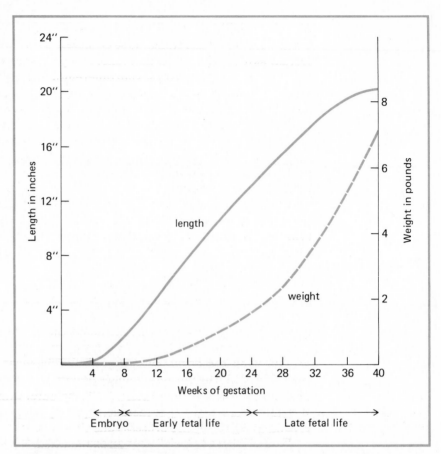

**Figure 2.6** The greatest gain in length of the fetus occurs earlier in fetal development than does weight gain. If you look at this graph, you can get some idea of the length and weight of infants born prematurely, at 28 or 32 or 36 weeks. (*Source:* Smith, 1978, p. 54.)

creted by the rudimentary testes in the embryo. If this hormone is *not* secreted, the embryo will develop as a physical female, even if genetically it is XY. If by some accident male hormone is present at this stage of development of an XX embryo, the infant may have ambiguous genitalia—that is, some characteristics of a male and some of a female.

There is now growing evidence, particularly from studies of other animals, that the prenatal hormones secreted by the male embryo affect not just the development of genitalia; they also appear to affect the pattern of brain development (Hines, 1982), influencing such functions as the pattern of growth-hormone secretions in adolescence or the relative dominance of the right and left hemispheres of the brain. Our knowledge of the mechanisms is still very sketchy, but the possibility of differential brain patterning for boys and girls becomes important when we look at such things as sex differences in certain kinds of intellectual skills. Might such differences be patterned prenatally?

The two-step process of sexual differentiation (genetic programming plus hormone influence) is a good example of the difference between a *genotype* and a *phenotype.* Geneticists use the word *genotype* to refer to the specific set of characteristics described by the information in a particular organism's genes. This is the basic map for later development we each inherit. But our *actual* characteristics are a product both of the basic map and of our experiences from conception onward. Geneticists refer to the actual characteristics of any individual as his phenotype. In the case of an XX embryo that accidentally receives male hormone (such as from drugs the mother may have taken), the genotype is female, but the phenotype may have elements of both male and female, such as ambiguous genitalia or increases in such "male" behavior as aggression.

## EXPLANATIONS OF THE NORMAL SEQUENCE OF DEVELOPMENT

One of the most important points about the child's prenatal development is how remarkably regular and predictable it is. If the embryo has survived the early, risky period, development usually proceeds smoothly, with the various changes occurring in what is apparently a fixed order, at fixed time intervals. To be sure, things can go wrong. But in the vast majority of instances (perhaps 90 percent of recognized pregnancies), the entire process runs off in a predictable, fixed pattern.

We don't have to look far for an explanation. Whenever there is that much regularity in a fixed sequence, maturation seems the obvious answer. The fetus doesn't learn to grow fingernails. She doesn't have to be stimulated from the outside to grow them. Rather, the fingernails, along with all the other parts of the complex system, apparently are controlled by the developmental codes contained in the genes. This sequence of development is not immune to modification or outside influence. A defect in the genes themselves could obviously have a significant effect, as may external conditions such as diseases in the mother. But it takes a fairly sizable intervention to make very much difference.

A second important point is that the effect of any outside influence depends heavily on the *timing* of that intervention or interference. This is an example of a *critical period*, or *sensitive period*, as I described in Chapter 1. The general rule is that each organ system—the nervous system, heart, ears, reproductive system, and so on—is most vulnerable to disruption at the time when it is developing most rapidly (Kopp & Parmelee, 1979). At that point it is "sensitive" to outside interference, whether that be from a disease organism that passed through the placental barrier, inappropriate hormones, drugs, or whatever. Since the most rapid development of most organ systems occurs during the embryonic and early fetal periods (up to about 12 weeks of gestation), this is the period of greatest risk.

Before I begin talking about the things that can go wrong, I want to emphasize that the maturational system is really extremely robust. Normal prenatal development requires an adequate environment, but "adequate" seems to be a fairly broad range. *Most* children are quite normal. The list of things that *can* go wrong is long (and getting longer as our knowledge expands), but many of these possibilities are quite rare. More important, a very great number of them are partially or wholly preventable, and many of the remaining problems do not have permanent consequences for the child. As I go along, I'll try to point out the sort of preventive action that is possible in each instance, and I'll return to the question of long-term consequences of prenatal difficulties at the end of the chapter.

## GENETIC INFLUENCES ON THE NORMAL SEQUENCE

The first point at which something can go wrong is at (or even before) the moment of conception. There are two main types of problems that can occur at this stage: (1) improper chromosome division and (2) single-gene defects, in which a disease or physical problem is passed on through either a dominant or a recessive gene or on the X chromosome.

### Chromosomal Problems

Abnormalities of the chromosomes appear to occur in 5 to 10 percent of all fertilized ova, but the great majority of these "conceptuses" are spontaneously aborted. Only about 1 in 200 newborns has such abnormalities.

The particular chromosomal anomaly you've probably heard most about is **Down's syndrome** (also called mongolism and trisomy 21), in which the infant has a particular eye-fold pattern, a flattened face, and often heart defects or other internal malformations and is usually mentally retarded to some degree. You can see some of the distinctive facial features in the photo in Figure 2.7.

This pattern, which is seen in about 1 out of every 600 births (Reed, 1975), occurs because the twenty-first chromosome does not separate properly during meiosis. One of the resulting germ cells ends up with two number 21 chromosomes, while the other has none. The cell with too few chromosomes ordinarily does not survive, but the cell with an extra one may. When this germ cell (either ovum or sperm) is combined with another germ cell at conception, the result is three number 21 chromosomes (hence the label "trisomy 21"). The risk of this deviant

**Figure 2.7** A Down's syndrome girl. Note the distinctive eye characteristics and the flattened face.

pattern is far greater for mothers over 35 than for younger mothers. Among women 35 to 39, the incidence of Down's syndrome is about 1 in 280; among those over 45 it is 1 in 65 births (Mikkelsen & Stone, 1970). The father, too, can contribute to this defect: In about 25 percent of the cases, the original improper cell division is in the sperm and not the ovum (Magenis, 1977).

Other types of genetic anomalies may occur if there is an incomplete or incorrect division of the sex chromosome. Several abnormal patterns occur (each apparently in about 1 out of 2000 births). An XXY pattern, called Klinefelter's syndrome, produces children who develop as boys, usually with mild mental retardation. Those with a "double Y" pattern have XYY and also develop as boys, typically unusually tall. Among girls, both an X pattern (called Turner's syndrome) and an XXX pattern may occur. Those with Turner's syndrome develop as girls (although with stunted growth), while XXX girls are of normal size and physical development but characteristically have markedly poor verbal abilities (Rovet & Netley, 1983). Many, *but not all*, individuals with these abnormal genetic patterns are mildly mentally retarded.

## Single-Gene Defects

*Dominant-Gene Defects*   Some physical abnormalities, diseases, or other unfortunate outcomes are caused by a dominant gene. For a child to inherit such a problem, she can receive that particular gene from *either* her mother or her father. In every instance, the parent who passes along the problem *also* has the same disorder. An example of a problem of this type is a form of blindness called retinoblastoma.

Fortunately, dominant-gene defects, although numerous in variety, are not all that common. There are two reasons. First, the number of defective genes in the population is simply not very large. More important, many people who inherit serious dominant-gene defects do not have children and so do not pass on the problem to the next generation.

The situation is quite different in the case of recessive-gene defects, which may be passed on to children quite unknowingly.

*Recessive-Gene Defects*   A sizable number of crippling or fatal diseases is carried on recessive genes. I've listed some of the major diseases inherited in this way in Table 2.2.

It is important to understand two points about recessive-gene diseases. First (unless the disease is carried on the X chromosome), *both* parents must carry the recessive gene for it to be expressed in the child. And second, even if both parents carry the gene, on average only one in four of their children will inherit the disease. (Actually, since many defective fetuses are spontaneously aborted, fewer than one in four live children of such parents may show the disorder.)

## Sex-Linked Defects

The third category of single-gene defects includes those that are carried on the X chromosome and are also recessive. Since a boy has only one X chromosome, inherited from his mother, any genetic disorder she carries on that X chromosome will be passed on to the son, without being overruled by information on the Y chromosome. For the girl, the likelihood of inheriting such a disorder is very much smaller, since she would have to inherit the defective gene from both the father and the mother.

TABLE 2.2

**Some of the major inherited diseases**

| Phenylketonuria | A metabolic disorder; the child is unable to digest many types of food, including milk. If not placed on a special diet shortly after birth, the child usually ends up quite retarded (IQs of 30 and below are not uncommon). Can usually be diagnosed at birth (such diagnosis is standard at most hospitals), but not before. |
|---|---|
| Tay-Sachs disease | An invariably fatal degenerative disease of the nervous system; virtually all victims die within the first three to four years. This gene is most common among Jews of Eastern European origin. Can be diagnosed prenatally. |
| Sickle-cell anemia | A sometimes fatal blood disease, with joint pain, increased susceptibility to infection, and other symptoms. The gene for this disease is carried by about 2 million Americans, most often blacks. Can now be diagnosed prenatally. |
| Cystic fibrosis | A fatal disease affecting the lungs and intestinal tract. Many children with CF now live to adolescence, a few to adulthood. The gene is carried by over 10 million Americans, most often whites. Cannot be detected in parental blood or diagnosed prenatally. |

The most famous example of a sex-linked recessive defect is the blood disorder hemophilia, which affects the clotting of the blood. Queen Victoria (Queen of England, 1837–1901) was a carrier of this disease and passed it on to some of her sons and to her daughters as carriers (one of whom then passed it on to the family of the Russian czars).

## Diagnosing Chromosomal Anomalies and Single-Gene Defects

I pointed out in Table 2.2 that phenylketonuria (PKU) can be diagnosed immediately after birth and then treated. Most of the other anomalies and some of the single-gene defects can be diagnosed before birth by the use of a process called **amniocentesis.** A sample of the amniotic fluid is taken at about 15 weeks after conception, and a chromosomal analysis of the cells in the fluid is then done. If there is some abnormality present, and if it is consistent with their moral judgment, the parents may elect to abort the fetus at this stage. Down's syndrome and all the sex-chromosome anomalies can be diagnosed in this way, as can Tay-Sachs disease.

Our increased knowledge about genetic abnormalities and inherited diseases, along with improved diagnostic technology, has made it possible to reduce the number of children born with crippling problems. But there are also very difficult ethical and practical problems for individual couples (and for society as a whole) embedded in this new technology, some of which I have discussed in Box 2.1.

BOX 2.1

# GENETIC COUNSELING: BETTER INFORMATION BUT DIFFICULT DECISIONS

Not so many years ago, when a child was conceived, that child was born with whatever good or bad qualities happened to come along. But modern science has made such incredibly rapid strides in the past decade or two that many new options and decisions are now built into this process. Couples who have been unable to conceive at all may now consider the option of test tube fertilization. And for virtually every couple, it is now possible to take specific steps to reduce the risk of disease or abnormality in a child. Each of these steps may involve difficult and soul-searching decisions, so the new technology and the new information are not an unmixed blessing. But many of you will want to consider one or more of these options before and during a future pregnancy.

There are basically three decision points. First, before conceiving, both parents can have blood tests done that will tell them whether they are carriers of recessive genes for specific diseases. This can be done for Tay-Sachs and for sickle-cell anemia (described in Table 2.2), for example. Cystic fibrosis, however, *cannot* be diagnosed in this way. One couple I know had the

tests done because they were both Jewish, of Eastern European extraction, and knew that their risks of being carriers of the recessive gene for Tay-Sachs disease were higher than normal. To their dismay, they found that they *were* both carriers.

What are their options? They could decide not to have any children at all or to adopt children. Or they could figure that they had a three out of four probability of having a normal child and take a chance (since the child would have Tay-Sachs only if he received this recessive gene from each parent, and that would happen, on average, only 25 percent of the time). Or they could conceive and then use any one of several new techniques for diagnosing disease or abnormality prenatally. If such techniques revealed a problem, they could choose to abort the fetus.

The best-known of these prenatal diagnostic strategies is probably amniocentesis, but several others are becoming more widespread. *Ultrasound* involves the use of sound waves to provide an actual "moving picture" of the fetus. Some kinds of spinal cord abnormalities can be diagnosed with ultrasound, for example. A new

## ENVIRONMENTAL INFLUENCES ON PRENATAL DEVELOPMENT: DISEASE, DRUGS, AND DIET

So far I have talked only about the sorts of deviations from normal development that can occur at the chromosomal level, at the time of conception. But there are also important "environmental" influences from the mother that can affect prenatal development. Most of these can be classified as the "three Ds": disease, drugs, and diet.

### Diseases of the Mother

Most diseases contracted by the mother cannot be passed through the placental membrane to the embryo or fetus, but there are a few excep-

procedure (not yet widely available), called *chorionic villi sampling* (CVS), is similar to amniocentesis, in that a sample of cells is taken from the developing embryo, but it can be done earlier in the pregnancy (perhaps at the sixth or seventh week). The cells are taken from those that later develop into the placenta. All the same genetic anomalies that can be detected with amniocentesis can be detected with CVS, including Tay-Sachs disease, Down's syndrome, and even sickle-cell anemia. Each of these types of disorder poses a different set of decisions for parents, none of them easy. (As an illustration of the complexity of the dilemma that can arise, consider the recent case of a woman who conceived twins. Amniocentesis revealed that *one* of the twins had Down's syndrome. What would you do?)

The case of cystic fibrosis (CF) illustrates the third decision point that may face some parents. Carriers of CF cannot be identified ahead of time, and the disease cannot be diagnosed prenatally by any presently available technique. Only those couples who have already had one child with CF know that they both carry the recessive gene. For them, the decision is whether to have more children, knowing that the risk in each pregnancy is one in four that the child will have CF.

There are obviously tough ethical and religious decisions embedded in this process. Should you make an effort to find out if you carry any diseases? If you do so, are you tampering in some way with the natural order? And if you undergo amniocentesis and find that the fetus has an abnormality or an inherited disease, are you prepared to abort? Many people have very strong moral feelings about abortion. Others have equally strong feelings about the morality of bringing handicapped individuals into the world, especially those who require long-term care. But what about diseases such as sickle-cell anemia, which can occur in mild or moderate forms that may not interfere greatly with the child's chance of a full and rewarding life? Are we moving slowly toward the day when only "perfect" fetuses will be allowed to survive? Some parents have even used amniocentesis as a method of determining the sex of the fetus and have chosen to abort the fetus if it is not of the desired gender. Such applications go well beyond the intended diagnostic use of amniocentesis, and they raise troubling questions, not only for individual parents but for society as a whole.

As genetic counseling becomes more common, as diagnostic techniques become still more sophisticated, these will become compelling questions for future couples—including many of you.

tions in which the disease agent is small enough to pass into the child's system. **Rubella** and rubeola (both forms of measles), syphilis, diphtheria, influenza, typhoid, serum hepatitis, and chicken pox all may be passed to the child in this way. In addition, it is possible for the child to contract other diseases (such as herpes simplex) during birth itself, when the fetus comes into contact with the mucous membranes in the birth canal. Of this list, probably the riskiest diseases for the child are rubella and syphilis, although recent evidence suggests that herpes also may have serious side effects.

*Rubella*   Rubella (also called German measles) is most risky for the child if the mother contracts it in the first three months of the pregnancy, especially during the first month (Berg, 1974). The particular organ systems most affected by rubella are the ears, eyes, and heart—all of which are developing rapidly during the first three months of gestation. The single most common effect is deafness in the child.

Fortunately, rubella is preventable. Vaccination is available and should be given to all children as part of a regular immunization program. Adult women who were not vaccinated as children can be vaccinated later, but it must be done at least three months before a pregnancy to provide complete immunity. (Those women among you who are not sure whether you have ever had German measles or have not been vaccinated for rubella should be checked for immunity. If you are not immune, you should be vaccinated, but only if you are sure you are not pregnant at the time of vaccination. A vaccination for rubella during the first three months of a pregnancy may have the same effect on the embryo/fetus as does the disease itself—although this effect is now in dispute among epidemiologists.)

*Syphilis*    This disease, too, may cause significant problems, including deafness, blindness, or mental retardation. Again, however, there is a preventive measure available. If a woman who has syphilis receives treatment and the disease is cleared up within the first 18 weeks of pregnancy, the fetus is unlikely to be infected.

*Herpes Simplex*    Herpes has received a great deal of press lately, so most of you know that, once contracted, this disease is not curable (at least not at the present state of medical science). If a pregnant woman is in the active phase of the disease during delivery, it is possible that the child will contract it during birth. Not only will the child then experience the genital sores periodically, but other complications are also possible, most notably meningoencephalitis (a potentially serious and often fatal inflammation of the brain and spinal cord). Because of this increased risk, many physicians now recommend surgical delivery (cesarean section) of infants of mothers with herpes, although vaginal delivery is possible if the disease is inactive.

## Drugs Taken by the Mother

Try sitting down and making a list of all the "drugs" you have taken in the past month or the past year. I'm not talking here about such illegal drugs as marijuana or cocaine (although they, too, affect the developing infant) but about everyday, legal drugs like aspirin, decongestants, vitamins, sleeping pills, or tranquilizers. Equally common in the everyday lives of most of us are alcohol, tobacco, and caffeine. Ours is a drug-taking culture, and this is no less true of pregnant women. The average pregnant woman takes six to seven prescribed drugs and another three or four over-the-counter drugs (such as aspirin) during the course of her pregnancy. And many pregnant women also smoke and drink alcohol, coffee, tea, and other caffeine-containing liquids. What are the effects of such drugs on the embryo or fetus?

Some drugs prescribed specifically for pregnant women have later been found to have significant negative effects. *Thalidomide*, for example, was a tranquilizer prescribed fairly often (particularly in West Germany and England) from 1958 to 1962. Some years later it was found that this drug, if taken during the first 52 days of pregnancy, greatly increased the risk of a particular kind of physical deformity in which the infant was born with foreshortened or missing limbs. Another drug, *diethylstilbestrol* (DES), was quite widely prescribed during the 1940s and 1950s to help prevent miscarriages (spontaneous abortions). No obvious deformity or disability was produced in the offspring, but recent evidence points to a number of possible subtle and long-term effects, including increased risk of vaginal cancer among girls whose mothers received DES during their pregnancies (Henley & Altman, 1978).

Discoveries like these have made physicians and pregnant women a great deal more cautious about drugs during pregnancy. Current findings suggest that antibiotics such as tetracycline, anticoagulants, antihistamines, amphetamines, and tranquilizers can all have negative effects on the developing embryo or fetus. Even caffeine has come under suspicion lately, although the findings are mixed on this one. (That is, some studies show a small increase in birth defects for women who drink a lot of coffee; other studies show no effects.) Obviously, given this list, any pregnant woman would be well advised to consult her physician before taking *any* medication, particularly "over-the-counter" drugs.

On a day-to-day basis, though, the drugs most of us have most contact with are not antihistamines or anticoagulants but alcohol and nicotine. Should a pregnant woman drink or smoke?

*Smoking*   The most clearly demonstrated effect of smoking on prenatal development is that it reduces the birth weight of the infant (U.S. Department of HEW, 1979). On average, the difference is about 200 g (a bit less than half a pound). This may not seem like a very sizable difference, but this reduced size appears to be produced by a reduction of placental blood flow (nicotine constricts the blood vessels), so the fetus suffers from a loss of nutrition. In addition, women who smoke are about 30 percent more likely to have stillborn infants or infants with some kind of malformation (Tanner, 1978; Naeye, 1978).

Long-term consequences for the infants of mothers who smoke are much harder to pin down. Several longitudinal studies point to higher rates of learning problems in school-age children of mothers who smoked during pregnancy (Nichols, 1977; Butler & Goldstein, 1973; Dunn et al., 1977), but other researchers have not found such long-term effects (Lefkowitz, 1981).

Despite the inconsistencies in the studies on long-term effects, though, the moral to be drawn from this research seems clear: Do not smoke during pregnancy. If you cannot quit entirely, then at least cut back, since all these studies show a relationship between the "dose" (the amount of nicotine you are taking in) and the severity of consequences for the child.

*Drinking*  An equally clear moral emerges from a look at the recent work on the effects of maternal alcohol ingestion on prenatal and postnatal development.

In the early 1970s, Kenneth Jones and his colleagues (1973) identified a syndrome characteristic of children born to alcoholic mothers, which they labeled **fetal alcohol syndrome (FAS)**. Infants with this syndrome are generally smaller than normal, with smaller brains; their faces are distinctively different (as you can see in Figure 2.8), and they ordinarily show mild to moderate mental retardation.

Since the first identification of this syndrome, extensive evidence has accumulated showing major negative effects of alcoholism or regular heavy drinking on the child's development (Rosett & Sander, 1979; Abel, 1981).

The recent evidence also points to at least some effects of "moderate" drinking. In one of the most comprehensive and best-designed studies, Ann Streissguth and her colleagues (1980, 1981) have found

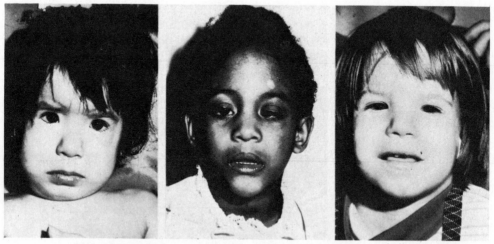

**Figure 2.8** These three children, from three racial backgrounds (from left: American Indian, black, and white), all have been diagnosed as having fetal alcohol syndrome (FAS). All are mentally retarded. Note the short nose, the low nasal bridge, and the relatively small head—all of these are typical of FAS children. (*Source:* A. P. Streissguth et al., *Science* 209 (July 18, 1980): 355, Figure 2; copyright 1980 by the American Association for the Advancement of Science.)

that women who average 1 ounce of absolute alcohol per day (or more) during pregnancy (equivalent to about two beers or one and a half 6-ounce glasses of wine or one or two 1-ounce drinks of liquor) are more likely to have sluggish, hard-to-arouse babies, often of lower birth weights and with lower scores on infant development tests at 8 months of age, than are women who do not drink at all or drink very little. The results of the infant development tests are shown in Table 2.3, so you can see for yourself the relationship between the amount of alcohol and the children's performance.

Whether there is any "safe" level of alcohol consumption during pregnancy I can't tell you, given the evidence we have today. Probably it matters when in the pregnancy the drinking occurs and how much you drink on any one occasion. And the total "dose" obviously makes a difference. But it seems clear that the *safest* course is not to drink at all.

## The Mother's Diet

Obviously, it matters what sort of drugs you ingest while you're pregnant. But does it matter what or how much you eat? Clearly it does, although no one knows *exactly* what is the best diet or what are the precise effects of too much or too little.

I've explored some of what we know about a "good diet" in Box 2.2. The other half of the spectrum is what we know about the effects of unusually poor diets. When there is severe malnutrition during pregnancy, there is a greatly increased risk of stillbirths, low birth weight, and infant death during the first year of life.

Zena Stein and her colleagues (1975) have done some of the most

TABLE 2.3

**The relationship between alcohol intake during pregnancy and the mental development of infants**

| Average Ounces of Absolute Alcohol[a] Ingested by Mother Per Day During Pregnancy | Child's Score on Measure of Mental Development at 8 Months |
|---|---|
| Less than .10 oz. | 116 |
| .10 to less than 1.0 oz. | 116 |
| 1.0 to 2.0 oz. | 114 |
| 2.0 to 3.0 oz. | 109 |
| 3.0 to 4.0 oz. | 101 |
| 4.0 oz. or more | 98 |

[a]One ounce of absolute alcohol per day is equivalent to approximately two beers or one to two glasses of wine or one to two drinks of liquor.
*SOURCE:* A. P. Streissguth, H. M. Barr, D. C. Martin, & C. S. Herman. Effects of maternal alcohol, nicotine, and caffeine use during pregnancy on infant mental and motor development at 8 months. *Alcoholism: Clinical and experimental research*, 1980, *4*, 152–164; used by permission.

BOX 2.2

# DIET AND EXERCISE DURING PREGNANCY

Life-styles have been changing; slimness and fitness in women are perhaps more highly valued now than before, especially among younger women of childbearing age. And all women want to give their unborn child the best possible start in the world. So questions about weight gain, diet, and exercise during pregnancy are of vital concern to many women. The quality of the evidence does not quite match the concern in every case, but at least there is more that I can tell you now than was true four years ago when I last wrote about this.

## WEIGHT GAIN

For many years, physicians thought that the fetus acted as a sort of "parasite" on the mother's body, taking whatever nourishment it needed, even at the expense of the mother. Recent research by Pedro Rosso (1977a, 1977b), however, has challenged this assumption as well as other customs about nutritional needs in pregnancy.

Rosso's research shows that if the mother is even a little underweight or malnourished, the fetus may not compete successfully for nourishment and may be born underweight, with increased risk of disease or disorders. The old rule of thumb was that a woman should gain 2 pounds per month during the pregnancy.

Rosso's work indicates that this is not nearly enough. The current advice is for a gain of approximately 25 to 30 pounds for a woman who is at her normal weight before pregnancy and a slightly greater gain for a woman who is underweight before pregnancy. Even overweight women need to gain at least 20 to 24 pounds in order to support the optimum development of the infant. Women who gain less than this may have infants who suffer from some fetal malnutrition and are usually born underweight for their gestational age (Winick, 1980; Brown, 1983).

Furthermore, it matters *when* the weight is gained. During the first three months of the pregnancy, there need be only minimal weight gain (2 to 5 pounds). But for the last six months, the woman should be gaining at the rate of about 14 ounces (350 to 400 g) per week in order to support fetal growth (Pitkin, 1977; Winick, 1980). One practical consequence of this is that a woman who has gained 20 pounds or so during the first four or five months should *not* cut back in order to hold her weight gain to some magic total number. Restricting caloric intake during those final months is exactly the wrong thing to do.

## A GOOD DIET

Pure poundage is not enough to ensure optimal development for the child. It also matters *what*

careful studies of these effects. They looked at the impact of a period of extreme famine in Holland toward the end of World War II (1944–1945), when whole sections of the country were allotted only about 1000 calories or less per person per day. By going back and looking at hospital, birth, and death records, they could trace the effects of the famine. Since the diet had been adequate both before and after this particular period, they could not only isolate the impact of poor diet from other kinds of social or physical disorders, they could also see whether malnutrition had a greater effect if it occurred early or late in the pregnancy.

the mother eats. Caloric requirements go up 10 to 20 percent (perhaps 300 calories a day beyond the woman's maintenance level), but protein needs appear go up much more markedly. The current recommendation (Winick, 1980) is that a pregnant woman of 19 or older needs to take in 1.3 g of protein per kilogram (2.2 pounds) of her weight. As an example, this would mean that a woman weighing 125 pounds would require about 75 g of protein per day. For teenagers, because they are still growing, the protein requirement is still higher—perhaps 1.5 or 1.7 g per day per kilogram of weight. (Since one egg has about 7 g of protein while one cup of cottage cheese has 33 g, even this heightened requirement is not difficult to meet.) Requirements for most vitamins and minerals also increase during pregnancy. Calcium needs rise 50 percent (from 800 mg to 1200 mg daily), and iron is also normally needed in increased amounts—perhaps 75 mg daily (Winick, 1980).

### EXERCISE

Two questions about exercise during pregnancy are relevant: Is it safe for the fetus, and does it make labor and delivery easier? The tentative answer to both questions seems to be "yes," but I am not satisfied that we have nearly enough research on these questions yet.

Since blood oxygen levels seem to remain fairly constant in exercising pregnant women, the fetus does not appear likely to suffer from any oxygen deprivation. Furthermore, the few existing studies comparing babies born to mothers who exercised and those who did not show no differences in birth weight, length, or healthiness at birth (Leaf, 1982). However, this is true *only* if the exercising woman gains a sufficient amount of weight. Not long ago I read a letter to the editor in *Runner's World* magazine from a man who bragged that his wife maintained a schedule of running 30 to 40 miles per week during her pregnancy and gained only 2 pounds in nine months! Such low weight gain is *not* desirable. I suspect, however, that such lower-than-optimal weight gain may be more common among women who exercise heavily in pregnancy simply because the caloric needs are increased both by pregnancy and by exercise. Furthermore, some kinds of complications of pregnancy may preclude exercise—something that should be discussed with your physician.

Aside from maintaining physical fitness during pregnancy, the main argument for exercise is that it *may* shorten labor to some degree (Leaf, 1982). I say "may" because the evidence here is scanty. I do not offer guarantees!

It is heartening to have at least some research on questions like these. But the answers are still tentative, and each of you will need to make the best decision you can, given the available information.

What Stein found was that in general the effects of malnutrition were worse if it occurred during the last half of the pregnancy, particularly in the final three months. These babies were lighter at birth and had a greatly increased risk of dying during the first year. You can see one of the patterns in Figure 2.9. Famine during the first three months (point *E*) had essentially no effect; but if the mother was malnourished during the final three months (point *B*), there was a big effect.

When you think back to the general rule I gave earlier—that interference with prenatal development has the biggest impact during the time of maximum growth of any system—this pattern makes good

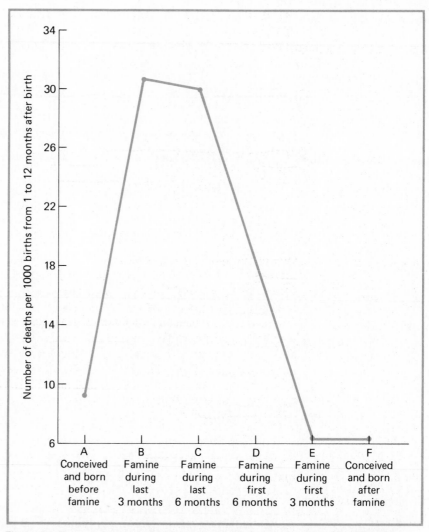

**Figure 2.9** These results from Stein's study on the famine in Holland show that the number of deaths between 1 and 12 months of life was much greater for infants whose mothers had experienced malnutrition during the last part of the pregnancy. (*Source:* Adapted from Zena Stein, Mervyn Susser, Gerhart Saenger, & Francis Marolla, *Famine and human development: The Dutch hunger winter of 1944–1945,* p. 161. Copyright © 1975 by Oxford University Press, Inc. Reprinted by permission.)

sense. The final three months is when the major gain in weight occurs (recall Figure 2.6), so we'd expect these babies to be small, as they are, and therefore perhaps more vulnerable to disease.

The final three months of gestation is also a time of rapid growth of the nervous system, so we might expect that malnutrition then would have some impact on the brain or nerves. And this is exactly what has been found, most clearly in research with animals. Malnutrition seems to result in fewer connective links between the nerve cells in the brain and in slower development of the sheathing around the nerves in the developing fetus (Lewin, 1975).

## Characteristics of the Mother that Affect the Normal Sequence

Aside from diet, drugs, and diseases, there are three characteristics of mothers that seem to make a difference in prenatal development: the mother's age, the number of children she has already had, and her overall emotional state during the pregnancy.

### The Mother's Age

One of the particularly intriguing trends in modern family life is the increasing likelihood that women will postpone their first pregnancy into their late twenties or early thirties (Giele, 1982). Of course there are many reasons for such decisions, chief among them being the increased need for second incomes in families and the desire of young women to complete job training and early career steps before bearing children. For our purposes in this chapter, though, the key question is the impact of maternal age on the developing child. Does it matter how old a woman is when she is pregnant? Are there any extra risks associated with pregnancy in a woman's thirties (or forties) as opposed to her twenties?

*Older Mothers*    Although the optimum age for pregnancy seems to be during a woman's twenties, the age of 35 is usually given as the definition of "older" pregnancies—the age past which risks increase notably. In particular, two kinds of risks appear to go up. First, I have already mentioned in discussing Down's syndrome that the risk of this chromosomal anomaly rises with increasing maternal age, particularly over 35. (In fact, women beyond this age are now quite routinely urged to undergo amniocentesis to check for this disorder.)

Second, for a *first* pregnancy over 35, there is an increased chance of stillbirth (fetal death) and longer labor (Kessner, 1973). However, it is important to emphasize that these heightened risks (except for the chance of a Down's syndrome child) are more likely for older mothers from poverty environments, which suggests that age is not the only factor. Rather, the mother's overall physical health is probably critical. Older mothers, particularly if they live in poverty, are likely to be less healthy. But older women who maintain good fitness appear to be able to reduce the risks of pregnancy considerably. So if you are going to have a late baby, the message seems to be: Stay in shape.

*Young Mothers*   At the other end of the age range, there are also added risks of a low–birth-weight infant, stillbirth, or difficulties during delivery (Kessner, 1973; Monkus & Bancalari, 1981). These effects are particularly evident for mothers 15 or younger. You can see the relationship between maternal age and the likelihood of a low–birth-weight infant or a stillbirth in Figure 2.10.

Teenage pregnancies represent a large (and possibly growing) percentage of all births in the United States (Scott, 1980). Something on the order of 17 to 20 percent of all births are to teenagers, of which about a third are to girls under 17. Perhaps 30,000 babies are born each year to girls 15 or younger. Given the fact that such very young mothers have not completed their own growth and thus have extra nutritional needs of their own, we should probably not be surprised that such pregnancies are at higher risk for low birth weight or fetal death.

But as is true for pregnancies in older women, teenage pregnancies appear to be risky mostly because teenagers who get pregnant are more likely to be poor (and thus probably have poor nutrition) and because

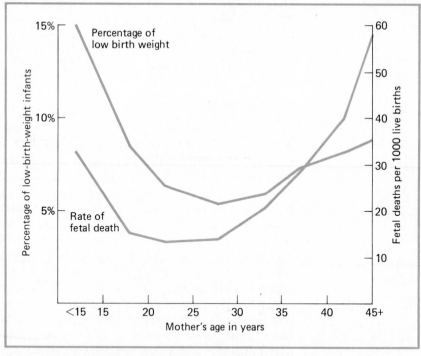

**Figure 2.10** Both younger and older mothers are more likely to have low–birth-weight infants or to have infants who die within a year of birth, as you can see clearly from these curves. But a great deal of this pattern is caused by the fact that younger mothers receive poorer prenatal care and that older mothers are likely to be generally less healthy. (*Sources:* Reproduced from D. Kessner, *Infant death: An analysis by maternal risk and health care,* 1973, p. 100, with the permission of the National Academy of Sciences, Washington, D.C.; and Keller, 1981, p. 8.)

teenagers are less likely to get decent prenatal care. When pregnant teenagers *do* have proper diets and adequate prenatal care, they are no more likely to have problems with the pregnancy or delivery than are women in their twenties (Robertson, 1981; Chilman, 1980).

Overall, while the mother's age can help us to predict problems in a pregnancy, it is probably not the age itself that is most critical; rather, it is the general physical and nutritional condition of the mother that matters the most.

## Number of Pregnancies

As a general rule, women who have had more than four pregnancies are at greater risk (as are their offspring) than are women who have had fewer. Their babies are more likely to be stillborn and to be smaller at birth (Kessner, 1973). Eleanor Maccoby and her colleagues (1979) have also found that any child after the first, especially if the pregnancies are closely spaced, has lower levels of hormones in his blood at birth. In particular, firstborn boys in this study had much higher levels of testosterone (the male hormone) at birth than did later-born boys. We don't know yet what the implications of such a difference may be for development, but this study does point to the possibility of some kinds of physical "depletion" in the mother as a result of pregnancy that can affect the physical development of later-born children.

## The Mother's Emotional State

Finally, the mother's state of mind during the pregnancy seems to have some effect. Arnold Sameroff and Michael Chandler (1975) have concluded that a woman who experiences prolonged or severe anxiety during her pregnancy—for whatever reason—has increased risk of a difficult pregnancy, including more nausea and vomiting, miscarriage, premature delivery, and longer and more difficult labor.

It doesn't seem quite fair that the women who are the most anxious are more likely to have their worst fears confirmed, but that's the way it seems to work. Furthermore, the mother's nervousness or anxiety also seems to affect the infant after birth. Infants born to tense or anxious mothers are more irritable, cry more, and are more likely to spit up or have intestinal problems—a pattern called *colic* (Lakin, 1957). There may be a kind of "self-fulfilling prophecy" here—mothers who expect to have more trouble with their infants may in fact have more troublesome babies because of the way they respond to their children. But the connection may be physiological rather than purely psychological. Prolonged anxiety during the pregnancy changes the chemical composition of the mother's blood, which may have some effect on the developing fetus that would account for the child's later irritability.

Of course, not all women who are anxious or unhappy about their pregnancy have difficulties or have colicky babies, and we don't know why this relationship holds only for some women and not for others. Some women may be anxious and upset for most of their pregnancy, others only for a short while. Some may eat poorly or drink or smoke more because of their nervousness, while others may not react to their anxiety in this way. We don't understand the links yet, but staying calm and unstressed during pregnancy seems like a useful thing to do—if you can manage it!

## AN OVERVIEW OF RISKS AND LONG-TERM CONSEQUENCES OF PRENATAL PROBLEMS

Every time I write this chapter I am aware that the list of "things that can go wrong" seems to get longer and longer and scarier and scarier. Physicians, biologists, and psychologists keep learning more about both the major and the subtle effects of prenatal environmental variations, so the number of "warnings" to pregnant women seems to increase weekly. One of the ironies of this is that too much worry about such potential consequences can make a woman more anxious, and anxiety is on the list of warnings! So before you begin worrying too much, let me try to put this information into better perspective.

First, let me say again that *most* pregnancies are normal and largely uneventful, and most babies are healthy and normal at birth.

Second, there are specific preventive steps that any woman can take to reduce the risks for herself and her unborn child. She can be properly immunized; she can quit smoking and drinking; she can watch her diet and make sure her weight gain is sufficient; and she and the child's father can have genetic counseling. In addition, she can get early and regular prenatal care. It is *very* clear from a number of studies, including Kessner's major study of pregnancies in New York City (1973), that mothers who receive adequate prenatal care reduce the risks to themselves and their infants.

The third positive point is that if something does go wrong, chances are good that the negative consequences to the child will be short-term rather than permanent.

Some negative outcomes *are* permanent and have long-term consequences for the child. Chromosomal anomalies, including Down's syndrome or deviations in sex chromosome patterns, are permanent and are nearly always associated with lasting mental retardation or school difficulties (Pennington et al., 1982). Physical defects cannot be altered (although many can be treated successfully after birth). Permanent effects are also caused by "environmental" influences, such as alcohol abuse (which causes fetal alcohol syndrome) or certain maternal diseases (such as rubella, which causes deafness) or drugs (such as thalido-

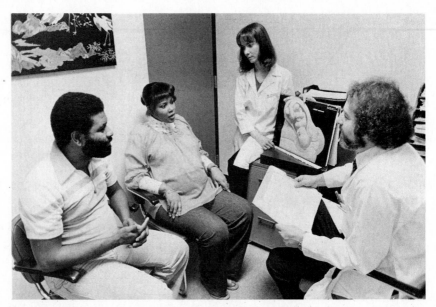

**Figure 2.11** This woman, by seeking out prenatal health care, is reducing the risks both for herself and for her infant.

mide). And as we'll see in Chapter 3, *very* low–birth-weight infants—those under about 1500 g (approximately 3½ pounds)—have an increased risk of persisting, long-term learning problems or low IQ, regardless of the richness of the environment in which they are reared.

But many of the effects I have talked about in this chapter may be detectable only for the first few years of the child's life and then only in certain families.

The relationship between prenatal problems and long-term outcomes, in fact, is a perfect example of the kind of interaction effect I talked about in Chapter 1 (recall Figure 1.10). As Horowitz (1982) points out, low–birth-weight infants or those with poor prenatal nutrition or other problems are likely to show persisting problems if they are reared in unstimulating or unsupportive environments. The same children reared in more rich and varied environments typically catch up to their healthier peers by school age, if not before. So it is not the prenatal problem by itself that is the cause of long-term negative effects; it seems to be a combination of a prenatal problem and a relatively poor early environment.

As one example, a number of researchers have found that low–birth-weight infants (at least those between about 3 and 5½ pounds) are only at a long-term disadvantage when they have also been reared in a poverty environment. For example, Emmy Werner and her colleagues (1967) found that the average IQ of a group of

2-year-olds who had experienced some sort of problem during gestation or birth and been reared in middle-class families was 91. Children from the same community, with the same level of complications, who had been reared in economically poor families had average IQs of 61.

The study of prenatally malnourished children by Zeskind and Ramey (1981) that I described in Chapter 1 (see Table 1.2) is another good example of the same interactive process.

Studies like these persuade me that problems experienced by the embryo or fetus may make an infant more vulnerable to later stresses or problems or may mean that the child requires a better family environment to develop normally. But in many cases such normal development *is* possible. So don't despair when you read the long list of cautions and potential problems. The story isn't as gloomy as it first seems.

## SEX DIFFERENCES IN PRENATAL DEVELOPMENT

Since nearly all prenatal development is controlled by maturational codes that are the same for all members of our species—male and female alike—there aren't very many sex differences in prenatal development. But there are a few, and they set the stage for some of the physical differences we'll see at later ages.

1. As I've already pointed out, boys secrete testosterone during the early months of gestation, which leads to the "fixing" of the brain so that the proper male hormones are secreted at the right time later in life. Girls do not secrete any equivalent hormone prenatally.
2. Girls are a bit faster in some aspects of prenatal development, particularly skeletal development. They are about three to four weeks ahead in bone development at birth.
3. Despite the more rapid development of girls, boys are heavier and longer at birth.
4. Boys are considerably more vulnerable to all kinds of prenatal problems. Many more boys than girls are conceived—on the order of about 120 to 150 male embryos to every 100 female—but more of the males are spontaneously aborted. At birth, there are about 105 boys for every 100 girls. Boys are also more likely to experience injuries at birth (perhaps because they are larger), and they have more congenital malformations.

The difference in vulnerability is particularly intriguing, especially since it seems to persist. Older boys are more prone to problems as well. One possible explanation for this may lie in the basic genetic difference. The XX combination affords the girl some protection against "bad" genes that may be carried on the X chromosome, since she would have to inherit the same one from both parents in order to develop some specific problem. The boy, on the other hand, could inherit a disorder by receiving the gene for it only from his mother, since he has only the one X chromosome. This may be the explanation of greater male susceptibility to infectious disease, since a gene that affects such susceptibility is carried on the X chromosome and is not matched by a "blocking" gene on the Y chromosome (Brooks-Gunn & Matthews, 1979). Whatever the cause, the difference in vulnerability is striking.

## SOCIAL CLASS DIFFERENCES IN PRENATAL DEVELOPMENT

I will be talking much more fully about social class differences in development in Chapter 13, but I cannot leave this chapter without saying a word about the impact of social class on the risks of pregnancy and birth.

The basic sequence of fetal development is clearly no different for children born to poor mothers than children born to middle-class mothers. But many of the problems that can negatively affect prenatal development are more common among the poor. For example, mothers who have not graduated from high school are about twice as likely as mothers with a college education to have a low–birth-weight infant or to have an infant stillborn (Kessner, 1973).

This difference appears to be primarily due to life-style, and particularly to the lack of prenatal care among many poor women. Among the poor, women are more likely to have their first pregnancy earlier and to have more pregnancies overall; they are less likely to be immunized against such diseases as rubella; and they seek prenatal care much later (if at all) in their pregnancies.

We have evidence that the lack of prenatal care is one of the keys, because when major public health efforts have been mounted, with low-cost or free prenatal care made easily available to the poor, the infant mortality rate has dropped sharply (Kessner, 1973). So we know that many of the social class differences we see can be prevented. If we were willing to devote the resources needed for such an effort, we could significantly reduce not only the rate of infant death but also the rate of physical abnormalities and perhaps even mental retardation. Unfortunately, in these times of government belt tightening, programs for pregnant women have been among the items cut from federal, state, and local budgets. If you will forgive me for getting up on my soapbox for a moment, I want to say what a monumentally false economy that seems to me—not just financially (since it is far more expensive to treat and care for a damaged child than it is to prevent that damage) but morally as well. It is hard for me to understand how, in a society like ours, we can justify anything less than a total effort to provide the best possible nutrition and prenatal care for all pregnant women. (End of soapbox speech!)

SUMMARY

1. Conception occurs when the male sperm penetrates the female ovum, ordinarily in the fallopian tube.
2. At conception 23 chromosomes from the sperm join with 23 from the ovum to form the 46 that will be reproduced in each cell of the new child's body.
3. The child's sex is determined by one of the 23 pairs of chromosomes, XX for a girl and XY for a boy.
4. Chromosomes are made up of genes, which are in turn made up of deoxyribonucleic acid (DNA).
5. Individual genes may be either dominant or recessive. If dominant, they will "win" in any mixed pairing of genes from the father and mother.
6. During the first days after conception, the initial cell divides (mitosis), travels down the fallopian tube, and is implanted in the wall of the uterus.
7. Over the next weeks, cell differentiation takes place, with the placenta, umbilical cord, and amniotic cavity all formed.
8. From 2 to 8 weeks, the developing organism is called the embryo; from 8 to 40 weeks, it is called the fetus.
9. Most organ systems are developed in rudimentary form during the embryonic period; the fetal period involves enlargement and refinements.
10. During the embryonic period, the XY embryo secretes the hormone testosterone, which stimulates the growth of male genitalia and shifts the brain into a "male" pattern. Without that hormone, the embryo develops as a girl.
11. The normal sequence of development prenatally seems heavily determined by maturation—a "road map" contained in the genes.
12. Problems in prenatal development can begin at conception if a genetic abnormality, such as Down's syndrome, occurs or if the child receives recessive genes for an inherited disease from both parents.
13. Prior to conception, it is possible to test for the presence of genes for many inherited diseases. After conception, amniocentesis may be used to diagnose diseases and genetic abnormalities prenatally.
14. Some diseases contracted by the mother may affect the child, most notably rubella, syphilis, and (more common recently) herpes. These may result in disease in the child or in physical abnormalities.
15. Both alcohol and nicotine have harmful effects on the developing fetus; the greater the dose, the greater the potential effect.
16. The mother's diet also makes a difference, particularly if she is severely malnourished. In that case, there is an increased risk of stillbirth, having a low–birth-weight infant, and infant death during the first year of life.

17. Older mothers and very young mothers, along with those who have borne four or more children, also run increased risks, but these risks are greatly reduced if the mother is in good health and receives adequate prenatal care.
18. The mother's emotional state may also affect the developing child. The more anxious the mother, the more difficult her pregnancy and delivery and the more irritable her infant is likely to be.
19. Some difficulties in prenatal development can produce permanent disabilities or deformities, such as Down's syndrome or deafness from rubella. Some produce lasting problems, as in the case of very low birth weight. But many disorders associated with prenatal problems can be overcome if the child is reared in a supportive and stimulating environment.
20. Sex differences in prenatal development (few in number) include variations in hormone secretions, rate of skeletal development, size, and vulnerability to disorders and deformities. Boys are slower, bigger, and more vulnerable.
21. Nearly all potential problems of prenatal development are more common among poor women, but these increased risks can be greatly reduced with good diet and adequate prenatal care.

## KEY TERMS

**Amniocentesis**   A medical test for genetic abnormalities in the embryo/fetus that may be done at about 15 weeks of gestation.

**Autosomes**   The 22 pairs of chromosomes in which both members of the pair are the same shape and carry parallel information.

**Blastocyst**   The name used for the small mass of cells, about two weeks after conception, that implants itself into the wall of the uterus.

**Chromosomes**   The portion of each cell in the body that contains genetic information. Each chromosome is made up of many genes.

**Crossing over**   The process that occurs during meiosis in which genetic material from pairs of chromosomes may be exchanged.

**Deoxyribonucleic acid**   Called DNA for short, this is the chemical of which genes are composed.

**Dominant gene**   A gene that "wins out" over a recessive gene in cases in which the individual inherits mixed signals from the father and the mother.

**Down's syndrome**   A genetic anomaly in which there are three number 21 chromosomes rather than two. Children born with this genetic pattern are usually mentally retarded and have characteristic physical features.

**Embryo**   The name given to the organism during the period of prenatal development from about two to eight weeks after conception, beginning with implantation of the cell mass into the uterine wall.

**Fallopian tube**   The tube down which the ovum travels to the uterus and in which conception usually occurs.

**Fetal alcohol syndrome (FAS)**   A pattern of physical abnormalities, including mental retardation and minor physical anomalies, found often in children born to alcoholic mothers.

**Fetus**   The name given to the developing organism from about eight weeks after conception until birth.

**Germ cells**   Sperm and ova. These cells, unlike all other cells of the body, contain only 23 chromosomes rather than 23 pairs.

**Meiosis**   The process of cell division that produces germ cells in which only one member of each chromosome pair is passed on to the new cell.

**Mitosis**   The process of cell division common for all cells other than germ cells, in which both new cells contain 23 pairs of chromosomes.

**Ovum**   The germ cell produced by women that, if fertilized by a sperm from the male, forms the basis for the developing organism.

**Placenta**   The organ that develops during gestation that lies between the fetus and the wall of the uterus and through which the mother's blood is filtered.

**Recessive gene**   A gene that "loses out" in competition with a dominant gene. When two recessive genes for the same characteristic are inherited, however, that characteristic will develop.

**Rubella**   A form of measles that if contracted during the first three months of a pregnancy may have severe effects on the embryo or fetus.

**Uterus**   The female organ in which the blastocyst implants itself and within which the embryo/fetus develops (popularly referred to as the womb).

## SUGGESTED READINGS

I have not found any highly readable, recent, general books or articles about prenatal development, so many of the sources on this list are somewhat older than what I usually recommend. But these are still good places to look for more information.

Apgar, V., & Beck, J. *Is my baby all right? A guide to birth defects.* New York: Trident, 1972.
An excellent source for more information about any of the genetic and environmental sources of defects described in this chapter.

The Boston Women's Health Collective. *Our bodies, ourselves: A book by and for women* (2d ed.). New York: Simon & Schuster, 1977.
Although this book is really focused on the adult female's body, it has an excellent discussion of health during pregnancy. You may not be entirely in sympathy with all of the political views included, but there is no better compact source of information on pregnancy.

Lewin, R. Starved brains. *Psychology today* 9, no. 4 (1975): 29–33.
If you are interested in the problems of malnutrition and diet, this is an excellent place to start.

Nilsson, L. *A child is born.* New York: Delacorte Press, Seymour Lawrence, 1977.
This book is full of marvelous photographs of the embryo and fetus. It also has a good basic text describing prenatal development and problems of pregnancy.

Smith, D. W.; Bierman, E. L.; & Robinson, N. M. *The biologic ages of man* (2d ed.). Philadelphia: Saunders, 1978.
This book was prepared for the use of first-year medical students at the University of Washington, so some of it is more technical than you may want. But the descriptions of pregnancy and prenatal development are extremely clear and interesting, with many good charts and photographs.

# 3.

# *birth and the newborn child*

Imagine (if you can) that you are a woman nine months pregnant with your first child. The long months of prenatal life are over, and the baby is about to be born. If you are like many of today's mothers, you and your partner have looked into alternative locations or "styles" of delivery; both of you may have taken prenatal classes, and you have tried to prepare yourselves for what the baby will be like and how the advent of this new member of the family will change your lives. You are a little apprehensive about the process of delivery and a bit uncertain about what to expect from the baby and about your own abilities to cope, but you are eager for the whole adventure to begin.

In this chapter I want to try to answer some of the questions that new parents reasonably ask about birth and about newborn babies. I have already talked about some of the things that matter during pregnancy. What things matter about birth? Does it make a difference whether the baby is born in a hospital or at home? Does it matter if the father is present or not? What happens if the birth is too early or if something else goes wrong? What can you expect of your baby during the first weeks of life? What can she do, what can she perceive?

Beyond giving some basic practical information, my second purpose in this chapter is to describe the beginnings of the child's independent life so that you can be clearly aware of the starting point for the long developmental journey. In the past few decades, researchers have discovered a great many things about newborns, and we now realize that these apparently helpless creatures really have a wide range of quite remarkable abilities. This knowledge has not only changed the information given out to new parents, it has also changed our theories of development.

## BIRTH

### The Normal Process

Physicians and midwives divide the period of labor into three unequal parts.

*The First Stage of Labor*   The first stage is the longest. Uterine contractions begin, initially spaced quite widely apart and later more frequent and rhythmical, Two important processes are going on in this stage: **dilation and effacement.** The cervix (the opening at the bottom of the uterus) must open up like the lens of a camera (dilation) and also flatten out (effacement). At the time of actual delivery of the infant, the cervix must normally be dilated to about 10 cm (approximately 4 inches). At the end of the first stage of labor, about 7 to 8 cm of dilation has been reached.

This part of labor has been likened to putting on a turtleneck sweater with a neck that is too tight. You have to pull and stretch the neck of the sweater with your head in order to get it on. Eventually the neck is stretched wide enough so that the widest part of your head can pass through. It is this widening and stretching that occur in the first stage of labor.

*Transition Stage*   At the end of the first stage, there is a period (usually brief) in which the final 2 to 3 cm of dilation are achieved. This period is very uncomfortable for many women, since the uterine contractions come quite close together and very strongly. Following this comes the urge to help the infant out by pushing. When the *birth attendant* (a phrase I will use to refer to the physician or midwife) is sure the cervix is fully dilated, she or he will encourage this pushing, and the second stage of labor begins.

*Second Stage of Labor*   The second stage is the actual delivery, when the baby's head moves past the stretched cervix, into the birth canal, and finally out of the mother's body. Most infants are delivered head first, facing the floor (if the mother is lying on her back). A few babies are born feet first or bottom first, and in these deliveries the birth attendant must often take a more active role, perhaps using medical instruments to aid the baby's descent.

*The Third Stage of Labor*   The final stage is the delivery of the placenta and other material from the uterus. You can see all of these steps schematically in Figure 3.1.

## The First Greeting: Parents and Newborns

The brief description I've just provided may give the bare details, but it certainly does not convey the emotions of the mother or father. Some of the amazement and joy parents often feel are captured in a wonderful set of tape recordings, collected by Aiden Macfarlane (1977), of conversations between mothers and fathers immediately following delivery, after the baby had been given to the mother to hold. Here's one excerpt (pp. 64–65):

> *Mother:* Hello darling. Meet your dad. You're just like your dad (baby yells).
> *Father:* I'm going home!
> *Mother:* Oh, you've gone quiet (laughs). Oh darling, she's just like you—she's got your little tiny nose.
> *Father:* It'll grow like yours.
> *Mother:* She's big, isn't she? What do you reckon? (Doctor makes a comment). Oh look, she's got hair. It's a girl—you're supposed to be all little. Gosh. Oh, she's lovely. Oh, she's opened her eyes (laughs). Oh lovely (kisses baby).

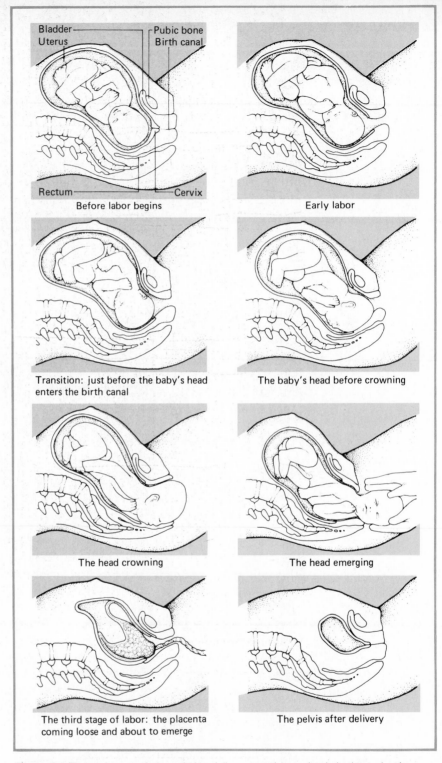

Before labor begins

Early labor

Transition: just before the baby's head enters the birth canal

The baby's head before crowning

The head crowning

The head emerging

The third stage of labor: the placenta coming loose and about to emerge

The pelvis after delivery

**Figure 3.1** The sequence of steps during delivery are shown clearly in these drawings. You can see the dilation stage, transition, the delivery itself, and the delivery of the placenta.

Notice both the pleasure the mother shows here and her concern about the child's physical features. Klaus and Kennell (1976) as well as Macfarlane have found that most parents are intensely interested in having the baby look at them right away. They are delighted if the baby opens her eyes and will try to stimulate her to do so if she doesn't. Klaus and Kennell also noticed that mothers (or fathers) would first touch the infant rather gingerly with the tip of the finger and then proceed gradually to stroking with the full hand. All of this seems to be part of the acquaintance process that occurs immediately after birth, whenever the parent first has an opportunity to hold and examine the infant.

## Conditions during Birth: Where, Who, and What

In perhaps 90 percent of all births (Macfarlane, 1977), the delivery occurs with few (or no) complications. The whole process is normal and satisfying to the mother, and the infant emerges from the process looking quite healthy. Still, there are many decisions about the delivery that can affect the child's health or the mother's satisfaction with the delivery. These decisions are made by a variety of people in the system—the parents, the birth attendant, the hospital staff, to name just a few. Since many of you will face these decisions at some point in the future, I want to give you the best current information I have.

*Drugs during Delivery*    One key decision concerns the use of drugs during delivery. This decision is normally made both by the woman and by the birth attendant, although hospital policies also enter in.

The obvious purpose of the drugs has been to reduce the discomfort of labor for the mother. But what about the infant? Questions about the potentially harmful effects of obstetrical medications on the infant have been raised only in the past 10 to 15 years, primarily by developmental psychologists (such as Yvonne Brackbill, 1979). There is still a great deal to be learned about such effects, but let me at least describe the current state of our knowledge.

First of all, despite a move toward "natural" (largely drug-free) childbirth among some groups of women, the use of drugs is still the norm rather than the exception. Brackbill (1979) estimates that approximately 95 percent of deliveries involve some drug administration.

Three types of drugs are commonly given during labor and delivery: (1) *analgesics* (such as Demerol), which are given during the first stage of labor to reduce pain; (2) *sedatives* or *tranquilizers* (such as Nembutol, Valium, or Thorazine), given during stage 1 labor to reduce anxiety; and (3) *anesthesia*, given during transition or the second stage of labor to block pain either totally (general anesthesia) or in portions of the body (local anesthesia). Many women receive all three types of drugs; others may receive only one or two of them. Because of the wide variability of drug combinations and dosages, it is very difficult to design research that sorts out specific effects, but some preliminary answers are emerging.

Nearly all drugs given to the mother during labor pass through the placenta and enter the fetal bloodstream. So the infant is obviously going to show some short-term effects. Infants whose mothers have received any type of drug are ordinarily found to be more sluggish, to suck less vigorously, to gain less weight in the days and weeks immediately after delivery, and to spend more time sleeping (Brackbill, 1979). In one recent study, Ann Murray and her colleagues (1981) found that babies whose mothers had received anesthesia were less predictable in their awake or sleepy state immediately after birth. A month later, the mothers of these babies thought the infants were harder to care for and less sociable. The mother who was given medication may thus find herself becoming acquainted with a less-responsive baby, which may introduce a slight "bias" into the developing mother-infant interaction pattern.

We know less about the long-term effects. Most physicians and psychologists assumed that the effects of delivery medication would wear off during the first few days and weeks as the drugs were eliminated from the child's bloodstream. But there are now hints that this may not be the case. Brackbill (1979), who has reviewed all the existing evidence, reports that there are now several studies in which infants have been followed for the entire first year. In a number of cases, the effects of the delivery medication can still be detected at these later ages. For example, 8-month-old children whose mothers were given anesthetic scored more poorly on tests of motor development—they sat and stood a little later, among other things. This effect was not as evident for infants whose mothers had been given only analgesics or sedatives.

If there *are* long-term effects (and so far we don't know whether there are), it is possible that the process is an indirect one: The sluggishness or unpredictability of the medicated newborn may affect the mother's first interactions with the infant. Many mothers will adapt to these qualities in their babies, but a few mother-infant pairs, as a result of the greater difficulty of their first encounters, will develop long-term patterns of interaction that are less optimal. The infant's development may be affected as result.

What does all this mean for the individual mother? I think it means two things. First, the most cautious choice is to have as little medication as possible during delivery—consistent with your level of tolerance. Second, if you have received medication, particularly anesthesia, bear in mind that the child is also drugged and that this will affect his behavior in the beginning. If you *allow* for this effect (and realize that it will wear off), the chances are that your relationship with your child will not be significantly affected.

*The Location of Birth: Home versus Hospital*   A second decision parents must make has to do with where the baby is to be born. Home deliveries are on the increase, as are nontraditional delivery settings in hospitals. "Rooming-in" arrangements, in which the mother and newborn can be together continuously after delivery, are now more common again (as they were several decades ago), and **"birthing rooms"** in hospitals are also being developed (see Figure 3.2). These are rooms designed to be as like a home as possible, in some cases with a nurse-midwife rather than a physician in attendance.

The arguments made for home or birthing-room deliveries are primarily that they are more natural, that they treat pregnancy and delivery as a normal process (rather than as an illness), and that the birth is less likely to be traumatic if the mother is in a comfortable, familiar setting. The counterargument (particularly against home deliveries) is that they are less safe. If anything should go wrong, full hospital facilities may not be available quickly enough. Clearly, a

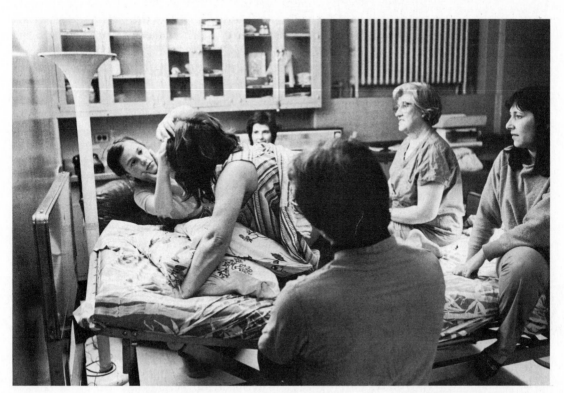

**Figure 3.2** Birthing rooms, like this one in a modern hospital, are becoming increasingly common as mothers and birth attendants search for an alternative that has the naturalness and comfort of home but the safety of the hospital. The father is usually present during the entire labor and delivery and may serve as the mother's "coach."

birthing room in a hospital is an attempt at a middle ground in this controversy.

Parents are obviously concerned with these issues of safety for the mother and the infant. Ease or comfort for the mother and father may also be critical ingredients in the decision. As a developmental psychologist, though, my concerns are somewhat broader. I also want to know whether the location or conditions of the delivery have a direct impact on the long-range development of the child. Or could the location of delivery have an indirect effect, by influencing the parents in some way that changes how they interact with the child?

I think these are important questions, and I wish I could give you firm answers to them. But I cannot. It is clear that no greater physical risk for the child *necessarily* accompanies home delivery. For example, in Holland, home deliveries are still extremely common; any woman who shows no signs of prenatal difficulty and has no history of such difficulty can have her baby at home. The rate of problems in these home deliveries is *very* low (Macfarlane, 1977), so it can obviously be done safely for the child. But whether babies born at home or in birthing rooms are *better* off than infants born in more traditional hospital settings is simply not clear from the information we have. One of the difficulties (at least for the researcher trying to answer such questions) is that women who choose home delivery or a birthing room are different in other ways from women who opt for accustomed procedures. They may have used fewer drugs during pregnancy or eaten differently or have different attitudes about delivery and motherhood. If we found that home-delivered infants were better off, we couldn't be sure that it was the delivery location and not one of these other differences that was the cause.

The indirect effect is even harder to pin down. Aiden Macfarlane (1977), in his discussion of this issue, reports that women who have home deliveries are less likely to be depressed in the days after giving birth than are women delivering in a hospital. But whether the depression accompanying hospital deliveries is long-lasting or whether it has any long-term effect on the mother's relationship with her infant we do not know. Given all this ignorance, and barring any signs of trouble in the pregnancy, the decision about the location of the delivery seems to be very much a matter of personal choice.

*The Who of Delivery: The Presence of Fathers*   A third important decision has to do with who should be present at the delivery. In particular, how important is it that the father be present?

Participation by fathers in the delivery room—as "coach" or merely as observer or emotional supporter of the mother—is clearly on the increase but still varies widely from one hospital to another and from one part of the country to another. In one survey of eight midwestern hospitals, James Garbarino (1980) found that most physicians and hospitals were *willing* to have the father present at delivery but did not actively *encourage* this practice.

Given the available evidence, this is a somewhat disappointing (although perhaps not surprising) attitude. Having the father present clearly seems to be beneficial for the mother as well as for the father's involvement with the infant.

Mothers report that having the father present is a great help, particularly if he has gone through prenatal classes with her. In one study, William Henneborn and Rosemary Cogan (1975) found that mothers who had their husbands present during delivery reported less pain and used less medication than did mothers whose husbands were not present—both highly desirable effects.

The most important effect, though, may be on the father's attachment to his infant. Fathers who are present at delivery or who are given a chance to hold and greet the baby immediately after delivery appear to become more *engrossed* in the infant—to use Greenberg and Morris' term (1974)—and to be more involved in the child's care throughout the first weeks and months of life than are fathers who have lacked this early contact (Peterson, Mehl, & Leiderman, 1979; Greenberg & Morris, 1974; Yogman, 1982). The engrossment of the fathers is visible to an observer, but the fathers themselves are also aware of their preoccupation with the infant. They say they want to touch and hold the infant, are absorbed by the baby's movements and skills, are more comfortable holding the baby, and think they are better at distinguishing their own infant from others in the newborn nursery than are fathers who lacked early contact.

I should point out that the father's presence at the actual delivery does not seem to be critical for this early "bond" to be formed. Very early contact outside of the delivery room seems to work as well. But given the benefits to the mother of having the father present at delivery, it seems to me to be the optimum procedure for both purposes. As James Garbarino (1980) points out, having the father participate in the delivery also underlines the fact that childbirth is a *family* process, not just a female process.

*Other Elements of the Conditions of Birth*     There are other elements in the complex of decisions surrounding delivery. As you will see in Chapter 11, a setting in which it is possible for the parent(s) to handle and observe their infant immediately after birth seems to help form a strong first attachment from parent to child. Many parents will want to seek out a birth attendant and setting in which such early contact is possible. Another element is the "gentleness" of the birth conditions, which I have discussed in Box 3.1. Each of you, as a prospective parent, needs to give these choices some careful thought, so that you will be prepared when your own children are born.

BOX 3.1

# GENTLE BIRTHS: ARE THEY IMPORTANT?

Still another new direction in childbirth procedures has been suggested by a French obstetrician, Frederick Leboyer (1975). Leboyer is convinced that the process of birth is extremely traumatic and painful for the baby. He describes the experience as "hell and white hot" because of the bright lights, noise, and rough handling. He argues that physicians need to try to reduce the stress as much as possible. Deliveries done using the **Leboyer method** are usually referred to as "gentle" births and involve a number of changes from "typical" delivery procedures.

In a "Leboyer birth" no pressure is placed on the head during stage 2 of labor, while the head is being delivered. The room is darkened as much as possible, and the birth attendants speak quietly or in whispers. Sometimes there is soothing or quiet music played. After the baby is delivered, she is placed on the mother's abdomen immediately. No effort is made to stimulate the infant's crying or breathing, except that the infant's mouth and nose are cleared if they are blocked. The umbilical cord is clamped only after the baby begins to breathe on her own and after the cord has stopped pulsing. A few minutes later, the baby is placed in a deep, warm bath, where she remains for five to six minutes. This recreates the sensations of the warm liquid she has been accustomed to in utero and soothes the infant still further.

Many physicians, while agreeing that births can and probably should be made more gentle, do not buy all of Leboyer's arguments and do not think that every change he suggests is essential. For prospective parents, this may be an important dispute, since many of you are "shopping around" more now, searching for the conditions of delivery that seem best to you. So just how right is Leboyer?

First of all, is the baby really traumatized at birth? Opinions differ. Some psychoanalytically oriented theorists, such as Otto Rank (1929), have been convinced that birth is traumatic. Rank went so far as to suggest that "birth trauma" left an emotional scar that lasted throughout life. Other observers, including Macfarlane

## Some Things that Can Go Wrong

While it is true that most deliveries are quite normal, as with prenatal development there are some things that can go wrong.

*Anoxia: Lack of Oxygen*    Sometimes during the process of delivery, the newborn has her oxygen supply cut off for a short while. (Such a loss of oxygen is called **anoxia**.) Most often this occurs because the umbilical circulation system fails to continue the supply of blood oxygen until the baby breathes or because the umbilical cord has been squeezed in some way during delivery. In severe cases, where the loss of oxygen has been prolonged, there can be brain damage. Many cases of *cerebral palsy,* a major motor disability that may involve loss of muscle control over the legs and arms or head, are linked to anoxia at birth or prenatally.

Fortunately, recent evidence points to a considerable ability on the part of the newborn to survive lack of oxygen without damage (Tanner,

(1977), have been struck instead by how capable and adaptable the newborn is. The baby seems to adjust rapidly to the demands of the environment he finds himself thrust into. Obviously, this is a difficult question to study systematically, so opinions are about all we will have to go on.

A second important question is whether the "gentle" method has any lasting effect on the child or on the parents and their relationships with the child. Do "Leboyer children" turn out better in later months or years? Do they respond differently to their parents?

Given the potential importance of these questions, I have been astonished that there has been so little decent research comparing children who experienced gentle births with those who have had more normal treatment. Comparing the outcomes for mothers who *chose* Leboyer birth methods with those for mothers who did not simply won't give us the answers, since these two groups are so different in other ways. Only by randomly assigning some mothers to Leboyer deliveries and others to "normal" deliveries can we really make the comparison. I know of only one such study (Nelson et al., 1980; Saigal et al., 1981), and in this case no differences were found between Leboyer-delivered babies and moderately gentle, normal hospital-delivered babies on any measures up through 8 months of life.

Despite this surprising lack of evidence, I suspect that Leboyer's methods, or at least portions of them (such as placing the infant on the mother's stomach immediately, delaying the cutting of the cord, even softer lighting and less noise), will become fairly widely accepted. Leboyer's arguments called the attention of obstetricians to the *possible* impact of some of their accustomed practices, and many physicians and nurse-midwives have consequently taken another look at the conditions of birth. Then, too, many parents find the conditions recommended by Leboyer to be soothing, and that is no small argument. Were I giving birth today, I would certainly search for a birth attendant who was sensitive to these questions. But since I am not convinced that the full "Leboyer method" is critical for the child or the parent, I would not search high and low for that rare birth attendant who follows the entire Leboyer procedure. You will have to make your own choice.

1978). Short-term anoxia at birth does not seem to have permanent effects in most cases (Sameroff & Chandler, 1975). And many of the significantly bad consequences (such as cerebral palsy) that used to be attributed to anoxia at birth are now seen often as the result of prenatal damage. Thus, a newborn may not be damaged because he failed to start breathing quickly at birth but may fail to start breathing because he is already damaged.

*Cesarean Section*    In some cases, because the mother's pelvis is shaped so that normal delivery is difficult, or if the mother has an active case of herpes II virus (see Chapter 2), or if new fetal monitoring systems show that the fetus is experiencing distress during delivery, the baby may be delivered through an abdominal incision rather than vaginally. This is called a **cesarean section**—a name that derives from the legend that Julius Caesar was delivered in this way.

C-sections (as they are usually abbreviated) are becoming remarkably common in the United States, amounting to as many as 15 percent of all deliveries (Bottoms, Rosen, & Sokol, 1980). The short-term effect of such deliveries may well be a healthier infant. But there is conflicting evidence about the long-term effect of C-section delivery on the mother-infant interaction.

On one side, there are reports that child abuse is more common at later ages among children delivered by C-section than among vaginally delivered children (Helfer, 1975). On the other hand, several investigators have found no major differences in the patterns of interaction of C-section mothers with their infants versus vaginally delivered mothers and infants (Field & Widmayer, 1980; Pedersen et al., 1981). Interestingly, fathers of C-section infants may be *more* involved in the care of the infant during the first year of life than are fathers of normally delivered babies, presumably because the mother is less able to care for the infant in the early weeks while she recovers from the surgery (Pedersen et al., 1981).

I am not sure how to make sense of these conflicting reports. It may be that in families that are otherwise at high risk for abusing a child, a C-section delivery simply stresses the system still more. But most families that experience a C-section delivery do not abuse their infants in any case, and they discover ways to adapt to this change in the normal delivery process.

*Low Birth Weight*   A potentially more serious complication is to have an infant born weighing less than the normal or optimum amount, a condition generally labeled as **low birth weight**. The cutoff point for this designation is generally 2500 g (about 5½ pounds).

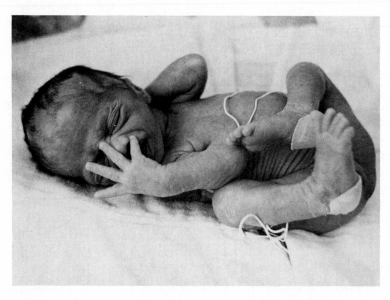

**Figure 3.3** This low–birth-weight baby looks fairly typical. He has the body hair and slightly puffy appearance found in most full-term babies but is smaller. Like many newborns, he is not overly attractive!

Infant weight is the single best predictor of infant mortality. For example, in one very large study of all the births in New York City during one year (Kessner, 1973), the mortality rate was 609 per 1000 for infants who weighed less than 1500 g (about 3¼ pounds). For babies who weighed between 1500 and 2500 g (3¼ to 5½ pounds, approximately), the mortality rate was 55 per 1000. By contrast, babies with optimum weight (between 3500 and 4500 g) had a risk of mortality of only about 6 per 1000. Present-day methods of care for the very low–birth-weight infant have reduced these mortality rates considerably, but birth weight is still a critical factor in the infant's short-term prognosis.

All lightweight babies used to be lumped into a single group, often called "**premature**." It is now clear, though, that it is very important to distinguish between several groups or types of low–birth-weight infants. Some infants have low birth weight because they are born too soon, usually called **preterm**, or short-gestation, infants. If the infant is below 1500 g, he would probably be called a **very low–birth-weight** infant. 3¼ lb

A second important type of low–birth-weight infant is the **small-for-date** baby. These are infants who are unusually light, given the number of weeks of gestation they have completed. They may even have completed the full 40 weeks of gestation but be under 2500 g. Infants in this group appear to have suffered from some kind of malnutrition or constriction of blood flow (from smoking, among other things) or other significant problem prenatally, while the preterm infant is merely early and may be developing normally in other respects (Tanner, 1978).

All low–birth-weight infants share some characteristics, including markedly lower levels of responsiveness at birth and in the early months of life (DiVitto & Goldberg, 1979; Barnard, Bee, & Hammond, 1984a). They are also all at higher risk of experiencing respiratory distress in the early weeks and may be slower in motor development than their normal-weight peers.

When we look at really long-term consequences of low birth weight, however, the distinction between preterm and small-for-date infants becomes very important. Preterm infants above 1500 g who are normal-sized for their length of gestation generally catch up to their normal peers within the first few years of life, particularly if they are reared in stimulating and supportive families. But both very low–birth-weight infants and small-for-date infants show much higher rates of long-term problems, including lower IQs, smaller size, and greater problems in school (Kitchen et al., 1980; Parkinson, Wallis, & Harvey, 1981). In one study of very low–birth-weight infants, Jane Hunt (1981) found that 14 percent of the children scored in the mentally retarded range on an IQ test at age 4 to 6 years, and a full 46 percent showed some form of learning disability at that same age.

Similar findings are now emerging from studies of small-for-date infants.

These findings underline the importance of paying attention to all the prenatal choices and behaviors that can affect the infant's weight—including smoking and diet. But they also emphasize the fact that a preterm birth, particularly if the infant is over 1500 g, although riskier for the baby, need not imply long-term problems. Preterm babies take a while to recover and catch up. But many of them *do* catch up and develop normally.

## THE NEWBORN: WHAT CAN HE DO?

The baby has been born. He cries, breathes, looks around a bit. But what else can he do in the early hours and days? On what skills does the infant build?

### Reflexes

Infants are born with a large collection of **reflexes**, which are automatic physical responses triggered involuntarily by a specific stimulus. Many of these reflexes are still present in adults, so you should be familiar with them—the knee jerk the doctor tests for, your automatic eye blink when a puff of air hits your eye, or the involuntary narrowing of the pupil of your eye when you're in a bright light are all examples.

In addition to these long-lasting reflexes, the newborn has a set of primitive reflexes, some of which are useful for his survival. I've listed some of the more helpful and interesting of these in Table 3.1.

**TABLE 3.1**

**Major reflexes in the newborn baby**

| Reflex | Description |
| --- | --- |
| Rooting | An infant touched on the cheek will turn toward the touch and search for something to suck on. |
| Sucking | When she gets her mouth around something suckable, she sucks. |
| Swallowing | This reflex is present at birth, though it is not well coordinated with breathing initially. |
| Moro | This is also called the "startle reflex." You see it in an infant when she hears a loud noise or gets any kind of a physical shock. She throws both arms outward and arches her back (see Figure 3.4). |
| Babinsky | If you stroke an infant on the bottom of his foot, he first splays out his toes and then curls them in. |
| Grasp | A baby will curl his fingers around your hand or any graspable objects. The signal for this is a touch on the palm. |
| Stepping | If you hold a very young infant up so that her feet just touch the ground, she will show walkinglike movements, stepping her feet alternately. |

Clearly, the rooting/sucking/swallowing reflexes are essential if the baby is to get fed, and the Moro reflex is helpful in moving the baby away from unpleasant things. The Babinsky and grasp reflexes, though, are less useful. They are primitive reflexes, governed by the midbrain—the part of the brain that develops earliest. Both of these drop out at about 6 months or so, when the more complex parts of the brain begin to dominate. Any of these primitive reflexes, if present *past* this age, however, may be signs of some neurological difficulty. Tests for these reflexes are thus often used in older infants, children, or adults as part of neurological diagnostic examinations.

### Perceptual Skills: What the Infant Sees, Hears, and Feels

Again, I've summarized what we know about the abilities of the newborn in a table (Table 3.2), but I want to expand on a couple of these points.

First of all, each item of information in the table represents more than one study—in some cases, there are dozens of studies involved. I've given references where the study is a "classic"—such as Wilton Chase's study of color vision in the infant or Kai Jensen's study of taste perception—or where there is a good recent study or review.

Second, I've carefully put a "maybe" in some statements, where the evidence is just not complete or not consistent. Testing newborn babies is extremely difficult. They aren't awake much and aren't very responsive during the first few days. So getting any kind of accurate informa-

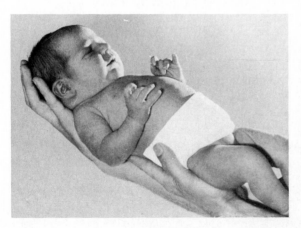

**Figure 3.4** These two photos show the Moro reflex very well. In the left photo the baby is fairly relaxed, but when the adult drops the baby suddenly (and catches him again—), the baby throws his arms out in the first part of the Moro reflex. This baby will later close his fingers, too. This reflex may be left over from our ape ancestors; young monkeys do this when their mother lets go briefly. The result is that the baby grabs hold of a bunch of fur and thus clings. In human babies this reflex has little usefulness but can be seen for the first six months or so.

TABLE 3.2

**Perceptual skills of the newborn**

| Sense | The Baby Can . . . |
|---|---|
| Sight | Focus both eyes on the same point; the best focus point is about 8 inches away (Haynes, White, & Held, 1965). Follow a moving object with the eyes; this skill is not well developed at birth but improves rapidly (Kremenitzer et al., 1979). Discriminate some colors; this can clearly be done by 2 weeks (Chase, 1937) and *may* be possible earlier (Bornstein & Teller, 1982). |
| Sound | Respond to various sounds, particularly those in the pitch and loudness range of the human voice. Make discriminations among very slightly different linguistic sounds, like *pah* and *bah* (Morse & Cowan, 1982). Locate the source of a sound (Clifton et al., 1981). If already crying or fussing, may respond to rhythmic sounds like heartbeats by being soothed (Salk, 1960). Discriminate the mother's voice from other voices on the first day or within a few days of birth. |
| Smell | React strongly to some smells, such as ammonia or anise (licorice). Discriminate the smell of the mother's breast pad from that of a strange woman, beginning at about 1 week of life (Macfarlane, 1975). |
| Taste | Tell the difference between salty and sweet tastes and prefer sweet tastes. Tell the difference between sour and bitter (Jensen, 1932). |
| Touch | Respond to touches over most of the body, especially on the hands and mouth. |

tion is a hard job indeed, and sometimes we just don't have clear answers yet. Other times the findings are simply inconsistent.

A third really intriguing thing about the perceptual skills of the newborn is how well adapted they are for the interactions the baby will have with the people in her world. Perhaps because of all their experience with the sound of voices (particularly the mother's) in utero, babies can discriminate between individual voices (mom's versus others) either at birth or shortly thereafter, and they generally respond best to sounds that are about in the pitch and loudness range of the human voice. They also focus their eyes best at a distance of approximately 8 inches, which is just about the distance between the infant's eyes and the mother's face during nursing. Helpless though the baby is in so many ways, she nonetheless comes equipped with the perceptual abilities needed to see, hear, and touch the people around her.

Newborns are also soothed by sounds and movements that are easily made by mothers and fathers, especially those that are something like the sounds or movements the baby experienced prenatally. For example, Lee Salk first reported in 1960 that babies were soothed by the sound of a heartbeat, presumably because it was like the conditions of the womb. More recently, Rosner and Doherty (1979) have reported that recordings of intrauterine sounds (including heartbeat but also sounds of digestion) were soothing to crying newborns. Rocking motions also appear to be soothing, again perhaps because they are like the movements the baby experienced before birth when the mother walked.

Mothers and other caregivers have certainly known about these soothing actions for centuries. Rhythmic sounds and movements—lullabies and rocking chairs, for example—are mostly used to soothe babies who are distressed. Heartbeat sounds or uterinelike sounds may be equally effective for that purpose. So keep singing those lullabies and holding the baby close!

## Motor Skills: Moving Around

In contrast, the motor skills of the newborn are not very impressive. He can't hold up his head; he can't coordinate his looking and his reaching yet; he can't roll over or sit up. The newborn baby does move a lot, but we don't know whether these movements of the arms and legs and head are attempts by the baby to explore the world around him or whether they are more like reflexes—automatic movements in response to sounds or sights or other stimulation.

During the early weeks, there are fairly rapid improvements in motor ability. By 1 month, for example, the baby can hold his chin up off the floor or mattress (Figure 3.5). By 2 months, he is beginning to swipe at objects near him with his hands. Still, by contrast with perceptual abilities, the baby's motor abilities are primitive and develop only slowly during the first year of life.

## Learning and Habituation

Both the perceptual abilities and the child's motor skills seem to be heavily influenced by maturation. At birth, seeing and hearing have matured, while the neurological structures and muscles required for

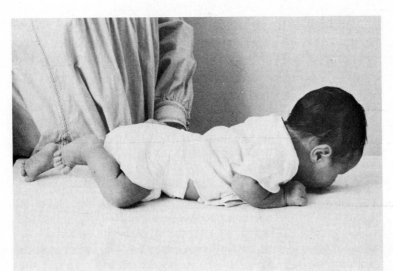

**Figure 3.5** Newborn infants have very poor motor control. Their heads must be supported when they are held; they cannot even raise their heads off a mattress. This baby, who is about 1 month old, has just developed enough muscular strength to lift his head a little bit.

moving have not. But what about learning? How early can the baby learn from her environment? For the theorist, these are important questions because they touch on the general issue of maturation versus learning. For the parent, they are equally important. The baby begins to learn before birth and then very rapidly after birth. Given this capacity, it makes sense to talk to and try to stimulate the baby—to give her things to learn from and learn about.

*Classical Conditioning*  Researchers are still arguing about whether newborn infants can be conditioned classically. Arnold Sameroff, for example (Sameroff & Cavanaugh, 1979), insists that the evidence shows that newborns learn but that they don't do so through standard classical conditioning. Other researchers, however, are equally convinced that they have been successful in classically conditioning newborns' sucking responses and even heartbeat (Lipsitt & Kaye, 1964; Stamps, 1977). My own conclusion from this research is that the newborn *can* be classically conditioned but that it is very hard to do. By 3 or 4 weeks of age, though, classical conditioning is quite easy to demonstrate in an infant. So the conditioned emotional responses I talked about in Chapter 1 may begin to develop as early as the first weeks of life.

*Operant Conditioning*  There is no disagreement about whether newborns can learn through operant conditioning. They can and do. In particular, the sucking response and head turning have both been successfully increased by the use of reinforcements such as sweet-tasting liquids (Sameroff & Cavanaugh, 1979).

The fact that conditioning of this kind can take place means that whatever neurological "wiring" is needed for learning to occur is present at birth.

*Schematic Learning*  The fact that babies can recognize voices and heartbeats in the first days of life is evidence that another kind of learning is going on as well, sometime referred to as schematic learning. The concept of a *schema* emerged from Piaget's theory (which I discussed briefly in Chapter 1). The baby is organizing her experiences into expectancies, into "known" combinations. These schemas or expectancies are built up over many exposures to particular experiences but thereafter help the baby to distinguish between the familiar and the unfamiliar.

*Habituation*  A related concept is that of **habituation**—the automatic reduction in the strength or vigor of a response to a repeated stimulus. An example would probably help: Suppose you live on a fairly noisy street (as I have done at several points in my life). The sound of cars going by is repeated over and over during every day. But after a while, you not only don't react to the sound, you quite literally *do not hear* *it* or don't perceive it as being as loud. The ability to do this—to dampen down the intensity of our experience of some repeated stimulus—is obviously vital in our everyday lives. If we reacted constantly to every sight and sound and smell that came along, we'd spend all our time responding to these repeated events and not have energy or attention left over for things that are new and deserve attention.

It turns out that the capacity to habituate is present in the newborn (Lipsitt, 1982). He will stop looking at something you keep putting in front of his face; he will stop showing a startle reaction (Moro reflex) to loud sounds after the first few presentations. This is not a voluntary process; it is entirely automatic. But the fact that the newborn is equipped with this capacity means that he can, in some way, "recognize" familir experiences (thus, he has a "schema" of some kind). It also means that he can respond each hour or each day to the genuinely novel things that are occurring.

## Social Skills

All of the skills of the newborn I have described so far are important for the baby's comfort and survival. But human newborns, unlike those in many other species, are a very long way from being independent. If they are to survive, someone must provide consistent care, over an extended period. So the infant's capacity to entice others into the caregiving role is critical. It is here that the "social" skills of infants come into play.

When you think about a newborn baby, you probably don't think of her as particularly social. She doesn't talk. She doesn't flirt. She smiles, but not often during the first weeks. Normal newborns nonetheless have a collection of behaviors that are remarkably effective for attracting and keeping the attention (and attachment) of adults. What is more, as I just pointed out in talking about the baby's perceptual skills, the social interaction process is very much a two-way street: Adult faces and voices are remarkably effective for attracting and keeping the baby's attention, too. There is even some intriguing evidence that newborn babies actually imitate the facial gestures of adults, such as movements of the tongue or widening of the eyes (Meltzoff & Moore, 1983). In fact, it seems as if the adult and the baby are "programmed" to join in a crucial social "dance," one that forms the root of the developing relationship between parent and child and that is critical for the formation of the parent's attachment to the child.

The baby's repertoire of social behaviors is quite limited, but these few behaviors appear to be very effective in eliciting care. He cries when he needs something, which ordinarily brings someone to him to provide care. And then he responds to that care by being soothed, which is very reinforcing to the caregivers. He adjusts his body to yours when you pick him up; after the first few weeks, he gets quite good at meeting your eyes in a mutual gaze or smiling—both of which are very powerful "hooks" for the adult's continued attention.

One other thing the baby does from the beginning, which seems to be critical for any social interaction, is to take turns. As adults, we take turns in a range of situations, including conversations and eye contacts. In fact, it's very difficult to have any kind of social encounter with someone who does *not* take turns. Kenneth Kaye (1982) argues that the beginnings of this "turn taking" can be seen in very young infants in their eating patterns. As early as the first days of life, the baby sucks in a "burst-pause" pattern. He sucks for a while, pauses, sucks for a while, pauses, and so on. Mothers enter into this "conversation," too, often by jiggling the baby during the pauses. The eventual conversation looks like this: suck, pause, jiggle, pause, suck, pause, jiggle, pause. The rhythm of the interaction is really very much like a conversation and seems to underlie many of the social encounters among people of all ages. The fascinating thing is that this rhythm, this turn taking, can be seen in an infant one day old.

## THE DAILY LIFE OF INFANTS

What an infant can see and hear, what she can do, are important parts of the picture of the newborn. But from a parent's perspective, the key question is really what the baby does with her time. How is the infant's day organized? What sort of natural rhythms occur in the daily cycles?

**Figure 3.6** Newborn babies are very skilled at attracting and keeping the attention of adults—a useful trait, since they need to be cared for so continuously. They can meet your gaze after the first few weeks, can smile, "take turns" during feeding, snuggle, be consoled, cry.

What can you expect from the baby as you struggle to adapt to and care for this new person in your life?

Researchers such as Heinz Prechtl and his colleagues (Prechtl & Beintema, 1964), who have studied newborns, have described five different **states of consciousness**—states of sleep and wakefulness in infants, which I've summarized in Table 3.3.

You can see that the baby spends more time sleeping than doing anything else; and of the time awake, only about two to three hours is "quiet awake" or unfussy, active awake.

The five main states tend to occur in cycles, just as your own states occur in a daily rhythm. In the newborn, the basic period in the cycle is about one and a half or two hours. Most infants move through the states from deep sleep to lighter sleep to fussing and hunger and then to alert wakefulness, after which they become drowsy and drop back into deep sleep. This sequence repeats itself about every two hours. Before very long, though, the infant can string two or three of these periods together without coming to full wakefulness, at which point we say that the baby can "sleep through the night." One of the implications of this rhythm, by the way, is that the best time for really good social encounters with a young infant is probably just after he is fed, when he is most likely to be in a quiet awake state.

Let's take a somewhat more detailed look at some of the major states.

TABLE 3.3

**The basic states of infant sleep and wakefulness**

| State | Characteristics | AVERAGE AMOUNT OF TIME SPENT IN STATE | |
| | | At Birth | At 1 Month |
| --- | --- | --- | --- |
| Deep sleep | Eyes closed, regular breathing, no movement except occasional startles. | 16–18 hr. | 14–16 hr. |
| Active sleep | Eyes closed, irregular breathing, small twitches, no gross body movement. | | |
| Quiet awake | Eyes open, no major body movement, regular breathing. | 6–8 hr. | 8–10 hr. |
| Active awake | Eyes open, with movements of the head, limbs, and trunk; irregular breathing. | | |
| Crying and fussing | Eyes may be partly or entirely closed, vigorous diffuse movement, with crying or fussing noise. | | |

*SOURCE:* Based on the work of Prechtl & Beintema, 1964; Hutt, Lenard, & Prechtl, 1969; Parmelee, Wenner, & Schulz, 1964.

## Sleeping

Sleeping may seem like a fairly uninteresting part of the infant's day. Parents obviously find the child's sleep periods helpful, particularly as they develop into a pattern with a long nighttime sleep. But there are two other aspects of an infant's sleep that are intriguing to psychologists.

First, irregularity in a child's sleep patterns may be a symptom of some disorder or problem. You may remember that I mentioned in Chapter 2 that one of the characteristics of babies born to drug-addicted mothers is that they seem unable to establish a pattern of sleeping and waking. Brain-damaged infants have the same kind of difficulties in many cases, so any time an infant fails to develop clear sleep/waking regularity, it *may* be a sign of trouble.

The other interesting thing about sleep in newborns is that they show the same external signs of dreaming as do older children or adults. In adults, the outward sign of dreaming is a fluttering of the eyeballs under the closed lids, called **rapid eye movement (REM) sleep**. Newborn infants also show REMs during active sleep. Even premature babies as young as 32 weeks of gestational age show REM sleep. In fact, Howard Roffwarg and his associates (Roffwarg, Muzio, & Dement, 1966) have found that newborns spend about half of their sleep time in REM sleep. In young adults, by contrast, only about 20 percent of sleep time is REM sleep.

Whether the newborn is "dreaming" in an adult's sense of the word during this REM sleep I haven't the faintest idea. One possibility is that this is time spent in "processing" new experiences—sounds, sights, sensations. And since the newborn (and the baby in the womb as well) is experiencing an *immense* amount of new stimulation, there is a great deal to process. Whatever the cause, it does seem to be the case that during the infant's REM sleep, there is a kind of intense stimulation of the central nervous system.

## Crying

For many parents, the infant's crying may be mainly a disturbing or irritating element, especially if it continues for long periods and the infant is not easily consoled. But crying can serve important functions for the child, for the physician or psychologist, and for the parent-child pair.

Newborns actually cry less of the time than you might think. Anneliese Korner and her colleagues (1981) monitored all the crying and noncrying activity of a group of normal newborns in the first three days of life and found that they cried only 2 to 11 percent of the time.

To be sure, there are quite wide individual differences in crying patterns. In particular, about 15 to 20 percent of infants develop *colic*, which is a pattern of daily, intense crying (three or more hours a day) that appears at about 2 weeks of age and then disappears spontaneously at 3 or 4 months of age. The crying is generally worst in late afternoon or early evening (a particularly inopportune time, of course, since it is usually when the parents are tired and needing time with each other, too). Physicians do not know the cause of colic. It is a difficult pattern to live with, but the good news is that it *does* go away.

Normal physical development seems to require at least some crying. Crying helps to improve lung capacity (since the baby gulps in more air between cries) and helps to organize the workings of the heart and respiratory system. The actual sound quality of the baby's cry may also turn out to be a useful diagnostic sign for the physician or psychologist. A number of very intriguing recent studies have shown that babies with some kind of physical problem—small-for-date babies, preterm infants, babies who experienced complications at delivery—have more piercing, grating, unpleasant cries than do physically normal infants (Zeskind & Lester, 1978, 1981; Friedman, Zahn-Waxler, & Radke-Yarrow, 1982). So it isn't necessarily the parents' imagination that some babies' cries are especially hard to take. Eventually, it may be possible for physicians to use the presence of such a grating or piercing cry sound as a signal that there may be some underlying physical problem with the infant.

The most important function of the baby's cry, though, is as a signal of distress. For caregivers, it is absolutely vital to know when the child is in need in some way, and most babies are very good at passing on this information in the form of a cry.

Most parents quite naturally respond quickly to these signals—feeding the baby, changing diapers, holding and cuddling the infant. But there is a dilemma, too, for many parents. If you pick up your baby immediately every time she cries, will you be reinforcing crying? Or is such quick responding essential if the child is to learn, in some way, that his needs will be met? (See Figure 3.7.)

There has been a splendidly wordy theoretical dispute about this question in the child development literature over the past decade (e.g., Ainsworth, Bell, & Stayton, 1972; Gewirtz & Boyd, 1977). But the one fact on which everyone seems to agree is that infants who are picked up or cared for quickly when they cry, cry *less* than do infants whose caregivers delay in responding. There is disagreement about *why* that should be the case, but the message for parents or other caregivers seems clear: Parents who are sensitive to the infant's cues and respond appropriately and quickly are likely to have an infant who cries less.

### Eating

Eating is not a "state," but it is certainly something that newborn babies do frequently! Given the approximately two-hour state-change

**Figure 3.7**

cycle, babies may eat as many as 10 times a day. By 1 month, though, the average number of feedings is about five-and-a-half, which drops to about five per day by 4 months (Barnard & Eyres, 1979). From the parents' perspective, one of the critical decisions about feeding is whether to breast-feed or bottle-feed. There are arguments on both sides, which I've summarized in Box 3.2.

## INDIVIDUAL DIFFERENCES AMONG BABIES

Most of my emphasis in the past few pages has been on the ways in which infants are alike. Barring some kind of physical damage, all babies have similar sensory equipment at birth and can experience the same kinds of happenings around them. But I have dropped a few hints, as well, of the sort of variations there can be in infant behavior or responsiveness. Such individual variations in style and pattern of responding are usually called **temperament**.

Babies range from placid to vigorous in their responses to any kind of stimulation. They also differ in their rates of activity, irritability, and restlessness (including crying) and in cuddliness. Some babies seem to enjoy being cuddled and adjust their bodies right away to the person holding them. Others seem to squirm from the beginning and to do less body adjusting.

It turns out that these differences are frequently found in clusters. The vigorous baby is often less cuddly, for example, and more irritable and restless. The placid baby is often cuddly and less irritable. Alexander Thomas and Stella Chess (1977), who have done the best-known studies of temperamental differences among infants, describe three basic types of babies.

*The Easy Child*  Easy children approach new events positively. They try new foods without much fuss, for example. They are also regular in biological functioning, with good sleeping and eating cycles, are usually happy, and adjust easily to change.

*The Difficult Child*  By contrast, the difficult child is less regular in body functioning and is slow to develop regular sleeping and eating cycles. These children react vigorously and negatively to new things, are more irritable, and cry more. Their cries also have a more "spoiled," grating sound than do the cries of "easy" babies (Boukydis & Burgess, 1982). Thomas and Chess (1977) point out, however, that once the difficult baby has adapted to something new, he is often quite happy about it, even though the adaptation process itself is very difficult.

*The Slow-to-Warm-Up Child*  Children in this group are not as negative in responding to new things or new people as is the difficult child. Rather, they show a kind of passive resistance. Instead of spitting out new food violently and crying, the slow-to-warm-up child may let the food drool out and may resist mildly any attempt to feed her more of the same. These infants show few intense reactions, either positive or negative, although once they have adapted to something new, their reaction is usually fairly positive.

These differences in temperament can be seen in very young infants and seem to persist to at least some degree throughout childhood (as you can see in Figure 3.8). Thomas and Chess (1977) have also found that temperament makes a difference for the child's later adjustment to school. Children with difficult temperaments are more likely to have school problems and are also more likely to show excessive aggressiveness, tantrums, speech problems, or stuttering in later childhood (Rutter, 1978a).

## Ethnic Differences in Temperament

Until the past few years, most psychologists assumed that differences in temperament among infants and children were essentially randomly distributed. There was no reason to suppose that children of particular ethnic or social class groups might have characteristic temperaments. But Daniel Freedman's research (1979) calls this assumption into question. Freedman has found systematic differences in the re-

BOX 3.2

# *BREAST-FEEDING VERSUS BOTTLE-FEEDING*

Many people get pretty heated over the question of breast-feeding versus bottle-feeding. Advocates of breast-feeding argue that it is the only "natural" way to feed a baby. Those who prefer bottle-feeding are just as passionate in defense of their choice. In fact most women *do* breast-feed their infants. In developing countries, 90 percent or more do so, and in the United States and in Western Europe, perhaps 60 percent do so for at least a few months (a number that has been rising in recent years). For the mother, the decision has important practical ramifications. For me, as usual, the key questions concern the potential effect of the type of feeding on the baby or on the interaction of the infant and the mother. Some of the answers to these questions may help you make your own decision when the time comes.

### EFFECTS ON THE BABY

There are several potent arguments in favor of breast-feeding. First and foremost, breast milk seems to provide important protection for the infant against many kinds of diseases. The baby receives antibodies from the mother—antibodies that he can't produce himself but that help to protect him against infections and allergies. For example, breast-fed infants have fewer respiratory and gastrointestinal infections than do bottle-fed babies (Marano, 1979).

Second, breast milk is easier for the baby to digest than is cow's milk or formula based on cow's milk. In particular, the fat in breast milk is almost entirely absorbed by the baby, while only about 80 percent of the fat in formula is absorbed. This is particularly relevant for low-birth-weight infants, who have difficulty digesting fats. The high-cholesterol fats in breast milk may also have a long-lasting benefit. Isabelle Valadian (cited in Marano, 1979) has found that adults who were exclusively breast-fed for at least two months have lower cholesterol levels than those who were given formula.

Third, there *may* be a slightly higher risk of obesity or overweight in bottle-fed babies (Taitz, 1975). As you'll see when you get to Box 4.2, there is some disagreement about whether infant fatness is predictive of later obesity. But some researchers are still convinced that bottle-fed babies have slightly increased risks of this prob-

sponses of newborns from different ethnic groups. He and his colleagues have observed and tested Caucasian, Chinese, Navaho, and Japanese infants. Of the four groups studied, the Caucasian babies were the most active and irritable and the hardest to console (the most "difficult" in Chess and Thomas's terms). Both the Chinese and the Navaho infants were relatively placid, while the Japanese infants responded vigorously but were easier to quiet than the Caucasian infants.

These differences were visible in newborns, so they cannot be the result of systematic shaping by the parents. The long-term persistence of these ethnic differences in temperament, though, is undoubtedly a joint result of the child's basic pattern and the responses of the parents. For example, William Caudill (Caudill & Frost, 1972) observed Japanese mothers and their infants and found that these mothers talked much less to their infants than did Caucasian mothers. Studies by

lem. The most likely explanation of any such connection is that the breast-fed infant has more control over the amount that he eats. When he is no longer hungry, he stops sucking. The mother doesn't really know how much milk he's taken, but she watches for the cues he gives her that he's had enough. The mother of the bottle-fed baby, on the other hand, may feel that the baby should take all the milk in the bottle and keep urging her to continue even though she's giving signals that she's no longer hungry. So bottle-fed babies may more often be overfed, and such overfeeding may set the baby into a persisting pattern of greater weight. This is obviously not something that happens with every bottle-fed baby. Sensitive parents can and do read satiation cues in their bottle-fed infants. But the risk of overfeeding seems to be somewhat higher than for breast-fed babies.

### MOTHER-INFANT INTERACTION

While the physical effects on the infant argue in favor of breast-feeding, no such advantage seems to be found when we look at patterns of mother-infant interaction. Bottle-fed babies are held and cuddled in the same ways as are breast-fed babies, and their mothers appear to be just as sensitive and responsive to their babies as are the breast-fed infants' mothers. Tiffany Field (1977), for example, looked at the kind of "turn taking" that Kenneth Kaye (1982) describes (and that I discussed in the section on social skills in infants). Field found that both breast-feeders and bottle-feeders entered into the "dialogue" equally well.

### ADVICE?

The dietary evidence argues for breast-feeding if it is at all possible and if the mother remains in good health and continues to eat a good diet. Many pediatricians are now urging this choice on their patients. But for some mothers this option is not possible. They may need to be away from their infant for long stretches each day, may be in poor health, or may want to share the feeding with the infant's father, to encourage his participation in the child's care. If any of these reasons is true in your own case, you should know that your infant can receive his basic dietary requirements from formula and that your relationship with your infant will not be adversely affected. When circumstances or philosophy permit, however, breast-feeding seems to be the best option for the child's short-term, and perhaps long-term, health.

Freedman and his colleagues show the same thing. Chinese mothers talked less and were much less likely to stimulate their infants. These differences in the mothers were present from their first encounter with their infants, so obviously the mother is bringing her own temperament (and training) to the interaction. When the mother and infant are of the same temperamental bent, they tend to reinforce each other's pattern so that the differences between the groups become more marked over time.

### The Effects of Infant Temperament on Parents

I do not want to overemphasize the importance of temperamental differences. The great majority of babies are "easy" or fairly easy in temperament. Only about 10 percent are "difficult." So most parents find themselves interacting with a baby who adapts quite readily and who

**Figure 3.8** These two pictures show consistency in temperament very graphically. Both are of the same pair of identical twins, in the same order. The child on the right in both pictures was consistently of a more "difficult" temperament, while her sister on the left was consistently "easy."

responds in a reinforcing way to their caregiving. But when the infant *does* present a more difficult temperament, the emerging parent-child interaction pattern may be tilted or shifted into a different pathway. Michael Rutter (1978a), for example, finds that difficult children are more often criticized by their parents, presumably because the child's behavior *is* more troublesome. The combination of the troublesome behavior and the parents' higher rate of criticism can greatly increase the likelihood that the child will subsequently develop some form of school difficulty or behavior problem.

The sequence of difficult temperament/later problem is not inevitable, however. A skilled parent (especially the parent who correctly perceives the child's "difficultness" as a temperamental quality and not as something caused by the parent's ineptness or by some willfullness of the child) can avoid some of the pitfalls and guide the temperamentally difficult child into a more adaptive pathway. But in many parent-child pairs, "difficult" behavior in the child can easily start the entire interaction system off on the wrong foot. So while temperament is not the most hugely significant element in child development, it can be one important ingredient in the *system* of factors influencing the child's pattern of growth.

## SEX AND SOCIAL CLASS DIFFERENCES IN EARLY INFANCY

Remarkably enough, there aren't many sex or social class differences among young infants. There are a few exceptions to that broad statement. As was true at birth, girls continue to be a bit ahead in some aspects of physical maturity, and boys continue to be more vulnerable. For example, more boys die during the first year of life. In addition, more of the boy's body is made up of muscle tissue than is true for girls.

Similarly, poor babies are more likely to be born with low birth weight and to have more problems at birth—a fact that's related to all the prenatal problems I mentioned in the last chapter. But if we look just at healthy babies, there are no differences between poor and middle-class babies in perceptual skills, motor development, or anything else I've discussed in this chapter (Bayley, 1965).

The most interesting thing about these facts is that boys and girls do not differ on the temperamental dimensions Thomas and Chess (1977) talk about. Boys are not more often "difficult" in temperament, and girls are not more often "easy," even though that is what our stereotypes might lead us to expect.

Having said that, I have to note two cautions. First, there haven't been very many studies of temperament in infancy, so we can't be completely sure about the lack of sex differences. More important, most of the information we have about babies' temperaments comes from descriptions of infants by their parents. Since parents, like the rest of us, have stereotyped expectations about what boys and girls ought to be like, it is possible that they are simply more tolerant of "difficult" behavior in a boy than in a girl and don't think it's noteworthy enough to mention. Boys and girls might really be different on such dimensions as activity or acceptance of new things but the differences could be masked by the way the parent *perceives* the behavior. It will take additional direct observations of young boys and girls to settle this question. For the moment, however, I think it is important to emphasize that at this stage we have no persuasive evidence for sex differences in temperament.

## SUMMARY

1. The normal birth process has three parts: dilation, delivery, and placental delivery.
2. The first "acquaintance" process after delivery may be an especially important one for parents. Most parents show an intense interest in the baby's features, especially the eyes.
3. Most drugs given to the mother during delivery pass through to the infant's bloodstream. They have short-term effects on infant responsiveness and on feeding patterns. They may have some long-term effects as well.
4. The location of the delivery (home versus hospital) *may* make some difference, but we know little yet about the effects of location on the baby or on the parent-infant bond.
5. The presence of the father during delivery appears to help reduce the mother's discomfort and may enhance the father's attachment to the infant.
6. Several types of problems may disturb the normal delivery process. The child may have a reduced oxygen supply (anoxia), or conditions may require a cesarean section (abdominal delivery).
7. Another potential problem is low birth weight, either from premature delivery or because of insufficient growth during the normal gestational period.
8. Low–birth-weight infants have higher risk of death during the first year of life, but if they survive, many catch up to full-size peers by school age. Those with birth weights below 1500 g or who are very small for date are more likely to show lasting problems.
9. The newborn has far more skills than most physicians and psychologists had thought, including excellent reflexes, good perceptual skills, and effective social skills.
10. The important infant reflexes include feeding reflexes, such as rooting and sucking, and the Moro reflex.
11. Perceptual skills include focusing both eyes, tracking slowly moving objects, some color vision, discrimination of sounds and sound direction, and responsiveness to smells, tastes, and touch.
12. Motor skills, in contrast, are only rudimentary at birth.
13. Social skills, while rudimentary, are sufficient to bring people close for care and to keep them close for social interactions. The baby can meet a gaze and smile within the first month of life.
14. Newborns can learn from the first days of life, most easily by operant conditioning but possibly also through classical conditioning.
15. Newborns also habituate to repeated stimulation.
16. Young infants spend the majority of their days sleeping and are

in an awake and alert state only a fraction of the time. Rhythms and daily cycles of sleeping, waking, crying, and eating are established early.

17. Babies differ from one another on several dimensions, including vigor of response, general activity rate, restlessness, irritability, and cuddliness. These temperamental dimensions—which can be grouped into "types," such as "difficult," "easy," and "slow-to-warm-up"—appear to persist into childhood and to affect the responses of those around the child.

18. Male and female babies differ at birth on a few dimensions. Girls are more mature physically. Boys have more muscle tissue and are more vulnerable to stress. No sex differences are found, however, on temperamental dimensions, such as cuddliness or sootheability.

19. No consistent differences between middle-class and poor infants are found on the usual measures of infant development.

## KEY TERMS

**Anoxia**  A shortage of oxygen. If it is prolonged, it can result in brain damage. This is one of the potential risks at birth.

**Birthing room**  An arrangement, becoming more common in hospitals, with a homelike atmosphere for delivery.

**Cesarean section**  Delivery of the child through an incision in the mother's abdomen.

**Dilation**  The first stage of childbirth, when the cervix opens sufficiently to allow the infant's head to pass into the birth canal.

**Effacement**  The flattening of the cervix, which, along with dilation, allows the delivery of the infant.

**Habituation**  An automatic decrease in the intensity of a response to a repeated stimulus, which enables the child or adult to ignore the familiar and focus attention on the novel.

**Leboyer method**  A "gentle" birth method proposed by Frederick Leboyer, including darkened lights and quiet, slow-paced birth.

**Low birth weight**  The phrase now used (in place of the word *premature*) to describe infants whose weight is below the optimum range at birth. Includes infants born too early (preterm, or short-gestation, infants) and those who are "small for date."

**Premature infant**  The term formerly used to describe short-gestation infants.

**Preterm infant**  Descriptive phrase widely used to label infants born before a full gestation period has been completed.

**Rapid eye movement (REM) sleep**  One of the characteristics of sleep during dreaming, which occurs during the sleep of newborns, too.

**Reflexes**  Automatic body reactions to specific stimulation, such as the knee jerk or the Moro reflex. Many reflexes remain among adults, but the newborn also has some "primitive" reflexes that disappear as the cortex is fully developed.

**Small-for-date infant**  An infant who weighs less than is normal for the number of weeks of gestation completed.

**States of consciousness**  Five main sleep/awake states have been identified in infants, from deep sleep to active awake states.

**Temperament**  Collections of typical responses or style of response to experiences that seem to be stable over time and that differentiate infants and young children from one another.

**Very low–birth-weight infants**  Phrase now commonly used to describe infants who weigh 1500 g or less (3¼ pounds or less) at birth.

SUGGESTED READINGS

Brazelton, T. B. *Infants and mothers: Differences in development.* New York: Dell, 1969.
Not a new book, but a lovely one, written by a remarkably observant and sensitive physician. It describes the first year of life in some detail and also chronicles the progress of three infants who differ in basic temperament.

Leboyer, F. *Birth without violence.* New York: Knopf, 1975.
Those of you interested in delivery options may find Leboyer's book about "gentle" birth of interest.

McCall, R. *Infants: The new knowledge.* Cambridge, Mass.: Harvard University Press, 1979.
This is an excellent newish book about the abilities and characteristics of infants, written in an easy style. McCall describes a fair amount of research but does so in a manner that can readily be understood by nonscientists.

Macfarlane, A. *The psychology of childbirth.* Cambridge, Mass.: Harvard University Press, 1977.
Again, not a brand-new book, but lovely nonetheless. Macfarlane presents research information as well as opinions, both expressed in very clear and readable language.

Pines, M. Baby, you're incredible. *Psychology today* 16 (February 1982): 48–52.
A lively description of some of the skills of newborns, written by one of the best science writers around.

Restak, R. M. Newborn knowledge. *Science 82* 3 (January 1982): 58–65.
Another good, recent, brief description of some of the skills of newborns. Very nice pictures, too.

Trotter, R. J. Baby face. *Psychology today* 17 (August 1983): 14–20.
An interesting description of some of the latest research on emotional expression in newborns and young infants.

PROJECT 3.1

# Observation in a Newborn Nursery

Despite the changes in birth practices, most hospitals still have newborn nurseries, and you can go and look through the window at the infants. However, you *must* obtain permission before you do so, especially if there are a number of students who wish to observe. Newborn nurseries are busy places, but they cannot tolerate an additional 5 or 10 or more people crowding around the window. If your instructor has assigned this project to the whole class, he or she will need to schedule times through the hospital administration and the nursing staff in the newborn nursery. If you are going on your own, at the very least you should call the head nurse in the obstetrics and newborn section of the hosptial. She (or he) may also require you to obtain more formal hospital permission.

Once you have obtained the necessary permission and arranged a time that will be least disruptive of the hospital schedule, I would like you to observe the infants (through the window) for approximately half an hour. Proceed in the following way:

**Score sheet**

| 30-Second Intervals | BABY'S STATE | | | | |
| --- | --- | --- | --- | --- | --- |
| | Deep Sleep | Active Sleep | Quiet Awake | Active Awake | Crying, Fussing |
| 1 | | | | | |
| 2 | | | | | |
| 3 | | | | | |

1. Set up a score sheet that should look something like the one shown above.
   Continue the score sheet for sixty 30-second intervals.
2. Reread the material in Table 3.3 until you know the main features of the five states as well as possible. You will need to focus on the eyes (open versus closed and rapid eye movement), the regularity of the baby's breathing, and the amount of body movement.
3. Select one infant in the nursery and observe that infant's state every 30 seconds for a half hour. For each 30-second interval, note on your score sheet the state that best describes the infant over the preceding 30 seconds. Do *not* select an infant to observe who is in deep sleep at the beginning. Pick an infant who seems to be in an in-between state (active sleep or quiet awake), so that you can see some variation over the half-hour observation.
4. If you can arrange it, you might do this observation with a partner, each of you scoring the same infant's state independently. When the half hour is over, compare notes. How often did you agree on the infant's state? What might have been producing the disagreements?
5. When you discuss or write about the project, consider at least the following issues: Did the infant appear to have cycles of states? What were they? What effect, if any, do you think the nursery environment might have had on the baby's state? If you worked with a partner, how much agreement or disagreement did you have? Why?

# part two
## the physical child

# 4.
# *physical growth and development*

Some years ago, when my daughter was about 8½, a lot of well-rehearsed family routines seemed to unravel. She was crankier than usual, both more assertive and more needful of affection, and alternately compliant and defiant. What on earth was happening? Had I done something dreadfully wrong? Was there something going on at school? I mentioned my problems to several colleagues and began to hear tales from other parents about the special difficulties they had had with their daughters between the ages of 8 and 9.

Nothing in any of the developmental research or theory I had ever read suggested this ought to be a particularly stressful time. But I began, slowly, to put some faith in my observations and to search for an explanation. Having been trained with a heavy emphasis on environmental influences on development, that's always where I look first. But that didn't offer me much in the way of answers. The 8- or 9-year-old has been in school for two or three years, and no major new adaptation seemed to be demanded. It was only when, belatedly, I began to think about physical changes that an explanation occurred to me: Girls of 8 or 9 are actually beginning **puberty**! The first hormone changes begin at about this age, and many of the inconsistent and uncomfortable behaviors I was seeing could easily be a response to the changing hormones in the system.

## WHY STUDY PHYSICAL DEVELOPMENT AT ALL?

It may amuse you to think of the clever psychologist being stumped by something so obvious. But in fact, developmental psychologists have often placed too little emphasis on physical growth. We describe it briefly and then take it for granted. But I am convinced both by the research literature on the effects of physiological change and by my observations as a parent that an understanding of physical development is an absolutely critical first step in understanding children's progress, for at least four reasons.

### The Child's Growth Makes New Behaviors Possible

Specific physical changes are needed before the infant can crawl or walk; others are needed for the child to acquire full control of the anal sphincter muscle (required for toilet training); still other physical changes lie behind an older child's growing skill at running, kicking a ball, or jumping rope; and at adolescence, the development of full reproductive capacity is based on a complex sequence of physical changes. Many researchers studying language and cognitive development are also beginning to suggest that changes in the brain lie behind major milestones in these areas as well.

The flip side of this is that the *lack* of a particular physical development sets limits on the behaviors the child is capable of. An infant of

10 months cannot be toilet trained, no matter how hard parents may try, because the anal sphincter muscle is not yet fully mature. Toddlers cannot easily pick up raisins or Cheerios from their high chair trays until the muscles and nerves required for thumb-forefinger opposition have developed.

It seems to me that such limits deserve far more attention than they normally receive—by parents, teachers, and others. Think, for example, about children who participate in PeeWee League football or Little League baseball. I have several times watched coaches reduce their young charges to tears by demanding levels of coordination and skill that 5- and 6-year-olds (or 10- and 11-year-olds) are simply unlikely to be able to show.

## The Child's Growth Determines Experience

The range of physical capacities, tendencies, or skills a child shows at any given age can also have a major indirect effect on cognitive and social development by influencing the range of experiences she can have with the world around her.

For example, an infant who cannot crawl can only explore things that are brought to her or are within easy reach. When she begins to crawl, her horizons are opened, and the range of objects and experiences she will encounter rises enormously. Similarly, a child who learns to ride a bike (a skill that depends on a whole collection of physical developments) widens his horizons still further, as he explores his neighborhood on his own, perhaps for the first time.

## The Child's Growth Affects Others' Responses

The effect of these changes in the child's skills works both ways: Not only do they change the child's experiences, they also change the way the people around the child respond to her. For example, nearly all parents become more restrictive and punitive toward their infants when they reach about 18 to 30 months of age, because the child gets into *everything*. The child is mobile enough to get into trouble in a heck of a hurry, so many parents find that they are more likely to put things out of reach or to limit the places the child can explore. As it happens, it seems to matter just how much restriction parents enforce at this age. In some of my own research (Barnard, Bee, & Hammond, 1984a), my colleagues and I have found that the more the parents restrict the child at 24 months or punish his attempts to assert himself and to explore, the less well the child is likely to do in school six years later, when he is in second grade.

Adults' expectations for children are also affected by the child's size and physical skills. As a general rule, the larger or more developed a child, the more "adult" his behavior is expected to be, which may or

**Figure 4.1** As soon as babies are able to scoot or crawl, they begin to explore much more widely, including a lot of "no-nos," and parents face a battle with a nonverbal child over what is permitted and what is not. This is a perfect example of the effect of the child's physical development on the pattern of family interactions.

may not match his actual skill. Yvonne Brackbill (Brackbill & Nevill, 1981) has shown this effect clearly in a recent study. She gave a group of parents of 11-year-olds, a group of elementary school teachers, and another group of female undergraduates all a list of names and descriptions of children who were enrolled in a summer camp. The (imaginary) children varied in height, weight, and age. Each adult was asked to assign camp chores to these children by whatever system they thought would work best. As it happened, the adults were more influenced by height than by age: The taller the child, the more difficult the task assigned to him or her by the adults. The point is that those around the child are affected by the child's changes in physical size and skill in a host of ways; and the child is, in turn, affected by the adults' responses to her new features and abilities.

### The Child's Growth Affects Self-Concept

The final reason for us to pay close attention to physical development is that physical skills (or lack of them) can have a profound effect on the child's self-concept (which I'll be talking about much more fully in Chapters 9 and 10). A personal example may help emphasize this point. As a child, I was unusually tall for my age. I was nearly 5 feet 6 inches at age 12, and when I finally stopped growing, I was just under 6 feet. There are some distinct advantages to being that tall: I can see over people at movies; I can reach into the top cupboards in kitchens and the top shelves of bookcases. But at age 12, the advantages weren't so obvious. During that two-year stretch when the girls all grew before the boys did, I was taller than everyone; and even when the boys grew,

**Figure 4.2** These children are the same age, but you'd never guess it by looking at them. Most adults will automatically assign the larger child more complex tasks, expect more, and perhaps even talk in a more adult way to this child.

most did not catch up to me. I felt gawky and conspicuous and socially inept as a result, all of which became parts of my self-concept (30 years later I describe this as my "moose" feeling!). Now I wouldn't trade an inch; there are too many good things about being tall. But my self-concept, and my behavior as a consequence, was greatly affected for many years by experiences resulting from physical changes.

For all of these reasons, I think it is important to begin our exploration of development with a fairly detailed look at physical growth and change. What are the underlying changes in the nervous system, in the musculature, and in the hormone system that form the substrate of behavior? What is the child physically able to do at various ages? How is he affected by his own perceptions of his physical qualities and by the reactions of others to his pattern of development?

## FIRST DESCRIPTIONS: BASIC SEQUENCES AND COMMON PATTERNS

### Changes in Height, Weight, and Shape

Babies gain in both height and weight very rapidly for the first two years. The usual rule of thumb is that an infant will double his birth weight by 5 months and triple it in the first year. The typical infant also adds about 10 to 12 inches in length within the first year (Provence,

1979). By age 2, most toddlers are already *half* as tall as they will be as adults—something many adults find hard to visualize.

After this rapid growth during the first two years, the child settles down to a slower but steady addition of 2 to 3 inches and about 6 pounds per year until adolescence, when another period of rapid growth occurs (as you can see in Figure 4.3). During this adolescent "growth spurt," the child may add 3 to 6 inches a year, after which there is again a period of much slower height gain until final height is reached in the late teens.

At the same time, the *shape of the body is changing*. The body proportions shift markedly. In an adult, the head is about one-eighth or one-tenth of the total height. But the toddler isn't built like that at all. In the 2-year-old, the head is about one-quarter of the total body length.

Individual body parts do not all grow at the same rate, either. This is particularly striking at adolescence. Hands and feet grow to full adult size earliest, followed by the arms and legs, with the trunk usually the slowest part to grow. We often think of an adolescent as "awk-

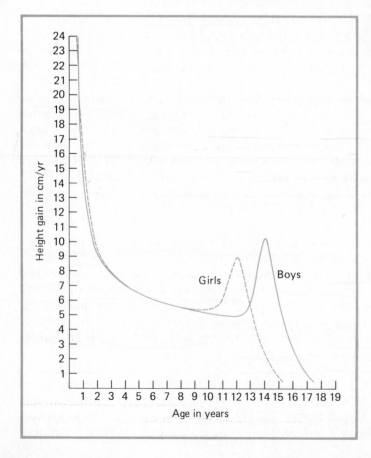

**Figure 4.3** These curves show the gain in height for each year from birth through adolescence. You can see that infants grow a tremendous amount but that after that the rate of increase drops way off, until the "growth spurt" at adolescence. (*Source:* Tanner, 1978, p. 14.)

Height gain in cm/yr

Girls     Boys

Age in years

ward" or uncoordinated. That turns out to be an inaccurate description. I think what people see in teenagers that may look like awkwardness is just the asymmetry of the different body parts. The child's body looks "leggy" and has proportionately large hands and feet. (My daughter, at age 12, had feet as large as mine, even though she was nearly a foot shorter.)

Children's heads and faces also change from infancy through adolescence. The size and shape of a child's jaw change when the permanent teeth come in (during the elementary school years mostly) and again in adolescence, when both jaws grow forward and the forehead becomes more prominent. This often gives teenagers' faces (especially boys') an angular, bony appearance, and it sometimes takes a while for these changes to "settle" into the final adult form.

## Development of Bones

Bones change in three ways with development: they increase in number, become longer, and grow harder.

*Number of Bones*  The parts of the body that show the greatest increase in the number of bones are the hand, wrist, ankle, and foot. For example, in the wrist of an adult, there are nine separate bones. In the 1-year-old, there are only three. The remaining six bones develop over the period of childhood, with complete growth by adolescence.

There is one part of the body, though, where there is fusing rather than a differentiation of bone. This is the skull, where the infant has several bones separated by spaces called **fontanels**. Fontanels allow the head to be compressed during the birth process without injury, and they also give the brain room to grow. In most children, the fontanels are filled in by bone by about age 2. (Although the originally separate parts of the skull retain distinctive names, the skull becomes one connected piece of bone.)

*Hardening of Bones*  In the infant, some bones are still mostly cartilage (like the bridge of your nose); and all bones are softer, with a higher water content than will be true later. The process of bone hardening, called **ossification**, occurs steadily from birth through puberty.

However, the rate of ossification varies for different parts of the body. The bones of the hand and wrist harden quite early, as do the bones of the head. By contrast, the long bones of the leg do not harden completely until the late teens.

The bone-hardening process may seem quite uninteresting, but it has practical ramifications. Because of the greater pliability of his body, the infant can work himself into all sorts of postures (he can suck on his toes or put his foot behind his head, for example). But that very lack of stiffness is one of the reasons the baby has difficulty sitting up or holding up his head. As the bones stiffen, the baby is able to manipulate his body more surely, which increases the range of exploration he can enjoy.

*Increased Size of Bones*   While the composition of the bone changes and the number of bones increases, the shape is also changing. This is particularly noticeable in the long bones of the leg and arm, which get steadily longer throughout the years of childhood. Growth of these bones stops only when the ends of the bones (called *epiphyses*) finally harden completely, which does not occur until the middle or late teens.

*Skeletal Age*   Because the several kinds of changes in the bones I have been describing are extremely regular and predictable, it is possible to estimate a child's or adolescent's overall level of maturational progress by assessing *skeletal age*, which is simply an estimate of how far along the sequence of bone changes a child has progressed. This is normally done by using X-ray pictures or careful physical examination of the wrist or knee (Chumlea, 1982; Tanner et al., 1975). Because the various sequences of maturation tend to be related in individual children, skeletal age turns out to be a much better predictor of other maturational change (such as the timing of puberty) than is actual chronological age.

## Development of Muscles and Fat

*Muscles*   Unlike the bones, which are not all present at birth, by shortly after birth the baby has virtually all the muscle fibers she will ever have (Tanner, 1978). What changes is the length and thickness of the muscle fibers. Like bones and height, muscle tissue increases fairly steadily until adolescence, when it, too, accelerates in rate of growth. One of the clear results of this rapid increase in muscle tissue is that adolescents become quite a lot stronger in just a few years. Both boys and girls show this increase in muscle tissue and strength, but as you can see in Figure 4.4, the increase is much greater in boys. Among adults, about 40 percent of the final body mass of a male is muscle, while for women it is only about 24 percent.

Some of you may be asking yourselves at this point whether this is an inevitable physiological difference or whether the greater levels of physical exercise typical of teenage boys (from sports as well as simply greater body movement) may not be contributing to the greater growth of muscle tissue, and hence greater strength. My hunch is that some of the strength differences are due to lack of muscular fitness in girls compared to boys. Until comparisons of equally fit teenagers are made, we won't know for sure. But the sheer amount of muscle tissue appears to me to be a real physiological sex difference, generated by differing amounts and patterns of hormones in the blood. Even ex-

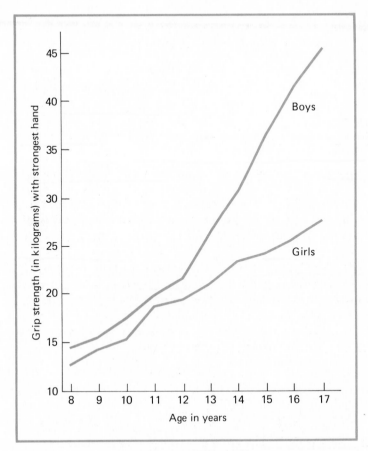

**Figure 4.4** Both boys and girls get stronger over the years of childhood and adolescence, but boys show a much larger change, particularly at puberty. Some of this might be caused by greater exercise by boys at this age, but some of it seems to be due to the effects of hormones. (*Source:* Adapted from Montpetit, Montoye, & Laeding, 1967, from Tables 1 and 2, p. 233.)

tremely fit teenage girls or adult women appear to have less muscle tissue than equally fit males.

*Fat*   Another major component of the body is fat, most of which is stored immediately under the skin. This *subcutaneous fat* (sometimes called "baby fat") is first laid down beginning at about 34 weeks prenatally and has an early peak at about 9 months after birth. The thickness of this layer of fat then declines until about age 6 or 7, after which it rises pretty steadily until adolescence.

Again, though, there is a very large sex difference in these patterns. From the beginning, girls have more fat tissue than boys do, and this difference becomes very much larger at adolescence. Among girls, about 20 to 24 percent of body weight is made up of fat at the beginning of puberty, and this *rises* to perhaps 28 percent at age 17; among boys, in contrast, only about 17 to 20 percent of body weight is made up fat at the beginning of puberty, and this *declines* to perhaps 10 to 12 percent at age 17 (Chumlea, 1982; Forbes, 1972). Girls develop more fat cells, and their individual fat cells are larger than are boys'.

Of course, as with muscle tissue, this sex difference in fat may be partially a life-style or activity-level effect; girls and women who are extremely athletic (long-distance runners, ballet dancers, and the like) typically have much lower body fat levels (perhaps as low as the average boy). But very fit boys have still *lower* fat levels, suggesting that sex difference in fat is a "real" physiological difference.

## Development of the Nervous System

Growth in height and weight involves changes you can see. Even the changes in muscles, bones, and fat can be "seen" fairly easily in the child's longer legs, greater strength, or softness or leanness of body. But there are two enormously important types of changes in the body that are not so easy to perceive. The first of these is change in the nervous system.

I mentioned in Chapter 2 that the nervous system is not "finished" at birth. Other body systems, like the lungs and the circulatory system, are fully operative at birth, but the nervous system still has a lot of developing left to do.

*Brain Development*   At birth, the parts of the brain that are most fully developed are those contained in what is usually called the **midbrain**. This section, in the lower part of the skull, regulates such basic things as attention and habituation, sleeping, waking, and elimination. As you saw in the last chapter, these are all things the newborn does pretty well.

The least-developed part of the brain at birth is the **cortex**, which is the convoluted gray matter that wraps around the midbrain and is involved in perception, body movement, and all complex thinking and language. The cortex is present at birth, but the cells are not yet well connected; impulses are not transmitted readily from one cell to another. Increases in size of brain cells and the addition of impulse-carrying connective tissue takes place rapidly in the first two years of life and then much more slowly through adolescence. The process is about half complete by 6 months and about 75 percent complete by age 2.

Within the cortex, though, the development is not even. The parts of the cortex that govern simple movements, touch sensitivity, and vision are fairly well developed at birth, with the area controlling sound perception coming along very quickly. Areas of the cortex that appear to be involved in more complex sensory integrations or problem solving develop much more slowly—matching the rate of the development of those skills in the child.

Another aspect of cortical development that has intrigued physiologists and psychologists is *hemispheric specialization*. The cortex is divided into two halves, or hemispheres, each of which seems to be "in charge of" somewhat different aspects of thinking and perceiving. The left hemisphere (which controls the actions of the *right* side of the body for the majority of us) is involved in all aspects of language (both speaking and understanding) and in most logical, sequential thought. The right hemisphere (which controls the actions of the *left* side of the body) specializes in spatial information—where things are located in space, how they are related to one another spatially. Most artistic activities require right-brain activity, as do many tasks labeled "creative." Most traditional schoolwork is heavily left-brained.

Physiologists are still arguing about whether this hemispheric specialization is already in place at birth, but the current thinking is that full specialization is not complete until adolescence (Wolff, 1981). Furthermore, there are hints that there may be sex differences in both the degree and timing of such specialization, which in turn may affect the development of verbal and spatial skills—a possibility I'll be returning to in Chapter 6.

*Myelinization*   Another important process in the development of the nervous system is the formation of sheaths around individual nerves, which insulate them from one another and make it easier for messages to pass down the nerves. This sheath is called **myelin**; the process of developing the sheath is called **myelinization**. At birth, for example, the spinal cord is not fully myelinized, which is one of the reasons for the slower development of muscular control over the lower trunk and legs. The process of myelinization of the nerves leading to and from the brain occurs rapidly during the early months and years and is almost complete by the time the child is 2. In the brain itself, however, both myelinization and growth of connective tissues continue into adolescence and perhaps adulthood.

To understand the importance of myelin, it may help you to know that *multiple sclerosis* is a disease in which the myelin begins to break down. The individual with this disease gradually loses motor control, with the specific symptoms depending on the portion of the nervous system affected by the disease.

## Hormonal Changes

The second "invisible" set of changes we need to look at is in *hormones*—secretions of the various **endocrine glands** in the body. Hormones govern growth and physical changes in several ways, which I've summarized in Table 4.1.

Of all the endocrine glands, the most critical is the **pituitary**, since it provides the trigger for release of hormones from other glands. For example, the thyroid gland only secrets thyroxine when it has received a "signal" to do so in the form of a specific thyroid-stimulating hormone from the pituitary.

TABLE 4.1

**Major hormones involved in physical growth and development**

| Gland | Hormone(s) Secreted | Aspect(s) of Growth Influenced |
|---|---|---|
| Thyroid | Thyroxine | Affects normal brain development and overall rate of growth. |
| Adrenal | Adrenal androgen | Involved in some changes at puberty, particularly the development of secondary sex characteristics in girls. |
| Testes (in boys) | Testosterone | Crucial in the formation of male genitals prenatally; also triggers the sequence of primary and secondary sex characteristic changes at puberty in the male. |
| Ovaries (in girls) | Estrogen | Affects development of the menstrual cycle and breasts in girls but has less to do with other secondary sex characteristics than testosterone does for boys. |
| Pituitary | Growth hormone<br>Activating hormones | Affects rate of physical maturation.<br>Signal other glands to secrete. |

*Prenatal Hormones*  Thyroid hormone (thyroxine) is present from about the fourth month of gestation and appears to be involved in stimulating normal brain development. Growth hormone is also produced by the pituitary beginning as early as 10 weeks after conception. Presumably it helps to stimulate the very rapid growth of cells and organs of the body. And as I mentioned in Chapter 2, testosterone is produced in the testes of the developing male and influences both the formation of male genitals and some aspects of brain development.

*Hormones between Birth and Adolescence*  The rate of growth in these years is governed largely by the thyroid hormone and by the pituitary growth hormone. Thyroid hormone is secreted in greater quantities for the first two years of life and then falls to a lower level and remains steady until adolescence (Tanner, 1978). This pattern of rapid early development followed by slower and steadier secretions obviously matches the pattern I already described of rapid early change and slower later change in height and weight between birth and adolescence.

Secretions from the testes and ovaries, as well as adrenal androgen, remain at extremely low levels during this period.

*Hormones in Adolescence*  These low levels of the sex hormones change markedly at adolescence. In fact, of course, the hormone changes surrounding puberty actually begin some while before we see any obvious physical changes like growth spurts or pubic hair or breast development in girls. (And it was this early hormone change that I think was behind some of the *behavioral* changes I was seeing in my 8- to 9-year-old daughter.)

The sequence of hormone changes and their effects is complex. So to help you sort it out (and to help *me* sort it out), I've put together a chart showing the hormones involved and their effects (Figure 4.5).

The key is again the pituitary (although its actions are in turn triggered by signals from a portion of the brain called the *hypothalamus*). At some point in late childhood (the age varies a lot from one child to the next), the pituitary gland (at a signal from the hypothalamus) begins secreting increased levels of **gonadotrophic hormones** (two in males, three in females). These, in turn, stimulate the development of the glands in the testes and ovaries, which then begin to secrete more testosterone or **estrogen**. At the same time, the pituitary also secretes three other hormones that affect growth and that interact with the specific sex hormones.

As you can see in Figure 4.5, the interaction is a little different for boys and girls. In particular, the growth spurt as well as pubic hair development in girls is less influenced by estrogen and more influenced by androgen (produced by the adrenal gland). Curiously, androgen is chemically very similar to testosterone, so it takes a "male"

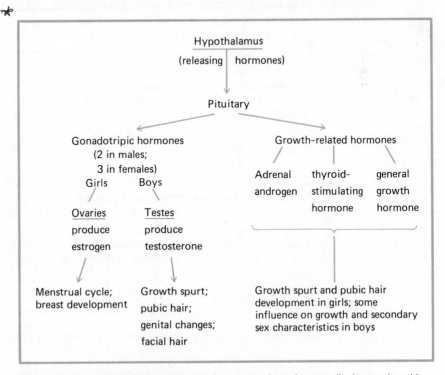

**Figure 4.5** The action of the various hormones at puberty is exceedingly complex; this figure oversimplifies the process but gives you some sense of the sequence and the differences between the patterns for boys and girls.

hormone to produce the growth spurt in girls. For boys, the adrenal androgen is less significant, presumably because they already have "male" hormone in the form of testosterone floating about in their bloodstreams.

Just how this hormonal process is turned off (or toned down) at the end of puberty is much less clear (Dreyer, 1982). But in some fashion the level of both growth hormones and gonadotrophic hormones produced in the pituitary drops to a lower level, and the rate of body change gradually tapers off at the adult levels.

## Development of Sexual Maturity

The physical result of the hormonal changes that take place during puberty is not only a spurt in height but, more important, a set of physical changes that brings about full sexual maturity. These changes are normally divided into two groups: development of **primary sex characteristics**, which are those necessary for reproduction, such as the testes and penis in the male and the ovaries, uterus, and vagina in the female. The **secondary sex characteristics** are those that are not necessary for reproduction, including breast development, pubic hair growth, lowered voice pitch, and hair growth on the face and underarms.

For each of these physical developments, it is possible to describe a specific sequence of changes. The progress of an individual teenager can then be described as a point along that sequence. Following the work of J. M. Tanner (1978), these sequences are customarily divided into five stages, with stage 1 always representing the preadolescent condition, stage 2 the first signs of pubertal change, stages 3 and 4 the next steps, and stage 5 the final adult characteristic. (To give you a more concrete sense of these stages, Table 4.2 describes the steps in pubic hair development.) These stages have proved to be extremely

---

TABLE 4.2

**The five stages of pubic hair development**

| | |
|---|---|
| 1 | There is no pubic hair at this first stage. (In all of Tanner's series of five stages, stage 1 always represents the *pre*pubertal level.) |
| 2 | A few pubic hairs appear, usually long, slightly pigmented hair that is either straight or slightly curly. This first growth is normally at the base of the penis or along the labia. |
| 3 | Pubic hair in stage 3 is not only denser but darker, coarser, and more curled. It is also spread over a larger area. |
| 4 | The pubic hair now resembles that of an adult in quality but covers a smaller area. There is no spread to the thighs, nor is the full triangle completed. |
| 5 | Adult pattern of pubic hair, in both distribution and quality. |

*SOURCE:* Adapted from Petersen & Taylor, 1980.

helpful not only in describing the normal progress through puberty but also in identifying the rate of development of individual youngsters.

*Primary Sex Characteristics: Girls*   For both boys and girls, changes in the reproductive organs are gradual, but for girls the first menstruation (called **menarche**, and pronounced menarkee) is a clear single event that is often taken as a measure of sexual maturity. In fact, however, although some girls do conceive shortly after menarche, for most girls no ovum is produced during the first several menstrual cycles. Then for a while only some cycles are fertile, until full fertility is achieved about a year after menarche.

For most girls in the United Stages and Western Europe, the average age of menarche is between 12½ and 13, with 95 percent of all girls experiencing this event between the ages of 11 and 15 (Garn, 1980; Tanner, 1978). In about three-quarters of girls, menarche occurs soon after the peak growth spurt and after breast development is already at stage 4 (close to adult shape and size), so it is typically a fairly late development in the sequence, as you can see in Figure 4.6.

*Primary Sex Characteristicxs: Boys*   In boys, there are major changes in reproductive organs beginning at about age 11 to 12. The first signs of change are an enlargement of the testes and scrotum, with the penis beginning to enlarge a little later. The entire process normally takes three to four years to complete. The stages of this sequence are outlined in Table 4.3.

Precisely when in this sequence the boy achieves reproductive maturity is very difficult to determine. The first nocturnal emission is a private event (unlike menarche, which normally occasions both discussion and assistance), and it is hard to tell just when the seminal fluid begins to contain viable sperm. For most boys, real fertility seems to occur sometime between 12 and 16.

TABLE 4.3

**Stages in genital development in boys**

| | |
|---|---|
| 1 | Preadolescent stage: no change yet in testes, scrotum, or penis. |
| 2 | The first change is in the scrotum and testes, which become slightly enlarged. The skin of the scrotum also changes color, becoming reddened. |
| 3 | The penis shows its first enlargement at stage 3, mainly an increase in length. The testes and scrotum also show further enlargement. |
| 4 | The penis continues to show further growth, in breadth and in the development of the glans. Testes and scrotum, too, continue their growth. |
| 5 | Adult level of genital development. |

*SOURCE:* Petersen & Taylor, 1980.

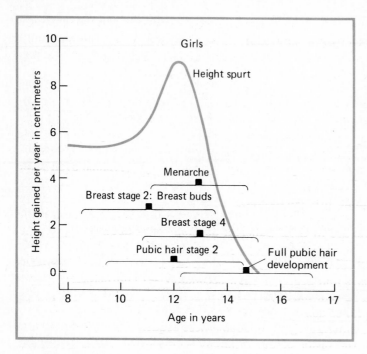

**Figure 4.6** This figure, which shows the pubertal changes for girls, should give you some sense of the sequence of events that is most common. The box on each line represents the average attainment of that change, while the line indicates the range of normal times. (*Sources:* Information from Tanner, 1978; Garn, 1980; Chumlea, 1982.)

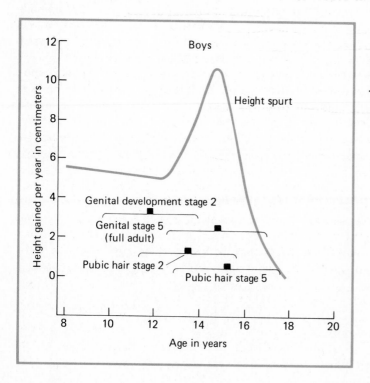

**Figure 4.7** The sequence of pubertal changes for boys. If you compare this figure with the pattern for girls (above), you can see clearly that all the changes are about two years earlier for girls. (*Sources:* Tanner, 1978; Chumlea, 1982.)

Figure 4.7 shows the sequence of changes for boys. As you can see, the changes in testes and penis normally begin before the boy shows the maximum growth spurt. But like girls, the point of reproductive fertility probably occurs after the height spurt.

*Secondary Sex Characteristics*     I have included several of the important secondary sex characteristics in Figures 4.6 and 4.7, so you can see how they occur in the normal sequence. Other than pubic hair, new body hair (such as under the arms) typically develops only after stage 4 of pubic hair development. Facial hair in boys develops even later, as does the breaking of the voice.

Two things are particularly interesting about these sequences. First, if you compare the two figures, you will see just how much ahead of boys girls are in their pubertal development—about two years for most shared sequences. (Most of you remember that period in late elementary school or junior high when all the girls were suddenly taller than the boys and began to show secondary sex characteristics while the 11- and 12-year-old boys were still definitely prepubertal. A painful time for a lot of us.)

A second intriguing thing about these sequences of development is that while the order of development seems to be highly consistent *within* each sequence, there is quite a lot of variability *across* sequences. A boy may be in stage 2 of genital development but already in stage 5 of pubic hair development. And different young people may experience the set of changes in somewhat different orders. So far physiologists have not figured out why this occurs. I've given you the averages in the tables and figures, but if you are trying to predict the development of an individual child, you should remember that the pattern may be quite different from the norm.

*Other Changes Accompanying Puberty*     Aside from the changes in primary and secondary sex characteristics and in height, musculature, and fat, there are some important changes in the body organs that seem to be triggered by the same hormones. In particular, the heart and lungs increase markedly in size, and the heart rate drops. Both of these changes are more pronounced for boys than for girls—another of the factors that increase the capacity for sustained effort for boys relative to girls. Before about age 12, boys and girls have similar physical strength, speed, and endurance; after puberty, boys have more of all three.

Obviously, children's bodies change enormously over the first 15 years of life. The brief picture I have provided of these changes should give you some sense of the alterations in muscles, fat, internal organs, and nervous system. But what this description does not tell you is how the changes affect the way the child can *use* his body—to crawl, walk, run, catch, throw or kick balls, pick up objects, and all the rest. What, in other words, are the implications of physical change for the child's *activity?*

## PUTTING THE CHANGES TOGETHER: MOTOR DEVELOPMENT

Psychologists usually use the phrase *motor development* to describe the complex changes in the child's body activities and movements. For parents or teachers, this is often the most noticeable part of physical development. The baby's first step, after all, is a big milestone, as is the first bike ride. But it's important to keep in mind that when the child learns to skip or ride a bike, those new skills are built upon a great many less obvious or totally invisible changes in body composition or chemistry.

Robert Malina (1982) suggests that we can divide the wide range of motor skills into three rough groups: *locomotor* patterns (such as walking, running, jumping, hopping, and skipping), *nonlocomotor* patterns (such as pushing, pulling, and bending), and *manipulative* skills (such as grasping, throwing, catching, kicking, and other actions involving receiving and moving objects). Nearly all the basic skills in all three areas are complete by about 6 or 7 years of age. After that, change is mostly improvement in performance as the child refines the basic skills and integrates them into more and more complex movement sequences. So 6- and 7-year-olds can kick soccer balls or dribble basketballs, but they do not do so skillfully or smoothly.

### Some Basic Sequences

Many of the key developments in motor skills take place during the first two years—a sequence I've listed briefly in Table 4.4. You may get a better sense of the changes, though, with pictures than with words.

TABLE 4.4

**Some major milestones in motor development, birth to 2 years**

| Age | Motor Skill |
| --- | --- |
| 1½ mo. | Lifts chin when on stomach |
| 3 mo. | Lifts chest; holds head erect when held |
| 5 mo. | Turns from side to back |
| 7–8 mo. | Sits with support, and then sits alone |
| 9 mo. | Stands with help |
| 10 mo. | Crawls |
| 11 mo. | Walks with support |
| 14 mo. | Stands alone |
| 15 mo. | Walks alone |
| 20 mo. | Runs |
| 24 mo. | Walks well |

Figure 4.8 shows a key locomotor sequence, that of walking (along with balancing and skipping). Figure 4.9 shows an important manipulative sequence, that of grasping—a skill that is essential for so many of the child's encounters with the toys and other objects in his world. The baby moves from grasping things with the fingers pressed against the palm to finally using the thumb in opposition to the forefinger—a sequence that is complete by about age 2.

I've explored some of the practical implications of all these changes in Box 4.1. There are less obvious, but enormously significant, implications for the child's mental and social development as well. As the child is able to sit up, crawl, walk, and ride a bike, she can explore her world more fully, which is critical for intellectual growth. At the same time, she becomes steadily more independent, which affects her relationships with her parents and peers. It is a remarkable day when your child first hops on her bike and casually announces, "I'm going to ride over to Julie's house to play." Things are never quite the same again!

## SECOND DESCRIPTIONS: BIG OR FAST VERSUS SLOW OR SMALL— SOME INDIVIDUAL DIFFERENCES

So far I have been concentrating on sequences of development—on patterns of physical development that are *common* to virtually all children. But I am sure you have gathered from several brief comments (as well as from your own observation of children) that there are wide individual differences in the *rate* and *timing* of the physical changes I have been describing. Not only are these differences interesting in their own right, they may also affect a child's relationships with his peers or his general contacts with the world around him.

### Differences in Rate

Children vary widely in the speed with which they go through all the body and motor changes I have described. Some children walk at 7 or 8 months; others not until 18 months. Some are skillful soccer players at 5 or 6, others not until much later. These differences are most striking at puberty, when young people of the same age may range from stage 1 to stage 5 in the steps of sexual maturation—as you can see very vividly in Figure 4.10.

As a general rule, a child is consistently early or average or slow in physical development. The child who shows slower bone development is also likely to walk later, to show slower motor development, and to have later puberty (Tanner, 1978). Similarly, tall infants tend to be taller teenagers and taller adults. There are exceptions to both of these generalizations, but what Tanner calls the *tempo of growth* is a powerful element in development.

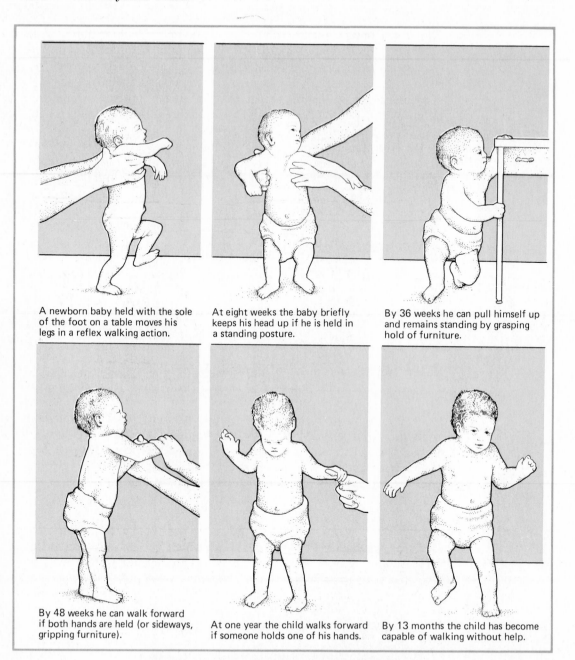

A newborn baby held with the sole of the foot on a table moves his legs in a reflex walking action.

At eight weeks the baby briefly keeps his head up if he is held in a standing posture.

By 36 weeks he can pull himself up and remains standing by grasping hold of furniture.

By 48 weeks he can walk forward if both hands are held (or sideways, gripping furniture).

At one year the child walks forward if someone holds one of his hands.

By 13 months the child has become capable of walking without help.

**Figure 4.8** These drawings show one of the key locomotor skill sequences, from standing to walking, and then to more complex skills. (*Source:* The Diagram Group, *Child's body: An owner's manual.* New York: Paddington Press, 1977, section D-13.)

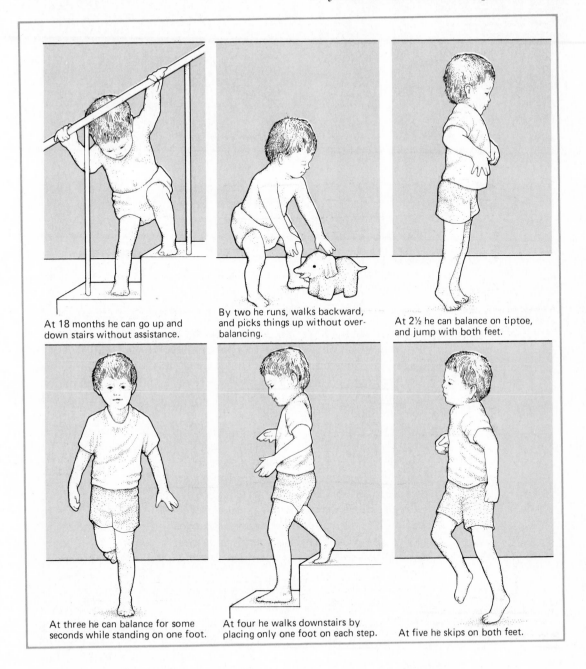

At 18 months he can go up and down stairs without assistance.

By two he runs, walks backward, and picks things up without over-balancing.

At 2½ he can balance on tiptoe, and jump with both feet.

At three he can balance for some seconds while standing on one foot.

At four he walks downstairs by placing only one foot on each step.

At five he skips on both feet.

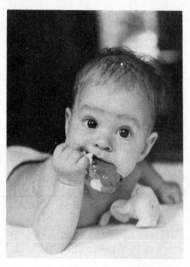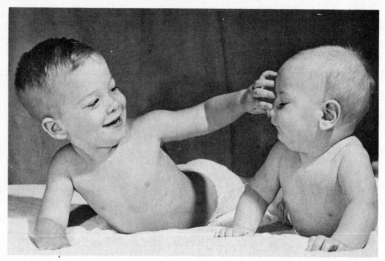

**Figure 4.9** These two photos show the transition from whole-hand grasping to thumb-forefinger opposition. Once the child has reached the final step, he can pick up small objects, turn doorknobs more easily, and perform many other tasks requiring fine motor coordination.

*Effects of Differing Rates on Mental Development*  These differences in rate of development appear to have at least some small link to a child's mental development, too. The general rule is that children who are more rapid in physical development are also slightly ahead in mental development. So if we compare children of the same age, those with the "oldest" skeletal or pubertal development or the most coordinated motor skill are also likely to score higher on an IQ test or to do slightly better in school (Wolff, 1981; Westin-Lindgren, 1982; Tanner, 1978; Pollitt, Mueller, & Leibel, 1982). It is also true that physically larger children of any given age tend to score higher on IQ tests. None of these differences is terribly large. (As an example, in one study, Tanner found an average difference of nine IQ points between 10-year-olds in the top 25 percent of height for their age versus those in the bottom 25 percent.) But the relationship is found consistently.

Some of this relationship between rate of growth and mental development may be due to the direct impact of brain growth; some may reflect differences in diet or differences in confidence or self-esteem between the larger, fast-developing children and the slower developers. And some may be due to differences in the responsibilities or opportunities offered by the people around the child (such as more challenging or more difficult tasks assigned to bigger children in summer camp). The thing I find interesting about this pattern is not so much that a difference exists in childhood (when the physical variations between fast and slow developer are apparent) but that it persists into adulthood. That is, adults who were early developers as children still have a slight intellectual advantage over their slower-developing peers, even though the latter group has caught up in height, brain growth, and physical skill. Presumably this carry-over into adulthood is a consequence of the psychological effects of earliness or lateness rather than of the physiological effects.

*Effects of Differences in Rate on Personality*    Faster-developing children also have somewhat different personalities. This effect is particularly apparent at adolescence, when we see differences between early maturers and late maturers in a number of personal qualities. One of the curious aspects of the research in this area, though, is that the effects of early or late maturing seem—at least at first look—to be quite different for boys and girls.

For boys, early puberty generally carries an advantage. Early-maturing boys are rated by others (parents and peers) as more poised, relaxed, good-natured. They are popular with their peers and tend to be leaders. In contrast, the late-maturing boy is likely to be rated as more tense, restless, talkative, attention-seeking, and less popular with his peers (Jones, 1957; Mussen & Jones, 1957; Savin-Williams, 1979). Mary Cover Jones (1965) and Harvey Peskin (1967, 1973) later followed one group of early- and late-maturing boys into adulthood and found that some of these differences persisted. As adults, early maturers were described as more responsible, cooperative, and sociable but also as more rigid, humorless, and conforming. Late maturers, on the other hand, were described both as more impulsive and assertive and as more insightful, creative, and playful.

Among girls, the results are much less clear. My own reading of the evidence is that *very* early maturing (such as menarche in the fifth or sixth grade) seems to be a negative experience for girls (Ruble & Brooks-Gunn, 1982; Peskin, 1973). Not only do very early maturers experience more physical and psychological symptoms accompanying menarche, they are also described as having less poise and lower popularity. Within the average or normal range of pubertal development, though, early development does seem to carry some advantages. So among seventh or eighth graders, girls who show clear breast development or other signs of maturity are more popular than are those who are still physically immature (Savin-Williams, 1979). Interestingly, though, Peskin concluded that in adulthood it was the very early-maturing girls—those who appeared to struggle the most in adolescence—who made a better adult adjustment.

It seems to me that one way to make sense out of the apparently conflicting findings for boys and girls is by remembering that "early" and "late" mean different things for the two sexes. Although girls develop sooner than boys do, there is a period of years—from perhaps 12 or 13 to about age 15 or 16—that is the "normal" range of ages for puberty for both sexes. Young people who develop in this normal range seem to have an advantage over those who are atypical. The difference is that for girls, the "atypical," or "out of range," development is very

BOX 4.1

# MOTOR DEVELOPMENT AND TOYS

If you have ever tried to buy a toy for a child, you know how bewildering it can be to walk into a store and see aisles and aisles of bright, attractive items. You want to find something that is right for your child's skills, but how do you know what makes a good toy and what toys are good at what ages? The answer to these questions can come partly from what we know about a child's motor development.

## BIRTH TO 6 MONTHS

Little babies use their hands and their eyes to play, so a good choice is something that is bright, safe to hold on to, and hooked to the crib so it won't fall. Mobiles and "cradle gyms" fit the category and so do soft toys tied to the sides of the crib.

## 6 TO 12 MONTHS

Older babies are more mobile and are interested in toys that let them try out their new large-muscle skills. Sling seats that hang from doorways and let babies jump are good, and so are "walkers," similar seats set on frames with wheels. Probably the best thing for a child this age is to "childproof" your house (removing hazards like sharp objects and poisons) so the child can explore freely. Playpens (now usually called "play yards") are probably not as good, although they may sometimes be necessary for safety reasons.

Infants of this age also enjoy stacking and nesting toys. Measuring cups and pots and pans are often better for this than expensive baby toys.

## SECOND YEAR

Give a toddler an expensive toy, and chances are he will show at least as much interest in the box it came in as in the toy itself. (Big boxes that can be crawled into I have found to be a particular hit.) At the other end of the size scale, since he can now pick things up with his thumb and forefinger, smaller objects (but not so small that they can be swallowed) are often favorites.

Toddlers like toys with wheels, but *push* toys are better than *pull toys* because the child can see the object while it moves. Near the end of the year, toward the second birthday, the child can sometimes handle a big crayon or pencil and may enjoy "drawing." For obvious reasons, washable colors are preferred!

---

early puberty; for boys, the "out of range" development tends to be late puberty. In other words, I am suggesting that children and teenagers pay a price for being *different,* whether that difference is very early or very late.

One additional element probably enters the equation for boys: Since athletic ability is highly valued among teenage boys, and since early-developing boys tend to have greater motor skills and coordination (as well as greater size for football or basketball), relative earliness for boys carries a special bonus. It will be interesting to see whether the recent emphasis on competitive sports for junior high school girls—such as basketball or volleyball, both of which call for height—will begin to confer some of the same advantages on

*THIRD YEAR*

When in doubt, get something with wheels. Kiddie cars, tricycles, and other riding toys are favorites among large toys, and cars and trucks (for both sexes) among small ones. Building toys start to be interesting, especially those with many possibilities, like large wooden blocks (and again, homemade are just as satisfactory as expensive kits from a store).

Coloring and drawing are usually great favorites, as are those messy classics, painting and playdough. As with younger children, "washable" is an important label to look for.

*FOURTH TO SEVENTH YEAR*

Small-muscle coordination develops rapidly during this period, and the child can manage toys like beads (to be strung on a string) and more accurate cutting (although typical children's scissors are too dull for much accuracy; a sharp pair of scissors is a great gift for a child old enough to use them safely).

Large-muscle skills are improving, too, and smaller balls (baseball- or tennis-size) can be used as well as large ones. By the end of this period, the child can often manage a bicycle or at least start on one with training wheels.

*ELEMENTARY SCHOOL*

Coordination is well developed by this age. Children 7 and 8 years old can usually ride a bicycle easily and can skip rope and play most games that require hitting, kicking, or throwing a ball. I should emphasize that children as young as 3 can do most of these things, too, *if* a large enough ball, a wide enough hockey stick, or a light enough racket is used. From age 3 through at least age 10, the development of play and athletic skills is more one of degree than of kind. So if you are interested in having your child develop specific abilities needed for later organized sports, you can begin quite early, as long as the materials are sized properly for the child's ability and you do not press for perfect coordination too early.

Practice in small-muscle coordination over the earlier years also makes the elementary-school–age child much more skillful with model building, arts and crafts, and even sewing—all of which may make excellent toys/games/gifts for children this age.

As a general rule, at every age steer clear of expensive, complex toys that do only one or two things (especially all those wretched toys that require batteries!). I am thinking here of toys like robots that whirr and walk. Children are intrigued the first time but rapidly lose interest, and such toys are not adaptable to other forms of play.

early-developing girls. I suspect, in fact, that it will not. At least at present, among girls it is the *late* developers—the small, very lean girls—who tend to persist with athletic effort in such sports as gymnastics or track. But we will have to see.

## Social Class and Racial Differences in Physical Development

As a group, poor children grow a bit slower and are a bit shorter than middle-class children, most probably because of dietary differences. The same social class (or income or education) differences show up in comparisons of menarchal age in poor versus more affluent women.

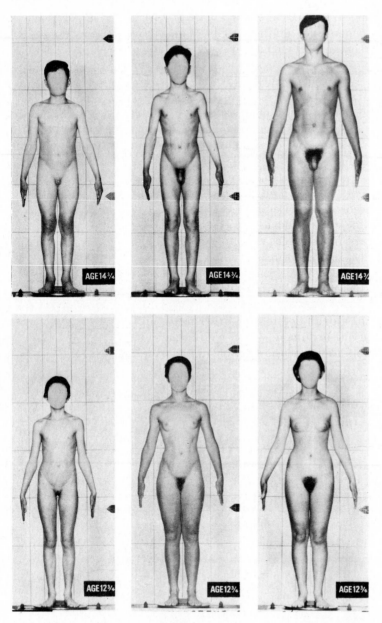

**Figure 4.10** Teenagers vary enormously in the timing and speed of pubertal changes, as you can see very clearly from these photographs. (*Source:* J. M. Tanner, Growth and endocrinology of the adolescent. In L. J. Garnder [Ed.], *Endocrine and genetic diseases of childhood and adolescence,* 2nd ed. © 1975 by W. B. Saunders Co., Philadelphia, Penn., p. 28.)

Stanley Garn (1980), using reports collected in 1968–1970 from over 5000 black and white women in 10 states, found that women and girls from families that are at the median income or better experience menarche about half a year earlier than do those from poverty-level families. This difference was clearer in the white group but was also present among black women.

Some of the variations in pattern and rate of growth that we see between different racial groups are undoubtedly partially the result of differences in income or diet rather than race itself. But there are also genuine racial differences, too.

Black infants and children appear to be slightly ahead of white children in some aspects of physical development. In fact, the gestational period for the black fetus seems actually to be slightly shorter than for the white fetus (Smith & Stenchever, 1978). Black babies also show somewhat faster development of motor skills, such as walking, and are slightly taller than their white counterparts (Bayley, 1965), with longer legs, more muscle, and heavier bones (Tanner, 1978). At puberty, black girls have slightly earlier menarche as well (on the order of about three months on average, according to Tanner). Thus, the tempo of growth appears to be slightly faster in black children than in white.

Asian children (Chinese, Japanese, and others) also have a relatively rapid growth tempo but are smaller, with long upper bodies but shorter final height.

## Sex Differences in Physical Growth

I have mentioned a number of sex differences in physical growth as I've gone along in this chapter, but let me pull together all the bits and pieces for you here. Table 4.5 summarizes the major findings.

TABLE 4.5
**Summary of sex differences in physical growth**

| Characteristic | Nature of Difference |
| --- | --- |
| Rate of maturation | Girls are on a faster timetable throughout development; this difference is about six weeks at birth and about two years at adolescence. |
| Predictability or regularity of maturation | Girls' physical growth is more regular and predictable, with fewer uneven spurts. It is easier to predict the final height of a girl, for example, than of a boy. |
| Strength and speed | There is little difference until adolescence, but after puberty, boys are stronger and faster. |
| Heart and circulation | At adolescence, boys develop a larger heart and lungs and a greater capacity for carrying oxygen in the blood than do girls. |
| Fat tissue | Girls from birth on have a thicker layer of fat tissue just below the surface of the skin and have a larger percentage of body weight devoted to fat after puberty. |
| Motor skills | In the preschool years, girls are better at tasks requiring jumping, hopping, rhythmic movement, and balance. In elementary school and later, boys are better at activities requiring running, jumping, and throwing, while girls are better at hopping. |

*SOURCES:* Tanner, 1978; Archer, 1981; Malina, 1982.

As you can see from the table, most physical differences between males and females become more pronounced after puberty. Preadolescent girls and boys are about equal in strength and speed. After adolescence, boys become stronger and faster as well as larger. One of the implications of this is that a 12-year-old girl is probably just as strong and just as good at throwing balls and stealing bases as a 14-year-old boy, since they are both at about the same point in pubertal development. At this age, girls should be able to compete effectively in Little League or other sports. A few years later, though, it will be the unusual girl who is able to compete successfully with boys in sports that call for considerable strength or speed. This is not an argument against athletics for girls. On the contrary. .Everything I know about the effect of maintaining fitness for adult health and longevity points to the importance of encouraging both boys and girls to develop athletic interests and skills that will carry forward into adult life. But it *is* an argument against mixed-sex competitive teams in high school.

Despite the general differences listed in the table, you should keep in mind that the distributions overlap. There are many girls with excellent speed and strength (see Figure 4.11) and many boys who are less physically developed.

## EXPLANATIONS OF PHYSICAL DEVELOPMENT

So far I have been answering "what" questions. I have been describing common developmental patterns and individual differences in rate or pattern. But "why" questions are equally important. Why does physical development occur as it does, and what can affect it?

### Maturation

It seems very clear that some set of internal signals governs most of the growth patterns I have described. While the *rate of development* varies from one child to the next, the *sequence* is virtually the same for all children, even those with marked physical or mental handicaps (Kopp, 1979). For example, Down's syndrome infants are often slower in motor development than are normal children; they nonetheless move through the sequence from sitting to standing to walking in the same order (Carr, 1975; Dicks-Mireaux, 1972).

The precise mechanisms by which such regular sequences of development are controlled are not fully understood. We presume that the signals are contained in the genetic code in some way and are thus shared by all members of the species.

**Figure 4.11** While it is true that the average teenage girl is not as strong or as fast as the average boy, there are many girls who are very swift and very strong.

## Heredity

Our genetic heritage is individual as well as species-specific. In addition to being programmed for the basic sequences, each of us also receives instructions for unique growth tendencies. Both size and body shape seem to be heavily influenced by such specific inheritance. Tall parents tend to have tall children; short parents tend to have short children (Garn, 1980). And there are similarities between parents and children in such things as hip width, arm length (some ancestor certainly passed on a gene for long arms to me!), and sitting height (long or short trunk).

An interesting phenomenon known as *regression to the mean* also operates in the genetics of growth (or other genetic patterns). For example, *very tall parents typically have children who are shorter than they are*, since the set of genes required for extreme height is quite rare and is not likely to be passed on to the children in precisely the same form.

The same process occurs when two very short people reproduce: their children are generally taller than they are.

*Rate* or tempo of growth as well as final shape or size seem to be an inherited pattern, too. Parents who were themselves early developers, as measured by such things as bone ossification or (for mothers) age of menarche, tend to have children who are faster developers, too (Garn, 1980). The age of menarche is itself strongly influenced by specific heredity. Tanner (1970) describes several studies of identical twin sisters, non-twin sisters, and random pairs of girls. Menarche is virtually the same for identical twins, somewhat similar in sisters, and not at all alike in random pairs of girls. This is precisely the pattern we would expect if there were one or more genes controlling the timing of physical changes.

## Environmental Effects

But as usual, nothing is completely one-sided. There are potent external influences on physical growth as well.

*Practice*   If a child were completely immobilized and given no opportunity to practice crawling, walking, or grasping, would those skills develop anyway? Is the underlying growth of bones and muscles all that is needed? Or does the baby have to have a chance to try out the coordination of muscles, bones, and senses?

There's still a good deal of disagreement about the answers to these questions. On the one hand, there is quite a lot of evidence that practice plays only a small role in the development of such skills as walking and climbing stairs. Several older studies of pairs of twins by Gesell and Thompson (1929) and McGraw (1935) were focused on this question directly. In each case, one twin of the pair was given a lot of early practice on the particular skill. Later, the second twin was given a brief period of practice, and then the two twins were tested. In general, if the "untrained twin" had been given even the briefest practice, the two children performed almost equally well on the task. For at least these early motor skills, then, a little bit of practice late is as good as a lot of practice earlier, presumably because physical changes have taken place in the intervening time.

Still, practice does matter. In the twin studies, the babies had at least some opportunity for normal physical exploration and body movement. The untrained twin was not kept completely immobile; she could practice parts of the acts of walking or crawling, even if special practice was not given. But when such opportunities for exercise and movement are *greatly* restricted, there *is* some retardation in motor development. A study by Wayne Dennis (1960) of children raised in Iranian orphanages is a good example (as is parallel re-

**Figure 4.12** Most babies love to stand and totter a few steps as soon as they are able; and most parents love to help them practice. But does this kind of practice really speed up the sequence so that the child walks sooner? Probably not—though that's no reason to stop doing it!

search on orphanage-reared children by Provence and Lipton, 1961). The babies in one of the institutions Dennis observed were routinely placed on their backs in cribs with very lumpy mattresses. They had little or no experience of lying or moving on their stomachs as a normal baby would and even had difficulty rolling over because of the hollows in the mattresses. These babies almost never went through the normal sequence of learning to walk—presumably because they didn't have enough opportunity to practice all the on-the-stomach parts of the skill. They did learn to walk eventually, but they were about a year late.

Thus, although many aspects of physical development are heavily

BOX 4.2

# OBESITY IN CHILDREN

In the United States, obesity has become a major national health problem. At least 15 percent of adults (and possibly many more) are more than 20 percent over the standard weight for their height. Life expectancy is reduced for people who are significantly overweight, and they are more prone to a number of disorders, including high blood pressure.

Perhaps because we've all become aware of fatness in adults, there has been a recent interest in obesity in children as well. Do fat children become fat adults? What contributes to overweight in children?

### DO OBESE CHILDREN BECOME OBESE ADULTS?

The answer to the question of whether childhood obesity leads to obesity in later life depends on the age of the children when you measure their fatness. Obese *infants* have only a slightly higher risk of obesity in adulthood, compared to leaner babies. But obesity in older children—beginning at age 4 or 6, for example—is

quite strongly predictive of adult fatness (Roche, 1981; Grinker, 1981). So while chubby babies don't necessarily become chubby adults, fat children usually do become fat adults.

Of course, the correlation is by no means perfect. Many fat adults were lean as children and only became overweight later in life; and some overweight children became much leaner adults. There has been a considerable amount of discussion among physicians and researchers about the possibility of there being two "types" of fatness—one kind that is present in childhood (which usually persists) and a different kind that appears only in adulthood. My reading of the recent research leaves me doubting this idea, but the data are not all in yet.

### WHAT CAUSES OBESITY IN CHILDREN?

To oversimplify a bit, there seem to be three causes for childhood obesity. First, children can inherit a tendency to fatness or leanness. Jean Mayer (1975) found in one study that only 7 percent of children of normal-weight parents were

determined by basic maturation, the process is much more complex than that. Some minimum amount of practice is needed just to keep the system working as it should. And complex combinations of basic actions, such as those required for kicking or throwing objects, improve markedly with practice. It is even possible that some chance to move and practice individual movements is necessary to stimulate the development of the brain, particularly the myelinization of the nerves. That is, the effects may work both ways—from brain development to better motor skill and from practicing movements to faster brain development. Exactly this argument, by the way, lies behind special therapies for physically handicapped children that consist of passive stimulation of body movements.

*Diet*   Another major influence on physical growth is the child's diet. Poorly nourished children grow more slowly and then don't end up as

obese, but 80 percent of those with two obese parents were themselves seriously overweight. Adopted children raised by obese parents, in contrast, are less likely to be overweight.

A second contributor is exercise. Again, some of the most interesting research comes from Jean Mayer. He found that obese children simply don't move as much, even while doing the same things. For example, normal-weight girls were in motion about 90 percent of the time while playing tennis; obese girls moved only 50 percent of the time. Meyer found, in fact, that he could help the obese girls reduce simply by introducing a regular exercise program, without changing their diet.

Just why some children move less vigorously is not so clear. It may be a basic temperamental difference; it may reflect differences in basic body type; or it may be that already-heavy bodies simply require more effort to move around, so that the overweight child moves less and less vigorously. Whatever the reason, lack of exercise appears to be an important element in overweight in children and adults.

A third element in the equation is obviously the child's diet and the family's eating patterns. Some researchers (e.g., Garn, Clark, & Guire,

1975) have argued that diet in infancy and early childhood is particularly critical because these are the years when fat cells are being added. Overfeeding an infant may thus increase the number of fat cells, and the child will then be stuck with this larger number, with added risk of later obesity. There is a good deal of dispute about this "fat cell number" theory (Roche, 1981) but little dispute about the general importance of diet in influencing fatness or leanness in children (and adults).

The family's attitude toward food, however, may turn out to be as important as the actual diet. A child whose family treats food as an antidote to boredom or unhappiness will acquire a very different set of classically conditioned emotional responses to food than will a child whose family treats food largely as a source of nourishment.

For some children, these several elements may work in combination to predispose the child strongly to obesity. The child may inherit a tendency to add fat cells and may also be of a generally placid temperament. If the child is then regularly fed more than required (especially when upset or bored) and remains inactive, the problem is compounded.

large. More important, malnutrition in the early years may have a permanent effect on some parts of the brain and nervous system.

As I pointed out earlier, the period of maximum brain growth is in the final three to five months of pregnancy and the first two to three years after birth (particularly the first six months after birth). Severe malnutrition during that time, even if the child later has an adequate diet, may still produce a lasting slow rate of physical and motor development (Malina, 1982). Such children may show some catch up in height or growth rate but are typically shorter and slower than their peers. Research with animals (and some parallel studies of the brains and nervous systems of malnourished children who have died) shows that the main physical effects of malnutrition are to reduce the amount of connective tissue between individual brain cells and to slow the rate of myelinization (Lewin, 1975; Dickerson, 1981). As a consequence, the cortex does not become as heavy. If the child is given a better diet during these early years, he seems to be able to catch up in brain development. But if the child's diet continues to be bad for the first two or three years, the effects appear to be permanent.

The impact of more mild malnutrition or "subnutrition" is harder to detect and has not been widely studied. We really don't know how poorly the child must be nourished before we see the effects in growth rate or motor coordination. It does appear, however, that chronic subnutrition affects the child's level of energy, which in turn can affect the nature of the interactions the child has with both the objects and the people around him (Barrett, Radke-Yarrow, & Klein, 1982). Just how this might affect social or intellectual development is a question I'll return to in later chapters.

At the other end of the diet continuum—obesity—we can also see effects of environment on the child's physical growth and psychological development. I've explored this important question in Box 4.2.

*Illness*    A third type of experience that can affect a child's growth is a long-term illness. Usually a sick child grows more slowly during the illness, perhaps because she is less active, or her diet has changed, or because of the operation of the disease itself. But after she recovers, her growth jumps ahead, and she shows something Tanner calls "catch up" (Tanner, 1970, 1978). He describes the case of one child, as an example, who had had a tumor on the adrenal gland from ages 1 to 3 (Prader, Tanner, & Von Harnack, 1963). By age 4, the child was extremely small—only about 30 inches tall, which is smaller than the average 2-year-old. When the tumor was removed, however, the child shot up. She grew about 8 inches in the next two years, and by adolescence she was within the normal range. She was still smaller than average, so the catch up wasn't total. But after several years of rapid growth, she returned to the *pace* of development she had shown before her illness.

Generally speaking, the earlier in a child's life an illness or malnutrition occurs, the more lasting the effect and the less successfully the child catches up to fully normal development. This is another example of a *sensitive period*, of the kind I discussed in Chapter 1.

*Secular Trends: An Example of Environmental Influence*    A striking example of the cumulative effect of all these potential environmental influences is a set of findings described as **secular trends**. In the United States, in Europe, in Japan and in other countries, average heights have been climbing steadily in each generation. In Sweden, for example, where accurate health records have been kept for over 100 years, the average height has gone up 3 to 4 inches since 1883 (Ljung,

Bergsten-Brucefors, & Lindgren, 1974). During those same years, there has been a steady decline in the age of menarche. Figure 4.13 shows this drop in menarchal age for one large sample of women in the United States (Garn, 1980). You can see that menarchal age has dropped a year or more in this century. In many European countries, the drop has been even more striking (Roche, 1979). Since menarchal timing is frequently taken as a measure of rate of maturation, what these trends tell us is that children are developing faster these days and ending up bigger.

But this does not mean that by the next century girls will begin menstruating at 11 and boys will all be 6 feet 4 inches. Most of these changes seem to be due to improvements in standard of living, particularly diet, and the rate of change has definitely leveled off—as you can see in Figure 4.13.

## THE SHAPE OF PHYSICAL DEVELOPMENT: A LAST LOOK

Of all the facets of development I'll describe in this book, physical development is probably least influenced by specific experience and most governed by underlying maturational patterns. But it is a mistake to conclude that environment has only minor effects. The strength and coordination required to throw a basketball high enough to reach the basket undoubtedly does develop in predictable ways over the early years without much intervention. But to develop the skill needed to get the ball through the hoop with regularity, from different angles and

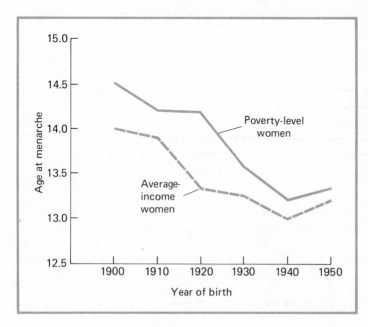

**Figure 4.13** Average age at menarche has been dropping steadily in the United States (and elsewhere in the world) for the past century, as these data show. The trend can be seen both for poor women and for more affluent women, although the menarchal age is consistently earlier for the middle-class women. This is an example of a "secular trend." (*Source:* Garn, 1980, p. 133.)

*consistency*

distances, requires endless practice. The development of really smooth, coordinated skill in virtually all complex motor tasks requires practice. It also requires an adequate enough diet to maintain the system and decent health. More important, the rate and pattern of the child's physical development also affect his self-image, his personality, his interactions with the world around him. So physical development influences experience as much as the reverse.

## SUMMARY

1. It is important to know something about physical growth and development because specific new behaviors are triggered by physical changes, because physical skills affect the kinds of experiences the child can have, and because her feelings about her own body can affect self-concept and personality.
2. Changes in height and weight are rapid during the first two years, then level off to a steady pace until adolescence, when there is a sharp "growth spurt."
3. Bones develop in a similar pattern, with rapid early growth and another rapid growth at adolescence. There are also increases in the number of bones and in the hardening of the bones, which occurs in a sequence.
4. Muscle tissue increases primarily in density and length of fibers, with a much larger increase at adolescence for boys than for girls.
5. Fat cells are added in the early years and then again rapidly at adolescence, in this case more for girls than for boys.
6. The brain is not fully developed at birth; over the first two years, connective tissue and the myelin sheath covering the nerves develop. Within the cortex, the portions governing vision, hearing, and basic motor movements are most fully developed in early infancy.
7. Hormones are vital influences throughout growth, particularly during adolescence. The pituitary gland secretes triggering hormones at the beginning of puberty, which stimulate the development of sex hormones. These, in turn, trigger the development of primary and secondary sex characteristics.
8. Pubertal changes begin as early as 8 or 9 in girls and continue until the midteens. In boys, the changes begin about two years later. In both sexes, the physical changes occur in reliable sequences, with beginning changes in secondary sex characteristics first visible, followed by the growth spurt, with reproductive maturity late in the sequence.
9. Developing motor skills—walking, running, bending, picking things up, throwing, and the like—reflect all the underlying changes. Most basic motor skills are present by about age 6; practice is required for further refinements.
10. Children differ markedly in the rate with which all these changes

take place. In general, rapidly developing children have advantages over slower-developing children in intellectual skill and in confidence and popularity.

11. Some social-class and racial differences can be detected, too, with children from poverty-level environments developing more slowly.

12. Males and females also differ in both rate and pattern of physical development. Girls are accelerated in physical growth, but at adolescence, boys develop more muscle tissue and a larger heart and circulatory system than do girls.

13. Maturation is the most important process underlying physical growth and development. Most sequences require only minimal environmental support. However, specific heredity, diet, and illness affect both the rate and pattern of development in individual children.

## KEY TERMS

**Cortex**  The convoluted gray portion of the brain that governs most complex thought, language, and memory, among other functions.

**Endocrine glands**  These glands—including the adrenals, the thyroid, the pituitary, the testes, and the ovaries—secrete hormones governing overall physical growth and sexual maturing.

**Estrogen**  The female sex hormone secreted by the ovaries.

**Fontanels**  The "soft spots" in the skull present at birth. These disappear when the several bones of the skull grow together.

**Gonadotrophic hormones**  Hormones produced in the pituitary gland that stimulate the sex organs to develop.

**Menarche**  Onset of menstruation in girls.

**Midbrain**  The section of the brain below the cortex that develops earlier than the cortex and regulates attention, sleeping, waking, and other "automatic" functions.

**Myelin**  The sheath around all the nerves of the body. This sheath is not completely developed at birth.

**Myelinization**  The process by which myelin is added.

**Ossification**  The process by which soft tissue becomes bone.

**Pituitary gland**  One of the endocrine glands that plays a central role in controlling the rate of physical maturation and sexual maturing.

**Primary sex characteristics**  Sexual characteristics related directly to reproduction, including development of the uterus and testes.

**Puberty**  The collection of hormonal and physical changes at adolescence that brings about sexual maturity.

**Secondary sex characteristics**  Sexual characteristics not directly involved in reproduction, including breast and body hair development and changes in body size and proportions.

**Secular trends**  Changes in the timing or pattern of development from one generation to the next.

## SUGGESTED READINGS

The Diagram Group. *Child's body.* New York: Paddington Press, 1977.
   This is a nifty book, designed as a parents' manual and full of helpful information about physical development, health, and nutrition.

Lewin, R. Starved brains. *Psychology today* 9 (1975): 29–33.

This is not a new source, but it is still the most comprehensible and readable description I can find of the effect of malnutrition on children's developing brains.

Smith, D. W.; Bierman, E. L.; & Robinson, N. M. (Eds.). *The biologic ages of man: From conception through old age* (2d ed.). Philadelphia: Saunders, 1978.

Like Tanner's book (listed below), this volume contains a wealth of useful (if somewhat technical) information about physical growth and change over the life span.

Tanner, J. M. *Fetus into man: Physical growth from conception to maturity.* Cambridge, Mass: Harvard University Press, 1978.

A detailed but very thorough and remarkably understandable small book that covers all but the most current information about physical growth.

White, B. L. *The first three years of life.* Englewood Cliffs, N.J.: Prentice-Hall, 1975.

For practical advice about toys, games, and other commercially available products for children, this is an excellent source.

PROJECT 4.1

# Plotting Your Own Growth

This project will work only if your parents are among those who routinely stood you up against a convenient doorjamb and measured you—and if you still live in the house with the marked-up doorjamb. But those of you who can meet both conditions might find it interesting to go back and plot your rate of growth over the years of childhood. Calculate the inches you grew each year (estimating when needed), and draw a curve similar to the one in Figure 4.3.

How does your curve compare to the averaged data in the figure? When was your maximum height spurt (the year in which you grew the most inches)? During elementary school, did you grow about the same number of inches per year? If you are female, add to the graph a point that represents your first menstruation (to the best of your recollection). Where did menarche fall on the curve? Does it match the pattern shown in Figure 4.6? That is, did menarche occur *after* your major growth spurt?

If you do not have access to such data for your own growth, you may want to inquire among your friends or neighbors, to see if someone else has doorjamb data. It really is fun to go back and look!

# 5.

# *perceptual development*

Several years ago, I went sailing for the first time. In the beginning, everything was extremely strange and difficult. I kept calling things "ropes" only to be told that they were not ropes but "lines" or "sheets" or "halyards" or something else complex or obscure-sounding. I had to learn to notice the differences so that I could tell what to reach for when I was given an instruction. I had to learn to read all the various gauges and other markers, too, and to figure out what was important to watch for in the waves. I enjoyed myself immensely, but I learned only a fraction of what I would need to know to be a good sailor. Still, it's a good example of **perceptual learning**. I did not have to learn *how* to look; but I had to learn *what* to pay attention to, which discriminations were important and which irrelevant, and then focus my attention so that I could make the needed discriminations.

When we study the development of perception in children, a great deal of what we need to talk about is perceptual learning of this sort—learning what to pay attention to and what to ignore and making discriminations. But to talk about all of this as "learning" is misleading, especially when we study perceptual development in the young infant. Many of the basic perceptual skills are built in at birth or develop as the brain matures. Often it is impossible to tell whether a particular perceptual ability in an infant or young child is something that develops automatically or has been "learned" on the basis of experience.

This should be a familiar difficulty by now, since this is really just a restatement of the nature/nurture argument. Among researchers and theorists studying perceptual development, there has been a historical split between **nativism**, which stresses the importance of heredity and maturation, and **empiricism**, which stresses the importance of environment and experience. If a child were raised in a black box without any visual or auditory experience but were fed and cared for, would she develop normal visual and auditory skills? Alternatively, can the child's experiences after birth account for all the perceptual abilities she develops?

In fact, no psychologist I know of would take either extreme position today. But it is still important to ask how much inborn or maturationally determined skills contribute to the child's improving perceptual abilities and how much is contributed by later experience.

You can see that, as usual, we have both "what" and "why" questions to answer. What is the developmental course of basic perceptual skills? What does the child pay attention to, and how do those attentional patterns change with age? And why or how do those changes take place? Let me again begin with basic descriptions and save the theoretical arguments until the end.

I should alert you ahead of time to the fact that most of what I will describe is about the development of visual skills during infancy. Partly because visual information appears to be a highly significant source of data for infants and partly because researchers figured out how to study vision in infants fairly early on, we know a lot more about this particular sense than we do about hearing or touch or smell or taste. And because perceptual skills change rapidly in the early months of life and then show relatively little change in older children, researchers have focused their attention on the period of greatest change. This does not mean that perceptual learning does not continue into later childhood or adulthood. Clearly, it does, as my experience on the sailboat shows. But the basic processes seem to be laid down quite early, and it is the basic processes I will try to describe to you.

## VISUAL DEVELOPMENT

### Acuity

The word **acuity** refers to how well or how clearly you can perceive something. When you go to apply for a driver's license and take the "eye test" that involves reading the letters on one line of a large chart, that's a test for visual acuity. The usual standard for visual acuity in adults is "20/20" vision. This means that you can see and identify properly something that is 20 feet away that the average person can also see at 20 feet. If you have 20/15 vision (and are thus "farsighted"), it means that you can see at 20 feet objects or letters that the average person has to be 15 feet from to see or read clearly. A "nearsighted" person is one who has to be quite close to something before it is clear. A person with 20/100 vision has to be as close as 20 feet to see something that the ordinary person can see at 100 feet. In other words, the higher the second number, the poorer the person's visual acuity.

Newborn babies have quite poor acuity—about 20/800 (Dobson & Teller, 1978), but it improves rapidly during early infancy. Most 4-month-olds have acuity ranging between 20/200 and 20/50, and acuity improves steadily thereafter (Figure 5.1), with most children reaching 20/20 by about age 10 or 11.

What does it mean to a baby to have such limited acuity? Obviously, one thing it means is that she can't see things that are far away, and even nearby things will not be as clear and crisp as they are for older children or adults. Still, she *can* see things within a narrow field around her, and her abilities improve rapidly. Parents and other adults who work with very young babies should keep this limitation in mind when they hold the infant or rattle some object nearby or design cribs or toys.

### What Babies and Children Look At

If you think of the human eye as like a camera, then visual acuity is a measure of how well the camera can focus. But to be useful, the camera has to be aimed at the right things—it has to be used skillfully to

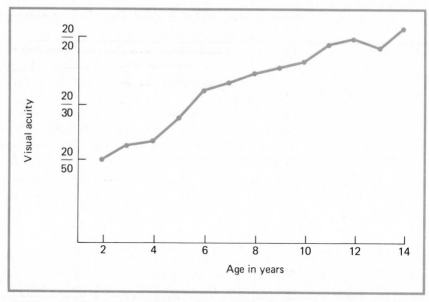

**Figure 5.1** Children's visual acuity improves over the first 10 to 12 years, as you can see from this figure. Children younger than age 2 have still poorer acuity—20/800 or so at birth, improving to 20/100 by about 4 months. (*Source:* Weymouth, 1963, pp. 132 & 133.)

provide the child with the maximum amount of information. Researchers have become extremely clever at devising ways of discovering what babies look at. Robert Fantz (1956) is credited with a strategy called the *preference technique,* in which infants (propped up in infant seats) are shown two pictures or objects that vary in some interesting dimension, like shape or size or symmetry or number of edges. The babies' eye movements are then watched carefully to see which of the two pictures or objects each baby looks at the most. In this way, researchers have been able to figure out what "rules babies look by" (to use Marshall Haith's phrase, 1980). More recently, sophisticated new equipment has even made it possible to see what babies do with their eyes in the dark or what happens to their heartbeats or brain waves when they look at stimuli with various characteristics. Some interesting conclusions have emerged.

*Scanning and Attention in Newborns*   The rule of thumb—suggested by several researchers, such as Gordon Bronson (1974) and Philip Salapatek (1975)—is that for the first six to eight weeks of life, the baby's visual attention is focused on *where* objects are in his world. Marshall Haith (1980) has even shown that newborns exhibit visual search in the dark. In the dark, babies open their eyes widely and scan the whole area, as if looking for light or for some object. If the lights are on, the baby searches until he finds an edge—some place in his range where there is a big contrast between light and dark. Once he finds such an edge, he stops searching and moves his eyes back and forth across and around the edge. Babies will also follow moving objects with their eyes. But for the first six to eight weeks, babies don't spend much time looking at the specific *features* of objects other than their edges.

An exception to this general rule may be human faces. Newborns may spend most of their time looking at edges or at places of sharp contrast (such as eyes or mouths), but they notice enough to tell the difference between a photograph of a real face and one that has had the features scrambled (Goren, Sarty, & Mu, 1975). And as I mentioned in the last chapter, as early as the first few weeks of life, babies will imitate behaviors like tongue protrusion or mouth opening (Meltzoff & Moore, 1983; Field, 1982), such as in Figure 5.2. Obviously, if babies can do this, they have to be paying *some* attention to the actual features of the faces around them.

*The Shift at 2 Months of Age*    At about 8 weeks of age, after the cortex has developed more fully, the emphasis changes. The baby's attention now shifts to *what* an object is rather than merely where it may be located. Put another way, the baby seems to move from a strategy designed to *find* things to a strategy designed to *identify* things.

Researchers are only beginning to chart the various "rules" that

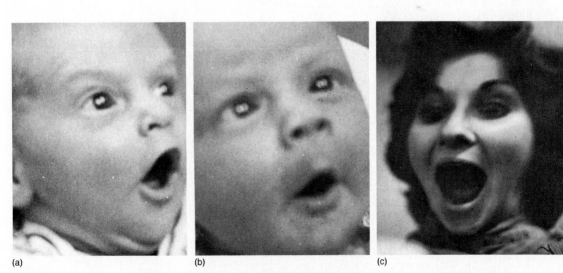

(a)                    (b)                    (c)

**Figure 5.2** These 1-day-old babies are obviously paying attention to the relevant parts of the adult's face, since they are partially imitating the expression—an amazing ability, when you think about it. So the basic rule that the baby looks mostly at edges apparently doesn't hold entirely for the human face. The baby's attention is caught by the movement of the mouth and eyes. (*Source:* T. M. Field, Social perception and responsivity in early infancy. In T. M. Field, A. Huston, H. C. Quay, L. Troll, & G. E. Finley [Eds.], *Review of human development.* Copyright John Wiley & Sons, 1982, p. 26.)

seem to operate after 2 months of age, but a few examples will give you a sense of the way the baby examines his world. Infants now move their eyes back and forth within the edges of some picture or object rather than getting stuck on the edges. Further, babies seem to prefer (spend more time) looking at curved rather than straight-lined figures (Fantz, Fagan, & Miranda, 1975). They also spend more time looking at figures with more elements and at those with larger-sized elements than at objects or pictures with few pieces (Fantz & Fagan, 1975). Recent work by Susan Linn and her colleagues (1982) also shows that children in the first year of life pay attention to whether elements are horizontal or vertical.

Linn first showed groups of babies (aged 5 months and 10 months) the picture at the top of Figure 5.3 and then showed them the original picture along with one of the other stimuli shown in Figure 5.3. What Linn wanted to see was which of the other pictures the babies would treat as "the same" as the original one by looking at them less and which ones the babies would look at more, indicating that they saw them as different. It turned out that one of the pictures the babies paid the most attention to was stimulus number 3, suggesting that a shift from horizontal to vertical bits was particularly salient to the infants. They also looked more at pictures 2 and 8, in which the size of the dots has been varied. One possible explanation of this, by the way, is that babies pay particular attention to eyes in faces and quickly develop (or may be born with) an expectation that the eyes will be a certain size and in horizontal configuration. Babies then quickly notice any violation of that expectation.

Whatever the reasons for babies' special attention to some features of objects, it is extremely interesting that such "rules" can be found. Infants do not just learn to pay attention to common things in their own environments; they seem to share basic strategies for examining the world around them.

*Attention in Older Children*  We know far less about the rules that govern attention in older children, but Eleanor Gibson (1969) has suggested four basic dimensions on which attentional patterns change from infancy through childhood and adolescence.

1. *From capture to activity.* Gibson argues that there is a general shift from "automatic pilot" rules to intentional activity in the infant and older child. Haith's work suggests that even newborns' attention is not entirely "captured" by faces or objects around him. Babies scan systematically even in the dark, when there is nothing to capture their attention. But Gibson is probably correct that as children get older, the built-in rules become less dominant, and their own inter-

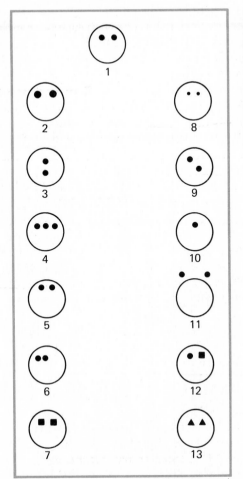

**Figure 5.3** These are the stimuli that Linn used in her study of attention in babies. The infants were shown the figure at the top for a few seconds and then shortly after that were shown that "standard" figure along with one of the others. Babies looked longest at stimuli numbers 2, 3, and 8, indicating that the size of the dots and the horizontal/vertical placement of the dots were particularly significant to the infants. (*Source:* Linn, Reznick, Kagan, & Hans, 1982, p. 652.)

est and intention become the more potent forces in determining attention.

2. *From unsystematic to systematic search.* Actually this would be better stated as "from less systematic to more systematic search." Babies follow a kind of system in examining things visually, but the strategies get more and more complete and systematic as children get older. For example, older children are better at recognizing things they have seen or played with before, presumably because they examined the object more completely the first time.

3. *From broad to selective pickup of information.* Older children get better and better at focusing their attention on a single aspect of a complex situation. In a classroom, the child has to be able to pick out and pay attention to the teacher's voice above the babble of other voices and noises or, at an intersection, to select the red and green

lights out of all the myriad visual signals around. Children become increasingly good at this selective attention right up to adolescence.

4. *Ignoring irrelevant information.* It may seem as if I just talked about this. After all, isn't focusing on one thing the same as ignoring everying else? Not quite. The young child in the classroom may be able to focus well enough to hear the teacher's voice but may still hear the words of the other children. What I'm talking about here, then, is really *distractibility.* Very often it isn't necessary to shut out everything else; but in complex situations, the child will do better at a task if she can concentrate so fully on one set of information that she literally doesn't see or hear anything else. Remember the last time you took an important test, such as perhaps the college board tests. You needed to be able to shut out everything else—the student sneezing next to you, the sound of the air conditioner, the sunshine coming in through the window—and focus all your attention on the questions and answers. Although infants and young children may show this sort of nondistractible focus of attention during some activities (such as nursing, for example), the ability to do so voluntarily develops gradually up to and through adolescence (Lane & Pearson, 1982).

Overall, the child's attentional processes seem to become more voluntary and more focused as he gets older.

## Ignoring Visual Cues: The Perceptual Constancies

I have been describing what the infant and young child pays attention to, but there is an equally important set of cues that the child must "learn" to ignore. (I put the word learn in quotation marks because I do not know whether the child learns this through experience or whether some of this "knowledge" is built in or develops as the brain grows.) Specifically, the child must acquire a set of rules we call **perceptual constancies**.

When you see someone walking away from you, the image of the person on your retina actually becomes smaller. But you don't see the person getting smaller. You see him as the same size but moving farther away. When you do this, you are demonstrating **size constancy;** you are able to see the size as constant even though the retinal image has become smaller or larger.

Other constancies include the ability to recognize that shapes of objects are the same even though you are looking at them from different angles, which we call **shape constancy**, and the ability to recognize that colors are constant even though the amount of light or shadow on them changes, which we call **color constancy**.

Taken together, the several specific constancies add up to the larger concept of **object constancy**, which is the recognition that objects remain the same even when they appear to change in certain ways. The evidence we have suggests that babies may be born with rudimentary forms of several constancies but that the constancies become more fully established over the first several years.

*Size Constancy*   In infants, the most studied aspect of size constancy is **depth perception**. For example, when you see a man walking away from you, in order to maintain your size constancy you have to be able to judge how far he has gone, which requires depth perception. Next time you're in an airplane, look out the window just before landing or just after taking off. The usual experience is that the cars on the ground look like toys and the people look miniature. Because you have no way of estimating the distance, you have difficulty maintaining your size constancy. You know they are real people and cars, but they look smaller to you.

For the infant, depth perception is obviously not only an essential ingredient in size constancy, it is also essential for other everyday tasks, like aiming the hands properly to reach a toy, mobile, bottle, or breast. Can the baby judge depth?

One of the earliest (and still one of the cleverest) studies of infant depth perception was the work of Eleanor Gibson and Richard Walk (1960), who built an apparatus called a *visual cliff.* You can see from the picture in Figure 5.4 that it consists of a large glass table with a sort of runway in the middle. On one side of the runway there is a checkerboard pattern immediately below the glass; on the other side—the "cliff" side—the checkerboard is several feet below the glass. If a baby had no depth perception, she should be equally willing to crawl on either side of the runway, but if she could judge depth, she should be reluctant to crawl out on the "cliff" side. From the baby's perspective, the cliff side would indeed look like a cliff, and she should stay away.

The original study by Gibson and Walk used babies 6 months old and older (since they had to be able to crawl to be tested on this apparatus). By and large these infants did *not* crawl out on the cliff side but were quite willing to crawl out on the shallow side. In other words, 6-month-old babies have depth perception.

But what about younger infants? How early is this perceptual ability present? The traditional visual cliff procedure can't give us the answer, since the baby must be able to crawl in order to "tell us" whether he can judge depth. Joseph Campos and his colleagues (Campos, Langer, & Krowitz, 1970) solved the problem by attaching equipment to younger infants to allow the recording of their heart rates while they were on the visual cliff apparatus. He put babies out on the cliff side and on the noncliff side and watched to see if their hearts responded differently. As it turned out, they did. In babies as young as 2 months of age, the heart rate went down a little when they were over the cliff

**Figure 5.4** The "visual cliff" apparatus used by Gibson and Walk in their studies of depth perception in infants. In this photo, the mother is trying to coax the baby out onto the "cliff" side. (*Source:* Gibson & Walk, 1960, p. 65.)

side and didn't change when they were placed on the noncliff side. So they were noticing some difference between the two. One-month-old infants, though, did *not* show any different reactions to the two sides. This could mean that young infants do not yet have the ability to respond to the cues of depth perception, or it could mean that their acuity is simply not good enough yet to detect the depth cues in this situation.

To sum up, 6-month-old infants clearly have depth perception, and 2-month-old babies seem to have at least some form of it. Researchers are still debating about whether newborns respond to depth. If they do, of course, it would be a point for the "nativists," but we simply don't have the answers yet.

*Shape Constancy*  Shape constancy is extremely important for the baby. She has to realize that the bottle is still the bottle even though it is turned slightly and thus presents a different shape, or that her toys are the same when they are in different positions. Researchers interested in studying shape constancy have generally used a variation of an operant conditioning experiment as the basis for their study. They reinforce babies for performing some behavior (usually head turning or sucking) when they see a particular shape, such as a rectangle. They then vary the shape they present and see if the baby still shows the same head turn or sucking response. If the baby does, then we can conclude that the infant sees the new shape as "the same" as the original one.

In Thomas Bower's classic study of this type (1966), 2-month-old infants responded to tilted or turned rectangles as if they were the same as the original rectangle, even though the retinal images cast by these tilted rectangles were actually trapezoids. So babies as young as 2 months appear to have at least some shape constancy, but we don't know how much earlier the precursors of this skill may be present.

*Color Constancy*    Results from similar studies by Marc Bornstein and his colleagues (Bornstein, Kessen, & Weiskopf, 1976) make it clear that most babies have at least some color constancy by the time they are about 4 months old and perhaps sooner.

Taken together, the evidence indicates that by 4 months at least (and possibly much sooner), infants have mastered the basic elements of object constancy. That is, they can judge depth to some degree, and thus can achieve size constancy, and can use color and shape constancy in their perceptions of objects in their world. All of these constancies improve over the first year of life, but it is extremely interesting to find such complex responses present as early as 2 or 4 months of age.

## Learning about Objects

Babies not only have to figure out where things are, what shape or color they may be, or how large they are. They also have to learn to tell one object or person from another consistently, a process we normally call *discrimination*.

*Visual Discriminations*    How early can a baby use all the visual (or tactual or other) cues to tell a rattle from a ball, or a bottle from a mobile? For parents, the most important variant of this question is how early can the baby tell the difference between mom or dad and a stranger or between mom and dad?

The answer seems to be definitely by 3 months and possibly earlier (Olson, 1981). In the first two to three months of life, babies can clearly discriminate the mother from a stranger in natural surroundings when the visual cues are combined with voice, touch, and smell. Infants of this same age also show different body movements and facial expressions when first confronted by another baby, compared to their reaction to the first sight of mom (Fogel, 1979). But it is not so clear that babies can make a *purely visual* discrimination between mother and a stranger (or between mother and dad) before about 3 months (Hayes & Watson, 1981). (That is, if the *only* cue is the sight of the mother's face, newborns are not as good at telling the difference between mom's face and a stranger's face.) By 3 months, however, nearly all babies can make such a visual discrimination. Maria Barrera and Daphne Maurer (1981), for example, showed 3-month-old babies photographs of their mother's face and the face of a stranger and found that babies looked longer at mom than at the stranger, which clearly means that they can tell the difference.

*The Object Concept*    Besides learning to tell one person from another or one object from another, the infant has to learn at least three other basic things about objects. She has to learn that objects remain the same even when they appear to be different (object constancy). But she also has to develop the **object concept,** which has two facets. The infant must learn that objects (or people) continue to exist even when she can't see or feel them any longer—that when her mother goes out of sight through a doorway, the mother continues to exist or that when a toy disappears beneath the sofa, it still exists. This understanding is usually called **object permanence**. Finally, the infant has to learn that individual objects retain their unique identity from one encounter to another. When the mother goes away and then comes back again, it is the same mother both times; the crib is the same object each time she is placed in it; and so on. This understanding is usually called **object identity**.

These understandings about objects and people may seem so basic that you may not be able to imagine that the child does not have them. But she does not, at least not at first. To the infant in the first few months of life, a rattle seems to be "something that makes sound when I move my hand" or "something I can get my hand around." It is not a constant object with describable properties that can be recognized time and again and that exists even when the baby isn't looking at it.

These several understandings develop over the first year or two of life. While object constancies such as size and color constancy are present in some rudimentary forms in the very young infant, object identity, by contrast, seems not to be present in the very young infant at all. It apparently develops first at about 5 months of age. For example, Thomas Bower (1975) has studied infants' reactions in a situation in which the infant, seated in an infant seat, looks at his mother through a window. The mother's image is then artificially multiplied so that the infant sees three mothers. Young infants show no signs of surprise at this multiple image. If anything, they seem to be more delighted with three mothers than with one. But at about 22 to 24 weeks of age, infants begin to be extremely upset at this multiple image, which suggests that they have in some sense understood that there should be only one, and the multiple image violates this expectation.

This finding, by the way, is another example of the child's development of what Jerome Kagan (1971) calls *schemas.* The baby either develops through experience or has at birth certain generalized expectations—images of the way things *should* be. When these expectations are violated, the baby shows surprise. Since the development of such schemas is both a cognitive and a perceptual process, it is very difficult to study these two aspects of development in isolation from each other.

Object permanence also develops over the first year or two of life, apparently through a series of moderately distinct stages. In the first months of life, there is little evidence that infants respond to anything that is not immediately present, visible, touchable, or hearable. By about 2 months, there are some signs that the infant is developing a rudimentary notion of object permanence. If you have an infant of this age look at a toy, then put a screen between the child and the toy, remove the toy, and then remove the screen, the 2-month-old will show some surprise, as if she had some expectation that the toy would continue to be there (a schema). But infants of this age show no signs of searching for a missing toy they may have dropped over the edge of the crib or that has disappeared beneath a blanket (see Figure 5.5).

Between 6 and 8 months, another breakthrough seems to take place. Now babies *will* look over the edge of the crib for the dropped toys or for food that was spilled. (In fact, babies of this age may drive their parents nuts playing "dropsy" in the high chair!) Infants this age will also search for partially hidden objects. If you put a favorite toy under a cloth but leave part of it sticking out, the infant will reach for the toy, which suggests that in some sense the infant "recognizes" that the whole object is there even though she can see only part of it. But if you cover the toy completely with the cloth, the infant will stop looking at it and will not reach for it, even if she has seen you put the cloth over it.

This changes again somewhere between 8 and 12 months; infants this age will reach or search for a toy that has been covered completely by a cloth or hidden by a screen (Dunst, Brooks, & Doxsey, 1982). There are further refinements of object permanence that appear during the second year of life, but by 12 months, most infants appear to grasp the basic fact that objects continue to exist even when they are no longer visible.

These changes in the child's understanding of the nature of objects have profound effects on the child's relationships with the people in his world. In particular, some kind of object permanence is probably required before the baby can become attached to an individual person, such as his mother or father. Babies younger than 6 months may be more sootheable by someone familiar with their habits and may smile more at mom and dad than at strangers; but the full-fledged attachment of the baby to a single other person (which I'll describe in more detail in Chapter 11) doesn't seem to take place until about 6 or 7 months, just about the time that the child begins to understand that mom continues to exist even when she is out of sight.

**Figure 5.5** These photos show very graphically the response of a 5- to 6-month-old infant in an object permanence test. The baby stops reaching for or searching for the toy when it is hidden from him. An older baby would keep searching or push the screen aside to reach for the toy.

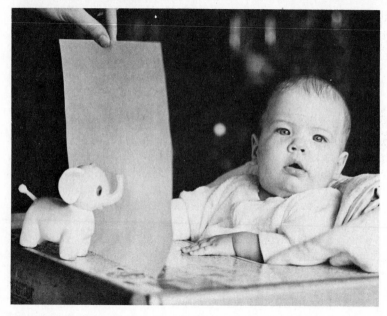

## AUDITORY DEVELOPMENT

### Acuity

Although children's hearing improves up to adolescence, newborns' auditory acuity is much better than their visual acuity. Current research evidence suggests that within the general range of pitch and loudness of the human voice, newborns hear as well as adults do, although adults have better hearing of quiet sounds (Sinnott, Pisoni, & Aslin, 1983). As they get older, children become able to hear softer and lower-pitched sounds (Morse & Cowan, 1982).

### Detecting Locations

Another basic auditory skill that improves with age is the ability to determine the location of a sound. You can tell roughly where a sound is coming from because your two ears are separated from each other, so that the sound arrives at one ear slightly before the other. If the sound comes from a source equidistant from the two ears (the "midline"), then the sound arrives at the same time at both ears. Newborns have some primitive ability to judge the general direction from which a sound has come and then get better quite quickly. By 6 months, most infants are quite good at making judgments of this kind (Bower, 1977a).

### Making Discriminations

As was true with vision, if we are to understand the child's perceptual development, we have to go beyond basic acuity and ask when the child is able to tell the difference between various sounds, such as discriminating between voices or between individual speech sounds.

Probably babies can discriminate individual voices before they can consistently discriminate faces—a finding that makes sense when you remember that auditory acuity is a good deal better than visual acuity in the first weeks of life (and that babies have quite a lot of auditory experience in utero, too). For example, *talking* faces can be discriminated by 4 to 5 weeks of age, while silent faces or photographs aren't discriminated till about 3 months (Olson, 1981). One researcher has even reported that in the first days after birth, babies prefer to listen to their mother's voice rather than to a stranger's (DeCasper & Fifer, 1980).

Similarly, the baby's ability to respond differently to very similar speech sounds appears quite remarkably early. In most of the research on this, babies first listen repeatedly to a particular sound (such as *ba*) until they habituate. Then slight variations of the sound are given, and the experimenter checks to see if the infant responds differently, such as by turning his head toward the sound or sucking harder on a nipple.

Research of this kind shows that as early as 4 to 6 weeks of age, infants can distinguish individual speech sounds like *ba* and *ga*. Soon after, they can discriminate two-syllable "words" like *bada* and *baga*. They can even respond to a syllable that is hidden inside a string of other syllables, like "ti*bat*" versus "ko*ba*ko" (Morse & Cowan, 1982).

This somewhat amazing ability to make discriminations among sounds is obviously critical for language development. It also tells us that it really is worthwhile to talk to babies from very early on. In fact, as you'll see in Chapter 8, when I talk about language development, parents who begin talking to their infants very early have children whose language development is more rapid.

## DEVELOPMENT OF OTHER SENSES

### Smell and Taste

The senses of smell and taste have been much less studied than either vision or hearing, but we do have some basic knowledge. As with adults, the two senses are intricately related—that is, if you cannot smell for some reason (like having a cold), you cannot taste, either. Taste is detected by the taste buds on the tongue, which can register only four basic tastes: sweet, sour, bitter, and salty. Smell is registered in the mucous membranes of the nose and has nearly unlimited variations.

Newborns appear to respond differentially to at least three of the basic flavors—sweet, sour, and bitter. Some of the clearest demonstrations of this come from a very simple (but very clever) set of studies by Jacob Steiner (1979; Ganchrow, Steiner, & Daher, 1983). Newborn infants, who had never been fed, were photographed before and after flavored water was put into their mouths. By varying the flavor, Steiner could determine whether the babies reacted differently. As you can see in Figure 5.6, babies respond to the sweet liquid with a relaxed face and an expression that looks a lot like a smile. The response to the sour liquid is pursed lips, while to the bitter liquid the baby responds with an arched mouth with sides turned down and an expression of disgust. The fact that babies show such different expressions in response to different flavors tells us that they do in fact taste different to the infant. Furthermore, babies 1 to 3 days old can discriminate between sugar waters of varying sugar concentrations (Cowart, 1981), which tells us that the taste system is well developed at birth.

### Touch

If you think back to the list of reflexes in the newborn I gave you in Chapter 3, you'll realize that the newborn has at least some sensitivity to touch. A touch on the cheek triggers the rooting and sucking reflexes; a touch on the bottom of the foot triggers the Babinsky reflex. Babies appear to be especially sensitive to touches on the mouth, the face, and the hands, with less sensitivity in other parts of the body. Probably the sense of touch becomes more finely tuned over the early years of life, with the child able to detect and respond to more subtle differences in the form or location of stimulation, but that is supposition. There has been little research on touch perception in infants or children.

## COMBINING INFORMATION FROM SEVERAL SENSES

If you think about the way you receive and use perceptual information, you'll realize quickly that you rarely have information from one sense at a time. Ordinarily, you have *both* sound and sight, or touch and

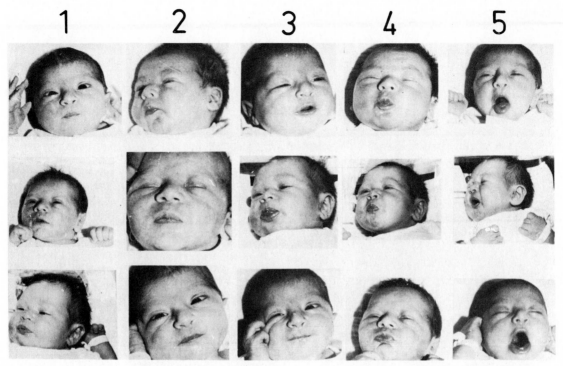

**Figure 5.6** These are three of the babies Steiner observed in his experiments of taste responses. You can see the marked similarity in the facial expressions of these infants when given liquids of various flavors: Column 3 shows response to sweet taste; column 4, to sour; and column 5 to bitter taste. (*Source:* J. E. Steiner, Human facial expressions in response to taste and smell stimulation. In H. W. Reese & L. P. Lipsett [Eds.], *Advances in child development and behavior,* Vol. 13. New York: Academic Press, 1979, Figure 1, p. 269.)

sight, or still more complex combinations of smell, sight, touch, and sound. Adults coordinate this information in complex ways. For example, if we have seen an object but not touched it, we can usually still pick it out from a batch of objects using only touch cues (that is, we know what it *ought* to feel like, based on what we saw). And if we see a drum being beaten in a particular rhythm, we expect to hear that same rhythm. But do babies coordinate information from their different senses in these ways?

Apparently, they do, at least after the first few months of life. If you put a 3- to 4-month-old baby in a situation in which she can see both father and mother and can hear a tape-recorded voice of one of them, she will look toward the parent whose voice she hears (Spelke & Owsley, 1979). In several delightfully clever experiments, Elizabeth Spelke has also demonstrated that 4-month-old infants can connect sound rhythms with movement (1979). She showed the babies two films simultaneously. One film showed a toy kangaroo bouncing up and down, the

BOX 5.1

# BLIND BABIES CAN "SEE" WITH THEIR EARS

One of the most fascinating—and practically relevant—sets of studies of infant perception I have seen in recent years is a series of observations by T. G. R. Bower of blind infants who have been equipped with a special ultrasonic device that allows them to perceive the world around them. Figure 5.7 shows what the apparatus looks like.

The system works in a way that is similar to the echolocation system of dolphins or bats. The transmitter continuously irradiates the environment with ultrasonic waves, which bounce off the objects—toys, walls, people, and the like—around the baby. The bounced-back sound is received by the headset and transmitted to the infant's ears through the speakers. The whole thing is remarkably sensitive to variations in the shape, distance, and size of objects.

The pitch of the sound the baby hears tells her how far away the object may be. Low pitches signal a nearby object, while high pitches signal farther-away objects.

The loudness of the sound tells the baby how big the object is. Loud sounds signal large objects; softer sounds signal smaller objects.

The clarity of the sound tells the baby something about the texture of the surface. Very clear sounds indicate a hard surface; fuzzy sounds indicate a soft surface.

The right/left source of the sound tells the baby where the object is located in space, since the two ears receive signals at different times, depending on the object's location. Objects on the right make sounds that arrive at the right ear fractionally sooner than at the left ear, while objects on the left do the reverse.

So far, this apparatus has been tested on six blind babies, ranging in age from 5 to 16 months. The results are fascinating.

First of all, even the 5-month-old baby was able to learn to use this device very quickly—within hours or days. The babies quickly begin to reach accurately for objects, to crawl or walk through doorways, even to hold out their hands and move them around (which changes the sound). These actions are accompanied by signs of great joy and delight.

All of these behaviors are strikingly similar to what we see in sighted infants, who begin reach-

other a donkey bouncing up and down, with one of the animals bouncing at a faster rate. Out of a speaker located between the two films came a tape of a rhythmic bouncing sound that matched one of the two rates. In this situation, babies spent more time watching the film that had the rhythm matching the sound they were hearing. Amazing!

Connecting information from touch and vision seems to come a bit later, beginning between 6 and 12 months (Acredolo & Hake, 1982). After this age, children begin to be able to identify by sight objects that they have previously explored only tactually, or vice versa.

A really lovely example of the ability of infants to use information from one modality to replace information from another comes from a

ing for objects within the first two to three months and show visual regard of the moving hand in the early months as well. What Bower's experiments show is that blind infants can glean essentially the same information about the environment from auditory cues as sighted infants do with visual cues. I am sure that these early experiments will be quickly followed by widespread use of such devices for blind babies—a wonderful breakthrough for these handicapped infants—based on new engineering techniques and knowledge of perceptual development from developmental psychologists.

But there are some equally fascinating theoretical implications. Bower has found that the *younger* babies actually have an *easier* time learning to use this apparatus than the older babies do. And adults have a very difficult time with it—taking weeks or months to learn what an infant learns within a few hours or days. Why might this be so?

Bower argues that the very young infant is really not treating the stimulus input as "sound." Rather, he is treating it as a description of the world around him, much as sighted people perceive light. Light is a background variable that gives us information, but it is not usually a property of objects. Blind infants treat the sounds the same way—as if they told about the world "out there." This suggests that, for the infant, auditory and visual information are essentially interchangeable.

But the older infant (and the adult)—starting as early as about 12 months of age—perceives the sounds as *part of* the objects in some way. So the 13-month baby Bower tested with the apparatus kept putting the toys and objects up to her ear, as if the sound were being made by the object rather than telling her where the object was. This older infant (and the adults who have been tested) appears to treat sound and sight as distinct sources of information, rather than as interchangeable sources as the younger infant does.

On the basis of evidence like this, Bower argues that babies are operating on very abstract perceptual principles. Over time, however, perceptual information becomes more and more specific, more and more differentiated. Obviously, we need to use perceptual information in such differentiated ways in order to make discriminations, to recognize objects or people and the like. But one of the prices of that developmental "advance" is that we lose the baby's rapid ability to use the information interchangeably. The practical implication of this finding is that blind babies should begin training with the ultrasonic device as early as possible.

series of studies of blind infants by Thomas Bower, which I've described in Box 5.1.

## LEARNING TO READ: AN APPLICATION OF THE BASIC PRINCIPLES

Many of the small bits of information I have been giving you in the last few pages, while interesting in themselves, become still more interesting when we apply them to a complex, practical task: learning how to read. Reading is very largely a perceptual process, involving discriminations among visual forms (letters) and coordination of information from two senses (hearing and sight). Reading normally begins long

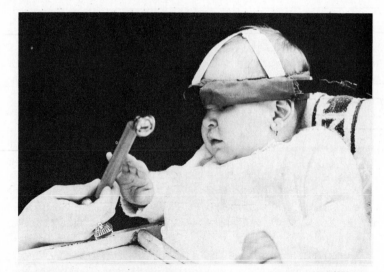

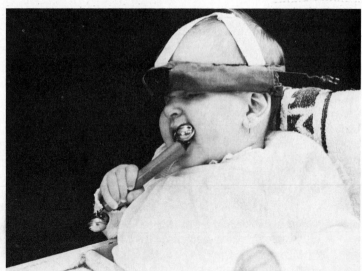

**Figure 5.7** A blind baby using the special sonic guide Bower has studied. Notice how she reaches accurately for the object, much as a sighted infant does using visual cues. (*Source:* T. G. R. Bower, Blind babies see with their ears. *New scientist,* 1977, *73,* p. 255, photographs by Ric Gemmel.)

after the early years of life on which I have focused so much of my discussion, but many of the basic perceptual processes enter into the task of learning to read.

## Some Perceptual Issues in Reading

One of the particularly interesting things about reading is that the child has to *unlearn* some of the shape constancy she has so carefully acquired during infancy. For the first four to five years of life, the basic rule is that an object is the same whether you see it right side up, upside down, turned around to the left or the right. But when you learn to read, that old rule has to be modified. Letters like *b* and *d* are the same shape, except with the direction reversed. The letters *p* and *q* are the same kind of pair, and *p* and *b* are the same except that one is "upside down." So in order to learn to read (at least the Latin alphabet), the child must now learn to pay attention to something she'd learned to ignore—namely, the rotation of the letter in space.

If this is a correct analysis of at least part of what goes on when a child learns to read, then we ought to find that children would have the most difficulty with the reversal pairs of letters or with words that make sense whether they are read from either end, like *saw* and *was*.

Another kind of shift of attention has to take place in learning to read. The child of 5 or 6 has been learning to understand and speak *oral* language. But when he begins to read, he has to look at the *written* language—to notice the visual information and not just the sounds or the logic of the word sequence. That's a major change in the focus of attention. In the early stages, when a child learning to read came to a word he didn't know, we might expect to hear him put in a word that could fit logically into that oral sentence, regardless of what the little squiggles on the paper might show. Later on, when the child has figured out that reading involves decoding the squiggles, we might expect him to make more mistakes in which he *misreads* the word.

## The Basic Steps in Learning to Read

Research by Eleanor Gibson and Harry Levin (1975), among others, suggests that children go through three basic steps in learning to read that do in fact reflect these perceptual issues. We can see these steps most clearly by watching what children do when they try to read and come upon a word they don't know. The first (earliest) strategy seems to be to try to make the written sentence make oral sense. Children using this strategy substitute words that are totally unlike the ones on the page but that make sensible sentences. Children at this stage aren't really "reading" all of what is on the page.

In the next step, however, the child figures out that what she reads out loud has to have *some* connection to the letters on the page. At this stage, when she comes to a word she doesn't know, she is likely to stop short. She may stop reading or just leave out that word. Finally, in the last step, instead of staying silent, the child will begin to try to decode the word—to figure out what it must be on the basis of the letters in it. So the kind of mistakes the child makes depends on what she's paying attention to—the sense of the sentence, the letters on the page, or both.

To take this one step further, Andrew Biemiller (1970) has found that children who reach the no-response phase (step 2) early are better readers by the end of first grade. As Gibson and Levin say:

**Figure 5.8** When children are first learning to read, they often "read" words that would make sense in the sentence but have no connection to the letters on the page.

Many children start school with the notion that reading is speaking with books open in front of them. The speech is not nonsensical. Still, the earlier the realization by the child that what he says must be determined by what is printed, the better the prognosis for early reading achievement (Gibson & Levin, 1975, p. 282).

Once the child *does* begin to pay attention to the individual letters, though, she still has to figure out that reversals like *b* and *d* are really different from each other. Eleanor Gibson's research on this shows that 4- and 5-year-old children still treat reversals as "the same" but that 6- and 7-year-old children rapidly learn that *p* is not the same as *b*. In the process of learning this "exception" to the shape constancy rules, the child initially makes a lot of reversal mistakes in her reading, but these drop out naturally as she begins to pay attention to the direction of the letters.

### "Whole-Word" Versus "Phonics" Methods for Teaching Reading

You will notice that so far I have steered clear of that hotly debated issue of how reading should be taught. Should children learn whole words in one chunk? After all, it is whole words that we read, not individual letters in isolation. So maybe it is better to emphasize whole words from the beginning. Alternatively, perhaps children would learn more readily if the teacher emphasized the sounds associated with individual letters or letter combinations, a procedure called *phonics training or decoding*.

Advocates of these two basic approaches among both researchers and teachers (such as Liberman and Shankweiler, 1977, on the phonics side and Perfetti and Lesgold, 1977, on the "whole-word" side) often feel very strongly about their particular positions. But the issue is obviously complex and has no single answer. I can't settle the issue here, but let me give you a few pieces of information to illustrate the complexity.

The type of instruction that works best seems to depend partly on the child's position in the three steps I have just described. In the early stages, when the child is focused more on the meaning than on the actual letters, the whole-word method works fine, especially if the words are short. It may be a good method for getting the child started on reading. But Jeanne Chall (1967), in her review of reading programs, concluded that some phonics training is essential for the child to move to the final step of decoding the individual words. By the second or third grade, children who have had no phonics training have fallen behind children trained in decoding. In particular, they are less skillful at reading new words. This debate has not ended; both educators and psychologists will no doubt still be arguing about whole words versus phonics at the turn of the next century. But practically speaking, the debate may not be so important, since virtually all current reading programs sensibly include both types of training. Despite the best efforts of educators, however, many children have great difficulty learning to read, a problem I've discussed in Box 5.2.

## INDIVIDUAL DIFFERENCES IN PERCEPTION

### Perceptual Styles

So far I've talked as if all infants and children were pretty much alike in the way they perceive things. That's true. But it is also true that there are some fascinating differences in the *style* with which people (including infants) examine the world around them. If you went to a museum and watched the visitors, you could get a glimpse of such differences in style: Some children or adults stand close to the exhibits and look at them carefully for a long time; others stand back and examine them more generally, glancing from one to another more quickly. (In fact, it is quite maddening to go to a museum with someone whose style is very different from your own!)

*Reflection Versus Impulsivity*    One way of describing this dimension of individual differences is in terms of **reflection** versus **impulsivity**. These two terms define the two ends of a dimension Jerome Kagan calls **conceptual tempo** (Kagan et al., 1964; Kagan, 1971).

Evidence of conceptual tempo can be seen in quite young infants (Kagan, 1971). Babies with slower tempo will remain still and look at something new with fixed concentration, while the faster-tempo baby

BOX 5.2

# WHEN THE NATURAL PROCESS BREAKS DOWN: PROBLEMS IN LEARNING TO READ

As many as 15 percent of children in the United States have significant difficulty learning to read. A small segment of this group has obvious brain damage or is generally retarded in development. But the majority of children with reading problems show essentially normal development in other respects. They have no obvious brain damage, frequently do well in school in subjects other than reading, and show no substantial emotional disturbance. Two labels have been applied to children in this larger group. Most frequently today they are described as having a **specific learning disability.** A somewhat older term for this syndrome, still in use, is **dyslexia**.

What might account for this type of problem? After years of debate and a great deal of research, the one thing that is clear is that there is no *single* explanation of reading problems that will account for all children's difficulties. There seem to be several potential sources of difficulty, one or more of which may enter into the problem experienced by a given child:

1. *Visual perception problems.* Some children seem to have trouble decoding the visual information, possibly because of some minimal (and nonobvious) brain damage. This does not, however, seem to be a major cause of difficulty for most children.
2. *Integrating visual and auditory information.* Reading involves, in part, matching the sound of a word with the sight of it. This is particularly true in the early years of reading, when children are asked to read aloud a lot. Herbert Birch (Birch & Lefford, 1963), among others, has argued that poor readers just don't integrate information from these two senses very effectively. In fact, this does seem to be the case for many poor readers.
3. *Hearing the parts of words.* Perhaps some children have difficulty because they genuinely don't hear words as strings of *separate* sounds. So when they have to decode new words by breaking apart the words into separate sounds, they have great difficulty. Isabel

will thrash around, become excited, gurgle, and look away after only a short period of examination. In preschool and school-age children, the task most often used to measure tempo is a picture matching game, using pictures like the one in Figure 5.9. The child's job is to find which of the six pictures at the bottom *exactly* matches the picture at the top. A "reflective" child looks carefully at all the alternatives before making a choice. Not surprisingly, he makes very few errors. An "impulsive" child, on the other hand, looks over the options quickly and chooses one—which is frequently incorrect.

This dimension of style is at least somewhat stable during childhood. In one longitudinal study, Kagan and his colleagues Deborah Lapidus and Michael Moore (1978) compared measures of tempo made when children were 8 months old with measures made at age 10 and found a significant correlation. That is, reflective infants were likely to become reflective children, and impulsive infants to be impulsive children. Kagan has also found that reflective children have a some-

Liberman and her colleagues (1976) have found that preschool children who have the greatest difficulty "hearing" the separate sounds in words do in fact have the hardest time learning to read.

4. *Problems with remembering.* Another critical element seems to be the child's basic memory ability. The child has to be able to remember what that combination of letters was the last time she read it, what the previous words were in the sentence being read so that the meaning of the sentence can be kept in mind, and the like. Thomas Hess and Robert Radtke (1981) have found that children with poorer general memory ability are also likely to be poorer readers.

5. *Problems with language.* Finally, we have to remember that when we read, we read *language,* so that any child who is having difficulty with language may have difficulty with reading as well. Frank Vellutino (1977), for example, argues that this is the *major* source of problems for most poor readers. "Our findings indicate that when dyslexics call *b* 'd' or *was* 'saw,' it is not because these figures are literally misperceived, but because dyslexic children cannot remember their names" (Vellu-

tino, 1977, pp. 337–338). A reading problem, then, may be just one facet of a broader language problem (or a broader memory problem).

The important point is that each of these explanations is probably true for *some* poor readers, but not all. This makes the teacher's problem extremely difficult, since she must try to diagnose, and then solve, a wide range of potential difficulties. It is precisely because of this diversity that well-trained special education teachers are so important. Diagnosing the problem early and designing appropriate remedial programs can not only help the child learn to read, it can also save the child (and the family) a great deal of anguish and failure. If I can get up on my soap box again, it seems to me that given the number of children affected by such problems, and the social and emotional costs involved, it would be money very well spent for school districts to provide well-trained diagnosticians and special education teachers. Regrettably, these are often the first people cut when budgets get tight.

what easier time learning to read, which makes sense when you think about the sort of careful examination of letter forms that is needed in the early stages of reading (Kagan, 1965).

But don't jump to the conclusion that reflectiveness is always best. Many (if not most) tasks in everyday life do not require careful examination or search. A quick look is enough, and someone who is "reflective" may take far longer than the task requires. If you store all your canned food in one cupboard, you don't have to examine each can carefully as you take it out of the grocery bag to decide where it should go. Or if you're driving down a street looking for a sign that says "Connecticut Avenue," you don't need to stop at every corner and carefully examine the street sign. You can tell just by the length of the name whether it could be "Connecticut" or not. In other words, any time a simple glance is enough, the impulsive person will be more efficient. It is only when a detailed examination is needed to make a discrimination or a judgment that the reflective style is helpful.

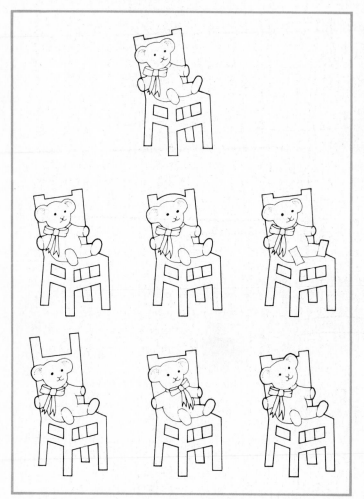

**Figure 5.9** A sample item from Kagan's test of "reflection versus impulsivity." The child taking the test must try to select the picture from among the bottom six that exactly matches the figure at the top. (*Source:* J. Kagan, B. L. Rosman, D. Day, J. Albert, & W. Phillips. Information processing in the child: Significance of analytic and reflective attitudes. *Psychological monographs,* 1964, *78* [1, Whole No. 578], p. 23. Copyright 1964 by the American Psychological Association. Reprinted with permission.)

*Field Dependence and Independence*    Another categorization of perceptual styles, emerging originally from studies of adults, has been suggested by H. A. Witkin and his associates (1962). Witkin was intrigued by the fact that some people's perceptions seemed to be heavily influenced by the background environment, while other people's did not. People who could ignore the irrelevant background material Witkin called **field-independent**, and those who were influenced by the context or background he called **field-dependent**.

In children, field dependence/independence has most often been measured with the *Embedded Figures Test*. In this task, the subject is shown a simple figure, such as a square or a pie shape, and then asked to find a figure exactly like that in a complex drawing. The problem is for the subject to ignore the other features of the drawing (the field) and pay attention only to the abstract shapes. (You might want to see how good you are at this yourself. One of the items from a children's version of the Embedded Figures Test is shown in Figure 5.10. The adult version is considerably harder.)

Generally speaking, children become more and more field-independent as they get older, which is certainly what we'd expect in view of the basic developmental changes in perceptual learning strategies I've described so far. But at any given age, there are still individual differences, with some children more field-independent, others more field-dependent.

*Conceptual Styles and Personality*    Conceptual styles appear to affect the way we look at things. But could they also reflect more basic aspects of personality or temperament? Witkin has argued all along that field-dependent individuals are also more dependent in other ways. There has been little research on such a link, but at least one study by Stanley Messer and David Brodzinsky (1979) shows a partial link between conceptual tempo and aggressiveness. They found that among fifth graders, impulsive children were rated by their teachers and by other children as more physically aggressive than were reflective children. Research like this raises some intriguing questions about the possible existence of very basic personal "styles" that may cut across our traditional categories of analysis.

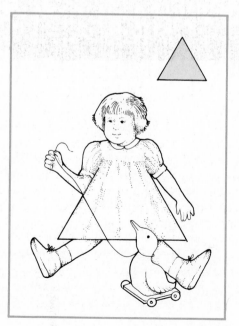

**Figure 5.10** A sample item from the Coates Preschool Embedded Figures Test, a measure of field dependence versus field independence. The simple figure at the upper right must be located in the complex figure below. How long does it take you to find it? (*Source:* Coates, 1972.)

### Sex Differences

As nearly as I can determine, there are fewer sex differences in perceptual skills than in any other area of development. Boy babies and girl babies do not seem to have different levels of acuity or discrimination ability. And they do not appear to differ in the rate of acquisition of such basic concepts as object identity or object permanence.

Measures of field independence/dependence, however, commonly do show a sex difference, with boys being more field-independent and girls more field-dependent. Possibly this difference occurs because many measures of this dimension involve some aspect of spatial visualization. Boys as a group are generally better at tasks that require visual-spatial skills. (More about that in Chapter 6.) On tests of conceptual tempo (reflection versus impulsivity), in contrast, no consistent sex differences have been found.

### Social Class Differences

There are no consistent social class differences that I know of in the basic maturation of perceptual skills. Middle-class children do not shift from looking at contours to looking at the middle of pictures any sooner than do poor children, for example. But in older children, there are differences in conceptual tempo, with poor children more often being impulsive and middle-class children being more reflective. I don't have any very good hunches about why this might be so, but this difference may help explain why poor children have more difficulty learning to read. Of course, there are many other reasons for greater reading difficulties among the poor, including less experience with books and reading in the home. But an impulsive visual-search style also makes it more difficult to examine the words carefully.

## ANSWERING THE "WHY" QUESTIONS: EXPLANATIONS OF PERCEPTUAL DEVELOPMENT

I began this chapter by pointing to the underlying theoretical argument between the *nativists* and the *empiricists*. Does the baby have to learn what to pay attention to, how to see depth, and so on? Or are these skills present at birth or based on preprogrammed development of neural structures? Such either/or, black/white statements of theoretical dilemmas can be (often are) helpful, but the truth usually turns out to be more the color of an elephant—gray. Still, it is helpful to see just what shade of gray our elephant may be this time.

## Arguments for Nativism

In the case of perceptual development, the arguments on the nativist side are quite powerful. The more skillful researchers have become in figuring out ways to test infants' percpetual skills, the more skillful the newborns appear to be. Babies have considerable perceptual acuity, some depth perception, and some rudimentary constancies. More important, babies do not have to be taught what to look at. There are "rules" for looking (and presumably for listening and touching, too) that can be detected at birth. As Kagan puts it: "Nature has apparently equipped the newborn with an initial bias in the processing of experience. He does not, as the nienteenth-century empiricists believed, have to learn what he should examine" (Kagan, 1971, p. 60). These "biases" change with age, but these later changes, too, seem to be strongly related to maturation of the nervous system. The shift in visual attention patterns at 2 months, for example, occurs at about the same time as a parallel change in the visual perception area of the cortex. In general, as a number of current researchers have pointed out (e.g., Allik & Valsiner, 1980), specific experiences do not seem to be required to stimulate the development of the relevant parts of the brain.

## Arguments for Empiricism

On the other side of the ledger, however, is a great deal of evidence from research with other species that some *minimum level* of experience is necessary to *maintain* the perceptual systems. Animals deprived of light show deterioration of the whole visual system and a consequent decrease in perceptual abilities (e.g., Riesen, 1947; Rasch et al., 1961). Wayne Dennis's study of orphanage babies in Iran, a study I've touched on before, suggests that the animal research may be generalizable to human subjects as well. The infants who didn't have a chance to look at things, to explore objects with hands and eyes and tongue, and who were deprived of the opportunity to move around freely were retarded in the development of both perceptual and motor skills.

Juri Allik and Jaan Valsiner (1980, p. 41) suggest an interesting analogy to computer hardware (the computer itself) and software (the programs). The perceptual "hardware"—specific neural pathways, sensitive periods for development of particular functions, and the like—may be preprogrammed genetically. But the "software" of the child's functioning in real environments depends on specific experience. A child is *able* to make visual discriminations between people or objects within the first few months of lfie. That's built into the hardware. But the specific discriminations she learns and the number of separate objects she learns to recognize will depend on her experience.

The basic system is thus adapted to the specific environment in which the child finds herself.

SUMMARY

1. Visual acuity is quite poor at birth but improves rapidly in the first few months.
2. Visual attention appears to follow definite rules, even in the first hours of life. Newborns search for objects and focus on the edges or on points of dark/light contrast. After two months of life, babies look more at *what* the object is, examining the middle as well as the edges.
3. The overall development of attention may be guided by four major principles suggested by Gibson: (1) "capture" to activity, (2) unsystematic to systematic search, (3) broad to selective pickup of information, and (4) inability to ability to ignore irrelevant information.
4. Babies must also learn to disregard certain perceptual information in order to operate with perceptual constancies, such as size, color, and shape constancies. Such constancies have been detected in infants as young as 1 to 2 months.
5. Babies learn to discriminate objects from one another fairly early, although visual discrimination may lag behind auditory or olfactory (smell) discrimination. By 3 months, infants can discriminate one face from another.
6. Object identity and object permanence are other properties of objects the child must learn in the first several years. By 6 to 8 months of age, most children have the rudiments of object permanence and realize that objects continue to exist even when they are out of sight.
7. Auditory acuity is better at birth than is visual acuity. Shortly after birth, babies are good at hearing sounds in the range of the human voice, detecting the location of sounds, and making fine discriminations between individual speech sounds.
8. Smell and taste sensitivities are also present in very young babies, as is response to tactual stimulation. Like all perceptual skills, however, the infant's acuity and discrimination ability increase over the early years of life.
9. Combining information from several senses is more difficult. Integration of visual and auditory information occurs quite early, with integration of visual and tactual information appearing later in the first year of life.
10. The basic principles of perceptual learning may be applied to the study of reading. Children have most difficulty discriminating letters that are reversals of one another, since this is a violation of shape constancy acquired earlier.

11. Difficulties in learning to read may arise because of perceptual problems, problems with integration of visual and auditory information, or problems with language.

12. Individual differences in perceptual style include the dimension of reflection versus impulsivity (tempo) and field independence versus dependence.

13. There are no consistently found sex differences in basic perceptual skills, although girls are frequently found to be more field-dependent than are boys.

14. Social class differences in perceptual abilities are also scarce, although poor children tend to have a faster conceptual tempo (be more "impulsive" in style) than do middle-class children.

15. Both the empiricists and the nativists are correct to some extent about the origin of perceptual skills. Many basic perceptual abilities, including strategies for examining the objects around one, appear to be built into the system at birth or develop as the brain develops over the early years. But specific experience is required both to maintain the underlying system and to learn fundamental discriminations.

## KEY TERMS

**Acuity**  Sharpness of perceptual ability—how well or clearly one can see or hear or use other senses.

**Color constancy**  The ability to see the color of an object as remaining the same despite changes in illumination or shadow. One of the basic perceptual constancies that make up "object constancy."

**Conceptual tempo**  A dimension of individual differences in perceptual/conceptual style suggested by Kagan, describing the general pace with which objects (or people) are examined or explored.

**Depth perception**  The ability to judge the distance of an object from your body, based on a number of cues.

**Dyslexia**  Term used to describe a significant difficulty in learning to read that is unaccounted for by mental retardation or substantial brain damage.

**Empiricism**  Opposite of nativism. The theoretical point of view that all perceptual skill arises from experience.

**Field dependence**  One end of a dimension of individual difference in perceptual style proposed by Witkin. Field-dependent individuals are heavily influenced by the context in which objects appear.

**Field independence**  The other end of the field dependence dimension. Field-independent individuals can ignore the context or distracting cues around objects.

**Impulsivity**  One end of the continuum of conceptual tempo described by Kagan. Impulsive individuals examine objects or arrays quickly, with rapid scans, and may make more errors if fine discriminations are required.

**Nativism**  See *empiricism* above. The view that perceptual skills are inborn and do not require experience to develop.

**Object concept**  A general term including the concepts of object permanence and object identity.

**Object constancy**  The general phrase describing the ability to see objects as remaining the same despite changes in retinal image.

**Object identity** Part of the object concept. The recognition that objects remain the same from one encounter to the next.

**Object permanence** Part of the object concept. The recognition that an object continues to exist even when it is temporarily out of sight.

**Perceptual constancies** A collection of constancies, including shape, size, and color constancy.

**Perceptual learning** An increase in the ability to extract information (via the senses) from the environment, as a result of practice or experience.

**Reflection** The other end of the "tempo" dimension of perceptual style. Reflective individuals examine objects or arrays very carefully and slowly. When fine discriminations are required, they normally perform better than impulsive individuals.

**Shape constancy** The ability to see an object's shape as remaining the same despite changes in the shape of the retinal image. A basic perceptual constancy.

**Size constancy** The ability to see an object's size as remaining the same despite changes in the size of the retinal image. A key element in this constancy is the ability to judge depth.

**Specific learning disability** The phrase commonly used to describe children with no obvious brain damage or mental retardation who show significant problems learning to read or doing other school tasks.

## SUGGESTED READINGS

There are not a lot of good, "chatty" sources on perceptual development. Even the current summaries of the literature are quite technical. Of the technical ones, the best is the paper by Linda Acredolo and Janet Hake, which is listed in the references at the end of the book. The only source I know of that is really intended for the nonprofessional reader is the following:

Bower, T. G. R. *The perceptual world of the child.* Cambridge, Mass.: Harvard University Press, 1977.

This brief book (about 85 pages) covers in readable fashion most of the major aspects of perceptual development during the early years.

PROJECT 5.1

# *Development of the Object Concept*

For this project, you will need to locate an infant between 6 and 12 months of age. Obtain permission from the baby's parents, assure them that there is nothing harmful or difficult in the tasks you will be doing, and inform them that you would like one of them to be there while you're presenting the materials to the baby.

Obtain from the parents one of the baby's favorite toys. Place the baby in a sitting position or on his stomach in such a way that he can reach for the toy easily (similar to the photos in Figure 5.5). Then perform the following steps:

Step 1: While the baby is watching, place the toy in full view and within easy reach. See if the infant reaches for the toy.

Step 2: In full view of the infant, cover part of the toy with a hand-kerchief, so that only part is visible. Does the baby reach for the toy?

Step 3: While the infant is reaching for the toy (you'll have to pick your moment), cover it completely with the handkerchief. Does the baby continue reaching?

Step 4: In full view of the child, while the child is still interested in the toy, cover the whole toy with the cloth. Does the baby try to pull the cloth away or search for the toy in some way?

You may need to use more than one toy to keep the baby's interest and/or spread the tests over a period of time.

Continued reaching when the toy is partly covered (as in steps 2, 3, and 4 above) should develop in the order listed. Jackson, Campos, and Fischer (1978) report that the first step (continuing to reach for the partly covered toy) is "passed" at about 26 weeks, the next at about 28 or 29 weeks, and the final step (reaching for the toy that has been fully covered) at about 30 or 31 weeks. The closer to these ages your infant is, the more interesting your results are likely to be.

Did your subject's performance conform to those expectations? If not, why do you think it was different? You might read the Jackson, Campos, and Fischer paper to see some of the reasons they give for differences in results from several studies. Do you think it mattered, for example, that a familiar toy was used? Did it matter that the mother or father was present?

# part three
## *the thinking child*

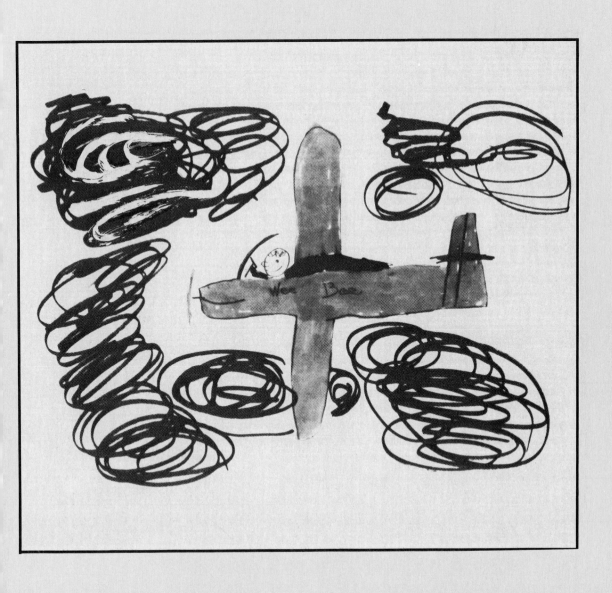

# 6.

# *cognitive development I: cognitive power*

Among the many tasks on my agenda for yesterday was preparing a casserole for a potluck dinner. Since I did not have all the ingredients on hand, I decided I would stop at the store after work. I made a list of the needed items, plus some other things I knew I had to buy, and put the list where I would be sure to take it with me. Of course, what happened was that I forgot to take the list. When I got to the grocery store, nine hours later, I wracked my brain to remember what had been on the list. My strategy was to remember the recipe I would be using and run through the list of ingredients in my mind as I wheeled the cart around the store. In the end I managed to reconstruct the full list in my head—all except the box of herb tea that had been on my written list but was not part of the recipe, and thus was not covered by my memory strategy.

All of us do things like that all the time. We plan, organize, remember, and use complex strategies to help in the process. These activities are part of what we normally describe as *cognitive functioning* or "intelligence." What I will be exploring in this and the next chapter is how we have acquired the ability to do these things. How do cognitive skills develop? And do all children (and all adults) use cognitive skills equally well?

Answering these questions turns out to be remarkably complicated, in part because there are really three different "theories" or "views" of cognition or intelligence, each of which has led to a distinct and huge body of research and commentary. Blending the three is a tricky task—one that I don't want to attempt until I have first presented each view separately.

## THREE VIEWS OF INTELLIGENCE

Historically, the first approach to studying cognitive development or intelligence was focused on individual differences. The incontrovertable fact is that people differ in their intellectual skill, their ability to remember lists for the grocery store, the speed with which they solve problems, the number of words they can define, their ability to analyze sequences or complex situations. When we say someone is "bright" or "very intelligent," it is just such skills we mean, and our label is based on the assumption that we can rank-order people in their degree of "brightness." It was precisely this assumption that led to the development of intelligence tests, which were designed simply to give us a way of measuring such individual differences in **intellectual power**.

This "power" definition of intelligence held sway for many years. But it has one great weakness: it does not deal with the equally incontrovertible fact that "intelligence develops: Behavior becomes increasingly complex and abstractly organized with age" (Butterfield, Siladi, & Belmont, 1980). If you give a 5-year-old a mental list of things to remember to buy at the grocery store, not only will she have trouble remembering more than a few of them, she also will not use many good strategies to aid her memory, such as rehearsing the list or organizing the items into sets (like my recipe strategy). An 8-year-old would remember more things and probably would rehearse the list under his breath or in his head as he was walking to the store. So not only does the child's skill (intellectual power) increase with age, the mental strategies, techniques, and types of logic applied to the problem also change as the child gets older.

This inescapable fact forms the foundation of the second great tradition in the study of cognitive development, the *cognitive-developmental* approach of Jean Piaget and his many followers. The focus here is on the development of cognitive **structures** rather than on power, on patterns of development that are *common* to all children rather than on individual differences.

These two traditions have lived side by side for some years now, rather like not-very-friendly neighbors who smile vaguely at each other when they meet but never get together for coffee. In the past few years, though, the two have developed a mutual friend—a third approach that at least partially integrates the first two. Proponents of this third view—such as Robert Sternberg (1981, 1982), Earl Butterfield (Butterfield, Siladi, & Belmont, 1980), and Robert Siegler (Siegler & Richards, 1982)—argue that what is needed is an understanding of the fundamental processes or strategies that make up all cognitive activity. What are the building blocks, the underlying elements, such as memory processes or problem-solving techniques? Once we have identified such basic processes, we can then ask if or when they change with age (a link to Piaget's theory) and whether people differ in their speed or skill in using them (a link to the traditional individual-differences view). This third approach has come to be called **information-processing** theory, and it is very much the new kid on the block.

Each of these three views tells us something useful and different about intelligence or cognitive development, so we need to look at all three. In other chapters, I nearly always begin by talking about developmental changes (changes in structure) and then turn to a discussion of individual differences (power). But in this case, I will follow the historical pattern and begin by describing the oldest of these three traditions—the measurement of intelligence. In the next chapter I'll talk about Piaget's views of developmental changes in intellectual structure and about information processing.

## MEASURING INTELLECTUAL POWER: IQ TESTS

Intelligence tests have a certain mystique about them, and most of us have a greatly inflated notion of the permanence or importance of an IQ score. If you are going to acquire a more realistic view, it's important for you to know something about what such tests were designed to do and something about the beliefs and values of the men and women who devised them.

## The First IQ Tests

Although there had been some earlier attempts to develop a global test of intellectual functioning, the first modern intelligence test was published in 1905 by two Frenchmen, Alfred Binet and Theodore Simon. The work of Binet and Simon was based on the generally held belief that individuals differed in mental ability and that it would be desirable to have a way of measuring these individual differences. Binet was asked by the French government to devise such a test in order to identify retarded children—those who were not profiting from regular school programs and who might be helped by remedial work. In the American version of this test, Louis Terman (Terman, 1916) expanded this goal and aimed for a test that would predict across the full range of school performance.

The selection of tasks to be included on the tests was heavily influenced by Binet's and Simon's thinking about the nature of intelligence. They believed that intelligence is basically judgment:

> It seems to us that in the intelligence there is a fundamental faculty.
> . . . This faculty is judgment, otherwise called good sense, practical
> sense, initiative, the faculty of adapting oneself to circumstances. To
> judge well, to comprehend well, to reason well, these are the essential
> activities of the intelligence (Binet & Simon, 1916, p. 24).

The tests they devised, not surprisingly, were composed of measures of comprehension, reasoning, vocabulary, memory, and the like: Can the child describe the difference between wood and glass? How many of a set of 30 pictures that a child views briefly can he later recall? Can the young child touch his nose, his ear, his head? Can the child tell which of two weights is heavier?

Similar types of tests were later used by Terman and his associates at Stanford University (Terman, 1916; Terman & Merrill, 1937), when they translated and revised the test for use in the United States (a test referred to as the **Stanford-Binet**). It consisted of a series of individual tests for children of each age. There were six tests for 4-year-olds, six tests for 5-year-olds, and so on. A child taking the test was given these age tests beginning below her actual age and continuing "upward" until a level was reached at which she failed them all.

This procedure led to something called the **intelligence quotient**, which is where **IQ** comes from. It was originally a comparison of the child's actual age (chronological age) with his **mental age**. For example, a child who could solve the problems for a 6-year-old but not those for a 7-year-old would have a mental age of 6. The formula used to calculate the IQ was

$$\frac{\text{Mental age}}{\text{Chronological age}} \times 100 = \text{IQ}$$

This results in an IQ above 100 for children whose mental age is higher than their chronological age and an IQ below 100 for children whose mental age is lower than their chronological age.

This old system for calculating the IQ is not used any longer, even in the modern revisions of the Stanford-Binet. Nowadays, IQs from any type of test are calculated by comparing a child's performance with the performance of a large group of other children his own age. The "average" child of any age is automatically given a score of 100; any child who does better than that average has an IQ above 100, with the precise score determined by the degree of deviation from the average.

The majority of children achieve scores that are right around the average of 100, with a smaller number scoring very high or very low. Figure 6.1 shows the distribution of IQ scores that we would see if we gave the test to hundreds or thousands of children, along with the labels typically attached to different ranges of scores.

## Modern IQ Tests

Two of the tests used frequently by psychologists today are the Stanford-Binet and the Weschler Intelligence Scales for Children, usually called the **WISC**, which was developed originally by David Wechsler (1949). Because the Binet has items designed for testing preschool-age children, which the WISC does not, the Binet is more often used with 3- to 6-year-olds, while the WISC is more commonly used with older children. To give you some idea of the sort of items included in tests like these, I've described the WISC in some detail in Box 6.1.

*Infant Tests*   Neither the Binet nor the WISC can be used with infants much younger than about 3. Infants don't talk well, if at all, and the usual childhood tests rely heavily on language. So how do we measure "intelligence" in an infant? This becomes an important question if we want to be able to identify, during infancy, those children who are likely to have intellectual or school difficulties later on. If we had a good "infant intelligence test," perhaps it would be possible to locate such children in infancy, when remedial programs might be of real help.

Several attempts have been made. The most frequently used current infant test is the Bayley Scales of Infant Development (Bayley, 1969), which yields separate scores for mental development and motor development. Included among the mental items are such tasks as

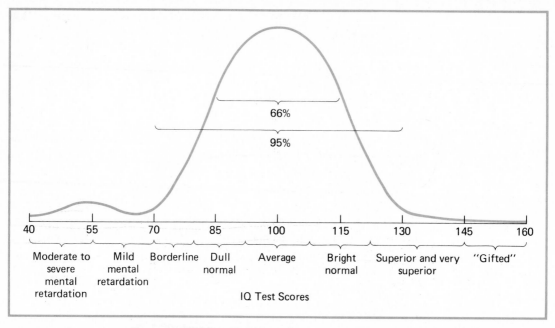

**Figure 6.1** The approximate distribution of IQ scores on most modern tests. The tests are *designed* so that the average score is 100, and two-thirds of the scores fall between about 85 and 115. Because of brain damage or genetic anomalies, there are slightly more low-IQ children than there are very-high-IQ children.

reaching for a dangling ring (3 months), uncovering a toy hidden by a cloth (8 months; obviously measuring an aspect of object permanence), putting cubes in a cup on request (9 months), or building a tower of three cubes (17 months). Nearly all infant tests are constructed to be very like the later **IQ** tests—they include a series of items of increasing difficulty that are intended to tap or demand basic cognitive processes.

Very recently, several researchers operating from an information-processing perspective (Fagan & McGrath, 1981; Lewis & Brooks-Gunn, 1981) have suggested that tests like the Bayley are not assessing the really fundamental processes. They argue that a better test of early processing skill, or "intelligence," is the rapidity with which an infant habituates to a repeated visual stimulus or "recognizes" some repeatedly presented picture. No standardized test to measure such behavior has been developed, but as I'll describe in the next chapter, this approach seems very promising.

*Culture-Fair Tests* Because most of the items on the Binet or the WISC require the child to read or use language in some way, some psychologists, such as Florence Goodenough (1926), thought that these tests might well be culturally biased. Verbal tests may underestimate the ability of children who come from cultural backgrounds in which language is not stressed or who speak a different dialect. So-called **cul-**

BOX 6.1

# THE WECHSLER INTELLIGENCE SCALE FOR CHILDREN (WISC)

Unlike the Binet, which has separate tests for children of each age, on the WISC all children are given the same 10 types of problems, with each type running from very easy to very difficult items. The 10 subtests are divided into two groups: those that rely heavily on verbal abilities and a group called performance tests, which involve less language ability and test the child's perceptual skills and nonverbal logic. The 10 tests, with examples of items similar to those on the actual tests, are as follows:

### VERBAL TESTS

*General information:* "How many eyes have you?"

*General comprehension:* "What is the thing to do when you scrape your knee?"

*Arithmetic:* "James had 10 marbles and he bought 4 more. How many marbles did he have altogether?"

*Similarities:* "In what way are a pear and an orange alike?"

*Vocabulary:* "What is an emerald?"

### PERFORMANCE TESTS

*Picture completion:* The child is shown pictures of familiar objects in which a part has been left out. He has to identify the missing part, such as a comb with a tooth missing.

*Picture arrangement:* Pictures like the frames of a comic strip are laid out in the wrong order in front of the child. The child has to figure out the right order to make a story.

*Block design:* Sets of blocks that are red, white, blue, and yellow on different sides, and half-red/half-white or half-blue/half-yellow on the other sides are given to the child. Using these blocks, she has to copy designs. The first problems involve only four blocks; harder problems include nine blocks.

*Object assembly:* Large pictures of familiar objects like a horse or a face have been cut up into pieces—rather like a jigsaw puzzle, except bigger pieces. The child has to put them together in the correct configuration as rapidly as possible.

*Coding:* A series of abstract symbols like balls and stars are each shown with a paired symbol, such as a single line. The child then has several rows of the first set of symbols and must fill in the paired symbol next to each one.

### USES OF THE WISC SCORES

One of the reasons many educators prefer the WISC to the Stanford-Binet is that it allows you to look at the variation in a child's performance. Gifted children typically do well on all the tests. Very retarded children typically do poorly on all the tests, although they may do a little better on the performance tests than on the verbal ones. But children with some kind of learning disability or brain damage may show a lot of variability. For example, children who have difficulty learning to read nearly always do better on the performance tests. But they may often do quite well on the vocabulary subtest and very poorly on the coding subtest (Sattler, 1974). So it isn't just words that are the problem.

The key point is that significant *unevenness* in a child's performance on the WISC (or on any other IQ test) may alert the teacher to a specific learning problem. Two children with the same total IQ scores may have very different patterns of test performance and may need very different kinds of special help.

|  |  |  |
|---|---|---|
| Score 7 | Score 25 | Score 47 |
| Mental age 4.75 years | Mental age 9.25 years | Mental age 13.00 years |

**Figure 6.2** Examples of children's drawings of the human figure and the score they were given on Goodenough's draw-a-person test. The drawing on the right—which includes the plaid of the suit, a cigarette, and a moustache—gets a higher score than the drawing in the middle. (*Source:* From *Measurement of intelligence by drawings,* by Florence L. Goodenough. Copyright 1926 by Harcourt Brace Jovanovich, Inc.; renewed 1954 by Florence L. Goodenough. Reproduced by permission of the publisher.)

**ture-fair** tests were developed to get around this problem by using tasks with which all children might reasonably have equal familiarity.

The most famous of the culture-fair tests is probably Goodenough's **Draw-a-Person** test, which simply requires the child to draw a picture of a man or a woman. You can see some examples of children's drawings in Figure 6.2. The child's drawing is evaluated in terms of the normal amount of detail and elaboration found in the drawings of children that age. Since all children have observed people, it is assumed that they all have the basic experience necessary to perform this task. Scores on these tests are moderately correlated (around .50) with scores on the Binet or WISC, so these rather different measures seem to be tapping some of the same skills. But scores on the Goodenough test are *not* at all strongly related to school achievement (Scott, 1981). Among other things, this means that such culture-fair tests are of no real use for screening children to identify those who are likely to do poorly in school.

## Achievement Tests

Finally, let me say a word about a very familiar type of test, the **achievement test**. Nearly all of you have taken these tests in elementary and high school. They are designed to test *specific* information learned in school, using items like the ones in Table 6.1. The child taking an achievement test doesn't end up with an IQ score. But his performance is still compared to that of other children in the same grade across the country. Often the scores are reported in *percentiles*. A child who does just as well as the average child in his grade would be at the fiftieth percentile; one who did better than 90 percent of the other children would be at the ninetieth percentile; and so forth.

How are these tests different from an IQ test? The original idea was that an IQ test was measuring the child's basic capacity (her underlying **competence**) while the achievement test was supposed to measure what the child had actually learned (her **performance**).

This distinction between competence and performance, between "ability" and "achievement," is an important one. Each of us presumably has some upper limit of ability—what we could do under ideal conditions, when we are maximally motivated, well, and rested. But of course, everyday conditions are rarely ideal, so we typically perform below our hypothetical ability.

But important as this distinction is, it is a great mistake to assume that the IQ test somehow measures the child's basic ability, or competence. It is *not* a benchmark against which you compare the child's day-to-day performance in the classroom. If you use it in that way, you are led into some interesting logical fallacies.

Suppose, for example, that a child's IQ test score is higher than his

TABLE 6.1

**Some sample items from a fourth-grade achievement test**

| Vocabulary | Reference Skills |
|---|---|
| *jolly* old man | Which of these words would be first in ABC order? |
| 1. angry | 1. pair |
| 2. fat | 2. point |
| 3. merry | 3. paint |
| 4. sorry | 4. polish |

Spelling

Jason took the *cleanest* glass.

right _____ wrong _____

Mathematics Computation

$$\begin{array}{cc} 79 & 62 \\ +14 & \times\ 3 \end{array}$$

Language Expression

Who wants _____ books?
1. that
2. these
3. them
4. this

$$\begin{array}{c} 149 \\ -87 \end{array}$$

Mathematics

What does the "3" in 13 stand for?
1. 3 ones
2. 13 ones
3. 3 tens
4. 13 tens

*SOURCE:* From Comprehensive Tests of Basic Skills, Form S. Reprinted by permission of the publisher, CTB/McGraw-Hill, Del Monte Research Park, Monterey Calif. 93940. Copyright © 1973 by McGraw-Hill, Inc. All rights reserved. Printed in the U.S.A.

BOX 6.2

# *THE USES OF IQ TESTS IN THE SCHOOLS*

## *THE SORTING FUNCTION*

The dominant use of IQ tests in public school systems today is for what Lauren Resnick (1979) calls the "sorting function." This is very much the purpose that Binet had in mind when he designed the first tests, and they are still used in this way.

Children who seem to be learning slowly in class may be given an IQ test to see if they might be "retarded." The test score would then be one of several pieces of information used to decide if the child should be in a special class. Or a child who is having difficulty learning to read but is otherwise doing okay may be given a test like the WISC or other special tests designed to diagnose specific learning disabilities or brain damage.

IQ tests are also sometimes used before school starts as a type of "readiness" test. When my daughter was not quite 5, she was given an IQ test because we wanted her to enter school at an age a few months younger than the official school cutoff point. The school psychologist used the IQ test to help him determine if she would be able to handle the work of kindergarten.

All of these uses of the tests are for diagnosis and sorting. They help the teacher or the school to know which children need special help (either because of poor performance or because of very high performance), and they help to pin down the sort of help that may be most useful.

I should point out that not all educators or parents approve of this use of IQ tests. As you'll see later in this chapter, it is possible that standard IQ tests are not equally "fair" for children from all racial or social class groups. If the tests alone are used as the basis for assignment to special classes, too many minority-group children end up being assigned (more than one would expect given the distribution of scores on the tests). In fact, one federal court judge recently ruled that IQ tests could not be used as a basis for special-class assignment of black children in California. I should emphasize, however, that a single IQ test score is almost *never* used as the sole basis for any special-class assignment in any school system. A child is normally given several tests, and his classroom functioning is also observed. Only when all the signs point in the same direction would a child be placed in a special class. Still, the court ruling

achievement test scores and higher than his grades. If you assume that the IQ test measures his "real" ability, this child may be called an "underachiever" and there may be parent conferences, much finger wagging and head scratching. Why is this basically "bright" child not doing well in school? How can he be motivated to do better?

That seems fairly logical, doesn't it? But now turn it around. What happens if the child's school performance is *better* than his test score would suggest? These children are sometimes called "overachievers," and again, the parents may get called in for a conference. Are they pushing the child too hard at home? But think about the logic. If the IQ test measures real capacity, then these "overachievers" are doing better than they are able to do. How is this possible?

The basic point, as John Horn states it flatly, is that "intelligence

shows the type of concern that has arisen recently about the use of IQ tests for sorting.

### THE ACCOUNTABILITY AND JUSTIFICATION FUNCTION

More recently, IQ tests are beginning to be used in another way as well—to justify educational practices to the public. *Accountability* is becoming a watchword in public life, and public schools are affected by the need to justify their actions, just as are other government groups. In many states, achievement tests are being used for this purpose. All the children in one or more grades may be given the same test, and then the results are made public. If the children in a given state are doing well by national standards, then all the educators pat themselves on the back. But if the children do poorly, what happens?

Poor performance by a group of children in a given class or a given school might come about because the school or the teacher just isn't doing a very good job. That's what parents are likely to conclude if they see low test scores, and they may pressure the schools to improve. In the face of pressure like this, some educators have fallen back on the IQ test as a measure of competence. If the children in a school have been given IQ tests and have performed relatively poorly, then how can the school be expected to teach them as readily?

It should be obvious from what I've already said that I think this is fallacious reasoning. But I know it happens, because I have seen it in the small school district on whose school board I served for several years. In one year, our fourth graders did poorly on the statewide achievement tests. The school psychologist suggested that we give them all IQ tests to see if they were "really" not very bright. The school board did not take his advice (I won that round!); but I suspect this use of IQ tests, as justification or legitimization of school policy, will become more prominent as schools come under increasing pressure.

### IQ TESTS AND CURRICULUM

One area of education on which IQ tests have had little impact—perhaps surprisingly—is curriculum. Schools rarely set out to "teach to the test." On the other hand, many schools do design their curriculum around the content of *achievement* tests, especially if they know that a particular test will be used as a basis for judging the quality of the school instruction. This is one reason that the score on an IQ test is usually considered to be a better measure of a child's basic cognitive skill than is a score on an achievement test, which may be more influenced by what happened in the classroom the day before.

tests are achievement tests" (Horn, 1979, p. 237). The difference between tests called IQ tests and those called achievement tests is really a matter of degree. The intelligence tests include items that are designed to tap fairly fundamental intellectual processes like comparison or analysis, and they *may* come closer to measuring maximal performance; the achievement tests call for specific information the child has learned in school (or elsewhere). But *both* measure aspects of a child's performance and not competence.

If that's so, why bother with IQ tests at all in the schools? Some educators, in fact, don't think that IQ tests add anything useful. But there are specific ways in which IQ tests are used in schools that you should know something about. I've described some of the main ones in Box 6.2.

## WHAT IQ TESTS PREDICT

The fact that IQ tests do not fully measure "basic ability," or "competence," as they were originally intended to do, does not mean that they are useless. For most psychologists, the critical question is what the tests predict. If IQ test scores can help us make predictions about future problems or success, then such tests may still be useful tools.

### School Performance

In the case of IQ tests, psychologists have most often looked at predictions of school performance. After all, Binet designed the first tests specifically to predict school success, and that is still the major use of the tests. The research findings on this point are quite consistent: The correlation between a child's test score and her grades in school or performance on other school tests is about .60 (Sattler, 1974). This is a strong, but by no means perfect, correlation. It tells us that, on the whole, the children with top IQ scores will also be among the high achievers in school and those who score low will be among the low achievers. Still, some children with high IQ scores don't do all that well in school, and some low-IQ children do well.

IQ scores not only relate moderately well to *current* grades, they can also predict *future* grades. Preschool children with high IQ scores will tend to do better when they enter school than those with lower scores; children in fourth or fifth grade who test well are likely to be performing well in high school.

There is also a consistent finding that the higher a child's IQ, the more years of school she's likely to complete (Brody & Brody, 1976). Children with lower scores are more likely to drop out of high school or to complete high school but not go on to college. And of those youngsters who *do* decide to try college, those with lower IQ scores have more trouble finishing. So the test scores do predict school performance reasonably well.

I am *not* saying here that IQ *causes* good or poor performance in school—although that is one possibility, and one that has been widely believed. All we know is that the two events—high or low IQ scores and good or poor school performance—tend to go together so that we can use one to predict the other.

### Later Job Success

Once a person gets out of school, does his IQ still predict anything important? Do people with higher IQs get better jobs, or do they do better in the jobs they hold? The answer is a cautious "yes."

There is a relationship between IQ and the types of jobs people hold as adults. Most doctors and lawyers, for example, have fairly high IQs, while cooks and salesclerks have lower average IQs (Brody & Brody, 1976). This happens partly because occupations like medicine or law have "entrance requirements" including IQ-like tests, while jobs like mechanic, cook, or salesclerk do not. So jobs in the latter group are open to people with less training or lower achievement. Even with entrance requirements, though, the relationship between IQ and occupation is far from perfect. In one longitudinal study, Dorothy Eichorn and her colleagues (Eichorn, Hunt, & Honzik, 1981) found that IQ scores obtained at age 17 to 18 for a group of 117 men were correlated only .46 with the status of the men's occupations when they were in their forties. So there is quite a lot of "give" in the system.

At the same time, once a person is in a job, his IQ doesn't tell us very much about how well he will succeed. Doctors with IQs of 150 don't make more money or have more satisfied patients than doctors with

**Figure 6.3** The job of secretary is one for which the IQ score predicts success. This job has no "entrance requirements"—that is, you don't have to have a high IQ to get into this occupation. Once in it, however, adults with higher IQs are more successful than those with lower IQs.

IQs of 120. And high-IQ carpenters don't hammer straighter nails than low-IQ carpenters. Only in those occupations where there are no entrance requirements and where there are intellectual demands, such as secretarial work or bookkeeping, does IQ predict performance.

## STABILITY OF IQ TEST SCORES

One of the bits of folklore about IQ tests is that a particular IQ score is something you "have," like blue eyes or red hair. This notion is based on the assumption that IQ scores remain stable over time—that a child who achieves a score of, say, 115 at 1 year of age will continue to score in about the same range at age 6 or 12 or 20. The fact that IQ scores can predict future school performance certainly tells us that there is *some* stability, but scores on IQ tests are quite a lot less stable than you probably think.

First of all, scores from "infant IQ tests" given in the first 12 or 18 months of life have only a limited resemblance to scores on tests given to the same children later (Kopp & McCall, 1982; McCall, 1981a).

Let me give you a concrete example from some research of my own (Bee et al., 1982). We have studied a group of 193 families since before the birth of their first child through the child's seventh year. Among many other things, we administered the Bayley test of infant mental development when the children were 12 months old and again at 24 months. At age 4 we tested them with the Binet, and at age 8 we gave them the WISC. When we looked at the correlations between the early infant IQ test scores and later IQ scores, we found the results in Table 6.2. As you can see, the test given at 12 months was only very weakly related to later test scores, so many children who had done poorly at 12 months later looked much better and vice versa.

Past about age 2 or 3, the consistency of performance on IQ tests becomes better. If two tests are given within a fairly short space of time—say, weeks or even months apart—the scores do tend to be quite similar. Nonetheless, over the years of childhood, *most* children show wide fluctuations in their scores. Robert McCall and his colleagues (McCall, Appelbaum, & Hogarty, 1973), for example, looked at the test

TABLE 6.2

**Relationship between infant IQ test scores and IQ at ages 4 and 8**

| | INFANT IQ TEST SCORES (BAYLEY TEST) | |
|---|---|---|
| *IQ Predictions* | *At 12 Months* | *At 24 Months* |
| 4 years (Binet) | .21 | .53 |
| 8 years (WISC) | .15 | .39 |

*SOURCE:* Bee et al., 1982, and unpublished data for 8-year WISC scores.
*NOTE:* The sample involved children of working-class and middle-class families. The higher the correlation, the stronger the relationship. Thus, the infant IQ test score at 12 months is only very weakly related to later IQ measures, while the 24-month score is more strongly related.

scores of a group of 80 mostly middle-class children who had been given IQ tests at regular intervals from the time they were $2\frac{1}{2}$ until they were 17. The *average* amount of variation in IQ scores in this group (the difference between the highest and the lowest score achieved by each child) was 28 points, and one child in seven showed a shift of more than 40 points. Thus, a child might achieve a test score in the "dull normal" range at one point and at another point test at a "superior" level. Such large fluctuations are more common in young children. The general rule of thumb is that the older the child or the closer to adulthood, the more stable the IQ score becomes.

Obviously, this type of shifting up and down in test scores is a very good argument against using any single IQ test score as some kind of "upper-limit" measure of a child's ability.

There are really two questions here. First of all, we need to understand why any one child's score may fluctuate from one testing to the next. But more generally, we need to determine why some children quite consistently do better on IQ tests than others do.

This second question is at the heart of the now-familiar nature/nurture question. How much of the difference among children's test scores is the result of inherited, built-in differences (nature), and how much results from different experiences or different opportunities to learn (nurture)?

When Binet designed the early IQ tests, he did not make the assumption that he was measuring some fixed, inborn quality. He assumed instead that a child's intelligence could be modified. All he wanted to do was to measure it at a particular time. But in the United States, the psychologists who devised and revised intelligence tests by and large *did* assume that intelligence was inherited and thus fixed at birth. This assumption somehow got attached to the tests in many people's minds, so that most nonpsychologists (and many psychologists, I should add) are convinced that you inherit an "amount" of intelligence that remains constant all your life.

How valid is that assumption? How much of a role do nature and nurture play in test scores?

## INFLUENCE OF HEREDITY ON IQ

### Direct Effect of Heredity on IQ: A Journey into Some Classic Research

The arguments about the heritability of IQ have been going on now for at least 50 years, and there is still no good agreement among the psychologists who do research in this area. Among current researchers and theorists, Arthur Jensen (1980, 1981) has taken one of the strongest genetic positions. He argues that as much as 80 percent of all variation among IQ scores is due to direct genetic differences. On the other end of this spectrum, Leon Kamin (1974, 1981) has taken an extreme environmentalist position. He contends that very little, if any, of the variation among people in IQ test scores is due to genetic influence.

In between these two extremes (and probably closer to the truth) are psychologists such as Robert Plomin (1978; Plomin & DeFries, 1980) and Sandra Scarr (1978; 1981a; Scarr & Weinberg, 1983), who argue that genetic and environmental influences are both present.

I cannot settle this theoretical argument here. What I can do is take you on a brief journey into this complex and fascinating literature and give you my own current synthesis.

*Searching for Hereditary Influences*   There are two basic ways of searching for a genetic influence on IQ (or on any other trait, for that matter). You can study identical and fraternal twins or you can study adopted children. Identical twins share exactly the same genetic patterning, while fraternal twins do not. So if identical twins turn out to be more like each other in IQ than do fraternal twins, that would be evidence for the influence of heredity on IQ.

In the case of adopted children, the child is being raised by someone other than her natural (genetic) parent. If the child's IQ should turn out to be more closely related to her *natural* parents' IQs, even though she didn't grow up with them, that would again be a point for the influence of heredity.

Both of these types of studies sound quite straightforward; but in fact, they are *extremely* difficult to do well, and the results are confusing.

*Twin Studies*   Identical twins *do* have IQs that are more alike than fraternal twins (Loehlin & Nichols, 1976; Wilson, 1977, 1978, 1983). Robert Plomin (Plomin & DeFries, 1980), combining the results of all the studies of IQ in twins, estimates that the correlation between IQ scores of identical twins who have grown up together is .86 (a *very high* correlation), while the correlation between scores of same-sex fraternal twins reared together is about .60—lower, but still fairly substantial. Score one point for heredity.

But wait a minute. Isn't it possible that identical twins are *treated* more alike than are fraternal twins, too? Maybe they are dressed alike, spend more time together, are disciplined alike, have more similar toys, and so on. In fact, this does seem to be true (Lytton, 1977), which means that at least some of the similarity between twins that has been ascribed to heredity may really be caused by the environment.

Studying a special subgroup of identical twins—those who have been reared *apart* from each other—can help us sort out these two influences. If such twins are *still* like each other in IQ, even though they have not been together, that would surely show a hereditary effect.

As you might imagine, there aren't many pairs of identical twins who have been reared in different families. But there are a few, and psychologists who have studied them (e.g., Shields, 1962) have generally found that the twins' IQ scores are still quite similar. Once again, though, the apparent support of a hereditary view that these data provide has been challenged by more recent analyses.

Leon Kamin (1974) went back and looked carefully at the cases involved in all studies of twins raised apart and found that, in the majority of instances, both twins were reared by relatives of the parents, such as two aunts or the grandmother and an aunt. In most cases, the children knew each other, went to the same schools, and knew they were twins. In those cases in which the twins were reared by unrelated families, ordinarily both children were placed in families of the same general social class. If we look at the correlation between the scores for identical twins raised in unrelated families only, we find that it is considerably lower (about .50 in the Shields study). Susan Farber (1981) has pursued this analysis still further and found that when the IQs of identical twins who were reared in the least-similar environments and for whom reliable and accurate data had been reported were compared, their IQs were the least similar as well. Thus, the twin data, which first appear to show an extremely strong hereditary influence on IQ, are not as clear-cut as they seem.

*Adoption Studies*  Results from adoption studies are equally two-sided. The most common finding is that adopted children's IQs can be predicted better from knowing the IQs or the level of education of their *natural* parents than from knowing the IQs or education of their adoptive parents (Horn, 1983; Scarr & Weinberg, 1983; Plomin & DeFries, 1983; Skodak & Skeels, 1945). Again, that sounds like a clear point for a genetic influence, but as usual, there are some confusions.

First of all, when two adopted children are raised in the same family, their IQs turn out to be more similar than you'd expect by chance, even though they have *no* shared inheritance at all (Scarr & Weinberg, 1977). The environment, in this case, seems to be moving both children in the same direction.

Second, adopted children, as a group, tend to have *higher* IQs than do their natural parents. The effect of most adoptive environments seems to be to raise the child's IQ 10 or 15 points over what it probably would have been if he had been raised by his natural mother (Scarr & Weinberg, 1977; Skodak & Skeels, 1945). So obviously, the adoptive environment has a major impact.

*Summing Up the Journey: The Direct Role of Heredity in IQ*  Confusing, isn't it? After reading all of this research and all the heated comments by theorists on both sides of the issue, my own conclusion is that, as usual, neither extreme position is correct. On the one hand, as Sandra Scarr says, "The evidence for some genetic individual differences in behavior is simply overwhelming" (1978, p. 336). On the other hand, I am convinced that the genetic component in measured IQ is far smaller than the 80 percent Jensen suggests and may even be less than the 50 percent Plomin proposes. In sum, we do appear to inherit particular characteristics or skills that have a significant influence on the speed or efficiency with which we can perform intellectual tasks. But the environment we grow up in plays a major role as well.

### Indirect Effects of Heredity on IQ

So far I have been describing a *direct* effect of heredity on IQ scores. Presumably each of us inherits some combination of genes that affects brain function, memory, reaction time, and the like, and these combine to influence the IQ score. But there is a second, *indirect* way that heredity could influence IQ scores. Children might inherit temperamental characteristics or personality traits that affect the way other people respond to them or the experiences they seek out. These differences in experiences may, in turn, affect the IQ score.

We know little about such potential indirect effects, but recently Michael Lamb (1982a) has suggested that a child's *sociability* may be part of such an indirect pathway of influence. There is now quite a lot of evidence that more friendly, sociable infants and young children obtain higher scores on infant IQ tests and on tests given in toddlerhood. (Whether the same relationship holds for older children I can't say, since it has not been studied.) Such a link could be interpreted several ways. Friendly infants and children may simply be better "test takers." The adult examiners may like them better, work harder at getting optimum responses from them, or score them higher. A second possibility, however, is that friendliness or sociability is an inherited temperamental trait and that infants high in this quality simply elicit more stimulation from the people around them.

Lamb argues that both of these explanations may be partially true. It is an intriguing possibility and is one more example of the potential impact of infant temperament on the child's experiences and performance.

## INFLUENCE OF THE ENVIRONMENT ON IQ

The other major source of influences on IQ is the environment in which the child is raised. I do not at all mean to imply that heredity and environment do not interact. Obviously, they do, as Lamb's work on sociability and IQ suggests. But we can identify some specific variations in environments that are strongly related to IQ. Let me begin at the most global level, with social class differences, and work my way "down" to more specific kinds of experiences.

## Social Class Differences

One of the most consistent findings in studies of IQ is that children from poor or working-class families have lower average IQs than do children from middle-class families. This relationship is vividly illustrated in Figure 6.4, which is based on data from a *huge* national study of over 50,000 children born in 12 different hospitals around the United States between 1959 and 1966 (Broman, Nichols, & Kennedy, 1975). I have given you the results only for white children who were tested with the Stanford-Binet at age 4, a total sample of over 11,800 children. The social class breakdown was based on the occupation, income, and education of both the father and the mother. As you can see in the figure, the average IQ of the children rises as the social class rises and as the mother's education rises.

These differences are *not* found in infancy (Golden et al., 1971), but after age 3 social class differences appear to widen steadily (Farran,

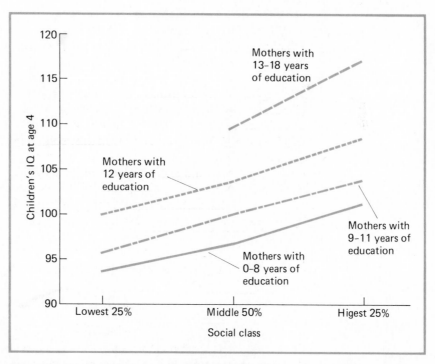

**Figure 6.4** These results from a very large national study of test scores of 4-year-old children show very clearly that IQ is related to the social class of the child's family and the education of the child's mother. Each line represents the scores for children with mothers at a particular education level living in three different social class environments. (There are too few cases of low–social class mothers with 13 to 18 years of education, though, so there are no data for this point.) Higher social class and higher education are each related to higher IQ. (*Source:* Broman, Nichols, & Kennedy, 1975, p. 47.)

Haskins, & Gallagher, 1980), producing what is sometimes called a **cumulative deficit.**

There are about as many ways to explain such findings as there are psychologists, as you might imagine. The difference could be hereditary (brighter parents presumably have more education and earn more money and also pass on their "bright" genes to their children). It could be due to differences in prenatal risks, diet, or general health or to differences in the actual patterns of interaction or stimulation provided in poor families versus middle-class families. Or it could be (probably is) the result of complex combinations of these effects. For example, brighter parents (who may also be in a higher social class) provide more enriched environments for their children, which then magnifies any basic genetic difference.

The key point, from my perspective, is that simple comparisons of IQ scores in different social class groups will never tell us *why* there are such differences. Studies like Broman's tell us that there *is* a difference, which is important. But to understand it, we will have to do more detailed observations of what is going on in families between parents and children.

## Specific Family Characteristics and IQ

There is now a very extensive body of research on the link between early parent-child interactions and the child's later IQ. My reading of this research has led me to the following list of five general characteristics of families whose children achieve higher IQ scores:

1. They provide *appropriate* play materials for the child. It is not the sheer quantity of play materials that is significant; rather, it is the appropriateness of the play materials for the child's age and developmental level that seems to be critical. A set of nesting pots or pans to play with is just as good as an expensive toy, so long as the child has access to it.
2. They are *emotionally responsive* to and *involved* with their child. They spend time with the child; encourage the child's play and problem-solving; and respond to the child's questions, actions, or activities. They smile at the child, speak warmly to her and about her.
3. They *talk to their child*, using language that is descriptively rich and accurate.
4. They *avoid excessive restrictiveness* or punitiveness, instead giving the child room to explore, even opportunities to make mistakes.
5. They *expect their child to do well and to develop rapidly*. They emphasize and press for school achievement.

Of all the studies I have drawn on in reaching these conclusions, the most influential and interesting are probably those of Bettye Cald-

**Figure 6.5** Parents who spend time with their child, encourage exploration, provide appropriate toys, and use complex language have children who later perform better on IQ tests.

well and her colleagues Robert Bradley and Richard Elardo (Elardo, Bradley, & Caldwell, 1975; Bradley & Caldwell, 1976, 1977, 1978; van Doorninck et al., 1981).

Caldwell has devised a measure of the environment she calls the HOME Inventory (Home Observation for Measurement of the Environment). An interviewer/observer visits a home, talks with the parent about a typical day in the family, and observes the kinds of materials available to the child and the kind of interactions the parent has with the child. The observer then scores "yes" or "no" for each of a series of specific items about that family. Some examples of items from this scale are shown in Table 6.3.

In Elardo, Bradley, and Caldwell's original study, they observed and

TABLE 6.3

**Some sample items from the HOME Inventory**

| | | |
|---|---|---|
| The mother spontaneously vocalizes to the child at least twice during the visit (excluding scolding). | Yes__ | No__ |
| When speaking of or to child, mother's voice conveys positive feeling. | Yes__ | No__ |
| Mother does not shout at child during visit. | Yes__ | No__ |
| Child gets out of house at least four times a week. | Yes__ | No__ |
| Child has push or pull toy. | Yes__ | No__ |
| Family provides learning equipment appropriate to age—mobile, table and chairs, high chair, play pen. | Yes__ | No__ |
| Mother structures child's play periods. | Yes__ | No__ |
| Mother reads stories at least three times weekly. | Yes__ | No__ |

*SOURCE:* Caldwell & Bradley, 1978.

scored the homes of 77 children from poor and working-class families. The homes were first observed when the children were 6 months old and again at 24 months. The children's IQs were tested when they were 3 and again at $4\frac{1}{2}$. What they found was that the two were correlated, as you can see in Table 6.4: Mothers who were emotionally responsive to their 6- or 24-month-old infants, provided appropriate play materials, spent time with their infants, and provided variety in the child's experience had children who later had higher IQs. The correlations are by no means perfect. Some mothers who do these things have children with moderate IQ scores, and some mothers who do not do these things have children who test well. But the relationship is remarkably strong considering how little time was spent observing each family.

My colleagues and I at the University of Washington (Bee et al., 1982) have replicated these findings in the longitudinal study I mentioned earlier (see Table 6.2). In still a third parallel study, Craig Ramey and his colleagues at the University of North Carolina (Ramey, Farran, & Campbell, 1979; Yeates et al., 1983) have also partially replicated the Caldwell results. In Ramey's research and in our own, the mother's level of punishment and restriction emerged as a more critical ingredient in the "environmental recipe" than was true in Caldwell's study. Mothers who were more physically restrictive and more punitive toward their children, especially right around 24 months of age, had children who had *lower* IQs later on.

Using a quite different strategy to study parents and children, Patrick Dickson (Dickson et al., 1979) has been able to identify one of the aspects of the mother's language to the child that also seems to be important. Dickson had white American mothers and Japanese mothers (in Tokyo) each describe a photograph to her 4-year-old child. The child was then shown four photos and had to pick out the one his mother had described. Obviously, for the child to be able to do this successfully, the mother had to have described the photo fully and accurately. Two years later, the children were tested with either the Binet or the WISC. Dickson found that those mothers whose language to the child at age 4 had been accurate and complete had children who had higher IQs at age 6.

In what I have just said about specific family characteristics, I have implied that these are *causal* relationships—that appropriate toys, in-

TABLE 6.4

**Correlations of the Caldwell HOME Inventory and the child's IQ scores**

| | CORRELATIONS WITH IQ AT | |
|---|---|---|
| *HOME Inventory* | *3 Years* | *$4\frac{1}{2}$ Years* |
| Scored at 6 months | .50 | .44 |
| Scored at 24 months | .70 | .57 |

*SOURCES:* Elardo, Bradley, & Caldwell, 1975, pp. 73–74; Bradley & Caldwell, 1976, p. 1173.

volved parents, complex and accurate language all *cause* higher IQ. And that is one possibility. But other interpretations are possible, too. Maybe genetically bright children bring out more stimulating environments; maybe parents with higher IQs (who may have passed on their "high-IQ genes" to their children) are simply more likely to do all these "good" things. Each of these alternatives has some merit and is doubtless partly true. But I am convinced by our own data and by the results of others (e.g., Yeates et al., 1983) that the specific qualities of the child's environment also contribute directly to her developing intellectual power.

*Birth Order and Family Size*  Another aspect of family experience that seems to have some connection to measured IQ is the size of the family and the child's position among the siblings. On the average, the more children there are in the family, the lower the average IQ of the children. And if the children are closely spaced, first-born children have the highest IQs, with average IQs declining steadily as you go down the family (Zajonc & Marcus, 1975; Zajonc & Bargh, 1980; Zajonc, 1983). One set of data (see Figure 6.6) that shows both family size and birth-order effects very clearly comes from a study of nearly 400,000 young men in Holland—the entire male population of the Netherlands who turned 19 between 1963 and 1966. You can see in the figure that IQs declined as the family size went up and that within each family size, later children had lower scores.

Robert Zajonc's explanation of these patterns, referred to as the **confluence model**, makes use of the concept of *family intellectual climate.* This "climate" is defined as the average of the intellectual *level* of the family members with whom the child interacts. Zajonc does not mean the average IQs of the family members. He is referring instead to the intellectual "structure" or level. A first-born has only grown-ups around her in the early years, so she's exposed to fairly advanced kinds of thinking and problem solving. But a second child has not only the adults but also a somewhat older sibling, whose intellectual level is quite low. Thus, for the second- or later-born child, the average intellectual level is lower than for the first-born. If the children are very widely spaced, however, the later-born child may have the advantage. In that situation, the younger child interacts not just with parents but also with relatively mature older siblings.

Zajonc also proposes that earlier-born children have a second advantage: They may serve as tutors to the younger children, which will—in the long run—stimulate their own intellectual development. In the short run, such tutoring means the older child spends a good deal of time with another child whose intellectual level is lower than her own, which may have the effect of temporarily reducing the level of stimulation to the older child and result in a temporary slowing of the older child's rate of intellectual growth.

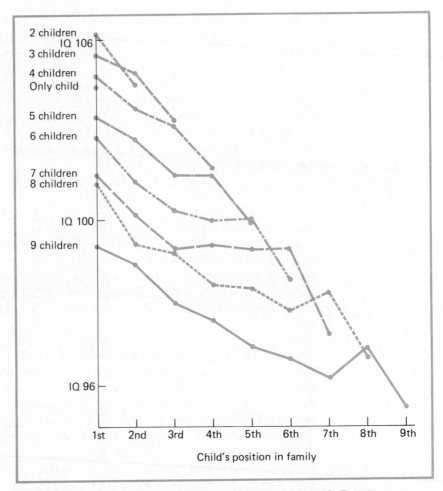

**Figure 6.6** The relationship between birth order, family size, and IQ. Each line represents a family of a particular size, and each dot represents the average IQ of the first, second, third, or *n*th child in a family of that size. Clearly, the larger the family, the lower the scores for all the offspring. And later children in any-sized family have lower scores than those born earlier. (*Source:* Zajonc, 1975, p. 43. Reprinted from *Psychology Today Magazine.* Copyright © 1975, Ziff-Davis Publishing Company.)

Zajonc's model makes good intuitive sense, and he has been able to account for patterns of IQ scores in families that may be difficult to understand otherwise. But I still have questions. For example, Elardo's study shows that toys, materials, and variety in stimulation help to increase IQ. Why would a second or third child have fewer toys or less variety? In other words, I think that more specific elements than the average intellectual level of the family members are involved in this process. Furthermore, patterns of IQ scores in families do not always match Zajonc's predictions (Galbraith, 1982). Still, Zajonc's hypothesis is intriguing and has led to a collection of new research on the effect of siblings on children's intellectual growth.

## School Experience and Special Interventions

Obviously, family experiences affect the child's intellectual development. But children also spend an enormous amount of time in school, in preschool, in day care, or in other group settings. How much effect do these environments have on the child's intellectual growth? Do children who have been to preschool do better on IQ tests?

Most of our answers to the first of these questions come from a series of studies of specially enriched preschools in which children from poverty environments have been enrolled. Since we know that children from such backgrounds are likely to show a "cumulative deficit" in IQ scores (or school achievement) without such intervention, many researchers and policymakers in the early 1960s conceived the idea of special preschools for such children. Several other researchers argued that if preschool was a good thing, then perhaps enriched environments for poor children beginning much earlier—in infancy—would be even better.

*Preschool Interventions*    Early results from Head Start and from more experimental preschool programs were somewhat discouraging. Children who had been enrolled in such programs at age 3 or 4 showed IQ gains of about 10 points during the preschool year, but the effect seemed to fade once they were in regular schools (Klaus & Gray, 1968; Weikart, 1972; Bissell, 1973). More recent news, though, has been more encouraging. There seems to be a "sleeper effect" in the impact of enriched preschool programs: If you keep track of the children into late elementary, junior, or even senior high school, you find that the children who had attended the special preschool are doing better than are those from similar backgrounds who did not have the preschool experience.

This conclusion emerges from a combined analysis by Irving Lazar and Richard Darlington (1982) of the results of 12 different longitudinal studies of children who had been in specially enriched preschool programs. The "experimental group" children (those who had been in the special preschools) compared to the "control group" children (those without the preschool experience) showed higher mathematics achievement test scores and somewhat higher reading achievement. (You can see the achievement test results from one of these 12 projects in Figure 6.7.)

Lazar and Darlington also found that children who had had preschool experience were less likely to be assigned to special remedial classes or to be held back a grade. For example, over the 12 studies,

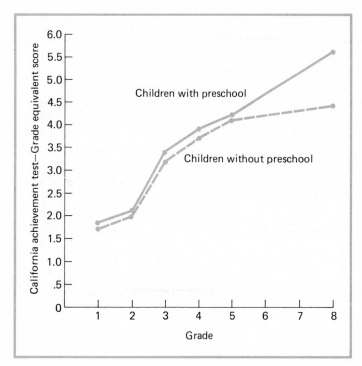

Children with preschool

Children without preschool

California achievement test—Grade equivalent score

Grade

**Figure 6.7** The effect of a preschool enrichment program on children's performance in grade school. Note that the children who had had preschool are very slightly ahead on achievement test scores all along, but the difference increases from sixth grade on. This is the "sleeper effect" of preschool. (*Source:* Bulletin of the High/Scope Foundation, 1977, p. 5. Reprinted with permission of High/Scope Educational Research Foundation, 600 N. River St., Ypsilanti, Mich. 48197.)

only about 13 percent of the experimental group children were placed in special education classes, compared to nearly 30 percent among the control groups. So although the children with preschool experience don't *test* a whole lot higher (and do *not* differ in IQ), they *function* better in school.

*Infancy Interventions*  Even bigger environmental effects have been found when researchers have provided highly enriched environments for children from poverty families beginning in early infancy. The most famous of the infancy interventions is probably Rick Heber's study in Wisconsin (Heber 1978; Garber & Heber, 1982), but there is an equally interesting one recently reported by Craig Ramey and Ron Haskins from North Carolina (Ramey & Haskins, 1981a, 1981b; Ramey, MacPhee, & Yeates, 1982). In both studies, small groups of children from poverty families, with low-IQ mothers, were enrolled in all-day–care programs, five days a week, beginning in early infancy (6 to 12 weeks of age). Heber's program appears to have been more intensive than Ramey and Haskins', with more adults, more emphasis on specific cognitive skills (such as early reading), and more training for the mothers. Heber's program also lasted longer—till school age, rather than to age 36 months as in the Ramey program. But both programs involved very much the kinds of "optimum" stimulation for children that I described in the last section, and both studies included a control group of infants

from highly similar backgrounds who did not receive the special enriched program.

The IQ scores of the children in both programs are shown in Figure
6.8. In both cases, the children who had been in the special program
had significantly higher IQ scores than the control group children, even
several years after the end of the enrichment program. Without intervention, many of the children from the "control" families are testing
at a level that would be considered subnormal or retarded. Interestingly, Heber found that the brothers and sisters of the experimental group
children also had higher IQ scores than the control group children, indicating that the mothers had actually changed in their mode of interacting with all their children.

These results do *not* mean that all mental retardation could be
"cured" by providing children with heavy doses of special education

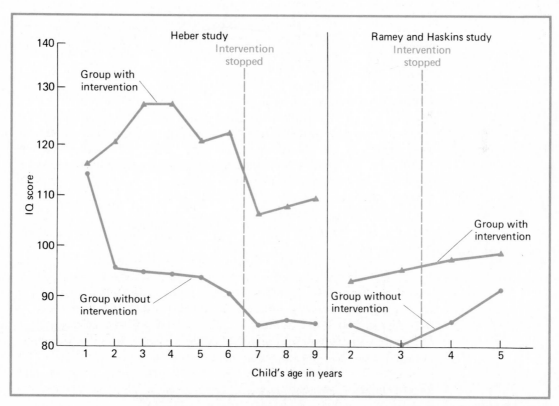

**Figure 6.8** The impact of special intervention programs, begun in infancy, can be seen
in the results of two separate studies. The Heber study involved a more intensive
intervention, including the mothers as well as the children, and appears to have had a
larger effect, but in both programs the children who had the special preschool are still
achieving higher IQ scores several years after the intervention stopped. (*Sources:*
Heber, 1978, p. 59; Ramey & Haskins, 1981a, p. 13, Figure 1, and 1981b, Table 1,
p. 42.)

in infancy. They do show that the intellectual power of those children who have the "environmental deck" stacked against them (poverty environment, less-stimulating parents) can be significantly increased if richer stimulation is provided in day care.

I have given you a fair amount of detail about the results of these studies because, taken together, I think they show that the child's early environment has a potent effect on IQ and school functioning.

### The Testing Situation

The final set of circumstances that can affect a child's test score is the specific conditions under which the test is given.

Two things seem to matter. First, children are likely to achieve higher scores if they are tested by a familiar, friendly examiner. With young children, this may make as much as 10 to 15 points difference in the score (Sacks, 1952). Second, higher scores are also typically found if children are given extra encouragement, extra time to respond, and if the hard items are mixed in with easier ones so that the child has regular successes amid the failures (Zigler & Butterfield, 1968).

Findings like these underline the fact that you must be very cautious about interpreting a score from a single test given to a child on a particular day. Did the child know the examiner? Was the child feeling well that day? Was the examiner warm and encouraging? In other words, is the child's test score representative of how well he can do under fairly optimal conditions, or is it a kind of lower limit of his performance under standard or even discouraging conditions? If the test was given in the first place because a decision is being made about placing the child in a special class, then caution in interpreting a single score is even more critical.

## GROUP DIFFERENCES IN IQ: RACE AND SEX DIFFERENCES

So far I have been talking about possible hereditary and environmental influences on IQ test scores for "children." I have talked a bit about the effects of poverty as a major environmental variable, but I have sidestepped two "hot" issues —namely, racial and sexual differences in IQ or cognitive power. The honest truth is that I would rather sidestep them completely—some things are nearly too hot to handle! But that is not fair to you. You need to see what we know, what we don't know, and how we are trying to explain both kinds of differences.

### Racial Differences in IQ

The basic troublesome fact is that on the average, black children achieve IQ test scores about 10 to 15 points lower than do whites. You can see this difference in Figure 6.9, based on data from the same large national study (Broman, Nichols, & Kennedy, 1975) from which I took the data in Figure 6.4. There are nearly 12,000 white children and over 14,000 black children in this study, from all areas of the country, tested with the Stanford-Binet at age 4 under reasonably standardized conditions. Since proportionately more black families live in poverty than is true for whites, I have given you the results with parents' education and income roughly matched. As you can see, there is a racial difference at each social class level.

Two other interesting facts about this racial difference are important for you to know. This difference is *not* found among infants. Black children show somewhat faster motor development in infancy, but there are no differences in total scores on IQ tests until about age 2 or 3.

A second interesting fact is that school performance is about equally well predicted by IQ scores in each group: Black children who have high IQ scores are more likely to do well in school than are black children with low scores, just as is true among whites.

How can we explain these differences?

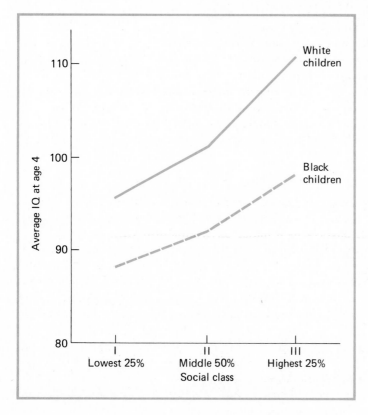

**Figure 6.9** The difference between black and white children in IQ scores appears even when the two groups are roughly matched for family social class. These results are from the same large national study (over 20,000 children) shown in Figure 6.4. (*Source:* Broman, Nichols, & Kennedy, 1975, p. 47.)

*Genetic Differences?*   The most controversial explanation of these findings is that there is a genetic difference between the two racial groups, with black parents simply having fewer "good-IQ genes" of their own, and thus a lower chance of passing on such "good-IQ genes" to their children. After all, I have already concluded that at least some of what we measure with an IQ test is influenced by heredity. Why shouldn't racial differences be partially hereditary, too? Logically it is possible that they may be. Arthur Jensen (1980), among others, is convinced that they are. But other scholars whose opinions and analysis I trust—perhaps most notably Sandra Scarr (1981c)—are equally convinced that such a conclusion is premature or unwarranted: "So far, I see no evidence for the hypothesis that the average difference in intellectual performance between U.S. whites and blacks results primarily from genetic racial differences" (Scarr, 1981c, p. 528). Instead, it seems much more likely that cultural differences in patterns of parent-child interaction and communication are the significant factors.

*Environmental Differences?*   But just what are the differences in environment that might be critical? I cannot answer that precisely because the needed research has not been done, but I can emphasize that major differences exist between American black culture and American white culture. Detailed comparisons of these two cultures from the perspective of the child's intellectual development are only beginning, but

> we know so far that the affective and communicative styles of
> parent-child interactions differ, as do probably the cognitive content,
> permission to explore the environment, interest in material objects as
> opposed to interpersonal contact, and possibly many other factors that
> affect the skills and knowledge that children bring to tests constructed
> by psychologists from the majority culture (Scarr, 1981b, p. 516).

Furthermore, when black children are placed in special enrichment programs, such as the Ramey or Heber programs I described earlier, their test scores rise markedly. For both these reasons, I am persuaded that cultural differences are a much more likely source of the difference in measured IQ than heredity.

*Test Bias?*   Of course, a third potential source of the difference may lie in the very fact that the tests were constructed by whites, and middle-class whites at that. The tests may thus be **biased** in some way that contributes to the observed black/white difference in test scores. Perhaps there are words on the vocabulary test that are not used in the black subculture. Perhaps the "correct" answers to other questions do not match what black children are taught.

I think there is some truth to the "test bias" argument. It is true that there are items on most IQ tests that are not equally accessible to blacks and whites. Williams (1970) gives an example: An item on the Stanford-Binet requires the child to answer the question "What's the thing for you to do if another boy hits you without meaning to do it?". Maximum credit is given if the child responds "Walk away" or some equivalent. But in many black neighborhoods (or poor neighborhoods of any ethnic characteristic), staying and confronting the other boy may be the only reasonable alternative. The child who answers the test question by saying "Hit him back," however, would get no credit on the Binet, even though that is a reasonable response within his own culture.

But I do not think that test bias can account for all the observed racial differences in IQ, for two reasons. First, when systematic efforts are made to eliminate such bias, by testing children in their own language or dialect, using only vocabulary words that all children might have had a chance to hear, and rescoring items like the one I've just described, social class and racial differences are still found (Lesser, Fifer, & Clark, 1965). Second, I must come back to the fact that *within* the black culture, it is still true that IQ scores predict other performances (such as school performance) about as well as they do among whites. So we can't say that the tests are *invalid* for blacks, even though the level of scores may be lower, partly because of the specific items included.

*Adding It Up*   Lacking complete evidence, I cannot totally reject the possibility of a genetic difference. But I would argue that the socially and ethically responsible position is to adopt a working hypothesis that the observed differences are largely environmental in origin or reflect test bias. That is, in the absence of stronger evidence to the contrary, let us presume that all racial groups have equal intellectual potential. That may seem to you to be mixing science with politics, but such a mixture is inevitable. I conclude, in other words, that cultural differences between the races are far more important than any genetic differences between them.

## Sex Differences in IQ

In contrast to comparison of racial groups, comparison of total IQ test scores for boys and girls do *not* reveal any consistent differences. It is only when we break down the total score into several separate skills that some patterns of sex differences emerge. I've summarized the major findings in Table 6.5.

Two crucial points need to be made about the differences described in the table. First, these are *average* differences. On *every* measure, there is a great deal of overlap between the scores of males and females. There are many girls good at spatial visualization and many boys good at verbal reasoning.

TABLE 6.5

**A summary of sex differences in intellectual abilities**

| Type of Ability | Nature of the Difference |
| --- | --- |
| Spatial visualization (ability to manipulate abstract shapes, to visualize three-dimensional spaces from two-dimensional drawings, and so forth) | Boys are quite consistently better at this from adolescence on. *No* consistent difference is found among younger children. |
| Arithmetic computation (basic adding, subtracting, counting) | Young girls (up to about age 8) are slightly better at this. |
| Mathematics (more complex problems; high school math) | Boys have a slight advantage, based on measures of math achievement given in high school or college. For example, on the college board tests, boys score higher than girls on the quantitative test. |
| Numerical reasoning (word problems involving numbers and the like) | Boys again have a slight advantage. |
| Verbal abilities | Girls are a bit more talkative and use a bit longer sentences in very early language and to some extent in later language. |
| Verbal reasoning (e.g., anagrams) | Girls are a bit better, starting at about adolescence. |

Second, as Robert Plomin and Terry Foch (1981) have pointed out, the *absolute size of the differences is very small*. For example, even though it is true that in most studies girls do better, on average, on measures of verbal skill, sex accounts for only about *1 percent* of the variation in scores. So knowing a child's gender tells you next to nothing about her likely performance on a test of verbal skill. The largest differences are found on measures of spatial visualization, where perhaps 5 to 10 percent of the variation among high school or college students' performances can be accounted for by gender (Sanders, Soares, & D'Aquila, 1982).

The large overlap in the distributions and the small absolute size of the differences mean that these differences have little practical importance for such real-life situations as job qualifications. But the consistency of the findings still leaves us with something to explain. Probably there are both environmental and biological forces at work. In particular, the difference in spatial skills seems to have some biological underpinning, perhaps having to do with hormone patterning. For example, both Deborah Waber (1977) and Nora Newcombe and Mary Bandura (1983) have found that girls who go through puberty later are better at spatial tasks than are girls who are early developers, which suggests that hormones may play some role. (Of course, it is also possible that late developers are more likely to take part in activities that require spatial skills, and thus get more practice. I have already pointed out that early- and late-developing teenagers have somewhat different personalities, so this is not totally implausible.)

In contrast, there appear to be no reasonable biological explanations of the small sex differences in mathematical or verbal reasoning. There is, instead, considerable evidence that girls' and boys' attitudes about mathematics are systematically shaped by parents and by schools. Jacquelynne Parsons and her colleagues (Parsons, Adler, & Kaczala, 1982), for example, found that parents of fifth to eleventh graders thought their daughters were less good at math and had to work harder to achieve well in math than did their sons, despite the fact that the students actually did not differ in math achievement. Doris Entwisle and David Baker (1983) found virtually the same pattern among first and second graders. At this age both the boys and their parents thought they would do better at math than did the girls and their parents.

The effect of these differences in expectation shows up in high school, when both boys and girls who have positive attitudes toward mathematics do better on math tests (Paulsen & Johnson, 1983). In part, then, the small sex differences in test scores are being perpetuated by subtle family and school influences on children's attitudes. It will be interesting to see if the sex differences in test scores disappear over the next decades as some of these subtle messages are altered.

## OVERVIEW OF IQ TESTING

One of the questions that students often ask at about this point is whether, given all the factors that can affect a test score, it is worth bothering with IQ tests at all. I think that these tests do assess some important aspects of children's intellectual performance and that they can be helpful in identifying children who may have difficulties in school. (Certainly, the IQ test is a *better* method of selecting such children than are the strategies that would replace the tests—most particularly teacher evaluations, which are more "biased" than the tests are.) But it is important to keep in mind that these tests do *not* measure a lot of other things we may be interested in, such as the structure of the child's thinking, her motivation to achieve, her creativity, or her persistence. They also tell us next to nothing about critical social skills that make up an important part of the child's overall competence (to use Burton White's term, 1975), such as skill at getting and holding the attention of adults, or using adults or other children as resources for problem solving, or expressing emotions clearly, or being a leader in a group. An IQ test is a specialized tool, and like many such tools, it has a fairly narrow range of appropriate use. I don't want to throw out this tool, but you have to keep its limitations very firmly in mind when you do use it.

## SUMMARY

1. When we study the development of "intelligence," we need to distinguish between measures of intellectual "power" and measures of intellectual "structure." IQ tests are intended to measure "how much" intelligence a child or adult has. They tap individual differences in intellectual power.

2. The most commonly used individually administered tests are the Stanford-Binet and the Wechsler Intelligence Scales for Children (WISC). The most common "infant IQ test" is the Bayley.

3. Both IQ tests and school achievement tests measure a child's performance, not capacity or underlying competence. Achievement tests, however, test much more specific school-related information than do IQ tests.

4. Psychologists are still arguing about whether or how much IQ test scores are influenced by heredity. Most psychologists would agree that something like 50 percent of the variation in scores among people is due to heredity.

5. Environmental influence, however, is also substantial: Poor children consistently test lower than do children from middle-class families; first-born and early-born children, on average, have higher scores; and children whose families provide appropriate play materials and encourage the child's intellectual development have children who score higher on IQ tests.

6. Environmental influence is also shown by increases in test performance among children who have been in special enriched preschool or infant day-care programs.

7. A consistent difference of about 10 to 15 points on IQ tests is found between white and black children. It seems most likely that this difference is due partially to "test bias" and partially to differences in the family environments of the two racial groups.

8. Males and females do not differ on total IQ test scores but do differ in subskills. Males are better at spatial visualization and mathematical reasoning; females are better at verbal reasoning and some other verbal tasks.

## KEY TERMS

**Achievement test**   A test usually given in schools, designed to assess a child's learning of specific material taught in school, such as spelling or arithmetic computation.

**Bias**   Aspects of a psychological test, such as dependence on language or cultural experience, that may influence the scores of some subjects more than others.

**Competence**   The behavior of a person as it would be under ideal or perfect circumstances. It is not possible to measure competence directly.

**Confluence model**  Zajonc's term for his explanation of family size and ordinal position effects on IQ. Assumes that a child's IQ is partially determined by the average intellectual level of the family members with whom the child has contact.

**Culture-fair test**  A test whose items are chosen so as to minimize test bias. That is, a test on which children from different cultural backgrounds would be expected to score equally well.

**Cumulative deficit**  Any difference between groups in IQ (or achievement test) scores that becomes larger over time.

**Draw-a-Person test**  Nonverbal (and ostensibly culture-fair) test of intelligence that requires the child to draw a picture of a human figure.

**Information processing**  Phrase used to refer to a new, "third" approach to the study of intellectual development that focuses on changes with age in fundamental intellectual skills as well as individual differences in those skills.

**Intellectual Power**  That aspect of intellectual skill that has to do with how well or how quickly a child can perform cognitive tasks.

A dimension of individual difference in intellectual skill.

**IQ**  Intelligence quotient. Originally defined in terms of a child's mental age and chronological age, IQs are now computed by comparing a child's performance with that of other children of the same chronological age.

**Mental age**  A way to describe the level of mental tasks a child can perform. A child who can perform tasks normally done by 8-year-olds but not tasks done by 9-year-olds would have a mental age of 8.

**Performance**  The behavior shown by a person under actual circumstances. Even when we are interested in competence, all we can ever measure is performance.

**Stanford-Binet**  The best-known American intelligence test. It was written by Louis Terman and his associates, based upon the first tests by Binet and Simon.

**Structure**  That aspect of intellectual skills that changes with age and is shared by all children. Focus is on *how* the child arrives at a particular answer rather than on the correctness of the answer.

**WISC**  The Wechsler Intelligence Scale for Children. Another well-known American IQ test that includes both verbal and performance (nonverbal) subtests.

## SUGGESTED READINGS

Bane, M. J., & Jencks, C. Five myths about your IQ. *Harper's* 246 (February 1973): 28–40.
This is an excellent discussion of some of the same issues I have raised in this chapter. Not new, but representing a particular, mostly environmental, point of view.

Detterman, D. K., & Sternberg, R. J. *How and how much can intelligence be increased?* Norwood, N.J.: Ablex, 1982.
This is not an easy book, but it is well worth the effort. It includes the most current reports of both the Heber study and the Ramey and Haskins study, as well as thoughtful papers by a number of other experts.

Farran, D. C.; Haskins, R.; & Gallagher, J. J. Poverty and mental retardation: A search for explanations. In J. J. Gallagher (Ed.), *Ecology of exceptional children.* New Direc-

tions for Exceptional Children, No. 1. San Francisco: Jossey-Bass, 1980.
The best current review I know about the link between poverty and IQ. Somewhat, but not overpoweringly, technical.

Jensen, A. R. *Bias in mental testing.* New York: Free Press, 1980.
Jensen has been the most consistent spokesman for a "hereditary" position on IQ differences. This is a massive and fairly difficult book, but it is the very best source for understanding this viewpoint.

Zajonc, R. B. Birth order and intelligence: Dumber by the dozen. *Psychology today* 8 (1975): 37–43.
A highly readable account of Zajonc's argument concerning birth order and IQ.

# 7.
# *cognitive development ɪɪ: cognitive structure*

Imagine the following scene: Your 5-year-old, John, and your 8-year-old, Anne, come into the kitchen after playing outside, both requesting a drink. With both children watching, you take two identical small cans of juice from the refrigerator and pour each into a glass. As it happens, the glasses are not identical; one is narrower than the other, so the juice rises higher in that glass. The 5-year-old, having been given the fatter glass, complains, "Anne got more than I did!" To which Anne replies (with the wonderful grace of the 8-year-old to her sibling), "I did not, you dummy. We both got the same amount. The two cans were just alike." To restore family harmony, you get out another glass identical to Anne's and pour John's juice into this new glass. The level of the liquid is now the same, and John is satisfied.

If this were an item on an IQ test, we'd say that Anne was "right" and John was "wrong." But such an emphasis on "rightness" or "wrongness" misses an essential point about this interchange: There is a *developmental* change, a shift in the way the child sees or understands the world and the relationships of objects. John is not being pigheaded or "dumb." He is merely operating with a different kind of reasoning from Anne's. A year or two from now, John will sound like Anne does now.

If we are to understand children's thinking, we need to understand these changes in the *form* or *structure* of that thinking as well as differences in power. How do children come to understand the world around them? What assumptions do they make? What kind of logic do they use, and how does it change over time?

These were precisely the kinds of questions that Jean Piaget asked in his many years of research on children's thinking. As a result, the whole "structural" approach to studying cognitive development bears Piaget's strong theoretical stamp. In fact, 12 years ago, when I first wrote this chapter, it was fair to say that Piaget's theory was the dominant theoretical influence on our thinking about cognitive development.

Piaget's ideas are still enormously important, but now it would be more accurate to say that he is no longer the intellectual "father" of current researchers but their "grandfather" or "great-grandfather." The lineage is still there, the family resemblance is still visible (like a distinctive nose or premature baldness that is passed on from one generation to the next), but a whole lot of other influences have entered the picture. To do justice to both the ancestry of the ideas (Piaget) and the current variations, I will use Piaget's ideas as a basic framework, but I will also describe the current work and the changes in the theory that have emerged in recent years.

## PIAGET'S BASIC IDEAS

Piaget's early training was in biology, but in his student days he worked briefly for Alfred Binet on the development of some of the early

IQ tests. His job was to give the same items to a whole series of children and to determine whether or not each child had given the "correct" answer on each item. But Piaget soon discovered that the "wrong" answers were often more interesting than the "correct" ones (teachers take note). In particular, he noticed that children of the same age often gave the *same* wrong answers.

Piaget drew a number of important conclusions from these early observations. First, he argued that to understand the child's thinking, we have to shift our attention from *how much* the child could do and look instead at the *quality* of his problem solving. We should look not at what answer he gave but at how he arrived at that answer.

Second, he suggested that when we begin to look at the quality of thinking, we will find that children of different ages have uniquely different ways of going about solving problems. It was not just that younger children learned things more slowly; they approached problems differently. To understand "intelligence" in children, Piaget argued, we would need to understand these changes in strategies, not just individual differences in speed or "power."

What has evolved from all of Piaget's work (and that of others, too) has been a set of basic assumptions about the development of thinking in the child. Let me try to put those assumptions in simplified form.

## The Central Assumptions

*Inborn Strategies*   Every child is born with certain strategies for interacting with the environment. The normal newborn can see, hear, touch, suck, and grasp. More important, from the beginning, the child's use of these skills appears to follow basic rules, like the "look at edges" rule that seems to dominate children's visual searching in the early days of life (see Chapter 5).

*Changes in Strategies*   These primitive strategies are the beginning points for the development of thinking. But the strategies change gradually as a result of the child's encounters with the world around her. The baby learns to grasp in several different ways, after she has had a chance to handle square, round, oval, and different-shaped things; her sucking becomes more skillful and more specific to the thing sucked on. From such humble beginnings, understanding gradually develops.

*Voluntary Exploration*   In the beginning, the child's reactions to the world around him are more or less reflexive. But over the early months and years, he begins to explore and examine with purpose and direction, trying out new combinations, new experiments. In this way, each child "rediscovers the wheel." Each child discovers that objects are

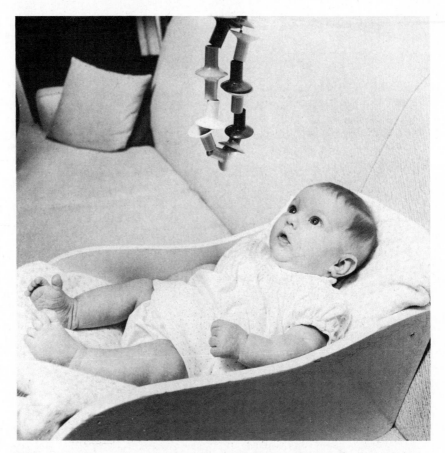

**Figure 7.1** Babies appear to be born with a collection of basic strategies for exploring the world around them, such as the "search for objects and scan the edges" strategy we see in very young infants like this one. These strategies—or *schemes*, to use Piaget's word—keep the baby focused on the objects in the world around him.

constant, that they can be grouped and classified, that things can be added to and subtracted from, and so on and on.

*Sequences and Stages*   Piaget observed that these discoveries appeared to occur in particular sequences. For example, the child can't discover the principles of adding and subtracting until she has figured out that objects are constant. Progress through the sequence of discoveries occurs slowly; and at any one age, the child has a particular general view of the world, a particular logic or "structure" that dominates the way she explores and manipulates her world. The basic logic changes as she encounters objects or events that don't fit into the system she has constructed, but the change is slow and gradual. Nonetheless, we can divide the sweep of changes into broad periods, or *stages* (listed in Table 7.1), which describe major shifts in the structure of the child's thinking.

## Piaget's Terminology

I introduced several of Piaget's terms and concepts in Chapter 1, so I have merely summarized the terminology here in a table (Table 7.2). (You may want to go back and review the section on *adaptation* in Chapter 1.) The key is to realize that Piaget assumes it is the nature of the human organism to organize experience and adapt himself to what he has experienced. *Assimilation* and *accommodation* are aspects of the adaptational process. *Equilibration* is part of the process of **organization**—a process of maintaining balance, particularly a balance between what has been experienced (assimilation) and the "understanding" of that experience (accommodation). It is this fundamental push toward equilibrium that Piaget sees as essential in moving the child from the somewhat workable, but primitive, views of the world we see in younger children to the more complex, abstract concepts we see in elementary and high-school–age youngsters.

With that background in mind, let's take a look at what Piaget and more recent researchers have to say about each of the major stages of development.

TABLE 7.1

**Piaget's stages of cognitive development**

| Stage | Age | Description |
|---|---|---|
| Sensorimotor | Birth–2 years | The baby "understands" the world in terms of what she can do with objects and of her sensory information. A block is how it tastes, feels to grasp, looks to the eye. |
| Preoperational | 2–6 years | By about 18–24 months, the child can represent objects to himself internally and begins to understand classification of objects into groups and to be able to take others' perspectives. Fantasy play appears, as does primitive logic. |
| Concrete operational | 6–12 years | The child's logic takes a great leap forward with the development of powerful new internal mental operations, such as addition, subtraction, class inclusion, and the like. The child is still tied to specific experience but can do mental manipulations as well as physical ones. |
| Formal operational | 12 years + | The child becomes able to manipulate ideas as well as events or objects in her head. She can imagine and think about things that she has never seen or that haven't yet happened; she can organize systematically and exhaustively and think deductively. |

TABLE 7.2
**Piaget's major concepts**

| Concept | Description | Examples |
|---|---|---|
| Adaptation | The basic process of all human activity, including assimilation and accommodation. | Chameleons "adapt" to their environment when they change color to fade into the environment; we adapt when we adjust the size of the lens of the eye when the light changes, or when we eat, or when we change the way we talk to adjust to the person we are talking to. |
| Assimilation | "Taking in" and adapting experience or objects to one's existing strategies or concepts; "construing reality." | A baby assimilates when she reaches for a toy. In Piaget's language, she "assimilates the toy to her reaching scheme." You assimilate when you classify a new object as a vase or a new person as a Democrat. |
| Accommodation | Modifying and adjusting one's strategies or concepts as a result of assimilation of new experiences or information. | When the baby changes the way he holds his hand as he reaches for round things as opposed to square things, he has accommodated. When you change your concept of what a Democrat is after talking with several self-proclaimed Democrats, you have accommodated. |
| Equilibration | The process of balancing assimilation and accommodation; refers particularly to major changes in internal organization after a buildup of experience that does not "fit" well in the old system. | A child shows equilibration when she gives up one strategy that may work fairly well for one that works better, such as moving from trial and error to systematic search. A researcher shows equilibration when he gives up an old theory because the evidence refutes it and builds a new theory that handles the evidence better. |
| Scheme | The "action" or "strategy" or "skill," either internal or external, to which the child or adult assimilates. The word *operation* Piaget uses to refer to complex internal schemes. These schemes are what is changed as a result of accommodation. | In the infant, sucking, grasping, reaching, and other overt actions are all schemes. In older children and adults, classifying, adding, subtracting, categorizing, searching systematically, rehearsing to help memory are also all schemes. |

## THE SENSORIMOTOR STAGE: FROM BIRTH TO AGE 2

### Piaget's View of the Sensorimotor Stage

Piaget's own observations of babies in the first two years of life led him to conclude that they operate almost entirely with overt, visible schemes: with sensory actions such as looking and touching and motor actions such as grasping and sucking—hence, the name **sensorimotor stage**.

*The Substages*   Piaget divided the sensorimotor period into six substages, which I've summarized in Table 7.3. Progress through these substages is continuous and gradual; there are no *abrupt* shifts. But it may still be fruitful to look at some of the underlying changes that seem to mark the transitions from one substage to the next.

The shift from substage 1 to substage 2 (from reflexes to "primary circular reactions," in Piaget's language) corresponds roughly to the shift I described in Chapter 5 from the early, apparently automatic scanning of edges and movement to the more careful examination of objects. A second important transition occurs between substages 2 and 3, at about 4 months of age, when the baby begins to make a distinction between his own body and other objects. The most visible sign of this is the baby's attempt to repeat actions that have resulted in interesting things happening with toys or other objects.

Piaget's own observations of his son Laurent illustrate this shift (Piaget, 1952). When Laurent was about $2\frac{1}{2}$ months old, he accidentally hit the mobile hanging above his crib; it moved, and Laurent became excited, thrashed around, and gurgled happily. But he didn't

TABLE 7.3

**Substages of the sensorimotor period proposed by Piaget**

| Substage | Age | Piaget's Label | Characteristics of the Stage |
|---|---|---|---|
| 1 | 0–1 month | Reflexes | Almost entirely practice of built-in reflexes, such as sucking and looking. These reflexes are modified (through accommodation) as a result of experience. |
| 2 | 1–4 months | Primary circular reactions | The infant tries to make interesting things happen again with her body, such as getting her thumb in her mouth. Visual and tactual explorations are more systematic. But infants in this stage still do not appear to distinguish between body and outside objects or events. They do not link their own actions to results outside themselves. |
| 3 | 4–10 months | Secondary circular reactions | The infant tries to make external interesting things happen again, such as moving a mobile by hitting it. He also begins to coordinate information from two senses and develops the object concept. He understands, at some level, that his own actions can have external results. |
| 4 | 10–12 months | Coordination of secondary schemes | The infant begins to combine actions to get things she wants, such as knocking a pillow away in order to reach for a toy. She uses familiar strategies in combination and in new situations. |
| 5 | 12–18 months | Tertiary circular reactions | "Experimentation" begins; the infant tries out *new* ways of playing with or manipulating objects. Improved motor skills make wider exploration possible, too. |
| 6 | 18–24 months | Beginning of thought | Internal representation is now readily apparent; the child uses images, perhaps words or actions, to stand for objects. |

**Figure 7.2** The opportunity to manipulate objects—put them in the mouth, roll them around, or turn them upside down—is crucial for the development of the child in the sensorimotor period. You can see just that sort of exploration in the play of these babies.

seem to try to make it happen again. Several days later, Piaget attached a string to Laurent's hand and to the mobile so that when Laurent waved his arms, the mobile moved. Laurent was delighted but still did not figure out that his arm movements controlled the movement of the mobile. But at about $3\frac{1}{2}$ months, Piaget observed that Laurent would move only the arm to which the string was attached. If Piaget switched the string to the other arm, Laurent shifted his movement to the new arm-with-string. Over the course of a month, then, Laurent had begun to respond to objects as distinct from himself and as things that could be affected by him.

*Internal Representation*   The transition from substage 5 to substage 6, when Piaget first observed internal representation, is also particularly fascinating.

In your thinking, you have a word for an object and a mental picture of it. You can use that word and image in various ways. You can remember the object, compare it mentally with something else, or figure out how to fix it—all in your head. Piaget thought that this ability to form and manipulate mental images was not present in the infant until the sixth sensorimotor stage, sometime in the second year of life. One of Piaget's observations, this time of his daughter Lucienne, illustrates this transition. At the time of this observation, Piaget was playing with Lucienne (who was 16 months old) and had hidden his watch chain inside an empty box. He describes what happened then:

> I put the chain back into the box and reduce the opening to 3mm. It is understood that Lucienne is not aware of the functioning of the opening

and closing of match box and has not seen me prepare the experiment. She only possesses two preceding schemes [strategies]: turning the box over in order to empty it of its contents, and sliding her fingers into the slit to make the chain come out. It is of course this last procedure that she tries first: she puts her finger inside and gropes to reach the chain, but fails completely. A pause follows during which Lucienne manifests a very curious reaction. . . . She looks at the slit with great attention; then, several times in succession, she opens and shuts her mouth, at first slightly, then wider and wider! [Then] . . . Lucienne unhesitatingly puts her finger in the slit, and instead of trying as before to reach the chain, she pulls so as to enlarge the opening. She succeeds and grasps the chain (Piaget, 1952, pp. 337–338).

What an enormous discovery this child has made! Faced with a new situation, instead of going immediately to trial and error, she paused and appeared to discover the solution through some kind of analysis. Piaget saw this behavior as a sign of the very beginning of the child's ability to manipulate and combine, to experiment and explore, with images instead of real objects.

## Current Work on the Sensorimotor Stage

Many of Piaget's observations about the young infant were made before the development of newer, sophisticated research techniques for studying babies. As a result, he appears to have underestimated the infant in a number of important respects.

*Imitation* If infants do not distinguish between own-body and other-things until substage 3, then they oughtn't to be able to imitate other people's actions, such as tongue protrusion or mouth opening. Such imitation seems to imply a distinction between "you" and "me." But in fact, as I pointed out in Chapter 5, babies *do* show such imitation, as early as 2 or 3 days of age (Meltzoff & Moore, 1983). Such extremely early imitation may simply reflect "innate releasing mechanisms"—an automatic response to certain visual stimuli, much as mating rituals in birds involve strings of automatic (wired-in) responses. But it is also possible that the newborn has a greater capacity to integrate information from different senses (seeing the adult's face and feeling the movement of his own face) than we had supposed.

Babies also show *deferred imitation* a great deal earlier than Piaget thought they did. Deferred imitation involves a delay between the observation of the model and the child's copying of that model. To delay imitation, the baby would have to have some method of storing the image in memory—that is, some form of representation. Piaget did not think this was possible until the sixth substage, at about 18 months. But research by Kenneth Kaye (Kaye & Marcus, 1981; Kaye, 1982) shows that babies display deferred imitation perhaps a year earlier than Piaget thought. The researchers demonstrated such specific behaviors as touching the ear with the hand or clapping four times and found that 9- to 11-month-old infants who did not imitate the clapping when it was being shown would sometimes clap later in the session when the experimenter was showing ear touching. The clapping behavior seems to have been "stored" in memory in some fashion.

*Internal Representation*    Other recent evidence also shows that infants as young as 8 to 10 months seem to remember what they see and to organize their memory according to certain features, such as shape (Caron & Caron, 1982). For example, Leslie Cohen (1979) found that 5-month-olds who had repeatedly seen a three-dimensional Styrofoam figure responded differently to that particular shape 24 hours later than to an unfamiliar shape. That is, they seemed to "remember" that shape and found it less interesting than a new and differently shaped figure. But they did not "remember" the color of the original figure in the same way.

Even more amazing, there are now a number of indications that what young infants remember is not a specific object—not a particular rattle or a particular blanket, for example—but a *prototype,* some general scheme that represents a typical rattle or a typical blanket (Strauss, 1979; Caron & Caron, 1982).

## Overview of the Sensorimotor Period

In a number of important respects, Piaget seems to have underestimated the ability of infants to store, remember, and organize sensory and motor information. But these findings do not necessarily mean that Piaget was wrong in his overall ideas about the sensorimotor period. In general, the sequences that Piaget described seem to hold up quite well on close scrutiny. Piaget also seems to have been correct in his observation that babies do little planning or intentional direction of action in the early months of life. His image of the infant as a little scientist is very much in keeping with the recent evidence. The infant assimilates information to his existing schemes (actions, skills, "prototypes") and modifies (accommodates) the schemes as he goes along. By the time the infant has reached the age of 18 or 24 months, his perceptions and actions are already quite well organized.

## PREOPERATIONAL THOUGHT: FROM AGE 2 TO AGE 6

In many ways, Piaget's approach to this second major stage, the **preoperational stage**, was oddly negative. He focused on what children this age *cannot* do or on deficiencies in their thinking and reasoning. (Even Piaget's label for this period is faintly negative: it is called *pre*operational because the child does not yet use the powerful mental strategies

Piaget calls **operations**, which appear in children's thinking at about age 5 or 6.) More recent work has changed this emphasis, and we are now aware of the many skills toddlers and preschoolers bring to cognitive tasks. I can contrast the two views most clearly by describing several key dimensions of the toddler's thinking, first through Piaget's eyes and then through the eyes of recent researchers.

## Piaget's View of the Preoperational Period

*Perspective Taking: Egocentrism*   Even though the preschool child has understood his separateness from others, Piaget saw him as still very much centered in his own perspective. Very young children do not even realize that there *are* other ways of looking at things. Piaget used the word **egocentrism** to describe this quality of "self-centeredness" on the part of the child.

Piaget saw this quality in the children's language as well as in their thinking. In their conversations, 2- and 3-year-old children do not seem to take into account the needs of the listener. They talk as if the listener could see the things they see and know the things they know. (They talk *at* people rather than *with* them.) In the child's thinking, you see egocentrism in his difficulty understanding that you do not look at the physical space from the same perspective. If the child is standing in front of a chair and you are standing behind it, the child may not realize that you don't see the same parts of the chair that he sees.

In Piaget's view, one of the key tasks of the preoperational period is for the child to become "decentered"—to shift from the self as the only frame of reference. As Herbert Ginsburg and Sylvia Opper (1969, p. 111) put it:

> The [preoperational] child decenters his thought just as in the sensorimotor period the infant decentered his behavior. The newborn *acts* as if the world is centered about himself and must learn to behave in more adaptive ways. Similarly, the young child *thinks* from a limited perspective and must widen it.

*Understanding Identities*   In a similar way, Piaget sees a new "layer" of understanding of the identity of objects that must be addressed by the preschool child. The sensorimotor infant eventually understood that objects continue to exist even when they are out of sight and learned (or came equipped with) color and size and shape constancies as well. But there are other aspects of objects that also remain constant—that are *conserved*, in Piaget's language—and these new constancies baffle the preschool child. For example, the number of buttons you have is not changed if you move them around in different arrangements; an amount of lemonade is not changed if you pour it into a different container; the weight of a lump of clay is not changed if you make it into a hot dog shape.

Piaget's observations and experiments convinced him that most children do not understand these new constancies, these **conservations,** until about age 5 or 6. One of the classic experimental situations Piaget devised to test this is shown in Figure 7.3. The child is shown two equal balls of clay. Then, in her full view, one of the balls is squished into a pancake, and the child is asked if the two have the same amount of clay. A preschool child will nearly always tell you that the ball and the pancake have different amounts—even if she agreed originally that the two balls were the same. But by age 6 or 7, children will nearly always tell you that the pancake and the ball are still the same, saying things like:

"If you put it back into a ball it would be the same."

"It's bigger around, but it's thinner, so it's the same."

"You haven't added any or taken any away, so it must be the same."

It was a problem of conservation that confronted Anne and John

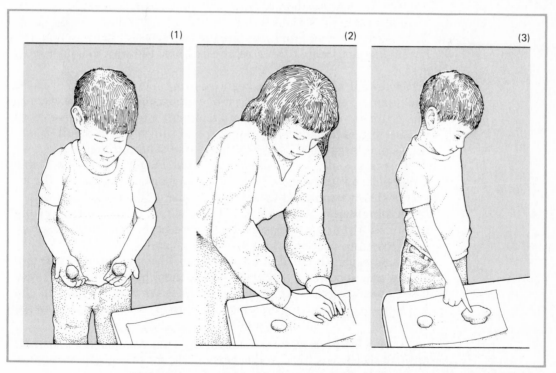

**Figure 7.3** In the classic conservation experiment using balls of clay, the child first holds both and agrees they are the same. The experimenter then squishes one of the balls into another shape (picture 2) and asks the child whether they are the same or different (picture 3).

and their juice glasses. John—aged 5—had not yet achieved a full understanding of conservation of quantity, while Anne had. Instead, John's attention was focused on the height of the liquid in the glass, which is a classic "error" for the preschooler. In order to achieve conservation (at least according to Piaget), the child must learn how to coordinate several bits of information instead of focusing on just one.

*Classification*   A third area Piaget describes is the child's ability to classify objects—to put things in sets or types and to use abstract or formal properties such as color or shape or even verbal labels as a basis for such classification.

Piaget studied this by giving young children sets of objects or picture cutouts of people, animals, or toys and asking them to put together the things that "go together" or "are similar" (Piaget & Inhelder, 1969). Two- and 3-year-old children, faced with such an array, will usually make designs or pictures. And if a child this age starts out sorting things into groups, he seems to shift his basis for grouping partway through or makes the whole thing into a picture. One 3-year-old Piaget observed put some circles into a pile, then some squares next to the circles, and continued with other groups of objects. "Aha!" you say. "Classification." But then the child looked at it and said "A train!" To be sure, the child *had* put the circles together, and the squares, but he had not treated these as abstractions, the way the older child does.

Somewhat older children begin showing more systematic sorting and grouping of objects, using first one dimension (e.g., shape, such as round things versus square things) and later two or more dimensions at once (e.g., size *and* shape: small round things versus small square things and large round things versus large square things).

This is a really big advance over what Piaget saw in the 2- and 3-year-olds, but there is still some distance to go. In particular, the aspect of classification that the preoperational child has not yet grasped is **class inclusion**: He does not understand that some classes are fully contained within other classes. Collies are part of the larger class of dogs; roses are part of the class of flowers; and so forth.

Piaget usually studied this by having children first create their own classes and subclasses and then asking them questions about them. One 5½-year-old child, for example, had a set of flowers made up of a large group of primroses and a smaller group of other mixed flowers.

Piaget: "If I make a bouquet of all the primroses and you make one of all the flowers, which will be bigger?"
Child: "Yours."
Piaget: "If I gather all the primroses in a meadow will any flowers remain?"
Child: "Yes" (Piaget & Inhelder, 1969, p. 108).

The child understood that there are other flowers than primroses but did *not* yet understand that all primroses are flowers—that the smaller, subordinate class is *included in* the larger class. This understanding does not come (at least in Piaget's view) until about age 7.

*Reasoning*   Piaget's daughter Lucienne announced one afternoon when she had not taken her nap, "I haven't had my nap so it isn't afternoon." This is a very good example of the kind of reasoning you'll hear in the preschool-age child. Lucienne knew that afternoon and nap usually go together, but she had the relationship between them wrong. She thought that the nap "caused" the afternoon. Another example, from a 3-year-old Russian boy: "Daddy, please cut down this pine tree—it makes the wind. After you cut it down the weather will be nice and mother will let me go for a walk" (Chukovsky, 1963, p. 22).

Piaget calls this **transductive reasoning**. Others, such as Carl Bereiter (Bereiter, Hidi, & Dimitroff, 1979), call it *intuitive* reasoning, which is an easier term to remember. Whatever the label, the basic characteristic of this type of reasoning is that the child sees that two things happen at the same time and assumes that one is the cause of the other. (A lot of superstitious behavior in adults is based on the same "logic." If the baseball manager wore green socks the day his team won a key game, he may wear the same green socks every day his team plays after that "for luck." He's showing a kind of transductive reasoning. Researchers sometimes do it, too, when we move from correlational results to statements about causality.)

Preoperational children's thinking is also rigid. They see things in black and white, good and bad terms. Rules of games are absolute and cannot possibly be changed; the more toys you break, the "worse" the action, regardless of whether you did it on purpose or not. More important, they do not yet have the ability to *examine* their own thoughts, conclusions, or strategies.

Obviously, Piaget sees the child from 2 to 6 making significant strides in a number of important areas—in logic, in understanding some of the abstract properties of objects, such as the classes they belong to. But in Piaget's view, children of this age still lack many of the really powerful cognitive understandings and strategies, including conservation, class inclusion, and the other skills he calls *operations*.

## Current Work on the Preoperational Period

As was true for the sensorimotor period, the current work on the preoperational period shows us that children in the 2 to 6 age range are probably a good deal more skillful than Piaget supposed.

*Perspective Taking*   I'll be talking more about current research on perspective taking in Chapter 12, but let me just say here that there is now a great deal of evidence that children as young as 2 and 3 have at least *some* ability to understand that other people see things or experience things differently.

John Flavell has devised a number of clever ways to show this (Flavell et al., 1981). Suppose you make up a card with a picture of a dog on one side and a picture of a cat on the other. You show the child both sides and then hold it vertically between you and the child, so that he can see either the cat or the dog and you see the other animal. You ask the child which animal you are looking at. Three-year-old children have no trouble understanding that you see something different from what they see. Children of this same age also talk in simpler sentences when they talk to a 2-year-old than when they talk to an adult (Shatz & Gelman, 1973), which again shows that they have some awareness of the different needs of the listeners.

But if you are *both* looking at the *same* thing from a different angle, those same 3-year-olds have a much harder time understanding that you have a different viewpoint. For example, Flavell put a picture of a turtle down on the table between the child and himself, with the head toward the child and the tail toward the experimenter. The child had to say whether the experimenter saw the turtle "right side up" or "upside down." Most 3- to 4-year-olds could *not* answer this correctly.

The preoperational child thus seems to be less egocentric than Piaget thought but still considerably more tied to her own perspective than will be true a few years later.

*Understanding Identities*    Here, too, researchers have found hints of conservation earlier than Piaget suggested. For example, Rochel Gelman (1972), in a widely quoted study, showed that children as young as 3 could display a form of number conservation. She showed 3-year-olds two plates, one with a row of three toys (two mice and a truck) and one with a row of two toys. On each trial, the plates were shuffled, and the child had to pick one plate as "the winner." The child had to learn that the plate with three toys was always "the winner."

After the child had learned this, the experimenter rearranged the three toys so that they were pushed together and presented the two plates again. What Gelman found was that the 3-year-olds still picked the three-toy plate as "the winner," showing that they realized the arrangement of the toys on the plate did not change the number. But children of the same age cannot do Piaget's typical conservation of number experiment, which involves larger numbers of M&Ms or poker chips in rows. Why the difference?

Part of the difference seems to lie in how many objects there are (Wellman, 1982). Three-year-olds can count to 3, and they already understand that if two sets of things can be counted and you arrive at the same number, they are the same. But they aren't good at counting to higher numbers and have not yet grasped the basic *principle* that shifting things around doesn't *ever* change the number. Thus, their judgment of equality or inequality is still based on counting rather than on the principle of conservation. What Gelman has shown, then, are some of the first steps that build toward a more general concept of conservation.

An equally clever study by Rheta DeVries (1969) also shows important beginning understanding of identities in 4- and 5-year-olds. De Vries had children aged 3 to 6 play with a live cat—an apparently very friendly and docile beast named Maynard. After each child had petted the cat and was comfortable with him, DeVries took the cat to a table, hiding the front end of him behind a box. The child was told to watch the "tail end" and that the cat would look different later. Behind the box, DeVries put a very lifelike dog mask on Maynard's head and then brought out the transformed creature to face the child (see Figure 7.4). What DeVries wanted to know was whether the child understood that Maynard hadn't fundamentally changed. So she asked the child whether Maynard could now bark, whether he would eat dog food or cat food, whether the new animal would play like a cat or a dog, and so on.

The 3-year-olds in this study understood very little about the constancy of Maynard. They thought that with a dog mask on, Maynard had essentially become a dog. But by age 5, the children were doing very well. They knew that the mask was something external that didn't change the *basic* characteristics of the cat, just as putting on different clothes does not make you a different person. This turns out to be an

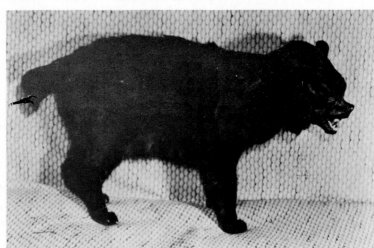

**Figure 7.4** Maynard the amazing cat, with and without the dog mask. Young children thought that with the mask on, Maynard had essentially become a dog and could bark and do other dog things. But 4- and 5-year-olds understood that Maynard was still a cat. (*Source:* R. DeVries, 1969, pp. 8, 9. © by the Society for Research in Child Development, Inc. All rights reserved)

important basis for the child's understanding of gender, as we'll see in Chapter 10. The child of 5 or 6 understands that she won't change into a boy just by putting on boys' clothes or doing "boy things."

*Classification Skills*  This ought to sound like a familiar refrain by now: Young children classify better than Piaget thought, at least if you simplify the task so that they are not distracted by irrelevancies. Ellen Markman (Markman, Cox, & Machida, 1981), for example, found that 3- and 4-year-old children could form quite consistent groupings of toys such as furniture or vehicles if they placed each toy in a bag rather than laying them out on a table in full view. When they can see the toys as they are sorting them, children get distracted from the sorting task and make pictures or tell stories with the toys. In other words, the basic understanding that things-go-together-in-groups is present at this age, but whether the child can show this understanding will depend on the way you set up the task. Piaget happened to pick a relatively "hard" version of the task, so he ended up underestimating the child's understanding.

Still, Piaget does not seem to have been wrong about class inclusion. Recent research by Ann McCabe and her colleagues (1982) shows that real understanding of class inclusion does not appear until age 7 or 8, just as Piaget originally suggested.

*Reasoning*  The old refrain: 2- to 6-year-olds are not consistently as primitive in their logic as Piaget thought. For example, Merry Bullock and Rochel Gelman (1979) have shown that children as young as 3 understand that a cause has to come *before* an effect rather than after it—a remarkably sophisticated level of logical understanding at so early an age. Still, Piaget was quite correct in saying that 4-year-olds are less skillful in their logic than 7-year-olds.

## Overview of the Preoperational Child

If we add up the different bits of information I've just given you, we come up with a picture of a child who is a lot more logical than Piaget had thought—perhaps more logical than many preschool teachers had thought. In general, Piaget seems to have been pretty accurate in describing the *sequences* in which various understandings develop, but recent researchers have been able to show that the first steps in these sequences may occur earlier than Piaget had thought.

It is important to emphasize, though, that in order for the preschool child to demonstrate these relatively advanced forms of thinking, you usually have to make the task quite simple—remove the distractions, use simple materials, or the like. The very fact that young children are easily distracted is, of course, one of the important properties of their thinking. They have a harder time than do older children keeping track of more than one thing at a time. They have difficulty with conservation problems partly because they are distracted by the change in the shape of the clay or the height of the water in the glass. If you remove the distraction, they may show you some conservation, but they cannot yet do so as a *general principle.* It is precisely a switch from "sometimes" or "under special conditions" to general "rules" that Piaget saw as so very significant at about age 6 or 7, when the child moves into the concrete operational period.

## CONCRETE OPERATIONAL THOUGHT: FROM AGE 6 TO AGE 12

### Piaget's View of Concrete Operations

The new skills we see at age 5, 6, or 7 build on all the small changes we have already seen in the preschooler, but from Piaget's perspective there is a great leap forward that occurs when the child "discovers" or "develops" a set of immensely powerful, abstract, general rules or strategies for examining and interacting with the world. Piaget calls the new set of skills **concrete operations**, with the term *operation* used specifically to refer to powerful, *internal* manipulations, such as addition, subtraction, multiplication, division, and serial ordering. The child now understands the *rule* that adding something makes it more and subtracting makes it less; she understands that objects can belong to more than one category at once and that categories have logical relationships. Pretty heady stuff!

Even more important from Piaget's perspective is that the child now grasps the fundamental rule or operation of **reversibility.** The child understands that a basic property of actions is that they can be undone or reversed—either physically or mentally—and that you will then get back to the original position. The ball of clay can be made back into a ball; the water can be poured back into the shorter, fatter glass. This understanding of the basic reversibility of actions lies behind many of the gains made during this period.

Signs of this shift in "mental gears" can be seen in myriad areas, such as the change in children's understanding of "where babies come from," shown in Table 7.4. But let me be more specific by following some of the same lines of development I described in the last section: identities, classification, and logic.

*Identities in the Concrete Operations Period* It is in this period that the child grasps the principle of conservation. However, the child does not go from no-principle to full-principle in one leap. Instead, the child seems to come to understand each of *several* conservations separately over the course of several years. Conservation of number is understood early (about age 5), but conservation of weight (changing the shape of an object does not change its weight) is not understood till about age

BOX 7.1

# YOUNG CHILDREN'S PLAY

Go to a preschool sometime and watch the children during an unstructured time—when they are not eating or napping or being "organized" by the adults. What are the youngsters doing? They are building towers out of blocks, moving dolls around in the doll house, making "tea" with the tea set, racing toy trucks across the floor, dressing up in grown-up clothes, putting puzzles together. They are, in a word, *playing.* This is not trivial or empty activity; it is the stuff on which much of cognitive development seems to be built.

Any parent who has watched the development of his child during the preschool years knows that play changes in very visible ways during the years from 1 to 7. When psychologists have attempted to describe these changes, a series of "steps" or "stages" emerges. These changes flow together; children show several of these kinds of play at any one time. But we can still see at least the following seven different kinds of play, in something like this order.

*Step 1: "Sensorimotor" play.* The child of 12 months or so spends most of her play time exploring and manipulating objects using all the sensorimotor schemes in her repertoire. She puts things in her mouth, shakes them, stacks them, moves them along the floor. In this way she comes to understand what objects can do. Much older children continue to show this kind of play with *new* toys or objects, but this type of play diminishes in frequency sometime in the second year of life.

*Step 2: First pretend play.* The really big advance is when children first use objects to *stand for* something else. The first sign of this is usually something like a child using a toy spoon to "feed" himself, or a toy comb to comb his hair. The toys are still used for their actual or typical purposes (spoon for feeding), and the actions are still oriented to the self, but there is pretend involved.

*Step 3: Elaboration with objects.* The child is still using objects for their usual purposes, but now the pretend is more complicated, like feeding a doll with the toy spoon. Children of 18 to 24 months show a lot of this kind of play (Ungerer et al., 1981). Dolls are especially good toys for this kind of pretend, since it is not a very large leap from doing things to yourself to doing things with a doll. So children dress and undress dolls, feed them imaginary food, comb their hair.

8, and conservation of volume (an object takes up the same amount of space even if you change its shape) is not understood until about age 11 or 12. So although we can talk about the concrete operational child as having "principles" or "rules," these rules are not initially used nearly as abstractly or as broadly as they will be at age 11 or 12.

The child can arrive at the understanding of conservation by using any one of a number of operations: He can apply reversibility ("If I changed it back, it would be the same"); he can apply addition or subtraction ("You didn't add any, so it has to be the same"); or he can pay attention to more than one thing at a time ("It's bigger around, but it's thinner, so it's the same").

*Step 4: Substitute pretend play.* Somewhere around age 3, children make another big change in their play and begin to use objects to stand for something altogether different. They may comb the doll's hair with a baby bottle while saying that it is a comb or use a broom to be a horsie or make "trucks" out of blocks. The earlier forms of play, in which toys are used for their "real" purposes (such as using blocks to build towers), do not disappear. But among 4- and 5-year-olds, as much as 20 percent of free play involves this new, complicated kind of pretending (Field, De Stefano, & Koewler, 1982).

*Step 5: Sociodramatic play.* At about age 4 or 5, children also begin to play parts, or take roles. They play "daddy and mommy" or "cowboys and Indians" or "doctor and patient" or "train conductor and passenger." Sometimes the stories that are acted out are very elaborate, and children clearly get great delight out of these fantasies. Equally important, by playing roles, pretending to be someone else, they also become more and more aware of how things may look or feel to someone else, and their egocentric approach to the world declines.

*Step 6: Awareness of the roles.* Six-year-olds not only create elaborate "dramas," they will also describe or label the roles they are playing. They plan the play ahead of time or assign people to different roles rather than merely drifting into a new set of roles in the process of play. This change seems to reflect a big cognitive advance and is not usually seen until about age 6 or later—at about the time that we see the transition to concrete operations.

*Step 7: Games with rules.* At elementary school age, pretend play begins to wane and is replaced by complex games with specific rules—jacks or marbles or baseball or kick the can or something equivalent. Earlier forms of play may involve spontaneously created rules, but in elementary school, children more and more play games that have persisting, agreed-upon rules.

As adults, most of us associate the word *play* with "goofing off," or nonproductive activities. But in some very real ways, play is children's "work." Opportunities to manipulate and experiment with objects, pretend with them, play parts and roles all seem to be important ingredients in the child's cognitive and social development (Fein, 1981; Piaget, 1962). The key point is that children need to have *time* for play—time when they are not watching TV, not organized, not required to do anything "constructive."

*Classification* The big change is one I have already described: the understanding of the principle of *class inclusion*. A good way to illustrate this is with the game of 20 questions (which you can try out in Project 7.1). In one of my favorite older studies, Frederic Mosher and Joan Hornsby (1966) showed 6- to 11-year-old children a set of 42 pictures of animals, people, toys, machines, and the like. The experimenter said he was thinking of one of the pictures, and the child was to figure out which one by asking questions that could be answered "yes" or "no."

Many of you have played this kind of game before and already know that there are several ways to go about it. One way, especially with a set of pictures, is simply to start at one end of a row and ask "Is it this

TABLE 7.4

**Development of children's concepts of "where babies come from":
An example of the transition from preoperational to concrete
operational thought**

| | |
|---|---|
| Level 1: Preoperational stage (ages 3–4) | Children answer as if the question were one about geography: "You go to a baby store and buy one." "From tummies." |
| Level 2: Preoperational stage (ages 4–5) | Children believe that babies are manufactured, like cars: "When people are already made, they make some other people. They make the bones inside, and blood. They make skin. They make the skin first and then they make blood and bones. They paint the blood, paint the red blood and the blue blood." |
| Level 3: Transitional stage (ages 5–7) | Children are more practical; they stick to things that can actually happen physically, but they don't understand the causal connections completely: "The sperm goes into the mommy to each egg and puts it, makes the egg safe. So if something bump comes along, it won't crack the egg. . . ." |
| Level 4: Concrete operations (ages 7–8) | Children are able to think logically and understand cause and effect; they can consider past and future. Explanations at this stage are based on concrete physiology: "The sperm reaches the eggs. It looses 'em and brings 'em down to the forming place, I think that's right, and it grows until it's ready to take out." |

*SOURCE:* Bernstein, A. C. How children learn about sex and birth. Reprinted from *Psychology Today Magazine,* 1976, *9* (No. 8), 31–35. Copyright © January 1976 (APA). Excerpts from pp. 32, 33, and 34.

one?" about each one in turn until you hit on the right one. Mosher and Hornsby called this strategy "hypothesis scanning." A second way is to classify the pictures mentally into a hierarchy of groups and then ask first about the highest level in your hierarchy. If you notice that among the objects there are red and blue toys, you could start by asking "Is it a toy?" If the answer is "yes," you might then ask about the subcategories: "Is it a red toy?" Mosher and Hornsby called this second strategy "constraint seeking." To use this second strategy efficiently, the child must not only classify but also use the principle of class inclusion.

You can see in Figure 7.5, which shows the main results of this study, that 6-year-olds almost never used a constraint (classification) strategy. They relied essentially on guessing. By age 8, however, the majority of children's questions reflected a constraint strategy, and by age 11, that strategy strongly dominated.

*Logic in the Concrete Operations Period*   Piaget argued that, during these years, the child develops the ability to use **inductive logic**. He can go from his own experience to a general principle. For example, he can go from the observation that when you add another toy to a set

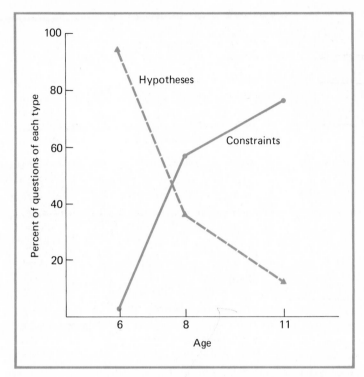

**Figure 7.5** Six-year olds, when they play 20 questions with pictures, use nearly all guessing (hypotheses), but 8-year-olds, who are into the period of concrete operations, use a strategy (constraints) that involves organizing the pictures into classes and hierarchies. (*Source:* Mosher & Hornsby, 1966, p. 91.)

and then count it, it always has one more to a general principle that adding always makes it more. In science, we use inductive reasoning a lot. We make systematic observations and then try to figure out why things turned out the way they did.

Elementary school children are pretty good observational scientists and will enjoy cataloging, counting species of trees or birds, or figuring out the nesting habits of guinea pigs or the mating habits of spiders. What they are not yet good at is going from a general principle to some anticipated experience (like going from a theory to a hypothesis), a process that requires **deductive logic**. This is harder than inductive logic because it requires imagining things that you may never have experienced—something the concrete operations child typically does not do. We do not see deductive reasoning until the period of formal operations in junior high or high school.

## Current Work on the Concrete Operations Period

Unlike the newer research on the sensorimotor and preoperational periods, the current research on the thinking of elementary school children has not been much focused on the question of whether Piaget underestimated or overestimated the thinking of children of this age or stage. Instead, attention has mostly been on two issues: (1) What is the sequence in which the several concepts develop in these years, and (2) do children show consistent skill across tasks? There has also been a good deal of research on areas of children's abilities that Piaget touched on only briefly but that now appear to be highly significant, such as children's memory strategies. I'll save the question of memory strategies for the discussion of the **information-processing** approach, but let me say at least a few words about sequences and consistency across tasks.

*Sequences of Development in the Concrete Operations Period*   The best study of sequences I know of was done by Carol Tomlinson-Keasey and her colleagues (1979). They studied a group of 38 children from kindergarten through third grade, testing them with five traditional concrete operations tasks each year: conservation of mass (there's the same *amount* of clay after you squish a ball into a pancake), conservation of weight, conservation of volume, class inclusion, and hierarchical classification (organizing classes into hierarchies). You can see from Figure 7.6 that the children got better at all five tasks over the three-year period, with an especially noticeable spurt between the end of kindergarten and the start of first grade—about the age that Piaget thought that concrete operations really began. More important, the different tasks were not equally easy. Conservation of mass was easier than conservation of weight, with conservation of volume the hardest of the three. Class inclusion was also generally harder than conservation of mass. In fact, they found that conservation of mass seemed to be a necessary precursor for the development of class inclusion.

Equally interesting, Tomlinson-Keasey found that a child's skill on these tasks, relative to that of the other children, stayed approximately the same throughout the three years of testing. A 6-year-old who developed conservation of mass early continued to be ahead of other children later on; a late-developing child went through the same sequence about two years later.

There is certainly a good deal of confirmation of Piaget's observations in this study. In particular, it shows that each step in the sequence of cognitive development builds from what has gone before and that the sequence remains the same, regardless of the rate of progress the child may show.

*Consistency Across Tasks*   The more difficult question, though, is whether we can talk about a child generally being "at" concrete operations or "at" formal operations. Do children perform at about the same "level" on a whole series of tasks? The very fact that Tomlinson-Keasey found that the traditional concrete operations tasks developed in a sequence rather than all at once demonstrates that, at least in the early years of this stage, children show complex or abstract thinking on some problems and not others. Others have found the same thing (Marto-

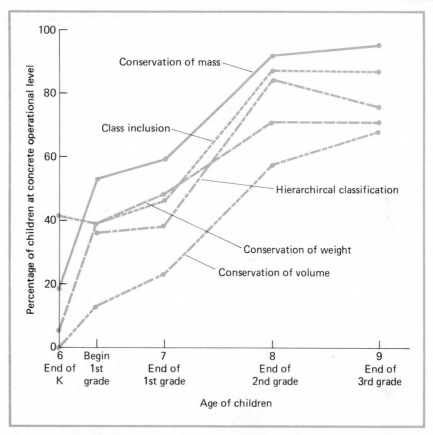

**Figure 7.6** These results are from a longitudinal study in which the same children were given a set of concrete operations tasks five different times, beginning in kindergarten and ending in the third grade. As you can see, the percentage of children "solving" each type of problem increased, particularly at about age 7. But the tasks differed in difficulty, too. (*Source:* Tomlinson-Keasey et al., 1979, adapted from Table 2, p. 1158.)

rano, 1977; Roberge & Flexner, 1979). Piaget recognized this lack of simultaneity of development of the concrete operations (using the phrase **horizontal decalage** to describe it). But acknowledging it does not explain why it occurs.

## Overview of the Concrete Operational Child

My own sense of this period is that Piaget is correct about the general character and significance of the shift in children's thinking that takes place between about age 5 and 7. Children do seem to be able to step back a bit from compelling, immediate sensations or experiences and work out the beginnings of general rules, general strategies. We see the ramifications of this change in an enormous number of ways. For example, youngsters of about this age get a lot better, a lot more sys-

BOX 7.2

# PIAGET'S THEORY AND EARLY EDUCATION

Piaget's theory is really not a theory of teaching. He has said only a little (Piaget, 1970) about how a teacher confronted daily by a classroom full of children can apply his ideas. But a great many preschool and elementary school educators have tried to apply at least some of Piaget's concepts in their teaching (e.g., Lavatelli, 1970; Weikart, 1972; Kamii & DeVries, 1974; Appel, 1977).

The most common application of Piaget's theory has been based on the sequence of changes from preoperational to concrete operational thinking. Preschool educators map out the steps involved in such concepts as classification and then try to move the child along that sequence by presenting materials that "lead" the child from where he is "up" to the next step. You can see some elements of this in "Sesame Street" (which I urge you to watch occasionally, by the way) when they "teach" classification by having children figure out which things go together. You can see it in preschool programs like David Weikart's (1972), in which concepts are taught by first using sensorimotor experience,

with more abstract experience added later. The word *boat*, for example, might be introduced by having the children play in a life-sized rowboat (sensorimotor), then with a toy boat that stands for the larger boat, then with pictures of boats, and finally—with much older children—with the written word *boat*.

This same use of the basic sequences can be seen in certain mathematics and science programs now used in some elementary and high schools. Marilyn Appel (1977) describes one science program called PASE (Personalized Approach to Science Education). Science projects are arranged in a sequence from preoperational (involving basic classification, for example) through the transition to concrete operations (involving reversibility or conservation tasks, for example) and on upward in complexity. At each level, there are many different experiences, and the child chooses which one she wants to work on. A child may work on many at one level before moving on to the next group of experiments.

tematic, at searching for lost toys, and their understanding of classes helps them learn beginning mathematics.

It also seems clear that during this period the child moves through a sequence or series of sequences, developing one concept or "operation" after another and applying each operation to more and more abstract tasks.

At the same time, I also think that these new skills are much more narrowly applied than Piaget's original view would lead us to believe. The child is still tied to his own specific experience to a very marked degree. Five- and 6-year-olds may be good at putting blocks in order from large to small if they have had a lot of time playing with those blocks or with objects like them. But they may not show the same ability to put things into serial order with less-familiar material, such as sets of sticks (Achenbach & Weisz, 1975). Or a child may be better at creating hierarchical classes out of toys he has played with than out of a group of totally new toys. In other words, the 7-year-old *does* show some impressive new cognitive skills. But this time Piaget may have

All of these efforts to "translate" Piaget into practical classroom procedures seem useful to me, but there are some pitfalls—some misunderstandings of Piaget that lead to misapplication of the theory. Let me mention just two.

First, from Piaget's point of view, the child's thinking is not created from the outside; it is *constructed* by the child. And this construction comes about through the child's own play and exploration (see Box 7.1). So as Joseph Lawton and Frank Hooper (1978) point out, merely presenting concepts in the "correct" sequence is not sufficient; it is the child's *activity* with materials that is critical. The teacher can help this process by providing things to play with and explore that are at a level of difficulty that will foster further growth in the child. Or the teacher might ask questions that will cause the child to rethink old concepts (accommodate). But in Piaget's view, the teacher cannot *force* the child along the sequence. (Nor, in Piaget's view, is there any particular purpose in trying to speed up the process, either. He regarded this desire to push children along faster to be a very curious American preoccupation.)

It seems to me that the PASE science pro-gram, focused as it is on the child's own activity, avoids this particular misapplication of Piaget's theory, but many other Piaget-based educational systems do not.

Second, American educators seem to be particularly vulnerable to the trap of paying attention to the "right" answers. We want children to say that the two balls of clay are the same in the conservation experiment, for example. Piaget has always been more interested in *why* a child says something and not in whether the answer is right by some adult standard. Our preoccupation with rightness may lead teachers to listen too little to the child's logic and to focus instead on teaching the child the right words to say. In Piaget's views, the right words don't necessarily mean that the child has achieved the fundamental understanding.

Overall, American educators have seized on the stages Piaget describes and have tried to overlay them onto educational practice and onto curricula. But in the process, we have often missed the subtleties of Piaget's theory.

*over*estimated the child. The skills seem to be less generally applied than Piaget suggests.

## FORMAL OPERATIONAL THOUGHT: FROM AGE 12 ON

### Piaget's View of Formal Operational Thought

The final step of cognitive development proposed by Piaget, the development of **formal operations**, is taken during adolescence, beginning at about age 12 and continuing into early adulthood. The major task of this period, according to Piaget, is to develop a new, still-more-powerful set of cognitive skills ("formal operations"), organized into a structure that allows you to think about *ideas* as well as about objects. Ideas can be classified and organized, just as objects can. In fact, they can be manipulated much more flexibly.

Piaget does *not* say that this new level of abstraction is achieved all at once one morning on a child's twelfth birthday, just as concrete operations do not develop suddenly, either. There are steps and sub-stages, with fully consolidated formal operations probably not completed until about age 15 or later. But he did believe that there was a fairly rapid "spurt" of development over a period of several years, when the major elements of this new level of abstract thinking were acquired. Let me describe some of those major elements.

*From the Actual to the Possible*   One of the first steps in this process is for the child to extend her reasoning abilities to objects and situations that she has not seen or experienced firsthand or that she cannot see or manipulate directly. Instead of thinking only about real things and actual occurrences, she must start to think about possible occurrences. She can also now begin to think about the "ideal," such as the "ideal parent." (This new ability can sometimes be a source of conflict between parents and children, since few of us are ideal parents!)

A study of class inclusion by Ellen Markman (1978) shows some aspects of this shift quite well. I've already said that concrete operational children develop the concept of class inclusion (there are more flowers than primroses). But it turns out that 8- or 9- or even 11-year-olds can only do this well when they have the objects right in front of them. When you put the problem in an abstract form, they have difficulty.

In one test Markman developed, she showed children four toy couches and two toy chairs, collectively labeled as "furniture." But then Markman hid all the toys behind a screen and said that she was going to take some of the furniture away. Then she asked, "Without seeing what I took away, can you tell for sure whether there is more furniture left or more couches left?" To answer this question correctly, the child must either be able to imagine the couches, chairs, and furniture behind the screen and manipulate these mental pictures entirely in his head, or he must understand the basic *logical* relationship between the different classes. This change essentially makes this a formal operations task, and Markman found that 11-year-olds—presumably still in concrete operations—had trouble with it. I would expect that 15-year-olds, in contrast, could perform this task well because they can manipulate the ideas as well as the objects.

Incidentally, an interesting implication of the teenager's new ability to consider unseen possibilities is that youngsters of this age should be able to consider the *future* much more systematically—something that our culture, in fact, expects of them at just about this age. Catherine Lewis (1981), in an interesting recent study, has found just such an increase in future orientation in teenagers' decision making. She had teenagers listen to tape recordings of other teens talking about decisions they were facing—like whether to have an operation to remove an unsightly lump on the face. The listening teenager was then asked to give the decision maker some ideas about things to keep in mind in making the decision. Two of the results are shown in Figure 7.7. As you can see, twelfth graders nearly always talked about the risks as well as the benefits of each choice, while only about half of the younger students gave such a balanced view. Twelfth graders were also much more likely to talk about the future as well as the present.

One twelfth grader, on the subject of the cosmetic surgery, said: "Well, you have to look into the different things . . . that might be more important later on in your life. You should think about will it have any effect on your future and with, maybe, the people you meet. . . ." In contrast, an eighth grader said: "The different things I would think about in getting the operation is like if the girls turn you down on a date, or the money, or the kids teasing you at school . . ." (Lewis, 1981, pp. 541–542). Obviously, then, this ability to go beyond the actual to the possible has very important practical implications for teenagers and for their ability to plan their own futures and make reasonable decisions. (And the relative *inability* of junior high school youngsters to do the same thing makes the practice of vocational interest testing or vocational counseling in junior high school seem questionable.)

*Systematic Problem Solving*   Thinking up and organizing possible solutions to a problem still does not solve the problem, though. In order to do that, the child must learn to test each of the possible solutions mentally until he finds one that works. So another important feature of the stage of formal operations is the ability to search systematically

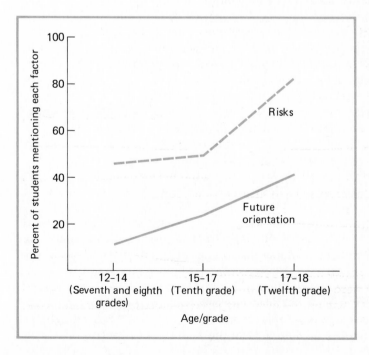

**Figure 7.7** One of the changes that happens in adolescence as youngsters begin using formal operations is that they are more likely to think about the future and consider future problems. These results are from a study of decision making among adolescents and indicate that the twelfth graders were considering the risks more carefully and considering the future more. (*Source:* Lewis, 1981, adapted from Table 1, p. 541.)

and methodically for the answer to a problem. This aspect of formal operations was extensively studied by Piaget and his colleague Barbel Inhelder (Inhelder & Piaget, 1958).

Inhelder and Piaget presented adolescents with complex tasks, mostly drawn from the physical sciences. In one of these tasks, the youngsters are given varying lengths of string and a set of objects of various weights that can be tied to the strings to make a swinging pendulum. They are shown how to start the pendulum by pushing the weight with differing amounts of force and by holding the weight at different heights. The subject must figure out which one or combination of these four factors (length of string, weight of object, force of push, or height of push) determines the "period" (amount of time for one swing) of the pendulum. (In case you have forgotten your high school physics, the answer is that only the length of the string affects the period of the pendulum.) If you give this task to a concrete operational child, she will usually try out many different combinations of length and weight and force and height in an inefficient way. She might try a heavy weight on a long string and then a light weight on a short string. Since both string length and weight have changed, there is no way to draw a clear conclusion about either factor.

An adolescent, in contrast, is likely to try a much more organized approach. The formal operations youngster apparently recognizes that the only way to solve the problem is to vary just one of the four factors at a time. So he may try a heavy object with a short string, then with a medium string, then with a long one. After that, he might try a light object with the three lengths of string. Of course, not all adolescents (or all adults, for that matter) are quite this methodical in their approach. But there is a very dramatic difference in the overall strategy used by 10-year-olds and 15-year-olds that marks the shift from concrete to formal operations.

*Logic*   Another facet of this shift is the appearance of deductive logic in the child's repertoire of skills. As I mentioned earlier, the concrete operational child is able to do inductive reasoning, which involves arriving at a conclusion or a rule based on a lot of individual experiences. The more difficult kind of reasoning, deductive reasoning, involves "if X, then Y" relationships: "If all people are equal, then you and I must be equal."

A great deal of the logic of science is of this deductive type. We begin with a theory and propose, "If this theory is correct, then I should observe such and such." In doing this, we are going well beyond our observations. We are conceiving things that we have never seen that *ought* to be true or observable. We can think of this process as being part of a general decentering that began much earlier in cognitive development. The preoperational child gradually moves away from his egocentrism and comes to be able to take the physical perspective of others.

During formal operations, the child takes the next step by freeing himself even from his reliance upon specific experiences.

## Current Work on Formal Operations

There has been less systematic post-Piagetian research on the formal operations period than on any of the other stages Piaget described, but the evidence has been expanding rapidly in the past 5 to 10 years. Most of this work has centered around three questions: (1) Is there really a change in the child's thinking at adolescence, and if so, when does it happen? (2) Why can't we see this change in every youngster? (3) How general are these new abilities?

*Is There Really a Change?*   All the recent research tells us that the answer to this question is clearly "yes." As Edith Neimark says (1982, p. 493), "An enormous amount of evidence from an assortment of tasks shows that adolescents and adults are capable of feats of reasoning not attained under normal circumstances by . . . children, and that these abilities develop fairly rapidly during the ages of about 11 to 15."

A large cross-sectional study by Susan Martorano (1977) is a good illustration. She tested 20 students (all girls) at each of four grades (sixth, eighth, tenth, and twelfth) on 10 different tasks that require one or more of the formal operations skills. Some of her results are shown in Figure 7.8. You can see that older students generally did better, with the biggest "spurt" between eighth and tenth grades (between age 13 and age 15). This is somewhat later than Piaget originally proposed but consistent with all the other recent findings. You can also see that the problems are not equally difficult. Problems that required the child to consider two or more separate factors simultaneously were harder than problems that simply required the child to search for the logical possibilities. For example, the easiest problem, called "colored tokens," asks the child how many different pairs of colors can be made using tokens of six different colors. This requires only thinking up and organizing possible solutions. The hardest problem was the "balance" problem, which tests the youngster's ability to predict whether or not two weights on either side of a scale will balance. This might sound easy, but the weights may be hung at different distances from the center point of the scale, which means that the child must consider both weight and distance at the same time, just as she must consider string length and pendulum weight simultaneously in the pendulum problem.

*Does Everybody Reach Formal Operations?*   The answer to this question seems to be "no." In Piaget's original studies, there were signs that unlike concrete operations, formal operations was not a universal achievement. Those early hints have been repeatedly confirmed in

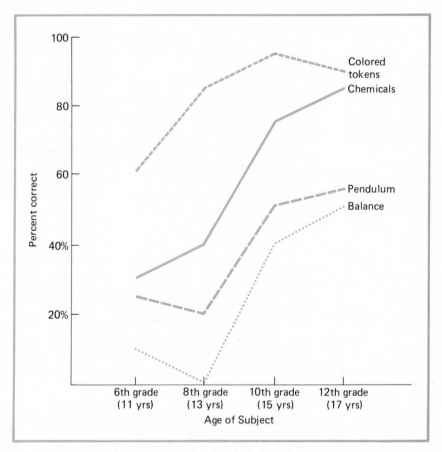

**Figure 7.8** The development of formal operations in adolescence is shown by the response of groups of American girls to four different formal operations tasks. As was true for concrete operations, we can see a big spurt in correct solutions during one age period (between 13 and 15, in this case), but the problems differed consistently in difficulty, depending on the number of different formal "operations" the child had to apply at once. (*Source:* Martorano, 1977, p. 670. Copyright by the American Psychological Association.)

more recent research. Only about 50 to 60 percent of 18- to 20-year-olds seem to use formal operations at all, let alone consistently (Keating, 1980). You can see this in Martorano's results, which I just described. Only 2 of her 20 twelfth-grade subjects showed formal operations on all the problems, and none of the younger children did.

Why? There are several possibilities. One is that the usual methods of measuring formal operations are simply extremely difficult or unclear. Fred Danner and Mary Carol Day (1977) found that they could greatly increase the rate of formal operations thinking by providing prompts or hints or rules. For example, the experimenter would name any variable the child had not tested and ask him to test it (such as the weight of the pendulum if the child had not varied that), or a verbal rule was given (such as "A good way to find out what makes a difference in how fast the weights go back and forth is to make sure that everything is the same except the one thing you're testing"). When children who had heard such prompts and rules were tested on a totally new formal operations problem, many more showed good skill at the task. These prompts may simply have made it much clearer to the teenager what she was expected to do.

A second possibility is that most of us have managed to work our way through the early steps of formal operations but that we have not organized all these skills into an integrated structure that applies to everything. In other words, we can reason this way some of the time, in areas with which we are familiar, but not in all areas. For example, I do a lot of formal operations reasoning about psychology because it is an area I know well. But I am a lot less skillful at applying the same kind of reasoning to fixing my car—about which I know next to nothing. I don't even ask very good questions when I talk to the mechanic!

Still a third possibility is that most of our everyday experiences and tasks do not require formal operations. Concrete operations is quite sufficient most of the time. So we get into a cognitive "rut," applying our most usual mode of thinking to new problems as well. We can kick our thinking "up a notch" under some circumstances, especially if someone reminds us (as in the Danner and Day experiment), but we simply don't rehearse formal operations very much.

A fourth possibility is that formal operations is related to the cognitive/perceptual styles I described in Chapter 5. Edith Neimark, in several studies (1975, 1981), has found that "reflective" children (who examine possibilities carefully) and "field-independent" children (who are able to disregard the immediate context) are more likely to show formal operations than are otherwise equally "bright" children who are "impulsive" or "field-dependent."

*How General Are These Abilities?*   I have already partly answered this one: "somewhat, but not perfectly." Some people do seem to use formal operations logic a good deal of the time; others do so rarely or never. In between, there are a lot of adults who use such skills on some problems but not on others (Neimark, 1982).

None of that sounds much like Piaget's description, of course. In his view, once the new structures are in place, they ought to be applied fairly generally. The fact that they are not—at least not for many people—is a troublesome finding for his theory to handle.

## OVERVIEW OF THE STAGES OF COGNITIVE DEVELOPMENT

The child comes a long way in only about 15 years. He moves from having very rudimentary abilities to being able to represent things to himself with images and words, to classifications, to conservation, to abstract, deductive logic. As Piaget sees it, the progress along this chain is continuous but marked off into stages, with each stage characterized by particular kinds of logic. In broad outline, that seems to be true; but there are some distinct problems with Piaget's theory, many of which have been evident in what I have already said. Since these problems are, in part, what has led to the new information-processing approach, let me be explicit about several of the key difficulties.

## PROBLEMS WITH PIAGET'S THEORY

There have been criticisms of Piaget's theory from the earliest days (Charles Brainerd's many critiques come to mind, 1974, 1978). But of late, the criticisms have been rising to a greater crescendo. As I read it, there are really three types of criticisms, two of which I consider relatively unimportant, and one of which I think is a serious difficulty.

### Individual Differences

One of the unimportant problems (in my opinion) is that Piaget hasn't said very much about why children don't all seem to develop at the same rate. Research like Tomlinson-Keasey's (Figure 7.6) shows that by age 6, some children are as much as two years ahead of others in their rate of progress through the sequence Piaget describes. The plain fact is that Piaget was simply not very interested in this question. He was interested in the sequence itself, not in the timing of it. But there is nothing to prevent other researchers from studying this problem and adding to the theory.

### The Timing of the Stages and Sequences

The second less-important question is the issue of just when the various stages or sequences occur. Sometimes Piaget seems to have underestimated children, as we saw in the research on the preoperational period, and sometimes he seems to have overestimated them, as at formal operations. I find it interesting that it is possible to see the early signs of concrete operations in children as young as 3. This research enriches our knowledge of the steps in the sequences the child passes through in her understanding of individual concepts. But I do not think that this body of research fundamentally refutes Piaget's basic theory.

### Consistency of Development: Are There Really Stages?

The one question that in my opinion does go to the heart of the theory is whether there are really stages at all. Piaget has taken what has come to be called the *structuralist* position: He argues that the child does not just develop a set of *independent* skills or abilities but that these abilities are organized into *structures*—into coordinated principles or rules or strategies that are applied across problems or tasks. This is particularly true of the way Piaget has described concrete and formal operations. He does say, of course, that neither concrete nor formal operations is developed all at once, but we should still find that a child who can ask good strategy questions in the 20 questions game ought to be able to solve other multiple-classification problems, too. In other words, a given skill should not be entirely task-specific. If there really is some internal organization or structure, skills ("operations") ought to be general.

It is *very* hard to test this proposition really well, and I am not at all sure that we have the information to settle this question. But as is clear from what I have already said, the information we have does *not* show that children are very consistent in their "level" or "strategy" of performance across tasks (Uzgiris, 1973; Martorano, 1977; Fischer, 1980; Keating & Clark, 1980; Flavell, 1982a, 1982b). Children not only do not do equally well on presumably same-stage problems, sometimes they do not even do equally well on different measures of the *same* task, such as measures of serial ordering using colors and sets of sticks (Achenbach & Weisz, 1975).

This lack of consistency across tasks is not a trivial matter. It calls into question the whole concept of "stages" or "structures." For example, John Flavell, a one-time student of Piaget's and a major interpreter of his work, has concluded that "human cognitive growth is generally *not* very 'stage-like'" (1982b, p. 17). That is, there is little *horizontal* consistency or structure at any given age.

What there is, instead, is *vertical* consistency or structure. There are sequences of development. Within any given cognitive "task"—such as understanding of conservation, number, classification, or the like—there do seem to be predictable sequences shared by nearly all children. As Flavell puts it (1982b, p. 18): "Sequences are the very wire and glue of development. Later cognitive acquisitions build on or are otherwise linked to earlier ones, and in their turn similarly prepare the ground for still later ones."

Thus, Piaget seems to have been very much on-target in talking about sequences but was probably off-target in proposing integrated structures or stages. This weakness in the theory has opened the door for a whole new set of questions: What are the observed sequences based on, if not structures? Can we find "basic" skills or strategies, such as memory strategies, that change over time and that may lie behind some of the sequences we observe? Those theorists in the information-processing tradition have been attempting to answer just such questions.

INFORMATION PROCESSING: A "NEW" APPROACH

The information-processing approach is a fascinating blend of a number of theoretical "fathers" or "grandfathers." The most important ancestor is the research on adult intellectual performance, particularly computer simulations of adult intelligence. If we use the computer as a metaphor, we can think of the "hardware" of intelligence (the physiology of the brain—the "wiring," if you will) and the "software" of intelligence (the program that uses the basic hardware). We can increase the speed or efficiency of a computer either by increasing the actual processing capacity of the machine itself or by writing better programs. If we apply this same idea to the study of the development of children's thinking, we could think of changes in children's skills with age either as the result of basic increases in the capacity of the system (the hardware) or as the result of improvements in the "programs" or strategies the child is using. What emerges from this line of reasoning is a search for the basic "building blocks" of intellectual functioning, such as processes of recognition, of memory, of analysis. We can then ask how early and how well the child uses these fundamental skills and how the "program" changes with age.

Interestingly, other researchers had arrived at a very similar point from different directions—with different theoretical ancestors. As I mentioned a bit ago, cognitive-developmental theorists, such as John Flavell (1982a, 1982b), have been persuaded that it is sequences and not stages that are really critical in development. Analyzing the basic processes in intellectual activity and describing the sequence in which each is acquired seemed like the next logical step.

Finally, there are some interesting links to the traditional individual-differences approach, too. If we assume that the development of intelligence involves both changes in the underlying capacity of the system ("hardware" changes) and changes in the efficiency of the strategies we all use to learn and remember information ("software" changes), then we may be able to define more precisely just what it is that makes one person more "intelligent" than another. It could be either a difference in the basic capacity (the "power" of the computer) or a difference in the "program" or both.

The convergence of these views has led to a real explosion of fascinating research on both the possible changes in processing *capacity* and on changes in *strategies* for learning, remembering, or solving problems. This work is mostly quite new, and there is no single integrative theory that ties it all together, so there is a somewhat "scattered" quality to this area of research. But let me sample briefly from the richness.

## Changes in Processing Capacity

Lyndon Johnson once said of a political foe, "He can't walk and chew gum at the same time." Most of us *can* manage to walk and chew gum, but it doesn't take much introspection to realize that there is a very distinct limit to the number of different items or tasks you can remember or perform at the same time. About seven "things" is the most that most adults can work with at any one time (Miller, 1956). But what about children? Do they have a smaller capacity (a less "powerful" computer, to use that analogy one more time)?

Maybe. When children and adults are given simple memory tasks, like repeating strings of numbers backward, the typical finding is that very young children can remember fewer than can adults (Dempster, 1981), as you can see in Figure 7.9. That *may* mean that 2-year-olds can only handle two "bits" of information at a time, while adults can handle seven. Given what we know about the growth of the brain during the first years after birth, some systematic growth in physiological capacity seems plausible. But it could also simply mean that children have had much less experience with numbers, so they don't have any "tricks" to help them remember. We are back, then, to the same problem that plagued us with IQ tests: We cannot measure capacity. We can measure performance, but performance is a product of a lot of things besides capacity. All I can say at the moment is that it is reasonable to assume that there are some changes with age in the processing capacity of the infant and child but that researchers haven't been able to figure out a way to demonstrate it unequivocally.

## Changes in Strategy

What we *can* say is that children develop increasingly complex and powerful strategies for using the capacities they have.

If you are confronted with a long list of things to remember or a complex problem to solve, you probably approach it by figuring out some way of *reducing* the load on your processing system—just as in the incident at the grocery store I described at the beginning of Chapter 6. I used the recipe I would be following as a way to help organize a list I needed to remember. As adults, we have a very large repertoire of such strategies. Young children have very few, but the number increases rapidly over the early years. Thus, we can think of cognitive development as a process of figuring out more and more helpful strategies for analyzing, remembering, or processing information and of extending those strategies to a wider and wider range of experiences (Brown et al., 1983). If we find (as we do) that these strategies are acquired in a particular sequence and that they are first applied quite

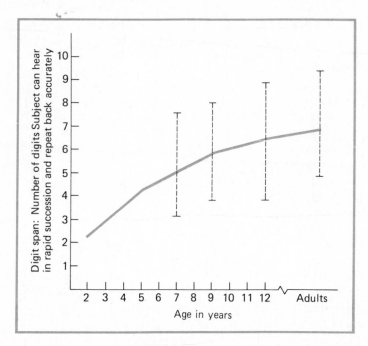

**Figure 7.9** One way psychologists have tried to measure the basic "capacity" of the brain to process information is to study very basic memory operations, such as remembering lists of things for short periods of time. Strings of digits are the most common items used, and you can see that the number of numbers that can be repeated goes up steadily with age. (*Source:* Dempster, 1981, Figure 1, p. 66.)

narrowly, then this research can be linked up very nicely with many of Piaget's observations.

Studies of children's mental strategies have become the most common sort of research in cognitive development in the past few years. A great deal of this work has been on strategies for remembering and for solving problems like searching for lost objects, and this work will give you some of the flavor of the information-processing research.

*Strategies for Remembering*   One strategy that works a lot of the time is *rehearsal*. When you look up a telephone number, you may find yourself repeating it under your breath or in your mind before you dial. Children do this, too, but most do not do so spontaneously before about the age of 5.

Much of the early work on children's use of rehearsal strategies was done by John Flavell and his students (Flavell, 1970). In one typical study (Keeney, Cannizzo, & Flavell, 1967), they showed children a row of seven pictures and told them to try to remember the pictures and the order in which they were laid out. Then a space helmet was placed over the child's head for 15 seconds, hiding his eyes but allowing the experimenter to see the child's mouth so that he could observe any muttering or quiet rehearsal. In this study, and in dozens like it, the standard finding is that 5-year-olds almost never use any kind of rehearsal, while 8- or 10-year-olds do. Regardless of age, children who used rehearsal remembered more of the cards, so it is an efficient strategy for this problem.

The really interesting thing is that when 5-year-olds are *taught* to rehearse, they can use this strategy and can remember better. But if you now give them a new problem and don't remind them to rehearse, they will slip back to the nonrehearsal pattern. Thus, they are *able* to use the strategy but do not do so spontaneously—a pattern Flavell called a **production deficiency**. It is as if the child does not recognize that it is an appropriate strategy for this type of task.

Rehearsal is not the only way to help remember things. If you have a list to recall, you can organize it into sets or groups. A grocery store list could be organized (in your head) into fruits, vegetables, canned food, dairy products, and the like. Or you could organize it by the aisles of the grocery store where you usually shop. This kind of "chunking" reduces the number of pieces of information you have to keep in mind at once and is a very helpful strategy.

Interestingly, children as young as 2 show some signs of using such organization of things to be remembered (Goldberg, Perlmutter, & Myers, 1974), but children get steadily better at this strategy up through adolescence. And again, if you teach young children a way of grouping things into sets, their memory improves, but they do not generalize the strategy well (Siegler & Richards, 1982; Brown et al., 1983).

Overall, from age 2 or 3 onward, three things seem to happen to children's memories: (1) children acquire more and more powerful strategies to aid memory; (2) they use these strategies more and more skillfully; and (3) they apply them to more and more different kinds of problems.

*Changes in Problem-Solving Strategies*   We see the same kinds of changes in problem-solving strategies. My favorite research in this area is Henry Wellman's work on children's search strategies (Wellman & Somerville, 1982).

When was the last time you misplaced your car keys? Think of how you went about searching for them. Did you retrace your steps? Did you think where you had seen them last and look there? Did you think of all the places they *could* be (or the people who could have taken them) and look in each place in turn? In other words, was your search logical or systematic? And could you think of alternate strategies if the first one did not work? Wellman has asked whether children do these things, too, and found some intriguing developmental progressions.

Two- and 3-year-olds do search for things in a somewhat logical way: They look first in the most likely place, for example, such as the place where the object was last seen. But it isn't until about age 4 or 5 that children show *exhaustive* and *systematic* search. In one study, Wellman (Wellman, Somerville, & Haake, 1979) had children search for a pair of scissors in a set of eight cupboards arranged in a row. An exhaustive search would require looking in all eight cupboards, and one way to be sure to do that is to start at one end and work from one to the next. Four- and 5-year-olds did that, but 3-year-olds did so much less frequently, as you can see in Figure 7.10.

Obviously, quite young children have pretty sophisticated strategies for searching. What they do not have, though, are good back-up plans. If the first strategy fails, they aren't so good at figuring out an alternative, while 8- to 10-year-olds are. In fact, the older child can tell you her plan in advance. For example, Mary Ann Kreutzer and her colleagues (Kreutzer, Leonard, & Flavell, 1975) asked children to imagine that they had lost a jacket at school. Most kindergartners could think of only one strategy for finding it, while most fifth graders could think of three or four ways they might search.

*The Role of Experience*   Age is not the only thing that matters in the use of good strategies for remembering or solving problems. Experience with the particular task or material is also enormously important. The more familiar you are with the area in which you are searching, for example, the easier it is to be systematic; the more familiar you are with the words or other items to be remembered, the easier it is to come up with ways of organizing them in your head.

In fact, when children have more experience than adults do, children's memory may actually be better than the grown-ups'. M. T. Chi

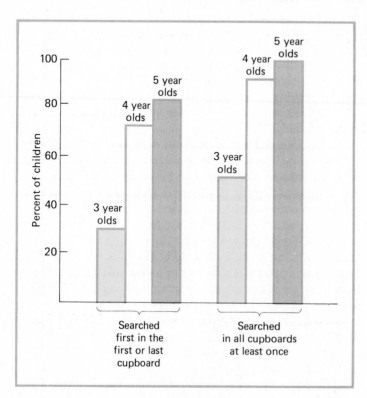

**Figure 7.10** Children's search strategies get more systematic and more exhaustive during the preschool years, as Wellman and Somerville found in this study. Children were trying to find a lost pair of scissors in one of eight adjacent cupboards. (*Source:* Wellman & Somerville, 1982, p. 64.)

(1978) showed this in a lovely study of memory for placement of chess pieces. She showed 10-year-olds and adults an organized arrangement of chess pieces on a board for 10 seconds and then covered them. The subjects had to try to reproduce the arrangement they had seen. The catch is that the 10-year-olds were all skilled chess players, while the adults were novices. Under these conditions, the children remembered better. But when Chi gave the same subjects a traditional digit-span task, she found that the adults could repeat back more of the numbers they had heard.

Of course, one of the big differences between very young children and older children (or adults) is that the preschooler has had much less experience with nearly everything. So the lack of memory strategies may not reflect lack of capacity at all, but merely lack of experience.

*Individual Differences in Information Processing*   The developmental changes I have been describing are widely shared among children. Virtually all children develop the ability to use the major strategies for remembering or solving problems. But it is quite clear that the rate with which children develop these and the flexibility with which they extend strategies to new tasks or problems vary from one child to the next. It may well be exactly this ability to develop and apply powerful strategies that we are measuring with an IQ test. As Robert Sternberg puts it (1981, p. 151), "intelligence . . . may in part be understood as the ability to acquire and reason with new conceptual systems." He goes on to suggest that it may be the child's interest in or willingness to find *new* strategies, new ways of solving problems, that distinguishes the very "bright" child from the less-intelligent child.

In fact, there is quite a lot of evidence that children with higher IQ scores are also more skillful at tasks demanding rapid information processing (e.g., Keating & Bobbitt, 1978). Furthermore, there is now some really intriguing evidence that measures of basic memory or attention in early infancy are quite remarkably correlated to later IQ. In one study (which I mentioned in Chapter 6), Joseph Fagan and Susan McGrath (1981) had tested a group of children on a "recognition memory" task when they were 7 months old. The infants had been shown pictures of two identical faces for 40 seconds and then shown a slide with one familiar face and one new one. If the infant looks more at the novel face, we can conclude that she "recognized" (remembered) the familiar one and chose to look at the novel face. Seven years later, Fagan and McGrath located some of these same children and gave them a verbal IQ test. They found that the children who had shown more recognition memory (spent more time looking at the novel faces) had higher IQs. The correlation between the two measures was .57, which is a great deal higher than what we usually see between measures of infant performance and later IQ.

This study and others like it (Lewis & Brooks-Gunn, 1981; Kopp &

Vaughn, 1982) at least raise the possibility that there may be basic in-formation-processing capacities that underlie what I have called "cog-nitive power" and that we may be able to identify those capacities in young infants. That does not mean that IQ is based entirely on the abil-ity to recognize familiar things. But it may mean that such recognition makes it easier to develop more complex strategies later on.

## Summing It Up

The information-processing approach is proving to be a very fruitful one. It seems clear from the research so far that children acquire new strategies in some fairly predictable sequence. But it appears to be a great mistake to think that the child "has" a particular strategy in some all-or-none fashion, just as it is a mistake to think that the child is "in" formal operations or concrete operations. Rather, the child first uses a particular strategy like rehearsal only in a few situations and easily forgets to apply it to new problems. Gradually, each new strategy is used more and more broadly. Development, then, involves acquiring new and more powerful ways of handling information, but it also involves a broader and broader generalization of those tech-niques.

Interestingly, many of the new strategies seem to be first visible in the 4- to 6- or 5- to 7-year period that Piaget saw as so critical. So there *is* something significant happening at about that age. But the new skills are still pretty specific, pretty isolated. It isn't until adolescence, really, that the child becomes fully aware of the techniques she has at her disposal and can *plan* the best strategy for solving any particular problem.

However, I do not want to leave you with the impression tht the information-processing approach is the ultimate theory in cognitive development. It is not. There are still *many* questions to be an-swered—including that troublesome "why." Why do children develop new strategies? Why do they give up earlier, less-efficient ones and figure out more general or more powerful ways of doing business? Piaget's notions of adaptation and equilibration are still useful for an-swering questions like these. We also need to understand much more fully just what the link is between information processing and cogni-tive power. There are certainly plenty of questions left for the next generation of developmental psychologists (like some of you) to an-swer.

## SUMMARY

1. The study of cognitive power does not tell us what we need to know about the shared changes in the *way* children think about the world around them. Piaget's studies of cognitive structure fill that gap.

2. Based on Piaget's ideas, most current researchers in the area of cognitive development would agree on basic assumptions that emphasize the child's active role in development and the sequential changes in her strategies for interacting with her environment.
3. The stages of development Piaget proposed are:
   a. Sensorimotor period, from birth to age 2, when the child moves from reflexive to intentional behavior. Current work places the development of internal representation earlier in this period than Piaget thought.
   b. Preoperational period, age 2 to age 6, when the child develops beginning forms of reasoning and classification and shows some primitive ability to see things from others' perspectives. Current work on children in this age range shows earlier signs of complex thought than Piaget had suggested.
   c. Concrete operations, age 6 to age 12, when the child acquires powerful new mental tools, called operations, such as addition, subtraction, multiplication, and serial ordering. Current work on this age period shows that these operations are applied less broadly by children than Piaget thought.
   d. Formal operations, age 12 and up, when the young person becomes able to manipulate *ideas* as well as objects and can approach problems systematically. Deductive logic appears. Unlike earlier stages, which virtually all children achieve, formal operations are achieved by only perhaps half of adolescents.
4. Although this sequence is a fairly good general description, Piaget's theory suffers from significant problems, most notably the fact that children are not consistent in their performance on tasks that appear to demand the same levels of cognitive skill.
5. Piaget's theory has had some effect on educational practices; but the application is more difficult than it appears to be, and the verdict is still not in on the question of the impact of Piagetian educational programs on the development of cognitive skills.
6. The apparent validity of *sequences* of development but the relative failure of the *stage* concept has been one force pushing psychologists toward a broader, "information-processing" approach to cognitive development.
7. Information-processing theorists describe development as a process of acquiring, and broadening the use of, basic strategies for remembering and organizing information and solving problems. For example, rehearsal as a memory strategy is used spontaneously by 7- and 8-years olds but is only used after a prompt by 5-year-olds.
8. Information-processing theory also offers some possibility of blending the cognitive power approach characteristic of IQ tests with descriptions of changes in cognitive structure or strategies, since the rate of acquisition of strategies or the breadth of their generalization may be an aspect of what is measured on an IQ test.

**Accommodation** The process hypothesized by Piaget by which a person adapts existing structures—actions, ideas, or strategies—to fit new experiences.

**Assimilation** The process of taking in a new experience or new information and adjusting it to fit existing structures. A cornerstone concept in Piaget's theory.

**Class inclusion** The relationship between classes in which a subordinate class is included in a superordinate class, as bananas are part of the class "fruit."

**Concrete operations** The stage of development proposed by Piaget for the ages 6 to 12, in which mental operations such as subtraction, reversibility, and multiple classification are acquired.

**Conservation** The concept that objects remain the same in fundamental ways, such as weight or number, even when there are external changes in shape or arrangement. The concept is achieved by children from 5 to 10 years of age.

**Deductive logic** Reasoning from the general to the particular, from a rule to an expected instance, or from a theory to a hypothesis. Characteristic of formal operational thought.

**Egocentrism** In Piaget's theory, the notion that children can see events only from their own points of view; the inability to take the perspective of another person.

**Formal operations** Piaget's name for the fourth and final major stage of cognitive development, occurring during adolescence, when the child becomes able to manipulate and organize ideas as well as objects.

**Horizontal decalage** Piaget's term for the in-

consistency of a child's performance across several similar tasks.

**Inductive logic** Reasoning from the particular to the general, from experience to broad rules. Characteristic of concrete operational thinking.

**Information processing** A way of looking at cognitive development that emphasizes acquisition of basic strategies for remembering and analyzing information or solving problems.

**Operation** Term used by Piaget for complex, internal, abstract, reversible schemes, first seen at about age 6.

**Organization** One of the two basic processes of human functioning, along with adaptation, proposed by Piaget.

**Preoperational stage** Piaget's term for the second major stage of cognitive development, from ages 2 to 6, during which the child develops basic classification and logical abilities.

**Production deficiency** A phrase used to describe a point at which a child *can* use some helpful strategy if reminded but does not do so spontaneously.

**Reversibility** In Piaget's theory, the understanding that physical and mental actions can be reversed (undone), such as subtracting after adding, thus returning one to the original starting position.

**Sensorimotor stage** Piaget's term for the first major stage of cognitive development, from birth to about 2 years, when the child moves from reflexive to voluntary action.

**Transductive reasoning** Reasoning from the specific to the specific; assuming that when two things happen together, one is the cause of the other.

Flavell, J. H. *Cognitive development.* Englewood Cliffs, N.J.: Prentice-Hall, 1977.
This is a first-rate basic text in the field, written by one of the major current figures in cognitive-developmental theory. Flavell has a fairly easy, anecdotal style, although the

book gets technical in places. A very good next source.
Furth, H. *Piaget for teachers.* Englewood Cliffs, N.J.: Prentice-Hall, 1970.
Not a new book, but an excellent discussion of the application of Piaget's theory to edu-

cation, written as a series of letters to teachers.

Piaget, J. Development and learning. In R. Ripple & V. Rockcastle (Eds.), *Piaget rediscovered.* Ithaca, N.Y.: Cornell University Press, 1964. Reprinted in C. S. Lavatelli & F. Stendler (Eds.), *Readings in child behavior and development* (3d ed.). New York: Harcourt Brace Jovanovich, 1972.

This relatively brief paper is one of the clearest and most "chatty" of Piaget's writings. It presumes that you know something about his terminology, so it is not really easy; but it is an excellent place to read about his view

regarding the role of maturation and experience in cognitive development.

Siegler, R. S., & Richards, D. D. The development of intelligence. In R. J. Sternberg (Ed.), *Handbook of human intelligence.* Cambridge, England: Cambridge University Press, 1982.

This is not at all an easy paper, but it is the best "introductory" description I can find of the information-processing approach to cognitive development. Happily, it also includes excellent discussions of the Piagetian view and the traditional IQ-measurement approaches.

PROJECT 7.1

# *The Game of 20 Questions*

*GENERAL INSTRUCTIONS*

The first step is to locate a child between the ages of 5 and 10. Tell the parents that you want to play some simple games with the child as part of a school project, reassuring them that you are not "testing" the child. Obtain their permission, describing the games and tasks if you are asked to do so.

Arrange a time to be alone with the child if at all possible. Having the mother, father, or siblings there can be extremely distracting, both for the child and for you.

Come prepared with the equipment you will need. Tell the child that you have some games you would like to play. Play with the child for a while to establish some kind of rapport before you begin your experimenting. At the appropriate moment, introduce your "game."

*THE TASK*

"I am thinking of something in this room, and your job is to figure out what I am thinking of. To do this, you can ask any question at all that I can answer by saying 'yes' or 'no,' but I can't give you any other answer but 'yes' or 'no.' You can ask as many questions as you need to, but try to find out in as few questions as you can."

Choose the door to the room as the answer to your first game. (If there is more than one door, select one particular door as correct; if there is no door, use a particular window.) If the child asks questions that cannot be answered "yes" or "no," remind her or him that you can't answer that kind of question and restate the kind of question that can be asked. Allow the child as many questions as needed (more than 20 if necessary). Write down each question verbatim. When the child has reached the correct answer, praise her and then say, "Let's try another one. I'll try to make it harder this time. I'm thinking of something in the room again. Remember, you ask me questions that I can answer 'yes' or 'no.' You can ask as many questions as you need, but try to find out in as few questions as possible."

Use your pencil or pen as the correct answer this time. After the child has solved the problem, praise him or her. If the child has not been successful, find something to praise. ("You asked some good questions, but it's a really hard problem, isn't it?") When you are satisfied that the child's motivation is still reasonably high, continue. "Now we're going to play another question-asking game. In this game, I will tell you something that happened, and your job will be to find out how it happened by asking me questions I can answer 'yes' or 'no.' Here's what happened: A man is driving down the road in his car; the car goes off the road and hits a tree. You have to find out how it happened by the way I answer questions you ask me about it. But I can only answer 'yes' or 'no.' Try to find out the answer in as few questions as possible. Remember, here's what happened: A man is driving down the road in his car; the car goes off the road and hits a tree. Find out how it happened."

If the child asks questions that cannot be answered "yes" or "no," remind him or her that you cannot answer that kind of question and that you can only answer "yes" or "no." If the child can't figure out the answer, urge her or him to try until you are persuaded that you are creating frustration, at which point you should quit with lots of positive statements. The answer to the problem is that it had been raining, the car skidded on a curve, went off the road, and hit the tree.

*SCORING*

Score each question asked by the child on each of the three problems as belonging to one of two categories:

1. *Hypothesis.* A hypothesis is essentially a guess that applies to only one alternative. A "yes" answer to a hypothesis solves the problem; with a "no" answer, all that has been accomplished is to eliminate one possibility. In the first two problems, a hypothesis would be any question that applied to only one alternative, only one object in the room—for example, "Is it your hair?" or "Is it the picture?" In the third problem, a hypothesis would be any question that covers only one alternative: "Did the man get stung in the eye by a bee?" "Did he have a heart attack?" "Was there a big snowbank in the middle of the road that the car ran into and then skidded?"

2. *Constraint.* A constraint question covers at least two possibilities, often many more. A "yes" answer to a constraint question must be followed up. ("Is it a toy?" "Yes." "Is it the truck?") A "no" answer to a constraint question allows the questioner to eliminate a whole class of possibilities. On the first two problems, any of the following

would be constraints: "Is it in that half of the room?" "Is it something big?" "Is it a toy?" "Is it something red?" (assuming there is more than one red thing in the room). For the third problem, any of the following (or equivalent) would be constraints: "Was there something wrong with the car?" "Was the weather bad?" "Did something happen to the man?"

*DATA AND ANALYSIS*

For your own analysis or for an assignment to be turned in to a course instructor, you should examine at least the following aspects:

1. How many questions did the child ask for each problem?
2. On each problem, how many were hypotheses and how many were constraints?
3. Did the child do better (ask more constraints) on the "concrete operations" problems (the first two) than on the "formal operations" problem (the story)? Or was the performance the same on both?
4. Is the child's overall performance on this task generally consistent with the findings from Mosher and Hornsby's (1966) study? Does your subject behave in a way that would be expected on the basis of his or her age? If not, what explanation can you offer?

# 8.

# the development of language in children

A friend of mine listened one morning at breakfast while her 6-year-old and her 3-year-old had the following conversation about the relative dangers of forgetting to feed the goldfish versus overfeeding the goldfish:

*6-year-old:* It's worse to forget to feed them.
*3-year-old:* No, it's badder to feed them too much.
*6-year-old:* You don't say badder, you say worser.
*3-year-old:* But it's baddest to give them too much food.
*6-year-old:* No it's not. It's worsest to forget to feed them.

Young children's language is delightful. It is full of inventive constructions and wonderful "mistakes" like *baddest* or *worsest*. It reflects the fascinating logic of the preoperational child, too: "Bees eat bruises because people don't want them," or "The moon has melted! Did the wind blow it away?" Aside from the "poetry" of this early language, perhaps the most astonishing thing about it is how fast it changes. An 8-month-old is making sounds like *kikiki* or *dadada*. By 18 months the child will probably be using 30 or 40 separate words, and by 3 years children construct long and complex sentences, like those of the 3-year-old in the conversation about the goldfish.

From the beginning, children's language is *complex, abstract, creative,* and *rule-governed.* It is abstract in the sense that nearly all the individual words describe classes or categories of things rather than individual instances; it is creative in the sense that the child regularly combines words into patterns he has never heard; it is rule-governed in the sense that even the first two-word "sentences" follow certain rules. My friend's children were trying to apply the rules for creating superlatives and just happened to hit on an irregular version of that rule. But the fact that they were creating words that followed a logical pattern (even though by adult standards they were "wrong") shows that they were operating with a rule.

For psychologists, the puzzle is to explain how this complex, abstract process can occur in a 2- or 3-year-old, whose thinking is otherwise quite limited in abstractness, as I pointed out in the last chapter. We also need to figure out how the process comes to happen so similarly in widely varying environments.

In attempting to solve these mysteries, I'll follow my usual plan and begin with some answers to the "what" questions and turn later to attempts to answer the "why" questions.

The vast majority of the research on language development in the past two decades has focused on describing two aspects of structural change: changes in the *form* or grammar of sentences (which the linguists call **syntax**) and changes in word meaning (called **semantics**). I'm going to explore each of these in turn, but you should be forewarned that the distinction between the two has become fuzzier and fuzzier.

The forms of sentences are not independent of the meaning, and children do not learn them separately, either. But it will be a bit clearer for you if I keep them somewhat separated initially.

## WHAT IS LANGUAGE ANYWAY?

Let me begin at the beginning. What do we mean by language? Roger Brown has defined language as an arbitrary system of symbols

> which taken together make it possible for a creature with limited powers of discrimination and a limited memory to transmit and understand an infinite variety of messages and to do this in spite of noise and distraction. (Brown, 1965, p. 246)

The critical element in this definition is the phrase "infinite variety of messages." Language is not just a collection of sounds. Very young babies make several different sounds, but we do not consider that they are using language. Chimpanzees and other primates have "vocabularies" of sounds, each used in a particular situation. But they apparently do not *combine* the individual sounds into different orders to create new and different meanings.

There is presently a fairly hot debate among linguists about whether primates can be taught to use words or symbols in this creative way (Gardner & Gardner, 1980; Scanlon, Savage-Rumbaugh, & Rumbaugh, 1982; Terrace et al., 1980). They can, apparently, learn to use gestures (sign language) or geometric symbols in novel combinations to obtain things to eat or to play with. But it is not clear that they are really showing internal representation the way a child does. Whatever the outcome of this argument, we do know that humans use language creatively. Virtually all children, without special training other than exposure to language, develop complex and skillful language use within the first three to four years of life. Even deaf children can learn a "language" in Brown's sense of the word, since gestural languages like American Sign Language involve arbitrary symbols combined in creative, rule-governed ways. (More about deaf children's language later in Box 8.2.)

## THE DEVELOPMENT OF GRAMMAR IN CHILDREN

### Before the First Word

The sounds a child makes before 10 months or 1 year, when she speaks her first words, are really not language at all. Linguists (e.g., Dale, 1976) usually call this the **prelinguistic phase**. Within this period, however, there are several recognizable stages or steps that appear to occur in the same order in virtually all children (Kaplan & Kaplan,

**Figure 8.1** Chimps like Nim can learn individual signs or symbols for words quite easily. In this picture, Nim is signing the word *ears*. What linguists do not agree on is whether chimps or other primates can create new strings of signs or symbols to convey new meanings. (*Source:* Terrace, 1979.)

1971). The rate of progression through these steps varies from one baby to another, but the sequence seems to be consistent.

*Crying* From birth to about 1 month of age, just about the only sound an infant makes is a cry. As I pointed out in Chapter 3, crying helps to improve lung capacity and cardiovascular development (crying is the baby's aerobic exercise!), and it signals to the caregivers that the baby is in need. Infants seem to have several different cries to signal different kinds of discomfort or problems, and many parents become quite skilled in "reading" these cries to diagnose the baby's particular need at that moment. I also mentioned in Chapter 3 that sick or low–birth-weight babies or those rated as having "difficult" temperaments are likely to have more unpleasant or grating crying sounds. So the quality of the child's cry may turn out to be a helpful diagnostic tool for physicians or parents.

*Cooing* Starting at about 1 month, the baby begins to add some non-crying sounds to his repertoire, particularly vowel sounds like *uuuuuu*. For obvious reasons, this is called **cooing**. Sounds like this are usually signals of pleasure in babies—and delight parents as well.

*Babbling* By about 6 months the infant begins to use a much wider range of sounds, including a lot of what we would call consonants, such as *k* and *g*. Frequently, the baby combines a consonant sound with a vowel sound to produce a kind of syllable, such as *ba* or *gi* or *da* (a sound much loved by fathers!). Linguists call this kind of sound combination **babbling**. Interestingly, babies of this age in many different cultures (hearing many different languages) all seem to babble the same kinds of sounds (Oller, 1981), even though this means that they may be babbling sounds they have not heard someone around them make. But toward the end of the first year, at about 10 to 12 months, babies begin to babble more and more the sounds in the specific language they are hearing.

At about this same point (10 to 12 months), the babbling takes on a new feature: The baby frequently repeats particular syllables over and over, such as *dadadadada* or *gigigigigi*. This endlessly repetitive game is called **echolalia**: The child repeats (echoes) his own sounds and sounds made by others, apparently for his own pleasure.

One of the particularly fascinating aspects of this phase is that the child's sounds begin to take on some of the *intonational* patterns of adult speech. The baby may use rising inflections at the end of strings of sounds or use a speechlike rhythm, even though he is still babbling seemingly meaningless sounds.

### The First Words

Somewhere in the midst of all the babbling, the first words appear. The baby's first word is an event that parents eagerly await, but it's easy to miss. A *word,* as linguists define it, is any sound or set of sounds that

**Figure 8.2** Echolalia strikes again! (*Source:* Johnston, 1978, p. 8.)

is used with a consistent referent. But it can be *any* sound. It doesn't have to be a sound that matches words the adults are using. One little girl, named Brenda, studied by Ronald Scollon (1976), used the sound *nene* as one of her first words. It seemed to mean primarily liquid food, since she used it for milk, juice, and bottle. But she also used it to refer to mother and sleep. (You can see some of Brenda's other early words in the left-hand column of Table 8.1.)

Brenda's early vocabulary illustrates the two ways in which young children seem to use their first words. Some of the time they use words merely to label objects, such as cookie or doll. But a lot of the time they use a single word to convey an entire sentence of meaning, something linguists call **holophrases**. The combination of the word, gestures, intonation, and context tell the listener what the child means. Parents usually become very skillful at decoding these meanings.

*Adding New Words*    Once the milestone of the first word is reached, toddlers go through a period of slow vocabulary growth. Katherine Nelson (1973) found that it typically took three to four months for a child to add the next 10 words. But past the 10-word point, there was usually a very rapid increase in vocabulary, with a new word added every few days. Eighteen-month-old children typically have vocabularies of 40 to 50 words, and by 24 months the average is nearly 300 words. To give you some sense of this change, I've listed Brenda's vocabulary at 19 months on the right-hand side of Table 8.1. Obviously, there has been a huge change in just five months.

*Kinds of New Words*    The early words in children's vocabularies are most likely to be what Katherine Nelson (1973) calls *general nomi-*

Table 8.1
**Brenda's vocabulary at 14 and 19 months**

| 14 Months | 19 Months[a] | | |
|---|---|---|---|
| aw u (I want, I don't want) | baby | nice | boat |
| nau (no) | bear | orange | bone |
| d di (daddy, baby) | bed | pencil | checkers |
| d yu (down, doll) | big | write | corder |
| nene (liquid food) | blu (pu) | paper | cut |
| e (yes) | Brenda | pen | I do |
| maem (solid food)  . | cookie (kuki) | see | met |
| ada (another, other) | daddy | shoe | Pogo |
|  | eat | sick | Ralph |
|  | at | swim | you too |
|  | (hor)sie | tape | climb |
|  | mama | walk | jump |
|  | mommy | wowow | |

*Source:* Scollon, 1976, pp. 47 and 57–58.
[a]Brenda did not actually pronounce all these words the way an adult would; I have given the adult version, since that is easier to read.

*nals*—names for classes of objects or people, like *ball, car, milk, doggie, he,* or *that.* Over half the first 50 words of the eight children she studied were of this type (which we would normally call nouns), while only 13 percent were action words. Dedre Gentner (1982) has observed the same thing in her study of a little boy named Tad, whose early words are listed in Table 8.2. The pattern of nouns-before-verbs seems to be a robust one. Not only does the same order of early words hold in every language in which it has been studied—including Japanese, Mandarin Chinese, German, English, and Turkish (Gentner, 1982)—but children also *understand* words for things before they understand words for actions (Goldin-Meadow, Seligman, & Gelman, 1976). (In fact, of course, children generally understand a good deal more than they can say, and this is particularly true at this early point of development. Linguists generally label these two forms of language **receptive language** and **expressive language**.)

## The First Sentences

Interesting as these first words are (to parents as well as linguists), most of us are much more fascinated by the child's growing ability to string words into combinations—that is, to create sentences. The first two-word sentences usually appear at about 18 months (in fact, you can see two examples in the list of Brenda's 19-month vocabulary). For some months after this, the child continues to use single words as well

Table 8.2

**Words learned by Tad from 11 to 21 months of age**

| Age | Nominals ("Nouns") | | Predicates ("Verbs") | Expressive Words | Indeterminate Words |
|---|---|---|---|---|---|
| 11–16 mo. | dog<br>duck<br>daddy<br>mama | teh (teddy bear)<br>dipe (diaper)<br>car<br>owl | keys<br>cheese<br>eye | yuk | toot toot |
| 18–19 mo. | cow<br>cup<br>spoon<br>apple<br>knee<br>ball<br>jeep | truck<br>juice<br>bowl<br>teeth<br>elbow<br>block | kitty<br>bottle<br>towel<br>cheek<br>map<br>bus | hot<br>happy<br>down<br>up | oops<br>boo<br>hi<br>bye<br>uh oh | bath<br>pee pee<br>TV |
| 21 mo. | toe<br>moon<br>bird<br>water | happy sauce<br>bee<br>pole<br>cookie | tree<br>wheel<br>peach | stuck<br>off<br>down<br>out | | back (piggyback ride) |
| Percentage: | 68 | | 15 | 8 | 8 |

*Source:* Gentner, 1982, adapted from Table 11.1, p. 306.

as two-word sentences. Eventually, the one-word utterances drop out almost completely, and the child begins to use three- and four-word sentences and to create more complex combinations of words.

Following the lead of Roger Brown (1973a, 1973b), most linguists divide the developmental progression of these more complex grammatical forms into several stages. Each stage is defined by the average number of words (the **mean length of utterance**, or MLU in linguists' terminology) included in the child's sentences and by the complexity of the forms used.

*Stage 1 Grammar*    There are several distinguishing features of the earliest, stage 1 sentences: They are *short*—generally two or three words—and they are *simple.* Nouns, verbs, and adjectives are usually included, but virtually all the purely grammatical markers (which linguists call **inflections**) are missing. Children in stage 1 of grammatical development do not use the *s* for plurals or put the *ed* ending on verbs to make the past tense, nor do they use the *'s* of the possessive or auxiliary verbs like *am* or *is* or *do.*

Because only the really critical words are present in these early sentences, Roger Brown (Brown & Bellugi, 1964; Brown, 1973b) describes this as **telegraphic speech**. The child's language is rather like what we use when we send a telegram. We keep in all the essential words—usually nouns, verbs, and modifiers—and leave out all the prepositions, auxiliary verbs, and the like.

Children's imitations of adults' speech as well as their own spontaneous speech is telegraphic. If you ask a child of 20 to 24 months to say "I am playing with the dogs," the child is likely to say "Play dog" or "I play dog," thus omitting the auxiliary verb *(am),* the verb ending *(ing),* the preposition *(with),* the article *(the),* and the plural ending *(s).*

As was true earlier, children displaying stage 1 grammar understand a good deal more than they say. Kenneth Roberts (1983), for example, found that 2-year-olds can respond accurately to requests to kiss or hug or tickle another child or adult before they can use these verbs in sentences.

*The Grammar of Early Sentences*    Despite these limitations, it is important to understand that this earliest language is nonetheless *creative.* Just as you can create totally new sentences following the rules of adult grammar, so the very young child seems to construct totally new sentences as well, following another set of rules.

In the early days of studies of grammar in children—in the 1960s particularly—there was a good deal of enthusiasm for the idea that we could write a "grammar" that would describe the rules that very young children use. There seemed to be two simple word classes, which Martin Braine (1963) called *pivot words* and *X words*. Pivot words seemed to be the key terms that children used with a whole lot of other words, like the word *allgone* in sentences like "Allgone shoe," "Allgone egg," or "Allgone vitamins" or the word *big* in "Big boat," "Big bus," and "Big boss." *X* words were used less frequently and were combined with the pivot words. Braine thought that in stage 1, children operated with basically one "grammatical rule": "Pick a pivot word and then select any *X* word to go with it."

Descriptions like Braine's were a big advance over early comparisons of children's language to adults', but it became clear very quickly that even stage 1 sentences were *far* more complex than Braine had thought. In fact, they are so complex that linguists have pretty much given up the effort to write "grammars" to describe them (Bates et al., 1982).

One of the things that makes the early grammar complex is that children convey many different *meanings* with exactly the same sentence forms. If we are going to understand this early language, we have to pay attention to semantics as well as to grammar. For example, young children frequently use a sentence made up of two nouns, such as "Mommy sock" or "Sweater chair" (to use some examples from Lois Bloom's 1973 analysis). In a simple grammar like the one Braine proposed, the word *mommy* would probably be considered a pivot word. But such a classification misses what the child was saying in some instances. The child in Bloom's study who said "Mommy sock" said it on two different occasions. The first time was when she picked up her mother's sock, and the second was when the mother put the child's own sock on the child's foot. In the first case, "Mommy sock" seems to mean mommy's sock (a possessive relationship). But in the second instance, the child seems to convey "Mommy is putting a sock on me," which is an *agent* (mommy)–*object* (sock) relationship.

In fact, from the earliest two-word sentences, the child appears to be able to express a series of different meaning relationships. He can express location, as in "Sweater chair"; possessive, as in "Mommy coat"; recurrence, as in "More milk"; and so on. In adult language each of these different relationships is expressed with different grammatical forms. Since the young child often uses the same kinds of word combinations to express these different meanings, it is easy to miss the complexity. But if you listen to the child's language in context and watch the gestures, you can see that the child is indeed expressing a rich array of meanings from the very earliest sentences.

Stage 1 continues for about a year or less, depending on the overall rate of the child's linguistic development. During this time the child's sentences get longer (the mean length of utterance, MLU, goes up), but they do not get significantly more complex.

*Stage 2 Grammar*   The beginning of stage 2 is largely defined by the appearance of much new complexity—by the addition of any of the grammatical inflections, such as plurals, past tenses, auxiliary verbs, prepositions, and the like. Children differ markedly in the age at which they arrive at this stage and in the rate at which they move through it, as shown in Figure 8.3. The three children represented in the figure were studied by Roger Brown over a period of years, and as you can see, they differed widely in their rates of language development. The horizontal line at 2.25 MLU represents the approximate point at which each child shifted from stage 1 to stage 2 grammar. Eve made this transition at about 21 months, while Adam and Sarah passed over this point at about 34 to 35 months. (Moral: do not panic if your child is still using simple two-word sentences at age 3.)

You can get a better feeling for the sound of the change from Table 8.3, which lists some of the sentences of a little boy named Daniel, re-

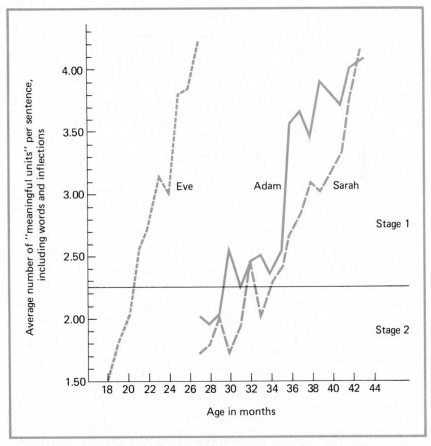

**Figure 8.3** This shows the rapidly increasing sentence length for three children studied longitudinally by Roger Brown and his colleagues. The division between stage 1 and stage 2 grammars occurs at about 2¼ words per sentence. As you can see, the pattern of change is very similar from one child to the next, but the ages at which the steps occurred differed markedly among the three children. (*Source:* Adapted from Brown, 1973, p. 55.)

corded by David Ingram (1981). The left-hand column lists some of Daniel's sentences at about 21 months of age, when he was still at stage 1; the right-hand column lists some of his sentences only 2½ months later (age 23 to 24 months), when he had just moved into stage 2.

Within stage 2 there are further regularities or sequences. The various grammatical inflections seem to appear in children's sentences in a fairly predictable order. Among English-speaking children, Brown (1973a) found that prepositions are added fairly early, as are plurals. Irregular verb endings also appear early (as in *went* and *saw*), while possessive forms such as *its* come later in the sequence. Stan Kuczaj (1979) has also recently found that, as a general rule, suffixes come before prefixes.

Another intriguing phenomenon of stage 2 grammar is **overregularization**, or overgeneralization. This is what the two little girls were doing in the conversation about the goldfish when they created new, "regularized" forms of superlatives *(badder, baddest, worser,* and *worsest)*. We can see the same thing in the use of past tenses as well. Children say "wented" or "goed" or "ated." Stan Kuczaj (1977, 1978) has

Table 8.3

**Examples of Daniel's stage 1 and stage 2 sentences**

| *Stage 1 Sentences (Age 21 Months)* | *Stage 2 Sentences (Age 23 Months)* |
| --- | --- |
| A bottle | A little boat |
| Broke-it | Cat there |
| Here (the) bottle | Doggies here |
| Hi daddy | Boat here |
| Horse doggie | Give you the book |
| Broke it | It's a boy |
| It a bottle | It's a robot |
| Kitty cat | It's cat |
| Oh a doggie | Little box there |
| Poor daddy | No book |
| Thank you | Oh cars |
| That hat? | Oh doggie |
| That monkey | Sit down |
| Want a bottle | This a bucket |
| Want bottle | That flowers |
| What that? | There's a boat there |
| | Those little boat |
| | What those? |
| | What's that? |
| | What this? |
| | Where going? |
| | Where the boat? |

*Source:* Ingram, 1981, adapted from Tables 6 and 7, pp. 344–345.

found that young children initially learn a small number of irregular past tenses and use them correctly for a short time. But then rather suddenly the child seems to discover the rule of adding *ed* and over-generalizes this rule to all verbs.

This type of "error," which is particularly common among children between the ages of 3 and 5, is wonderfully illustrated in a conversation of Christopher, the 4-year-old son of some friends. The children in Christopher's school had all seen the movie *The Wizard of Oz* the night before and were talking about it. Christopher's description of the story is very typical of language at this age:

> When Dorothy goed to her house and there was a tornado and it was pickin' up her house and then the wicked witch came and then her throwed fire at her cheeks. . . . And they came up and heard somethin' and the wicked old witch was standing on a house. Then her throwed fire way down at those guys. And they got dead. . . . A big lion came out and scared them and they didn't know what was happening. They they got to the Wizard of Oz castle and they goed on a big road. They goed on a little track. . . . They all saw the witch there. The witch goed right into the castle. Her zoomed right in. The witch landed on the tin man's hat. Her was a nice witch. The nice witch who was in a bubble landed right on his head.

It is important to emphasize the fact that this "error" only occurs be-cause the child is operating with a set of rules. If the child had no rules for forming words or sentences, we'd expect to see past tenses learned more or less one at a time, with the irregular forms used correctly at about the same rate as the regular forms. In fact, this "rule applica-tion" looks a great deal like many of the other cognitive strategies in the preschool child that I described in the last chapter.

There are also predictable sequences in the child's developing use of questions, negatives, or even passive sentences (e.g., "The wagon is pulled by the boy"). In each case, the child seems to go through periods when he creates types of sentences that he has not heard adults use but that are consistent with the particular set of rules he seems to be following. For example, in the development of questions, there is a point at which the child gets a *wh* word *(who, what, when, where, why)* at the front end of a sentence but doesn't yet have the auxiliary verb put in the right place, such as: "Why it is resting now?" Similarly, in the development of negatives, there is a stage in which the *not* or *n't* or *no* is put in but the auxiliary verb is omitted, as in "I not crying" or "There no squirrels."

Linguists have also begun to trace the order in which children begin using specific words. For example, Lois Bloom and her colleagues (Bloom, Merkin, & Wootten, 1982) listened regularly to one group of

BOX 8.1

# LEARNING TWO LANGUAGES: BILINGUAL CHILDREN

Not long ago I spent the evening with a group of parents of infants to answer some questions about day care and normal development. In one of the couples, the father was a native speaker of Lithuanian and wanted to know if he should try to teach his son Lithuanian along with English. This is an unusual combination of languages, but the question is relevant for a great many parents who may speak more than one language between them. If you want your child to grow up speaking both languages, how should you go about it? Will it have a detrimental effect? Language theorists have also been interested in these early bilingual children because of what they might tell us about the normal process of language development.

A related set of questions faces our school systems (and employers). In nearly every country there are some groups of children whose families speak a different language at home than the language used in the school. When these children reach school, they have to learn a second language. This has been the case for many Spanish-speaking children in parts of the United States, as well as other minority groups. Until recently, it was also frequently the case for French-speaking children in Canada. Educators have had to grapple with the task of teaching children a second language.

Despite these interests, there isn't a great deal of research on bilingual children. But let me summarize what we think we know at this stage.

There is both good news and bad news about children raised with two or more equal languages. On the negative side, their early language development seems to be a bit slower. It takes them longer to get to, and through, stage 1 grammar, for example. It seems to be easier for the child if the two languages are consistently spoken by *different* people, which helps the child to discriminate between the two, but if you speak two languages to your child, you should expect that the child will simply be slower in the early stages.

The good news is that such children seem to understand quite early that there is a distinction between a word and its meaning. Since a child learning French and English, for example,

seven children from age 2 to age 3 and found that there was a common order for using *wh* words: *where, what,* and *who* were used earliest (at about 2), followed by *how* and *why.* Questions using *which* or *when* were extremely rare, even at age 3.

This series of changes is delightful to listen to. But the changes are important, too, for theorists, who are impressed with the fact that the child creates sentences he could not have heard but that make excellent sense within the rules of his own grammar.

Incidentally, all of what I've said so far describes what happens when a child learns a single language. But what about children who are exposed to two or more languages from the beginning? How confusing is this for a child? And how can parents ease the process? I've discussed the problems of bilingual children in Box 8.1.

learns two words for dog *(dog* and *chien)*, he works out pretty early that a given meaning can be expressed several ways (Ianco-Worrall, 1972). This is a rather advanced concept and may aid the child's overall rate of cognitive growth.

Dan Slobin (1978) observed this process in his daughter Heida, who lived in Europe with her family from about age 2½. By age 3, she was asking for the words in other languages: "What does bread mean in German?" Sometimes she would even ask, in English, for the English translation, as in "What is spoon called in English?" It is as if she had understood that she was hearing several languages but did not realize that she herself spoke one of them (another example of egocentrism).

Perhaps because of this early understanding of the arbitrariness of words, and despite their slower language start, bilingual children do as well as or better than monolingual children on most IQ and other cognitive tests at school age (Segalowitz, 1981). Given this information, if I were in a position to raise a child with two languages, I would certainly do so. It helps to have as much separation between the two languages as possible—different people speaking them or different places in which they are spoken. But even without this, the child will eventually learn both and appears to benefit from the richness. In addition, of course, the child ends up with the wonderfully flexible skill of bilingualism.

Children learning the second language at school age or a bit earlier face a different problem, particularly if they must be taught in the second language. These children find the early grades in school very tough going indeed, and many of them never catch up later. Nicholas Anastasiow and Michael Hanes (1976) argue for two strategies in dealing with schoolchildren for whom English is a second language:

(1) Delay the teaching of reading until the child has mastered English, or preferably (2) teach the child to read [in his first language] and after the third or fourth grade switch to English. (Anastasiow and Hanes, 1976, p. 144)

Many school systems, faced with the need for bilingual education, have opted for the second strategy. They provide instruction in the child's native language while simultaneously teaching English as a second language. The results are not all in on this procedure, but given what we know about reading and about language development, it seems like a sensible option.

## Later Language Development

By age 5 or 6, a child's language is remarkably like that of an adult. She can construct most kinds of complex sentences and can understand most. Despite this excellent skill, however, there are some specific kinds of "errors" that still occur and some systematic changes that take place over the elementary school period. For example, children of 5 or 6 have difficulty with passive sentences (e.g., "The food is eaten by the cat"). They don't spontaneously produce many passive sentences at this age and have more difficulty understanding this construction than they do the active version of the same meaning ("The cat is eating the food"). Five- and 6-year-olds also still have some difficulty with "tag questions"—those questions we add on to the end of a declarative sentence to turn it into a question (e.g., "You can play the guitar, can't you?" or "They like Robert, don't they?"). Putting the correct tag onto a sentence is a fairly complex process, and children are not skilled at it until about age 8 or 9 (Dennis, Sugar, & Whitaker, 1982).

Obviously, language development does not end in first grade. Vocabulary continues to increase, and more complex sentence forms are learned later. But the really giant strides occur between 1 and 5 years of age, as the child moves from single words to complex questions, negatives, and commands.

## Overview of Grammatical Development

Let me pause for a brief summary of the key points about grammatical development before I move on to a discussion of word meaning.

1. Even children's earliest sentences show regularities and "rules." The rule system is not the same as for adult language but is nonetheless present in children's language.
2. The same rules seem to appear in children learning all sorts of different languages. We find something like a stage 1 grammar in children learning Russian or French or Japanese (Slobin, 1983).
3. The child's grammar changes gradually in a sequence that seems roughly the same for all children who have been studied. The *rate* of development varies, but the basic outline of the sequence seems to be shared, especially the early steps in the sequence.
4. Children's language is creative from the very beginning. The child is not just copying sentences he has heard; he is creating new ones according to the rules of his own grammar.

## THE DEVELOPMENT OF WORD MEANING IN CHILDREN

Although there is still some disagreement among linguists on the details of grammatical development, there is a great deal of agreement about the summary I have just given you. In the area of the development of word meaning, however, research is still in a much earlier stage, and both description and explanation are still in some dispute.

The questions that arise when you try to study the meanings children attach to their words overlap a great deal with what I've already said about cognitive development. Nearly all words describe or represent *classes* of things, so when we ask about children's word meanings, we are asking something about the kinds of classes they create.

If the child calls the family tabby a "cat," what other sorts of creatures or objects is the child likely to put into the same class, labeled with the same word? Are the early word categories very narrow, or are they extremely broad? Does the child generalize (extend the class) on the basis of the perceptual properties of the objects? For example, does he call all furry things or all four-legged things "cats"? Or does he generalize on the basis of what he can do with the object, such as "Cats are things you pet"? Answers to all these questions are still coming in, but let me take a look at some of the current ideas.

## Which Comes First, the Meaning or the Word?

The most fundamental question is whether the child learns a word to describe a category or class she has *already* created through her manipulations of the world around her (Nelson et al., 1977; Nelson, 1982) or whether she creates new cognitive categories to handle those things that are named with the same word (Clark, 1973). This may seem like a highly abstract argument, but it touches on the fundamental issue of the relationship between language and thought. Does the child learn to represent objects to herself *because* she now has language, or does language simply come along at about this point and make the representations easier?

The answer seems to be both (Greenberg & Kuczaj, 1982). In the early stages of language development, children seem to apply words (or even create words) to describe categories or classes they have already created in actions or images. Probably Brenda's word *nene,* which seemed to mean liquid food and the pleasure that goes with it, is an example of this. Put another way, in the early years concepts *precede* language in many instances. But it seems equally clear that children's classification systems are affected by the labels attached to objects, too. As Lev Vygotsky (a noted Russian psychologist) pointed out years ago (1962), there is a point somewhere in the child's second year when she "discovers" that objects have names. If children this age hear a strange word and see an unfamiliar object, they seem to figure out that the two go together (Kagan, 1981). In this way, the words help create new categories.

Another example would be a child who has never seen a horse and is taken to a county fair. He hears the word *horse* used several times, usually with mom or dad pointing at the large animal. The naming not only tells him that this creature is different from a dog, but when he sees several horses and hears the name applied, he begins to see the boundaries of the class.

In other words, the child's early thought shapes her language, but her later language shapes her thought as well.

## Extending the Class

Let me go back to the family tabby. Your 2-year-old is very likely to use the word *cat* correctly when referring to this animal. That certainly makes it easier for the child to talk to you, but it doesn't tell us much about the word meaning the child has developed. What does the word *cat* mean to the child? Does he think it is a name only for that *particular* fuzzy beast? Or does he think it applies to all furry creatures (in which case many dogs and perhaps sheep would be included in the category)? Does he think having a tail is a crucial feature? If so, then some breeds of cat that have no tails, like the Manx, might not be called "cats" by the child.

Our current information tells us that children *overextend* their early words more often than they *underextend* them, so we're more likely to hear the word *cat* applied to dogs or guinea pigs than we are to hear it used for just one animal or for a very small set of animals or objects. Some examples of the kind of overextensions that children create, collected by Eve Clark (1975), are shown in Table 8.4.

All children seem to show overextensions like these. But the particular classes the child creates are unique to each child. There doesn't seem to be any tendency for all children to use the word *cat* to apply to all four-footed animals or to all furry creatures or whatever. Each child overextends his words using his own distinct rules, and those rules change as the child's vocabulary grows.

Another way to look at the naming process is to realize that part of the child's problem is that she simply doesn't know many words. If she wants to talk about something, point out something, or ask for something, she has to use whatever words she has that are fairly close. So the child may appear to have quite broad or overextended categories when in fact she does not (Clark, 1977).

This possibility came back to me when I was recently in France, struggling with my highly primitive and rusty French. I spent most of one day trying to buy my mother a sweater. The problem was that

Table 8.4

**Examples of overextensions in the language of 1- and 2-year-old children**

| Word | Object or Event for Which the Word Was Originally Used | Other Objects or Events to Which the Word Was Later Applied |
|---|---|---|
| mooi | moon | cakes, round marks on windows, writing on windows and in books, round shapes in books, tooling on leather book covers, round postmarks, letter *O* |
| buti | ball | toy, radish, stone spheres at park entrance |
| sch | sound of train | all moving machines |
| em | worm | flies, ants, all small insects, heads of timothy grass |
| fafer | sound of trains | steaming coffeepot, anything that hissed or made a noise |
| va | white plush dog | muffler, cat, father's fur coat |

*Source:* Adapted from Eve V. Clark. Knowledge, context, and strategy in the acquisition of meaning. In *GURT 1975: Developmental Psycholinguistics: Theory and Applications.* Edited by Daniel P. Dato. Copyright 1975 by Georgetown University, Washington, D.C.; pp. 83 and 84.

I couldn't remember the word for sweater, so I used the closest word I did know, which was the word for blouse. Since I did remember the word for "wool," I started out asking for a "wool blouse," which created great amusement among the salespeople. It didn't take long before I was reduced to pointing, until I managed to pick up the word for sweater from the replies of the salespeople. It struck me that young children must often find themselves in a similar position—realizing that the word they are using is incorrect but simply not knowing the right word. As the child learns the words, the overextensions in the child's language begin to disappear.

Parents may actually contribute to a child's overextensions. Carolyn and Cynthia Mervis (1982) found that mothers give things labels that they think match the child's categories rather than using the more precise labels. So they may call leopards and lions "kitty cats" or a toy fire engine a "car." This may well aid communication between the mother and child, but it may also be one contributing factor in the child's "overextensions" of categories.

### Form versus Function: What Does the Child Attend To?

A third dispute among researchers studying the development of word meaning is whether the child initially creates categories based on what objects *look like* (form) or whether she bases her early classifications mostly on what you can *do with* the object (function).

Eve Clark (1973) originally took the first view, and if you go back and look at the overextensions in Table 8.4, this position makes a lot of sense. Children do seem to be basing their overextensions on the shape or sounds or textures of objects, all of which are *perceptual* qualities.

The second view has been proposed by Katherine Nelson (1973, 1982), who has been very much struck by the fact that the child's first words nearly always refer to objects that have particular functions or objects that the child can play with or move. The young child is more likely to learn the word *ball,* for example, than the word *sofa,* even though both are part of her world on a daily basis. But she *plays with* the ball and only *looks at* or sits on the sofa. Similarly, words that describe changes in state, like *dry* or *dirty,* are understood and spoken earlier by most children than are words that describe constant qualities, like *rough* or *square.*

Nelson concluded that children's concepts are most often organized around a "functional core"—a set of things that an object does or is. A ball *is* something round that rolls, bounces, and can be thrown. Extensions of this concept may be based on perceptual qualities, as Clark suggests. New round things may be labeled as balls, for example. But if the child discovers that the new round thing does not bounce, it would no longer belong in the same category.

As is so often true when two competing theories have been proposed, the evidence tells us that both theories are at least partially correct. Children's early word meanings seem to be based on both form and function. There is some indication, in fact, that what children do is to develop a sort of mental *prototype* (Greenberg & Kuczaj, 1982) and generalize to other examples based on how close the new instance is to the prototype. Adults do this, too. Think of a bird. Birds come in a very large variety of shapes, sizes, and colors. But probably when you first thought of a bird, a picture of a *particular* bird came to your mind. (If your prototype is anything like mine, probably something vaguely robinlike came to mind.) This is your prototype of a bird—a central example that "defines" the category for you. When you encounter some new creature that *might* be a bird, you compare it mentally to the prototype to see if it fits (Does it have wings? Does it have a beak? Does it have three toes?).

Children seem to do the same thing. Their early prototypes may be based on either form or function, and the prototype changes as the child has more experiences with instances and as the child learns new words for related categories. When the child learns the word *horse,* she stops calling horses "dogs" and develops a horse prototype as well as a dog prototype.

The whole process of developing word meanings is clearly complicated and seems to vary more from child to child than does the process of grammatical development. Obviously, what linguists are searching for are the rules that govern this process, so that we can understand how and why children use words the way they do. So far, a few general principles have emerged, but the study of semantics is still very much in the toddler stage.

## EXPLAINING LANGUAGE DEVELOPMENT

Since language is such a central aspect of human behavior, it has fascinated theorists as well as researchers. Obviously, any theory of language development must somehow account for the timing of the child's development of language, the regularity of the sequence, the form of early words, and all the other bits of evidence I've described to you. In fact, theorists from most of the major theoretical "types" I discussed in Chapter 1 have taken a crack at accounting for language.

### Early Ideas: Imitation and Reinforcement

*Imitation*   Probably your first idea about how a child learns language is that it is a process of imitation—an idea clearly consistent with social learning theory. Imitation obviously has to play *some* part, since the child does learn the language he is hearing and doesn't invent his own.

And imitation contributes to a child's learning of new words, too, when he copies the name for something first modeled by an adult (Leonard et al., 1983). In fact, recent evidence suggests that those babies who show the most imitation of actions and gestures in the first year of life are also the ones who later learn language more quickly, so the tendency to imitate may be an important ingredient in the process (Bates et al., 1982).

But if you think about all the facts I've given you about grammar and semantics, you can see that imitation just doesn't explain a lot of what actually happens. In particular, remember that children create types of sentences and forms of words that they have never heard. When a child regularizes the past tense and invents words like *goed* or *beated* or invents wonderful questions like "Why it can't turn off?" she is following her own grammatical rules, not imitating what she hears. Furthermore, when children do imitate adult sentences directly, they reduce them to a form that is like their own sentences.

The conclusion of linguists like Roger Brown (1973b) or David McNeil (1970), among many others, is that imitation plays some role in language development but that it is not the central process, no matter how much common sense says otherwise.

*Reinforcement*    A second possibility, also drawn from learning theory, is that children are *taught* language directly by their parents or others around them. B. F. Skinner, one of the major exponents of reinforcement theory, has attempted to apply the fundamental principles of learning to language (1957). He argued that adults around the child shape the child's first sounds into words, and then the words into sentences, by selectively reinforcing those that are understandable or "correct." When your child says "coo" while reaching for a cookie, and you say "No, say *cookie*" and withhold the cookie until the child says something close, you are shaping the child's language.

Although some parents do this sort of shaping occasionally, it is difficult to see how such a reinforcement view can account for the facts I have given you, particularly for the creative and rule-governed aspects of children's early language. Furthermore, when Roger Brown and his colleagues Courtney Cazden and Ursula Bellugi (1969) recorded actual exchanges between parents and children, they found that parents mostly responded to the "truth value" of their children's language rather than to grammatical correctness (Brown, Cazden, & Bellugi, 1969). As a general rule, parents seem to be remarkably accepting of children's language efforts. They try to interpret incomplete or primitive sentences and very rarely correct the child's grammar. Interestingly, there is one study by Katherine Nelson (1973) that shows that when parents are *not* accepting, when they systematically correct poor pronunciation of words and reward good pronunciation, their children develop vocabulary more *slowly.* Altogether, the whole process just doesn't sound much like shaping. In fact, the evidence for a reinforcement theory of language is so weak that this view has been widely discarded.

Before I cast the reinforcement explanations of language completely into outer darkness, however, I should note that shaping *is* used in programs designed to teach language to children whose language has been delayed for some reason, such as retarded children or those with a disorder known as autism. Such children may be taught both specific words and basic sentences through complex shaping programs (Lovaas, 1976), or they may be positively reinforced for speaking as part of a program to encourage greater language use (Reynolds & Risley, 1968). Such applications of reinforcement principles show that spoken language, like other behaviors, can be affected by basic reinforcement processes. But the vast majority of children do not require this kind of careful programming to learn language. Shaping or other kinds of reinforcement programs may thus be useful as back-up systems when the normal acquisition process fails, but they appear to play relatively small roles in the normal process.

### Linguistic Nativism: Innateness Theories

At the other end of the theoretical spectrum are theorists who take a "nativist" position very similar to the nativist position in perceptual development. Think back to what I said in Chapter 1 about maturation. Whenever we see a clear sequence of development that is shared by children in widely differing environments, it looks very much as if some physiological maturation may lie behind it. Early language development seems to meet both tests (sequences and consistency across cultures), so perhaps it is "built in" in some fashion. Noam Chomsky (1965, 1975) has been the theorist most strongly associated with this position. He argues that language is not learned; rather, it unfolds or emerges as part of the maturational process. Just as the maturation of physical skills such as walking requires a basic, supportive environment, so the maturation of language requires that the child hear language being spoken around him. The built-in mechanism, which David McNeill (1970) calls the **language acquisition device**, is not programmed especially for English or Swahili or Arabic. It is programmed for language in some more general sense—just as a computer program is designed to "read" certain kinds of input and analyze that input in specific ways. The particular language the child is hearing is passed through this system, and the child emerges with the appropriate set of rules for the language she hears and speaks.

*Transformational Grammar*   But what exactly could it be about language that is built into the "language acquisition device"? Chomsky argues that what is built in is **deep structure**. He proposes, in essence, that every sentence exists at two levels. The *meaning* of the sentence (i.e., what the person wants to say) is contained in the deep structure. That meaning is then transformed into **surface structure**, which is the sentence that we actually see or hear. The rules for turning basic meaning into sentences Chomsky calls transformational rules, and the whole system has come to be called **transformational grammar**.

Suppose, for example, that I have in my head a basic idea or meaning that is something like "I love chocolate." I can make this basic idea/meaning into many different kinds of sentences by using transformational rules. If I apply rules for forming questions, I can say something like "Do I love chocolate?" or "What do I love?" If I apply the rules for forming negations, I could say something (untrue) like "I do not love chocolate." I could even make it into a passive sentence, "Chocolate is loved by me."

Very young children, in Chomsky's view, have the same basic meanings to express but do not yet know the rules for transforming the meanings into sentences. But they are "programmed" (he thought) to attend to the language they hear in a way that will reveal the transformational rules.

If you think about the basic sequences of grammatical development I have already described, Chomsky's ideas make some sense. The earliest holophrases and two-word sentences seem to be very close to deep structure. The child uses a few words to convey whole meanings, and the adult listener fills in around the edges. As the child's language improves, what she seems to do is learn the transformational rules—the rules for turning those basic meanings into various kinds of complex sentences in the language she is hearing.

This approach can help to explain why children's language is rule-governed from the beginning and why we hear children create forms of sentences they have never heard. They are simply applying an incomplete set of transformational rules. When a child says "Why it can't turn off?" he is getting the *wh* word in the right place and has the negation rule in place but hasn't applied the rule that determines the location of the auxiliary verb. If we assume that children initially apply rules one at a time and then learn how to apply two or more at once, then a lot of what we hear children saying begins to make better sense.

In the late 1960s and early 1970s, this theory was enormously influential. Today, I think nearly all linguists would accept *some* innate predispositions as part of language development. Nonetheless, in its strong form, this theory has been superseded, just as reinforcement theory was before it. It does not tell us enough about exactly what it is that may be built in; it assumes more equivalence among children's early language attempts than seems to be true, and most important, it does not seem to place the child's own constructive activity in a prominent enough place in the system.

BOX 8.2

# LANGUAGE IN THE DEAF

Linguists have been interested in the language of deaf children for both practical and theoretical reasons. Can we use any of the information about basic language development to help the deaf child? And can the deaf child help us to understand the process of language development better? In particular, studies of the deaf have been used to address the question of a critical period in language development. Many deaf children do not learn any language during their early years. Does this interfere with their ability to learn language later? Does language *have* to be learned during the first few years for it to be acquired readily?

Let me tackle the practical and theoretical questions by beginning with a summary of what we know at this point about language in the deaf child.

1. The vast majority of deaf children (about 90 percent) are born to *hearing* parents and thus grow up in a world dominated by spoken language.
2. Most deaf children have major deficits in both spoken and written language. They have difficulty speaking; most do not lip-read well; and most read at only the most basic level. Hilde Schlesinger and Katheryn Meadow (1972), for example, found that the teenage deaf children in their study read at about the fourth-grade level.
3. Among the deaf, those with deaf parents usually do as well or *better* on measures of written and spoken language than do those with hearing parents (Liben, 1978).

It is this last fact that is the most surprising and that raises key practical and theoretical questions. Why would children raised by deaf parents have a better prognosis? Schlesinger and Meadow argue that the major reason is that these children are learning a language—in this case, sign language—at the normal time. Deaf parents use sign language with each other and with their children, so the children learn that language. And in their early use of signs, deaf children seem to go through the same stages as those we hear in the spoken language of hearing children. There is a kind of stage 1 grammar of signs, for example, and the inflections are added later, just as with spoken language.

This basic finding provides some support for the existence of a critical period in language development. Children who learn to sign are later able to learn spoken and written language fairly well. But deaf children who are not taught (or not allowed) to use signs when they are small and thus do not learn a language at the "normal" time have more difficulty later.

From the point of view of the parent of a deaf child, the message seems to be fairly clear: A combination of sign language and spoken language works well for the child and for the relationship between the child and the parent. Not only is the child exposed to a language at the normal time, but the child and parent can communicate with each other—something that is very difficult for the hearing parent who does not sign with a deaf child.

Not everyone who works with the deaf agrees with this conclusion. There are still those who argue for the "oral" method, particularly for elementary-age children, rather than the "total communication" method I am advocating here. But I find the evidence in favor of early signing persuasive.

## Cognition and Language: The Child's Role

Some "nativist" theorists talk about language as if it were developing all by itself, unconnected to anything else that is happening in the child or to the child. At first that made some sense, since the child's language seemed to be a whole lot more complex and abstract than his thinking. But as I pointed out in the last chapter, recent research shows us that 1- and 2-year-olds use more complex thought than we had supposed. And linguists' studies of early word meaning convinced them that language and thought were connected in important ways in the early years.

Piaget's theory, too, has had an important influence. He believed that language was merely one reflection of what was developing cognitively. If he is correct, we ought to find parallels between the speed or quality of the child's language development and his thinking in other areas, such as understanding object permanence or causal relationships. It begins to look as if that is *partly* true. For example:

Symbolic play (such as drinking from an empty cup, which I discussed in Box 7.1) and imitation of sounds or gestures both appear at about the same time as the child's first words. In children whose language is significantly delayed, both symbolic play and imitation are normally delayed, too (Snyder, 1978; Bates et al., 1982).

At about the point at which two-word sentences appear, we can also see children first begin to combine several gestures into a sequence in their pretend play (such as pouring imaginary liquid, drinking, then wiping the mouth). Among groups of children, those who first show this "sequencing" or "chunking" in their play are also the first to show two- or three-word sentences in their speech (Bates et al., 1982).

But not all aspects of cognitive development are linked to language. One notable nonconnection is that the child's understanding of object permanence (which I discussed in Chapter 5) is *not* related to her language development, which suggests that there may be a less generalized structure to the child's thought and language than Piaget hypothesized.

The moral seems to be that language is not merely unfolding in some maturationally determined way. The child's language also reflects, at least partially, broader understandings that he has developed through his interactions with the world. The connection is not perfect. Children's thinking and their language do not always match in complexity. But they match better than the "nativists" at first supposed.

This way of looking at language obviously places the child's own activity much more at the center of the process. But the child is not developing in a vacuum, either. People are *talking* to the child. Even though simple reinforcement and modeling theories don't seem to hold much water, it seems obvious that the richness or variety of language the child hears must make *some* difference. The search for such social bases of early language represents the other major thread in current theory.

## The Social World: What People Say to the Child

The basic idea is that some parents may make the child's language-learning job easier by talking often (thus providing "food" for the process), by using clear and understandable language, and possibly by emphasizing the critical features of the language, so that the child's attention is focused on the most relevant elements. It is still the child who is paying attention, listening, extracting regularities and meaning from the language she is hearing. But the amount and form of that language ought to make the job easier or harder. In fact, that seems to be true. Several elements of speech-to-the-child seem to matter.

*Talking to the Child*   It may seem a little silly to begin at this simple level, but it *does* matter how much adults around a child talk to him: Children who hear a lot of language develop vocabulary a little faster in the early years than those who are talked to less. In one study, Allison Clarke-Stewart (1973) observed and listened to a group of 36 infants and their mothers. You can see in Figure 8.4 that those mothers who talked to their children more in the early months of life had children who knew and used more words at 17 months. At the very least, we know that there is some *minimally sufficient* amount of exposure to language that is necessary for children to develop language at all. Beyond that minimal level, the effect is less clear, but it looks as if children who are exposed to more words, more different grammatical forms, may develop somewhat faster.

*Simpler Language to the Child*   Other than simply talking to the child, one of the most critical things that adults do that seems to aid the process of language development is to speak in very simple sentences to the child. Virtually all adults do this—apparently without a lot of conscious planning—when talking to young children. But since this simpler language is most often heard when mothers talk to their infants or toddlers, it has acquired the name of **motherese**.

Motherese has several key features (Snow & Ferguson, 1977; Schachter & Strage, 1982):

1. It is spoken in a higher-pitched voice and at a slower pace than is speech to adults, with clear pauses at the end of sentences (Jacobson et al., 1983).
2. The sentences are short and nearly always grammatical (unlike speech to adults, which is frequently ungrammatical).
3. The sentences are grammatically simple, with relatively few modifiers and few clauses. Mothers of 2-year-olds are more likely to say

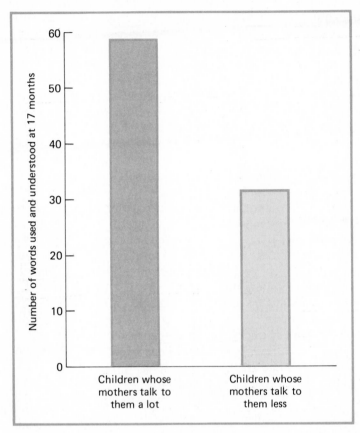

**Figure 8.4** Seventeen-month-old children whose mothers talked to them a lot had much larger vocabularies than children whose mothers talked to them less, which certainly shows that the "language environment" makes some difference for language development. (*Source:* K. A., Clarke-Stewart, 1973, p. 82. With permission of the Society for Research in Child Development, Inc.)

"Mrs. Smith was at the store today" than "I saw your preschool teacher, Mrs. Smith, when I went to the grocery store today."

4. It is highly repetitive. The adult tends to use the same sentences or minor variations of the same sentences over and over when talking to a young child (e.g., "Where is the ball? Can you see the ball? Where is the ball? There is the ball!"). The adult also repeats the child's sentences frequently—perhaps 10 percent of the time. Usually these are not perfect repetitions, but "expansions" or "recastings" of the child's sentence that turn the child's sentence into a more complete grammatical form. (If, for example, the child said "Mommy coat," the mother might say "Yes, that's mommy's coat.")

5. The vocabulary is concrete, nearly always referring to objects or people that are immediately present. The vocabulary is also limited; adults choose words they think the child will understand. In particular, when choosing nouns, adults are likely to pick the label for a category of intermediate generality, rather than either a specific term or a superordinate. For example, they will use the word *dog* rather than either *collie* or *animal* (Blewitt, 1983).

6. As the child's sentences become longer and more complex, the adults' language moves ahead slowly in length and complexity, always a notch or two ahead of the child (Phillips, 1973).

Obviously, mothers and fathers don't do all this in order to teach the child grammar. They do it in order to communicate with the child. But in fact, motherese may not only improve the child's understanding, it may also make the job of learning language a whole lot easier. The child hears simpler forms and hears them repeated and varied. She also hears her own simple sentences turned into more complex ones when the parent "expands" or "recasts" those sentences. It's hard to imagine that this doesn't help the child.

In the past few years, linguists have been hard at work trying to show that this sort of language is, in fact, an essential ingredient in the child's language development. It has turned out to be remarkably hard to study—partly because nearly every parent uses the same kind of motherese. But several researchers, most notably Keith Nelson (1977), have been able to show that special language stimulation can speed up the process. He worked with 2½-year-old children who were not yet spontaneously producing sentences such as negative *wh* questions (e.g., "Why doesn't it work?") or future tenses of verbs. He then gave the children five 1-hour training sessions over two months. In these sessions each child had either his questions or his verb forms "recast" by the adult—thereby giving the child a consistent model for these more complex forms. What Nelson found was that the children who heard the expanded questions showed rapid growth in their spontaneous use of questions, and those who heard complex verbs showed improvement in that area.

What this study demonstrates is that the speed with which children develop particular kinds of grammatical complexities may be very closely related to the ways in which adults speak to them. For parents, the morals seem to be fairly clear: Talk to your child early and often; use simpler language (which you'll do automatically anyway), but take opportunities to expand or recast the child's sentences into more complex forms, too, not to *correct* the child but merely to provide examples of the more adult version.

## A Combined View

I have described four different explanations of language development, each of which has some merit. But is there some way to combine them? I think so. Stan Kuczaj's formulation (1982) seems particularly helpful.

Language development appears to be influenced by three things: First, there are innate "organizing predispositions." I talked about apparently innate "scanning strategies" when I described perceptual development in Chapter 5. Newborns seem to be programmed to scan the edges of things and to look at movement. Piaget's sensorimotor schemes can also be thought of as "organizing predispositions." It seems equally logical to assume that there are built-in *listening* strategies, or "rules to listen by," such as attending more to the ends of strings of sounds (which would lead to attention to suffixes before prefixes, for example) or paying attention to the sequence of sounds.

A second critical influence is the *input,* the set of language experiences actually encountered by the child. A child who hears *no* language or only very limited language will not develop in the same way as does a child who encounters a rich array of sounds and sentences. Probably the particular pattern of language (such as repetitions and expansions) makes some difference, too.

The third crucial element is what the child *does* with the input. The child begins with strategies (rules), receives input (hears people talking), processes that sound according to her initial strategies, and then changes the strategies or "rules" to fit the new information. The result is a series of rules for understanding and creating language. Undoubtedly, this rule-making process is not unique to language. To some degree, very young children seem to develop broader strategies that are reflected in language. The strong similarities we see among children in their early language constructions come about both because all children share the same initial processing rules and because most children are exposed to very similar input from the people around them.

Obviously, what I've done in this summary is merely to combine pieces of three different theories. But even this, I am sure, is far too simple a view of what happens. If we know anything about development at all, it is that separate influences rarely just *add.* They combine and interact in important ways. What we need to understand now are the ways in which the child's "rules," his own processing of experience, and the quality of that experience interact to produce language. It is a tall order!

## INDIVIDUAL DIFFERENCES IN LANGUAGE DEVELOPMENT

### Differences in Rate of Language Development

I have said in a couple of places that although the sequence of language development is very similar from one child to the next, the rate of development varies a lot. (You can see this clearly in Figure 8.3, for example.) In other words, the *structure* may be similar, but the *power* differs. Let me hasten to add that the range of "normal" development is quite large, and the earliness of language is not strongly related to the eventual skill the child shows. Still, it is important to try to understand just where such differences in rate or in final skill may come from. As usual, we fall back on familiar explanations.

*Genetic Explanations*    One fairly obvious possibility is that the rate of language development may be something you inherit—in the same way that intelligence may be partially influenced by heredity. Certainly, if we assume that part of language is built into the brain, it makes sense to think that some children may inherit a more efficient built-in system than others.

Studies of language development in identical twins and fraternal twins (e.g., Munsinger & Douglass, 1976) do show that the final language skill at school age and adolescence is more strongly correlated among identical twins than among fraternal twins. That is, the language skill of identical twins is more equivalent than is the language skill of fraternal twins, which certainly shows that there may be an inherited element.

Studies of adopted children also point to some genetic influence. In the first year of life, children's language comprehension and production can be predicted better knowing the *natural* parents' cognitive ability than knowing the *adoptive* parents' skill (Hardy-Brown, Plomin, & De-Fries, 1981).

Unfortunately, we do not have any studies of language development in identical twins reared apart to help us sort out the effects of similar environments. But these first studies of the genetics of language development make it clear that we have to consider seriously the possibility that there may be an inherited element influencing both the rate of language development and the skill level finally achieved.

*Environmental Influences*    The other side of the coin is environmental influence. I have already pointed out that parents who talk to their children a lot have children with more rapid language development in the early years. This *could* be a disguised genetic effect: parents who have more language facility both talk to their children more and are more likely to pass on "good language" genes to them. But the language environment seems to be important by itself. In Karen Hardy-Brown's study of adopted children, the amount that the *adoptive* mother imitated the infant's vocalizations and the frequency of her "contingent vocal responses" to the baby were both related to the infant's language at age 1. Since this is the adoptive mother and not the natural mother, we can be sure that this is an effect of the environment and not a combination of heredity and environment.

As with IQ, it seems obvious that both the particular genes the child inherits and the environment provided for her contribute to the rate of language development the child shows.

## Differences in Style of Language Development

Differences in rate of development are fairly obvious and need explaining, but I find myself much more interested in differences in the way children use language and in the kinds of vocabulary they develop in the early stages. I've described one such difference in "style," **black English**, in Box 8.3. A broader look at style differences comes from Katherine Nelson (1981). She thinks there are two general "types" of early language learners: **expressive** and **referential**. I've summarized the differences in Table 8.5, but a few examples would probably help as well.

Children who use language referentially develop early vocabularies that consist primarily of names of individual objects—mostly "specific nominals," to use the terminology I introduced earlier. Their sentences tend to be short, and they don't seem to use language very much for social interactions with adults. In contrast, children who use language expressively seem to be focused much more on the communicative aspect of language. They also seem to learn more from imitation. Their early sentences often include whole "chunks" of adult sentences, spoken without any pauses or inflections, as if the word strings were single words. One child of 18 months that Nelson describes used the phrase *I-don't-know-where-it-is* in this way. If we look only at the complexity of the sentence, we might conclude that this child was in stage 2 grammar, but Nelson thinks not. Rather, the child has learned this "formula" as if it were a single word.

Most children use a mixture of these two "styles." But Nelson's observations suggest that some children seem to use primarily one mode or the other in their early language. In Nelson's studies, "referential" children were likely to come from families in which the mother did a lot of naming and used a lot more nouns than pronouns. So perhaps the child's style is basically imitative of the parents' style. Alternatively, it could reflect a more fundamental individual difference in chil-

---

Table 8.5

**Some differences between "expressive" and "referential" language users in their early vocabulary and sentence structure.**

|  | Expressive | Referential |
|---|---|---|
| Types of words learned and used initially | Vocabulary is diverse, with many "personal social" words as well as nominals. High rate of pronoun use compared to referential children. | Many more general nominals (names for things) than expressive children and fewer pronouns. |
| Types of early sentences | Many "social routines" used in their entirety (e.g., "I want it" or "Stop it"). | Few social routines. |
|  | Many "formulas" or "rote strings" of words inserted into sentences in their entirety, such as "What do you want?" or "I don't know where it is." | Very few rote strings. As a result, the referential child's early sentences may be shorter than those of expressive children. |

*Source:* Based on Nelson, 1981.

BOX 8.3

# BLACK ENGLISH

Many black children in the United States speak differently from whites. Until fairly recently, teachers and others who dealt with black children assumed that this "difference" was really a "deficit," that the children just hadn't learned properly. But a number of linguists, most notably William Labov (1972), have argued that what black children learn is a perfectly legitimate dialect of English. Anastasiow and Hanes give a lovely example:

A petite five-year-old black girl sits across from an experimenter. He asks her to repeat a sentence spoken in typical school English and played on a tape recorder. The tape recorder plays the sentence: "I asked him if he did it and he said he didn't do it." She smiles, presses down the folds of her thin dress and says, "I asks him if he did it and he says he didn't did it but I knows he did." (Anastasiow & Hanes, 1976, p. 3)

This child has simply translated the standard English sentence into black English.

When linguists have analyzed black English, they have found that there are very specific differences, particularly in the use of verbs. In the Green Road Housing Project in Ann Arbor, Michigan (a largely black neighborhood), the children say "He be gone" when they mean "He is gone a good deal of the time." They say "He been gone" when they mean "He's been gone for a long while." Other translations are from such sentences as "He is going home" into "He going home" or "Every day when I come, he isn't here" into "Every day when I come, he don't be here."

The black English versions are predictable enough so that it is quite possible for someone to learn the dialect. But is the black English dialect less complex? Philip Dale (1976), among others, argues that it isn't. When the black child says "She come home" in place of "She came home," it doesn't mean that there is no past tense in black English; rather, it means that both the present and the past tense are formed with the word *come*.

Putting all this together, we find that the English spoken by most school-age black children is about as complex *within its own rules* as is the standard English spoken by whites. It is a different dialect, but it is as subtle and varied as standard English.

Virtually everyone—educators and linguists—now agrees on this basic point. The argument now is over whether the black child should be allowed or encouraged to use the black English dialect in school or whether he should be required to use standard English. Parents in the Green Road Housing Project went to court to force the Detroit school system to provide better training for its teachers so that the children could use their dialect in school. They won the suit (*Time,* August 20, 1979).

Some of you will have noticed the parallel between this issue and the problem of bilingual education for children who come to school speaking an entirely different language (Box 8.1). Perhaps we ought to apply the same argument to the black English dialect and begin the teaching of reading and other school subjects using the child's primary language. Standard English could then be taught later as a second language.

The other side of the argument is taken by many black leaders, who emphasize the fact that, like it or not, standard English is the basic language of the culture, and black children need to become skillful in its use. They think that children should use the standard language from the beginning.

At the moment, we simply lack the evidence that would permit us to choose. The whole issue will no doubt be with us for a long time to come.

dren's orientation toward objects versus relationships. It would be extremely interesting to see whether "expressive" children interact differently with other children than do "referential" children or whether their play with toys is qualitatively different. Until such research is done, these style differences in language remain merely intriguing suggestions or hints.

## SUMMARY

1. From the earliest use of two-word sentences, children's language is complex, abstract, productive, and rule-governed.
2. Language can be defined as an arbitrary system of symbols that permits us to say and to understand an infinite variety of messages.
3. The "prelinguistic" phase, in the first year of life, can be broken up into steps: crying, cooing, and babbling.
4. At about 1 year of age, the earliest words appear. The child begins to use sounds with consistent referents. These early words are normally used to convey whole sentences of meaning.
5. By age 2, most children have a vocabulary of 50 or more words, and the first two-word sentences normally appear between 18 and 24 months.
6. Grammatical development can be divided into two broad stages. In stage 1, the child may construct two- or three-word sentences but omits all the grammatical inflections. Stage 2, which normally begins about a year later, is marked by the beginning use of such inflections.
7. During stage 2, the child progressively adds questions, negatives, superlatives, past tenses, and other grammatical forms.
8. The development of word meanings (semantic development) follows a less predictable course. Children appear to have concepts or categories before they have words for them. When they begin to use words, they also "overextend" their usage.
9. Children's early word meanings seem to be based both on what they can do with objects (function) and on the perceptual properties of the objects (form). There are also hints that children form "prototypes" as the central meaning of words, just as adults do.
10. Several theories have been offered to explain language development. Early ideas that language was learned through imitation or reinforcement have been largely set aside. "Nativist" theories, positing maturing language-learning devices, had their heyday in the 1960s and 1970s but are accepted today in only weak forms.
11. Current theories focus on the role of the child's more general cognitive development and on the impact of the language heard by the child. The most logical current theory is one that combines nativist, cognitive, and social elements.
12. Children differ in the rate of development of both vocabulary and

grammar. There is some support for a theory of genetic contribution to such differences, but environmental explanations also seem valid.

13. Some differences in language style have also been noted in young children. Some children's language can be described as "referential," with heavy use of nouns. Other children's language is more "expressive," with more pronouns and more "rote strings" of words.

14. Despite these variations in early patterns, most children learn to speak skillfully by about age 5 or 6.

## KEY TERMS

**Babbling**   The repetitive sounds, usually involving at least one consonant and one vowel, shown by the baby from about 6 to 12 months.

**Black English**   The dialect of standard English spoken by many black children and adults in the United States.

**Cooing**   An early stage during the prelinguistic period when vowel sounds are repeated, particularly the *uuu* sound.

**Deep structure**   The underlying meaning of a sentence—a concept first proposed by Noam Chomsky.

**Echolalia**   A characteristic of the babbling period. The child repeats (echoes) the same sounds over and over.

**Expressive language**   The term used to describe the child's skill in speaking and communicating orally.

**"Expressive" language style**   One of two language styles described by Nelson, including high use of social routines, pronouns, and "rote strings."

**Holophrases**   The expression of a whole idea in a single word. Characteristic of the child's language from about 12 to 18 months.

**Inflections**   The grammatical "markers," such as plurals, possessives, past tenses, and their equivalent.

**Language acquisition device**   A hypothesized brain structure that may be "programmed" to make language learning possible.

**Mean length of utterance**   Usually abbreviated MLU; the average number of meaningful units in a sentence. Each basic word is one meaningful unit, as is each inflection, such as the *s* for plural or the *ed* for a past tense.

**Motherese**   The word linguists often use to describe the particular pattern of speech by adults to young children. The sentences are shorter, simpler, repetitive, and higher-pitched.

**Overregularization**   The tendency on the part of children to make the language regular, such as using past tenses like "beated" or "goed."

**Prelinguistic phase**   The period before the child speaks his first words.

**Receptive language**   Term used to describe the child's ability to understand (receive) language, as contrasted to her ability to express language.

**"Referential" language style**   The second style of language proposed by Nelson, including high use of object labels (nouns) and low use of pronouns and "rote strings."

**Semantics**   The study of word meaning.

**Surface structure**   The phrase used by Chomsky to describe the actual grammatical construction of a sentence. Surface structures are created from deep structures by use of transformational rules.

**Syntax**   Grammar or sentence structure.

**Telegraphic speech**   A characteristic of early child sentences in which everything but the crucial words is omitted, as if for a telegram.

**Transformational grammar**   The phrase used broadly to describe Chomsky's theory of language and language development. It describes the rules by which deep structure (meaning) is transformed into surface structures (actual sentences).

## SUGGESTED READINGS

Brown, R. Development of the first language in the human species. *American psychologist.* 1973, *28,* 97–106.

A wonderful, brief description of some of the major findings in language development, written in Roger Brown's usual clear style. (A more recent summary might be more informative, but I can't find one that is even half as readable as this one. Most of the current material is simply extremely tough and complex.)

Pines, M. The civilizing of Genie. *Psychology today,* September 1981, *15,* 28–34.

Genie was a girl raised under conditions of extreme deprivation who had almost no language when she was found at the age of 12. Maya Pines describes the attempts by linguists to teach Genie language—an attempt that raised important theoretical and practical issues about language development.

Schachter, F. F., & Strage, A. A. Adults' talk and children's language development. In S. G. Moore & C. R. Cooper (Eds.). *The young child: Reviews of research* (Vol. 3). Washington, D.C.: National Association for the Education of Young Children, 1982.

This whole book is full of really good chapters on current issues about children, all intended to be read by students or educated laypeople. Schachter & Strage's chapter discusses what we know about "motherese."

Terrace, H. S. How Nim Chimpsky changed my mind. *Psychology today,* 1979, *13,* 65–76.

This is the paper that has sparked a renewed controversy about whether chimps "really" create complex sentences or not. Very interesting.

## PROJECT 8.1

# *Beginning Two-Word Sentences*

Some of you have been around young children a lot and already have some sense of the delightful quality of early language. But you'll get a much better "feel" for it if you do some systematic listening. I would particularly like you to locate a child who is still in stage 1 or just beginning stage 2, since that will be easier for you to analyze. This is most likely to be a child of 20 to 24 months, but a child between 24 and 30 months may do fine, too. The one essential ingredient is that the child be speaking at least some two-word sentences. If you are unsure, ask the parents; they can nearly always tell you whether the child has reached this stage or not.

Arrange to spend enough time with the child at his or her home, in a day-care center, or in any other convenient setting, so that you can collect a list of 50 different utterances, including both one-word utterances and two- or more-word sentences. Write them down in the order in which they occur and stop when you have 50. It may take several sessions with the child before you get this many, and you will very probably find it helpful to have the child's mother or someone else play with the child while you listen and write things down. (Children this age are likely to clam up if you try to get them to talk, but if they are playing, the language will occur spontaneously.) Whenever you can, make notes about the context in which each sentence occurred so that you can judge the meaning more fully.

When you have your list of 50 utterances, take a crack at describing the child's language in any terms emerging from this chapter. For example, is the child at stage 1 or stage 2? How can you tell? What is the mean length of utterance? (If you want to calculate this precisely, follow the rules suggested by Brown, 1973b, p. 54, or by Dale, 1976, p. 19.) How many different meanings can you detect, such as subject-object relationships or attribution (e.g., "big boat")? Does this child's language seem to be "referential" or "expressive" in style?

If you are completing this project for a class assignment, turn in your record of the child's sentences along with a page or two of comment.

PROJECT 8.2

# *Conversation between Mother and Child*

This time I would like you to focus on the social environment—what is said *to* the child as well as the child's response. Again, find a child somewhere in the second year of life—though it's okay to go up to about $3\frac{1}{2}$. (It can be the same child you listened to in the last project, but you should collect the two sets of observations separately.)

Arrange to spend some time with the child while the mother is around. If you are working in a nursery school or day-care center or have access to such a setting, it is all right to study a child and the teacher. But you'll have to get the teacher alone with the single child for a period of time.

Record the conversation between the mother (or teacher) and the child, making sure that you have the sentences of the two people in the right order. Continue to record the conversation until you have at least 25 sentences for each. You may use a tape recorder if you wish, but you'll find it helpful to write down the sentences as they occur as well.

When you have collected the sentences, reread the sections of this chapter on the social environment. See if you can detect any of the following patterns in your adult-child conversation:

1. *Expansions.* Were there any instances in which the adult repeated what the child had just said but expanded it into a complete adult

grammatical sentence? How often did it occur? What about exact repetitions of what the child said?

2. *Motherese.* Did the adult's language conform to motherese, as I described it in the chapter?

3. *Child's imitations.* Did the child imitate the adult exactly or with some kind of simplification of the adult's sentence? How often did this happen?

4. *Reinforcement from the adult.* Is there any instance in which the adult reinforced the child for the *form* of the sentence or the accuracy of the pronunciation?

If you are completing this project for a class assignment, turn in your record of the conversation along with a page or two of analysis and comment.

# part four
## the social child

# 9.
# *personality development: alternative views*

If you could be a fly on the wall of a kindergarten classroom on the first day of school, you would be treated to a wonderful example of the differences in children's ways of coping with stress and novelty. Probably at least one child would cling to his mom, perhaps weeping and begging her not to leave him alone. Some children would say good-bye to mom, walk right into the room without a backward look, and begin talking to other children immediately. You might see another child standing quietly in the back of the room, not crying but not joining in easily, either. Another child is probably busily exploring the whole room right away, looking at the blocks and storybooks, the coat closet, and the water fountain, trying out several different chairs and desks for size.

If you came back to the same classroom six months later, when the situation was no longer scary and new, some of these differences would be less obvious, but the children's styles of approaching their world and the nature of their relationships with other people are still likely to be recognizable. The "shy" child who waited at the back of the room is likely to have one or two pals in the class but not to be the center of the crowd. The child who could hardly bear to let mom leave may

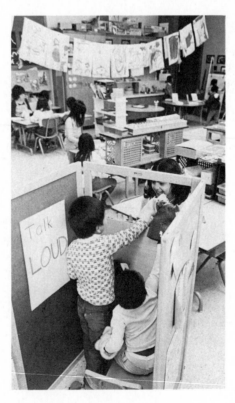

**Figure 9.1** By kindergarten age (if not considerably sooner), children already have highly recognizable and individual patterns of interacting with one another and with the world around them. Where do these differences in "personality" come from?

be sitting right up near the teacher; the gregarious, talkative child is probably still the center of attention, the one who decides what game they will all play at recess.

All of these differences in patterns of behavior are usually included under the term **personality**.

## WHAT DO WE MEAN BY PERSONALITY?

The term *personality* is one of the slipperiest in all of psychology—maybe even worse than the term *intelligence*. In fact, the two terms have a good deal in common. Both are concepts designed to help us describe or explain *enduring individual differences* in behavior. The concept of intelligence was invented to describe enduring individual differences in intellectual ability or competence. *Personality* describes a broader range of individual characteristics, mostly having to do with the typical ways each of us interacts with the people and the world around us. Whether we are gregarious or shy, whether we plunge into new things or hold back, whether we are independent or dependent, whether we are confident or uncertain—all of these (and many more) are usually thought of as elements of personality.

Underlying the concept of personality is the assumption that these tend to be *persisting* aspects of the individual—that a shy child is likely to become a shy adult or that a confident 5-year-old will still have some element of confidence 40 years later. Obviously, this assumption matches our own experience with ourselves as well as with the people we know. We see in other people a coherence, to use Alan Sroufe's term (1979), and a continuity of behavior patterns. We sense the same coherence and continuity in our own behavior as we age. I am not the same as I was when I was 5 or 10, but there are ways in which my behavior, my attitudes, my beliefs about myself, my style of responding are similar.

Unlike the concept of intelligence, however, the concept of personality is not reduced to numbers like an IQ score. Children do not have an *amount* of personality; they have a *kind or type of personality*—a style or pattern of interacting with the world around them. The dimension of personality that is most analogous to intellectual "power" is *healthiness*. Some children seem to have developed patterns of interacting with the people and world around them that are adaptive, positive, and supportive of the child's own needs. Other children behave in ways that irritate others or that interfere with loving or supportive contacts with other people. As was true for the study of intelligence, which was originally spurred by an interest in children who did *not* function well in school, a great deal of the interest in the development of personality in children arose from a desire to understand how some children came to have "unhealthy" or "nonadaptive" patterns of interaction with others. I find elements of this same concern today in research on day care or divorce or child abuse. Will experiences like these have a permanent (negative) effect on the child's personality? How much of the child's characteristic "healthy" or "unhealthy" pattern of interaction is shaped by these early experiences? How does that happen?

One of my tasks in the next few chapters is to examine what we know about the origins of those unique and consistent patterns of individual behavior that we call personality. What have various theorists said about how those differences might come about?

But it is a mistake to cast all of the discussion of children's relationships with others in the language of individual differences. As we did with cognitive development, we also have to look at *shared* developmental patterns—at changes in the "structure" of the child's relationships. For example, you can probably think of some adult you know who is highly dependent on others. We'd call that an aspect of his or her personality. But *all* of us were clinging and dependent when we were infants and toddlers. So there seem to be both *enduring characteristics* and *developmental patterns* shared by all children.

It is not always possible to disentangle these two questions when we talk about personality and social development (just as questions of "power" and "structure" get tangled in descriptions of cognitive development). But let me approach the problem (as I did in talking about cognitive development) by beginning with the question of the origins of individual differences in personality. How do children come to have distinctive and enduring patterns of interacting with the world and the people in that world? Do they inherit these patterns? Are they "taught" their different styles of interacting? Do the patterns result from the child's interactions with the significant people in her life?

Unfortunately, there is no single body of research that addresses these questions. Unlike the area of IQ, there is no agreed-on basic description of personality differences in children. Instead, what we have are several distinctive theories of personality development, each of which casts the question differently and each of which has led to quite separate bodies of research. So in this case it makes sense to talk about the theories (the answers to the "why" questions) first, so that you can get some sense of the range of questions that fall under the general label of "personality." Then, with some understanding of the theoretical alternatives as background, I can explore what we know about the basic *developmental* patterns in children's self-concepts and social relationships in the following two chapters.

## THE MAJOR ALTERNATIVE VIEWS OF PERSONALITY

Three kinds of descriptions/explanations of individual differences in personality have existed side by side for some time: (1) biological explanations, based primarily on the assumption that differences are inherited; (2) learning explanations, based primarily on the assumption that each child's behavior patterns are shaped by reinforcement contingencies; and (3) psychoanalytic explanations, based on the assumption of an interaction between inborn impulses in the child and the response of the parents to the child. I also see signs of the emergence of a fourth view, based loosely on Piaget's cognitive-developmental theory.

To some degree, these different approaches are based on distinctly different assumptions about the nature of human development—different *paradigms,* to use Kuhn's term (1962). And to some degree they are fundamentally incompatible with one another (Reese & Overton, 1970). But my own reading of current thinking tells me that a beginning synthesis may be emerging—a new, "transactional" paradigm that includes at least some elements of all four approaches. Let me describe each approach separately and then try my hand at an integration.

## A BIOLOGICAL APPROACH: TEMPERAMENT

Temperament has become one of the "hottest" concepts in developmental psychology in the past 5 or 10 years and certainly represents the dominant (although not the only) biological approach to personality today (Goldsmith & Campos, 1982; Rothbart & Derryberry, 1981; Carey, 1981).

I talked about temperamental differences among infants in Chapter 3, so the concept is not new. As it is currently used, the term *temperament* refers to one facet of personality—the individual's "emotional reactivity or behavioral style in interacting with the environment" (Carey, 1981). The term thus describes *how* the child reacts rather than what he can do or why. Current temperament theories, though, have moved well beyond merely defining such a style dimension of personality. I can identify three basic propositions of this theoretical appraoch:

*Proposition 1: Each individual is born with characteristic patterns of responding to the environment and to other people.* Alexander Thomas and Stella Chess (1977) have emphasized such qualities as activity rate, rhythmicity, adaptability to new experiences, intensity of response, general mood, and persistence as being basic properties of temperament in infants and young children. Combinations of these properties create the several distinctive temperaments of "easy," "difficult," and "slow-to-warm-up" children that Thomas and Chess have described (and that I talked about in Chapter 3).

An alternative formulation of basic temperament has been offered by Arnold Buss and Robert Plomin (1975), who have identified the four main temperamental dimensions I've listed in Table 9.1 Obviously, there is not yet agreement on just what aspects of behavior we should label with the term *temperament*. There is agreement among temperament theorists, though, on the assumption that these temperamental qualities are inherited.

*Proposition 2: These temperamental characteristics affect the way any individual responds to people and things around him.* Temperamentally gregarious children seek out contact with others; lethargic children are more likely to choose sedentary activities like puzzles or board games than baseball. Thus temperament affects experience.

*Proposition 3: The individual's temperament also affects the way others respond to her.* Temperament affects the environment as well as the other way around. The gregarious child, who may smile more than the detached child, "shapes" the parents' behavior toward her. The parents may smile, pick her up, and talk to her more, simply because she has reinforced their behavior by her positive temperament. Thus, although this group of theorists emphasizes the inheritance of temperament, they are also emphasizing the fundamental importance of the *interaction* between the child's temperament and the response of the people around her. Temperament does not inevitably determine personality. Rather, it creates a kind of "bias" in the system toward particular patterns. It also acts as a kind of "filter" through which the environment must pass.

Table 9.1

**Four dimensions of temperament proposed by Buss and Plomin**

| | |
|---|---|
| Active versus lethargic | The active person is usually busy and in a hurry, with vigorous actions. |
| Emotional versus impassive | Intensity of reaction is involved; the emotional person is easily aroused and responds more intensely. |
| Gregarious versus detached | The gregarious person is more "affiliative," has more desire to be with others, and is more responsive to others. |
| Impulsive versus deliberate | Impulsive people respond quickly rather than inhibiting the response. (Note the similarity of this dimension to impulsive versus reflective perceptual styles discussed in Chapter 5.) The impulsive person is more likely to give in to urges and responds quickly rather than planning. |

*Source:* Adapted from Buss & Plomin, 1975, p. 8.

### The Evidence

All three of these propositions have been supported by the findings of recent research. Studies of the inheritance of temperament show that identical twins are quite a lot more alike in their temperament than are fraternal twins (Goldsmith, 1983; Buss & Plomin, 1975; Plomin & Rowe, 1979; Matheny et al., 1981). Since this result has been found even when the ratings of the child's temperament are made by separate observers for each twin (Goldsmith & Gottesman, 1981) rather than by the parents, it certainly makes it look as if there may be a hereditary piece in this puzzle. Sociability and activity level seem to be especially influenced by heredity.

Children's temperament also appears to be somewhat consistent over time. For example, Adam Matheny and his colleagues (1981) have found that both negative responding (such as the frequency of temper tantrums or irritability) and positive sociability (such as smiling or cuddliness) were somewhat stable over the first six years of life. Several other researchers have observed similar patterns, with activity level and such aspects of sociability as smiling and laughter being particularly stable.

What is more intriguing, from my perspective at least, are the findings that are beginning to emerge that show that children's temperaments affect the way people respond to them. Temperamentally "difficult" children are punished more, for example (Rutter, 1978c), which may help create a cycle in which the punishment increases the likelihood of their cranky, difficult behavior, which, in turn, triggers more punishment.

### Strengths, Weaknesses, and Implications

I see two great strengths in this approach to the origins of personality. First, it forces us to consider the role of heredity—an important theoretical antidote to the dominance of environmental explanations over the past decades. No temperament theorist is saying that *all* individual differences in children's behavior are the result of inherited temperament, but it does appear that each child begins life with *some* measurable and reasonably stable behavioral tendencies.

The second great strength is the emphasis in this theory on the interactions (or transactions) between the child's temperament and the responses of the people around her. This is not a purely biological approach; it is an interactionist approach, and that is very much the direction in which I think we need to go in our thinking about children's development.

On the other side of the ledger, I see three current weaknesses. The first is that neither a common definition nor a common method of measuring temperament has been agreed on by researchers in this area. So the concept is still fuzzy. Second, we simply don't yet have enough information, particularly about the impact of children's temperament on the responses of the parents and on the "pathway" of interaction that the child and parents are likely to enter. What is the effect of the parents' temperament or personality or expectations on this system? Are there some parents who can readily handle a "difficult" child, while others cannot?

Finally, I see a sort of bandwagon effect in the latest work on temperament. The idea of inherited temperamental differences has become the latest, favorite explanation for virtually everything infants do or do not do. I am convinced that there really is such a thing as temperamental difference, but I am not so sure it is the magic explanatory concept some would have us think.

## SOCIAL-LEARNING APPROACHES TO PERSONALITY

The emphasis shifts rather completely when we look at social-learning approaches. Instead of looking at what the child brings to the equation, learning theorists have looked at the reinforcement patterns in the environment as the primary cause of differences in children's patterns of behavior. In fact, most learning theorists do not use the word *personality* at all. They don't see the child as having an enduring trait or quality of gregariousness or shyness, activity or lethargy; rather, they would describe the child as showing friendly *behavior* or high rates of activity. Albert Bandura, who has developed perhaps the most systematic social-learning theory, puts the basic proposition flatly:

> Except for elementary reflexes, people are not equipped with inborn repertoires of behavior. They must learn them. New response patterns can be acquired either by direct experience or by observation. (Bandura, 1977, p. 16)

Bandura is not rejecting biology. He goes on to say that biological factors such as hormones or inherited propensities (such as temperament, presumably) can affect behavior. But he clearly comes down hard on the side of the environment as the major "cause" of the behavior we observe.

These are not new ideas. You have already read about them in Chapter 1 (and again briefly in Chapter 8). The question here is how to apply this theory specifically to such "personality" characteristics as dependency, nurturance, aggressiveness, activity level, or shyness. So let me restate the basic propositions of the theory and then see how they can be applied to the explanation of those relatively enduring patterns of behavior we call personality.

*Proposition 1: Behavior is "strengthened" by reinforcement.* If this rule applies to all behavior, then it should apply to attachment, shyness, sharing, or competitiveness, too. We'd expect that children who are reinforced for clinging to their parents, for example, would show more of this behavior than do children who are not reinforced for it, and such children are likely to be seen as being more "dependent." Similarly, a nursery school teacher who pays attention to children only when they get rowdy or aggressive should find that the children get steadily more rowdy and aggressive over the course of weeks or months.

*Proposition 2: Behavior that is reinforced on a "partial schedule" should be even stronger and more resistant to extinction than behavior that is consistently reinforced.* I talked about this phenomenon in Chapter 1 and have already given you some examples of the application of the principles of partial reinforcement (see Box 1.1). Parents are nearly always inconsistent in their rewards to their children, so most children are on partial schedules of some kind. Given the strong persistence of behavior rewarded in this way, if we want to understand how children develop distinctive and stable patterns of behavior—aggression or kindness or smiling or friendliness or whatever—we should look for what is being reinforced by the parents on a partial schedule.

*Proposition 3: Children learn new behaviors largely through* **modeling**. Bandura has argued that the full range of social behaviors, from competitiveness to nurturance, is learned by watching others perform those actions. Thus, the child who sees her parents making a donation to the local Cancer Society volunteer or taking a casserole next door to the woman who has just been widowed will learn generosity and thoughtful behavior. The child who sees her parents arguing or hitting each other when they are angry will most likely learn violent ways of solving problems.

Children learn from TV, too, and from their playmates, their teachers, and their brothers and sisters. A boy growing up in an environment where he observes playmates and older boys hanging around street corners, shoplifting, or stealing hubcaps is going to learn all those behaviors. His continuous exposure to such antisocial models makes it that much harder for his parents to reinforce more constructive behavior. Teenagers are often irate when their parents get concerned about the "crowd" they run with. But from Bandura's point of view, such parental concern is justified, since the child is learning from observing.

These three basic propositions describe the fundamental "rules" for learning any behavior, including behaviors that we typically think of as part of personality. According to this theory, children are gregarious, shy, aggressive, nurturant, generous, or stingy because they have been reinforced for behaving that way. The corollary, of course, is that if the reinforcement pattern were to change markedly, so would the child's behavior.

Recently, Bandura (1977) has also added a "developmental" aspect to this theory. He has recognized that what a child learns and how she behaves after observing a model will change with age. What the child pays attention to, understands, or remembers about what the model did will be affected by the child's overall level of cognitive development. This aspect of the theory seems to me to put the child back into the system; it is no longer a purely automatic, environmentally controlled process. Rather, it is an interactive process in which the child's own attention and information processing are an integral part.

## Some Evidence

There is an immense collection of studies supporting these basic propositions. For example, when experimenters systematically rewarded some children for hitting a Bobo doll (an inflated rubber clown) in the nose and then watched the children in a play situation, the children who were rewarded showed more hitting, scratching, and kicking than the children who hadn't been rewarded for punching the Bobo doll (Waters & Brown, 1963).

And "partial" reinforcement in the form of inconsistent behavior from parents also has the expected effect. For example, Sears, Maccoby, and Levin (1957) found that parents who allow their children to be quite aggressive (are *permissive toward it*) but occasionally react by

**Figure 9.2** These children clearly show aggressive behavior and postures learned through observation, probably on television. The fact that the "victim" is not actually killed does not mean that the children have not learned the full set of responses.

punishing quite severely have children who are more aggressive than are children whose parents are nonpermissive and nonpunitive.

Both these principles have also been used successfully in therapy with families of children with troublesome behaviors, such as tantrums, defiance, or extreme aggressiveness, as I've described in Box 9.1.

The impact of observational learning has also been demonstrated in literally hundreds of studies (Bandura, 1977, 1973). One interesting—and very practical—sidelight to the process of modeling has been the repeated finding that when there is a conflict between what a model does and what he says, it is the *behavior* that is likely to be imitated. In one study, Joan Grusec and her co-workers (Grusec, Saas-Kortsaak, & Simutis, 1978) found that telling children to be generous did little good, but showing them generosity led them to be generous, too. So the old adage "Do what I say and not what I do" doesn't seem to work. Another example of the operation of this principle is the fact that parents who smoke are more likely to have children who smoke, even if the parents tell the children that they wish they had never started.

## Strengths, Weaknesses, and Implications

Several implications of this theoretical approach are worth emphasizing. First of all, unlike temperament theorists, who expect at least a certain amount of consistency of behavior in different situations, learning theorists can handle either consistency or inconsistency in children's behavior. If a child is friendly and smiling both at home and at school, this would be explained by saying that the child was being reinforced for that behavior in both settings, not by assuming that the child had a "gregarious temperament." But it is equally possible to explain how a child could be the soul of helpfulness at school but never mind his mother at home, or do whatever his father asks but be disobedient to his mother. In cases like this, learning theorists merely go searching for the differing patterns of reinforcement in the different settings.

A related implication is that this view of behavior is a very hopeful one. Children's behavior can change if the reinforcement system changes, so "problem behavior" can be modified, as I described in Box 9.1. The same approach has been used in special training programs for shy children, who can be taught (through reinforcement) how to make better eye contact, how to listen intently, to smile more, and the like. Children who have been through such programs do become more popular with their peers (Ladd, 1981).

The great strength of this view of social behavior, in my opinion, is that it gives an accurate picture of the way in which many behaviors are learned. It is perfectly clear that children do learn through modeling; and it is equally clear that children (and adults) will continue to perform behaviors that "pay off" for them. The addition of

BOX 9.1

## USING SOCIAL-LEARNING PRINCIPLES TO MODIFY "PROBLEM BEHAVIOR" IN CHILDREN

Many forms of therapy have been used successfully to modify unwanted behavior in children. One widely used strategy is the systematic application of reinforcement principles, often described as **behavior therapy**. Gerald Patterson's descriptions (1975, 1980) of behavior therapy with children showing severe problem behavior is particularly fascinating. One case study will give you some of the flavor of this approach.

Erik was ten years old and a practiced monster. He not only hit his younger sister, but had completely alienated himself from children in the neighborhood as well. He was so bossy that other children avoided playing with him. He was likely to settle disagreements with an all-out attack. At home he made derogatory remarks about his mother and his sister. He was large enough

and aggressive enough so that his mother felt she could not handle him. . . . Eric was so skilled at noncompliance that neither the father nor the mother asked him to do anything. As is the case for most aggressive boys, both parents had been trained to believe that Erik *could not* mind or do chores. (Patterson, 1975, p. 130)

Having arrived at this awful state of affairs, what could Eric's parents do? Patterson's prescription follows distinct steps.

1. Select only *one* specific problem behavior to work on at a time, preferably beginning with one of the less awful. In this case, Eric's parents started with his noncompliance.
2. Observe and keep records. Eric's parents defined what they meant by "noncompliance" and then counted each time it occurred. At

the cognitive elements in Bandura's theory seems to me to offer the possibility of creating, eventually, a genuinely *developmental* social-learning theory.

The weakness of the theory, for me, is that too much emphasis is placed on what happens *to* the child and not enough on what the child is doing with the information she has. The theory is thus unbalanced and too mechanistic. Still, it offers immensely useful descriptions of one source of the child's developing pattern of behavior.

## PSYCHOANALYTIC THEORIES

The third theoretical approach, psychoanalytic theory, represents a considerable shift in emphasis from either temperament or learning approaches. From my perspective, these psychoanalytic theories are

the beginning of the treatment, Eric "noncomplied" about once every 10 minutes. (I guarantee you that such a rate of ignoring, disobedience, and outright defiance is horrifyingly hard to live with. Patterson has shown that mothers who live with children showing behavior like this become depressed and lose any sense that they can control their lives or their children.)

3. Describe your records to the child and tell him precisely what you expect and what he'll get in the way of a reward if he changes his behavior. Eric was told that he would get a "point," which he could exchange for things he wanted, each time he did what he was told. (Very small improvements earn points initially. Later the child may have to do a better job to earn credit.) Eric used his points to earn extra time to stay up in the evening and later accumulated enough points to have his father take him fishing. During this step, the parents do *nothing* if the child does not comply.

4. After point earning has been well established, the parents introduce a type of punishment called "time out" whenever the child doesn't do what has been asked. "Time out" involves having the child go to a separate room by himself for a specified period of time. In Eric's case, he had to spend five minutes alone in the bathroom each time he disobeyed and had minutes added to this "time out" if he yelled or screamed or kicked the door (all of which he did in the beginning).

5. Change the point programs as needed by adding other possible incentives or other goal behaviors. The possibility of a fishing trip with his dad was not introduced as a goal originally; it was offered later, after Eric had begun to comply more regularly.

Children exposed to programs like these often get worse before they get better, and it can be a terrific strain on the parents to maintain the new system. Frequently, the parents need the assistance of an outside therapist (such as Patterson) to help them maintain consistent responses to their child. But many types of problem behaviors that had been the despair of parents have been modified in this way. And many mothers have experienced a genuine boost in their confidence, self-esteem, and feeling of well-being when the child's behavior changes.

more "balanced," since they emphasize both inborn qualities in the child and particular environmental needs.

There is, in fact, a whole family of theories called "psychoanalytic," beginning with Freud's and continuing with theories by Carl Jung (1916, 1939), Alfred Adler (1948), and Erik Erikson (1963, 1964, 1974). The word *psyche,* in Greek, refers to the soul, spirit, or mind. So psychoanalysis is the analysis of the mind or spirit. All the theorists who share this general tradition have been interested in explaining human behavior by understanding the underlying processes of the mind and the personality. And nearly all psychoanalytic theorists have begun by studying and analyzing adults or children who are disturbed in some way. Many believed they could come to understand the normal processes by analyzing how they had gone wrong.

Of all the theorists in this large group, Freud and Erikson have dealt most thoroughly with the *developmental* questions about the ori-

**Figure 9.3** This child, the soul of helpfulness at nursery school, may be the despair of his mother's life at home. Social-learning theory can handle this kind of inconsistency across situations better than most other theories simply by arguing that the reinforcement contingencies may be quite different in the two settings.

gin of personality in infancy and childhood. Since the two theories differ in important ways, I want to describe them to you separately.

### Freud's Theory: Psychosexual Stages

Let me lay out the basic concepts in Freud's theory as a set of propositions, as I have done before.

*Proposition 1: All behavior is energized by fundamental instinctual drives.* Freud thought there were three such instinctual drives or motivating forces: *sexual drives,* which he called **libido**; *life-preserving drives*, including instincts such as hunger and pain; and *aggressive drives*. Of the three, he thought the most interesting—and perhaps the most important—were the sexual drives.

*Proposition 2: Throughout life, the child (and later the adult) is focused on gratification of these basic instincts.* The specific *form* of gratification sought and the strategies used to obtain it change with age, as we'll see later; but the inner push to obtain gratification remains.

*Proposition 3: Over the course of childhood, each of us develops three basic structures of personality that aid in gratifying the instincts.* These three structures Freud called the **id**, the **ego**, and the **superego** and suggested that they are developed in the order listed. The id is the basic storehouse of raw, uninhibited, instinctual energy. Freud thought that this was all that was present in the infant. The baby tries to gratify his needs very directly. He has no ability to delay. He wants what he wants when he wants it.

This basic instinctual push for gratification remains a part of the personality; but because gratification can frequently be achieved more successfully by planning, talking, delaying, and other "cognitive" techniques than by instant demands, the child gradually transfers energy from the id to the ego. In Freud's terms, the ego is the planning, organizing, thinking part of the personality. The child is still trying to get what she wants, but now she is trying to gratify her desires by using more reality-based strategies.

Finally, there is the superego, which is roughly the same as what we call the **conscience**. This is the part of the personality that "monitors" the rest, that decides what is right and wrong, that channels the basic energy into forms of gratification that are acceptable to parents and to society.

These three parts of the personality are, in some sense, at war with one another. The id says, "I want it now!" The ego says, "You can have it later," or "Take it easy; we'll get there eventually if we do it this way." The superego says, "You can't have it that way. That way's wrong. Find another way."

*Proposition 4: When conflicts arise between the different parts of the personality, the result is anxiety.* You all know the feeling of anxiety, so I don't need to try to define it for you. Many times the ego can handle the anxiety directly. If I send in a paper to a professional journal and have it rejected, I feel anxious. But I know what I'm anxious about and can handle it realistically by looking objectively at my paper to see how it could be improved, doing another study to prove the point I was trying to make, or doing something equivalent.

But sometimes (often, in fact) the anxiety is too much to be handled this way, so we resort to **defense mechanisms**—automatic, unconscious strategies for reducing anxiety. For example, I can *repress* the feelings when my paper is rejected and insist that I really don't mind at all. Or I can *project:* "The people who reviewed my paper are really stupid! They don't know what they're doing." In this way, I ascribe to the other people the qualities I fear may be true for me (stupidity, in this case).

The key things to realize about defense mechanisms, as Freud conceived them, are that they are unconscious, they involve self-deception, and they are quite *normal*. They can be taken to extremes, in which case they become neurotic. But Freud believed that defending yourself against anxiety is a normal process.

*Proposition 5: In the course of development, the child goes through a series of distinct psychosexual stages.* Two things develop in stages. First of all, the ego and the superego are not present in the infant and must be developed. And second, the goals of gratification change. At each stage, the sexual energy is focused on ("invested in," as Freud says) a single part of the body, which he called an **erogenous zone**, such as the mouth, the anus, and the genitals. The infant first focuses on stimulation in the mouth because that is the part of the body that is most sensitive. Later, when his neurological development progresses, other parts of his anatomy become sensitive, and his focus of sexual energy changes.

There is a strong maturational element in this part of Freud's theory. He thought that the transitions from one psychosexual stage to the next were determined largely by the changes in body sensitivity.

Freud proposed five developmental stages. I've summarized the stages very briefly in Table 9.2, but I need to describe them in more detail as well.

*The Oral Stage: Birth–1 Year* Freud emphasized that the oral region—the mouth, tongue, and lips—are the first center of pleasure for the baby. His earliest attachment is to the one who provides pleasure in the mouth, usually his mother. In Freud's view, normal development in the infant requires that the baby receive sufficient oral stimulation—not too much and not too little. If the needed amount of stimulation is not available or the child has had excessive oral stimulations, he may *fixate* on this form of gratification and continue to seek oral pleasures in later life. (Some of the proposed characteristics of adults who are "stuck" at the oral stage are listed in Table 9.2.)

*The Anal Stage: 1–3 Years* As maturation progresses and the lower trunk becomes more developed and more under voluntary control, the baby becomes increasingly sensitive in the anal region and begins to receive pleasure from bowel movements. At about the same time, her parents begin to place great emphasis on toilet training and show pleasure when she manages to perform in the right place at the right time. These two forces together help to shift the major center of sexual energy from the oral to the anal erogenous zone.

As was true in the oral period, the key to the child's successful completion of this stage is whether the parents allow the child sufficient anal exploration and pleasure. If toilet training becomes a major battleground (as it often does) or occurs too early (thus denying sufficient

**Table 9.2**

**Freud's stages of psychosexual development**

| Stage | Age | Erogenous Zone | Major Developmental Task (Potential Source of Conflict) | Some Adult Characteristics of Children Who Have Been "Fixated" at This Stage |
|---|---|---|---|---|
| Oral | 0–1 | Mouth, lips, tongue | Weaning | Oral behavior, such as smoking and eating; passivity and gullibility. |
| Anal | 2–3 | Anus | Toilet training | Orderliness, parsimoniousness, obstinacy, or the opposite (extreme untidiness, for example). |
| Phallic | 4–5 | Genitals | Oedipus complex; identification with parent of same sex | Vanity, recklessness (and the opposite). |
| Latency | 6–12 | No specific area; sexual energy quiescent | Development of ego-defense mechanisms | None: fixation does not normally occur at this stage. |
| Genital | 13–18 and adulthood | Genitals | Mature sexual intimacy | Adults who have successfully integrated earlier stages should emerge from this stage with a more sincere interest in others, realistic enjoyments, mature sexuality. |

time for anal pleasure), then some fixation of energy at this stage may occur—with the possible adult consequences of excessive orderliness, stinginess, or the opposite.

*The Phallic Stage: 3–5 Years*   At about 3 or 4 years of age, the genitals increase in sensitivity, ushering in a new stage. (One sign of this new sensitivity, incidentally, is that children of both sexes quite naturally begin to masturbate at about this age.)

According to Freud, the most important event that occurs during the phallic stage is the so-called **Oedipal crisis.** He described the sequence of events more fully (and more believably!) for boys, so let me trace that pattern for you.

The theory suggests that first the boy somehow becomes "intuitively aware of his mother as a sex object" (Rappoport, 1972, p. 74). Precisely how this occurs is not completely spelled out, but the important point is that the boy at about age 4 begins to have a sort of sexual attachment to his mother and to regard his father as a sexual rival. His father sleeps with his mother, holds her and kisses her, and generally has access to her body in a way that the boy does not. The boy also

**Figure 9.4** Most children are toilet trained at about age 2, which is during Freud's anal stage. For many parents and children, toilet training becomes a battleground, with the child enjoying both the anal sensations and the control he can exert over himself (and his parents); the parents, meanwhile, are doing their darndest to exert control over the child.

sees his father as a powerful and threatening figure who has the ultimate power—the power to castrate. The boy is caught between desire for his mother and fear of his father's power.

The result of this conflict is anxiety. How can the little boy handle this anxiety? In Freud's view, the boy responds with a process he calls **identification**: The boy "incorporates" his image of his father and attempts to match his own behavior to that image. By trying to make himself as like his father as possible, the boy not only reduces the chance of an attack from the father, he also takes on some of the father's power as well. Furthermore, it is the "inner father," with his values and moral judgments, that serves as the core of the child's superego or conscience.

A parallel process is supposed to occur in girls. The girl sees her mother as a rival for her father's sexual attentions and also has some fear of her mother (though less than is true for the boy, since the girl may assume she has already been castrated). The girl also carries forward her original loving attachment to the mother from the oral period. In this case, too, identification with the mother is the "solution" to the girl's anxiety, although Freud thought that since the anxiety was less, girls' identifications would be weaker than boys' (an expectation totally unsupported by later research, by the way).

*The Latency Stage: 5–12 Years*    Freud thought that after the phallic stage there is a sort of resting period before the next major change in the child's sexual development. The child has presumably arrived at some preliminary resolution of the Oedipal crisis, so that there is a kind of calm after the storm. Then, too, the child starts school during this period, and this new activity absorbs the energies rather fully.

During these years, the child's peer interactions are almost exclusively with members of the same sex. The identification with the same-sex parent at the end of the phallic stage is thus followed by a long period during which the identification and interaction extend to others of the same sex.

One of the significant events Freud saw in this period, however, is the development of a wider repertoire of defense mechanisms. Among those thought to be developed in the latency period are *denial,* in which the child simply denies that he feels or thinks a certain thing (e.g., "I am *not* tired" when he is clearly at the edge of exhaustion), and *repression,* in which unacceptable thoughts or feelings are simply forced out of conscious awareness. The child literally forgets unpleasant things.

*The Genital Stage: 12–18 and Older*   The further changes in hormones and the genital organs that take place during puberty reawaken the sexual energy of the child; and during this period, a more mature form of sexual attachment occurs. From the beginning of this period, the child's sexual objects are people of the opposite sex. Freud placed some emphasis on the fact that not everyone works through this period to a point of mature heterosexual love. Some have not successfully completed the Oedipal period, so they may have confused identifications that affect their ability to cope with rearoused sexual energies in adolescence. Some have not had a satisfactory oral period and thus do not have a foundation of basic love relationships. This, too, will interfere with full resolution of the conflicts of puberty.

What we see as the child's personality, then, is a complex result of all of these processes, depending on the particular stages at which the child may have become fixated, on the particular form of the child's identification with the parents, and on the defense mechanisms that the child adopts.

Many of these same themes—inborn drives, critical elements of early parent-child interaction, stages of development, and "fixation"—are part of Erikson's theory as well.

## Erikson's Theory: Psychosocial Stages

Erik Erikson belongs firmly in the psychoanalytic tradition, but he has focused his attention on the ego—the conscious self—rather than on the unconscious drives or instincts. He has always been much more interested in the cultural and social demands made on the child than in the sexual drives. So Erikson's stages are referred to as **psychosocial stages**, whereas Freud's are called **psychosexual stages**. Most broadly, Erikson has been interested in how the child (and later the adult) develops her *sense of identity*. In Erikson's view, this process takes a full lifetime. As usual, let me break down the theoretical concepts into a series of basic propositions.

*Proposition 1: Over the life span, each individual goes through a series of distinct developmental periods (stages), with a specific developmental task at each stage.* (See Table 9.3.) The central task of each period is the development of a particular "ego quality," such as trust, autonomy, or intimacy.

*Proposition 2: The developmental periods are defined partly by maturation and partly by the society in which the person grows.* A stage may begin at age 6 in our culture because that is when the child goes off to school. In a culture in which schooling was delayed, the timing of the developmental task might change as well. In this view, Erikson obviously differs from Freud, for whom maturation was the critical element in moving the child from one stage to the next.

*Proposition 3: The child's (or adult's) success in completing the task at each stage is heavily dependent on the interactions that take place between the child and his parents or the child and his teacher(s).* This is a heavily *interactive* theory, just as Freud's is. The child is a key part-

Table 9.3

**The eight stages of development proposed by Erik Erikson**

| Approximate Age | Ego Quality to Be Developed | Some Tasks and Activities of the Stage |
|---|---|---|
| 0–1 | Basic trust versus basic mistrust | Trust in mother or central caregiver and in one's own ability to make things happen. A key element in an early secure attachment. |
| 2–3 | Autonomy versus shame, doubt | Walking, grasping, and other physical skills lead to free choice; toilet training occurs; child learns control but may develop shame if not handled properly. |
| 4–5 | Initiative versus guilt | Organize activities around some goal; become more assertive and aggressive. Oedipal-like conflict with parent of same sex may lead to guilt. |
| 6–12 | Industry versus inferiority | Absorb all the basic cultural skills and norms, including school skills and tool use. |
| 13–18 | Identity versus role confusion | Adapt sense of self to physical changes of puberty, make occupational choice, achieve adultlike sexual identity, and search for new values. |
| 19–25 | Intimacy versus isolation | Form one or more intimate relationships that go beyond adolescent love; marry and form family groups. |
| 26–40 | Generativity versus stagnation | Bear and rear children, focus on occupational achievement or creativity, and train the next generation. |
| 41+ | Ego integrity versus despair | Integrate earlier stages and come to terms with basic identity. Accept self. |

ner in the exchange, but the responses of the people around him shape his development as well.

Proposition 4: *Any developmental task that is not successfully completed leaves a residue that interferes with later tasks*. Actually, Erikson thinks that no task is ever fully completed, so all adults feel at least occasional mistrust, doubt, guilt, or inferiority. There are always bits and pieces left over. But the number and size of those bits and pieces may be critical for later health. A child who has not formed a trusting first relationship, for example, will have greater difficulty completing every later task; a teenager who does not complete the task of developing her sexual or occupational identity will have a harder time later on entering into a fully intimate relationship at age 20 or 25. In this proposition, Erikson is obviously very like Freud, who also thought that truly "mature" or "healthy" adult functioning required the successful sequential resolution of all the different stages or tasks.

*Basic Trust versus Basic Mistrust: Birth–1 Year*   The first task (or "crisis," as Erikson sometimes says) occurs during the first year of life (Freud's oral period). What is at issue is whether the child will develop a sense of basic trust in the predictability of the world and in his ability to affect the happenings around him. Erikson believes that the behavior of the major caregiver (usually the mother) is critical to the child's successful or unsuccessful resolution of this crisis. Children who emerge from the first year with a firm sense of trust are those with parents who are loving and who respond predictably and reliably to the child ("contingent responsiveness" again). A child who has developed a sense of trust will go on to other relationships carrying this sense with him; but those infants whose early care has been erratic or harsh may develop *mis*trust; and they, too, carry this sense with them into the later relationships.

*Autonomy versus Shame and Doubt: 2–3 Years*   Erikson sees the child's greater mobility at this age as forming the basis for the sense of independence or autonomy. But if the child's efforts at independence are not carefully guided by the parents and she experiences repeated failures or ridicule, then the results of all the new opportunities for exploration may be shame and doubt instead of a basic sense of self-control and self-worth. The fact that toilet training occurs during this period (Freud's anal stage) may also create additional difficulties for the parents, since this is an area in which there are many taboos and more occasions when ridicule or failure may occur for the child.

*Initiative versus Guilt: 4–5 Years*   This phase (Freud's phallic stage) is again ushered in by new skills or abilities in the child. The 4-year-old is able to plan a bit, to take initiative in reaching particular goals. The child tries out these new cognitive skills, tries to conquer the world around him. He may try to go out into the street on his own; he may take a toy apart, then find he can't put it back together and throw it—parts and all—at his mother. It is a time of vigor of action and of behaviors that parents may see as aggressive. The risk is that the child may go too far in his forcefulness or that the parents may restrict and punish too much—either of which can produce guilt.

*Industry versus Inferiority: 6–12 Years*   The beginning of schooling is a major force in ushering in this stage. The child is now faced with the need to win approval through productivity—through learning to read, do sums, and other specific skills. The task of this period is thus simply to develop the repertoire of abilities society demands of the child. The obvious danger is that for one reason or another the child may be unable to develop the expected skills and will develop instead a basic sense of inferiority. (Of course, the opposite problem can occur, too: The child who has too much emphasis placed on achievement and becomes a "workaholic.")

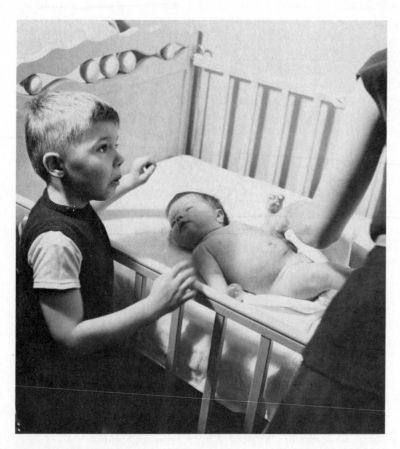

**Figure 9.5** This boy very clearly shows guilt—a quality that Erikson thought was central to the task for this age. The boy had been left alone with his infant brother and had played a bit roughly with him. When his mother returned, he pulled his hand back and turned toward her with this expression.

*Identity versus Role Confusion: 13–18 Years*   The task occurring during puberty (Freud's genital stage) is a major one, in which the adolescent reexamines his identity and the roles he must occupy. Erikson suggests that two "identities" are involved—a "sexual identity" and an "occupational identity." What should emerge for the adolescent from this period is a reintegrated sense of self, of what she wants to do and be, and of her appropriate sexual role. The risk is that of confusion, arising from the profusion of roles opening to the child at this age.

*Adult Stages*— As you can see in Table 9.3, Erikson proposed three further stages in adulthood (and he is thus one of the few theorists to offer a truly life-span theory): *intimacy versus isolation, generativity versus stagnation,* and *ego integrity versus despair.* Successful adult development thus requires the establishment of a truly intimate relationship, some form of "generativity" (bearing and rearing children, creative accomplishments, serving as mentor to younger colleagues, or the like), and a final reflective integration, resulting in acceptance of who you are and what you have done. (I find the idea of such continued opportunities for growth in adulthood to be an extremely comforting thought, by the way.)

## Some Evidence on Psychoanalytic Theory

There are no direct tests of the propositions of either Freudian or Eriksonian theory, mostly because both theories are general enough to make specific tests very difficult. But I can see the influence of psychoanalytic theories in a great many issues that are being studied intensively today. One example is the question of the impact on a child of being reared without a father. Given current divorce rates, there are obviously pressing social reasons for wanting an answer to this question. But there are important theoretical questions at issue, too, and psychoanalytic theory has been a dominant force in the thinking of many researchers who have studied divorce and its effects. I've explored some of these issues in Box 9.2.

A second research area that has its roots in psychoanalytic theory is the current work on the security or insecurity of children's early attachments. Specifically, both Erikson and Freud argue that the quality of the child's first relationship with the central caregiver will shape her relationships with other children and with other adults at later ages. I'll be talking a great deal more about early attachments in Chapter 11, but for now I want to point out that this particular aspect of psychoanalytic theory has received a good deal of support from recent studies, particularly the work of Alan Sroufe (e.g., Sroufe, 1978; Waters, Wippman, & Sroufe, 1979; Arend, Gove, & Sroufe, 1979). Children rated as being "securely attached" to their mothers (with a sense of basic "trust," in Erikson's terminology) at 12 or 18 months of age, com-

BOX 9.2

# BEING RAISED WITHOUT A FATHER: THE EFFECTS OF DIVORCE

Four out of every 10 children born during the 1970s (and perhaps more of those growing up in the 1980s) will spend at least part of their childhood in a one-parent family, most often with the mother (Hetherington, 1979).

What is the effect on the child of growing up without a father present full time? Freud thought that the impact could be substantial, even devastating. In particular, he thought that the damage would be greatest if the father was missing during the Oedipal period (age 3 to 5, approximately) when identification was taking place and that it would be greater for a boy. A girl still has her mother to identify with, so at least her sex-role identification is appropriate. But the boy, lacking a father, may never go through the identification process properly and may end up with a very confused sex-role orientation and perhaps a weaker superego.

From the social-learning point of view, too, divorce or father absence should have an effect. If the behavior of the remaining parent (usually the mother, although that is changing) is altered, the children's behavior should change as well. Mavis Hetherington and her colleagues (Hetherington, 1979; Hetherington, Cox, & Cox, 1978) have found that mothers become less affectionate and more inconsistent in their discipline in the first few years after a divorce. We might ex-

pect, as a result, that the children would become less tractable. Social-learning theorists also point to the lack of a male role model for the boy; this should affect the development of sex-role behaviors, particularly if the loss of the father occurs early.

The results of studies of children in divorced families (and raised without a full-time father) support some, but not all, of these depressing expectations.

First of all, virtually *all* children show at least short-term distress or disruption following a parental separation (Wallerstein & Kelly, 1980; Hetherington, 1979; Kurdek & Berg, 1983). In the first two years or so after a divorce, children typically become more defiant, more negative, often more depressed, angry, or aggressive. Their school performance typically goes down for at least a while (Mitchell, Hammond, & Bee, 1983), and they may be ill more often (Hess & Camara, 1979). This is a profoundly *disruptive* process for children, no matter what their age.

Second, the effects do seem to be greater for boys, particularly in the short term, just as both Freud and the social-learning theorists would expect (Hetherington, Cox, & Cox, 1978; Kurdek & Berg, 1983). Boys whose parents have been divorced show more distress, more negative and noncompliant behavior, and more school

pared to children with "insecure" attachments, have been found to be more friendly and outgoing with other children at age 2 and 3 and to be more persistent and curious in their play and in school. Some typical results from a more recent study in this same area by Donald Pastor (1981) are shown in Figure 9.6.

Pastor had rated a group of 18-month-old children on the security of their attachment to their mothers. Three to six months later, when the toddlers were 20 to 23 months old, he observed each child again in a standard situation while playing with another (strange) child. Ob-

problems than do girls from equivalent families.

Whether younger children are more severely affected is less clear. The *symptoms* children show differ, depending on their age when the parents split up. Wallerstein and Kelly, in their detailed study of 60 divorcing families (1980), found that 3- to 5-year-olds showed more fearfulness and more "regression" to infantile behavior than did older children, but the older children showed more sadness or anger. Over the long term, though, there was no indication that 3- to 5-year-olds had a more difficult time adjusting to the change. Other studies, though, hint at the possibility that the older the child at the time of the divorce, the easier the adjustment, perhaps because the older child has the cognitive capacity to make sense of the divorce while the younger child does not (e.g., Kurdek & Berg, 1983). There is no indication in these results, however, that there is something *uniquely* difficult for a child about having a parental separation during the Oedipal period.

So much for the bad news. The good news is that many of the worst effects seem to diminish after a year or two. Hetherington found that the mother's disorganization and the child's negativity both diminished. Findings on the long-term outcomes for children from divorced families are mixed; some children seem to show lasting consequences, while many appear to recover and function well.

What is encouraging about the recent work in this area is that we are beginning to get some sense of the elements in the family that help the child to recover from the initial shock and disruption. One key is for the child to have regular contact with the noncustodial father. Wallerstein and Kelly found that those youngsters who looked psychologically healthy five years after the divorce were usually those who had had regular, supportive contact with their fathers. Kurdek has also found that time spent alone with the father was a key element in children's adjustment.

Another related key seems to be the degree of continuing conflict between the separated parents. If the mother and father manage their new relationship amicably, then the children have an easier adjustment (Kurdek & Berg, 1983). Finally, anything that may decrease the mother's stress—keeping the same job rather than changing, having a secure income, having supportive friends—helps the child's adjustment as well as the parent's.

Overall, there is some support for both the Freudian and the social-learning theories in the findings on the effects of divorce, but the process is more complex than either theory describes. Children's responses to separation from the father are affected by their capacity to understand the loss (which is related to age), by the degree of disruption in the mother's life and her response to the child, and by the opportunity for continued contact with the "missing" father. It is never an easy process, but lasting negative consequences, while visible for some children, do not appear to be inevitable. The best news is that it is possible to help children deal with this crisis.

servers rated the behavior of the children in a number of ways, including their "sociability" (friendliness toward and cooperativeness with the mother and the other child) and "orientation to peer" (the degree of interest and attention the child showed toward the strange playmate). As you can see in the figure, toddlers who had earlier been rated as securely attached were more sociable and more strongly oriented toward the other child than were toddlers who had been rated as insecurely attached.

Sroufe and Pastor have not followed their subjects much past early

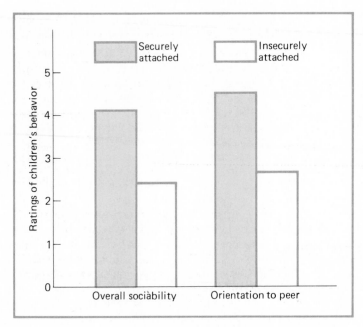

**Figure 9.6** A number of recent studies, like this one, have shown that children who are securely attached to their mothers in the first 12 to 18 months of life are more sociable and skillful in their interactions with peers than are less securely attached children. (*Source:* Pastor, 1981, from Table 1, p. 331.)

elementary school, so I don't know how lasting these differences may be. But this research suggests that the resolution of the first "stage" of psychosocial development may have a major impact on the child's subsequent relationships and thus on her personality, just as Freud and Erikson said.

### Strengths, Weaknesses, and Implications of Psychoanalytic Theories

Psychoanalytic theories like Freud's or Erikson's have several great attractions. First of all, they are *sequential* theories, and there is now increasing evidence (as I've described in earlier chapters) that sequences are built into many of the child's developing skills. Second, they focus our attention on the importance of the child's relationship with the caregivers. More important, both these theories suggest that the child's needs or "tasks" change with age, so that the parents must constantly adapt to the changing child. One of the implications of this is that we should not think of "good parenting" as if it were a global quality. Some of us may be very good at meeting the needs of an infant but quite awful at dealing with teenagers' identity struggles; others of us may have the opposite pattern. The child's eventual personality and her overall "health" thus depend on the interaction or transaction that develops in the particular family. This is an extremely attractive element of these theories, since more and more of our research is moving us toward exactly this conception of the process.

A third strength is that psychoanalytic theory has offered several useful new concepts, such as defense mechanisms or identification. The concept of identification, in particular, has been an influential one and has been widely adopted in one form or another. For example, Bandura's concept of modeling may be thought of as a variation of the identification concept.

These strengths have led to a resurgence of influence of psychoanalytic approaches in recent years, particularly Erikson's theory. Erikson has had a marked influence on the growing number of researchers studying adult development, since he offers one of the few frameworks for describing adult change. But his thinking about the early stages of development has also gained new respect.

The great weakness of the theory is its fuzziness. It is really a framework, a set of assumptions, rather than a precise description of causes and relationships. But it may turn out that this framework works in much the same way that the U.S. Constitution does: It is specific enough to be useful but flexible enough to be adapted to the changing times.

## A COGNITIVE ALTERNATIVE

The three theories I have just described represent the major, currently influential views of the origins of personality in early childhood. Neither Piaget nor his followers have offered a cognitive theory of personality development (although Lawrence Kohlberg, following this general tradition, has suggested a cognitive explanation of sex-role identity, as you'll see in the next chapter). But—undaunted by the general silence—let me offer a cognitive alternative.

The core of this alternative is the notion of the *self-concept*. By the age of 6 or 7, most children have very definite and clear ideas about themselves and their qualities. They know if they are a boy or a girl, if they are strong or weak, coordinated or clumsy, smart or not so smart, liked by other people or not, and on and on. This is a cognitive construction and can thus be thought of as a *scheme* in Piaget's sense. The child assimilates experiences and information to this scheme (to the self-concept), and the scheme changes (accommodates) over the early years of life. There are definable steps in the development of self-concept that are common to children (which I'll describe in the next chapter), but each child's self-concept has unique content. Once this unique "idea" of the self has developed, both the child's future thinking and her behavior are affected by the content of this scheme.

Remember from Chapter 7 that one of the characteristics of the process of assimilation is that new experiences or information are modified as they are taken into existing categories. So once the child has developed his self-concept scheme, new information is *interpreted* in light of the existing scheme. Once a child believes he is unpopular, for example, then the occasional times when he gets invited to a birthday party or someone chooses to sit next to him at lunch in the cafeteria are chalked up to other factors (there was no place else to sit; all the kids in the class got invited; etc.), and the underlying scheme isn't modified (accommodated) very much.

Thus, the self-concept, once well formed, serves as a central mediating process, leading to stable differences in behavior. It affects the activities the child will choose and his interpretations of the events that take place. It *can* be modified (accommodated) if the child accumulates enough experience or evidence that doesn't fit with the existing scheme. If the "unpopular" child noticed that classmates chose to sit next to him at lunch even when there were other seats available, eventually he might have to change the "unpopular" part of his self-concept. But since the child (like the adult) will choose activities or situations that fit his self-concept (e.g., sitting in the corner where no one is likely to see him or never giving birthday parties), he will be partially protected from such "nonconfirming" experiences.

This view of the self-concept bears a good deal of resemblance to the theory of "self-efficacy" recently proposed by Albert Bandura (1977, 1982), whose social-learning theory I have talked about in several places. (Obviously, the fact that Bandura has shifted to such "cognitive" grounds illustrates the fact that different theories are converging.) Bandura argues, basically, that each person's beliefs about what he can and cannot do affect his thought patterns, his actions, and his emotional reactions—in a word, his personality. Adults choose activities at which they believe they can do well and expend more effort trying to succeed at such activities. Both children and adults perform better on difficult tasks if they believe ahead of time that they can succeed.

This preliminary proposal is not yet a theory of personality development. Among other things, I have said nothing about the *origins* of a sense of self-efficacy or of specific self-concepts. But it does seem abundantly clear that the child's cognitive construction—her *idea* of who she is—shapes her behavior, her attitudes, her feelings, and her thoughts in pervasive ways.

## A TENTATIVE SYNTHESIS

I have given you four different views of the origins of those unique, individual patterns of behavior we call personality. Each view can be at least partially supported with research evidence, so it seems impossible to choose one of the four as the "correct" view. But can we combine them in any sensible way? There are those who argue that theories as different as these cannot ever be combined (Reese & Overton, 1970; Overton & Reese, 1973) because they make such different assumptions about the child's role in the whole process. I agree in part. I do not think we can simply add up the different sources of influence and say that personality is merely the sum of inborn temperament, reinforcement patterns, interactions with parents, and self-concept.

But more complex combinations seem fruitful to me. I have suggested one in Figure 9.7. In this model I am proposing that the child's inborn temperament is a beginning point—an initial bias in the system. Arrow number 1 shows a *direct* relationship between that inborn temperament and the eventual personality or behavior we see in a child.

I am suggesting a second direct effect in arrow number 2, between the pattern of the child's environment and his eventual pattern of behavior. Whether the parents respond reliably and contingently to the infant will affect his trust, which will show up in a range of behaviors later; whether the parents reinforce bratty behavior or friendly behavior will influence the child's future as well.

But most of what happens is much more complicated than that. The way the child is treated is influenced by her temperament (arrow 3), and both the basic temperament and the family environment affect the child's self-concept. The self-concept, in turn, helps to shape the behavior we see, the personality of the child.

The complexity of this system is nicely illustrated by a recent study by Susan Crockenberg (1981). She studied a group of 46 mothers and infants over the first year of the child's life. The child's irritability (an aspect of temperament) was measured when the baby was 5 to 10 days old, and the security of the child's attachment to the mother was mea-

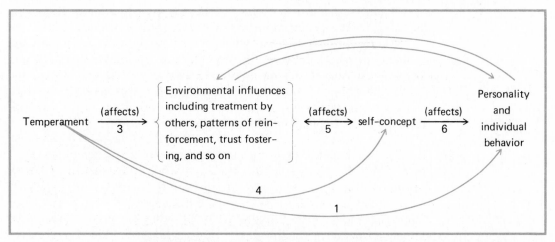

**Figure 9.7** A first try at a complex, interactive model to explain the formation of individual personality. Rather than merely adding, the environmental effects and the child's temperament both influence each other, and both affect the child's self-concept. What we think of as personality is a complex product of all three.

sured when the child was 12 months old. We might expect that irritable babies would be more likely to be insecurely attached, merely because they are more difficult to care for. In fact, Crockenberg found a small effect of this kind. But Crockenberg didn't stop there. She also measured the level of the mother's social support—the degree to which she had family and friends who were sufficiently helpful to assist her in dealing with the strains of a new child or other life changes she might be experiencing. The results of the study show that insecure attachment in the child was likely only when the mother had *both* an irritable infant *and* low levels of support. If the baby was irritable but the mother had good support, the child's attachment developed securely. Only when two difficult conditions occurred together did a poor outcome result for the child.

Finally, I have included arrow 7 in the diagram to underline the *transactional* elements of the system. Once the child's unique pattern of behaviors and attitudes (personality) is formed, it affects the environment she will encounter, the experiences she will choose, and the responses of the people around her, which, in turn, affect her behavior (Scarr & McCartney, 1983).

What we call personality is thus a blend of innate temperament with the patterns of stimulation and care the child receives from the parents and others. The parents are, in turn, influenced by the child's temperament and emerging personality, and their ability to respond supportively to the child is affected by a whole range of things in their own lives. All of these elements affect the child's self-concept, which, once formed, serves as a mediator for the system, directing the child's behavior and making change more difficult.

Obviously, this is only a very primitive synthesis. It is also a synthesis based on the assumption that the child is an active participant in the system, *constructing* his own self-concept and not merely reacting in an automatic way to reinforcements from the world around him. This assumption places me in the cognitive/psychoanalytic "camp" rather than in a narrow social-learning camp. But it seems to me that there are hardly any narrow social-learning theorists left! They are all beginning to sound like cognitive theorists. Whether my synthesis is on the right track or not, I think the field of developmental psychology is right on the edge of creating a model of personality development that blends elements from several of the approaches I have described to you in this chapter (Sroufe, 1979; Sameroff, 1982). It will be fascinating to watch a new consensus emerge in the next decade.

## SUMMARY

1. The word *personality* refers to a person's unique, individual, relatively enduring pattern of relating to others and responding to the world around her. *Personality* is a more general term than *temper-*

*ament,* since the latter refers primarily to inborn style of response to the environment.

2. The origins of personality differences have been described in three distinct theoretical approaches: temperament theory (primarily a biological approach), social-learning theory, and psychoanalytic theories.

3. Temperament theory proposes that each child is born with innately determined patterns or styles of reacting to people and objects. These patterns shape the child's interactions with the world and affect others' responses to the child as well.

4. Social-learning theorists assume that patterns of social behavior (what we normally call "personality") are learned through modeling. Because they are learned, they may be specific to particular situations; we should not necessarily expect consistency across situations or over time.

5. Current versions of social-learning theory, particularly Bandura's, have introduced some new cognitive elements. Bandura argues that a child's cognitive capacity (which changes with age) affects what she attends to and remembers of models' behavior.

6. Freud's psychoanalytic approach emphasizes a maturationally based developmental sequence of psycho*sexual* stages. In each stage, a particular erogenous zone is dominant. Of particular importance is the phallic stage, beginning at about age 4, when the Oedipal crisis is met and mastered through the process of identification.

7. Erikson's emphasis is on psycho*social* stages, each one shaped in part by social demands and in part by the child's physical and intellectual skills. Each of the major stages has a central task or "crisis," each relating to some aspect of the development of identity.

8. Recent research on such topics as the impact of the quality of a child's early attachment on her peer relationships and exploration has provided support for some aspects of the psychoanalytic view.

9. A cognitive-developmental theory of personality is also possible. The self-concept can be thought of as a scheme to which information is assimilated. Once well formed, the self-concept serves as a mediator, affecting the child's choice of activities, behaviors, and feelings.

10. Elements of all four views can be combined into an interactionist approach to personality development. Temperament may serve as the base from which personality grows, both by affecting behavior directly and by affecting the way others respond to the child. Both the temperament and the specific pattern of response from the people in the child's environment affect the child's self-concept, which then helps to create stability in the child's unique pattern of behavior.

**Behavior therapy**  A therapeutic intervention based on principles of reinforcement.

**Conscience**  Roughly equivalent to the term *superego*. The part of the personality (according to Freud) that monitors one's behavior, judging it to be acceptable or unacceptable.

**Defense mechanisms**  Strategies of the ego, in Freudian theory, for coping with anxiety, including denial, repression, identification, projection, and many others.

**Ego**  That portion of the personality in Freudian theory that organizes, plans, and keeps the person in touch with reality. Language and thought are both ego functions.

**Erogenous zones**  Portions of the body that in Freudian theory are thought to be sequentially the seat of heightened sexual awareness, such as the mouth, the anus, and the genitals.

**Id**  The first, primitive portion of the personality in Freud's theory; the storehouse of basic energy, continually pushing for immediate gratification.

**Identification**  The process of taking into oneself ("incorporating") the qualities and ideas of another person, which Freud thought was the result of the Oedipal crisis at age 3 to 5. The child attempts to make himself like his parent of the same sex.

**Libido**  The term used by Freud to describe the pool of sexual energy in each individual.

**Modeling**  Bandura's term for the process of learning through observation.

**Oedipal crisis**  The pattern of events Freud believed occurred between the ages of 3 and 5 when the child, because of fear of possible reprisal from the parent of the same sex and "sexual" desire for the parent of the opposite sex, identifies with the parent of the same sex.

**Personality**  The collection of individual, relatively enduring patterns of reacting to and interacting with others that distinguishes each child or adult.

**Psychosexual stages**  The stages of personality development suggested by Freud, including the oral, anal, phallic, latency, and genital stages.

**Psychosocial stages**  The stages of personality development suggested by Erikson, including trust, autonomy, initiative, industry, identity, intimacy, generativity, and ego integrity.

**Superego**  The "conscience" part of personality proposed by Freud, which is developed as a result of the identification process. The superego contains the parental and societal values and attitudes incorporated by the child.

*SUGGESTED READINGS*

Bandura, A. *Social learning theory.* Englewood Cliffs, N.J.: Prentice-Hall, 1977.
   Not easy reading, but the most up-to-date statement of Bandura's theory.
Erikson, E. H. *Identity and the life cycle.* New York: Norton, 1959 (reissued 1980).
   The middle section of this book, "Growth and crises of the healthy personality," is the best description I have found of the psychosocial stages of development.
Patterson, G. R. *Families.* Champaign, Ill.: Research Press, 1975.
   As a general rule, I don't lean much toward behavior modification approaches, but this is a wonderful book—clear, easy to understand, and very helpful, particularly if you are struggling with a child whose behavior stymies you.
Sroufe, L. A. The coherence of individual development. *American psychologist,* 1979, *34,* 834–841.
   A brief, readable paper that reflects much of what I see as the current thinking about personality development.

# 10.
# *the concept of self in children*

Try an experiment: Before you read any further, write down 20 separate answers to the question "Who am I?".

Now look over your list. Have you included descriptions of your appearance (e.g., "I have brown hair"); what you can do ("I play the guitar"); your beliefs ("I am a Protestant"); your skills, problems, or behavior patterns (e.g., "I have trouble getting along with bosses," or "I am a loner"); or your roles (e.g., "I am a parent," or "I am a psychologist")? And did you include some statement about your gender in the list somewhere ("I am a male" or "I am a female")?

My hunch is that you didn't have a lot of trouble thinking of 20 things to say about yourself and that you probably included some descriptions in most of the categories I mentioned. Each of us carries around a detailed, pervasive set of ideas about ourself—what we can and can't do, how we look and feel, how we compare to others—collectively called the **self-concept**. I mentioned in the last chapter that this set of ideas affects our behavior, our choices, our relationships with other people and may well be one very important root of what we call "personality."

In this chapter I want to talk about how children develop these ideas about themselves. Can we identify steps or sequences in the content or organization of children's self-concepts? The child's self-concept profoundly affects her social interactions, but it is a *cognitive* accomplishment as well—an *understanding* of the self. So we ought to see some parallels between the child's concept of the self and the themes of cognitive development I traced in Chapter 7.

William Damon and Daniel Hart (1982) have suggested (based on the work of William James, 1892) that there are two parts to the self-concept that may develop somewhat differently. There is the sense of *me*, the definition of the self that includes all our individual characteristics—what we look like, what we know or can do, what we like and don't like. This is what Michael Lewis and Jeanne Brooks-Gunn (1979; Lewis, 1981) call the **categorical self**. It is a definition of the self by category, by comparison with others.

The second part is the *I*, the sense of "self as knower," the awareness of self as a continuous entity, the self as having the capacity to choose. This is similar to what Lewis and Brooks-Gunn call the **existential self.** Thus, the sense that I exist, that I am separate from others, is part of the "I," while my ideas about my specific qualities are part of the sense of "me." Most of what I have to say in this chapter will deal with the "me" part of the self-concept, the "categorical self." I'll talk more about the "I" part in Chapter 12, where the links between cognition and social development will be traced more fully. But the early awareness of the self as a separate and unique entity is the first step in the whole process of developing the self-concept.

Let me begin by tracing the developmental sequence.

## DEVELOPMENTAL CHANGES IN THE SELF-CONCEPT

### Infancy

Both Piaget and Freud have emphasized that in the first months of life the infant does not distinguish between himself and other people. Freud talks about the **symbiotic** relationship between the mother and the infant in which the two are joined together as if they were one. For the infant, the first step in creating a self-concept must be to develop some primitive sense of a separate self. Lewis and Brooks-Gunn (1979; Lewis, 1981) argue that the basic underpinnings of this sense of separateness are the contingent interactions the baby has with the people around him. When he cries, someone picks him up; when he drops his rattle, someone returns it to him; when his mother smiles, he smiles back. By this process the baby slowly begins to grasp the basic difference between self and other. I have already pointed out the importance of contingent responsiveness for the development of both language and cognitive skills in the infant and young child. This same pattern may also be critical for the development of the concept of the separate self as well.

As nearly as we can tell (it is very hard to study!), this first primitive step in the development of the self-concept takes place sometime between 12 and 18 months (Damon & Hart, 1982). Because babies can't answer questions like "Who am I?" researchers have had to be clever about devising ways to check on the baby's self-awareness. One of the cleverest approaches has been to observe babies watching themselves in a mirror (Amsterdam, 1972). First the baby is placed in front of a mirror, just to see how she behaves. Most infants of about 9 to 12 months will look at their own images, make faces, or try to interact with the baby in the mirror in some way. After allowing this free exploration for a time, the experimenter, while pretending to wipe the baby's face with a cloth, puts a spot of rouge on the baby's nose and then again lets the baby look in the mirror. The crucial test of self-recognition, and thus of awareness of the self, is whether the baby reaches for the spot on her *own* nose (not the nose on the face in the mirror).

The result from one of Lewis's studies using this procedure is shown in Figure 10.2. As you can see, none of the 9- to 12-month-old children in this study touched their noses, but by 21 months, three-quarters of the children showed that level of self-recognition. The figure also shows the rate at which children refer to themselves by name when they are shown a picture of themselves. You can see that this development occurs at almost exactly the same time as self-recognition in a mirror.

In other studies, Lewis and Brooks-Gunn (1979) found that 15- to 18-month-old children smiled and looked more at pictures or video-

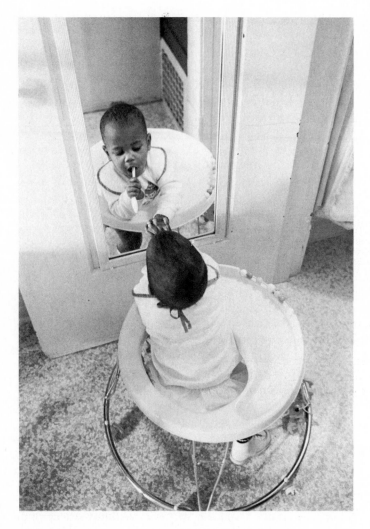

**Figure 10.1** One of the signs that a child has understood his own separateness is that he recognizes himself in a mirror. Research by Lewis and others shows that a child of 18 or 20 months normally can do this, although some rudiments of self-recognition may come earlier.

tapes of themselves than at pictures or videotapes of other children, so the ability to "recognize" the self and distinguish it from others is apparently present somewhere in the middle of the second year of life.

There is some indication that this developing understanding parallels the child's grasp of the object concept (Chapter 5): While the baby is figuring out that the bottle he handles continues to exist from day to day, even when it is out of sight, he is also figuring out that he exists separately and continuously, too. This link is particularly clear in a study by Bertenthal and Fischer (1978), who tested 6- to 24-month-old infants on the traditional object constancy tests involving hidden objects and also used several tests of children's recognition of themselves in a mirror. The researchers identified seven steps in each development

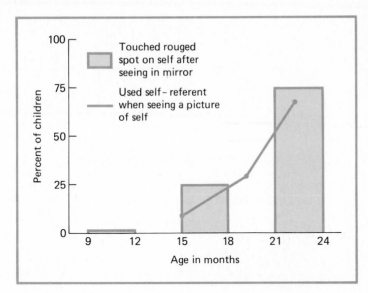

**Figure 10.2** Both the growth of children's use of self-references in their language and their recognition of themselves in a mirror show that the basic sense of a separate self is well established in most children by 18 months to 2 years of age. (*Source:* Lewis & Brooks, 1978, pp. 214–215.)

(object concept and self-awareness) and found that most children were about one step further ahead in understanding the object concept than they were in self-awareness, as you can see in Figure 10.3. Whether the object concept is *necessary* for the development of the concept of self I don't know, but it is interesting that these understandings seem to develop in parallel.

## Early Childhood: The Categorical Self Develops

Once the infant has clearly understood that she is separate and distinct from others (has a beginning sense of "I"), the process of defining the self begins. This is a *comparative* process. The child must notice dimensions on which people differ and place herself somewhere along each dimension, such as age or gender or physical coordination or whatever. The kinds of dimensions (the categories) that are salient change with age, but the process of defining by comparison seems to be constant.

Some of the earliest dimensions children pay attention to are age, size, and sex (Damon & Hart, 1982), which seem to become significant at about 18 to 24 months, and children begin to label themselves and other people as "old" or "young," "big" or "little." Carolyn Edwards and Michael Lewis (1979), for example, found that when they asked 3- to 5-year-old children to sort photographs of infants, toddlers, children, and adults, they made separate groupings for "big children" and "little children" and for "parents" and "grandparents." The category of "little children" seemed to include everyone up to about age 5, while "big children" included those up to about age 13 or so. Everyone older

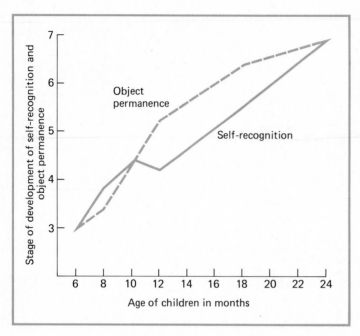

**Figure 10.3** In this study, Bertenthal and Fischer tested children's object permanence and their self-recognition separately. As you can see, they found that these two types of understanding develop at about the same rate in the early months of life, with object permanence coming perhaps slightly sooner. These results don't tell us that object permanece is *necessary* for the child's self-recognition, but the parallel is intriguing. (*Source:* Bertenthal & Fischer, 1978, Figure 1, p. 49.)

than that was a grown-up from the perspective of the preschool-age child.

These first comparisons seem to be based primarily on physical features of people. Children from 3 to 5 also define themselves by their actions, what they do and what skills they have. When Ann Keller and her colleagues (Keller, Ford, & Meacham, 1978) asked children this age to complete sentences like "(Child's name) is_____" or "(Child's name) is a boy/girl who_____", the most common answer was a description of an action: "sits and watches TV," "I can pick things up," "I help Mommy," "goes to school," "eats." About 30 percent of the responses of the 3-year-olds and 50 percent of the responses of the 5-year-olds fit this category.

### School Age

Self-definitions by physical features and by action continue into early elementary-school years, but some new elements enter as well. Six- to 12- year-old children begin to define themselves by what they like and dislike, and they make more explicit comparisons with others. You can see all these themes in the response of an 11-year-old girl to the "Who am I?" question I asked you to answer at the beginning of the chapter:

My name is A. I'm a human being. I'm a girl. I'm a truthful person. I'm not very pretty. I do so-so in my studies. I'm a very good cellist. I'm a very good pianist. I'm a little bit tall for my age. I like several boys. I

**Figure 10.4** Preschool-age children, like this boy, frequently insist on doing things for themselves. This may reflect aspects of autonomy (in Erikson's sense), but it may also reflect the child's emerging sense of self—an extension of the self to "things I can do." By trying out the boundaries of his skills, the child is defining himself.

like several girls. I'm old-fashioned. I play tennis. I am a *very* good swimmer. I try to be helpful. I'm always ready to be friends with anybody. Mostly I'm good, but I lose my temper. I'm not well-liked by some girls and boys. I don't know if I'm liked by boys or not. (Montemayor & Eisen, 1977, pp. 317–318)

Thus, as the child moves through the concrete operations period, her self-definition becomes more complex, less tied to external features, more focused on feelings, on ideas.

## Adolescence

This trend toward greater abstraction in the self-definition continues during adolescence. Compare the answers of this 17-year-old to the "Who am I?" question with the ones you just read:

I am a human being. I am a girl. I am an individual. I don't know who I am. I am a Pisces. I am a moody person. I am an indecisive person. I am an ambitious person. I am a very curious person. I am not an individual. I am a loner. I am an American (God help me). I am a Democrat. I am a liberal person. I am a radical. I am a conservative. I am a pseudoliberal. I am an atheist. I am not a classifiable person (i.e., I don't want to be). (Montemayor & Eisen, 1977, p. 318)

Obviously, this girl's self-concept is much less tied to her physical characteristics or even her abilities than are those of the younger child. She is describing traits or ideology, both of which are quite abstract. You can see the shift I'm describing graphically in Figure 10.5, based on the answers of all 262 subjects in the Montemayor and Eisen study. Each of the subjects' answers to the "Who am I?" question was placed in one or more specific categories, such as references to physical properties ("I am tall," "I have blue eyes") or references to ideology ("I am a Democrat," "I believe in God"). As you can see, older teenagers define themselves less by their physical properties and more by ideology.

*Identity in Adolescence*   This increasing preoccupation with ideology may reflect the central task of adolescence, as Erikson described it, of *identity versus role confusion.* The teenager's old definition of himself is called into question, in part because of the changes of puberty but also because of changing expectations on the part of his family and soci-

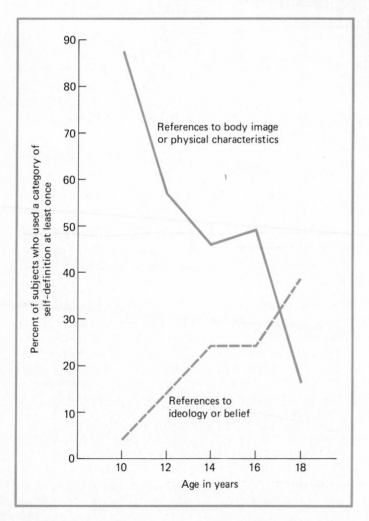

**Figure 10.5** With increasing age, children define themselves less and less by what they look like and more and more by what they believe or feel. (*Source:* Montemayor & Eisen, 1977, from Table 1, p. 316.)

ety. He is expected to be more independent, more responsible for himself. And he is expected to look to the future, to plan, to decide what or who he *will* be as well as what or who he is.

The changes in the self-concept that occur at adolescence are thus a reflection not just of greater cognitive abstractness but also of a search for a new understanding of the self. It is precisely this search that is referred to as the "identity crisis." In particular, the adolescent must develop an *occupational identity* (what will he *do* as an adult?), an *ideological identity* (what does he believe in?), and a *sexual identity* (what pattern of sexual behavior is acceptable? What sex role is desired?).

Nearly all the current work on the formation of these elements of the adolescent identity has been based on James Marcia's descriptions of identity statuses (Marcia, 1966, 1980). Following Erikson's basic formulation, Marcia argues that there are two key parts to any adolescent identity formation: a *crisis* and a *commitment.* By a "crisis" Marcia means a period of decision making when old values, old choices are reexamined. This may occur as a sort of upheaval—the classic notion of a crisis—or it may occur gradually. The outcome of the reevaluation is a commitment to some specific role, some particular ideology.

If you put these two elements together, as I have in Figure 10.6, you can see that four different "identity statuses" are possible.

**Identity achievement**: The young person has been through a crisis and has reached a commitment.

**Moratorium**: A crisis is in progress, but no commitment has yet been made.

**Foreclosure**: A commitment has been made without the young person's having gone through a crisis. No reassessment of old positions has been made. Instead, he has simply accepted a parentally defined commitment.

**Identity diffusion**: The young person is not in the midst of a crisis (although there may have been one in the past), and no commitment has been made. Diffusion may represent either an early stage in the process (before a crisis) or a failure to reach a commitment after a crisis.

The struggle for a new identity seems to occur quite late in adolescence—in late high school or the early twenties (Archer, 1982; Waterman, 1982). Some results from a study by Philip Meilman (1979), shown in Figure 10.7, illustrate this very clearly. He classified separate groups of 12-, 15-, 18-, 21-, and 24-year-olds using Marcia's categories. As you can see, it wasn't until age 18 that any significant number of young people in this study had reached the "achievement" status. In a similar

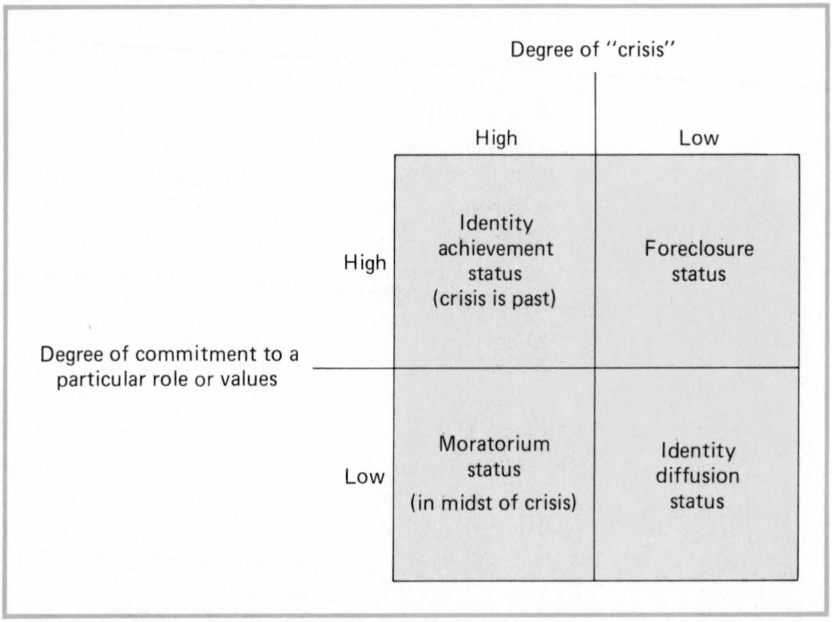

Degree of "crisis"

|  | High | Low |
|---|---|---|
| **High** | Identity achievement status (crisis is past) | Foreclosure status |
| **Low** | Moratorium status (in midst of crisis) | Identity diffusion status |

Degree of commitment to a particular role or values

**Figure 10.6** The four identity statuses proposed by Marcia. For a fully achieved identity, the young person must both have examined his or her values and have reached a firm commitment. (*Source:* Marcia, 1980.)

study, Sally Archer (1982) found that virtually all sixth and eighth graders were in the diffusion or foreclosure statuses and only a few tenth and twelfth graders could be classified as in moratorium or achievement statuses. Most young people seem to grapple with these issues first with reference to a future occupation and religious beliefs. Political ideologies and sex-role identities come later. (I can remember that religious and political ideologies were very much the topic of all those late-night sessions in the dorm when I was in college.)

Other studies using Marcia's categories (Waterman, Geary, & Waterman, 1974; Marcia, 1976) show that there is a developmental transition involved, with most college students moving from diffusion through moratorium to a final identity.

## Summary of Developmental Changes in the Self-Concept

Let me sum all this up for you. The young child first develops a primitive sense of her own separateness. This is followed quickly by beginning definitions of herself in terms of her physical properties (age, size, gender) and what she does. Over the period of concrete and formal operations (from age 6 through adolescence), the content of the child's self-concept becomes more abstract, less and less tied to external physical qualities. During late adolescence, the whole self-concept also ap-

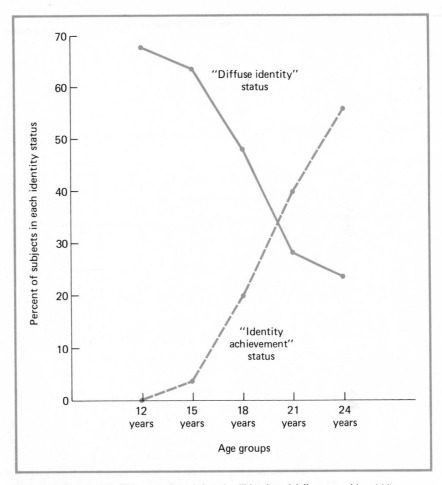

**Figure 10.7** Although Erikson believed that the "identity crisis" occurred in middle adolescence (perhaps at 15 or 16), these results from Philip Meilman's study are typical in showing that most young people do not reach "identity achievement" until they are in their late teens or early twenties. (*Source:* Meilman, 1979, p. 231. Copyright 1979 by the American Psychological Association. Reprinted by permission.)

pears to undergo a kind of reorganization, with a new future-oriented sexual, occupational, and ideological identity created.

## INDIVIDUAL DIFFERENCES IN THE SELF-CONCEPT

So far, I have talked about the self-concept as if there were no values attached to the categories by which we define ourselves. But that's clearly not the case. Look again at the self-descriptions given by the 11-year-old and the 17-year-old (quoted earlier). The younger child includes a lot of positive statements about herself, while the older child gives mostly negative descriptions. This evaluative, positive/negative dimension of the self-concept is usually referred to as **self-esteem**. Children who have "high self-esteem" are those whose definitions of themselves are primarily positive, while those who define themselves in mostly negative terms are said to have "low self-esteem."

You will find it encouraging to know that self-esteem generally rises during late elementary school and through adolescence: 18- and 20-year-olds usually think of themselves more positively than they did when they were 12 or 14 (O'Malley & Bachman, 1983; Simmons et al., 1983). But within this general developmental trend, there appear to be some persisting individual differences.

## Differences in Self-Esteem

What does it mean for a child to have high or low self-esteem? Table 10.1 lists some of the other characteristics of high–self-esteem children. It certainly appears that evaluating yourself positively is a good thing. It is associated with many other qualities that most of us see as valuable (such as doing well in school and having more friends). For those of you who are particularly concerned about fostering such positive feelings in your children, I've explored some of what we know about the kinds of families such children come from in Box 10.1.

Let me enter one note of caution about what I've listed in Table 10.1. If you read women's magazines or other "popular" press, you may have concluded that a child's or adult's self-esteem is the most central element in mental or emotional health. But the research on children's self-esteem (on which Table 10.1 is based) is inconsistent and messy (Damon & Hart, 1982; Wylie, 1979). There is not much good research, and the results of the studies are not consistent. This could mean that self-esteem is not nearly so significant a factor for children as we have thought, or it could mean that we have done a poor job of measuring self-esteem.

My own sense is that the child's beliefs about herself (her *total* self-concept) have a powerful effect on her behavior but that there may not be a global positive/negative quality to those beliefs. Most of us

Table 10.1

**Characteristics of children with high self-esteem compared to children with low self-esteem**

They get somewhat better grades in school and on achievement tests.

They see themselves as responsible for their own success or failure.

They have more friends.

They see their relationship with their parents more positively.

They may be more competitive (DeVoe, 1977).

As adolescents, they are more likely to have achieved "identity status" (LaVoie, 1976).

know that we are good at some things and bad at others, and children make these discriminations, too. What is needed now is some decent research in which the *content* of the child's self-concept and the positive/negative evaluation are measured separately. Then we may be able to figure out which element is the more important for the child's behavior.

## Differences in Identity Achievement

Research on differences in identity achievement is much newer, and here, too, the conclusions are only tentative. The findings so far suggest that teenagers and young adults who are in the identity achievement or moratorium statuses, compared to those in diffusion or foreclosure, are more independent and autonomous, get better grades in college, are more successful in establishing satisfying intimate relationships as young adults (Kacerguis & Adams, 1980; Hodgson & Fischer, 1979), and are higher in self-esteem (Marcia, 1980).

A particularly vivid picture of the characteristics of identity achievers versus nonachievers comes from a series of case studies of psychosocially "mature" and "immature" eleventh-grade boys and girls by Ruthellen Josselson and her colleagues (Josselson, Greenberger, & McConochie, 1977a, 1977b). Josselson has not used Marcia's categories but is clear that the "mature" young people in her studies are those who are either struggling toward or have reached a completed identity.

Among the boys, those with low maturity were heavily focused on the here and now. They made few plans for the future, and their behavior was guided by what other people thought of them or did for them. Someone else decided whether they should go to college or get a job after high school; their self-esteem was dependent on being liked by their friends. Many of these boys were popular, and many were actively involved in sports. Nearly all the boys in the "immature" group also had a steady girlfriend.

By contrast, high-maturity boys were very future-oriented. They thought about what they would do with their lives. For them, self-esteem arose from what they did more than from what other people thought. (Other recent research by Grotevant and Thorbecke, 1982, also shows that this quality of not caring what other people think is characteristic of teenage boys who have developed clear occupational identities.) Mature boys were also quite introspective and tried to understand other people's motivations.

One of the very interesting findings in this study was that among the boys, those who were *low* in maturity were the most popular, the most likely to be seen as leaders in their group. The low-maturity boys were very friend-oriented and cared a great deal about being accepted by and being part of the gang. The higher-maturity boys were often

BOX 10.1

# *REARING A CHILD WITH HIGH SELF-ESTEEM*

Where does high self-esteem come from? Is it something you just have, like blue eyes or black hair? Or are there some specific experiences that foster it? These questions have considerable personal relevance for at least two reasons. You may want to understand better where your own level of self-esteem came from, and you may want to rear your own children so that they have the benefit of high self-esteem.

All the evidence tells us that the child's self-esteem is rooted in family experiences. Stanley Coopersmith (1967), who has been one of the major researchers in this area, found that school-age children with high self-esteem had parents with high self-esteem, too—which may suggest that some work on your own self-esteem would be a good first step if you are concerned about your children. More important, in families in which the children liked themselves, the children were treated as responsible individuals. Mothers in these families were more accepting and positive toward their children, more affectionate, and more likely to praise the children for their accomplishments. They were interested in their children and showed it. They expected their children to have opinions and wanted them to share those opinions with others.

The parents of the children with high self-esteem also set fairly strict and clear limits for their children's behavior and applied those limits consistently. So such parents provide quite a lot of consistent guidance and discipline and are loving at the same time.

This combination of firm but reasoned control, positive encouragement of independence, and a warm and loving atmosphere shows up again in a particularly interesting study of preschool children by Diana Baumrind (1972). She selected children who were content with themselves, self-reliant, self-controlled, and explorative and compared them with children who had poor self-esteem, little curiosity and exploratory behavior, and little self-reliance. The children with the highest self-esteem, self-reliance, and explorative tendencies had parents with the same combination of traits that Coopersmith found in parents of children with high self-esteem. Baumrind calls this combination **authoritative parental style**, in contrast to either **authoritarian parental style** (detached, controlling, and less warm) or **permissive parental style** (noncontrolling and undemanding but quite warm and affectionate). In her study, the least self-reliant and effective children were likely to

active in school, but they were also more self-sufficient. Josselson's results suggest that "success" for a boy in the high school culture may not be a sign of overall health or growth.

Among girls, on the other hand, it was the *high*-maturity girls who were seen as popular and as leaders. These were girls "who [took] themselves seriously," as Josselson put it. They were introspective and had thought about who they were and where they were going. But their thinking was much less focused on an occupation than on their own inner nature. They wanted to find out *who* they were, not what they would do. So they differed from the high-maturity boys in their attitude about the future. Still, most of them had specific career plans and expected to work in addition to marriage.

have permissive parents; the most positive and competent children were likely to have authoritative parents, and the children of authoritarian parents fell in between.

Aside from the general style of discipline and the family warmth, two other things that parents do seem to affect the child's self-esteem. The first is simply how they label the child to herself. Children who are repeatedly told that they are "pretty" or "smart" or "a good athlete" are likely to have higher self-esteem than are children who are told that they are "dumb" or "clumsy" or a "late bloomer." I know of one mother and father who call their son "jerk" or "the jerk." And I remember vividly from my own childhood being called clumsy. When something was broken in our house, the question never seemed to be "Who broke the dish?" Instead, the question seemed (to me) to be "Helen, when did you break the dish?" I suspect that I did not break things more than other children, but I certainly came to believe that I did. My self-concept then and now includes a sense of physical clumsiness, and my self-esteem is lower as a result. The moral is that as parents we need to be very careful what sort of language we use to describe our children's behavior. What we say out of irritation, or even in an attempt at humor, may make a lasting impression.

For a girl, high self-esteem also seems to be helped by having a close, supportive relationship with her father. Highly successful, competent, self-confident women consistently report that their fathers treated them "like a son"—expecting them to do well, teaching them skills, spending time with them (Hennig & Jardim, 1976). What seems to emerge from this kind of treatment is a girl whose self-concept includes more masculine traits. Such girls (as you'll see in more detail later in the chapter) typically have higher self-esteem than do girls who define themselves in more traditionally feminine ways.

Such involved and supportive relationships between fathers and daughters are more common in families in which there are no sons. But there is certainly nothing to prevent a father from establishing this sort of relationship with all his children, boys and girls.

In sum, if you want your children to emerge from early childhood with a strongly positive view of themselves, both the mother and the father will need to love and respect the child as an individual, spend time with the child one-on-one, set clear limits and high expectations for the child's behavior, watch what they call the child or how they "explain" his behavior. As a parent, I know that this "formula" is easier to state than to put into practice, but it is worth the effort to try.

Outwardly, the low-maturity girls were very similar to the high-maturity girls. Both groups were involved in school activities; both had friends; and both dated. But inwardly there were differences in values. "The world of the low-maturity girls is dominated by two concerns; having fun and having things" (Josselson et al., 1977b, p. 152). As a group, these girls were outgoing, often cheerful, sometimes successful with their peers. But they were "diffuse" in Marcia's terms.

These results fit the current "popular" model of the key place of clear identity and high self-esteem in a young person's overall adjustment. But we know a lot less than I would like about the origins of these differences or how long they persist into adulthood.

## THE SELF-CONCEPT: A SUMMING UP

There are obviously many questions still to be answered. But I want to emphasize once again that a child's self-concept appears to be a highly significant mediating concept. Her beliefs about herself and her abilities color nearly all of her actions and interactions. The child who believes that she can't play baseball behaves differently from the child who believes that she can. She is likely to avoid baseballs, bats, playing fields, and other children who play baseball. If forced to play, she may make self-deprecating remarks like "You know I can't play," or she may play self-defeating games, such as refusing to watch the ball when she swings at it or not running after the ball in right field because she knows she couldn't catch it even if she did get there in time. (If you think all this sounds autobiographical, you're right! Those of you who were bad at baseball, as I believed I was, know that the poorest fielders are *always* put in right field.)

A child who believes that he can't do long division will behave quite differently in the classroom from the child whose self-concept includes the idea "I am good at math." He may not try to work long-division problems on the theory that if you don't try, you can't fail. Or he may try much harder, paying the price in anxiety about failure.

The point is that these beliefs are pervasive, and they develop early. Such beliefs do not seem to be easily changed. We need to know a good deal more about the origins of the child's self-definitions if we are to understand how to modify the inaccurate elements.

## THE DEVELOPMENT OF GENDER AND SEX-ROLE CONCEPTS

The element of the child's self-concept I have mostly left out of the discussion so far is the gender concept and the accompanying concept of sex roles. How do children come to understand that they are a boy or a girl, and when and how do they learn what behaviors are "appropriate" for their gender? I have saved this set of questions for a separate discussion partly because this has been an area of hot debate and extensive research for the past decade (so there is a lot to say) and partly because this set of questions has such central relevance for so many of us.

### Some Definitions

Before I can delve into these questions, though, I need to define some terms for you. These words and phrases often get used fuzzily or interchangeably, which only confuses things. I will use these terms and phrases this way:

The **gender concept** is the basic understanding of one's own gender. "Am I a boy or a girl?" "Will I stay the same gender for all my life?" This is a *cognitive* accomplishment.

**Sex roles** are the set of behaviors, attitudes, rights, duties, and obligations that are part of the "role" of being a boy or a girl, a male or a female. All roles have such collections of duties, rights, and expected behaviors. Teachers are supposed to behave in certain ways, as are employees or mothers or baseball managers. These are all roles. Sex roles are somewhat broader than most other roles in our culture, but they are nonetheless roles.

**Sex-role stereotyping** is a process of overextending the sex roles or applying them too rigidly. Any stereotype involves assigning people to rigidly defined categories without taking into account the individual qualities. When we say "Men are unemotional," we are expressing a stereotype. The male sex role may include "unemotional" as one of its qualities (that is, men are "supposed to be" unemotional to fit the role), but clearly many men show their emotions easily. Stereotypes thus go beyond statements of what is "supposed to be" to inaccurately broad statements about "what is."

**Sex typing** and **sex-role behavior** refer to the extent to which a child's behavior (or an adult's) matches the expectation for her or his sex role. A girl may know quite well that she is a girl and be able to describe the sex roles accurately but still behave in a tomboyish way. We would say that her behavior is not "sex-typed," whereas a girl who adopts more traditional play patterns would show "sex-typed behavior."

If we are going to understand the development of the child's concept of gender, we have to understand all of these elements. How does the child come to know what gender he is? How and when does he develop ideas about sex roles? Does sex-role stereotyping also occur in young children? And how well do children match their behavior to the sex roles or the stereotypes?

## Developmental Patterns

*The Development of the Gender Concept*   How soon does a child figure out that she is a girl or he is a boy? It depends on what we mean by "figure out." There seem to be three steps. First, there is **gender identity**, which is simply a child's ability to label his own sex correctly and to identify other people as men or women, boys or girls. Children seem to notice those features that differentiate male from female quite early—as early as 15 to 18 months. And by age 2, if you show them a set of pictures of a same-sex child and several opposite-sex children and say "Which one is you?" most children can correctly pick out the same-sex picture (Thompson, 1975). By $2\frac{1}{2}$ or 3, most children can correctly label and identify the sex of others as well (point out "Which one is a girl?" or "Which one is a boy?" in a set of pictures). Hair length and clothing seem to be the cues that children are using for these early discriminations (not a perfect guide to gender these days!).

Accurate labeling, though, does not signify complete understanding. As is true with all the concepts I talked about in Chapter 7, which show increasing subtlety and complexity over the preschool and early school years, the gender concept undergoes further refinements. The second step is **gender stability**, the understanding that you stay the same gender throughout life. Researchers have measured this by asking children such questions as "When you were a little baby, were you a little girl or a little boy?" or "When you grow up, will you be a mommy or a daddy?" Ronald Slaby and Karin Frey (1975) found that most children understood the stability aspect of gender by about age 4.

Finally, there is the development of true **gender constancy**, which is the recognition that someone stays the same gender even though he may appear to change by wearing different clothes or having different hair length. For example, girls don't change into boys by cutting their hair very short or by wearing boys' clothes. It may seem odd that a child who understands that he will stay the same gender throughout life (gender stability) can nonetheless still be confused about the effect of changes in dress or appearance on gender. But numerous studies show this sequence.

The underlying logic of this sequence becomes a bit clearer if we draw a parallel between gender constancy and the concept of conservation I described in Chapter 7. Conservation of mass or number or weight involves recognition that an object remains the same in some fundamental way even though it changes externally in some fashion. Gender constancy is thus a kind of "conservation of gender" and is not typically understood until about 5 or 6, when the other conservations are first grasped (Slaby & Frey, 1975; Marcus & Overton, 1978).

In sum, children as young as 2 or 2½ know their own sex and that of people around them, but they do not have a fully developed concept of gender until they are 5 or 6.

*The Development of Sex-Role Concepts and Stereotypes*    Obviously, figuring out your gender and understanding that it stays constant is only part of the story. Learning what goes with or ought to go with being a boy or a girl is also a vital part of the child's task.

Researchers have studied this in two ways—by asking children what boys and girls like to do and what they are like (which is an inquiry about stereotypes) and by asking children if it is *okay* for boys to play with dolls or for girls to climb trees or to do equivalent "cross-sex" things.

The youngest children who have been asked about their ideas about boys and girls or men and women are the 2½- and 3½-year-olds studied by Deanna Kuhn and her colleagues (Kuhn, Nash, & Brucken, 1978). They showed children paper dolls (a boy figure and a girl figure) and then made statements such as "I like to play with dolls." The children were to say whether the boy doll or the girl doll had made that statement. They found that nearly all the 2½-year-olds they studied could do this task and had remarkably similar ideas about the two sexes.

Both boys and girls thought that girls like to play with dolls, like to help mother, like to cook dinner, like to clean house, talk a lot, never hit, and say "I need some help." Both boys and girls thought that boys like to play with cars, like to help father, like to build things, and say "I can hit you."

In addition, each sex saw its own gender as having special positive qualities. Girls saw other girls as looking nice, giving kisses, and never fighting; boys saw other boys as working hard. At the same time, each sex had some negative perceptions about the other: Girls saw boys as liking to fight and as mean and weak. Boys saw girls as crying and being slow.

Obviously, a lot of these ideas match the adult sex stereotypes. In our society, adults see men as being competent, skillful, assertive, aggressive, and able to get things done. Adults see women as warm and expressive, tactful, quiet, gentle, aware of others' feelings, and lacking in competence, independence, and logic (Rosenkrantz et al., 1968). Two- and 3-year-olds already see girls as less aggressive and more nurturant.

The strongest stereotypes (most rigidly held) seem to be found among elementary-school children (Ullian, 1981). Deborah Best, John Williams, and their colleagues (Best et al., 1977; Williams, Bennett, & Best, 1975) found that fourth and fifth graders in the United States, England, and Ireland see women as weak, emotional, soft-hearted, sentimental, sophisticated, and affectionate. They see men as strong, robust, aggressive/assertive, cruel, coarse, ambitious, and dominant. Kindergartners in these studies showed some of these themes, but not as strongly, while in adolescence these stereotypes seem to become somewhat more flexible (Emmerich & Shepard, 1982; Huston-Stein & Higgens-Trenk, 1978).

This pattern of increasing and then declining sex-role stereotyping (ideas about what men and women *are* like) is matched by changes in children's ideas about what boys and girls *ought to* be like. This trend emerges particularly clearly in a lovely study by William Damon (1977). He told a story to children aged 4 through 9. In this story, a little boy named George likes to play with dolls. His parents tell him that only little girls play with dolls; little boys shouldn't. They buy him some other toys, but still George prefers dolls. The children were then asked a batch of questions about this:

Why do people tell George not to play with dolls? Are they right?
Is there a rule that boys shouldn't play with dolls?

What should George do?
Does George have a right to play with dolls?
What if George wanted to wear a dress to school? Can he do that?
(Damon, 1977, p. 242)

Four-year-olds in this study thought it was okay for George to play with dolls. There was no rule against it, and he should do it if he wanted to. Six-year-olds, in contrast, thought it was *wrong* for George to play with dolls. At this age, what boys (or girls) *do* has become transformed into what boys and girls *ought to do* or *must do*. They say things like:

> He should only play with things that boys play with. . . . If a boy is playing with something, like if a boy plays with a Barbie doll, then he's just going to get people teasing him, and if he tries to play more, to get girls to like him, then the girls won't like him either. (Damon, 1977, p. 255)

By about age 9, children have differentiated between what boys and girls usually do and what is "wrong." One boy said, for example, that breaking windows was wrong and bad but that playing with dolls was not bad in the same way: "Breaking windows you're not supposed to do. And if you play with dolls, well you can, but boys usually don't" (Damon, 1977, p. 263).

What seems to be happening is that the 5- and 6-year-olds, having figured out that she is permanently a girl and he is a boy, are searching for a *rule* about how boys and girls behave (Martin & Halverson, 1981). They pick up information from watching adults, from watching TV, from listening to the labels that are attached to different activities (e.g., "Boys don't cry"). Initially, children treat these as absolute, moral rules. Later they understand that these are social conventions, at which point sex-role concepts become more flexible and stereotyping wanes (although it does not in any sense disappear; sex stereotyping is very strong among adults).

One of the interesting sidelights in this research is that the male stereotype and sex-role concept seems to develop a bit earlier and to be stronger than the female stereotype and sex-role concept. More children agree on what men are or should be like than on what women are or should be. This might happen because children have seen women in more different roles (mother and teacher, for example) than they have seen men. Or it could mean that the female role in our society is more flexible than the male role. At any rate, it is clear that the qualities attributed to the male are more highly *valued* than are the female traits (Broverman et al., 1970). It is "good" to be independent, assertive, logical, and strong; it is less good to be warm, quiet, tactful, and gentle. Perhaps girls recognize, early, that the male role is seen more positively and aspire to some of the valued male qualities. That would lead to a female role perceived more broadly. Whatever the reason, it is an interesting finding—one with considerable relevance for understanding adult male and female sex roles and stereotyping.

*The Development of Sex-Role Behavior*　The final element in the equation is the actual behavior children show with their own sex and with the opposite sex.

We have several pieces of information. First of all, if you observe children while they play in a room stocked with a wide range of attractive toys, you'll see that children as young as 2 or 3 show sex stereotyping in their toy choices. Little girls play at various housekeeping games, including sewing, stringing beads, or cooking. Boys play with guns, toy trucks, fire engines, and carpentry tools (Fagot, 1974). You can see the same themes in requests of older children (about 4 to 9 years old) for gifts from Santa Clause in a study by John Richardson and Carl Simpson (1982). (Some sample results from this study are shown in Figure 10.8.)

Children also begin to choose same-sex playmates very early—as young as $2\frac{1}{2}$ or 3—and are much more sociable with playmates of the same sex at these ages (Jacklin & Maccoby, 1978). By school age, especially in early elementary school, the very strong pattern is for children to play in exclusively same-sex groups.

The other intriguing pattern is that children in early elementary school seem to pay more attention to the behavior of same-sex than opposite-sex adults or playmates and to play more with new toys that are labeled as being appropriate for their own sex (Ruble, Balaban, & Cooper, 1981; Slaby & Frey, 1975; Masters et al., 1979). Thus, although children are aware of gender quite early and are apparently influenced by gender in both toy and playmate choice, gender seems to become a still more potent force in guiding behavior and attitudes at around age 5 or 6.

## Theories of the Development of Sex-Role Concepts and Sex-Role Behavior

How can we explain this pattern? As you might expect, theorists of virtually every persuasion have tried their hand at explaining the development of sex roles.

*Social-Learning Explanations*　The major proponent of a learning explanation of the development of sex-role behavior has been Walter Mischel (1966, 1970). He has argued that children learn their sex roles by being reinforced directly for doing sex-appropriate things and for imitating same-sex models, particularly the same-sex parent. Mischel as-

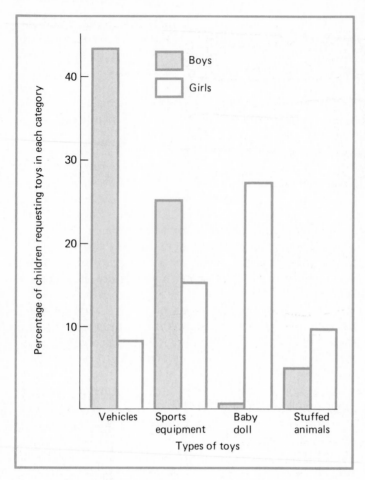

**Figure 10.8** *Sex typing of toy choice can be seen very clearly in children's requests for toys in letters to Santa Claus. Boys (aged about 4 to 9 years) request vehicles, military toys, robots, machines, and male dolls. Girls request female and baby dolls, clothes, educational and art materials, and stuffed animals. But both boys and girls ask for books, games, and musical toys. (Source: Richardson & Simpson, 1982, Table 2, p. 432.)*

sumes that parents pay more attention to children when they imitate the "right"-sexed person. In this way, the child learns the appropriate sex role.

There is a fair amount of support for this position. Starting in the early months of life, parents buy different kinds of toys for boys and girls. To study this, Harriet Rheingold and Kay Cook (1975) made an inventory of the toys in the rooms of children aged 1 month to 6 years and found that boys' rooms had more vehicles, sports equipment, toy animals, shape-sorting toys, and outer space toys, while girls' rooms had more dolls and more floral decorations. Boys' and girls' rooms did not differ in the number of books, musical objects, or stuffed animals they had. Since these differences were present in the rooms of young infants, it appears that the parents are systematically selecting these toys rather than responding to interests expressed by the child.

It is also true that parents may punish children for showing sex-inappropriate behavior. This is especially true of fathers of boys

**Figure 10.9** It's easy to tell just from looking whether this bedroom belongs to a boy or a girl. Partly this is because children *ask for* certain kinds of toys or decoration, but partly it's because parents buy different toys, different wallpaper, different kinds of furniture for boys and girls, starting when they are infants.

who show "girlish" behavior. Both mothers and fathers are far more tolerant of "tomboyish" behavior in girls. (This may be one reason that the male stereotype develops earlier and is stronger than is the female stereotype.)

The pattern of fathers' disapproval for girlish behavior is shown very clearly in a lovely study by Judith Langlois and Chris Downs (1980). Three- and 5-year-old children were given either a set of "boys' " toys (an army game with soldiers, cowboy outfits, cars) or a set of "girls' " toys (dollhouse, stove with pots and pans, and women's dress-up outfits). Half the boys and half the girls had a set of girls' toys; the other half had a set of boys' toys. Those who had boys' toys were told to "play with these toys the way boys do," while those who had girls' toys were told to "play with these toys the way girls do." After the child had been playing for a while, the mother or father came into the room. Langlois and Downs then watched to see whether the parent joined in or was supportive of the child's play or interfered or showed disapproval. What they found was that for mothers it didn't make much difference what kind of toys the child played with, but for fathers it mattered what their *sons,* but not their daughters, played with. Fathers showed some form of disapproval about 11 percent of the time when the boys played with girls' toys but less than 1 percent of the time when they played with boys' toys.

These findings certainly provide some support for a reinforcement theory of sex-role development. Parents do provide different environments for their boys and girls and are differentially tolerant of appropriately or inappropriately sex-typed behavior. But this approach simply can't account for all the facts I've given you. First of all, there is much less differential reinforcement than you'd expect. Eleanor Maccoby and Carol Jacklin (1974), in their comprehensive review of the research, could find little evidence that parents systematically reward boys for "boy behavior" and girls for "girl behavior." Yet girls begin to choose dolls to play with when they are 2 and 3, despite the fact that parents are quite tolerant of (and reinforce) play with many other kinds of toys.

In addition, there is little evidence that children imitate same-sex adults or children more than opposite-sex adults or children until they are 5 or 6 years old. In other words, we don't see differential imitation until *after* the child has already developed a strong set of ideas about sex roles. So the child does not seem to be learning the sex role by being rewarded for imitating same-sex adults. Some other mechanism appears to be involved.

*Psychoanalytic Theories of Sex-Role Development*   Freud saw the process of identification as the major vehicle for the child's acquisition of sex-role concepts and behavior. As you'll remember from Chapter 9, identification is the result of the Oedipal crisis, at about age 3 to 4. The child "takes in" (incorporates) all the qualities of the same-sex parent as a way of lessening his anxiety. If Freud is correct, then we should see children begin to imitate the same-sex parent and other same-sex adults pretty consistently, beginning at age 4 or so. But in fact we don't. Most children do not show such differential imitation until several years later. Freud's view also doesn't help us explain why children would show sex-typed toy choices or playmate choices as early as 2 or 3, before the Oedipal crisis has occurred. All in all, this theory has not been very helpful in explaining this particular developmental pattern.

*Cognitive-Developmental Theories of Sex-Role Development*   Lawrence Kohlberg (1966; Kohlberg & Ullian, 1974) has offered a third alternative, grounded in Piagetian theory. Kohlberg argued that we have to look at the cognitive part of the child's understanding of gender. Until the child has fully grasped the constancy of gender, we shouldn't see very much sex-typed behavior, and we certainly shouldn't see much imitation of same-sex models. Once the child has understood the gender concept, however, and realizes that he is a boy or she is a girl forever, then (in order to maintain cognitive consistency) it becomes highly important to learn how to behave in a way that fits the category one belongs to. Thus, Kohlberg predicts that we should see systematic same-sex imitation only *after* the child has shown full gender constancy.

In fact, that's what the research generally shows. Diane Ruble's recent study is a good example (Ruble, Balaban, & Cooper, 1981). She showed 4- to 6-year-old children a cartoon, with a "commercial" in the middle. The commercial showed either two girls playing with a toy or two boys playing with the same toy. After the cartoon was over, the child subjects were encouraged to play with any of the toys in the room, which included the toy they had seen during the commercial.

As you can see in Figure 10.10, children who had already achieved full gender constancy were much more influenced by the gender of the models in the commercial than were children who were at earlier levels of development of the gender concept. Other researchers have found that children who understand gender constancy are more likely to watch same-sex adult models (Slaby & Frey, 1975). This result is not found in every study (e.g., Herzog et al., 1982), but the finding is consistent enough to provide good support for this aspect of Kohlberg's theory. I think these are fascinating and important findings, since they link the child's cognitive progress with some critical elements of her social development.

Despite the accuracy of this key prediction, however, Kohlberg's approach still has weaknesses, the most glaring of which is the fact that children show clear signs of sex-typed behavior quite a long while before they have fully grasped gender constancy. Two- and 3-year-olds show sex-appropriate toy and playmate choice at a point when they can barely label their own and others' genders accurately. Obviously, something else, such as parental reinforcement for certain toy choices, is at work in the early years.

*A New Alternative: Gender Schemas* The most plausible alternative (at least at the moment) seems to me to be one offered by Carol Martin and Charles Halverson (1981, 1983), based on an information-processing model of cognitive development. "The basic idea [is] that ste-

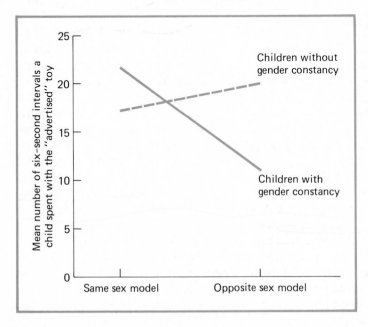

**Figure 10.10** Results from Ruble's study show that children who had already achieved gender constancy were much more likely to imitate the same-sex model than the opposite-sex model, which suggests that once children figure out that gender is permanent, they spend a lot of time trying to determine just what they are supposed to do in order to be a boy or a girl—figuring out the "rule." (*Source:* Ruble, Balaban, & Cooper, 1981, adapted from Figure 1, p. 670. Copyright by The Society for Research in Child Development, Inc.)

reotypes are 'schemas,' or naive theories that are relevant to the self, and function to organize and structure experience by telling the perceiver the kinds of information to look for in the environment and how to interpret such information" (Martin & Halverson, 1983, p. 563). The gender and sex-role "rule" or "schema" is developed gradually over the first six to eight years of life and affects the child's attention, memory, and behavior.

After figuring out their own gender, 2- and 3-year-olds begin with a basic "rule" that organizes objects and people into two big groups: "own sex" and "other sex." Some of the information for forming this first rule comes from comments by parents or from specific reinforcements; some comes from observation. When the child later understands the permanence of gender (at about 5 or 6), information about gender-appropriate behavior becomes a great deal more salient to the child, and she develops a more elaborated rule or schema of "what people who are like me do." Initially, the child of this age treats this "rule" the same way she treats other rules—as absolutes. Later, she understands that these are social conventions (Carter & Patterson, 1982). The child's knowledge of the "gender rule" continues to develop, but her application of it becomes more flexible. (She knows that most boys don't play with dolls but that they *can* do so if they like, for example.)

Martin and Halverson emphasize that such rule learning is absolutely normal and so is the rigid "stereotyping" that we see in elementary-school children's ideas about sex roles. Many of us, committed to the women's movement, have seen children's early sex stereotypes as evidence that we have made little progress toward equality. But I think that Martin and Halverson are quite correct; children are searching for order, for rules that help them make sense of their experiences. And a rule about "what men do" and "what women do" is a helpful schema for children. Like grammatical rules, children first apply this new rule too rigidly and then later learn the exceptions. But the rule-learning process seems to be an integral part of both cognitive and social development.

Obviously, the particular rule about sex roles that a child will develop depends on the kinds of models she encounters and the reinforcement pattern she experiences. In our culture, a key source of this rule-generating information is TV and children's books—a subject I have explored in Box 10.2.

### Individual Differences in Sex Typing and Sex-Role Stereotypes

The developmental patterns I have been describing seem to be true for virtually all children, but children do differ quite a lot in the rigidity of the "rule" they develop or in the sex typing of their behavior.

As a group, boys usually have stronger (more rigid and more traditional) sex-role stereotypes (Angrist, Mickelsen, & Penna, 1977; Best et al., 1977). Among both boys and girls, however, children whose mothers work outside the home have *less* stereotypic views (more flexible rules) (Broverman et al., 1972; Powell & Steelman, 1982). This makes perfectly good sense if you think about the origin of children's sex-role schemas. Presumably children learn "what women do" partly from observing their mother; if their mother does the same sort of work as their father, their schemas are bound to include this greater equality.

*"Cross-Sex" Children*    Children with cross-sex preferences—girls who would rather be boys and boys who would rather be girls—also seem to have less distinctly different sex-role stereotypes (Nash, 1975; Kuhn, Nash, & Brucken, 1978).

Such cross-sex children are particularly interesting. How does a child come to prefer to be the other sex or to choose cross-sex playmates or toys?

One possibility is that these children are trained that way. They may have been specifically reinforced for aspects of the opposite sex's role. Some girls are given trucks and carpentry tools and taught football by their fathers (or mothers). They may come to wish to be boys. In fact, there are far more girls who say they would like to be boys than there are boys who say they would rather be girls (Nash, 1975), which makes sense from a social-learning point of view. Tomboy behavior is more accepted and reinforced than is girlish behavior in a boy. Also, as I've pointed out before, male behavior is more highly valued than female, so it's logical that more girls would want to adopt the role that has the higher status.

But could there also be a biological element, such as a different hormone pattern, in the cross-sex choice of some children? Again, maybe. There are some bits of information that support a biological view. Most striking are several studies of girls who have experienced heightened levels of androgen prenatally. (Recall from Chapter 4 that androgen is largely a male hormone.) These "androgenized" girls, in comparison to their normal sisters, were later more interested in rough-and-tumble play, more often preferred to play with boys, and thought of themselves as tomboys (Ehrhardt & Baker, 1974).

But John Money, who has done a good deal of the research on the impact of prenatal hormones on sex typing, argues that biology is not destiny (1975). He thinks that the child's experiences—particularly the gender *label* that is applied by the parents, with all the accompanying differences in treatment—override hormone patterning. He thinks that it is the sex of *rearing* and not the genetically determined gender or the hormone-determined gender that governs behavior. His evidence for this somewhat sweeping assertion comes primarily from a series of case studies of children who, because of ambiguous genitals or other accidents, were assigned a gender that did not match their

BOX 10.2

## TV AND BOOKS AS SOURCES OF INFORMATION ABOUT SEX ROLES

If children are searching for information about what men and women do, as part of the creation of their sex-role "rules" or "schemas," then TV and children's books may have a major impact on them. Certainly children watch a lot of TV—three to six hours per day by current estimates (Murray, 1980). In fact, many children spend more time watching TV than they spend in school or playing or talking with their parents. So the portrayals of men and women, boys and girls, in TV programs are bound to be a very important source of data for the child's emerging sex-role concept.

What researchers have found when they looked at sex roles on TV (and in children's books) is that men and women are portrayed in highly stereotypic ways. This may help the child make a clear distinction between the two, but it is *not* an accurate reflection of the behavior of men and women.

Terry Saario, Carol Jacklin, and Carol Tittle (1973) analyzed the roles of males and females in children's reading books and found that there were very few major female characters at all and those that were included tended to be weaker, less able to solve problems on their own, and more dependent on male characters. The boys and men in the children's books are shown as strong, dominant, and problem-solving. In one reading book, for example (O'Donnell, 1966), a little girl is shown having fallen off her roller skates. The caption said, " 'She cannot skate,' said Mark. 'I can help her. I want to help her. Look at her, Mother. Just look at her. She is just a girl. She gives up.' "

Fortunately, blatant examples like this have disappeared from children's reading books, partly as a result of the efforts of parent groups. But on TV, women (and men) are still portrayed highly stereotypically. Not long ago Jane Trahey (1979) went through an issue of *TV Guide* and picked out the descriptions of the female charac-

genotype. The parents reared these children according to the assigned sex, and the children's behavior, toy preferences, and playmate choices matched the assigned sex, not the biological sex.

Money is making an important point. Clearly, the child's specific experience and what he *thinks* he is have a powerful effect on the sex role he adopts and the behavior he shows. (They affect the *schema* he develops.) But at the risk of being unpopular, I want to say that I don't think all the evidence is in yet on hormone effects. I'm still not convinced that hormones are totally overridden by experience; I think we just don't know very much yet about their possible effects. Whatever the source of the difference, we need to know more about children who would prefer to be the other sex, since that might well tell us a great deal about how most children come to prefer to be their own gender.

*Androgyny*  A very different approach to the study of "cross-sex" sex typing has emerged in the past decade in the study of **androgyny**. Until quite recently, psychologists had thought of "masculinity" and

ters: Heartbroken housekeeper, misguided housewife, restless housewife, student-victim, old flame, invalid wife, do-good nun, natural mother, rich society deb, nurse, and stage-struck singer. In the same issue, the male roles were described as venerable physician, country-music veteran, private eye, lawyer, teacher, and handsome dentist.

When researchers have systematically counted the roles and behaviors of men and women on TV, they have supported Trahey's brief sampling. Both George Gerbner (1972) and Sarah Sternglanz and Lisa Serbin (1974) found that women were more conforming, less effective, more dependent, and less physically active. They are most often in "handmaiden" roles—they hand the male character his coat, type his reports, and listen to his troubles.

A continuous exposure to these stereotyped males and females does seem to affect a child's vision of men and women and their roles. Terry Frueh and Paul McGhee (1975) found that elementary-school children who watched more than 25 hours of TV a week had much more "traditional" views of sex roles than did children who watched less than 10 hours a week. Even more

persuasive is an experiment by Emily Davidson (Davidson, Yasuna, & Tower, 1979), who found that 5- and 6-year-old children who were shown highly sex-stereotyped cartoons gave more stereotyped answers to questions about the qualities of men and women than did children who had seen cartoons depicting men and women in more equal roles.

Clearly, TV and children's books are having an impact on children's ideas about men and women (just as those same sources influence their aggressive behavior). I am persuaded that children of 5 to 8 are going to develop quite rigid rules or schemas about male and female roles as a normal part of their search for regularity in the world around them. But sex-role portrayals on TV seem to foster even more stereotyped (and thus inaccurate) sex-role concepts in children and reinforce such stereotyped concepts well into elementary and high school ages. If we showed men and women in more equal roles on TV, we might make it more difficult for the 5- or 6-year-old to develop a simple sex-role schema, but we would be reflecting reality far more. Of course, you could turn off the TV set. . . .

"femininity" as opposite ends of the same continuum. A person could be one or the other but couldn't be both. Lately, though, Sandra Bem (1974), Janet Spence and Robert Helmreich (1978), and others have argued that it is possible for a person to express *both* masculine and feminine sides of herself, to be both compassionate and independent, both gentle and assertive. In the language I have been using in this chapter, this would mean that a child or adult's self-concept could include elements of both male and female sex roles.

In this new way of looking at sex roles, masculinity and femininity are conceived of as two separate dimensions. Any person can be high or low on either one or on both. The terms used to describe the four possible "types" created by this two-dimensional conception are shown in Figure 10.11. The two "traditional" sex roles are the masculine and the feminine combinations. But there are two new "types" that become evident when we think about sex roles in this way: *Androgynous* individuals are those who describe themselves as having both masculine and feminine traits, and *undifferentiated* individuals are those who describe themselves as lacking both. (These undifferentiated people sound to me a lot like those with a "diffuse" identity in Marcia's system.)

Notice that this categorization system says nothing about the accuracy of the child's or the adult's rule or schema about sex roles. What it tells us about is the degree of match between the traditional sex roles and how a person thinks of herself or himself.

I cannot find any research on androgyny in young children (perhaps because androgyny ought to be quite uncommon at early ages, when children are creating their rigid rules about sex roles). But there is a growing body of research on androgyny in adolescents, and the results are tantalizing.

First of all, about 25 to 35 percent of high school students can be described as androgynous (Spence & Helmreich, 1978; Lamke, 1982a). More girls than boys seem to show this pattern, and there are more girls in the "masculine" category than there are boys in the "feminine" group.

Second, for *both* boys and girls, either a masculine or an androgynous sex-role self-concept is associated with higher self-esteem (Lamke, 1982a, 1982b). Thus, a boy can achieve high self-esteem and success with his peers by adopting a traditional masculine sex role. For girls,

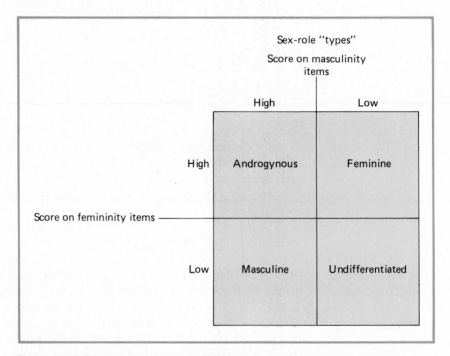

**Figure 10.11** The current view of masculinity and femininity is that each of us may express some amount of *each* of these qualities, which produces the four possible combinations of sex-role "types" shown here.

though, adoption of a traditional feminine sex role (without some balancing "male" characteristics) seems to carry a risk of lower self-esteem and even poorer relationships with peers (Massad, 1981).

Thus, although the creation of rigid rules or schemas for sex roles is a normal—even essential—process in young children, a blurring of those rules may be an important process in adolescence, particularly for girls, for whom a more androgynous self-concept is associated with positive outcomes.

## SUMMARY

1. The child's emerging self-concept has several elements, including the awareness of a separate self (the "I," or the "existential self") and the definition of the self in comparison to others (the "me" aspect, or the "categorical self").
2. In infancy, the child develops a sense of a separate self by about 15 to 18 months, as indicated by self-recognition.
3. In early childhood, the child begins to place herself in basic categories such as age, size, and gender. These early self-definitions appear to be based primarily on physical attributes and things the child can do.
4. At school age, the self-concept continues to include many actions but also includes likes and dislikes. In adolescence, beliefs and more general personality characteristics become part of the self-concept.
5. At adolescence, there is also a reevaluation of the self, a process Erikson talks of as the "identity crisis." Most adolescents move from a diffuse sense of future occupational or ideological identity through a period of reevaluation (moratorium) to a commitment to a new self-definition.
6. Another dimension of the self-concept (other than the content) is the positive or negative evaluation the child makes of himself—an aspect called self-esteem. Children with high self-esteem (positive self-concepts) appear to do somewhat better in school, see themselves in control of their own destiny, have more friends, and get along better with their families. These differences, however, are not as large as one might expect.
7. There are also individual differences in the speed or completeness of the identity reevaluation at adolescence. More mature girls appear to be more popular and more likely to be seen as leaders. Among boys, however, there are hints that the less psychologically mature may be more popular in high school.
8. Children with high self-esteem most often come from families in which their independent achievements are valued and praised, in which there is a warm, affectionate relationship between parents and children, and in which clear limits are set on the child's behav-

ior. For girls, high self-esteem appears also to be fostered by having an involved and stimulating father.

9. Gender identity is part of the self-concept, but the development of the child's understanding of what goes with being a girl or a boy (the sex-role concept) is a more pervasive process. Children generally acquire gender identity (labeling themselves and others correctly) by about age 2 or 3. They develop gender stability (knowing you stay the same gender throughout life) by about 4 and gender constancy (you don't change gender by changing appearance) by about 5 or 6.

10. Gender constancy is developed at about the same time that most children acquire other "conservation" concepts, such as conservation of number or mass.

11. Children's ideas about what males and females do and what they *ought* to do or be also begin to develop before school age, with the strongest stereotyping and the most rigid sex-role concepts apparent in children of 6 or 7. Older children are aware of the social conventions but do not treat them as incontrovertible rules.

12. Sex-typed behavior also appears at age 2 or 3, when children show sex-typed toy preferences and begin to choose same-sex playmates.

13. Theorists of several different traditions have attempted to explain these patterns. Mischel emphasizes the role of reinforcement and modeling and argues that children are reinforced for imitating same-sex models. Parents do appear to do some differential reinforcing (especially punishment of boys for "girlish" behavior), but not enough to account for the observed differences.

14. Freud's explanation rests on the concept of identification, by which the child comes to imitate the same-sexed parent, thus acquiring appropriate sex-typed behavior.

15. Kohlberg proposes a cognitive-developmental model: Children begin to imitate same-sexed models only after they have achieved gender constancy. There is some evidence to support this, but the theory does not explain sex-typed behavior at age 2 or 3.

16. Current theorists have proposed a "schema" or "rule" model: Children begin to acquire a rule about what boys do and what girls do as soon as they figure out the difference. After the development of gender constancy, however, the issue becomes more salient.

17. One important source of information for children's development of a sex-role rule is the portrayal of men and women on TV and in children's books. These portrayals are highly stereotyped.

## KEY TERMS

**Androgyny**  A self-concept including, and behavior expressing, high levels of both masculine and feminine qualities.

**Authoritarian parental style**  Pattern of parental behavior described by Baumrind, among others, including high levels of directiveness and low levels of affection and warmth.

**Authoritative parental style** Pattern described by Baumrind, including high control and high warmth.

**Categorical self** The definition of the self by comparing the self to others in one or more categories, such as age, gender, size, or skill.

**Existential self** Lewis and Brooks-Gunn's term for the most basic part of the self-concept, the sense of being separate and distinct from others.

**Foreclosure** One of four identity statuses proposed by Marcia, involving an ideological or occupational commitment without having gone through a reevaluation.

**Gender concept** The understanding of one's own gender, including the permanence and constancy of gender.

**Gender constancy** The final step in developing a gender concept, in which the child understands that gender doesn't change even though there are external changes such as in clothing or hair length.

**Gender identity** The first step in gender concept development, in which the child labels herself correctly and categorizes others correctly as male or female.

**Gender stability** The second step in gender concept development, in which the child understands that a person's gender continues to be stable throughout the lifetime.

**Identity achievement** One of four identity statuses proposed by Marcia, involving the successful resolution of an identity "crisis," resulting in a new commitment.

**Identity diffusion** One of four identity statuses proposed by Marcia, involving neither a current reevaluation nor a firm personal commitment.

**Moratorium** One of four identity statuses proposed by Marcia, involving an ongoing reexamination but without a new commitment as yet.

**Permissive parental style** A third style described by Baumrind, among others, which includes high warmth and low levels of control.

**Self-concept** The broad idea of "who I am," including the existential self, the categorical self, and a level of self-esteem.

**Self-esteem** The positive or negative evaluation of the self.

**Sex-role behavior** Exhibiting behavior that matches the culturally defined sex role, such as choosing "sex-appropriate" toys or playing with same-sex children.

**Sex roles** The set of behaviors, attitudes, rights, duties, and obligations that are part of the role of being a male or a female.

**Sex-role stereotypes** The overextension or too-rigid definition of sex roles or sex-role behavior.

**Sex typing** See **Sex-role behavior.**

**Symbiotic** Word used by Freud to describe the mutually interdependent relationship between the mother and infant during the earliest months of life. Freud believed the infant was not aware of being separate from the mother at this stage.

*SUGGESTED READINGS*

Baumrind, D. Socialization and instrumental competence in young children. In W. W. Hartup (Ed.). *The young child: Reviews of research* (Vol. 2). Washington, D.C.: National Association for the Education of Young Children, 1972.
An excellent and not very difficult paper describing Baumrind's research on the development of "competence" in young children.

Fagot, B. I., & Kronsberg, S. J. Sex differences: Biological and social factors influencing the behavior of young boys and girls. In S. G. Moore & C. R. Cooper (Eds.). *The young child: Reviews of research* (Vol. 3). Washington, D.C.: National Association for the Education of Young Children, 1982.
A very readable paper that touches on many of the issues I have raised. It also includes mention of the role of school and teachers in shaping sex-role concepts and sex-role behavior.

Hennig, M., & Jardim, A. *The managerial woman.* Garden City, N.Y.: Doubleday (Anchor Books), 1976.
This book is not primarily about children or childhood; it is about women in executive roles. But it describes the early childhood and adolescence of a group of highly successful women. I found it fascinating.

Maccoby, E. E. *Social development: Psychological growth and the parent-child relationship.* New York: Harcourt Brace Jovanovich, 1980.
An excellent basic text, which includes two chapters that touch on the material I have covered here.

Rivers, C.; Barnett, R.; & Baruch, G. *Beyond sugar & spice: How women grow, learn, and thrive.* New York: Putnam, 1979.
An excellent, very readable book on sex-role development in girls. Since the book was designed for a lay audience rather than for other psychologists, you will find it less technical than some of other other books and articles I have suggested here.

PROJECT 10.1

# *Sex Roles on TV*

You may want to combine this project with the one I will suggest at the end of Chapter 13, which involves watching for aggressive episodes on TV. Recording both aggression or violence and sex-role behaviors will give you a very good sense of the portrayals of "real life" given on TV.

For this project, you can select any one of several patterns of watching—I want you to get some practice designing your own project.

1. Watch at least eight hours of TV, spread over several time periods, and record the number of male and female characters and whether they are the central character or a minor character.
2. Watch four to six hours of TV, selecting among several different types of programs, and note the activities of each male and female character in the following categories: aggression, nurturance, problem solving, conformity, constructive/productive behavior, and physically exertive behavior.
3. Watch four to six hours of TV, selecting among several different types of programs, and focus on the consequences of various actions by male and female characters: positive outcome resulting from own action; positive outcome resulting from the situation or someone else's action; neutral outcome; negative outcome resulting from own action; negative outcome resulting from the situation or the action of others.
4. Watch and analyze the commercials on at least 10 programs, making sure that the programs cover the full range of types, from sports to soap operas. You might count the number of male and female participants in the commercials and the nature of their activity in each case, using some of the same categories listed in number 2.

Whichever one of these projects you choose, you must define your terms carefully and record your data in a manner that makes them understandable. In writing up your report, include the following: an *introductory* section, in which some of the background literature is described and your hypotheses are given; a *procedure* section, which must include details of the programs you observed, how you selected them, what specific behaviors you recorded, how you defined your behavioral categories, and any other details that a reader would need to understand what you actually did; a *results* section, in which the findings are reported, using graphs or tables as needed; and a *discussion* section, in which your results are compared to those of other researchers (as cited in this book or elsewhere) and any puzzling or unexpected findings are discussed and explained (if possible). You may also want to suggest additional projects that might help clarify the points of confusion in your own findings.

# 11.
# *the development of social relationships*

The other night at a gathering of friends, I watched two young friends, Mark and Marcie, with their 4-month-old son, Alexander. With very little effort, Alexander managed to attract everyone's attention. He looked around him, occasionally gave brief smiles, kicked his feet, shook a rattle, and cried once in a while. Those simple behaviors were enough to have all the adults in the room hovering over him, trying their best to entice a smile. I was not immune to his charms. I trotted out all my playing-with-baby tricks, raising my eyebrows, smiling broadly, calling his name, tickling him a bit on the cheek or on his feet, making clucking noises. My reward was one very small smile and a brief period of attention from Alexander.

But Mark and Marcie, after four months of practice, were a whole lot better than any of the rest of us at soothing, flirting with, and eliciting responses from young Alexander. Either mom or dad could get the baby to smile within just a few seconds; when he cried, either one of them could soothe him quite easily, after the rest of us (doting "aunts" or "uncles" or "grandparents" that we were) had failed in the attempt.

Nearly all of you have been involved in a similar situation, so you know the sense of pleasure that comes from watching parents being delighted with their children; you find yourself smiling from ear to ear. But psychologist that I am, I was struck by some other elements in the interaction between Alexander and his parents. First of all, even at 4 months, Alexander is really quite skillful in social exchanges. He can't do very many things, but what he does do is very successful in getting attention and care. The second point is that Alexander and his parents have developed a sort of "dance" that they do much more skillfully with each other than the baby does with other folks. They have *adapted* to each other.

I have described Alexander and his parents because their interaction focuses our attention on an aspect of development I have largely neglected so far—namely, the child's relationships with others. The self-concept is a critical element in the child's eventual "personality," but the self-concept and the style and pattern of the child's behavior emerge from and are displayed in social exchanges with others. If we are to have the barest grasp of the nature of the child's development, we have to describe and understand the ways in which the child's *social* behavior develops and changes. How does the first relationship with the parents change over time? What is the effect on a child of a supportive and well-adapted relationship with the parents compared to a maladjusted one? How and when does the child begin to be interested in other children? What about friendships in childhood and adolescence? These are all vital questions I will be exploring in this chapter.

One of the key concepts in the study of social relationships is that of **attachment**, a term used particularly in the theoretical work of John Bowlby (1969, 1973, 1980) and Mary Ainsworth (1972, 1982; Ainsworth et al., 1978).

**Figure 11.1** By the time babies are 2 or 3 or 4 months old, most mothers and fathers have become skillful and confident in their interactions and securely attached to the baby.

## ATTACHMENT AND ATTACHMENT BEHAVIOR: DEFINITIONS

As Bowlby has described it, an attachment is an important emotional link, an "affectional bond," between two people. The child or adult who is attached to another person uses her (or him) as a "safe base" from which to explore the world, as a source of comfort when distressed or stressed, and for encouragement. Attachment is an invisible, internal structure—perhaps even a "scheme" in Piaget's sense.

We know when an attachment exists by observing **attachment behaviors**, just as we infer the child's cognitive competence by looking at the way he solves problems. Attachment behaviors are all those behaviors that allow a child or an adult to achieve and retain proximity to someone else to whom he is attached. This could include smiling, making eye contact, calling out to the other person across a room, touching, clinging, crying. (Alexander showed many of these behaviors, didn't he?)

It is important to make clear that there is no one-to-one correspondence between the number of different attachment behaviors a child (or an adult) shows on any one occasion and the strength of the underlying attachment. A child with a strong, secure attachment to a parent may play happily in the same room with the parent, showing only occasional glances or other brief contacts. On another occasion, the same child may show high levels of attachment behaviors. It is the *pattern* of these behaviors, not the frequency, that tells us something about the strength of the attachment.

One of the useful features of the concept of attachment is that we can apply it equally to the parents' attachment to the child or the child's attachment to the parents. Let me begin by looking at how parents form their bond to the baby.

## THE ATTACHMENT PROCESS: PARENT TO CHILD

There seem to be two steps or two parts to the development of a parent's attachment to an infant. An initial bond may be formed in the first hours after birth, especially if the parent has an opportunity for early contact with the baby. The really critical element, though, for the parent's attachment is the opportunity to engage in mutual attachment behaviors with the baby.

### The First Step: The Initial Bond

If you read the popular press at all, I am sure you have come across articles proclaiming the absolute importance of immediate contact between mother and newborn. Until fairly recently, hospital practices in the United States (as elsewhere) involved an immediate separation of the baby and the mother after delivery—the baby to the nursery for 12 to 24 hours and the mother to the recovery room. Mothers didn't like this much, but since this seemed physically safer for the infant, not much change was made until two pediatricians, Marshall Klaus and John Kennell (1976), began a program of research designed to show that there was a "critical period" for the mother's development of an attachment to her infant in the first hours after birth. Mothers who were denied early contact, Klaus and Kennell thought, were likely to form weaker attachments and thus be at higher risk for a range of disorders of parenting.

Klaus and Kennell's work was almost immediately seized by parents' groups, by women's magazines, and by other media. Hospital practices actually began to change, too, with mothers and fathers encouraged to hold their newborns immediately after delivery. For many reasons this seems like a very good change to me—among other things, parents report that they find this first "acquaintance" time to be a joyful occasion. At the time I wrote the third edition of this book, it also looked as if Klaus and Kennell were correct in their idea that such early contact was also vital for the development of parent-child attachment. Recent research, though, indicates that early contact may be only minimally potent or critical for the long-term development of parents' attachment (Lamb & Hwang, 1982; Svejda, Pannabecker, &

Emde, 1982). These newer findings do not alter the conclusion that early contact is a positive and pleasant experience. But the recent work shows all of us (including me) that we need to be cautious about extending Klaus and Kennell's basic idea too far. Let me review some of the evidence.

*Short-Term Effects*   Mothers who have handled their newborn within the first few hours do often show more tender fondling and more gazing at the baby in the first few days than do mothers who did not have an opportunity to hold their newborn until later (e.g., Campbell & Taylor, 1980; Carlsson et al., 1979; de Chateau, 1980; Grossman, Thane, & Grossmann, 1981).

Not every researcher has found this kind of effect (e.g., Svejda, Campos, & Emde, 1980), and some have found it only for mothers with their firstborns (e.g., de Chateau, 1980), but I am reasonably well satisfied that there is at least a small short-term effect of early contact, perhaps especially for those mothers who are least experienced with infants or who have the least support from spouse or families.

It seems more and more doubtful, however, that this small short-term effect is based on some hormonal "readiness" of the mother. It seems more likely to me that it is the infant's greater alertness in the first hours after birth that is the key. Whatever the explanation, the effect is not nearly so large as Klaus and Kennell first proposed (or as the popular press would have you believe).

*Long-Term Effects*   The conclusions are still more tentative when we look at studies of longer-term effects of early contact. Several studies show a persisting effect (including Klaus & Kennell's own early work: Kennell et al., 1974; Ringler, Trause, & Klaus, 1976). But many do not (e.g., Grossman, Thane, & Grossmann, 1981).

My own current conclusion is that early contact has a small effect on a few maternal behaviors in the first days after delivery but little or no *lasting* effect on such specific maternal behaviors as the amount of smiling at the child or tender touching. Mothers who did not have very early contact show just as many of these behaviors in the long run. But we may detect some effect, for at least some mothers, if we look at broader measures of the mother's attitude toward her infant, her confidence in child rearing, or her attachment (Sostek, Scanlon, & Abramson, 1982). Such broader measures might include the number of months the mother chooses to stay home with her child before going back to work or global measures of the adequacy of her care. On measures such as these, for *some* mothers, we can still detect the impact of early contact versus no early contact as much as a year or two after the child's birth.

The one study I find most convincing in this regard is by Susan

O'Connor and her colleagues (1980). They have followed a large group of poverty-level mothers who were given both early and extended contact through a "rooming-in" arrangement in a Nashville, Tennessee, hospital. Other similar mothers in the same hospital were randomly assigned to a more traditional care arrangement, and these two groups have now been followed through the first 18 months of the children's lives. O'Connor's interest has been in a global measure of the mothers' behavior that she calls "adequacy of parenting." Inadequate parenting was indicated if the child was physically abused or neglected, if the child was repeatedly hospitalized, or if the parents relinquished custody of the child.

As you can see in Table 11.1, very few mothers in either the rooming-in or the normal-hospital group showed inadequate parenting, but the rate was higher for the group that had had less contact with the infant in the early days. These findings raise the possibility that early contact may help *prevent* later parenting problems among mothers who may be at especially high risk for abuse. For the majority of mothers, however, early or extended contact does not seem to be an essential ingredient in the long-term attachment process.

## The Second Step: The Meshing of Attachment Behaviors

Much more critical for the establishment of the parents' attachment to the child is the opportunity to interact with the child over the early months of life. Over that early period, the parents and child develop a mutual, interlocking pattern of attachment behaviors. The baby signals her needs by crying or smiling; she responds to being held by soothing or snuggling; she looks at the parents when they look at her. The parents, in their turn, enter into this two-person "dance" by coming near the baby when she cries or gurgles, by picking her up, by waiting for and responding to her signals of hunger or other need, by smiling

Table 11.1

**"Parenting inadequacy" and abuse**

|  | "Rooming-in" Group (143 Cases) | Regular Hospital Care Group (158 Cases) |
|---|---|---|
| Number of mothers who showed any kind of parenting inadequacy in first 18 months | 2 | 10 |
| Number referred to Children's Protective Service for suspicion of abuse | 1 | 5 |
| Number of children hospitalized for illness or for "failure to thrive" | 1 | 8 |

*Source:* Study done in Nashville by O'Connor et al., 1980, from text pp. 356–357.

at the baby when she smiles, by gazing into her eyes. It was this smooth "dance" that I could see between Mark and Marcie and 4-month-old Alexander.

One of the most intriguing things about this process is that we all seem to know how to do this particular dance. In the presence of a young infant, most adults will automatically shift into a "baby-play act," which includes smiling, raised eyebrows, very wide open eyes, and a quiet, high-pitched voice (see Figure 11.2). The baby runs through his half of the dance pretty automatically, too. But while we can perform all these attachment *behaviors* with many infants, we do not become *attached to* every baby we coo at in the grocery store. I can run through my baby routine with Alexander, but I am not attached to him.

For the adult, the critical ingredient for the formation of a genuine

**Figure 11.2** Virtually every adult, when interacting with a young baby, shows this "mock surprise" expression, including the raised eyebrows, wrinkled forehead, and open mouth or wide smile. This combination of features is, in fact, quite likely to elicit a smile from a young baby.

attachment seems to be the opportunity to develop real mutuality—to practice the dance until the partners follow one another's lead smoothly and pleasurably. This takes time and many rehearsals. The parents of a newborn, especially if it is a first child, may feel clumsy or awkward with their infant. They don't read the baby's cues easily, and the interaction may be out of synchrony. But as they care for the infant, play with him, and talk to him, the synchrony improves. And the smoother and more predictable the process becomes, the more satisfying it seems to be to the parents and the stronger their attachment to the infant becomes.

This second step appears to be far more important than the initial bond at birth in establishing a strong attachment by the parents to the child. But this second process, too, can fail. I've explored some of the possible reasons for such a failure in Box 11.1.

## Attachments by Fathers

I have used the word *parents* in the discussion so far, but most of the research I have talked about has involved studies of mothers. Are all the same things true of fathers as well? Are fathers affected by early contact? Do they form attachments to their infants? The preliminary answer seems to be "yes" to both questions.

Fathers who are present at delivery or who have some other opportunity to hold and fondle the child shortly after birth report stronger feelings of attachment to the baby than do fathers lacking such early contact (Greenberg & Morris, 1974; Peterson, Mehl, & Leiderman, 1979). Whether this initial effect lasts I do not know, since I can find no study in which fathers who had extra early contact with their newborn have been followed beyond the first days or weeks of the child's life. But it is an intriguing question—and one with obvious practical relevance given the current emphasis on having fathers present during delivery.

We do have information now, though, about fathers' actual attachment behaviors toward their infants. This research shows that fathers' *initial* reactions to the newborn are virtually identical to mothers' reactions. Ross Parke, in several studies (Parke & Tinsley, 1981), has observed fathers and mothers with their newborns and finds that when fathers are actually holding their infants, they touch, talk to, and cuddle their babies as much as, and in the same ways that, mothers do. Mothers usually spend more time actually holding the baby, so the quantity of affectionate behavior shown to the infant by the father may be less, but the quality is the same. It certainly appears, then, that a father's initial attachment to his infant is as strong as is a mother's.

Past the early weeks of life, however, we see signs of a kind of "specialization" of parents' behaviors with their infants and toddlers. The

BOX 11.1

# WHEN MUTUALITY FAILS: CHILD ABUSE AND OTHER CONSEQUENCES OF FAILURE OF ATTACHMENT

The two-part system for fostering strong attachment by the parent to the infant is normally robust and effective. Most parents *do* become attached to their babies. But attachment is a process requiring two partners, both of whom have the necessary signals and skills and the energy to enter into the "dance." When either partner lacks the skills, the result can be a failure of attachment or a weaker attachment by the parent to the child. Child abuse or neglect is one possible consequence of such a failure.

## WHEN THE INFANT LACKS SKILLS

For the system to work, the baby has to possess the whole repertoire of attachment behaviors. If some are missing, real problems can ensue. For example, Selma Fraiberg (1974, 1975) has studied a group of blind babies, who smile less than sighted infants and do not show mutual gaze. Most parents of blind infants, after several months of this, begin to think that their infant is rejecting them, or they conclude that the baby is depressed. These parents feel less attached to their blind infants than to their sighted infants.

Similar problems can arise with parents of premature infants, who are usually separated from their parents for the first weeks or months (which *may* interfere with the first bond) and are then unresponsive for the first weeks after they are home from the hospital. Most mothers of premature infants work extra hard in those first months to stimulate their infants. In fact, such mothers show *higher* rates of involvement with and stimulation of their babies in the early months than do mothers of full-term babies (Field, 1977; Barnard, Bee, & Hammond, 1984a). But eventually the mothers withdraw somewhat from the interaction, since the babies so seldom respond with real mutuality.

Obviously, not all blind infants or premature infants or others who are "different" in some way end up being physically abused. Many parents manage to surmount these problems. But the rate of abuse is higher among prematures than among term infants. Klein and Stern (1971) found, for example, that about a quarter of the abused children in their study had been born prematurely, even though prematures represent only about 8 percent of the total population. (This does not mean, by the way, that a quarter of all prematures are abused. It does mean that they are overrepresented in the group of abused children.)

"mother role" seems to involve not only routine caregiving but also more talking and more quiet interactions. The "father role" involves more playfulness. Fathers do more physical roughhousing (Figure 11.3) with their children and are more likely to play a "game" of some kind with the child (Lamb, 1981). Their play also seems to be faster-paced than is mothers' (Arco, 1983). This does not mean that fathers are less attached; it does mean that the attachment behaviors they show toward the infant are somewhat different from those of mothers.

But where do such "parenting roles" come from? The possibility

## WHEN THE PARENT LACKS SKILL

The other partner in the "dance" is obviously the parent, and failure of attachment can just as well come from the parent's end of the system. A parent might lack "attachment skill" because she or he did not form a secure attachment with her or his own parents and did not learn the needed behaviors in later relationships. In fact, the majority of abusing parents were *themselves* abused as children, which makes this argument seem plausible. Or the parent could lack skill because he or she approaches the child-care task from an essentially *egocentric* stance. For example, Carolyn Newberger and Susan Cook (1983) have found that abusing parents are more likely to describe the task of parenting in terms of their *own* needs that may be met. They may thus be less sensitive or responsive to the child's signals.

Another factor that can affect a parent's ability to enter fully into the attachment process is the amount of other stress in her or his life. Parents who have many children, small living spaces, and uncertain incomes and who lack friends or other sources of emotional support are much more likely to abuse their children than are parents with lower levels of stress (Light, 1973; Garbarino & Sherman, 1980).

When these two elements are combined—a child who is less able to respond fully for some reason and a parent who is less skillful in forming attachments or who is experiencing heightened stress—the likelihood that there will be a failure of attachment and possibly neglect or abuse of the child is greatly increased.

## WHAT CAN BE DONE?

Fortunately, it's possible to intervene to help the unattached parent become more attached. Fraiberg (1974) found that she could help the parents of blind babies to "read" the child's hand and body movements instead of waiting for smiles or eye contact. After such training, the parents of the blind babies found their attachment to the infant was strengthened. Rose Bromwich (1976; Bromwich et al., 1981) has used a similar procedure with parents of children with other physical handicaps. She begins by finding some activity that the child and parent can do together that brings pleasure to both. When that level of basic mutual pleasure has been achieved, she then tries to help the parent become more attentive to the child's individual signals. Through this process, the parents' attachment to the child can be enhanced.

When actual abuse has already occurred, more extensive intervention may be needed. Henry Kempe and his colleagues in Denver (Kempe & Kempe, 1978), for example, report that they have had an 80 percent success rate with abusing families using a combination of a crisis hot line to help the parents deal with life stresses (among other things) and personal counseling to help them deal with their own early relationships and to develop the skills needed to relate to their child. This is not a simple or a quick process, but it can and does succeed.

that has probably occurred to you first is that the person who is doing the major physical caregiving is quite logically going to end up doing less playing. Since mothers do more caregiving (even in families in which both parents work), the "mother" and "father" roles may be really "caregiver" and "noncaregiver" roles. If that's true, then we should find the roles switched around in families in which the father is doing the major caregiving.

Interestingly, in the one study of such families that I know of, that's not what the researchers found. Michael Lamb and his colleagues

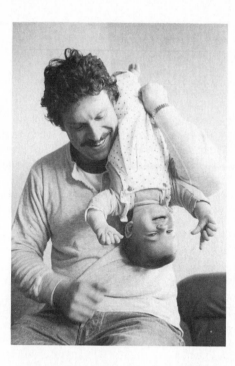

**Figure 11.3** At least in American and other Western cultures, the role of father with a young baby seems to involve a lot more play, including roughhousing or physical actions like these. Obviously, the baby is enjoying it immensely!

(1982) studied a group of caregiving fathers in Sweden, where the custom of "paternal leave" from work at the birth of a child is quite well established. Lamb located a group of families with 8-month-old children in which the father had spent at least one of the previous three months as the major caregiver. He compared the behavior of these fathers and mothers with that of parents in more traditional families during a home observation when both parents were present with the child. As you can see in Figure 11.4, mothers talked to and held the infants more and showed more affection and more physical care, regardless of whether they were or had been the major caregiver. This does not mean that males are biologically limited to the "play" role with a child. It does suggest, though, that these male and female roles with children are very strongly established in our culture.

## THE ATTACHMENT PROCESS: CHILD TO PARENT

The process of attachment formation for parents seems to begin with the development of an initial bond and then extends to more and more skillful attachment behaviors. For the infant, the process seems to begin with attachment behaviors and progress to the full attachment somewhat later.

Based on their research, Mary Ainsworth and her colleagues (1978) suggest that the emergence of a genuine attachment in an infant occurs in several steps.

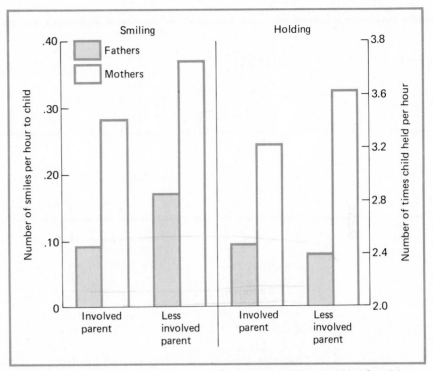

**Figure 11.4** Unexpectedly, Lamb and his colleagues found in their study of Swedish fathers and mothers that those fathers who had been the primary caregiver for a month or more in the first eight months of the child's life (the "involved" fathers) were *not* more likely to show the "mother style" of interacting with babies. (*Source:* Lamb et al., 1982, p. 218.)

## Phase 1: Initial Preattachment

During the first three to four months of life, the baby displays a wonderful range of attachment behaviors that Ainsworth describes as "proximity-promoting"—they bring people closer. As I pointed out in Chapter 3, the newborn can cry, make eye contact, cling, cuddle, and respond to caregiving efforts by being soothed. But because the child of this age shows no consistent preference for any one caregiver over another, we can't say that he is attached to any one person yet. This preattachment phase *may* be linked to the young infant's relative lack of skill in making visual discriminations between one person and another (see Chapter 5).

The importance of the visual cues in aiding the infant's discrimination is underlined by Selma Fraiberg's fascinating observations of blind infants (1975). Although such children do eventually establish clear attachments to their mothers or other caregivers, the process is considerably delayed, since the child must develop other methods for making reliable discriminations.

### Phase 2: Attachment in the Making

Sometime around 3 months, when the baby can tell the difference between familiar and unfamiliar faces, she begins to dispense her attachment behaviors more discriminatingly. She smiles more to the people who regularly take care of her and may not smile readily to a stranger. (Alexander was in this stage.) Still, this is not yet a full-blown attachment to a *single* figure; there are still a number of people who are favored with the child's "proximity-promoting" behaviors.

### Phase 3: Clear-Cut Attachment

Two important changes take place at about 6 to 7 months of age. First and most important, the child typically now has *one* person toward whom attachment behaviors are primarily directed. We can say for the first time that the child is genuinely *attached* to someone. Second, the dominant mode of his attachment behavior changes: He shifts from using mostly "come here" signals (proximity-promoting) to what Ainsworth calls "proximity-seeking" (which we might think of as "go there" behaviors). Because the 6- to 7-month-old begins to be able to move about the world more freely by creeping and crawling, he can move *toward* the caregiver as well as enticing the caregiver to come to him. We also see a child of this age using the "most important person" as a safe base from which to explore the world around him.

*Separation Protest and Fear of Strangers*   In many children (but not all), one of the striking signs of this strong single attachment is that the child may show both protest at separation from the preferred person and fear of strangers. Separation protest—if it occurs at all—is usually seen sometime around 6 to 8 months, after which it fades (Ainsworth et al., 1978). Fear of strangers begins to emerge at about 6 to 8 months and continues until about 18 months, after which it, too, gradually fades (Emde, Baensbauer, & Harmon, 1976). Such heightened fearfulness of strangers at about 12 months has been observed in children in a wide range of different cultures—e.g., Israeli, Guatemalan, and African Bushman (Kagan, 1976)—as well as in the United States, so the timing of this pattern appears to be species-typical.

But while the timing may be widely shared, the intensity of the fearful reaction varies widely from one child to another. Nearly all children show more fearfulness in stressful situations (e.g., the doctor's office, as in Figure 11.5), but some children show only a little wariness of strangers; others show more striking withdrawal, such as crying, clinging to the parent, or other signs of fear (Sroufe, 1977; Batter & Davidson, 1979). In the last few years, psychologists have been trying to figure out where such individual differences in fearfulness might come from. So far we have the following clues (summarized by Thompson & Lamb, 1982):

1. Children whose mothers rate them as being generally more fearful—not just of strangers but of other new things—are likely to show more fear of strangers, as are infants rated as "fussy" (Berberian & Snyder, 1982). Thus, the child's basic temperament may be part of the picture.
2. Children whose families have recently gone through some major change, such as the birth of a new sibling or a move or a parent changing jobs, show more fear of strangers than do children whose families have been more stable.
3. But there is *no* consistent relationship between the child's fear of strangers and the number of different caregivers he has experienced. You might expect a child who has been cared for by more different people to have less fear of new people. Several researchers have hunted for such a relationship, and no consistent finding has emerged. Day care (or other multiple-caregiving arrangements) apparently does not make children either more or less fearful of strangers.

### Phase 4: Multiple Attachments

The most intense single attachment normally occurs during the period from 6 to 12 months. After that time, most babies show a spread of attachments: to older siblings, regular baby-sitters, grandparents, or other regularly seen adults. These attachments appear to have the

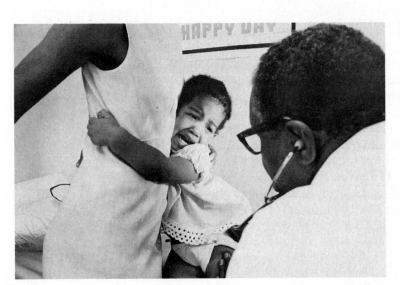

**Figure 11.5** By about age 2, most children show this type of clinging, unhappy form of attachment behavior only when they are under stress, such as visiting the doctor, as this little girl is doing. This same child is probably less likely to show such clear attachment behavior at home.

same qualities as the attachments to the principal caregiver: The child uses all of his preferred adults as a safe base for exploration, smiles more at them, and turns to any of them for comfort in distress.

### Attachments in Preschool and Elementary-School Children

During the preschool years, the overall level of the child's proximity seeking declines. A 12-month-old child stays pretty close to the safe base most of the time, remaining within sight of the mother or other caregiver. But by 2 or 3, children seem to be comfortable being on their own more (Clarke-Stewart & Hevey, 1981). This is made easier by the fact that the child can now talk well enough to call out to mom or dad from some distance away and still stay in contact. Children of 2 can even use a photograph of their mother in a strange situation as a safe base for exploration (Passman & Longeway, 1982).

This reduction in proximity seeking does not mean that the child is less *attached to* the caregiver. Rather it says that the attachment behaviors change and become less visible. We can still see clear attachment behaviors in 2- or 3- or 4-year-olds who are frightened, tired, or under stress. But in normal circumstances they move more freely from the safe base of their preferred person(s).

In elementary-school–age children, the attachment behaviors toward parents become still less visible (such as perhaps fewer occasions when the child comes to the parent for a hug), while involvement with peers becomes a much more dominant theme in the child's social world—a set of relationships I'll talk more about shortly.

### Parent-Child Relationships at Adolescence

Most of you can remember quite clearly the changes in your own relationships with your parents when you hit adolescence, so the research findings are not going to surprise you much. At first there is typically an increase in conflict. Laurence Steinberg (1981) found that this increase occurred at the very beginning of the pubertal cycle in a group of boys he studied over a yearlong period. At that point the boys questioned their parents more, interrupted more, disagreed more. But after the peak at the beginning of puberty, the conflict declined.

Another trend that is very clear is an increasing amount of time spent with peers. But neither the temporarily heightened conflict nor the increased involvement with the peer group signifies that the young person's attachment to the parent has disappeared or even greatly weakened. This fact is nicely illustrated in a recent study by Fumiyo Hunter and James Youniss (1982).

Hunter and Youniss had groups of fourth, seventh, and tenth graders and college students answer eight questions about their relationships with mother, father, and best same-sex friend. Each question was a statement like "My mother (father, best friend) gives me what I need" or "I like to talk to my mother (father, best friend) about my problems." Subjects answered each question on a four-point scale where 1 meant not very often and 4 meant almost always. Figure 11.6 shows the average score for those questions that dealt with the intimacy of the relationship ("we talk about problems," "the other person knows how I feel," "we talk over disagreements," "we do things together") and for questions about the nurturance of the relationship ("the other person gives me what I need and helps me solve my problems").

As you can see, during adolescence (the seventh and tenth graders), intimacy with the mother and father goes down, while intimacy with the friend goes up. But young people across this age range see their parents as consistently high sources of nurturing. So teenagers may be spending more time with their peers and may be developing very deep attachments to their friends, but they still turn to their parents for nurturance, for affection, for help.

## ATTACHMENTS TO MOTHERS AND FATHERS

I pointed out earlier that both fathers and mothers appear to become attached to their infants, although their behavior with infants varies

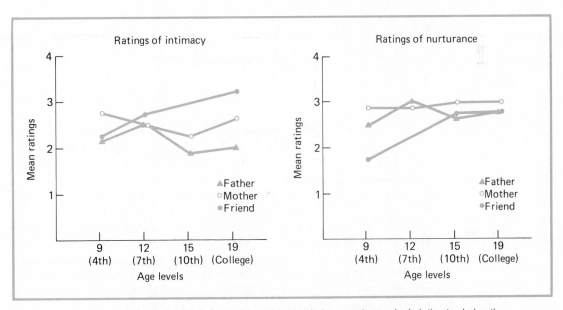

**Figure 11.6** Relationships with friends become increasingly intimate during the adolescent years; friends tell each other more about themselves, resolve disagreements, share activities. But young people continue to see their parents as a major source of nurturance throughout these years. (*Source:* F. T. Hunter & J. Youniss. Changes in functions of three relations during adolescence. *Developmental psychology,* 1982, *18,* Figures 2 & 3, pp. 809, 810. Copyright 1982 by the American Psychological Association. Reprinted by permission of the publisher and author.)

somewhat. But what about the child's half of this attachment? Are infants and children equally attached to their fathers and mothers?

In general, yes. From the age of 7 to 8 months, when strong attachments are first seen, infants prefer *either* the father or the mother to a stranger. And when both the father and the mother are available, an infant will smile at or approach either or both, *except* when he is frightened or under stress. When that happens, especially for a child between 8 and 24 months, the child typically turns to the mother rather than the father (Lamb, 1981).

As you might expect, the strength of the child's attachment to the father at this early age seems to be related to the amount of time the dad has spent with the child. Gail Ross (Ross et al., 1975) found she could predict a baby's attachment to the father by knowing how many diapers the dad changed in a typical week. The more diapers, the stronger the attachment! But greatly increased time with the father does not seem to be the only element, since Michael Lamb and his Swedish colleagues have found that infants whose father was the major caregiver for at least a month in the first year of the child's life (with an average of about three months) were nonetheless more strongly attached to their mothers than to their fathers (Lamb et al., 1983). One resolution of this apparent contradiction is that fathers who invest more time being attuned to the infant's signals are likely to have infants who are more strongly attached to them. But for the father to be consistently *preferred* over the mother would probably require essentially full-time paternal care. As this option becomes more common in our society, it will be possible to study such father-child pairs to see if a preference for the father develops.

Among older children, there is some indication (consistent with Freud's concept of identification) that girls form a stronger attachment to their mothers and boys to their fathers. In the Hunter and Youniss study (Figure 11.6), for example, across all ages, boys rated the father's nurturance higher than the mother's, while the girls did the reverse.

## INDIVIDUAL DIFFERENCES IN THE QUALITY OF ATTACHMENTS

Virtually all babies seem to go through the sequence I've described from preattachment to attachment. But the *quality* of the attachment they form to their parents differs. Mary Ainsworth (Ainsworth & Wittig, 1969; Ainsworth et al., 1978; Ainsworth, 1982) suggests that the best way to think about such differences in quality is in terms of the *security of attachment*.

Ainsworth developed a technique for measuring the security of the child's attachment that has come to be called the **strange situation**. It consists of a series of episodes in a laboratory setting in which the child is with the mother, with the mother and a stranger, alone with the stranger, completely alone for a few minutes, and then reunited

with the stranger and finally with the mother. Based on the child's reactions to this set of experiences, the child is classed as being **securely
attached** or as one of two types of **insecurely attached**. I've listed
some of the characteristics of each type in Table 11.2.

There is an obvious parallel between Ainsworth's distinction between secure and insecure attachment and Erikson's trust/mistrust
distinction. Erikson sees the first attachment as the model for later relationships, a view shared by current theorists studying attachment
(e.g., Sroufe, 1979; Lamb, 1982b). Because the present work on the security of attachments has so many theoretical and practical ramifications, I need to take some time to explore some of the issues and implications.

## Is It Just Temperament?

Erikson, Ainsworth, and others all assume that a secure or insecure
attachment is largely the product of the child's interaction with the
parents in the first 12 or 18 months of life. But is that the whole explanation? If you look again at the description of the insecurely attached
child—especially the "resistant/ambivalent" type—you may find that
it sounds a lot like Thomas and Chess's descriptions of temperamentally "difficult" children (discussed in Chapter 3). In fact, Chess and
Thomas have recently suggested (1982) that most of what is being measured in the strange situation is really temperament and not "security
of attachment" at all.

I am not persuaded by Chess and Thomas's argument. I think there
are two distinct processes here, but they may be linked in some cases.
Specifically, I think that temperamentally difficult infants are more
*likely* to develop an insecure attachment (Waters, Vaughn, & Egeland,

Table 11.2

**Behavior of securely and insecurely attached 1-year-old infants
in the strange situation**

| Group | Behavior |
|---|---|
| Securely attached | Baby seeks and maintains contact with or proximity to mother, especially when reunited with her after absence; clearly prefers mother to stranger; greets mother with smile or cry after separa-tion. |
| Insecurely attached: detached/avoidant | Child avoids or ignores mother at reunion; little tendency to seek contact with mother at any time; does not hold on if picked up; treats stranger about the same as mother. |
| Insecurely attached: resistant/ambivalent | Both actively resists contact with mother (particularly at reunion) and seeks contact and nearness; baby seems ambivalent, as if he wants contact but resists it when offered; baby very dis-tressed when separated from the mother. |

*Source:* Based on descriptions of Ainsworth et al., 1978, pp. 59–63.

1980), simply because parents respond differently to the difficult baby. But it is the different response of the parents, and not the difficult temperament per se, that produces the insecure attachment. The same "difficult" infant might develop a secure attachment if the parents were able to respond to her in a more sensitive and contingent fashion.

### Does a Secure or Insecure Attachment Last?

A more critical question is whether a secure or insecure attachment in a 12-month-old child persists into preschool or elementary school. Is a child "stuck with" whatever quality of attachment he achieved in the early years?

Most of what we know about this question involves very short-term comparisons in infancy, such as between security measured at 12 months of age and again at 20 or 24 months. We know far too little about the persistence of insecure attachments in school-age children or adolescents or even adults. But given the limits of our knowledge, my answer to the question is "yes and no."

When the child's family environment or life circumstances are reasonably stable, the security or insecurity of the child's attachment does seem to remain constant over short periods. For example, Everett Waters (1978) found that only 2 out of 50 infants changed their category of attachment from 12 to 18 months. But when the child's family circumstances change—mother going back to work, or the child entering a new child-care center, or grandmother coming to visit—the security of the child's attachment to the mother (or father) may also change, either from secure to insecure or the reverse (Thompson, Lamb, & Estes, 1982, 1983; Vaughn et al., 1979). In one study of abused children, for example, Brian Egeland and Alan Sroufe (1981) found that a child who had been insecurely attached at 12 months might become more securely attached after the grandmother had come to live with the family or when the family's level of stress went down.

From an applied point of view, results like these can be seen as very encouraging. It would appear that even a very poor early environment need not destine a child to a permanently insecure attachment. At least within the early years, the child can "recover" from an insecure attachment (or lose a secure one). Just how long this resilience may last I do not know. Can a child who had a consistently insecure attachment for the first three to four years later develop a secure attachment to a kindergarten teacher or a stepmother? An important question, well worth further research.

### How Is a Secure Attachment Formed?

Just what is it that some parents do or don't do that seems to lead to a secure or an insecure attachment?

Mothers of securely attached infants are more supportive of their infants' independent play, more sensitive to their children's needs, and more emotionally expressive toward their babies. My favorite of the studies that show this relationship is one by Mary Blehar, Alicia Lieberman, and Mary Ainsworth (1977). They use the wonderfully descriptive phrase *contingent pacing* to characterize the behavior of the mother of the securely attached child. A mother who is using this type of interaction paces her actions "slowly and gently, modifying them in keeping with infant cues, pausing if needed to allow him time to mobilize a response" (p. 185). Moreover, these mothers encourage further interaction by allowing the baby enough time to respond during their play and are playful themselves. The mothers of securely attached babies are also rarely routine in manner with their babies and are rarely silent or unsmiling. They are, in a word, "dancing" well with their babies.

It is important to remind you at this point of the research on day care I discussed in Chapter 1. It would be an easy thing to assume that mothers who place their infants in day care would have less opportunity to develop smoothly synchronized pacing with their infants and that as a consequence infants in day care might be less securely attached. You'll remember that that is *not* what investigators have found. Secure attachment does not seem to require *constant* contact between mother and infant, just as the infant's attachment to the father does not require his constant presence. What I do not know, however, is what impact the separation between mother and child has on the *mother's* attachment to the child. Curiously, in all our research on day care, this last question has not been asked—an oversight I hope will be remedied in the next few years.

## Long-Term Effects of Secure/Insecure Attachment

As I mentioned in Chapter 9, there is now a growing body of research showing long-term effects of the security or insecurity of the child's first attachments. Those children who are rated as securely attached when observed in the strange situation at 12 or 18 months are found to be more sociable and more skillful with peers several years later and more emotionally "mature" in their approach to school and other non-home settings. There is even a recent finding that securely attached children later explored a new space more independently and thoroughly than did children who had been rated as insecurely attached at 12 months (Hazen & Durrett, 1982), presumably because a securely attached child can wander farther and more comfortably from the safe base of the mother's location.

If, as I have suggested here, these differences are not merely inborn temperamental differences in new forms and are reasonably stable over time, then this entire body of research offers considerable support for Erikson's or Freud's general view of the importance of the primary relationship.

## BEYOND THE FIRST ATTACHMENT: CHILDREN'S RELATIONSHIPS WITH OTHER CHILDREN

So far I have talked almost exclusively about the child's relationship with his father and mother, with only occasional references to other adults, such as day-care workers or grandparents, and even more fleeting mention of same-age friends. But beginning in the preschool years, other children play an increasingly central role in the child's social world.

Most of the work on children's social interactions with one another has focused on the two ends of a positive-negative continuum. On the positive end, researchers have looked at children's friendships, at popularity, and at helpfulness or generosity among peers. On the "negative" end, psychologists have looked at aggression among peers and at dominance in play groups. For both convenience and clarity, I will divide my own discussion in a similar way. But I want to emphasize at the outset that "positive" versus "negative" is an overly simplistic way of describing the complex social interactions we see among children (or among adults). There are signs of a shift of emphasis in some recent research; ideas like "cohesiveness" or "synchrony" in children's relationships are appearing in the literature. I will try to use such concepts wherever I can to give a richer description of the quality of children's relationships with one another.

### Positive Social Interactions among Children: Developmental Patterns

*Early Peer Interactions*    Children first begin to show some positive interest in other infants as early as 6 months of age. If you place two such babies on the floor facing each other, they will look at each other, touch, pull each other's hair, imitate each other's actions, and smile at each other (Vandell, Wilson, & Whalen, 1981; Hay, Nash, & Pedersen, 1983). By 10 months these behaviors are even more evident (Eckerman & Whatley, 1977). Children this age apparently still prefer to play with objects but will play with other little bodies if no toys are available. By 14 to 18 months, we begin to see two or more children playing with each other and with toys at the same time, as Joseph Jacobson's work shows (Figure 11.7). Jacobson observed a group of children in a series of 20-minute episodes from the time they were 10 months till they were 14 months old. As you can see in the figure, play interactions centering around a common toy increased sharply over the four-month period, while interactions involving no toy leveled off.

**Figure 11.7** Recent research, like this study by Jacobson, shows that even very young infants will play with one another if left alone, but in the second year of life (14½ months in this study), their play is increased if a toy that they both enjoy is also around to play with. (*Source:* Jacobson, 1981, p. 623. © The Society for Research in Child Development, Inc.)

Besides the steady increase in social exchanges, two facets of this developmental change deserve some emphasis. First, the quality of children's play interaction changes, shifting from what Piaget calls **parallel play** to **cooperative play**. In parallel play, two children may be using the same materials or the same toys, but each is playing independently, such as two children each painting a picture. In cooperative play, the children join in a common project (see Figure 11.8). Some play involving common themes or "shared meaning" can be seen occasionally in children as young as 12 or 18 months (Brenner & Mueller, 1982), but cooperative play becomes much more common in children 3 and 4 years of age.

Another interesting aspect of children's early social exchanges is that to some extent young children seem to have to learn how to play with one another. Children who have had more experience with same-age peers are more skillful—they make more overtures, are more likely to respond appropriately to a play overture from another child, and the like (Mueller & Brenner, 1977). I am intrigued, though, with a hint in a recent study (Vandell, Wilson, & Whalen, 1981) that young children who are around older children a lot—older siblings or older day-care children, for example—may learn to be more passive in their interactions with peers. They are accustomed to having the older child

**Figure 11.8** These two photos illustrate parallel play (on the top) and cooperative play (bottom). During the preschool years, there is a shift from a predominance of parallel play to a predominance of cooperative play.

make the first move and thus have not learned the *mutual* play skills we see in children who spend time with same-age peers.

While 1- and 2-year-old children show real social interactions, they do not appear to have *attachments* to other children. The first signs of "best friends" are seen at about age 3 or 4 (Hartup, 1975). These early friendships are fairly fragile. They are based mostly on proximity and shared play interest (the child next door or the child down the street who likes to ride a trike with you), and they form and shift from week to week. But even these early relationships have some of the features of attachments. Three- and 4-year-old children are more positive toward their friends than toward nonfriends; they show greater pleasure and more exploratory behavior when they are in a strange environment with a friend than with a nonfriend; and they comply with the friend's wishes or suggestions more than with a nonfriend's (Doyle, 1982). I am reasonably sure that children this age would turn to a parent rather than to a friend-peer under real stress, but there are at least the beginnings here of true attachments.

Children as young as 2 or 3 also show another type of positive social behavior, **altruism**. They will offer to help a child who is hurt, offer a toy, or try to comfort another (Zahn-Waxler & Radke-Yarrow, 1982). The fact that such young children behave in this thoughtful and helpful way toward one another is especially interesting in light of what we know about the typical "egocentrism" of children at this age. Such children have only a beginning understanding of the fact that other people feel differently from themselves. But they obviously understand enough to respond in supportive and sympathetic ways when they see other children (or adults) who are hurt or sad.

It turns out, though, that children vary a lot in the amount of such altruistic behavior they show at this early age. For those of you interested in knowing more about how helpful children come to be that way, I've explored some of the research in Box 11.2.

*Positive Social Interactions at School Age*    Individual friendships play a large role in the social patterns of elementary-school–age children. In one study, John Reisman and Susan Shorr (1978) found that second graders named about four friends each; by seventh grade this had increased to about seven friends each.

There are some curious inconsistencies in the information we have about the quality of these relationships. On the one hand they are more stable than are the friendships of younger children (Berndt, 1981a). On the other hand, elementary-school–age children treat friends and strangers more alike than do younger children (Berndt, 1981b; Gottman & Parkhurst, 1980).

At the moment, the most reasonable resolution of this apparent contradiction seems to be that older children are simply more "polite" to strangers. They show many of the same positive, sharing, considerate behaviors toward strangers that they show toward friends. But school-age children *do* make clear distinctions between friends and nonfriends among those children they know well. So it is not that 5- to 12-year-old children treat all other youngsters alike. They don't. They have stable, positive friendships that play important roles in their lives. But they have also learned the "proper" or "polite" way to act toward others more thoroughly than have 2- to 5-year-olds, and we see this polite behavior with strangers in first encounters.

Another striking thing about peer relationships in elementary school is that the groups children form then are almost exclusively

BOX 11.2

# *REARING HELPFUL AND ALTRUISTIC CHILDREN*

I have said that children as young as 2 or 3 will show helpful and kind behavior toward one another at least occasionally. This is quite true, but some children show much more altruism and kindness than others. Since most of us would *like* our children to behave in this way toward us, toward their brothers and sisters, and toward other children, it's worthwhile to take a look at what we know about the kind of family environments that seem to foster this type of positive social interaction.

Several things parents can do seem to make a difference.

*CREATING A LOVING AND WARM FAMILY CLIMATE*

It shouldn't surprise you to learn that parents who behave in loving, nurturing, and supportive ways toward their children have children who are more helpful, more empathic, and more thoughtful of others (Zahn-Waxler, Radke-Yarrow, & King, 1979). Undoubtedly, this is partly the effect of modeling. But it may also reflect the effect of a more secure attachment of the child to the parent or even the effect of a good mood. Studies with adults show that we are more likely to help someone in distress if we are in a good mood, and this may be true for children as well.

Other adults (such as teachers) can enhance a child's helpful or altruistic behavior, too, by listening intently to the child's conversation and by being supportive and encouraging (Staub, 1971).

*EXPLAINING WHY AND GIVING RULES*

A second significant element in the equation is to be clear to children about what your rules and standards are. The combination of clear rules and loving support is what Baumrind calls "authoritative" parental style. It certainly seems to be a pattern that fosters several "good" things in children, such as high self-esteem and popularity. It reappears in studies of altruism in children as well. This shows up particularly clearly in research by Carolyn Zahn-Waxler and her colleagues (Zahn-Waxler, Radke-Yarrow, & King, 1979; Zahn-Waxler & Radke-Yarrow, 1982).

They asked a group of 16 mothers of young children to keep daily diaries of every incident in which someone around the child showed distress, fear, pain, sorrow, or fatigue. For example, John's mother described an incident in which her 2-year-old son was visited by a friend, Jerry:

sex-segregated. Obviously, in many schools children interact with peers of both sexes, but in their own chosen play groups, girls play with girls and boys with boys. Perhaps in recognition of this preference, most organized children's activities at these ages (e.g., Boy Scouts or Girl Scouts) are also sex-segregated. Interestingly, this is not an isolated Western-culture phenomenon. Such sex segregation of groups has been observed in widely varying cultures (Rubin, 1980).

It is worth noting in passing that this maximum sex segregation of children's groups occurs during the period Freud called *latency,* when sexual energies were thought to be relatively quiescent. It is also the period after children have fully grasped the permanence of gender,

Today Jerry was kind of cranky; he just started completely bawling and he couldn't stop. John kept coming over and handing Jerry toys, trying to cheer him up, so to speak. He'd say things like "Here, Jerry," and I said to John: "Jerry's sad; he doesn't feel good; he had a shot today." John would look at me with his eyebrows kind of wrinkled together like he really understood that Jerry was crying because he was unhappy, not that he was just being a crybaby. He went over and rubbed Jerry's arm and said "Nice Jerry" and continued to give him toys. (Zahn-Waxler, Radke-Yarrow, & King, 1979, pp. 321–322).

Zahn-Waxler found that mothers who both explained the consequences of the child's actions ("If you hit Susan, it will hurt her") *and* who stated the rules clearly, explicitly, and with emotion ("You mustn't hit people!") had children who were much more likely to react to others with helpfulness or sympathy. Research with older children, too, shows that stating the *reason* for generosity or helpfulness increases the likelihood that a child will behave in a kind or helpful manner (Grusec & Arnason, 1982).

Many of us, as parents, spend a lot of time telling children what *not* to do. The research on altruism in children points to the importance of telling children *why* they should not do things (especially explaining how they will affect others). Equally important is stating *positive* rules or guidelines (e.g., "It's always good to be helpful to other people," or "We should share what we have with people who don't have so much").

### HAVING CHILDREN DO HELPFUL THINGS

A third thing that fosters helpfulness is giving children a chance to do really helpful things—around the house or in school (Staub, 1979). Children can help cook (a nurturing activity), take care of pets, make toys to give to hospitalized or poor children, assist in making a casserole to take to the recently widowed neighbor, teach younger siblings how to play games (or even how to "share"), and the like.

### MODELING THOUGHTFUL AND GENEROUS BEHAVIOR

The fourth key—perhaps the most significant—is to demonstrate to your children exactly the generous, thoughtful, and helpful behavior you would like them to show. If there is a conflict between what you say and what you do, children will imitate your actions (Grusec & Arnason, 1982). So stating the "rules" or guidelines clearly will do little good if your own behavior does not match what you say.

when they seem to be focused on learning their "appropriate" sex roles and are maximally stereotyped in their sex-role concepts.

*Positive Social Interactions at Adolescence*   Although I am sure you remember your elementary-school years as a time when friendships with your school chums were important, it is the period of adolescence that most of us think of as being dominated by peer relationships. It is also part of our cultural stereotype of adolescents that they are overly influenced by peers.

To a considerable extent these recollections and stereotypes are based on fact. Adolescents report that they spend more time talking to peers than doing any other thing (Csikszentmihalyi, Larson, & Prescott, 1977), and this peer time may be an essential mechanism for making the transition from dependent child to independent adult. Relationships with peers (unlike the relationship with one's parents) are relationships among equals, so they allow the young person to practice many of the aspects of relationships that will be critical in a later marriage or on the job or with adult friends (Berndt, 1982).

The influence of the peer group on a teenager's ideas, customs, or behaviors seems to be at its peak between the ages of about 12 and 14 (Berndt, 1979) and then declines in later adolescence. At the peak point, teenagers are most likely to go along with the group ideas—about where to eat or what activity to choose or even to do something illegal like soaping windows on Halloween—even when they do not agree with those ideas. Dress customs and other "shared culture" are likely to dominate during this period as well, while youngsters in late high school are more willing to buck the crowd.

Over the same years the structure of the peer group changes, too. Dunphy's study (1963) of the several steps or stages in the shape and function of the peer group during adolescence is particularly fascinating. He observed the formation, dissolution, and interaction of teenage groups in a high school in Sydney, Australia, between 1958 and 1960. Two types of groups were visible. The first type Dunphy called **cliques.** They were made up of four to six young people who appeared to be strongly attached to one another. Cliques had strong cohesiveness and high levels of intimate sharing. In the early years of adolescence, these cliques are almost entirely same-sex groups—left over from the preadolescent pattern. Gradually, however, the cliques combine into larger sets called **crowds**, made up of several cliques. Ultimately, the crowd breaks down again into heterosexual cliques and finally into loose associations of couples (see Figure 11.9). The period of the fully developed crowd (at least in Dunphy's study) occurred at about age 13 to 15—the very years when we see the greatest conformity to peer pressure.

According to Dunphy, the crowd performs the highly important function of serving as a vehicle for the shift from unisexual to heterosexual social relationships. The 13- or 14-year-old can begin to try out her new heterosexual skills in the somewhat protected environment of the crowd; only after some confidence is developed do we see the beginnings of committed heterosexual pair relationships.

While these changes in peer groups are taking place, young people continue to have important individual friendships as well. These friendships are reasonably stable, lasting two to three months on the average (much longer in some individual cases, of course). These friendships also become increasingly intimate over the adolescent years (Berndt, 1982). Adolescents share their inner feelings and secrets with their friends more than do elementary-school children and are more knowledgeable about their friends' feelings as well. This trend contin-

**Figure 11.9** Dunphy's observations of Australian teenagers led him to suggest that there were two "phases" in teen group formation: cliques, which are closely knit groups of six or eight friends, and later crowds, which may be looser-knit associations of cliques. This group would probably qualify as a crowd. Does Dunphy's description fit with your own memory of the groups you were involved with in high school?

ues throughout the teen years, with intimate sharing reaching a peak in the early twenties (as Erikson suggested).

I think it is important for adults—especially parents—to understand the *function* of friendships and peer-group relationships for adolescents. Parents are often horrified at the conformity they see and at their reduced influence on their children. But the teenager is struggling with making a slow transition from the protected life of the family to the independent life of adulthood. Peer culture in adolescence is a *vehicle* for that transition.

## Individual Differences in Positive Interactions: Popularity

Peer relationships obviously play a key role in the child's daily life as well as in his development. But equally obviously, children are not all skilled at forming or maintaining satisfying relationships with their peers. In Table 11.3 I've listed some of the characteristics of popular children—those who are chosen as playmates or who are leaders of groups (Asher, Renshaw, & Hymel, 1982; Ladd, 1983; Rubin & Daniels-Beirness, 1983). Some of the items on this list are things that a child can't control, such as his physical size or attractiveness. These characteristics do make some difference, but the crucial element in popularity is how the child *behaves,* not how he looks. Popular children are those with good "social skills." They are positive, supportive, nonaggressive, and nonpunitive toward their peers; they pay attention to other children's ideas and actions; they make eye contact when you talk to them; they smile at you. It is not surprising that children who behave this way are well liked!

What kinds of families do popular children come from? I've already mentioned two elements: Families that foster secure attachment have children who show greater skill with peers in the preschool period, and this may well carry over to later years. Families that foster high self-esteem also have more popular children. Other research suggests several other aspects of families of popular children (Asher, Renshaw, & Hymel, 1982; Hartup, 1970): (1) they discourage aggression and antisocial behavior in their children; (2) they try not to frustrate the children and use little punishment; (3) they like their children and tell them so; (4) they make sure their children have plenty of opportunity to play with other children (play groups, picking up and delivering playmates, participation in children's groups like Scouts, etc.); and (5) they provide toys and materials to their children that foster pair or group interaction, such as dress-up materials or puppets. For a boy to be popular with his peers, a strong father figure—one who is warm and positive toward the son—also seems to be important.

**Table 11.3**

**Characteristics of "popular" children in elementary school and high school**

| | |
|---|---|
| Friendliness | The more friendly (and less negative), the more popular a child is. |
| Cooperativeness | Popular children are more likely to cooperate with the suggestions of others. |
| Outgoingness | Gregarious children are more popular than withdrawn children. |
| Success in school | Children who get better grades or have greater academic skill are more popular. |
| Family position | Youngest children in a family are usually more popular than firstborns. |
| Physical attractiveness | The more attractive the child, the more he is liked by peers. This element seems less important among preschoolers. |
| Physical size | Tall or physically mature children are more popular. |
| Specific task ability | Children who are very good at sports or at some other task valued by the group are more popular. |
| General social skills | In general, children who have good "social competence"— who smile more, make eye contact when you speak to them, listen when you talk, make good suggestions, ask questions —are more popular with peers. |

If you think back to what I said in Box 10.1, this combination of parental treatment sounds a lot like the pattern Baumrind calls "authoritative" child rearing. Thus, the origins of high self-esteem and the origins of popularity may have something in common. But children who lacked such an optimal upbringing can still learn the skills necessary for effective peer relationships. When children are coached on how to ask questions and on how to offer support to peers, their popularity increases as well (Asher, Renshaw, & Hymel, 1982; Ladd, 1981).

## Negative Social Interactions among Children

If you have watched children together, you know that all is not sweetness and light in the land of the young. Children do show affectionate and helpful behaviors toward one another, but they also tease, fight, yell, criticize, and argue over objects and territory. Researchers who have studied this "negative" side of children's interactions have looked mostly at aggressive behavior, which we can define as behavior with the apparent intent to injure some other person or object (Feshbach, 1970).

*The Development of Aggressive Behaviors*   Every child shows at least some **aggression**. The basic built-in "signal" for aggression in most instances seems to be frustration. Some early theorists (Dollard et al., 1939) argued that aggression *always* followed a frustration and that all aggressions were preceded by frustration. This extreme version of the "frustration-aggression hypothesis" turns out to be wrong, but it does seem to be true that the human child is born with a fairly strong natural tendency to behave aggressively after being frustrated.

Over the early years of life, the frequency and form of aggression change, as I've summarized in Table 11.4. When 2- or 3-year-old children are upset or frustrated, they are more likely to use physical aggression. As their verbal skills improve, however, there is a shift toward greater use of verbal aggression, such as taunting or name-calling.

*Individual Differences in Aggressiveness*   Go to a school playground or a day-care center and sit and watch for a while. It isn't hard to pick out some children who are consistently more aggressive than others. They get into more fights, yell more at other children, and generally make a nuisance of themselves. Other children play together for long stretches without getting into disputes. Where do such differences come from?

Of course, it could be partly a temperamental difference. But it seems to me to be more likely a result of the reinforcement patterns the child has experienced. In nursery schools with a "permissive" approach to child behavior, children who come to school with relatively

Table 11.4

**A summary of developmental changes in the form and frequency of aggression in children**

|  | *2- to 4-Year-Olds* | *4- to 8-Year-Olds* |
|---|---|---|
| Frequency of physical aggression | At its peak from 2 to 4 | Declines over the period from 4 to 8 |
| Frequency of verbal aggression | Relatively rare at 2; increases as the child's verbal skill improves | A larger percentage of aggression in this period is verbal rather than physical |
| Form of aggression | Primarily "instrumental aggression," which is aimed at obtaining or damaging an object rather than directly hurting someone else | More "hostile aggression" at these ages, aimed at hurting another person or another person's feelings |
| Occasion for aggression | Most often occurs after conflicts with parents | Most often occurs after conflicts with peers |

*Source:* Based on data from Goodenough, 1931; Hartup, 1974.

high rates of aggression simply get more that way over time. They find that aggression works—they get the toys they want or the first turn at the swing.

In families, the reinforcement pattern also seems to make a difference. In Chapter 9 I mentioned a study by Sears, Maccoby, and Levin (1957) that showed that the most aggressive children come from fami-

**Figure 11.10** Preschoolers are more likely to show this kind of hostile, physical aggression than are older children. Toddlers are more likely to fight over toys or objects; preschoolers fight with each other; elementary-school children call each other names.

lies high in both permissiveness and punishment for aggression. The sequence apparently runs something like this: The mother or father allows the child to beat up her brother or snatch a toy from her sister. But when the noise level becomes too high or the screams of agony too piercing, the parent steps in with some fairly severe punishment, such as spanking, sending the offending child to her room, or taking away a cherished privilege. The parents in such cases may think that they are being consistently severe toward aggression and may be mystified that their children are so aggressive. What the parents have done, though (in addition to modeling aggression to the child), is to allow aggression some of the time and punish it at other times—a kind of partial reinforcement schedule.

Another pattern that seems to increase aggressiveness is what Gerald Patterson (1980) describes as "coercion" by the child. When a child behaves in an aggressive or unpleasant way, the parent may simply get tired of the yelling and screaming and let the child have his way. This produces blessed (if temporary) quiet, which serves as a negative reinforcement for the parent, while the child has been positively reinforced for the angry or aggressive behavior.

Probably the quality of the child's first attachment to the parent makes a difference, too. One consistent finding in research on families is that those that are rejecting toward the child have more aggressive children. Often, of course, rejection is combined with high rates of physical punishment of the child. These children are unloved, frustrated, and see a model of aggressive behavior. It is not surprising that they show higher rates of aggression themselves.

Of course, an additional element in the equation is the child's exposure to other aggressive models, such as those on TV—a process I'll be talking about in Chapter 13.

*Competition and Dominance in Children*    A related, but quite separable, aspect of "negative" encounters between children is **competition** or **dominance**. Whenever there are too few toys for the number of children, not enough time with the teacher to go around, or some other scarcity of desired objects, there will be competition. Sometimes competition results in outright aggression. More often, though, competition results in the development of a clear **dominance hierarchy**, more popularly known as a "pecking order." Some children seem to be more successful than others at asserting their rights to a desired object, either by threats, by simply taking the object away, by glaring at the other child, or the equivalent.

Clear dominance hierarchies are seen in play groups of children as young as 2 to 5 years old (Strayer, 1980; Vaughn & Waters, 1981). That is, among 10 or 15 children who play together regularly, it is possible to predict who will "win" in any given competition over some desired object or space. Children high in the dominance hierarchy win out over nearly all other children; children at the bottom of the pecking order lose to everyone.

Recent work on dominance in young children has revealed some extremely interesting patterns. Among 2- to 5-year-olds, a child's place in the group dominance system is *not* related to popularity or to positive interactions to or from the child. But among elementary-school children, the dominance and popularity/friendship system may be linked. When Strayer (1980) observed 5- and 6-year-olds in play groups, he found that the dominant children were also the most popular. So among children this age, popularity may reflect both positive actions and perceived dominance.

Overall, the picture that emerges is that past the age of 4 or 5, *socially competent* children are those who are at the middle to higher end of the dominance hierarchy; who are positive, helpful and supportive of others; and who refrain from overt acts of physical aggression.

## SEX DIFFERENCES IN SOCIAL INTERACTIONS

So far I have steered clear of any discussion of sex differences in social interactions. But since this is an area in which the sex-role stereotypes are very strong, I need to face the question as squarely as I can. Take a look at Table 11.5. In the table, I've listed both the stereotype (the basic cultural expectation) and the actually observed differences, so you can see how well they match.

In many areas the match is not good. Girls don't seem to be more dependent or consistently more nurturant (the offering of care and concern to others) or more socially oriented. The pattern of social behavior boys and girls show does differ somewhat: Boys play in larger groups and appear to have less intimate individual friendships. But there are no differences in involvement with others. The one area in which the stereotype seems to be fairly accurate is in aggression, assertiveness, and dominance. As expected, boys show more of all three.

Where might such a difference in aggressiveness come from? Eleanor Maccoby and Carol Jacklin (1974), who have summarized all the studies done up to 1974, concluded that there is an important biological basis for the aggression differences:

Let us outline the reasons why biological sex differences appear to be involved in aggression: (1) Males are more aggressive than females in all human societies for which evidence is available. (2) The sex differences are found early in life, at a time when there is no evidence that differential socialization pressures have been brought to bear by adults to "shape" aggression differently for the two sexes. (3) Similar sex differences are found in man and subhuman primates. (4) Aggression is related to levels of sex hormones, and can be changed

Table 11.5

**Sex-role stereotypes and observed sex differences in social behavior**

| Behavior | Stereotyped Expectation | Actual Observed Behavior |
|---|---|---|
| Aggression/dominance/competitiveness | Boys are expected to show more of all three | Boys are quite consistently found to show more rough-and-tumble play in the early years (DiPietro, 1981) and aggression and competitiveness at virtually all ages (Maccoby & Jacklin, 1980; Berndt, 1982). |
| Risk taking | Boys are expected to show more | Boys are also more willing to try new and daring or faintly dangerous things, such as riding an elephant at the zoo (Ginsburg & Miller, 1982). |
| Dependency | Girls are expected to show more | No consistent sex difference has been found in such behaviors as clinging, being near, or attention seeking in young children (Maccoby & Jacklin, 1974). |
| Nurturance/helping/generosity | Girls are thought to show more of all three | Mixed results. Most studies show no difference, but when a difference is found, girls are usually slightly more generous or slightly more likely to help or nurture (Maccoby & Jacklin, 1974; Shigetomi, Hartmann, & Gelfand, 1981). |
| Interest in others/sociability | Girls are thought to show more | Results are mixed. Boys seem to be more peer-oriented in preschool (Maccoby & Jacklin, 1974). In elementary school, boys have more friends and play in larger groups; girls seem to have fewer but stronger friendships (Laosa & Brophy, 1972). In adolescence, some indication that girls' friendships are more intimate, but no difference in the number (Berndt, 1982). |
| Compliance | Girls are thought to show more | Preschool girls comply more with adult requests (Minton, Kagan, & Levine, 1971; Maccoby & Jacklin, 1974). Among older children there is no consistent tendency for girls to be more compliant, although very high levels of noncompliance are more likely to be found in boys (Patterson, 1980). |
| Crying | Girls are thought to do more | There is no consistent difference among children in the likelihood of tears. Among preschoolers, when there is a difference, it looks as if boys cry more (Maccoby & Jacklin, 1974). |

by experimental administration of these hormones. (Maccoby & Jacklin, 1974, pp. 242–243)

Other psychologists (including Maccoby and Jacklin in more recent writings) have emphasized that there are important social influences, at least in our culture, that also may foster higher levels of aggression in boys (Brooks-Gunn & Matthews, 1979; Tieger, 1980). For example, Margaret Snow and her colleagues (Snow, Jacklin, & Maccoby, (1983) have found that with children as young as age 1, fathers punish or prohibit behavior in their sons more than in their daughters.

It seems clear to me that both biological and environmental influences play a role. There probably are hormonal or other biological factors creating higher rates of aggressiveness in boys to begin with. But as I pointed out in Chapter 10, there is also pressure from parents (particularly fathers) for 4- and 5-year-old boys to adopt more "boyish" behaviors and attitudes, which includes playing physical games and being assertive with others. The manner in which parents respond to the child's aggression also helps to shape it, which shows clearly that aggression is not entirely determined by biology.

Despite this difference in aggressiveness, the striking thing about the evidence on sex differences in social behavior is how few of them are found consistently. Boys and girls are much more like each other than they are different in the quality and content of their encounters with each other.

## SUMMARY

1. Relationships with adults and peers are of central significance in the development of all children. Of particular importance is the formation of basic attachments to others in infancy and later childhood.
2. An important distinction is between *attachment behavior* and underlying *attachment*. The latter is the basic bond between two people. The former is the manner in which that bond is expressed in actual behavior.
3. The parents' attachment to the infant may develop in two phases: (1) an initial strong bond may be formed in the first hours of the child's life, and (2) a growing attachment may result from the repetition of mutually reinforcing and interlocking attachment behaviors.
4. The short-term strength of the first bond appears to be somewhat increased if the parents have immediate contact with the newborn, but the long-term effect of this early contact is small and seen only in some subgroups of parents.
5. Fathers as well as mothers form strong attachments to their infants. Some differentiation of interactive pattern occurs past the

early weeks of life, however, as fathers show a more playful interactive pattern with their children than do mothers.

6. The development of the infant's attachment to the parents begins with a period in which the baby shows attachment behaviors toward nearly anyone but shows no preferential attachment.

7. By 5 to 6 months, most infants have formed at least one strong attachment, usually to the major caregiver (most often the mother).

8. In toddlers and preschoolers, the basic attachment remains, but the form of attachment behaviors changes, becoming less clinging, except when the child is under stress, when the earlier forms reappear.

9. In adolescence, too, the basic attachment to the parents appears to remain strong, although the young person now spends considerably more time with peers than with parents, and parent-child conflict becomes more common.

10. Children typically develop strong attachments to both father and mother. Children 12 to 24 months old typically prefer the mother over the father in stressful situations.

11. Children differ in the security of their first attachments. The secure infant uses the parent as a safe base for exploration and can be readily consoled by the parent.

12. Secure attachment appears to be fostered by attentive, loving, "contingently paced" interactions between parent and child. Securely attached children appear to be more skillful in later years with peers and more curious and persistent in approaching new tasks.

13. Children's relationships with other youngsters become more and more central to their social development from age 1 or 2. Toddlers are aware of other children and will play with them; by 2 or 3, children show specific social approaches to others.

14. By age 4 or 5, children have formed individual friendships and show preferential positive behavior toward friends. Friendship becomes more common and more stable in the elementary-school years.

15. The peer group is particularly significant in adolescence, when it may serve as a "bridge" between the role of dependent child and that of independent adult. Teenagers are maximally influenced by peer pressure at around age 14, a time when large groups of teens ("crowds") may associate regularly. Individual friendships also are significant in adolescence.

16. Young children also show such negative social patterns as aggressiveness and dominance. Physical aggression peaks at 3 or 4 and is more and more replaced by verbal aggression among older children. Children who are reinforced for aggressiveness show more aggression with their peers; rejected children and those who are

permitted to be aggressive and then punished for it show heightened aggression.

17. Dominance patterns are visible in groups of toddlers as well as
older children.

18. Popularity among peers, in elementary school or later, is associated with greater intelligence, greater dominance, and greater attractiveness. But it is primarily associated with the amount of positive and supportive social behavior shown by a child.

19. The most consistent sex difference in social behavior is that boys
are more aggressive than girls. In other areas the similarities are
more striking than the differences.

*KEY TERMS*

**Aggression**  Usually defined as intentional
physical or verbal behaviors directed toward
a person or an object with the intent to inflict
damage on that person or object.

**Altruism**  Giving or sharing objects, time, or
goods with others, with no obvious self-gain.

**Attachment**  The positive affective bond between one person and another, such as the
child for the parent or the parent for the
child.

**Attachment behavior**  The collection of
(probably) automatic behaviors of one person
toward another that brings about or main-
tains proximity and caregiving, such as the
smile of the young infant; behaviors that reflect an attachment.

**Clique**  A group of six to eight friends with
strong attachment bonds and high levels of
group solidarity and loyalty.

**Competition**  Interaction between two or
more persons in which each person attempts
to gain control over some scarce resource,
such as toys, attention from a preferred person, or "success."

**Cooperative play**  Play between two children
in which both are joined in a common enter-
prise, such as building a block tower together.

**Crowd**  A larger and looser group of friends

than a clique, with perhaps 20 members; normally made up of several cliques joined together.

**Dominance**  The ability of one person consistently to "win" competitive encounters with
other individuals.

**Dominance hierarchy**  A set of dominance
relationships in a group describing the rank
order of "winners" and "losers" in competitive encounters.

**Insecure attachment**  Includes both ambiva-
lent and avoidant patterns of attachment in
children; the child does not use the parent as
a safe base and is not readily consoled by the
parent if upset.

**Parallel play**  A pattern of play in which two
or more children play next to each other but
each at his own game or task, with no mutual
activities.

**Secure attachment**  Demonstrated by the
child's ability to use the parent as a safe base
and to be consoled by the parent after separation, when fearful, or when otherwise
stressed.

**Strange situation**  A series of episodes used
by Mary Ainsworth and others in studies of
attachment. The child is observed with the
mother, with a stranger, when left alone, and
when reunited with stranger and mother.

*SUGGESTED READINGS*

Asher, S. R.; Renshaw, P. D.; & Hymel, S. Peer
relations and the development of social

skills. In S. G. Moore & C. R. Cooper (Eds.).
*The young child: Reviews of research* (Vol 3).

Washington, D.C.: National Association for the Education of Young Children, 1982.

A very nice discussion of social skills in children and some of the attempts that have been made to increase such skills in socially isolated children.

Maccoby, E. E. *Social development: Psychological growth and the parent-child relationship.* New York: Harcourt Brace Jovanovich, 1980.

A fine text including chapters on attachment, on aggression, and on sex differences in social behavior.

Oden, S. Peer relationship development in childhood. In L. G. Katz (Ed.). *Current topics in early childhood education* (Vol. 4). Norwood, N.J.: Ablex, 1982.

Another good current review of information on children's peer relationships and friendships, with a focus on the early years of life.

Rubin, A. *Children's friendships.* Cambridge, Mass.: Harvard University Press, 1980.

Zick Rubin writes wonderfully; this book is both delightful and informative.

Stern, D. *The first relationship: Infant and mother.* Cambridge, Mass.: Harvard University Press, 1977.

Another lovely book, full of good examples and clear descriptions of research.

PROJECT 11.1

# *Observation of Children's Play Groups*

Let me give you a tougher assignment than many of the earlier projects. This will really stretch your skills as an observer and researcher. Arrange to spend several hours in a day-care center or preschool that includes groups of children of about age 2 to 4. Be sure to do the observation during a time that includes some "free play"; if all you observe is snack time, nap, and organized play, you will not get a chance to observe the things I want you to look for.

Watch for about 15 minutes without writing anything down, making an effort to identify (to yourself) about 10 different children, about half of whom should be boys and half girls. Label them in some way that you can use as shorthand, and be sure to indicate whether each is a boy or a girl. Now begin your real observations. At the start of each three-minute period, note down which other child or children each of your 10 focal children is playing with at that moment. Note for each child: (1) How many other children there are in the play group, (2) the gender of all children in the play group, (3) the specific identity of any child in the group you can identify, and (4) the activity the children are engaged in (e.g., doll play, blocks, swings).

Continue this procedure for each three-minute period for at least an hour. Inevitably you will have some periods in which one or more of the focal children were not in sight (they are in the bathroom or elsewhere), and probably there will be some three-minute periods in which all the children are playing together in some activity organized by the teachers. In the former case, merely omit that child from the record for that interval. In the latter case (full-group activity), omit that three-minute period from your record entirely.

When you are done, you should have up to 20 notations for each of your focal children. For each child: (1) Compute the average size of the play group that child was in across the three-minute periods. (2) Determine the percentage of periods in which only same-sex playmates were present, only opposite-sex playmates, and mixed-sex groups.

Compute the same figures across all your focal children (average size of group and percentage of same-sex, opposite-sex, and mixed-sex groups). Also see if you can find any consistent pairs of children who seemed to play together frequently. Were these "friends" usually same-sex pairs?

How do your observations match the patterns of early peer associations I have described in the text? Are there consistent pairings of "friends"? Were some children consistently solitary in their activity, while others were in larger groups? Do children this age mostly choose same-sex pairs? How large are the groups typically formed? What kinds of activities were these groups engaged in?

What difficulties did you have in completing the assignment? Was it hard to determine who was "in" a particular group? This is a tough kind of observation to do, so don't be discouraged if you found it confusing. You may end up with more respect for the attention to detail required for researchers to do this type of study well.

# 12.
# *thinking about relationships: the development of social cognition*

Who is your best friend? Why is that person your friend? What are friends for? Try thinking of your answers to those questions and then compare your own answers to children's answers to similar questions.

What kind of person makes a good friend?
"Boys play with boys, trucks play with trucks, dogs play with dogs." (Selman, 1980, p. 136)

"Karen is my friend because she's nice. She gives me jewelry and candy, and I give her things, too."
"A friend is someone you can count on when you need her and the chips are down."
"Friends are people that you trust; you know that they won't take advantage of you or lie to you." (Damon, 1977, pp. 27, 29)

In the last chapter I talked about children's friendships—when they first develop, how many of them children seem to have, how stable and how intimate they are. But that is only part of the picture. Children's *understanding* of their relationships also changes with age.

If you look at the four "definitions" of a friend I just quoted, you may see at least three different kinds of reasoning. The first child defines a friend as someone like himself (boys play with boys). The second child defines friendship in terms of exchange of material goods or favors. Friends are people who do things for you and for whom you do things in return. The third and fourth young people define friendship less externally, but personal needs are still uppermost (a friend is someone who fills personal needs and does not betray you).

You will not be a bit surprised to learn that the first two answers were given by children younger than those who gave the last two answers. So it is not just the outward characteristics of friendships that change; children's ideas about friendship change at the same time.

There has been a real blooming of research on children's understanding of social relationships in recent years (a research area usually called **social cognition**), and the results are quite fascinating. In particular, this new research represents a significant blending of work on thinking and on relationships. By studying social cognition, we can begin to get a glimpse into the complex interweaving of thought and feeling, thought and action, thought and relationships.

## BASIC IDEAS ABOUT SOCIAL UNDERSTANDING

To put it most simply: The child's thinking about relationships affects those relationships, and her relationships affect her thinking.

**416**

## Thought Shapes Relationships

The key cognitive element in the child's growing understanding of relationships seems to be *perspective taking*. I talked about physical perspective taking in Chapter 7 and pointed out that 3- and 4-year-olds already have some ability to recognize that other people see or sense things differently from the way they do. If I am looking at a chair from the back and a 4-year-old is looking at it from the front, he is likely to realize that I do not see the same thing that he does. But *social* perspective taking is much more complex, since it requires the child to be aware of things that can't be seen, like the other person's thoughts or feelings. As you'll remember from Chapter 7, such awareness of nonvisible aspects of objects or situations does not normally appear first until age 5 or 6 or 7 and then undergoes still further refinements and abstractions at adolescence.

Obviously, such an ability to take the other person's view is critical in the development of mature, complex relationships. You know that your friends or your parents see things differently from the way you see them and take those differences into account; you expect them to do the same for you. Mature relationships thus require a *coordination of perspectives*. But young children do not yet have the ability to coordinate perspectives, so their relationships are very much more based on here-and-now elements and are much more likely to be self-oriented.

Thus, there is a sequence of cognitive changes that lies behind, or makes possible, many of the changes in children's relationships that I described in the last chapter.

## Relationships Shape Thought

But this is a two-way street. The "food" for this particular cognitive progression is not play with or manipulation of objects (as is the progression of cognitive changes described in Chapter 7); the "food" for changes in perspective taking and in social understanding is social interaction. In particular, Piaget (1970a) and Sullivan (1953) both argue that it is interaction with *peers* that is critical for the emergence of the child's understanding of alternative viewpoints.

Unlike relationships with parents, which are by definition unequal, relationships with peers are more equal. So children argue with each other, present their own views, hear other people's ideas, and so gradually come to understand that other children (and other adults) think about things and feel things differently from the way they themselves think about and feel them (Youniss, 1980).

Most of the research on children's emerging social understanding puts the cognitive horse before the social relationship cart, implying

**Figure 12.1** The youngsters in the lower picture are likely to have been friends for longer than the younger pair above; as I've already pointed out, friendships become more stable as children get older. But the older pair also has different *expectations,* different understandings of their relationship than do the younger children.

that it is the "understanding" part of the system that is paramount. I will inevitably foster this impression further in this chapter, since most of what I will describe will be research on the cognitive "side." But I will try to balance the scales a bit later on (in Box 12.1 and elsewhere).

## Selman's Theory of Social Understanding

The most integrated (and most influential) description of these changes in social understanding has been proposed by ~~Robert Selman~~ (1976, 1980). He has been very much influenced by Piaget's basic theory and by Piaget's open-ended exploratory method of probing children's ideas. So Selman devised a series of stories that describe relationships and dilemmas within relationships. Children hear (or read) these stories and are then asked to say what the child(ren) in the story should do or would do. Two of the stories (the first used with children under about age 10 and the second a story used with adolescents) are shown in Table 12.1.

Based on children's comments about stories like these, Selman proposes five stages or "levels" in children's social perspective taking (which I've summarized in Table 12.2). These levels are loosely associated with particular ages, but there is a good deal of individual variation in the speed with which a child moves through these levels (as is true in Piaget's theory as well, of course).

*Level 0: Undifferentiated and Egocentric Perspective Taking (about Age 3 to 6)* The child at this level does not yet really realize that other people feel or think things different from his own thoughts and feelings. He can recognize other people's feelings, such as knowing someone is "sad" if they cry, but has not yet gotten this external event hooked up to the internal emotion. These children are likely to judge someone else's actions by the consequences rather than by the intention of the actor.

*Level 1: Differentiated and Subjective Perspective Taking (about Age 5 to 9)* There are several big advances at this level. First, children now realize that other people have ideas and feelings that may be different from their own. Children at this level also understand that there is a difference between what someone does and what they think and feel, so youngsters at level 1 distinguish between intentions and consequences.

Despite these great advances, however, the level 1 child's understanding is still limited. He still thinks that he can figure out your feelings or thoughts by your facial expressions or other external cues, and he does not yet understand that *you* are also aware of his thoughts and

Table 12.1

**Examples of stories in Selman's studies of children's social understanding**

A story exploring children's understanding of individuals, for children below 9 or 10:

"Tom has just saved some money to buy Mike Hunter a birthday present. He and his friend Greg go downtown to try to decide what Mike will like. Tom tells Greg that Mike is sad these days because Mike's dog Pepper ran away. They see Mike and decide to try to find out what Mike wants without asking him right off. After talking to Mike for a while the kids realize that Mike is really sad because of his lost dog. When Greg suggests he get a new dog, Mike says *he can't just get a new dog and have things be the same.* Then Mike leaves to run some errands. As Mike's friends shop some more they see a puppy for sale in the pet store. It is the last one left. The owner says that the puppy will probably be sold by tomorrow. Tom and Greg discuss whether to get Mike the puppy. Tom has to decide right away. What do you think Tom will do?"

A story exploring children's understanding of friendship, for adolescents and adults:

"Charlene and Joanne have been good friends since they were five. Now they were in high school and Joanne was trying out for the school play. As usual she was nervous about how she had done, but Charlene was there to tell her she was very good and give her moral support. Still Joanne was worried that a newcomer in school would get the part. The new girl, Tina, came over to congratulate Joanne on her performance and then asked if she could join the girls for a snack. Right away Charlene and Tina seemed to hit it off very well. They talked about where Tina was from and the kinds of things she could do in her new school. Joanne, on the other hand, didn't seem to like Tina very well. She thought Tina was a little pushy, and maybe she was a bit jealous over all the attention Charlene was giving Tina.

"When Tina left the other two alone, Joanne and Charlene arranged to get together on Saturday, because Joanne had a problem that she would like to talk over with Charlene. But later that day, Tina called Charlene and asked her to go to Washington to see a play on Saturday.

"Charlene had a dilemma. She would have jumped at the chance to go with Tina, but she had already promised to see Joanne. Joanne might have understood and been happy that Charlene had the chance to go, or she might feel like she was losing her best friend when she really needed her."

*Source:* Selman, 1980, pp. 318, 322.

feelings. In the old infinite-regress game, children at level 1 can say "I know that you know" but cannot yet understand the next step—"I know that you know that I know."

*Level 2: Self-Reflective and Reciprocal Perspective Taking (about Age 7 to 12)* At this level, the child now does understand that other people also "read" his feelings and thoughts. For the first time at this stage, children see relationships as really reciprocal. They also begin to understand other people's motivations, feelings, and actions in much more complex ways. They realize that someone can be *both* frightened and curious or that someone might do something they did not intend or want to do. There is also some understanding of the fact that other

Table 12.2

**Selman's five levels of social understanding**

| Level | Approximate Age | Description |
|---|---|---|
| 0 | 3–6 | *Undifferentiated and egocentric perspective taking.* The child may realize that other people *physically* experience things differently but does not yet understand that other people *feel* or *think* differently. |
| 1 | 5–9 | *Differentiated and subjective perspective taking.* The child now realizes that other people feel and think differently and knows that people may act differently from how they feel but does not yet realize that other people also see the same things about him. |
| 2 | 7–12 | *Self-reflective and reciprocal perspective taking.* The child realizes that there is a two-way street—that each member of a pair knows the other may think differently (I know that you know that I know). Relationships are seen as truly reciprocal. |
| 3 | 10–15 | *Third-person and mutual perspective taking.* The child at this stage (early formal operations) is able to stand outside a relationship completely and view it as if he were a third person. Relationships involve mutual coordinations, mutual satisfactions. |
| 4 | 12–adult | *In-depth and societal-symbolic perspective taking.* The young person understands that other people's actions are influenced by their upbringing, by their enduring personalities, and by social forces and takes these factors into account. |

*Source:* Selman, 1980.

people may *disguise* their true feelings or thoughts by putting on a "social" face.

*Level 3: Third-Person and Mutual Perspective Taking (about Age 10 to 15)* At adolescence (at approximately the time that formal operations first appear), we see still further *decentering.* Young people at this level can now take a "third-person" perspective and consider both themselves and others simultaneously. This allows mutual coordination of perspectives. The adolescent sees herself, and friends or parents, as potentially engaging in a process of simultaneous adjustments to one another. Furthermore, they *expect* satisfying relationships to have this quality.

*Level 4: In-depth and Societal-Symbolic Perspective Taking (about Age 12 to Adulthood)* This final level will be clearer after I talk about some specific themes. Very abstract understanding of relationships is involved here. The young person understands that other people are enormously complex and that they are shaped by their society and by their own past—and that others themselves may not even understand why they do what they do. In relationships, the adolescent or adult at this level realizes that both he and his partner are affected by social systems, customs, and training.

If you think about this progression, you can see several threads that should sound very familiar from Chapter 7. The child is moving from a heavy reliance on external cues to greater and greater emphasis on invisible forces—a shift that we saw in the child's understanding of conservation, among other things. The child is also moving from an egocentric perspective to a mutual one to a still more abstract ("formal") ability to stand mentally outside of the system itself.

But Selman is *not* saying that the cognitive sequences I described in Chapter 7 are merely "applied" by the child to social relationships. The two threads of development are obviously related, but Selman thinks that the child must grapple with social understanding in social interactions. So let's take a look at some of the social relationships that Selman and others have studied, using his model, so that you can get a clearer grasp of just how the child's social understanding affects, and is affected by, relationships with other people.

## THEMES IN THE DEVELOPMENT OF SOCIAL UNDERSTANDING

### Understanding Individuals

A good deal of what I have already said about the overall qualities of Selman's five levels relates to the child's growing understanding of individuals. At level 0, the child does not differentiate thinking and acting, even for himself. He apparently believes that a person's thoughts must always be the same as his behavior. At level 1, he realizes that thinking and acting are separate and that different people may react quite differently to the same events.

At level 2, the child understands that people (including himself) may hide their thoughts and feelings—he understands that there is an "inner" self to each person that may not be visible at all. Finally, at levels 3 and 4, the young person begins to see others as possessing complex, organized personalities. At level 3, the child sees other people as having "traits"—certain pervasive and persistent qualities that will turn up again and again—like shyness or aggressiveness or verbal skill or physical coordination or liberal political attitudes. Young people at this level have a strong tendency to stereotype others, however. They generalize the "traits" too broadly, expecting complete consistency. Only at level 4 do we see the most complex understanding of others as made up of both unconscious and conscious thoughts and emotions, shaped by our culture and our upbringing.

One aspect of this shift is illustrated nicely in a study by Carl Barenboim (1981). He asked youngsters (aged 6, 8, and 10) to talk about three different people (other than family members) they knew well, saying "what kind of person" each was. A year later (when the children were 7, 9, and 11), he asked them again to do the same thing. Barenboim then searched in the children's comments for two kinds of things: (1) behavioral comparisons, like "Billy runs a lot faster than Jason," or "She draws best in our whole class"; (2) psychological constructs, in which general personality characteristics were mentioned, like "He's a real stubborn idiot!" or "Randy is always trying to boss other kids around."

These two types of description reflect precisely the kind of changes Selman is talking about. The child starts out focused on visible behavior in other people and only later figures out that there are "invisible" properties. Barenboim's results, which you can see in Figure 12.2, in fact show that descriptions of others in terms of psychological constructs rise sharply at about age 10, when children would be expected to be in Selman's level 2. And for all three groups, the number of psychological constructs mentioned rose from the first to the second testing a year later.

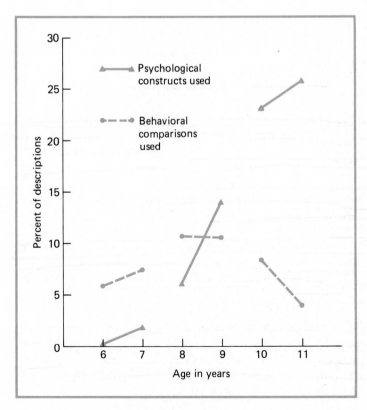

**Figure 12.2** When children talk about their friends, younger children are likely to compare them on some physical or behavioral dimension (Jake is bigger than Sam), but as they get older, psychological comparisons become more common—another sign of the child's growing awareness of the "insides" of other people. (*Source:* Barenboim, 1981, adapted from Figure 1, p. 134.)

This transition has some implications for parents and teachers. For example, if you are trying to explain to your 5-year-old child why a playmate was particularly selfish, a "situational" explanation (e.g., "Maybe he was tired today") will probably be understood better than an "internal attribution" (e.g., "He really likes his own way a lot").

## Understanding Friendships

Obviously, this shift in the way children "see" other people can't help but influence their friendships. At the higher developmental levels, we can understand our friends' behavior better, forgive peculiarities more easily, and expect the same comprehension from them in return. This shift should make friendships more intimate and more stable—which is precisely the change I described in the last chapter.

But children's specific understanding of friendship also undergoes change, as illustrated by the quotes I gave at the beginning of this chapter. I've summarized Selman's five levels of understanding of friendship in Table 12.3, but some illustrations will help.

One of the ways Selman (1980) has explored understanding of

Table 12.3

**Five levels in the child's understanding of friendships**

| | |
|---|---|
| Level 0 | *Close friendship as momentary physical interaction.* Children call those they may be playing with that day or that week "close friends." Friends are chosen by who shares an interest or who happens to be available. Not stable relationships. |
| Level 1 | *Close friendship as one-way assistance.* Friends are important or useful because they play with you, they fill needs (like the need to have nine players on a baseball team). The purpose of friends, in other words, is to fulfill a child's self-interests. |
| Level 2 | *Close friendship as fair-weather cooperation.* There is some reciprocity here (as there must be for level 2 understanding), but it is "fair-weather." We're friends as long as we continue to please each other. Friendships are seen as important for each person, to provide companionship and liking as well as playmates. |
| Level 3 | *Close friendship as intimate and mutual sharing.* Young people at this age talk about the "relationship" with their friend as if it existed separately and are concerned with behaving in ways that will maintain that relationship. Sharing of intimate concerns is one ingredient in maintaining the friendship. |
| Level 4 | *Close friendship as autonomous interdependence.* After the relationship-absorbtion of level 3, young people at level 4 are able to step back a notch and realize that there may be times when their own beliefs, choices, or tasks may require them to make new demands on a friendship or to go outside the relationship. They see relationships as constantly changing and adapting to new demands or growth in each of the parties to the relationship. |

*Source:* Selman, 1980.

friendship is to ask children what friends should do if they disagree: "What are some good ways to settle fights, arguments, or disagreements with a friend?" and "Can friends have arguments and still be friends?" (These are important questions for adult friendships, too, aren't they?)

At level 0, children typically say either to use physical force ("Punch her out") or to go away when they have a disagreement with a friend. They do not seem to realize that the anger or distress will continue when the two friends are apart. At level 1, children have some understanding that the feelings will continue, but they are still looking at it from only one perspective (usually their own). They see conflicts as *caused* by one person and *felt* by the other. Their solutions are usually to have the one "in the wrong" apologize or do something to make up.

> "Stop the fight and give him back what you took or take back what you called him."
> "Give him something nice that will make him feel better."
> "Around our way the guy who started it just says he's sorry."
> (Selman, 1980, p. 108)

This strategy works reasonably well when the conflict was, in fact, "started" by only one person. But this level of understanding will get in the way of conflict resolution if both people "started it" or are involved. (I suspect that you occasionally find yourself thinking this way, even as an adult! How often have you waited for the "other guy" to say she's sorry or to make a peace offering?)

At level 2, though, children understand that both people are involved in virtually all conflicts, so the solution has to satisfy both people as well.

> "Somebody wants to play one game and the other wants to play another game and you can settle it, but first we will play your game and then we will play my game." (Selman, 1980, p. 109)

Children in this stage also think that it isn't enough just to apologize—now you also have to *mean* it. This obviously reflects their new understanding that people can and do disguise their real feelings.

What is missing, here, though, is any sense that solving problems between friends requires *mutual* problem solving. This mutuality first appears at level 3, when young people first seem to understand that the conflict exists *within the relationship itself.* Note the really big difference in this 15-year-old's comment:

> "If you just settle up after a fight that is no good. You gotta really feel that you'd be happy the way things went if you were in your friend's

shoes. You can just settle up with someone who is not a friend, but that's not what friendship is really about." (Selman, 1980, p. 111)

*level 3*

What is more, adolescents and adults who are reasoning at this level realize that sometimes conflicts result from basic personality differences, not just momentary disagreements. They also see that conflict, if resolved carefully, may actually strengthen a relationship. The emphasis is on sharing, on active communication.

Finally, at level 4, young adults realize that sometimes problems between them result from each person's own individual problems, and they can accept that in each other. They no longer place such a total premium on complete sharing and "talking it out," either, but mention accepting each other's qualities or letting things "settle" on their own. Relationships among people at this stage may seem to be less intense because there is less constant sharing, but the level of understanding is more subtle:

> "Sometimes when a person's got problems of his own, he finds himself starting fights with all his friends. The best thing you can do is try to be understanding but don't get stepped on either." (Selman, 1980, p. 111)

Since the final steps in this sequence are often not taken until late adolescence or even adulthood, these descriptions should tell you something about your own relationships as well. When you have an argument with a friend, lover, or spouse, how do you resolve it? Would you place your own thinking at level 2, level 3, or level 4?

Virtually the same sequence of changes in children's understanding of friendships can be seen in studies by James Youniss (1980), who asked children about being kind to their friends. I've given some of their answers in Table 12.4, with the ages scrambled. Can you figure out the correct age sequence just by reading the comments? (The right answers are upside down at the bottom of the table.)

Table 12.4

**Examples of children's ideas about being kind to friends.
(Can you put the comments in order by age?)**

"Tell me a story in which a child your age does something kind for a friend."

- *A.*   She fell and hurt herself riding bikes. I took her home, washed her knee, and gave her a Band-Aid.
- *B.*   Play with him a lot.
- *C.*   Trusting them. Not lying to them.
- *D.*   When he fractured his finger, I comforted him and made him feel at home.
- *E.*   Being nice.

B & E, both age 7; A & D, both age 10; C, age 13.

*Source:* Youniss, 1980, pp. 87–88.

## Understanding Groups

Selman has also explored children's growing understanding of the uses and functioning of peer groups—a particularly interesting topic in early adolescence, when the peer group seems to be especially significant.

In the early stages, children's ideas about groups are very much like their ideas about friends. At level 0, children talk about groups as bunches of friends who happen to be available to play with each other—children who live on the same block or are in the same class. Children at this stage do not seem to have an idea of conscious or intentional collaboration.

At level 1, which Selman calls "unilateral relations," children see groups as ways to provide enough people for desired activities: "Clubs are good, because there are more people to do things with, so you can play more games." Children at this stage understand that it may be necessary to do nice things or cooperate in order to stay in the group but do not yet grasp the principles of group planning or coordinated actions to improve group solidarity or functioning.

By middle childhood (level 2), children have begun to understand the reciprocal nature of groups and use words like *teamwork* to describe the way they can work together for mutual goals. They also begin to argue that children in clubs or groups should share the same feelings ("They should like the same things"). But preadolescents still think of groups really as sets of interlocking friendships. Sullivan (1953) referred to these groups as "interlocking two-groups," a phrase that conveys the sense nicely.

Only at level 3 do young people begin to talk about the *group* as having special qualities of its own. They see peer groups as forming shared communities of common interests and think about the social structure of the entire group. To fit into such a group, it is not enough just to have one or two friends in the group; teenagers now think that they need to be like (and be liked by) the *whole* group and to conform to the group norms. Of course, this is precisely the point (about age 13 or 14) when we see the peak of conformity to groups, as I described in Chapter 11.

> "The team has to work together as a unit."
> "We decide on one thing everyone wants to do." (Selman, 1980, p. 146)

Finally, at level 4, this "Everyone is equal" and "We all have to agree" concept of the group gives way to a greater understanding of how individuals and groups can coexist (just as the idea that friends have to "talk everything out" gives way to greater acceptance of the other's qualities at stage 4). The young adult understands that while a group can be thought of as a community, there are different roles and needs within that community, so everyone doesn't have to think alike or behave alike to be part of the group.

> "Individual personalities of people, different from each other, will contribute to the group and make it more of an entity than it was before." (Selman, 1980, p. 147)

The importance of contracts or agreements for organizing the group is also recognized.

> "Rules serve as guidelines so an artificial order gives some structure to the group." (Selman, 1980, p. 147)

In the last chapter I suggested that one of the reasons we see the increased importance of the peer group in early adolescence is that such groups serve as a kind of bridge for the young person between the dependency of childhood and the independence of adulthood. But Selman's work gives us another insight: The peer group has the shape and quality that it does in early adolescence in part because young people's *ideas* about groups and their functions are maximally conformist and norm-oriented at that age. It is the combination of this cognitive construction with the social value of the group that seems to give teenage groups their special qualities.

### Understanding Parent-Child Relationships

The final dimension of the child's social understanding that Selman describes is the understanding of the relationship of parent to child. (This dimension may be particularly interesting to you as prospective parents: It may help you to understand how the child "sees" you in your role as parent at various points during childhood.)

Unlike friendships, the relationship with the parent is not one of equality. So the child must come to understand more complex relationships. At level 0, Selman finds that children perceive their relationship with parents as mostly a "boss-servant" link. The parent is the boss and tells you what to do. Parents are more powerful than children. They take care of children, but they also punish. Children this age are not clear about what causes what—whether bad behavior causes punishment or punishment causes bad behavior (an example of transductive reasoning, by the way)—but they are clear about who does the punishing.

This understanding of parents is slightly modified at level 1, which Selman describes as the "caretaker-helper" level. Children this age accept the parent not only as more powerful but also as more wise and

**Figure 12.3** Children of this age mostly see their parents as caretakers and helpers. Probably this child assumes that her parents love her and thinks her mother and father are very wise and knowing. But she doesn't yet see the relationship at all as a two-way street, nor does she yet understand that the parent may get some satisfaction (or problems) from the role.

knowing and as having good intentions toward children. Elementary-school children at this level think that parents have children because children are fun to be with and because children help with chores. The idea that there are *responsibilities* of parenthood has not yet entered the equation. Children at level 1 also typically believe that their parents love them but do not see this as a reciprocal system: Parents show their love by taking care of the child; the child shows her love by doing what she's told.

Reciprocal understanding defines the beginning of level 2, just as it does in the other social understandings I have been describing. Children this age understand that parents get some satisfaction from their role and also realize that "good" parents have given up things they might like to do for the sake of their children. The "role" of parent has changed in children's thinking, too. Parents are now seen mostly as "counselor" or need satisfier. A good parent is one who is "sensitive" to the child's needs.

In early adolescence, at level 3, a more intimate relationship based on mutual tolerance and respect is conceived by the child. The teenager hopes for love and closeness from the parent and believes that the lack of such love will cause problems for them later. But adolescents are also aware of the fact that parents still have more power so that there are bound to be disagreements and conflicts.

Selman has not explored level 4 in this sequence but thinks that it would involve both autonomy and interdependence, with fluctuations between the two over the rest of the life cycle.

### Links between Selman's Themes

Before going on to talk about the final theme of "moral understanding"—a discussion that will require exploring a different theoretical model—I need to pause and say at least a word or two about the consistency of children's understanding across these themes. Table 12.5 summarizes the five levels in each of the four themes I've just described. The obvious implication is that a child's social understanding will be pretty much the same in each theme. A child who understands reciprocal relationships in friendships ought to see groups and parent-child relationships in reciprocal ways, too. This issue should be familiar from Chapter 7, since this is another variation of the question of *stages* versus *sequences*. Obviously, Selman thinks that there is some overlap between these sequences. But is he right?

The preliminary answer seems to be "yes." Selman (1980) used his story method to inquire about children's ideas of individuals, friends, and groups in a sample of 225 people, aged $4\frac{1}{2}$ to 32 years. All a child's comments on stories that dealt with a single theme (individuals, friends, or groups) were scored by one person who didn't read the rest of the child's comments on other themes. When Selman then looked at the consistency *across* themes, he found several very interesting things.

First, as you can see in Figure 12.4, children move through the levels at almost identical rates on the three themes—although understanding of groups lags a bit behind. Second, most children gave an-

Table 12.5
**Selman's levels by "themes"**

| Theme | Stage 0<br>3–6 yrs. | Stage 1<br>5–9 yrs. | Stage 2<br>7–12 yrs. | Stage 3<br>10–15 yrs. | Stage 4<br>12–adult |
|---|---|---|---|---|---|
| Understanding of individuals | Physical entities | Intentional subjects | Introspective selves | Stable personalities | Complex self-systems |
| Understanding of friendships | Momentary physical interactions | One-way assistance | Fair-weather cooperation | Intimate and mutual sharing | Autonomous interdependence |
| Understanding of peer groups | Physical connections | Unilateral relations | Bilateral partnerships | Homogeneous community | Pluralistic organization |
| Understanding of parent-child relationships | Boss-servant | Caretaker-helper | Counselor, need satisfier | Tolerance, respect | Unknown |

*Source:* Selman, 1980.

swers at the same level, or very nearly the same level, across themes. In a subgroup of 48 children whose scores were analyzed fully, he found that you could easily identify an overall level of each child's social understanding and that nearly all of a child's individual answers were within "one-third of a stage" of that overall level.

In general, children's understanding of social relationships "radiates outward," moving from understanding individuals (including the self) to understanding pairs such as friends and, finally, to groups. But the spread of understanding appears to be quite rapid. At least under the conditions of Selman's study, it does seem to be fair to describe children's social understanding as being "at" a single, global level. I'll be returning to this question of consistency across domains later in the chapter, but for now it is intriguing that there is more "stagelike" reasoning here than researchers have been finding lately in the more traditional studies of cognitive development (Chapter 7).

### Understanding Right and Wrong, Good and Bad

Selman's work has focused mostly on children's understanding of *relationships* with other people. But social understanding also requires the child to think about or explain other people's *actions*. The facet of this that has most intrigued developmental psychologists is the child's judgment of the "morality" of actions. How does a child decide what is good or bad, right or wrong in other people's behavior and in his own behavior? When you serve on a jury, you are asked to make a judgment of this kind, but of course, you do this every day, too, when you decide if you should give the store clerk back the excess change she handed you or when you consider whether it is right or wrong to withhold part

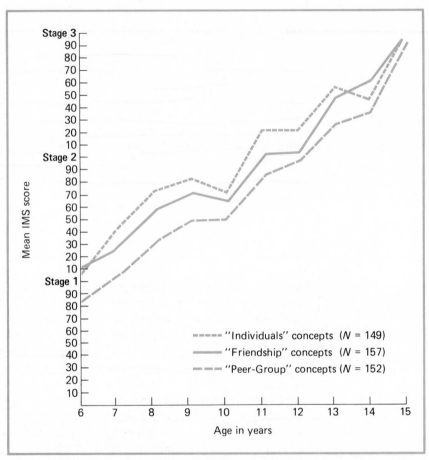

**Figure 12.4** Children who are read or asked to read stories about friends, about individuals, and about peer groups usually talk about those stories in very similar ways, just as these children in Selman's study did. But understanding of individuals is consistently slightly ahead of understanding of friends, with understanding of peer-group relationships lagging slightly behind. (*Source:* Selman, 1980, Figure 8.1, p. 180.)

of your income tax as an antiwar protest or when you are offered an "advance look" at a course exam by a friend.

The two men who have been most involved in studying these questions are Piaget (1932) and Lawrence Kohlberg (1964, 1976, 1980, 1981; Colby et al., 1983). Piaget described early steps in moral reasoning in preschool and elementary-school–aged children. Kohlberg's work grew out of Piaget's early studies and extended the stages of moral reasoning upward into adolescence and adulthood.

*Piaget's Early Ideas about Moral Judgments*  Piaget described two stages of children's reasoning about right and wrong. (These are going to sound very much like Selman's stages 0 and 1, but remember that

Piaget first described these ideas in 1932, so it is Selman who has been influenced by Piaget rather than the other way around.)

The first stage is **heteronomous morality**, also sometimes called **moral realism**, and it is characteristic of preschool children (3 to 6 or so, just like Selman's level 0). Children of this age are "moral absolutists." They think rules are absolute, fixed, and unchangeable. This is true for rules parents give and rules of games as well. They also believe that if you break a rule, punishment (from parents, teachers, or even God) will inevitably follow (called a belief in *immanent justice*). A third element is that children of this age generally judge the goodness or badness of other people's actions largely on the basis of the consequences rather than the intent. By this reasoning, a child who breaks five glasses accidentally is seen as worse than a child who intentionally throws one down and breaks it.

Obviously, this kind of "rule" for goodness and badness makes sense when we think of what else we know about children's perspective taking at this age. Selman's work shows that 3- to 6-year-olds have not yet made the distinction between actions and intentions and are still mostly focused on behaviors they can *see* in other people. And what you can see is how many glasses got broken.

At about 6 or 7, Piaget saw a change. He called the second stage **autonomous morality** or the **morality of reciprocity**. Children of this age accept social rules but see them as more arbitrary, more changeable. Rules of a game, for example, can be changed if the children playing the game agree on the change. The belief in immanent justice fades, too; rule violations are no longer thought to result in inevitable punishment. Most striking, the intent of the person performing some action is now taken into account in judging the morality of the action.

There is a great deal of support for this element of Piaget's theory (e.g., Ferguson & Rule, 1980, 1982). Children under about age 6 or 7 make most of their judgments based on the badness of the outcome, while children over 9 or 10 judge mostly on the basis of the intent, even if the consequences aren't so bad.

So, for example, if children hear a story about a child who purposely pushes another child off the monkey bars at school, the older children (9- and 10-year-olds) think this is naughty even if the pusher only means to cause *a little* damage, while younger children think that intending only a small hurt is not so bad as intending a big hurt (Ferguson & Rule, 1982).

*Kohlberg's Stages of Moral Development*    Kohlberg's description of moral development overlaps Piaget's but extends into adolescence and adulthood. Since virtually all the recent research on moral development has been based on Kohlberg's stages, I need to describe them and the procedures he uses to measure them in some detail.

In order to explore a child's or young person's reasoning about difficult moral issues, such as the value of human life or the reasons for doing "right" things, Kohlberg devised a series of dilemmas. One of the most famous is the dilemma of Heinz:

> In Europe, a woman was near death from a special kind of cancer. There was one drug that the doctors thought might save her. It was a form of radium that a druggist in the same town had recently discovered. The drug was expensive to make, but the druggist was charging ten times what the drug cost him to make. He paid $200 for the radium and charged $2000 for a small dose of the drug. The sick woman's husband, Heinz, went to everyone he knew to borrow the money, but he could only get together about $1000 which is half of what it cost. He told the druggist that his wife was dying, and asked him to sell it cheaper or let him pay later. But the druggist said, "No, I discovered the drug and I'm going to make money from it." So Heinz got desperate and broke into the man's store to steal the drug for his wife. (Kohlberg & Elfenbein, 1975, p. 621)

After hearing this story, the child or young person is asked a series of questions, such as whether Heinz should have stolen the drug. What if Heinz didn't love his wife? Would that change anything? What if the person dying was a stranger? Should Heinz steal the drug anyway?

Obviously, dilemmas like this are artificial, as a number of critics have pointed out (Baumrind, 1978). But in my opinion, the issues they raise are the same ones we all face in our day-to-day moral decisions. How can we weigh the value of laws and society against the rights of individuals? How do we weigh our own desires against the needs or values of the group? What Kohlberg is interested in is not the actual choice the child makes in resolving the dilemma but the *kind* of reasoning he uses in grappling with the problem.

On the basis of answers to dilemmas like this one, Kohlberg concluded that there were three main levels of moral reasoning—**preconventional**, **conventional**, and **principled**—with two substages within each level. I've summarized the stages in Table 12.6. (I'll bet you're all sick of lists of stages by now!) Obviously, Kohlberg's stage 1 is similar to Piaget's *heteronomous morality,* and Kohlberg's stage 2 is similar to Piaget's *autonomous morality.* The transition to stage 3, however (from level 1 to level 2 in Kohlberg's terminology), takes us into new territory. It represents a shift from judgments based on consequences and personal gain to judgments based on the rules and norms of the group the child belongs to. Kohlberg asked one 10-year-old, for example, why someone should be a good son. The boy answered, "Be good to your father and he'll be good to you." This is a stage 2 answer, at the preconventional level. You are "good" because it will bring a reward. But sometime in early adolescence, there is a shift for most young people. Andy, an older boy Kohlberg interviewed, said:

"I try to do things for my parents, they've always done things for you. I try to do everything my mother says, I try to please her. Like she wants me to be a doctor and I want to, too, and she's helping me get up there." (Kohlberg, 1964, p. 401)

Andy is at stage 3, at the conventional level. He is deciding what is good on the basis of the important relationships around him. What his family wants or thinks is right is what he wants and thinks is right.

In his early writings, Kohlberg proposed that most teens or young

Table 12.6
## Kohlberg's stages of moral development

|  |  |
|---|---|
|  | **Level 1: Preconventional morality** |
| Stage 1: Punishment and obedience orientation | The child decides what is wrong on the basis of what is punished. Obedience is valued for its own sake, but she obeys because adults have superior power. |
| Stage 2: Individualism, instrumental purpose, and exchange | The child follows rules when it is in his immediate interest. What is good is what brings pleasant results. Right is also what is fair, what's an equal exchange, a deal, an agreement. |
|  | **Level 2: Conventional morality** |
| Stage 3: Mutual interpersonal expectations, relationships, and interpersonal conformity | The family or small group to which the child belongs becomes important. Moral actions are those that live up to what is expected of you. "Being good" becomes important for its own sake, and the child generally values trust, loyalty, respect, gratitude, and keeping mutual relationships. |
| Stage 4: Social system and conscience, law-and-order orientation | A shift in focus from the young person's family and close groups to the larger society. Good is fulfilling duties you've agreed to. Laws are to be upheld except in extreme cases. Contributing to society is also seen as good. |
|  | **Level 3: Postconventional or principled morality** |
| Stage 5: Social contract or utility and individual rights | Acting so as to achieve the "greatest good for the greatest number." The child is aware that there are different views and values, that values are relative. Laws and rules should be upheld in order to preserve the social order, but they can be changed. Still, there are some basic nonrelative values, such as the right to life and liberty, that should be upheld no matter what. |
| Stage 6: Universal ethical principles | The young person develops and follows self-chosen ethical principles in determining what is right. Since laws usually conform to those principles, laws should be obeyed; but when there is a difference between law and conscience, conscience dominates. |

*Source:* Adapted from Kohlberg, 1976; Lickona, 1978.

adults make another major shift, to level 3 (stages 5 and 6), in late adolescence. The young person may begin to realize that there are some issues that just can't be resolved by relying on fixed laws. Hitler, after all, was obeying the laws of Germany when he ordered the confiscation of Jewish property and created the extermination camps. And the laws of many southern states in the United States in the early 1960s allowed poll taxes or required blacks to ride at the back of the bus. Faced with such a conflict between a law and individual rights and freedom, a young adult may reassess moral issues and come to the conclusion that while we need laws so that there won't be social chaos, the laws are changeable. Individual values are important, and the laws should reflect those values. But if they don't, then the laws should be changed.

As a final, "ideal" stage, Kohlberg thought there were a few rare individuals who go beyond even this reasoning and search for enduring ethical principles to guide all their actions. Gandhi and Martin Luther King are two who Kohlberg thought used stage 6 reasoning.

In Kohlberg's own longitudinal studies of moral reasoning, though, it is clear that even stage 5 reasoning is really quite rare. He and Anne Colby and their colleagues (Colby et al., 1983) have followed one group of 58 boys over a 20-year period—from the time they were between 10 and 16 to age 30 to 36. Figure 12.5 shows the percentage of subjects who showed each type of moral reasoning at each age over this long stretch of years. It's pretty clear from these results that (at least in this sample) conventional, *not* postconventional, moral reasoning is the dominant pattern in adults.

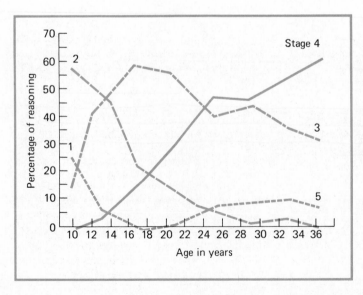

**Figure 12.5** This figure shows the relationship between age and young people's answers to Kohlberg's moral dilemmas. As you can see, stage 5 is not common at any age. For older teenagers and young adults, stages 3 and 4 (conventional morality) are by far the most common. (*Source:* Colby et al., 1983, Figure 1, p. 46. © The Society for Research in Child Development, Inc.)

## SOME QUESTIONS ABOUT SOCIAL UNDERSTANDING

After reading this far, I am sure you have some questions about all the stages and sequences I have been describing. You are not alone. Except for Piaget's and Kohlberg's work on moral reasoning, the study of the development of social understanding is really quite new, and there is a great deal we do not know yet. Let me focus on a few questions that I think are important: (1) Are there really *sequences?* I have described steps or levels, but do we know that children actually move through these steps or levels in the order in which they are described? (2) Are there *stages*? Do children and young people show common forms of reasoning about relationships, about right and wrong, about logical relations? I have delved into this question several times already (including earlier in this chapter), but it is an important one theoretically and deserves a further look. (3) Do children behave as well as they understand? What is the link between a child's understanding of relationships, or a teenager's level of moral reasoning, and her behavior? Are popular children more likely to be at higher levels in Selman's system? Are postconventional moral reasoners less likely to cheat on an exam than conventional or preconventional reasoners? (4) Can we apply any of this information to the real world, such as designing educational programs? (5) Finally, do boys and girls, men and women, show the same sequences and forms of reasoning?

The last of these questions I have explored in Box 12.1. Let me take up the other four in turn.

### Are There Really Sequences?

The answer to the question regarding the existence of sequences seems quite clearly to be "yes." Just as we can find clear sequences in the child's understanding of objects and relationships among objects (Chapter 7), so we find clear sequences in the child's social and moral understanding as well. The right way to study the existence of social and moral sequences is with longitudinal research—observing, interviewing, or testing the same children or young people repeatedly over time, to see whether the changes in their understanding follow the proposed sequence.

Selman has done this with a group of 48 boys he originally interviewed when they were in first through sixth grades. He reinterviewed them two years later (Selman, 1980) and then again three years after that (Gurucharri & Selman, 1982). At the time of the final interview, the boys ranged from 11 to 17 years of age and were from both working-class and middle-class backgrounds. All the boys responded to the same stories each time. Over the five-year interval between the first and the third testing, none of the 48 boys stayed at precisely the same

BOX 12.1

# VISIONS OF MATURITY: SEX DIFFERENCES IN SOCIAL UNDERSTANDING

One of the oddities of research on social understanding and moral judgment is that the majority of the children and adolescents who have been interviewed and studied have been boys. *All* of Kohlberg's subjects and most of Selman's subjects have been males. Girls' responses to the moral dilemmas are often judged as at a "lower" level, or they don't fit well into the categories at all. Could it be that the sequences I have described to you in this chapter are really patterns of *male* development and that a different model is needed for girls?

At least one eloquent author, Carol Gilligan (1982a, 1982b), thinks so. She argues that Kohlberg's description of moral development stages is a description of ideas about rights and justice and that it omits emerging ideas about relationships and connections. Boys, Gilligan says, follow the sequence Kohlberg lays out, but girls frequently do not.

Take, for example, the answers of two bright 11-year-olds, Jake and Amy, to the Heinz dilemma. Jake says:

"For one thing, a human life is worth more than money, and if the druggist only makes

$1000, he is still going to live, but if Heinz doesn't steal the drug, his wife is going to die. [*Why is life worth more than money?*] Because the druggist can get a thousand dollars later from rich people with cancer, but Heinz can't get his wife again. [*Why not?*] Because people are all different, and so you couldn't get Heinz's wife again." (Gilligan, 1982a, p. 203)

Jake's responses are scored as conventional, a mixture of stages 3 and 4, but he is clearly bringing some early formal operations logic to bear on this problem. In fact, Jake specifically compares the dilemma to a math problem and searches for the logical solution. He is grappling with the relationship between individual rights and society's rights and working out logical solutions.

Amy, in contrast, understands the question differently. As Gilligan points out, Amy does not focus on the question of whether Heinz *should* steal the drug but on whether he should *steal* the drug versus obtaining it by some other means, such as persuasion or negotiation. For her, the problem is to find a solution that recognizes and

---

level, and only 8 failed to move "up" at least one full level. (The rest showed some upward shift, but not a full level.) When their form of understanding changed, it always changed from "lower" to "higher" levels. At least for boys, then, the sequence seems to be a genuinely developmental progression, which is widely (perhaps universally) shared.

Anne Colby, Lawrence Kohlberg, and their colleagues (1983) have found a similarly striking developmental progression in their 20-year longitudinal study of 58 boys/men in the United States and in a shorter longitudinal study of boys in Turkey (Nisan & Kohlberg, 1982). In these studies no subject skipped a stage, and only 5 to 10 percent

protects the network of relationships. She says, in answer to the question about whether Heinz should steal the drug:

"Well, I don't think so. I think there might be other ways besides stealing it, like if he could borrow the money or make a loan or something, but he really shouldn't steal the drug, but his wife shouldn't die either. [If he stole the drug, she explains], he might save his wife then, but if he did, he might have to go to jail, and then his wife might get sicker again, and he couldn't get more of the drug, and it might not be good. So, they should really just talk it out and find some other way to make the money." (Gilligan, 1982a, p. 204)

Amy assumes that if the druggist really understood that Heinz's wife will die, he would be willing to help in some way. As Gilligan says: "Seeing a world comprised of relationships rather than of people standing alone, a world that coheres through human connection rather than through systems of rules, she finds the puzzle in the dilemma to lie in the failure of the druggist to respond to the wife" (1982a, p. 205).

Amy's responses are scored a full stage lower than Jake's. But rather than interpreting this as meaning that girls are less "morally mature" than boys, Gilligan argues that girls simply develop a different ethic, a different *basis* for morality. Boys rely on logical principles of justice; girls rely on a matrix or "web" of relationships.

I find Gilligan's ideas appealing for my own "web" of reasons. She is absolutely right that far too much basic research on development is done exclusively with boys or young men and then generalized to women. If girls do not perform in the same way or in the same sequence, they are judged to be "inferior" in some way. I am glad to hear voices raised questioning this strategy.

I am also struck by the interesting parallel between Gilligan's observations about girls' solutions to moral dilemmas and all the findings I described in Chapter 11 that show girls' actual friendships to be more intimate and lasting than are boys'. Intimate relationships thus may be more central to girls' development than they are to boys'. This might also mean that girls progress more rapidly through Selman's stages of social understanding, arriving at a sense of mutuality sooner than do boys. I will be interested to see if future research confirms this possibility.

Assuming that Gilligan is at least partially right, the real question is *why* such a difference in the basis for social/moral reasoning might emerge between boys and girls. Do you have any good hypotheses?

showed "regression" of a part of a stage. Since ordinary mortals score the subjects' answers and may make mistakes in the way they rate those answers, we could expect some such "reversals" just from error. The fact that there is so little "downward" movement in the level of the subjects' reasoning is very strong evidence indeed for the sequence Kohlberg has proposed.

But the developmental sequence seems to hold only up through stage 4 (the second stage of conventional reasoning). Since so very few adults ever do show true stage 5 reasoning (let alone stage 6), we can't really consider these steps to be part of the normal or expectable developmental progression.

## Are There Stages?

You'll remember from Chapter 7 that the question about stages is different from the question about sequences. To show sequences we need to show that all (or nearly all) children learn or develop skills or ideas in the same order. But to show real stages we have to show that clusters of conceptually related skills or ideas all develop at about the same time. It's obvious that the sequence of social understandings Selman proposes and the stages of moral development Kohlberg describes are very similar to each other. And both have some obvious connection to Piaget's stages of cognitive development (Chapter 7). I've already said that children seem to develop different facets of social understanding at about the same time. But does social understanding combine with moral reasoning and cognitive development to create "super stages"?

The answer seems to be "sort of." There is quite a lot of research that shows links between a child's social understanding, logical reasoning, and moral judgment (for example, Keasey, 1975; Selman & Damon, 1975; Selman, 1980). But recent evidence shows that what we may be seeing here are not structurally integrated stages but a set of "necessary but not sufficient" relationships. Specifically, Kohlberg (1976) has proposed that basic cognitive understandings (concrete or formal operations) underlie the social understandings and that both are necessary (but not sufficient) for changes in moral reasoning. For example, at least beginning formal operations and mutual perspective taking (Selman's level 3) may be necessary for the young person to move into the stages of conventional moral reasoning, and full formal operations and Selman's level 4 may be required for postconventional reasoning. That is, first the child figures out how to think logically, then applies this new kind of logic to relationships as well as objects, and only then applies this thinking to moral problems.

Table 12.7 shows the linked developments that Kohlberg is proposing. The idea is that each row in the table is based on or dependent on the developments in the row(s) above it. In fact, there is now pretty good evidence for this relationship. Lawrence Walker (1980) found that of a group of fourth to seventh graders he had tested on all three dimensions, half to two-thirds were reasoning at the same level across the different domains, which makes the whole thing look very "stagelike." But when a child was ahead in one progression, the sequence was always that he developed logical thinking first, then more advanced social understandings, and then the parallel moral judgments. Dennis Krebs and Janet Gillmore (1982) have found a similar sequence, although not quite so consistently.

What this research tells me is that there is *some* coherence in a child's or young person's thinking or reasoning about quite different problems. Children who have not yet understood principles of conservation are not likely to understand that other people may feel differently

Table 12.7

**Possible relationships between cognitive development, interpersonal understanding, and moral reasoning**

| Cognitive Stage | Social Understanding Level | Moral Judgment Stage |
|---|---|---|
| Preoperational | Level 0: egocentric | Stage 1: heteronomy; punishment and obedience |
| Early concrete operations | Level 1: differentiated and subjective | Stage 1: still see stage 1 at this point |
| Concrete operations | Level 2: self-reflective and reciprocal relationships | Stage 2: individualism, "naive hedonism," exchange |
| Beginning formal operations | Level 3: mutuality | Stage 3: mutual interpersonal expectations |
| Early basic formal operations (hypothetic-deductive reasoning used) | Level 4: in-depth societal understanding | Stage 4: social system and law-and-order orientation |
| Consolidated formal operations (used consistently and exhaustively) | Level 4: still greater understanding of symbolic interactions | Stage 5: social contract and individual rights |

*Source:* Adapted from Walker, 1980, Table 1, p. 132.

from the way they behave. But once conservation is understood, the child rapidly extends this principle to people and to relationships. Similarly, a young person still using concrete operations is unlikely to use postconventional moral reasoning. But the coherence is not automatic. The basic cognitive understanding makes advances in social and moral reasoning *possible* but does not guarantee them. Experience in relationships and with moral dilemmas is necessary, too.

The moral of this (if you will excuse the pun) is that just because a young person or adult shows signs of formal operations does *not* necessarily mean that the teenager or young adult will show sensitive, empathetic, and forgiving attitudes toward friends or family.

## Social Understanding and Social Behavior

An equally important question about consistency is whether children's and adolescents' behavior matches their social understanding or moral reasoning. Are children who think of friendships as mutual relationships more likely to have more friends? Are their friendships more intimate? Do teenagers who give stage 4 kinds of moral arguments cheat less on a test than those at less-mature levels of moral reasoning?

Again, the answer is "yes and no." It is simply not possible to predict *precisely* what a child will do in a real-life situation from knowing the form or level of his reasoning. But there are some important links between thinking and behavior.

For example, Martin Ford (1982) studied teenagers' empathy (the ability to understand and share another person's feelings, which is an aspect of social understanding) and their "social competence." Ford asked ninth and twelfth graders about six hypothetical situations that would demand real social skill, like the following:

> One of your school's best teachers has tragically died in an accident. The students in your grade have gotten together and decided to do something for the teacher's family. The class decides that someone should make a personal visit to the teacher's family. This person would bring flowers and try to tell the family how sorry the students were to lose such a good teacher and a good friend. Who in your grade do you think would be a good person to make the visit to the teacher's family? (Ford, 1982, p. 339)

Ford also asked each of the young people how well they thought they would do in a situation like that. These situations are hypothetical, but by having students rate *each other,* he could see which teenagers were perceived by their classmates as being particularly skillful or thoughtful in demanding social situations. What he found was that adolescents who are chosen by their peers as being the best in such situations also have more empathy and role-taking ability.

Studying second to fifth graders, Selman and his colleagues (1983) also found a link between reasoning and behavior. They observed groups of girls working together on after-school activities (such as constructing puppets or writing a play). The sessions were tape-recorded and later checked to see which children actually talked to each other in ways that reflected complex social understanding, such as:

> "I felt pretty bad because she was just sitting there all by herself looking like she was feeling sad and lonely." (Selman et al., 1983, p. 89)

Not only did they find that older girls talked this way more often, they also found that among girls of a given age, those who had exhibited more advanced forms of social understanding (in separate tests) showed more "communicative competence" in the groups, too. Children whose understanding of relationships is at the reciprocal or mutual level listen and talk to each other differently than do those at level 0.

In neither of these studies is the link between thinking and behavior at all perfect. Many children think "higher" or "better" than they show in their behavior—certainly not a surprising finding! After all, our behavior is influenced by a host of other conditions, including the specific relationships in the group we are in, shyness, popularity, and the pressures of the group. But it is important, I think, to realize that there is at least *some* connection between the level of maturity of a child's thought and her behavior.

Exactly the same kind of conclusion emerges from the research linking moral reasoning to moral action. In Box 12.2 I have discussed what we know about ways parents and schools can foster more "moral" behavior in children. Here I want to focus on just one possible element in the equation: the impact of the child's level of moral reasoning on behavior. Kohlberg has never said that there should be a one-to-one correspondence between the two. Reasoning at stage 4 (conventional reasoning) does not mean that you will never cheat or always be kind to your mother. But the form of reasoning a young person typically applies to moral problems should have at least *some* connection with real-life choices. In fact, it does (Straughan, 1983).

For example, Kenneth Keniston (1970) found that nonviolent Vietnam War protesters in the late 1960s were more likely to be using stage 5 moral reasoning than were nonprotesting college students. These students protested and marched, but they were prepared to go to jail for breaking the law in order to make their point—all characteristics of stage 5 reasoning.

Kohlberg, too, has found some connections. In one study (1975), he found that only 15 percent of students reasoning at the principled level (stage 5) cheated when they were given an opportunity, while 55 percent of conventional-level and 70 percent of preconventional students cheated.

A study of much younger children by Nancy Eisenberg-Berg and Michael Hand (1979) shows a similar link. The preschool children in this study who answered simple moral dilemmas with hedonistic reasoning (what feels good is right; what feels bad is wrong) were much less likely to share toys with other children in their nursery school than were youngsters who considered the needs of others in their moral reasoning.

Obviously, though, there is no direct and automatic relationship between moral reasoning and moral behavior. As Kohlberg points out about his own study, 15 percent of the stage 5 students *did* cheat. As he says, "One can reason in terms of principles and not live up to those principles" (Kohlberg, 1975, p. 672). (Ain't it the truth!)

But if the level of reasoning is not the only key, what else might matter? We don't have all the answers to that question yet, but some influences are clear. First, simple habits are involved—what Randy Gerson and William Damon (1978) call *habitual* moral reactions. Each of us faces every day small moral situations that we have learned to handle in a completely automatic way. Sometimes these automatic choices may be at a lower level of reasoning than we would use if we sat down and thought about it. (For example, I may make the same donation to a particular charity every year, automatically, without stopping to consider whether I could now afford more or whether that charity is really the place where my money could best be used.)

Second, and perhaps more important, the group we are in makes

BOX 12.2

# *FOSTERING MORAL BEHAVIOR AT HOME AND AT SCHOOL*

A lot of what I have said in this chapter may seem pretty abstract to you. Parents and teachers are usually much more concerned with whether a child can resist the temptation to cheat or obeys family rules when you're not in sight than with the abstract properties of the child's reasoning. Does Beth sneak a cookie as soon as you leave the room? Does Jason come home when you said he should? Does he tell you he came straight home from school even when he really stopped off at Mark's house to play? How can you, as a teacher or parent, encourage honesty, fairness, and resistance to temptation in children? More important, how can you instill or encourage in your children an *internalized* set of standards to guide their behavior?

Two kinds of actions by parents and teachers seem to be helpful.

1. Anything you can do to increase the child's role-taking ability, her empathy, or the level of her moral reasoning seems to help foster more honest or "moral" behavior. In preschoolers, this includes small-group activities and playacting or role playing (fantasy play is useful here) (Rubin & Everett, 1982). Chil-

dren's level of moral reasoning can also be raised by steadily exposing them to reasoning at higher levels than their own. So it is more helpful to explain reasons and actions to a young child by using conventional reasoning (or even postconventional) than by trying to aim your arguments to the child's own level. So saying to a child "You should come in when I tell you to because I'll send you to your room if you don't" merely reinforces stage-2 reasoning; explaining that you need to have the child come in when asked because you'll worry if she doesn't or even that people need to try to help each other out may encourage more advanced role-taking ability. More advanced role-taking skill, in turn, seems to support more "moral" behavior in the child.

A related strategy with older youngsters has been to include courses in moral judgment or ethics in high school curricula or even to create an entire school organized to foster a "moral atmosphere" (Lickona, 1978; Power & Reimer, 1978). Students in these classes or schools discuss real-life dilemmas occurring in their own school. The instructors encourage discussion, but they also consistently

a huge difference. Children, adolescents, and adults are all motivated, in part, by a desire to be liked by or accepted by the group. When faced with a dilemma, you may find yourself going along with the group consensus even though your own moral reasoning says that isn't right. Gerson and Damon found this very clearly in their study. One of the tasks they used was to have a group of four children divide up 10 candy bars. The candy was a reward for work the children had done on a project, and some of the group members had worked harder than others. Many children who would otherwise argue that the hardest-working child should have the greatest reward nonetheless agreed to divide up the candy into four equal shares. We might expect that in early adolescence, when the impact of the peer group is particularly strong, this

introduce forms of moral reasoning that are a notch or two higher than what the students initially use.

In one experimental school, the Cluster School (Power & Reimer, 1978), researchers and teachers attempted to organize the whole school as a laboratory for moral education. Students and staff jointly governed the school through weekly meetings. Thus, students became *responsible* for the rules and for enforcing them. Under these conditions, not only did the level of moral reasoning of the students shift upward, but the moral *atmosphere* of the school had changed. Stealing and other petty crime virtually disappeared, for example, after the students had repeatedly discussed the problem and arrived at a just solution.

2. When a child has broken some rule or "transgressed" in some way, **inductive discipline** works better than physical punishment or withdrawal of love. *Inductive discipline,* a term introduced by Martin Hoffman (1970), involves explaining *why* some particular behavior is "bad" or "good" and emphasizing the consequences of the child's actions for others. You may remember from Box 11.2 that exactly this same kind of explanation/discipline seems to foster helpfulness and compassion in children, too. Hoffman's research shows that inductive discipline also

fosters resistance to temptation—what many of us think of as a strong conscience.

In contrast, punishment—either physical or verbal—*without* explanations and reasoning does not produce children who resist temptation. In fact, the opposite is true. The more physical punishment parents use, the *less* resistance to temptation and the less guilt the child shows. Withdrawal-of-love discipline ("I don't like you when you behave like that," or "I don't want to be around you when you're like that") also does not seem to increase children's "good" behavior.

Induction is not pure reasoning. It includes strong feelings, too, and may also involve some form of punishment. But the key seems to be to emphasize why something should or should not be done and what the consequences will be. Of course, this strategy usually involves reasoning at a higher level than the child's own reasoning, so induction may work partly because it fosters greater perspective taking or greater empathy. It may also work because it helps the child internalize not just the "dos" and "don'ts" but the *reasons* for those dos and don'ts. The key thing to remember, though, is that punishment for "bad" behavior does not seem to result, in the long run, in a child who can be relied on to resist that bad behavior the next time.

group effect on moral actions would be especially strong, too. So youngsters this age may be most susceptible to group decisions to go joyriding or to sneak beer into a party or to soap the teachers' car windows on Halloween (Berndt, 1979).

Still, even at adolescence, every child is not equally vulnerable to this type of group pressure. There are some hints, for example, that young people who are reasoning at Kohlberg's stage 5 (postconventional reasoning) are less likely to be swayed by group pressure or pressure from authority than are youngsters reasoning at less-mature levels (Kohlberg, 1969).

I don't think we know nearly enough yet about a child's ability to resist group pressure. But at the very least, we know that the effect of the group is not automatic or uniform. The child's form of logic does seem to make a difference, and the type of discipline and explanations of moral behavior the child has been exposed to seem to make a difference, too (Box 12.2). But we badly need to know more, both about group pressure and about all the other factors that lead each of us to behave in ways that are less thoughtful, considerate, or fair than we "know how" to do. Answers to such questions would be important for the theories I have been talking about in this chapter, but they are still more important for understanding (and possibly changing) everyday relationships, everyday moral actions.

## SUMMARY

1. The study of social understanding and the field of *social cognition* in general have provided researchers with an important new link between cognitive development and social relationships.
2. The child's thinking has an impact on relationships with people as well as encounters with objects. In particular, the child's perspective-taking ability is central to emerging understanding of other people and of relationships.
3. The relationships the child encounters, however, also shape her thinking, particularly relationships with peers. Such relationships foster greater perspective taking.
4. Robert Selman's theory of social understanding has been particularly influential. He proposes five levels of development, from undifferentiated and egocentric (level 0) to differentiated/subjective (level 1) to reciprocal (level 2) to mutual (level 3) to societal-symbolic (level 4) perspective taking.
5. These levels of understanding can be seen in children's ideas about other people as well as in their understanding of friendships, of groups, and of parent-child relationships.
6. Two especially key levels for emerging relationships are the reciprocal level (approximately age 7 to 12) and the mutual level (about age 10 to 15). At the reciprocal level the child understands that other people feel or see things differently than he does and that others know the same thing about him. Relationships are seen as a two-way street. At the mutual level, the young person understands that relationships involve constant mutual adjustments.
7. Early research shows that children tend to display the same level of understanding across their ideas about relationships or groups.
8. Moral understanding or reasoning, primarily studied by Piaget and Kohlberg, follows a similar progression. Kohlberg proposes six stages, divided into three levels. The child moves from preconventional morality, dominated by punishment and "what feels good," to conventional morality, dominated by group norms or laws, to

postconventional (principled) morality, dominated by social contracts and basic ethical principles.

9. Longitudinal research shows that the first four stages occur in the order listed but that most teenagers and adults do not move past stage 4 (conventional morality). Similar developmental sequences for Selman's levels of social understanding have been shown from longitudinal research.

10. Connections between levels of social understanding, moral reasoning, and basic cognitive development have been more difficult to demonstrate. Current evidence suggests that the basic cognitive understanding forms the underpinning of social understanding and that both underlie moral judgment. Thus, beginning formal operations and level 3 social understanding may be necessary but not sufficient conditions for conventional moral reasoning.

11. Moral behavior or more skillful social behavior appears to be at least partially linked to the child's level of social understanding. Socially skillful or effective children typically show somewhat higher levels of social understanding; young people showing conventional or postconventional moral reasoning typically show greater resistance to group influence or to temptations to break the law or the moral code. But the relationship between reasoning and behavior is not at all perfect.

12. Parents and teachers can foster or encourage moral behavior by creating opportunities for children to learn perspective taking, by exposing them to higher levels of reasoning, by making them responsible for group actions and decisions, and by using *inductive discipline*—explaining why the child should not do some forbidden thing and describing the consequences to others.

## KEY TERMS

**Autonomous morality**  Piaget's second proposed stage of moral reasoning, developing sometime after age 7, characterized by judgment of intent and emphasis on reciprocity.

**Conventional morality**  The second level of moral judgment proposed by Kohlberg, in which the person's judgments are dominated by considerations of group values and laws.

**Heteronomous morality**  Piaget's first proposed stage of moral reasoning, characterized by moral absolutism and belief in immanent justice. Judgments are based on consequences rather than intent.

**Inductive discipline**  The form of discipline that includes clear statements of rules, the use of reason, and emphasis on the consequences of the child's actions.

**Morality of reciprocity**  Another description of autonomous morality.

**Moral realism**  Another description of heteronomous morality.

**Preconventional morality**  The first level of morality proposed by Kohlberg, in which moral judgments are dominated by consideration of what will be punished and what feels good.

**Principled morality**  The third level of morality proposed by Kohlberg, in which considerations of justice, individual rights, and contracts dominate moral judgment.

**Social cognition**   Term used to describe a relatively new area of research and theory focused on the child's *understanding* of social relationships.

*SUGGESTED READINGS*

Damon, W. *The social world of the child*. San Francisco: Jossey-Bass, 1977.
A very readable book discussing many of the developmental themes I have been talking about in this chapter.

Lickona, T. Moral development and moral education: Piaget, Kohlberg, and beyond. In J. M. Gallagher & J. A. Easley, Jr. (Eds.). *Knowledge and development* (Vol. 2): *Piaget and education*. New York: Plenum, 1978.
An excellent review of recent attempts to apply Kohlberg's work to moral education in the schools.

Rubin, K. H., & Everett, B. Social perspective-taking in young children. In S. G. Moore & C. R. Cooper (Eds.). *The young child: Re-views of research* (Vol. 3). Washington, D.C.: National Association for the Education of Young Children, 1982.
A very helpful integrated discussion of all aspects of perspective taking (social and physical) and of the implications of the research and theory for education.

Selman, R. L. *The growth of interpersonal understanding*. New York: Academic Press, 1980.
This is Selman's most comprehensive description of his theory. You may find some of this book fairly difficult, but Chapters 5 and 6 should be very helpful if you are interested in delving further into this topic.

PROJECT 12.1

# *Understanding of Friendship*

For this project you will need to locate a child between the ages of about 6 and 12. Arrange with the parents to spend some time with the child, explaining that you want to talk to the child for a school project and that this is not a "test" of any kind. Try to find a time and a place to be alone with your subject; it will not work as well if siblings or parents are present.

Say to the child something like, "I'd like to talk to you about friends. Let me tell you a story about some children who were friends." Then read the following story:

Kathy and Becky have been best friends since they were 5 years old. They went to the same kindergarten and have been in the same class ever since. Every Saturday they would try to do something special together, go to the park or the store, or play something special at home. They always had a good time with each other.

One day a new girl, Jeanette, moved into their neighborhood and soon introduced herself to Kathy and Becky. Right away Jeanette and Kathy seemed to hit it off very well. They talked about where Jeanette was from and the things she could be doing in her new town. Becky, on the other hand, didn't seem to like Jeanette very well. She thought

Jeanette was a showoff, but was also jealous of all the attention Kathy was giving Jeanette.

When Jeanette left the other two alone, Becky told Kathy how she felt about Jeanette. "What did you think of her, Kathy? I thought she was kind of pushy, butting in on us like that."

"Come on, Becky. She's new in town and just trying to make friends. The least we can do is be nice to her."

"Yeah, but that doesn't mean we have to be friends with her," replied Becky. "Anyway, what would you like to do this Saturday? You know those old puppets of mine, I thought we could fix them up and make our own puppet show."

"Sure, Becky, that sounds great," said Kathy. "I'll be over after lunch. I better go home now. See you tomorrow."

Later that evening Jeanette called Kathy and surprised her with an invitation to the circus, the last show before it left town. The only problem was that the circus happened to be at the same time that Kathy had promised to go to Becky's. Kathy didn't know what to do, go to the circus and leave her best friend alone, or stick with her best friend and miss a good time. (Selman, 1980, pp. 321–322)

After reading the child the story, you need to ask some open-ended questions and then probe the child's understanding of friendship:

OPEN-ENDED
QUESTIONS

1. What do you think the problem is in this story?
2. What do you think Kathy will do, choose to be with her old friend Becky or go with the new girl, Jeanette? Why? Which do you think is more important: to be with an old friend or to make new friends? Why?
3. Do you have a best friend? What kind of friendship do you have with that person? What makes that person your best friend?

Based on the child's answers, you may then want or need to probe as follows (you probably will not need to ask *all* these questions; be selective, depending on your child's comments):

PROBES

1. What kind of friendship do you think Kathy and Becky have? Do you think it is a good or close friendship? What is a really good, close friendship? Does it take something special to have a very good friendship? What kinds of things do friends know about each other?
2. What does being friends for a long time, like Kathy and Becky have, do for a friendship?

3. What makes close, good friendships last?
4. What kinds of things can good friends talk about that other friends sometimes can't? What kinds of problems can they talk over?
5. What makes two friends feel really close to each other?
6. What's the difference between the kind of friendship Becky and Kathy have and Kathy and Jeanette's friendship? Are there different kinds of friendship? What's the difference between "regular" and "best" friendship?
7. Is it better when close friends are like each other or different from each other? Why? In what way should good friends be the same? In what way should they be different?
8. Which is better to have (be with)—one close friend or a group of regular friends? Why? (Selman, 1980, pp. 321–333)

*SCORING*

Transcribe your child's answers as close to verbatim as you can (tape the conversation if that will help). Compare your child's answers to the levels of social understanding described in this chapter. At what level does the child appear to be reasoning? Are there contradictions or confusions about the scoring?

# part five
## the whole child

# 13.
## *the ecology of development: the impact of families, schools, and culture*

Thirty years ago, most child development texts and books of advice to parents emphasized the role of the parents in "molding" the child, as if the child were some sort of shapeless block of clay (Hartup, 1978). The term *socialization* was widespread; the parents' task was to socialize the child, to shape the child's behavior so that it fit well into the expectations and rules of society.

The first 12 chapters of this book certainly don't sound much like that. Instead, I have repeatedly emphasized that many dimensions of development appear to have their own internal timetables, their own inevitability. Given the most rudimentary environmental support, virtually all children do learn to walk and talk; they do figure out that they are separate people; they do develop more and more complex ways of analyzing and understanding the objects and people around them. Some of this powerful inner push comes from genetic instructions, which produce unfolding maturational timetables. Some seems to come from the child's own encounters with and manipulation of the environment. And for many purposes, a remarkably wide range of environments seem to be "good enough" to provide the child with the "food" for development (just as many different food diets are "good enough" to sustain physical growth).

My emphasis on *intrinsic* developmental processes comes about partly because that is what the current research is telling us and partly as an antidote to the older "clay-molding" view of development. But I would certainly be a great fool if I tried to persuade you that the child's family and the child's culture have no impact on the form or rate or content of his developmental pattern.

As we have gone along, I have talked about ways in which the parents' behavior makes a difference—in attachment, language, cognitive development, self-concept, and the like. But now I need to explore the role of parents much more systematically. Even more, we need to think about the impact on the child of other institutions, other forces within society. I talked about the impact of day care in Chapter 1, but what about the effect of schooling in general or of TV? What about the effects of such a broad cultural phenomenon as poverty? And what are the forces that influence children *indirectly,* through their impact on parents, such as the parents' jobs or their social networks or even the quality of the parents' relationship? In other words, we need to move our focus outward from the child in a series of steps—to the family, to the school, to the culture—and see how all these elements affect the child's development.

The field of developmental psychology is indebted to Urie Bronfenbrenner (1977, 1979) both for the phrase *ecology of development* and for insisting that we extend our gaze past the dyad of mother and child, past the family, and into the intricate network of cultural and personal relationships that forms the *system* or *ecological niche* in which the

**454**

**Figure 13.1** A lot of a child's development evolves from inner maturation and from the child's own explorations and manipulations. But to understand development, we must also understand the ways in which the family, the school, and other cultural forces shape the child as well.

child grows. Understanding how such interlocking and interpenetrating forces may influence or even shape the trajectory of a given child's development is an immensely complex task—one I can only begin to explore here. But let us plunge into the complexities and see where it can take us.

## THE INFLUENCE OF THE FAMILY

With rare exceptions, children grow up in families. (For many children these days, a "family" may consist of the child and one parent, but we still think of this as a family unit.) Describing the ways in which families behave is an astonishingly difficult job. Over the course of just the first few years of a child's life, the child and the parents have literally millions of conversations or encounters—feeding, changing diapers, dressing, undressing, providing names for objects, answering questions, rescuing the child from danger, and so on and on. In the midst of this richness and diversity, though, psychologists have identified several major *dimensions* on which families differ that seem to be significant for the child: the emotional tone of the family, the manner in which control is exercised, the quality and amount of communication, and the quality and quantity of cognitive enrichment provided.

## The Emotional Tone of the Family

The first key element for the child seems to be the relative **warmth versus hostility** of the home. *Warmth* is difficult to define, and psychologists have wrestled for decades with the problem of finding ways of measuring it. But intuitively and theoretically it is clear that it is highly important for the child. A warm parent cares about the child, expresses affection, frequently or regularly puts the child's needs first, shows enthusiasm for the child's activities, and responds sensitively and empathically to the child's feelings (Maccoby, 1980b). On the other

**Figure 13.2** I am sure it is obvious to all of you that loving a child is a critical ingredient in optimum development. But sometimes it helps to restate the obvious!

end of the continuum are parents who overtly reject their children—saying and expressing with their behavior that they do not love or want the child.

Few parents are constantly loving and warm toward their children (although many of us try), but it is possible to measure the typical level of warmth. When psychologists have done this, they have found that children in warm and loving families

1. Are more securely attached in the first two years of life (Ainsworth et al., 1978).
2. Have higher self-esteem (Coopersmith, 1967).
3. Are more empathic, more altruistic, more responsive to others' hurts or distress (Zahn-Waxler, Radke-Yarrow, & King, 1979).
4. Have higher measured IQs in preschool and elementary school (Barnard, Bee, & Hammond, 1984b; Bradley & Caldwell, 1976).

I suspect that the role of warmth in fostering a secure attachment of the child to the parent is one of the key elements in this picture. I've already pointed out (in Chapter 11) that secure children are more skillful with their peers, more exploratory, more sure of themselves. But as Maccoby (1980b) points out, warmth also makes children generally more responsive to guidance, so affection and warmth increase the potency of the things that parents say to their children and the efficiency of their discipline.

## Methods of Control

It is the nature of children that they will do things their parents do not want them to do, ask for things they cannot have, or refuse to obey their parents' requests or demands. From early days, parents are inevitably faced with the task of controlling the child's behavior. It is this dimension of parental behavior that people usually mean when they talk about *discipline*. It will help, though, to break this dimension apart into several elements.

*Clarity and Consistency of Rules*  One element of control is simply making it clear to the child what the rules are, what the consequences are of disobeying (or obeying) them, and then enforcing them consistently. Some parents are very clear and consistent; others waffle or are fuzzy about what they expect or will tolerate. Studies of families show conclusively that parents who are clear and consistent have children who are more obedient (which is wonderful reinforcement for the parents). But such clarity does not produce little robots. Children from families with consistent rules are also more competent and sure of themselves (Baumrind, 1967, 1971, 1973) and less aggressive (Patterson, 1980).

A related element is the level of expectations the parents have for the child's behavior. Is the child expected to show relatively more mature behavior, or does the parent feel it is important not to expect too much, too soon?

Here, as with clarity and consistency of rules, within limits more does appear to be better: Children whose parents make high demands on them, expecting them to help around the house or to show relatively mature behavior for their age, have higher self-esteem, show more generosity and altruism toward others, and exhibit lower levels of aggression. Obviously, this can be carried much too far. If the parent expects a 2-year-old to set the table every night or to tie his own shoes, that is totally unrealistic and will lead to painful and negative confrontations. The expectations need to be realistic to be helpful to the child. But if the parents do expect the child to be as independent and helpful as possible for his age, that does seem to foster a sense of competence in the child that carries over into other situations.

*Restrictiveness* Another element of parental control is the degree of **restrictiveness** imposed. This is not the same thing as clear or consistent rule setting. A parent can be relatively low in restrictiveness and still have clear rules. For example, you might have a rule that your 10-year-old can stop off at another child's house after school to play without arranging it ahead of time but must call you to tell you where he is if he does so. That would be a clear rule but relatively low restrictiveness. On the other hand, a parent who insists on keeping a child within eyesight at all times or who puts a toddler in a playpen for most of the day rather than risk having the child pull the drawers open or touch the stereo would be considered restrictive.

Restrictive parents also frequently use a distinctive form of language with their children—namely, *imperative* sentences, such as "Stop that" or "Come here" or "Do what I tell you." They are less likely to explain the rules to the child but instead use their own power to control her.

The other end of the continuum is usually termed *permissiveness,* which frequently also includes relatively few rules and few imperatives. Sometimes permissive parenting styles emerge from a sense of helplessness about controlling the child at all: the parent has given up. Often, though, permissiveness emerges from a specific philosophy of child rearing that emphasizes the child's need for freedom and opportunity to explore.

Evidence on the impact of restrictiveness and permissiveness is mixed. Highly restrictive parents are likely to have quite obedient, unaggressive children. But such children are also likely to be somewhat

**Figure 13.3** All parents impose some restrictions on a child. Children must be kept away from dangerous objects or places, and they have to follow basic rules. But too much restriction—such as having a child spend hours in a playpen—seems to have negative consequences.

timid and may have difficulty establishing close relationships with peers. Results from some of my own longitudinal studies (Barnard, Bee, & Hammond, 1984b) suggest that restrictiveness is also associated with lower IQ, particularly in middle-class children, possibly because of the lowered opportunity to explore freely.

Low restrictiveness, on the other hand, is also not a wholly positive strategy. Children with highly permissive parents—who may exert far too little control—are likely to show only moderate independence and to be relatively thoughtless of others. On this dimension, as on many others, the "ideal" appears to lie somewhere in the middle.

Overall, it seems clear that children respond very positively to clear rules consistently enforced, realistic demands and expectations, combined with only moderate restrictiveness.

*Punishment*    I have saved for last the one thing that probably comes to the mind of most of us when we think about "controlling" the child—namely, punishment. When a child does something you don't want (like writing on the wall or hitting her brother) or fails to do something you do want (like coming home on time or cleaning his room), most parents respond with some kind of punishment. I've talked about

BOX 13.1

# TO SPANK OR NOT TO SPANK

Since I seem to be giving a lot of advice in this chapter, I might as well carry on. The short, emphatic answer to the question "Should I spank my child?" is *no*. I am well aware that this is easier to say than to do (and I admit to having applied a hand to my own children's rear ends on one or two occasions, even knowing that it would do little good and some potential damage). But the information we have about spanking (and other forms of physical punishment) and its effects seems to me to be so clear that a firm answer to the question is possible.

In order to make the point clear, I need to distinguish between the short-term effects of spanking and the longer-term effects. In the short term, spanking a child usually *does* get the child to stop the particular behavior you didn't like, and it seems to have a *temporary* effect of reducing the chance that the child will repeat the bad behavior. Since that's what you wanted, it may seem like a good strategy. But even in the short term, there are some negative side effects. The child may have stopped writing on the walls or throwing water at you or swearing (or whatever behavior you had forbidden), but after a spanking he is undoubtedly crying, which is unpleasant. It is also a behavior that spanking does not decrease (it is virtually impossible to get children to stop crying by spanking them!). So you have exchanged one unpleasantness for another, and the second unpleasantness (crying) can't

**Figure 13.4** Spanking is probably the most common form of discipline used by parents, but it has many negative (even though usually unintended) side effects.

be dealt with by using the same form of punishment.

Another short-term side effect is that when the child stopped doing something unpleasant when you spanked him, *you* were reinforced for

the pros and cons of the "classic" form of punishment, spanking, in Box 13.1, but let me say just a few more words here.

As Gerald Patterson (1975) says, "punishment 'works.' If you use it properly it will produce rapid changes in the behavior of other people" (p. 19). Yelling at children to stop doing something usually does bring a *brief* change in their behavior (which thus reinforces the parent for yelling, by the way). The difficulty is that you are also modeling yelling to the child. Children who are yelled at yell back on other occasions. So to a considerable degree, you get back what you give out.

spanking. So the more effective the spanking is in reducing the child's unwanted behavior, the more you are being "trained" to use spanking again. A cycle is thus built up.

Whatever apparent benefits come in the short run from spanking disappear when we take a longer look. Three long-term effects are particularly significant:

1. The child observes you using physical force or violence as a method of solving problems or getting people to do what you want. You thus serve as a model for a behavior you do *not* want your child to use with others. Telling the child that it's okay for parents to behave this way but not for children is likely to have little effect, since children will do what you do, not what you say, when there is a conflict between the two messages.
2. By repeatedly pairing your presence with the unpleasant or painful event of spanking, you are undermining your own positive value for your child. Over time, this means that you are less able to use *any* kind of reinforcement effectively. Eventually even your praise or affection will be less powerful in influencing your child's behavior. That is a very high price to pay.
3. There is frequently a strong underlying emotional message going with spanking—anger, rejection, irritation, dislike of the child. Even very young children "read" this emotional message quite clearly. Spanking thus helps to create a family climate of rejection instead of warmth, with all the consequences I have described in the main part of this chapter.

I am *not* saying that you should never punish a child. I *am* saying that *physical punishment,* such as spanking, is rarely (if ever) a good way to go about it. Children whose parents use high rates of physical punishment are frequently highly aggressive (Bandura, 1973). Or they may be docile and obedient at home but unruly elsewhere. More important, their relationshps with peers are frequently less good than are those of children whose parents use other forms of control.

But what "other forms of control" will work? If you have been brought up in a family in which spanking was the standard method, you may simply not know other ways. If you find yourself in this position, I'd urge you to read Gerald Patterson's book *Families* (listed in the "Suggested Readings" for this chapter). A parenting class might also be of help. The key is to intervene *early* in problem sequences, to do so consistently, and to use the mildest possible form of punishment that will stop the behavior—taking away a favored toy, separating two children, sending the child to her room or to a special place for a "time out" period, withholding an anticipated privilege. Spanking typically happens when you have let things get well beyond this early stage and you are at your wit's end. The best way to avoid it is not to let yourself get to that point.

The most effective punishments—those that produce long-term changes in the child's behavior without the bad side effects—are those used *early* in some sequence of misbehavior, with the lowest level of emotion possible and the mildest level of punishment possible (Patterson, 1975; Johnston, 1972). Taking a desired toy away when the child *first* uses it to hit the furniture (or a sibling) or consistently removing small privileges when a child misbehaves will "work," especially if you are also warm, clear about the rules, and consistent. Waiting until the screams have reached a piercing level or until the fourth time your teenager has taken off without telling you where she's gone and then weighing in with yelling, loud comments, and strong punishments is far less effective.

## Communication Patterns

Two things about communication within the family seem to make a difference for the child: the amount and richness of language spoken *to* the child and the amount of conversation and suggestions *from* the child that the parent encourages.

*Talking to the Child*   I already pointed out in Chapter 8 that the child's language development is enhanced if the adults around the child speak more, using more complex and rich language. In fact, the language "climate" of the entire family—parents, older siblings, and other adults—seems to make a difference.

In an interesting recent study, Jacquelyn Norman-Jackson (1982) observed a group of 2- to 3-year-old children (from poor, black families) whose older siblings were either good or poor readers in second grade. The preschoolers from families with an older good-reading child spent more than twice as much time talking with their parents and older brother or sister than did the preschoolers whose older sibling read less well, as you can see in Figure 13.5. Five years later, the preschoolers from families with greater verbal interaction themselves were more likely to be good readers, too.

*Listening to the Child*   The other side of this coin is listening. I have in mind here more than merely having conversations with the child in which there is time for the child's response. When I say "listening" to the child, I also mean conveying to the child the sense that what he has to say is *worth* listening to, that he has ideas, that his ideas are important and should be considered in family decisions. This pattern of active involvement of the child in the family process is sometimes called **democratic child rearing**.

This is a complex pattern of interaction, and we are a long way from understanding all of its effects. In general, children from families with open communication are seen as more emotionally or socially mature (Bell & Bell, 1982; Baumrind, 1971, 1973). But there are some hints, too, of certain less-positive qualities. In early research, A. L. Baldwin (1948, 1949) found that children from more democratic families were likely to be leaders, to be good at planning, and relatively fearless but were also likely to be bossy and more aggressive. These children were highly involved socially but were used to getting their way. Understanding this mixture of effects requires looking at *patterns* of parental behaviors. But before I turn to that, let me list the one last element

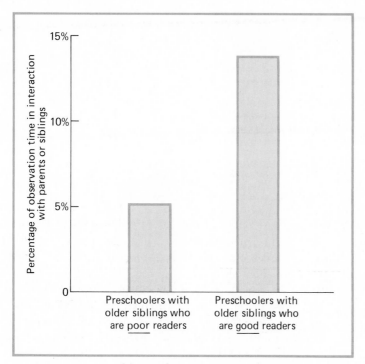

**Figure 13.5** Families that talk to their children often and encourage their children to talk to them in return have children who read better when they get to school. This particular study shows that it is not just the parents' behavior that matters; having an older sibling who talks to a younger one also helps. (*Source:* Norman-Jackson, 1982, from Table 2, p. 354).

of the family environment that seems to be of real importance for the child.

## Cognitive Enrichment

You are already familiar with this aspect of family environment from Chapter 6. Both the richness and the variety of the *inanimate environment*—toys, objects, varied experiences—and the responsiveness and variety of the *animate environment* make a difference (Wachs & Gruen, 1982). The effect can be seen most clearly in cognitive development and language, but I am sure that the impact of the richness of the environment spills over into other areas of the child's functioning as well.

## Patterns of Child Rearing

I have talked about four dimensions or facets of the family environment that can affect the rate or quality of a child's development or the style of interaction with others that she may develop. But in the real world these four dimensions don't occur in isolation; they combine into complex patterns or styles. Given the infinite complexity of human behavior and of family interaction, the number of different individual styles is probably infinite, too. But some combinations are more common than others, and it helps our understanding to look for some basic "types."

The most insightful and fascinating work on types or styles of parental behavior has been done by Diana Baumrind (1967, 1971, 1973, 1983), whose work I described briefly in Box 10.1 (page 354). Baumrind has observed several different groups of families with their preschool children. Each encounter between the parent and the child is rated by the observers for the amount of nurturance shown, the degree of control exerted, the openness of communication, and the level of maturity demanded. Each family eventually is given average or summary scores on each of these dimensions.

While there were many individual variations in level on these four aspects of parental behavior, three patterns emerged consistently enough to be thought of as real "types." Figure 13.6 shows the relative level on each aspect for the three types.

The **authoritarian child-rearing** pattern combines high control and high maturity demands with relatively low communication and low nurturance. These are the dictatorial parents who expect and demand obedience, but without a climate of warmth.

The **permissive child-rearing** pattern is essentially the reverse: high levels of warmth without much control. These are parents who provide loving, nurturant care but do not set clear standards or rules and do not enforce their rules consistently.

The **authoritative child-rearing** pattern is perhaps the most interesting. Parents in this group are high on all four dimensions. They

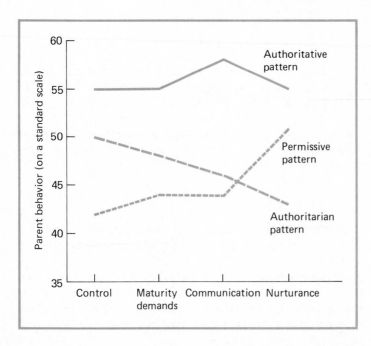

**Figure 13.6** The three patterns of child-rearing style, based on Baumrind's observations in the homes of preschool children, are clear in the figure. Authoritative parents are high on all four dimensions. (*Source:* Adapted from Baumrind, 1967, p. 73.)

have clear control, high expectations, listen to the child, and also provide a loving environment.

When the children from these families were preschoolers, Baumrind found that those from the authoritative families showed the greatest independence, leadership, social responsibility, originality, self-confidence, and achievement orientation. Children from the authoritarian families, in contrast, were low in independence, less confident of themselves but relatively more obedient and nonaggressive. Children of permissive parents were also not particularly independent (which may surprise you), lacked social responsibility, and were relatively low in self-confidence and high in anxiety.

When the children were 8 or 9, Baumrind found that the same differences persisted. Children whose parents showed authoritative child rearing when they were preschoolers were more self-confident and oriented toward achievement than were those from more permissive families.

Several conclusions from this research are important. First, it seems clear that children *are* affected by the family "climate" or style. Although we do not have the sort of longitudinal data needed to be sure, I suspect that these effects persist well into adulthood. Second, many of us are accustomed to thinking about family styles as if permissive and authoritarian patterns were the only options. But Baumrind's work shows clearly that one can be *both* affectionate and firm and that children respond to this combination in very positive ways. If that sounds to you like I am stating a "moral for parents," you're quite right. I am!

## INFLUENCES *ON* THE FAMILY

We all know, though, that parents do not operate in a vacuum. While it is doubtless true that each parent brings to the job of raising a child certain long-standing patterns and personality traits (such as an inclination to exert firm control or to be more permissive), our ability to live up to our own ideals as parents is strongly influenced by the actual dynamics of a particular family, by the stresses we are under, and by the kinds and amounts of outside support we may have.

### The Child's Characteristics

One of the first things that affects parents—and that illustrates the *transactional* nature of development—is the characteristics of each particular child.

A child's temperament is one example of a quality that is bound to interact with the parents' typical style (as I pointed out in Chapter 9). Parents dealing with temperamentally "difficult" children punish such children more than they do "easy" children (Rutter, 1978a), presumably because the child simply shows more negative and noncompliant behavior. One would suppose (although we do not yet have research on this) that a parent who is *already* inclined to be strict and authoritarian would be much more likely to show such behavior with a temperamentally difficult child. Other parents whose natural pattern is more permissive might react quite differently to the difficult child. Thus, the child's qualities and the parents' propensities combine to create a pattern of interaction that may be unique to that combination.

Whether a child is firstborn or later-born also makes a difference. In Table 13.1 I've summarized some of what we know about the ways parents treat their firstborns compared to the way they treat later children. Some of the differences are undoubtedly the result of simple lack of experience with the first child, so parents are more anxious, press a little harder to do everything right. But part of the difference also lies in the fact that the family configuration is simply different. The task of parenting is very different when there are two children than when there is only one. There is less time for highly individualized play or story reading or one-on-one interactions, and the children spend more time playing with each other.

Still a third characteristic of the child that affects the way parents behave is the child's age. This may seem so obvious that it is hardly worth stating, but I think the point is vital. As the child develops, very different demands are made on the parents. As any parent can tell you, caring for an infant is a different task than caring for a 2-year-old or a 12-year-old. The areas in which control will need to be exercised change; the degree of push for independence changes; the child's intellectual and language abilities grow, so that the child can "talk back" more effectively and argue her side more cogently.

Each of these changes in the child requires an adaptation by the parent, and some of those adaptations may be a lot easier than others. A parent who is very good at dealing with infants may find that the demands of toddlerhood are far more difficult to handle (a common ex-

Table 13.1

**How parents treat their firstborn, compared to their later-born, children**

| Firstborns receive: | More achievement pressure (they are expected to achieve better). |
|---|---|
| | More complex language and more total language, especially in infancy. |
| | More intrusive and restrictive child rearing. |
| | More anxiety from parents (Am I doing it right?). |
| | More child-centered environment: family activities center around the individual child more than with later-borns. |
| | More coercive discipline (more punishment of all kinds). |
| | Less skillful parenting. |

perience, by the way; hence, the label "terrible 2s" to describe the negativity and independence demands of 2-year-olds). A parental style that worked fine with a 7-year-old may be far less effective with a 14-year-old. The important point here is that we should not fall into the trap of thinking that parents have a consistent or permanent style or pattern of child rearing that is the same for all children in the family or the same for each child over time. There are threads of consistency that run through the variations, I am sure. But each parent-child system is an evolving one, to which both parties contribute.

## The Family Environment: Poverty and Wealth

A second, very different category of influences on the family is the total economic and social environment in which the family exists—the "ecological niche" of the family, if you will. Most often this is described in terms of the **social class** of the family. Most of the research, though, contrasts families in poverty circumstances with those in middle-class or more affluent circumstances. As Dale Farran and her colleagues define it (Farran, Haskins, & Gallagher, 1980), poverty is "a physical and sociopsychological environment in which individuals have severely limited amounts of power, money, and social status" (p. 47). People in this condition or position experience a very different network of social influences than do adults in more affluent circumstances.

I have talked about some of the characteristics and effects of poverty in several earlier chapters, so you know that whether a family lives in a poverty environment or in a working-class or middle-class environment is related to the child's development in a whole host of ways. Let me pull these several threads together for you here and add a few bits of new information along the way.

First of all, women in poverty circumstances have less access to prenatal and other health care. They are thus at higher risk for problems during pregnancy, and their children are more likely to be born with some sort of disability. Family diets also tend to be worse, for the children as well as for the mothers. One group of researchers (Read & Felson, 1976) has estimated that 20 to 30 percent of children under age 6 in the United States have too few calories on a daily basis, and most of these children are from poor families. About 30 percent of poor children are also anemic (inadequate iron intake).

Women at the lower end of the economic spectrum are also more likely to work than are middle-class mothers (although this is changing). Their children are thus more likely to be in day care, from earlier ages. And since family day care is usually cheaper than center care, children from poor families are likely to be cared for in unlicensed settings.

A third difference between poor and wealthier families is that poor families are larger (Broman, Nichols, & Kennedy, 1975), with children more closely spaced. They live in smaller and less adequate housing as well. Thus, the total environment experienced by the family, and by the child, because of poverty is very different from what is experienced by a child in a more affluent family.

Possibly because of this combination of circumstances, mothers and fathers living in poverty treat their children quite differently. They talk to them less, provide fewer age-appropriate toys, spend less time with them in intellectually stimulating activities, are stricter and more physical in their discipline (Farran, Haskins, & Gallagher, 1980). In Baumrind's category system, they are more likely to be *authoritarian* than authoritative or permissive. They use more imperative statements to control their children ("Stop that!" "Do what you're told") and explain things less often and less fully.

Some of this pattern of parental behavior is undoubtedly a response to the extraordinary stresses of the poverty environment (you, too, would probably be less permissive and less helpful to your children if six or seven of you lived on little money in a small, cold, drafty apartment in a dangerous neighborhood). Some of the pattern may also be simple imitation of the way these same parents were brought up in their own childhood; some may be a product of ignorance of children's needs. Poor parents with relatively more education, for example, typically talk to their children more and provide more intellectual stimulation than do equally poor parents with lower levels of education. But whatever the cause, children reared in poverty experience not only different physical conditions but quite different interactions with their parents.

Not surprisingly, such children turn out differently, as I have pointed out repeatedly in earlier chapters. Children from poverty environments have higher rates of birth defects and early disabilities; they recover less well from early problems; they are more often ill and malnourished throughout their childhood years. Typically, they also have lower IQs and move through the sequences of cognitive development described by Piaget more slowly. They do less well in school and are less likely to go on to college. Such children, in turn, are more likely to be poor as adults, thus continuing the cycle through another generation.

The effects of family poverty on children are thus both direct (such as poorer diet) and indirect (such as changes in the way parents treat the child). The combined effects, however, are very large indeed.

## Short-Term Family Stress

The system of influences I have just described is normally long-term and difficult to change. But most families, whether in poverty or relative affluence, also experience shorter-term upheavals or stresses. Moving to another city, changing jobs, having your own parent die, getting divorced—all of these are major life changes, major sources of stress. They not only have an impact on the parent directly, they also affect the way parents relate to their children.

The clearest example of this is the effect of separation or divorce on the parents' behavior toward their children. Mavis Hetherington and her colleagues (Hetherington, Cox, & Cox, 1978), who have done the most detailed observations of parents and children after divorce, find that the short-term effect of this major stress is to reduce parents' maturity demands, reduce the clarity and consistency of rules, reduce warmth, and reduce communication. These families are disorganized! Parents who used to impose regular bedtimes for their children stop doing so. They stop reading bedtime stories, even stop eating meals together on a consistent basis. This disorganization declines during the two years after the divorce, but the short-term effect is striking.

My hunch (not backed up yet by the right sort of research) is that most major life changes or stresses experienced by parents have a similar—if briefer—disorganizing effect on the way the parents interact with and discipline their children.

## Social Support for Parents

Do you remember those old movie Westerns, in which the brave settlers were surrounded by hostile forces and the cavalry came to the rescue at the last moment? Well this section might be subtitled "The cavalry returns!" Just when you are probably thinking that *everything* makes the task of raising children in a consistent and loving fashion nearly impossible, I will come to the rescue by telling you about the beneficial effects of a class of events that has come to be called **social support**.

The general point is fairly easy to state: Parents who are giving each other adequate emotional and physical support and who have friends and family members from whom they receive information, assistance, and affection are able to respond to their children more warmly, more consistently, and with better control (Cochran & Brassard, 1979; Crockenberg, 1983; Crnic et al., 1983).

The effect of social support on parents is particularly evident when they are experiencing stress of some kind (including poverty). In Chapter 9 I talked a bit about a study by Susan Crockenberg (1981) that illustrates the point nicely. She found that temperamentally irritable infants were very likely to end up with an insecure attachment to their mothers when the mother lacked adequate social support. When the mother felt that she had enough support, similarly irritable children were later securely attached. In a recent study, Lois Wandersman and Donald Unger (1983) have given us another link in the chain. They have shown that among teenage moms, those who have temperamentally difficult infants are able to provide more affectionate and stimulating environments (measured by Caldwell and Bradley's home inventory, which I described in Chapter 6) if they have good support from the father and from family members than if the support is inadequate.

Hetherington and her co-workers report a similar effect in their study of divorced parents. Those who had help and emotional support from friends or family members were much more able to maintain a stable and affectionate environment for their children than were those who grappled with the problem in isolation.

There are other sources of information and support than families and friends (some of which I have discussed in Box 13.2). And of course, not all "help" from families or friends feels like support (I'm sure you have all been given unwanted advice from your partners or in-laws or friends). The key is not the objective amount of contact or advice received but the parents' *satisfaction* with the level and quality of the support they are experiencing. The moral seems to be that at those times of greatest difficulty or stress—when a new child is born, when a child presents special difficulties, when the family moves or experiences major changes—you most need the emotional and physical support of others. But if you wait until that difficult moment to look around and see who is there to help, you may not find what you need. Social networks must be developed and nurtured over time. But they certainly seem to pay dividends for parents, and thus for children.

## BEYOND THE FAMILY: THE DIRECT INFLUENCE OF OTHER INSTITUTIONS ON CHILDREN

One of the curious things in the field of developmental psychology has been our blithe assumption that the family is the key to the child's development. We have spent a great many hours observing mother-infant and mother-child interactions (and more recently, father-child interactions). The work on social support has expanded our sights still further, to the larger family and circle of friends. But if you think about it, children past the age of 5 and 6 spend as much of their awake time in school as they do at home—or more. With the enormously rapid rise in mothers' employment, infants and preschoolers are also more and more spending their days outside of the family. And when children *are* at home, they spend an extraordinary amount of time sitting in front of a television set rather than interacting with live people. If we are to understand children's development, we must obviously understand the ways in which these other institutions or forces shape the child.

Research on the impact of television has been extensive, but until about 10 years ago, we knew remarkably little about the influence of day-care settings or schools on children's development or on their well-being. But of late, we have been scrambling to catch up.

Since I talked about day care at some length in Chapter 1 (and you may want to go back and reread those pages now), let me spend my

BOX 13.2

# PROFESSIONAL SUPPORT FOR FAMILIES

Assistance, advice, and emotional support from families and friends seem to be critical ingredients in good family functioning. But professionals and institutions can play a helpful role as well. I have to say that we don't know very much about the ways in which families use professional help or about the best way for such help to be offered. But there are at least some models that have been tried and that seem to work.

One of the most striking examples is the impact of the Parent Child Development Centers (PCDCs), which were created in the early 1970s as part of the "war on poverty." The centers were designed to support the optimum development of children in poverty environments by providing information and support to mothers. The centers offered classes for mothers (primarily mothers of preschool children) on child development and child rearing, home management, nutrition, how to use the social system to get what you need, and the like. There were some direct services for children as well, such as child care, but the main focus was on helping the families to become more knowledgeable and skillful with their children, reinforcing strengths and responding to individual needs.

Apparently, it worked. Not only did parents use these centers, they learned from them. Mothers who participated in these centers praised their children more, used more complex language, encouraged more conversation with the child, used more reasoning and less physical punishment than did mothers in equivalent neighborhoods that did not have PCDCs (Andrews et al., 1982). In other words, mothers who had had access to supportive and informative help from professionals shifted their child-rearing style quite markedly. And their children responded. Children of mothers who participated in the centers had higher IQs at age 3 and 4 than did children whose mothers had not been involved (Andrews et al., 1982).

A more focused, but similar, program offered to teenage mothers in Cincinnati by Earladeen Badger and her colleagues (Badger, 1981) has also had some success (as have researchers and program designers who have followed Badger's model —e.g., Slaughter, 1983). Badger operates within the context of a major hospital that serves most of the poverty-level mothers in the city. Teenage mothers are offered a chance to participate in a special series of weekly classes that last for the first year of the infant's life. In the classes, they learn about normal development, what to expect from their infant, how to read the infant's signals, specific parenting skills, and the like. Of course, there was also time for the mothers to share experiences, to get specific help with problems that had cropped up, and to provide emotional support for one another.

Badger has found that the infants of girls who have gone through this program (compared to a control group without the special program) show somewhat faster development in the first year of life. Perhaps more important, the mothers who have had these classes are more likely to continue their education and are less likely to get pregnant again within the next two years.

Of course, not every community has exemplary programs like these. But most communities *do* have resources for parents that are similar. Community colleges frequently offer classes on parenting skills, as may the public health department. It could take some digging to find such programs in your community, but these resources may be especially important to families who lack other sources of support. We know a lot less than we should about how to make information and help available to families in ways that are accessible, helpful, and genuinely supportive. But good programs *do* exist, and they can make a real difference for family functioning.

time here talking about the effects of two other major forces in the child's life: schooling and television.

## Schooling

What kind of effect does school have on children? I've already pointed out (in Chapter 6) that special preschools or compensatory education programs can affect IQ scores or school achievement or the likelihood of school problems. But what about regular elementary and high school experiences?

There are two ways to try to answer this question. First, we can look at children who do *not* attend school—for one reason or another—and see if they turn out differently from those who have had regular schooling. Second, we can study different *kinds* of schools and see whether they have different effects on children.

*Children without Schooling*   There are a number of societies or cultures in the world in which schooling is neither compulsory nor universally available. Studies of children in these cultures give us a chance to see what effect schooling might be having.

Nearly all of this research has focused on the effects of schooling on intellectual development. There is little I can tell you about the social or emotional development of children who do not attend school. But the cognitive effects are reasonably well established (Sharp, Cole, & Lave, 1979; Rogoff, 1981). Children or teenagers (or adults) who have been to school, compared to those who have not, are better able to go beyond specific information and look for general rules or broader strategies. In other words, they use more complex or more abstract information-processing skills. For many everyday tasks, like putting tools into their accustomed places or remembering the ingredients in a well-known recipe, complex processing is not required, and schooled and unschooled children or adults do not differ. But when the problem becomes more complex, differences emerge.

For example, when Donald Sharp and his colleagues (Sharp, Cole, & Lave, 1979) gave Mexican village children and adults a list of 20 words to remember that included animals, utensils, food, and clothing, they found that the more schooling a subject had had, the more likely he or she was to use the "chunking" strategy of organizing the list into the categories and repeating the items back in groups. As Sharp says in summary of their research, "It is not differences in the information . . . but differences in what people do with commonly available information that is critical" (p. 77). Children and adults with more schooling seem to have a larger repertoire of complex or abstract information-processing strategies available to them.

Presumably schooling may have such an effect because children are taught specific new methods of dealing with information or because in school children deal with things they have not experienced directly. They read about places they have never been, talk about situations they have never experienced. Such exposure may push children beyond the concrete to a search for more general rules.

*Different Kinds of Schools*    Studies of children without schooling may be interesting to anthropologists or theorists examining the reasons for cognitive development. But for most of you reading this book, the *real* question about schools is how to pick a school for your own child. Real estate agents constantly try to sell you on the idea that you should buy a house in a "good" school district, obviously assuming that differences between schools really matter. Most parents make the same assumption. But is it true?

The evidence is fairly new (and not yet fully evaluated or digested), but I think the answer is "yes," although perhaps not in the way you would expect.

The studies of school effects have been done primarily in England and the United States (wonderfully reviewed by Michael Rutter, 1983a). Essentially the strategy has been to search for unusually "effective" or "successful" schools, those in which the pupils consistently do better than you would predict knowing the kind of families or neighborhoods the pupils come from. By "better," I mean such things as higher scores on standardized tests, or better school attendance, or lower rates of disruptive classroom behavior or delinquency, or a higher rate of pupils who go on to college, or higher self-esteem in the pupils. If there are schools that consistently produce such "better" outcomes, then the next step is to ask how they are different in organization or functioning from schools in similar neighborhoods that have less-impressive track records.

Apparently, such effective schools really do exist (Rutter, 1983a). More important, some achieve good results consistently, year after year, so the effect is apparently not just chance variation. What are these successful schools like?

I've summarized the key characteristics of effective schools, compared to average or less-effective schools, in Table 13.2. If you look over this list, you may be struck (as I was when I read the literature) by the similarities between the qualities of effective schools and the qualities of "effective parents" that emerge from the discussion of parenting you just read. Effective schools sound a lot to me like *authoritative* schools rather than either permissive or authoritarian schools. There are clear goals and rules, good control, good communication, and high nurturance.

Another key is that it is the school *as a whole*—the ethos or climate of the school, if you will — that seems to matter. Individual teachers are important—as you can see in Box 13.3—but the overall effect seems to be greater than the sum of individual teachers. The school climate

Table 13.2

## Characteristics of unusually effective schools

| | |
|---|---|
| Qualities of pupils | A *mixture* of backgrounds or abilities seems to be best, although the key appears to be to have a large enough concentration of pupils who come to school with good academic skills. Too great a concentration of children with poor skills makes it more difficult for the rest of the things on this list to occur. |
| Goals of the school | A strong emphasis on academic excellence, with high standards and high expectations, characterizes effective schools. These goals are clearly stated by the administration and shared by the staff. |
| Organization of classrooms | Classes are focused on specific academic learning. Daily activities are structured, with a high percentage of time spent in actual group instruction (as opposed to planning and organizing for instruction or in behavior management). High expectations of performance are conveyed to pupils. |
| Homework | Homework is assigned regularly, graded quickly. Effective schools assign markedly more homework than do less-effective schools. |
| Discipline | Most discipline is handled within the classroom, with relatively little fallback to "sending the child to the principal" or the like. But in really effective schools, not much class time is actually spent in discipline, because these teachers have very good control of the class. They intervene early in potentially difficult situations rather than imposing heavy discipline after the fact. |
| Praise | High doses of praise for good performance, for meeting expectations, are given to pupils. These are structured, but warm schools. |
| Teacher experience | Teacher *education* is not related to effectiveness of schools, but teacher *experience* is, presumably because it takes time to learn effective class management and instruction strategies. It probably also takes specific guidance and training from experienced administrators or master teachers to help in this learning. |
| Building surroundings | Age or general appearance of the school building is not critical, but maintenance in good order, cleanliness, and attractiveness do appear to matter. |
| School leadership | Clear values, shared and regularly stated by school administrators, are a major key. The academic emphasis of the school must be apparent in all school activities, in allocation of funds, in priorities of time use. |
| Responsibilities for children | In effective schools, children are more likely to be given real responsibilities—in individual classrooms and in the school as a whole. |

*Source:* Rutter, 1983a.

is made up of the shared goals of the administration and staff, the dedication to effective teaching, and the concrete assistance provided for such teaching. It is reflected in respect for pupils, for parents, for the building.

Take note, though, of what is *not* in the list in Table 13.2: *money.* Within at least normal limits, the sheer amount of money spent in a school district or in an individual school seems to make little difference in the outcome for pupils. Schools with higher teacher salaries are not automatically better; those with newer or fancier buildings are not necessarily better. It is what happens *in* the classrooms and

**Figure 13.7** Each school has its own "climate," its own ethos. Recent research shows that the dozens of small ways in which the teachers, staff, and students express the school goals and values all affect children in important ways. An "authoritative" school (high in control and maturity demands, high in achievement expectations, with good communication and high warmth) not only increases students' academic achievement, it also affects their motivation, their attendance, and their behavior.

the school that matters, not the dollars spent. School boards trying to gain public support for tax increases or new buildings may not be happy to hear that!

On the other side, though, it is fair to say that money does have *some* relevance to the process of education. If salaries are so low that the really effective teachers cannot afford to stay in the profession or in that school, then money matters; if equipment is so inadequate that good science teachers throw up their hands (or their lunch!) in despair and quit, then money matters; if buildings are in such disrepair or so overcrowded that there is simply not enough time for good instruction, then

BOX 13.3

# THE REMARKABLE CASE OF "MISS A"

If you look at Table 13.2, you'll see that many of the characteristics of effective schools are qualities of individual classrooms. The total effect seems to be greater than the sum of individual teachers, but an individual teacher *can* make a difference. Such an effect of a very special teacher is strikingly shown in a fascinating report by Eigel Pederson and his co-workers (Pederson, Faucher, & Eaton, 1978).

These researchers had been looking at the long-term outcomes of a group of children who had all attended a single school in a poor neighborhood. In the course of their study, they came by accident on evidence of the effects of a remarkable teacher whom they call "Miss A."

Miss A taught first grade in the same school for over 30 years. Her teaching sounds very much like an optimum combination of the items listed in Table 13.2: she assumed that all the children could learn to read (high expectations), spent the majority of her class time actually instructing the children, was firm and loving at the same time.

Pederson was able to track her former pupils through the school system and was later able to interview 14 of them as adults, along with 44 others who had had different first-grade teachers. It seems clear from this study that Miss A had a lasting impact on her pupils.

The children in her classroom were more likely to show increases in IQ during elementary school. They were rated as more cooperative by their later teachers, and they got better grades throughout elementary school. They finished more years of schooling and were *much* more successful as adults. Not a single one of Miss A's pupils whom Pederson interviewed as an adult was in the lowest level of adult success defined in this study, despite the fact that most of the children in Miss A's classes came from poor families, many from minority families.

All of Miss A's pupils remembered her, even 20 or 30 years later, while adults who had had other first-grade teachers often did not recall their teacher's name or anything about her.

This is only one study of one teacher, and the number of people studied is not large. But if we combine this study with the evidence in Table 13.2, those of you planning a career in elementary education should take heart. It does seem to matter what you do with and for children in the early years of school. As Pederson puts it:

If children are fortunate enough to begin their schooling with an optimistic teacher who expects them to do well and who teaches them the basic skills needed for further academic success, they are likely to perform better than those exposed to a teacher who conveys a discouraging, self-defeating outlook. (Pederson, Faucher, & Eaton, 1978, p. 11)

money matters. But if these basic levels are reached, the money seems to be best spent on training teachers in more effective techniques and in providing support for teachers in their work.

One moral of this research appears to be that campaigns to improve schools by changing *what* is taught, such as "back to basics" programs, may be at least partially misdirected. The key seems to be *how* teaching is done and the overall climate of the school. A second moral is that it *does* matter what school your child attends and that it is worth your while to spend time visiting schools and classrooms, talking to principals. Some school districts may have traditionally good (or poor) track records, but it is the individual *school* in which your child will spend many hours over the years. The list in Table 13.2—preliminary though it may be—may help you to search for those qualities of schools that are likely to make a difference for your children.

## Television

Time spent watching television ranks right up there with school, sleeping, and play as central activities in children's days. Estimates vary, but it appears that preschoolers watch TV three to four hours a day (Singer, 1983; Liebert & Schwartzberg, 1977). This figure rises slightly among 6- to 9-year-olds, to perhaps four to six hours per day, and then declines through adolescence. Adolescents watch about three hours per day (Comstock et al., 1978). To be sure, some of the time the child may be playing with toys or talking to mom while the set is on, so this is not all intent watching time. Still, over the years of childhood, that is a *lot* of hours in front of the tube.

Just what are children seeing during all of those hours? Obviously, a great many things. Some of it is specifically educational, such as "Sesame Street" or "Mr. Rogers' Neighborhood." Much more of the programming, though, is "entertainment" in the form of cartoons, situation comedies, adventure programs, and the like. Given what I have already said about the process of modeling, it's reasonable to assume that children learn a great deal from the television they watch, including sex-role concepts (as I pointed out in Chapter 10). In the past few years, there has been an increase of interest in TV's impact on children's thinking, social behavior, and attitudes (Rubinstein, 1983). But by far the largest body of research has focused on the violent content of TV programs and the potential impact of such violence on children's aggression.

*Violence on TV* The inescapable fact is that TV is full of violence. George Gerbner and his colleagues have been systematically measuring the violence of TV programs for the past 15 years, defining violence as the "overt expression of physical force against others or self, or the compelling of action against one's will on pain of being hurt or killed" (Gerbner, 1972, p. 31). You can see the scores on their "violence index" for the period up to 1979 in Figure 13.8 (Gerbner, et al., 1980). Translated into real-life terms, this means that there are about 6 violent episodes per hour for prime-time programs and about 17 per hour for children's cartoons. (This level of violence has not declined in recent years, by the way, despite repeated congressional hearings and other hand wringing and public pressure.)

Even more disturbing is the fact that violence is concentrated in programs during the times of day when children are watching. Ronald Slaby and his colleagues (Slaby, Quarfoth, & McConnachie, 1976) found

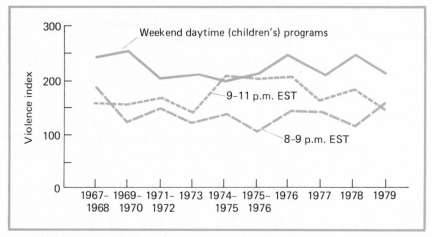

**Figure 13.8** Despite repeated attempts by Congress, through several major sets of hearings and waves of research, violence in children's programs and on prime-time TV is still remarkably high. (*Source:* G. Gerbner, L. Gross, M. Morgan, & N. Signorielli. The "mainstreaming" of America: Violence profile no. 11. *Journal of communication,* 1980, *30,* p. 13. Copyright 1980 by the Annenbey School of Communications.)

that TV violence was high in the early morning, when young children watch cartoons, dropped during "nap time" in the afternoon, and then rose again during the after-school and after-dinner hours.

I want to emphasize several points about the violence children (and adults) see on TV: (1) The numbers of violent episodes I have just listed involve *physical* aggression. If verbal aggression were counted, too, the rate of aggression on TV would be many times higher. (2) The "good guys" are just as likely to be violent as the "bad guys." (3) Violence on most TV programs is rewarded; people who are violent get what they want. In fact, violence is usually portrayed as the most successful way of solving problems. (4) The consequences of violence—pain, blood, damage—are seldom shown (although this is changing). The networks' own codes forbid the showing of such gore (except on the 6 o'clock news), so the child is protected from seeing the painful and negative consequences of aggression and thus receives an unrealistic portrayal of those consequences.

What effect does this barrage of violence have on the child viewer? Is she likely to be more aggressive because of all that exposure to aggression on TV? Can she tell the difference between the fantasy of television and the real-life encounters at home or school?

*The Effects of TV Violence*  There is a *vast* amount of research and commentary on this question, not all of it of high quality. Demonstrating a *causal* connection between watching violent TV and behaving violently is extremely difficult. For example, children who already behave aggressively may *choose* to watch more TV and more violent TV. And families in which TV is watched a great deal may also be more likely to use patterns of discipline that will foster aggressiveness in the child. Some of these difficulties can be counteracted by carefully designed experiments, in which children are exposed to specific TV programs under controlled conditions. But such experiments are, by definition, artificial. It is hard to generalize from experimental results to the real world. Because of these methodological difficulties (not unlike the problem of demonstrating a causal connection between smoking and lung cancer), there is still some debate going on about the impact of TV violence on children (e.g., Milavsky et al., 1982). But like the example of smoking and lung cancer, I think that the weight of the evidence in favor of a link between violence TV and aggressive behavior is very heavy indeed. As Eli Rubinstein (1983) says:

> Granted that the data are complex and that no single study unequivocally documents the connection between televised violence and later aggressive behavior, the convergence of evidence from many studies is overwhelming. (p. 821)

Let me summarize what I think are the basic points to emerge from this body of research:

First, children *do* learn specific aggressive actions from watching them—on TV or in real life. So children are learning about guns, knives, karate, and other aggressive actions from watching TV.

Second, children who watch violent TV *are* more aggressive with their playmates than are children who watch less-violent TV (Murray, 1980). A sample finding from a recent series of studies by Leonard Eron and his associates (Eron, 1982; Eron et al., 1983), shown in Figure 13.9, makes the point graphically. The subjects in this study were first-through fifth-grade students whose aggressive behavior had been rated by peers. The children also picked their favorite TV programs out of several lists of programs. Those children who preferred the more violent programs were also rated as more aggressive by their peers.

As I just indicated, results like this *could* mean that more aggressive children simply like violent TV, with no causal connection involved. But experimental studies in which some children are systematically exposed to violent TV show increases in aggression following such exposure. And field studies of towns both before and after TV first became available show that children's level of aggression rises in the months and years after TV is introduced (Joy, Kimball, & Zabrack, 1977).

Third, the effects of seeing violence on TV seem to be cumulative. The more violent programs a child sees, the more aggressive he seems to become (Steuer, Applefield, & Smith, 1971). Eron and his associates (Eron et al., 1983), in fact, have suggested that there is a cumulative

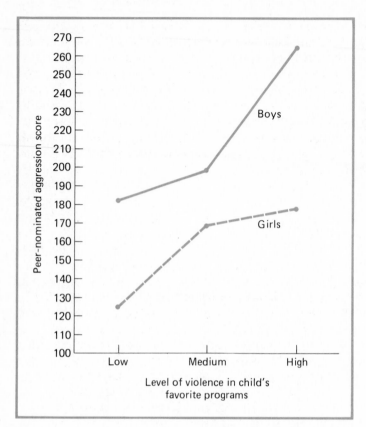

Peer-nominated aggression score

Low  Medium  High

Level of violence in child's
favorite programs

**Figure 13.9** When you ask children about the level of aggression of their classmates and then ask those rated as more aggressive what their favorite TV programs are, you find that the children whose favorite programs are more violent are rated as more aggressive by their peers. (*Source:* L. D. Eron. Parent-child interaction, television violence, and aggression of children. *American psychologist,* 1982, *37,* Figure 3, p. 203. Copyright 1982 by the American Psychological Association. Reprinted by permission of the author.)

effect over time as well as over numbers of programs, particularly during the late elementary-school years (about age 8 to 10). That is, the more violent TV a child watches during those years, the higher the aggression he or she will show *later,* in adolescence.

Fourth, children (and adults) who watch a lot of violent TV have different attitudes about aggression. They are more likely to think that aggression is a good way to solve problems, and they are likely to be more fearful and less trusting (Gerbner et al., 1980; Dominick & Greenberg, 1972).

Obviously, the best way to control all these effects is to turn off the violent programs on TV or (heaven forbid!) to turn off the TV altogether. Short of such a drastic step (which adults find more painful than children do, by the way), there are some ways to soften the impact of the violence the children see. One approach is simply to make clear your own disapproval of violence or aggression. Children from families that express such disapproval show a smaller effect from viewing violent TV. Another possibility is to watch TV with your children and comment on some of the action, perhaps pointing out some of the consequences of the violence. Pointing out the *unreality* of TV programs may also be useful ("It's only pretend. People aren't really like that"). Leonard Eron's work (1982) shows clearly that children who believe that TV is like real life or actually presents real life are more likely to be highly aggressive. Third, you can talk to your child about the effects of watching all that violent TV. When Eron (1982) had some children write paragraphs about the harmful effects of TV violence and videotaped them making a speech on the subject, he found that the aggression scores of these children declined over a four-month period, no matter how much violent TV they watched.

*Nonviolent Television*    I do not want to leave you with the impression that all TV is bad stuff. It is not. The important point, really, is that TV is an educational medium. Children are learning from what they watch. If they watch violent TV, they learn violence and behave more aggressively. But if they watch programs that emphasize sharing, kindness, and helpfulness, such as "Mr. Rogers' Neighborhood" or "Sesame Street" or even "Lassie," they show more kind and helpful behavior (Murray, 1980). If you choose to have a television set (and nearly everyone does), then I would urge you to think hard about what your children are watching and whether you want to limit or control it in some way. It seems to me that if you go to the trouble of worrying about good discipline and about good schools, it is just as important to worry about (and attempt to control) what your children learn from TV.

## FITTING THE INFLUENCES TOGETHER: THE EXAMPLE OF CHILD ABUSE

The particular pattern of development we see in an individual child—the rate or normality of development the child shows, the security or insecurity of the first attachment, the vulnerability or resilience of the child to stress or inadequate environment, and all the rest—is an enormously complex combination of all these influences. As an illustration of how the several pieces of the puzzle may fit together, let me go back to the issue of child abuse, which I first discussed in Chapter 11 (Box 11.1).

There is no *single* cause of abuse: It results from an interaction of many of the elements I have been talking about in this chapter. In particular, abuse is more likely to occur when there is a parent with a higher potential for abuse, living under heightened stress, lacking adequate social and material supports, with an "abusable" child. Generally speaking, abuse only occurs when these elements act *together* (Belsky, 1980).

Parents with a potential for abuse include those who were abused themselves as children, who thus may not have formed a secure early attachment or who may have learned abusive methods of control through modeling. This category also includes parents who lack good parenting skills and who thus have difficulty controlling their children through less-violent means. Like many of us, they resort to physical punishment when they have failed to achieve the desired results with other methods. As a group, abusing parents are also likely to have unusually high and unrealistic expectations for their child's behavior. They expect infants to stop crying if they are told to or 2-year-olds to come immediately when asked (Steele & Pollock, 1974).

But even parents at higher risk for abuse do not all abuse their children. Another critical ingredient seems to be a high level of stress, either short-term or chronic, combined with a low level of support. It is not poverty, per se, that is the causal agent here. James Garbarino's research shows that *among* parents living in poverty, it is only those who are *also* experiencing high life change (divorce, moves, job loss or job change, new people moving into the family, etc.) and who do not have adequate assistance who are likely to abuse their children.

Garbarino (Garbarino & Sherman, 1980) has uncovered some of the critical elements by comparing equally poor neighborhoods that have very high or very low rates of child abuse. Some of the characteristics of the high-risk neighborhoods are listed in Table 13.3. As you can see, there are very few supports available to parents in these neighborhoods: little child care available, few supportive contacts with neighbors, and many single working mothers whose need for support is heightened.

But even in such nonsupportive environments, with high stress, not all children are abused. And in any one abusing family, not every child is abused. As I pointed out in Box 11.1, the child's own qualities may

**Table 13.3**

**Characteristics of poor neighborhoods with high rates of child abuse, compared to equally poor neighborhoods with low rates of child abuse**

| In high-abuse neighborhoods: | There are more single, working mothers. |
|---|---|
| | Parents experience high levels of personal life change (e.g., people moving in and out of the household, job changes). |
| | Parents are more socially isolated: They have few people in family networks and do not have neighbors that they can ask for help. |
| | Child care is less readily available. |
| | Children play with each other less. |
| | People move in and out of the neighborhood frequently. |
| | Parents are less likely to be home when children get home from school. |
| | Parents see the neighborhood as a bad place to rear children. |

*Source:* Garbarino & Sherman, 1980.

contribute to the system as well. Children who are unusually difficult or physically handicapped or who make exceptional demands on the parents are more likely to be abused (Lewis & Schaeffer, 1981).

This one example makes it clear, I hope, that understanding or explaining the differing developmental pathways or trajectories of individual children is an immensely complex task. To complete it, we will need not only to look at the shared developmental patterns, common to all children, but to examine the context in which that development is occurring. The child, the family, the larger culture interact with one another, influence one another, and together shape each child's development.

## SUMMARY

1. Children develop within families, and families exist within larger cultural influences. This complex of forces has a significant impact on the child's development.
2. Within the family, several dimensions of parental behavior toward children seem to be particularly significant, including the emotional tone of the family, the method of maintaining control, the patterns of communication, and the degree of cognitive enrichment provided.
3. Families that provide high levels of warmth and affection, compared to those that are more cold or rejecting, have children with more secure attachments and better peer relationships.
4. Families that have clear rules and standards, relatively high levels of expectation or maturity demands for the child, and enforce those rules and expectations consistently appear to have children with the greatest self-esteem and the greatest competence across a broad range of situations.
5. Children who are talked to frequently, in complex sentences, and who are listened to in turn not only develop language more rapidly, they also have more positive and less conflicted relationships with their parents.
6. Parents who provide a rich array of inanimate stimulation (including toys and opportunities for new experiences) along with responsive and contingent animate stimulation have children who show the most rapid cognitive development.
7. These elements of parental behavior can be combined into several styles of child rearing, which Baumrind refers to as *authoritative* (high in warmth, control, communication, and maturity demands), *authoritarian* (high in control and maturity demands; low in warmth and communication), and *permissive* (high in warmth and communication; low in control and maturity demands). The authoritative style appears to be the most generally effective for pro-

ducing confident, competent, independent, and affectionate children.

8. Parents are, in turn, influenced by a series of factors, including the child's own temperament and developmental level.

9. The overall level of poverty or affluence of the family also has an impact on the family interaction, by affecting health and health care, diet, discipline patterns, and levels of stress and support.

10. Short-term stresses or life change also affect the way parents interact with their children. For example, immediately following divorce (or other major upheaval), parents show lower levels of control, lower maturity demands, less warmth, and poorer communication with their children.

11. The effects of poverty or short-term stress are mitigated by the presence of adequate social support for the parent or parents. Supporting each other is important, but having additional sources of emotional and material support from family and friends is critical as well.

12. Children are also influenced directly by schools and by television. Simply attending school appears to foster certain kinds of more abstract information processing. But the particular qualities of schools or teachers also have an effect on the child's attitude toward school, achievement in school subjects, and likelihood of attending college.

13. "Effective" schools have many of the same qualities as authoritative parents: They have clear and shared goals, including an emphasis on academic achievement; they have high levels of control without invoking heavy punishment; they are warm; and they have excellent communication, both among staff and between staff and students.

14. Children spend almost as much time watching television as they do in school. They learn significant new behaviors or skills from TV, particularly adult roles. Most research has focused on the impact of TV violence on children.

15. Children who watch a lot of violent TV show more aggression toward their peers, both in controlled experiments and in free interactions. The effect appears to be cumulative and to touch children's attitudes about aggression as well as their behavior.

16. We can see the combination of the total "ecological niche" in which the child is developing well illustrated in the research on child abuse. Children are most likely to be abused when there is a combination of at least three elements: a parent with the potential for abuse, a highly stressful family situation lacking in adequate social support, and a child who is particularly difficult or demanding. There is thus no single cause of abuse, just as there is no single

cause for most patterns of individual development we see in children. To understand development, we therefore need to understand the complex context in which it occurs.

## KEY TERMS

**Authoritarian parental style**   Pattern of parental behavior described by Baumrind, among others, including a high level of directiveness and a low level of affection and warmth.

**Authoritative parental style**   Pattern described by Baumrind, including a high level of both control and warmth.

**Democratic child rearing**   An older term used to describe a particular pattern of care that included high levels of warmth but particularly high levels of open communication and negotiation. Similar to Baumrind's group of permissive parents.

**Permissive parental style**   A third style described by Baumrind, among others; it includes high warmth but a lower level of control.

**Restrictiveness**   Term used to describe a particular pattern of parental control, involving limitation of the child's movements or options, such as by the use of playpens or harnesses in a young child or strict rules about play areas or free choices in an older child.

**Social class**   Term widely used to characterize broad variations in economic and social positions within society. Four broad groups are most often described: upper-class, middle-class, working-class, and lower-class (also called poverty-level). For an individual family, the designation is based on the occupations and education of the adults in the household.

**Social support**   Phrase now widely used to describe the emotional, material, and informational assistance available to any one individual from family and friends in times of need.

**Warmth versus hostility**   The key dimension of emotional tone used to describe family interactions.

## SUGGESTED READINGS

Bronfenbrenner, U. *The ecology of human development*. Cambridge, Mass.: Harvard University Press, 1979.

This book is sometimes tough sledding, but it is worth the effort. Bronfenbrenner has gone further than anyone in describing the many forces that affect the child's development and how those forces may connect to one another.

Maccoby, E. E. *Social development*. New York: Harcourt Brace Jovanovich, 1980.

Chapter 10, on child-rearing practices, is particularly clear and useful as an expansion on what I have said in this chapter. (In fact, you will easily detect Maccoby's influence on my own thinking.)

Patterson, G. R. *Families: Applications of social learning to family life*. Champaign, Ill.: Research Press, 1975.

Once again I suggest this book, particularly for those among you who are already parents and who may feel the need of very concrete guidance on how to establish clear and consistent control with your children.

Radin, N. The unique contribution of parents to childrearing: The preschool years. In S. G. Moore & C. R. Cooper (Eds.). *The young child: Reviews of research* (Vol 3). Washington, D.C.: National Association for the Education of Young Children, 1982.

Another very good chapter in a book I have recommended regularly in these "Suggested Readings" sections.

# Television Aggression

As I suggested earlier, you may want to combine this project with the one at the end of Chapter 10, which involved observing sex-role presentations on TV. If so, you or your instructor may wish to modify the following instructions somewhat. But if you are doing this in isolation, proceed as follows:

Using the definition of violence offered by George Gerbner ("the overt expression of physical force against others or self, or the compelling of action against one's will on pain of being hurt or killed"), select a minimum of four half-hour television programs normally watched by children and count the number of aggressive or violent episodes in each. Extend Gerbner's definition somewhat, however, to count verbal aggression as well as physical aggression.

You may select any four (or more) programs, but I would strongly recommend that you distribute them in the following way:

1. At least one "educational" television program, such as "Sesame Street" or "Mr. Rogers' Neighborhood."
2. At least one Saturday morning cartoon. I haven't watched these in a while, so I can't point you to particularly grisly examples. Select at random.
3. At least one early-evening adult program that is watched by young children: a family comedy, a Western, a crime film, or one of each.

For each program that you watch, record the number of violent episodes, separating the instances of verbal and physical violence.

In thinking or writing about the details of your observations, consider the following questions:

What kind of variation in the number of violent episodes is there among the programs that you watched?

Are some programs more verbally aggressive, some more physically aggressive?

Do the numbers of violent episodes per program correspond to the numbers found by Gerbner?

What about the consequences of aggression in the television films? Are those who act violently rewarded or punished? How often do reward and punishment occur?

What behaviors other than aggression might a child have learned from watching the programs you viewed? This question is particularly relevant for "Sesame Street" or "Mr. Rogers" but applies to more traditional entertainment programs as well.

In view of the material in this chapter and your own observations for this project, what rules or limits (if any) would you place on TV viewing for your own child? Why?

# 14.
# atypical development

Archie, who is 9 years old, seemed "different from other children even when he started school." Often he was "disoriented" or "distractible." Although he scored in the normal range on an IQ test, he had great difficulty learning to read. Even after several years of special tutoring, he could read only by sounding out the words each time; he didn't recognize even familiar words by sight. Archie also sometimes called people and objects by the wrong names (Cole & Traupmann, 1981).

Tommy, who is 4 years old, seems to be bright but is fearful and inhibited. He is both imperious and anxiously complying with the other children. His nursery school teacher is worried about him (Solnit & Provence, 1979).

Vickie is 11. "She absolutely loves to roller-skate, and like any other 11-year-old, she squeals with delight when she's careening down the sidewalk in front of her house. But Vicki doesn't speak . . . sucks her thumb . . . and has a great deal of trouble making eye contact with others" (*San Francisco Chronicle,* August 21, 1979).

When Jeffrey was 4, he couldn't walk or talk and spent most of his time in a crib. His parents fed him pureed baby food through a bottle. After six years with a loving foster family, at age 10 Jeffrey is now in a special class in a regular elementary school and is learning to print and read.

Each of these children is "atypical" in some way. In each, the normal developmental processes I have been describing in the past 13 chapters didn't quite work in the normal way. Archie has some kind of **specific learning disability**. Tommy shows some mild or moderate form of emotional disturbance, often called a **behavior problem**, while Vicki has a much more serious type of disorder, usually called **autism**. Jeffrey is a Down's syndrome child and is **mentally retarded**.

I have touched on some of the problems of atypically developing children in earlier chapters—problems in learning to read, problems of deaf children, and treatment of excessive aggressiveness in children. But in this chapter, I want to try to give you some sense of the range of problems that can occur, the causes of the problems, and the sort of treatments that are used. The topic is enormous, so I will of necessity be giving you breadth rather than depth. Still, I can alert you to some of the difficult issues and questions still facing us in understanding the reasons for atypical development and in designing successful treatments.

## DEFINITIONS AND CLASSIFICATIONS

Before I go further, I need to say a word or two about labels and classifications of children's problems. Most government and clinical agencies now use the classification system provided in the third edition of the

American Psychiatric Association's *Diagnostic and Statistical Manual of Mental Disorders*—usually abbreviated **DSM-III** (American Psychiatric Association, 1980). I've listed the broad categories of disorders from DSM-III in Table 14.1, and I will roughly follow this category system in this chapter. At the same time, I want to emphasize that many of the labels and terms that parents will hear used to describe their child may not match the DSM-III designations. Sometimes I will deviate from the DSM-III categories when this will make the more common language clearer, and in each case I will try to give you the everyday words as well as the technical ones.

Two other points about definitions are important. First, the definition of *atypical* is very much a matter of degree. How long does a period of depression or anxiety have to persist before a child is diagnosed as having an "anxiety disorder"? How poorly does a child have to do in school before she is called "learning-disabled" or "retarded"? At the extremes, there is little disagreement about diagnosing atypical development, but in every domain there is a fuzzy area in which the distinction between what is "normal" and what is "atypical" is a matter of judgment.

Second, children whose development is atypical in some respect are much more *like* normally developing children than they are unlike them. Blind and deaf and retarded children all form attachments in much the same way that physically and mentally normal children do; children with conduct disorders go through the same sequences of cognitive development that more adjusted children show. So the fact that a child is different in one way should not blind us to the fact that he is probably quite "typical" in many other ways.

Table 14.1

**Major diagnostic categories of child and adolescent emotional disorders**

| | |
|---|---|
| Attention deficit disorders | Includes hyperactivity as well as problems of attention without hyperactivity. |
| Conduct disorders | Includes "undersocialization" in children who may or may not also show aggression. Excessive aggressiveness and juvenile delinquency are typically classed in this group. |
| Anxiety disorders | Includes serious separation anxiety and any other form of excessive anxiety. |
| Eating disorders | Includes anorexia nervosa, bulimia, and other patterns of atypical eating. |
| Pervasive developmental disorders | Includes infantile autism, childhood-onset pervasive developmental disorder, and all learning disabilities. |

*Source:* Adapted from the third edition of the *Diagnostic and statistical manual of mental disorders* (DSM-III) of the American Psychiatric Association, 1980, p. 15.

## FREQUENCY OF PROBLEMS

How common are the various types of atypical development? *Most* children show at least some kinds of "problem behavior" at one time or another. For example, among more "everyday" disorders, parents report that 10 to 20 percent of 7-year-olds still wet their beds at least occasionally; 30 percent have nightmares; 20 percent bite their fingernails; 10 percent suck their thumbs; and 10 percent swear enough for it to be considered a problem. Another 30 percent or so have temper tantrums (Achenbach & Edelbrock, 1981). Problems like these are so common, in fact, that many of them—especially if they are short-term patterns—should be considered part of "normal" development.

More serious or more persisting problems are less common. Table 14.2 gives some recent guesses. I've taken these estimates from several different sources, and there is considerable overlap in the categories. For example, the children with serious learning disabilities (700,000 of them) are also a part of the group with significant reading problems. Similarly, there is probably some overlap between the group with severe emotional disturbance and those with milder emotional problems, since the two numbers come from two different places and the definition of *mild* and *severe* is bound to vary from one investigator to another.

Still, even if we allow for some overlap, the numbers are astonishing. Something like 15 to 20 percent of all the children in the United States (and presumably in other countries as well) show at least one form of atypical development. At least one in six, and probably as many as one in five, will require some form of special help in school, in a child guidance clinic, or the equivalent. When you think of these figures in terms of the demands this places on the school system and on other social agencies, the prospect is somewhat staggering.

Of course, some of the children reflected in Table 14.2 may have only short-term problems. Many children experience brief periods of intense emotional disturbance (just as adults do), which can be treated successfully or which fade without any intervention. Many children with speech or language problems can be helped, too, just as many children with reading problems can be assisted with special programs. But many of the children represented in the table have long-term handicaps, such as major physical disabilities, serious emotional disorders, or significant mental retardation. These problems may require continuous assistance.

For society as a whole and for the several helping professions in particular, there are at least three tasks involved in coping with these large numbers of children in need. First, we have to understand the nature and origins of the problems we are facing. Second, we need to develop effective intervention programs; and third, we need to consider

Table 14.2

**Estimated incidence of various types of atypical development in the United States**

| Type of Problem | Approximate Number of Children in the United States with the Problem | Approximate Percentage of All Children 0–18 |
|---|---|---|
| *Problems with language or cognition* | | |
| Significant reading problems | 8,000,000 | 12.0 |
| Speech and language problems, including delayed language, articulation problems, and stuttering | 2,400,000 | 3.5 |
| IQs below 70; mental retardation | 1,700,000 | 2.5 |
| Serious learning disabilities | 700,000 | 1.0 |
| *Problems in relating to others or to society* | | |
| Short-term behavior problems or relatively mild emotional disturbance | 5,000,000 | 7.5 |
| Relatively severe emotional disturbance | 1,400,000 | 2.0 |
| Juvenile delinquency (counting only those arrested) | 1,100,000 | 1.6 |
| *Physical problems* | | |
| Significant hearing impairment or deafness | 350,000 | 0.5 |
| All other problems, including blindness, cerebral palsy, and epilepsy | 120,000 | 0.2 |

*Sources: Profiles of Children,* 1970; Hobbs, 1975; Graham, 1979; Achenbach, 1982.

the possibility of prevention. Can any of these disorders be avoided if we provide proper prenatal care to mothers or special programs for children and families in early infancy? Most of what I'll say in this chapter speaks to the first of these tasks (description and understanding), but I will talk at least a bit about possible treatments and prevention.

## MENTALLY ATYPICAL DEVELOPMENT

### The Mentally Retarded

Of all the atypical children listed in Table 14.2, probably those studied most thoroughly are those labeled "retarded." Not too many decades ago, when mental ability was thought of as a fixed trait, mental subnormality was considered a kind of incurable disease. Labels like "idiot," "feeble-minded," "imbecile," or "moron" were used. But this older view has changed a great deal. Not only have the old negative labels been changed, but the basic assumptions about the nature of retardation have changed, too.

Mental retardation is now (correctly, I think) viewed as a *symptom* rather than as a disease. And like any symptom, it can change. A child's life circumstances or his health may change, and his IQ score may go up or down at the same time. Remember from Chapter 6 that *many* children's IQ test scores vary as much as 30 or 40 points over the childhood years. Of course, many children with low IQ scores will continue to function at a low level throughout life. But it is important for educators and parents to understand that a single low IQ score need not invariably mean that the child will function at that level forever. For many children, improvement is possible.

*The Assessment of Retardation*    Two criteria are usually used in deciding whether a given child is functioning at a mentally retarded level. First, an individual IQ test score is used. But second, some measure of the child's **adaptive behavior** is also used. Can the child dress himself and go to the bathroom alone? Can he get along with other children and adapt to the demands of a regular classroom by being quiet for periods and paying attention to the teacher? As Thomas Achenbach (1982) says, "Children doing well in school are unlikely to be considered retarded no matter what their IQ scores" (p. 214). It is only when a child copes poorly with the everyday demands of home or school life *and* achieves a low score on a standardized test that she is likely to be called retarded.

*Labels*    Low IQ scores are customarily divided up into several ranges, with different labels attached to each, as you can see in Table 14.3. I've given both the labels used by psychologists and those that may be more common in the school system. (There are no school system labels for children with IQs below about 35, since schools very rarely deal with children functioning at this level.)

The farther down the IQ scale you go, the fewer children there are. Seventy or 80 percent of all children with IQs below 70 are in the "mild" range; only about 2 percent of the low-IQ youngsters (perhaps 35,000 children in the United States) are profoundly retarded.

Table 14.3

**IQ scores and labels for children classed as retarded**

| Approximate IQ Score Range | Label Used by Psychologists | Label Often Used in Schools |
| --- | --- | --- |
| 68–83 | Borderline retarded | (No special label) |
| 52–67 | Mildly retarded | Educable mentally retarded (EMR) |
| 36–51 | Moderately retarded | Trainable mentally retarded |
| 19–35 | Severely retarded | (No special label) |
| Below 19 | Profoundly retarded | (No special label) |

*Cognitive Functioning in Retarded Children*   In recent years there has been a great deal of fascinating research on thinking and information processing in retarded children, much of it by Joseph Campione and Ann Brown (Campione, Brown, & Ferrara, 1982). This research has been a significant ingredient in the emerging information-processing approach to studying cognitive development in children. But it also tells us a good deal about the way retarded children think.

Several points have emerged from Campione and Brown's work. Retarded children

1. Have slower reaction times: They think more slowly.
2. Require much more complete and repeated instruction to learn new information or a new strategy (compared to normal-IQ children, who may discover a strategy for themselves or profit from incomplete instruction).
3. Do not generalize or transfer something they have learned in one situation to a new problem or task. They thus appear to lack those "executive" functions that enable older, higher-IQ children (or adults) to compare a new problem to familiar ones or to scan through a repertoire of strategies until they find one that works.

These children *can* learn, but they do so more slowly and require far more exhaustive and task-specific instruction.

The research that leads to these conclusions is fascinating, both because it tells us a great deal about the ways in which low-IQ children differ from normal-IQ children and because it opens the door to the possibility that we may soon be able to diagnose individual children's "information-processing deficits" much more precisely. This may, in turn, allow us to provide more appropriate training.

What are the causes of low IQ scores or inefficient information processing? Conventionally, the causes are divided into two broad categories: *physical causes* and *cultural-familial causes* (also called sociocultural causes).

*Physical Causes of Retardation*   About 25 percent of mental retardation (including nearly all the cases of profound and severe retardation) has an identifiable physical origin, including several kinds of inherited disorders and brain damage.

Many of the chromosomal anomalies I described in Chapter 2, such as Down's syndrome, are typically (but not invariably) accompanied by mild or moderate retardation. Down's children typically show fairly normal motor and mental development for the first six months, after which the rate slows down quite markedly. Most, however, show steady mental development until they reach approximately the level of functioning of a 4-year-old, following essentially the same sequence as we see in normal-IQ children but at a slower rate. But then their development seems to level off (Achenbach, 1982; Hanson, 1981).

A child may also inherit a specific (recessive-gene) disease or **inborn error of metabolism**, which can cause retardation if not treated. The best-known such inherited metabolism error is *phenylketonuria* (PKU). Children with PKU lack the liver enzymes needed to digest the amino acid phenylalanine. A metabolic chain reaction is set in motion that results in brain damage, hyperactivity, and mental retardation. Hospitals routinely check for the presence of this disorder when a baby is born, and children who have it (about 1 out of 15,000 to 20,000 births) are placed on a special diet of foods low in phenylalanine. If the special diet is begun within the first three months of life, the child usually develops normally.

Still a third physical cause of retardation is **brain damage**, which can result from a large number of causes. Diseases in the mother during pregnancy, such as rubella or syphilis, can produce damage to the brain; severe malnutrition in the mother during pregnancy can have a similar effect. Maternal alcoholism also frequently produces brain damage, as I pointed out in Chapter 2. Finally, the child's brain may be damaged during delivery or by some accident after birth (e.g., an auto accident or the child's falling out of a treehouse on her head).

Before you get discouraged at this long list of rather awful things that can cause retardation, you should remember that a great many of the things I've mentioned here are preventable. Some genetic disorders can be diagnosed in utero using amniocentesis; others, like PKU, can be treated effectively if diagnosed early; many maternal diseases

**Figure 14.1** Programs like the Special Olympics, in which Mark was participating when these pictures were taken, have helped to enrich the lives of Down's syndrome and other retarded children.

can be prevented by immunization. Good *preventive* health care, then, should help us to reduce the number of children with physically caused mental retardation.

*Cultural-Familial Causes of Retardation*   The remaining 75 percent of retarded children show no signs of any brain damage or other physical disorder. In almost all cases, such children come from families in which the parents have low IQs, where there is serious family disorganization, mental illness in the parents, or emotional or cognitive deprivation in the home. Often several of these factors (both genetic and environmental) operate simultaneously.

As I pointed out in Chapter 6, psychologists are still arguing about the extent to which heredity influences a child's measured IQ. But nearly all agree that there is at least *some* effect. So it is reasonable to assume that many children who score below 70 on an IQ test start out life with several strikes against them.

But genetic endowment is clearly not the only ingredient in this soup. When children from families like the ones I have just described are placed from early infancy in special enrichment programs, their IQs can be quite startlingly increased. Go back and reread the section in Chapter 6 about special enrichment programs, particularly the programs run by Heber and by Ramey. The children in Heber's study all came from families in which the mothers had IQs below 70, with little home enrichment. Without intervention, children from such families have a high chance of showing retarded development as well. But those in the special program function at a normal or above-normal level.

Research like this shows us the power of the environment in causing retardation in some children. It also seems to point the way to a solution. But before you leap to the conclusion that we should immediately begin intervention programs such as this for all children who are likely to function at a retarded level, I have to caution you.

First, we know amazingly little about the specific kinds of experiences that a child has to have to develop cognitive skills at the normal rate. I can give you a *general* prescription, including enough toys and materials for exploration, warm and responsive (and talkative) adults, and (within limits) a nonrestrictive and nonpunitive environment. But it is another matter to turn this general statement into specific programs for children. Even more, we know next to nothing about the *long-range* effects of special programs.

Second, enrichment programs like Heber's or Ramey's may work well for the child whose retardation is primarily environmental in origin. But they may work less well for children with some physical abnormality. This is not to say that we should ignore environmental enrichment or specific early training for children with physically caused retardation. Greater breadth of experience would enrich their lives and might improve their functioning. Certainly, efforts to provide special schooling for Down's syndrome children have done both (Hayden & Haring, 1976; Hanson, 1981). But even massive early interventions are not likely to make most brain-damaged or genetically anomalous children intellectually normal, although they may foster a level of functioning closer to the child's intellectual limits and permit the child to function much more independently.

Third, interventions of the type Heber and Ramey used are *expensive*. Obviously, if we knew more precisely just what kind of experiences a child needs for optimal growth, we could "aim" our programs more narrowly, and they would probably cost far less. In the meantime, we use a sort of "shotgun" approach, doing everything we think might help; and that costs money. In the long run, I think that such an investment would pay off handsomely, both for the child's happiness and for society. The cost to society over the lifetime of an individual child would be far less if he grew up to be a well-functioning, capable adult than if he emerged as a borderline retardate requiring public assistance. But even if we were sure that early interventions could have large and persisting effects (which, as yet, we are not), it is not at all clear to me that as a society we are prepared to pay the very high initial cost of intervening. It is even less clear to me that we have agreed that we have some shared responsibility to do so.

## Children with Learning Disorders

DSM-III places learning disorders in the category of "pervasive developmental disorders." But since children in this group have difficulty with one or another cognitive task, I have considered them in the broad category of mentally atypical development.

Some children with normal IQs and essentially good adaptive functioning nonetheless have difficulty learning to read or write or do arithmetic. There are a lot of labels for children with this kind of problem. The ones you are likely to encounter in a school include *learning disability* or *specific learning disability,* often abbreviated *SLD*. In theory, the SLD label is only applied if the child's problem is confined to a fairly narrow range of tasks, but in fact, the SLD label is used more broadly than that.

Some of the specific subtypes of learning disorder have acquired their own names, including **dyslexia** for problems with reading and **dysgraphia** for problems with writing. The term *dyslexia,* unfortunately, is also often used interchangeably with SLD to mean any form of learning disorder.

The largest group of children with learning disorders is made up of those who have difficulty learning to read (*correctly* called dyslexia). As I indicated in Table 14.2, about 1 percent of children have *serious* problems of this kind, while another 14 to 15 percent have more moderate difficulty. I have already talked about some of the possible explanations of difficulties with reading in Box 5.2, but let me emphasize a couple of points here.

The honest truth is that even after years of research, we don't really know why some children have such serious trouble learning to read (or write or calculate). Learning disability or disorder is nearly always a *residual* diagnosis. It is the label we apply when we have ruled out the other logical possibilities, such as general retardation or emotional disturbance or an undetected hearing or vision problem. Any of these may *also* produce problems with reading or writing, but even after these are examined and cast out as explanations, there are still significant numbers of children whose learning patterns are not normal.

Furthermore, among children given this residual label, the specific form of the problem varies widely, as I pointed out in Box 5.2. For some the difficulty seems to be in language, for others in visual processing, for others in auditory processing. Given such variability, we shouldn't be surprised that the search for causes has been unfruitful.

The most commonly offered explanation of specific learning disability—particularly by educators and parents—is that the child suffers from some kind of "minimal brain damage." Such children rarely show any outward signs of major brain damage, but perhaps there is some lesser damage, undetected by normal neurological tests, that nonetheless shows itself when the child is faced with a complex task like learning to read.

This may be a comforting hypothesis in many ways, since it avoids the label *mental retardation* and makes it clear that no one is at fault for the child's problem. But you should understand that this is a *hypothesis* and not a fact. Most children with specific learning disabilities do *not* show any signs of brain damage on any standard tests. It may well be that their brains *work differently* because of some chemical difference or an inherited tendency. Or parts of their brains may simply mature more slowly, thus giving a kind of unevenness of skill (Brumback & Staton, 1983). But these, too, are hypotheses.

Fortunately for parents and educators, the question of causes doesn't have to be answered before a child can be diagnosed and given special help for the learning problem. Obviously, alternative possibilities (such as vision or hearing problems or family discord or lack of stimulation) have to be ruled out first. And the complex job of determining the precise nature of the child's disability must be completed. But once that is done, special remedial programs that work around the child's problem are possible. I am sure that any parent of a learning-disabled child can tell you that the available programs do not begin to match the need. And psychologists can tell you that we do not yet have good enough diagnostic tools to describe each child's disability precisely. But recognition of the problem is a vital first step—one we *have* taken.

## The Gifted Child

I can't leave the topic of "mentally atypical development" without saying at least a word or two about the group of children on the other end of the distribution, the **gifted.** Statistically, these children are just as atypical as the mentally retarded. And like the retarded, they place special demands on both parents and school systems. Let me give you an extreme example, a child named Michael described by Halbert Robinson (1981):

> When Michael was 2 years and 3 months old, the family visited our laboratory. At that time, they described a youngster who had begun speaking at age 5 months and by 6 months had exhibited a vocabulary of more than 50 words. He started to read English when he was 13 months old. In our laboratory he spoke five languages and could read in three of them. He understood addition, subtraction, multiplication, division, and square root, and he was fascinated by a broad range of scientific constructs. He loved to make puns, frequently bilingual ones. (p. 63)

Michael's IQ on the Stanford Binet was in excess of 180 at age 2; two years later, when Michael was 4½, he performed on the test like a 12-year-old and was listed as having an IQ beyond 220.

*Definitions*   We can certainly all agree that Michael is astonishingly gifted. The term *gifted,* though, is used to describe a great many children whose gifts are not as remarkable as Michael's. Fundamentally, gifted children are those whose *rate* of intellectual development is greatly in excess of the norm (just as retarded children are those who are developing unusually slowly). Most often, the child's rate of development is measured with an IQ test, and giftedness is frequently defined simply as any IQ above some specific cutoff point—usually a score of 135 to 150 or higher. Recently, broader definitions have appeared, which include among the gifted those children who have unusual skill in a particular intellectual ability, such as memory whizzes or mathematical prodigies or children with exceptional spatial abilities. Robinson suggests that it may be useful to divide the group of gifted children into two sets: the "garden-variety gifted," with high IQs (perhaps 135 to 150) but without extraordinary ability in any one area, and the "highly gifted" (like Michael) with extremely high IQ scores and/or remarkable skill in one or more areas. These two groups of children may have quite different experiences at home and in school.

*Characteristics of Gifted Children*   A great deal of what we know about gifted children comes from a remarkable longitudinal study by Lewis Terman, who selected about 1500 children with high IQs from the California school system in the 1920s. These children—now adults in their sixties, seventies, and even eighties —have been followed regularly throughout their lives (Terman, 1925; Terman & Oden, 1947, 1959; Sears & Barbee, 1977; Sears, 1977).

Terman found that the gifted children he studied were better off than their less-gifted classmates in many other ways as well. They were somewhat healthier; they were interested in many things such as hobbies and games; and they were successful in later life. Both the boys and the girls in this study went on to complete many more years of education than was typical of children of their era and had successful careers as adults. More recent research has generally confirmed this rosy picture of the adjustment of very bright children. They are typically friendly, socially adept, popular with peers, and usually well adjusted (Gallagher, 1975).

Certainly these findings do not support the assumption that was common 50 years ago (and still is today in some circles) that gifted children are maladjusted or social misfits. But Robinson (1981) offers a cautionary note. The small group of highly gifted children—those with IQs above 165 or 170, for example—may not fare as well as the "garden-variety gifted." There is no suggestion that remarkable talent inevitably brings about maladjustment. But Robinson points out that such children are *so* different from their peers that they may be seen as strange or unsettling. For them, friendships with age-mates may be far harder to achieve than is true for the less strikingly gifted child.

*Families of Gifted Children*   Children with very high IQs are far more likely to come from middle-class or otherwise advantaged families than from working-class or poor families. Terman found this, and so have more recent researchers (Freeman, 1981; Robinson, 1981). Doubtless there is some genetic influence at work here: Very bright parents are not only more likely to have very bright children, they are also likely to be well educated and financially well off. But the environmental enrichment provided to the child is also an important ingredient in gifted performance. Joan Freeman (1981) suggests that what we call giftedness is most often a product of "good genes" *and* a stimulating environment. Even if "good genes" are equally distributed across social class groups, environmental enrichment is not, so a bright child in a middle-class family is more likely to receive that extra boost of stimulation that turns "bright" into "gifted." But there is little evidence from the research on the families of gifted children to show that these mothers and fathers are "pushing" their children. In fact, the parents nearly always express surprise at their children's remarkable achievements (Robinson, 1981).

Whatever the origin of their special gifts—and some remarkably gifted children come from poor or uneducated parents—these children obviously have an unusual potential for making significant contributions as adults. We need to know a good deal more about how such gifts can be supported and nurtured at home and in school.

## EMOTIONALLY ATYPICAL DEVELOPMENT

Problems in relating to others and in the child's emotional state can range from relatively minor (and basically normal) brief depressions or fears to broader or more lasting patterns of behavior, such as hyperactivity or excessive aggression, to still more severe problems (usually called *psychoses*) that affect all the child's encounters and make normal relationships virtually impossible.

### Mild or Moderate Problems

The term *behavior problem* is often used by school psychologists or teachers to describe many of the deviant patterns at the mild or moderate level. Several quite distinct syndromes or patterns are included, each with different origins and different prescribed treatment. Let me describe a few such patterns—those that are the most common or the most troublesome for parents and teachers.

*Hyperactivity*  The behavior pattern commonly called **hyperactivity** is included in the category of "attention disorders" in DSM-III. Such children are restless, impulsive, distractible, overactive, with a short attention span. They have difficulty concentrating on any one activity or any one task for very long. They may run about and climb on things, have a hard time staying seated for long, don't listen well, and are "on the go" all the time. Parents who live with such children and teachers who try to instruct them frequently describe them as "off the wall."

The diagnosis of hyperactivity has become a favorite one in the United States—something of a catchall to describe children who may be aggressive or who act up to receive attention or who are simply more energetic than a particular parent or teacher can tolerate. In controlled studies of large, randomly selected samples of children, the incidence of hyperactivity ranges from 1 to 3 percent (Trites & Laprade, 1983), which suggests that it is a common pattern, even if not quite so common as some teachers or parents may think. Some of these children are identified by parents in the preschool years, but the full diagnosis is most often made when the child reaches school.

Children who are diagnosed as hyperactive typically have low school achievement, even in adolescence, when the behavioral signs of hyperactivity have waned somewhat. Many children diagnosed as hyperactive in childhood "recover" from this problem and lead relatively normal adult lives, but as a group these youngsters are likely to show greater impulsive behavior, perhaps more drug use, and perhaps poorer social skills as adults (Hechtman & Weiss, 1983). Poor outcomes are especially likely for children who are both hyperactive and aggressive.

Attempts to figure out the origins of hyperactivity and to design effective treatment have been extensive. I am sorry to say, though, that the results are inconclusive (Achenbach, 1982). Hyperactivity appears *not* to be the result of any general brain damage, since most brain-damaged children are not hyperactive, and most hyperactive children (like learning-disabled children) show no overt signs of brain damage. There *may* be other neurological or physical causes, however, such as neurotransmitter deficiencies or habitually low levels of arousal (which the child overcomes by providing high levels of activity) or even food sensitivities or allergies. No one of these possibilities has been strongly supported by research, however. In particular, the hypothesis that sensitivities to artificial food dyes might be the cause—a proposal advanced with absolute certainty by one physician (Feingold, 1975)—has *not* been supported by controlled experiments (Harley et al., 1978).

Results of treatment studies are equally mixed. By far the most common treatment for hyperactive children is medication with a *stimulant* drug, most often Ritalin. Such medication does reduce the hyperactive behavior, but it does not affect the hyperactive child's typically poor academic performance or improve social relationships of the hyperactive child with her classmates. In addition, not all children respond well to the drug treatment, and there may be undesirable physical side effects, such as insomnia, weight loss, or increased heart rate or blood pressure (Achenbach, 1982; Quay & Werry, 1979). No doubt children who show this behavior will continue to be given medication, if only because it makes them much easier to live with. In the meantime, the long-term task for researchers is to uncover the causes of hyperactivity so that more effective treatments can be found.

*Aggressiveness*  A second behavior problem usually placed in the "moderate" category (and which often occurs along with hyperactivity, especially in boys) is excessive aggressiveness. In DSM-III, this is labeled as a *conduct disorder*. Juvenile delinquency is frequently included in the same category (although there are obviously forms of delinquency that are not aggressive). Children described as aggressive are argumentative, bullying, disobedient, irritable, threatening, and loud. They may throw temper tantrums or physically or verbally attack others (Achenbach & Edelbrock, 1982). Delinquent children go a step further and steal, cheat, swear, or lie.

Children who show these syndromes are not all alike, of course. But as a group, they most often come from homes in which the parents are themselves maladjusted and arbitrary, lax, or inconsistent in their discipline. The parents use a lot of physical punishment with their children, argue more with each other, and lack warmth and affection in dealing with their children (Hetherington & Martin, 1979; Patterson, 1980). In fact, the parents of highly aggressive children are often hostile and rejecting toward their children (a pattern that may well lead to insecure attachments, among other things). Through observation and direct reinforcement, the child has also learned a highly aggressive and violent pattern of relating to others. No one of these family elements alone is strongly associated with aggressiveness or delinquency, but the more of these conditions are present, the greater the likelihood that the child will be aggressive during childhood (McCord, McCord, & Zola, 1959; Patterson, 1980). And the more such antisocial behavior shown in childhood, the greater the chance for delinquent and criminal behavior in adolescence and adulthood (Loeber, 1982; McCord, 1982).

*Anxiety, Withdrawal, Sadness*   A third pattern of disturbed behavior that frequently results in a child's being seen by a psychologist or mental health clinic is some combination of depression, sadness, and anxiety. Such children may complain of being lonely, unloved, and worthless. They may also feel that they are picked on by others and that too much is expected of them. These children are nervous, high-strung, and fearful (Achenbach & Edelbrock, 1978). Sadness or depression is characteristic of perhaps 10 percent of children at least some of the time (Achenbach & Edelbrock, 1981), but it is the pervasive and lasting quality of sadness, anxiety, or depression that would lead a teacher or parent to seek help for a child.

Among elementary-school children, this pattern of feeling and behavior is also associated with suicidal thoughts or comments. Among adolescents, however, threats of suicide are not confined to this depressed group; they occur among groups of teenagers showing a wide variety of behavior problems. Suicide is one of the leading causes of death in late adolescence (about 5000 per year in young people aged 15 to 24), so it is troubling that we know so little of its causes.

There is not a great deal of information about the backgrounds of children who show this particular pattern of problem behavior. But it appears that withdrawn and anxious children tend to have parents who are similarly withdrawn and anxious. Usually at least one of the parents shows a consistently disturbed pattern, and there is generally conflict in the parents' marriage (Hetherington & Martin, 1979). Parents in these families are ordinarily not openly hostile and don't use a great deal of physical punishment, but they are restrictive, controlling, and not very loving.

One interesting exception to this pattern, however, comes from studies of children who have a specific fear of school, called *school phobia.* These children would ordinarily be classed with the withdrawn and anxious types, but their family background is likely to include *over*protection rather than restrictiveness (Waldron et al., 1975).

Some Causes of Mild or Moderate Behavior Problems

To understand the origins of problem behavior in children, we end up turning to familiar biological and environmental explanations. Children may inherit specific tendencies to respond to setbacks with aggression or withdrawal; there may be particular chemical or neurological patterns associated with hyperactivity or even with depression. At the same time, the family environment is clearly formative as well. The quality of the earliest attachment patterns may be particularly critical, along with the warmth and affection expressed to the child throughout the early years and the form and consistency of control methods used by parents.

The child makes a significant contribution, too, so we need a full *transactional* model and not just a simple additive or interactive one to understand the origins of deviant behavior. The child's temperament may be one such transactional element; difficult children receive more punitive upbringing and under adverse family circumstances are more likely to be insecurely attached.

But to understand the causes of behavior problems, we have to explore another category of influences, too: short-term stress.

*The Role of Short-Term Stress*    Many children who show significant behavioral disturbance come from families who look reasonably supportive and loving; other children growing up in what look like nonoptimal families show no disturbance at all.

James Anthony (1970) suggests that in any child, a behavior problem emerges only when there is some accumulation of risks or stresses above the threshold that the child can handle. We know that children experiencing *major* upheavals, such as their parents' divorce, show increased behavior problems—disobedience or depression or anxiety (Wallerstein & Kelly, 1980; Hetherington, Cox, & Cox, 1978). But an *accumulation* of stresses seems to be even worse. Michael Rutter (Rutter et al., 1975), for example, has found that in families in which there was only one stress at a time—such as marital discord or overcrowding or psychiatric disorder in one or both parents or the death of a family member—the children were no more likely to have behavior problems than were children from families with no stresses. But any *two* stresses occurring together enormously increased the possibility that the child would show serious symptoms.

The same pattern shows up in the study of school phobia by Waldron, Shreir, Stone, and Tobin (1975). Mothers of school-phobic children were more protective of their children, but about half of the phobic children had *also* experienced some significant stress in the family in the year just before the school phobia began.

The particular symptom the child shows in the face of too much stress—phobia, depression, aggression, or whatever—may be determined by the pattern of early attachment and later discipline. But the presence of any symptom may also reflect the presence of an excess of stress, as Anthony suggests. When the level of stress goes down, the child's symptoms often disappear.

I find the concept of stress to be a very helpful way to look at behavior problems in children. Anthony has shown that problems are especially likely at particular times in children's lives when stress is more likely to accumulate, such as during early elementary school (peaking at about age 9) and at adolescence (with a peak at about age 14). The concept of short-term stress can thus help us understand the ebb and flow of behavior problems that we see in children over time. It also helps to explain why behavior problems often go away without any special intervention—the stress has been eliminated, or the child has developed other methods of dealing with new circumstances.

Finally, the concept of stress raises the very interesting issue of differences in children's vulnerability. Why do some children show symptoms in the face of only a few stresses, while others can handle a much greater load? I've discussed this issue in Box 14.1.

## Severe Emotional Disturbance

Probably the majority of children show some form of behavior problem at one time or another. A far smaller number—perhaps 1 in every 1000 children (Achenbach, 1982)—shows really severe disturbance. In DSM-III these are called *pervasive developmental disorders*; such children show disturbance in virtually every aspect of their functioning—in their relationships, their thinking, even their language.

Clinicians who work with such severely disturbed children agree that there are several types of problems, but there is not yet perfect agreement on the labels that should be applied to the subgroups or even the characteristics of some of them. Three types seem most common: **autism, childhood-onset pervasive developmental disorder**, and childhood **schizophrenia**. I've listed some of the defining characteristics of each disorder in Table 14.4, but the really critical difference is in *when* the problem emerges. Autistic children show significant peculiarities or disorders from earliest infancy; schizophrenia, on the other hand, normally appears much later (most often in adolescence) and thus represents a *loss* of function. Severe disturbances that begin after infancy but before adolescence are nowadays put into the diagnostic grab bag of "childhood-onset pervasive developmental disorder." Let me say just a few further words about the two best-defined of these syndromes, autism and schizophrenia.

*Autism*  Autistic children are generally unresponsive to the people around them, do not cuddle or respond to affection as do normal infants, do not make eye contact regularly, and show significant retarda-

BOX 14.1

# VULNERABLE AND INVULNERABLE CHILDREN

Throughout the book, when I've talked about the impact of the environment on a child, I've generally talked as though the effect were equal for all children. But that is clearly not the case. Some children raised in the most punitive, rejecting, unstimulating homes turn out to be successful and distinguished adults; some children who face far fewer difficulties develop chronic emotional problems, delinquency, or other life problems. Why?

As I pointed out in Chapter 1, psychologists have only recently begun to ask about "invulnerable" children, so we have few answers. But there are bits and pieces I can pass on to you.

First, males seem to be more vulnerable to stresses than females are—a point I'll be coming back to later in the chapter.

Second, the child's temperament seems to make a difference. The "difficult" child is much more likely to show emotional problems during the preschool period than is the "easy" child. This could reflect an inborn vulnerability of the difficult child or an inborn invulnerability of the easy child. Or it could reflect differences in the patterns of interaction that develop between the child and the parent. The difficult child is more likely to be criticized by his parents, as one example (Rutter, 1979). So the developing transactions between a parent and child may simply aggravate an already existing tendency in the difficult child to react strongly to stress or to change.

Most important, the *in*vulnerable child—the child who seems later to be able to cope with life's stresses without lapsing into serious behavior problems—seems to have one important thing going for him. He nearly always has at least one good, strong, secure relationship with a parent or with another adult (Rutter, 1971, 1978a). The existence of this early secure attachment seems to "buffer" the child against the later slings and arrows of normal life.

I mentioned in earlier chapters that children with secure attachments have more successful peer relationships and better approaches to solving problems during the preschool years. Now we have another piece of the puzzle: Children with secure early attachments seem better able to cope with such life stresses as their parents' divorce or a death in the family.

Let me be careful here not to make the mistake of placing too much emphasis on the first attachment. Important as it seems to be, a child *can* recover from a highly stressed early relationship if the family situation improves. Note, however, that "improvement" in the family situation almost by definition means that the child now has some one person—a stepparent, a grandparent, an older sibling—with whom he can form a strong, supportive relationship. The fundamental point seems to be that for a child to be able to handle temporary stresses without showing serious behavior problems, he must have *some* close attachment. But it need not be the *first* attachment of infancy.

tion of language. Some do not develop language at all; others develop vocabularies and may even use two-word sentences, but they do not adapt their language to the person they are talking to and may develop their own words for common objects. They also typically show resistance to new events or to any changes in their environment and often show ritualistic or repetitive behavior (twirling, finger movements, or

Table 14.4

**Some of the symptoms of autism, childhood-onset pervasive developmental disorder, and childhood schizophrenia**

| | |
|---|---|
| Autism | Onset before 30 months of age. Pervasive lack of responsiveness to other people; gross deficits in language development, including excessive echolalia or other peculiar speech patterns. Resistance to change in the environment or schedule. Peculiar attachments to animate or inanimate objects. |
| Childhood-onset pervasive developmental disorder | Onset after 30 months and before 12 years. Sustained impairment in social relations, which might include inappropriate clinging or lack of appropriate emotional expression or asocial behavior. Any three of the following: sudden bursts of anxiety; extreme mood swings or inappropriate emotions; resistance to change in the environment; oddities in motor movement or posturing; abnormalities of speech, particularly intonation (such as monotonous voice); hypersensitivity to sensory stimuli; self-multilation. |
| Childhood schizophrenia | Deterioration from previous level of adequate or near-adequate functioning. Delusions, hallucinations, or disturbances in the form of thought. Disturbance in social relationships. Any of several specific symptoms, depending on the subtype of schizophrenia involved. |

*Source:* Adapted from American Psychiatric Association, 1980, pp. 89–91; Achenbach, 1982.

the like). All of these symptoms are typically present from the earliest months of life.

We are still a long way from understanding this pattern of deviance, but all the evidence I have read points to one clear conclusion: children are *born* with this disorder. It is not caused by poor parenting. Understandably, parents rearing autistic children may *become* less responsive or affectionate with the child, but there is simply no indication that parents are causing this problem by inadequate or unloving child rearing.

Instead, it seems most likely that these children are born with some basic cognitive deficit (Rutter, 1978b, 1983b). Another possibility is that they are in a chronic state of high physiological arousal in which every sound, every sight is overpoweringly strong (Hutt & Hutt, 1970). The cognitive-deficit hypothesis, proposed most strongly by Michael Rutter, seems to be gaining the most adherents.

Essentially Rutter argues that the autistic child suffers from some form of brain dysfunction that makes it difficult for him to make sense out of strings of sounds. Try to imagine what that would be like. So much of what happens around you, so much of what you understand about the world you live in, depends on sounds. What if the sounds just didn't make sense? If that were true, you might withdraw from people (who make confusing sounds), and you might find yourself arranging your time in very rigid ways so that you could create order out of chaos.

Language deficit or disorder does not explain all the symptoms autistic children show. But it fits with the fact that the best single predictor of an autistic child's long-term adjustment is whether he has developed useful speech by age 5. Autistic children who do not achieve useful

**Figure 14.2** This autistic child, who makes little eye contact and shows few signs of friendliness or involvement with others, is being treated in an operant conditioning program. Every time he shows one of the desired behaviors, he is quickly reinforced with some food he likes.

speech are likely to remain highly deviant throughout life (Rutter, 1978b).

*Childhood Schizophrenia* The definition of childhood schizophrenia is far looser. Some clinicians use this label to cover only adolescent-onset disturbances that include hallucinations or delusions; others use the schizophrenic label to cover virtually all severe emotional disturbances in children that develop after infancy. Because of this confusion about definitions, the research results are hard to add up. Different investigators may be studying very different types of children, even though they are called by the same name.

Nonetheless, some reasonable conclusions are possible. First, unlike autism, in the case of schizophrenia (or of childhood-onset pervasive developmental disorders), both specific heredity and family interaction patterns are implicated as causes. Children born to schizophrenic parents are much more likely to become schizophrenic themselves than are those born to nonschizophrenic parents, even if they are adopted and thus reared by adequate parents (Rosenthal et al., 1971). Furthermore, children reared by parents with schizophrenia or other severe emotional disorders are likely to develop one or another form of deviant behavior, including schizophrenia (Sameroff, Seifer, & Zax, 1983).

Arnold Sameroff (Sameroff, Seifer, & Zax, 1983) argues that a transactional process is set up: A child with some form of vulnerability (genetic or constitutional) is born into a family with disturbed or inadequate parents. In the process of mutual adaptation, in some families both the child and the parent develop symptoms or deviancies. Schizophrenia in the child is thus seen as an *adaptation* by the child to the family, given the inborn capacities or tendencies of the child. Not every child of schizophrenic parents will thus end up disturbed; similarly, reasonably effective parents may have a seriously disturbed child if the adaptation pattern goes awry.

## PHYSICALLY ATYPICAL DEVELOPMENT

If you look back to Table 14.2, you'll see that children with major physical problems —such as blindness, deafness, or significant motor dysfunction—are relatively rare, especially in comparison to the frequency of other types of problems. Although the numbers may be small, the degree of difficulty encountered by the physically atypical child may be very great indeed. Most of the children I'll be talking about here require special schooling or special facilities in school; many require continued assistance throughout life. Still, with improved instruction, intervention, and mechanical assistance, many children with significant physical handicaps are leading full and satisfying lives.

### The Deaf and Hearing-Impaired

Most children with hearing loss can function adequately with the assistance of a hearing aid. In fact, many physicians are now fitting **hearing-impaired** children (the phrase that is now used in place of *hard of hearing*) with hearing aids during infancy rather than waiting until the child is of preschool age. The situation is quite different, though, for the profoundly deaf—the child whose hearing loss is so severe that even with assistance his comprehension of sound, especially language, is significantly reduced. I raised some of the issues connected with the early rearing of deaf children in Box 8.2, and you may want to go back and reread that section at this stage. The basic point is that if the emphasis is placed exclusively on *oral* language, the deaf child has very great difficulty developing either speech or reading. But if the child is taught sign language *and* lip reading at the same time, the maximum benefit can be derived. Some such children can function in a normal school environment, but even with good early training, most deaf children require special schooling.

### The Blind Child

If I had asked you, before you read this chapter, to tell me which would be worse, to have been blind or deaf from birth, most of you would have said it would be far worse to be blind. Yet from the point of view of the child's ability to function in most normal settings, including school,

**Figure 14.3** These deaf children are being taught sign language. Research on the deaf shows that children who learn to sign as well as to lip-read and speak (as much as possible) when they are very young have the best prognosis.

blindness is a smaller handicap. The blind child can learn to read (with Braille), can talk with others, can listen to a teacher, and so on. Because of this greater academic potential, and because of the enormous role of language in forming and maintaining social relationships, there are more options open to the blind adult than to most deaf adults.

Still, there are obviously important limitations for the blind and important potential pitfalls. One of these lies in the earliest relationship with the parent, which I've discussed in Box 14.2. Later relationships may be impaired for the same reasons.

What does seem to be critical, for both the deaf and the blind child, is early intervention with the family as well as with the child. In Sameroff's terms, the transactional process between parent and child needs attention. The child can't be "cured," but many of the potential emotional and intellectual problems can be softened if there is early treatment.

## Other Physical Problems

Among the most heart-wrenching youngsters are those with multiple handicaps or with physical disabilities so severe that they are unable to communicate, move, or play. Some severely afflicted cerebral palsied youngsters, for example, are unable to move without assistance, cannot speak comprehensibly, and may be retarded as well. They require full-time care for their entire lives. Still, they *can* learn and love. Among the health care professionals dealing with severely or multiply handicapped children, the move today is toward very early intervention. The family is ordinarily involved from the beginning, not only learning how to care for and stimulate the child but also getting help in developing their own attachment to the child.

BOX 14.2

# BASIC ATTACHMENTS BETWEEN BLIND BABIES AND THEIR MOTHERS

In Chapter 11, I mentioned Selma Fraiberg's work with blind infants as part of the discussion of the parent's attachment to the child. Because Fraiberg's work is so fascinating, I want to expand on that brief discussion here.

Fraiberg (1974, 1975, 1977) found that blind babies begin to smile at about the same age as sighted babies (approximately 4 weeks) but that they smile less often. And at about 2 months, when the sighted baby begins to smile regularly at the sight of the parent's face, the blind baby's smiles become less and less frequent. The blind infant's smile is also less intense, more fleeting.

The other thing blind babies don't do is enter into mutual gaze. They don't look right at their parents, and everything we know about parents' responses to their babies underlines the importance of mutual gaze for the parents' feeling of attachment to the baby. When the blind baby does not look, the parents often report feeling "rejected."

Generally, the facial expressions of the blind infant are muted and sober. Many observers, including parents, conclude that the baby is depressed or indifferent.

Fraiberg found that most of the mothers of the blind babies in her studies gradually withdrew from their infants. They provided the needed physical care, but they stopped playing with the baby and gave up trying to elicit smiles or other social interactions. They often said they didn't "love" this baby.

Fortunately, it's possible to solve this particular problem. Fraiberg found that these mothers could be helped to form a strong bond with their infant if they could be shown how to "read" the baby's other signals. The blind child's face may be sober and relatively expressionless, but her hands and body move a lot and express a great deal. When the child *stops* moving when you come into the room, this means she is listening to your footsteps. Or she may move her hands when she hears your voice rather than smiling as a sighted child would do.

When parents of blind children learn to respond to these alternative "attachment behaviors" in their babies, then the mutuality of the relationship can be reestablished. And when this happens, and the parents are able to provide more varied stimulation, blind children develop more normal behavior in other ways. In particular, they don't show the "blindisms" so often observed in blind youngsters, such as rocking, sucking, head banging, and other repetitive actions.

Children with chronic diseases, such as muscular dystrophy or cystic fibrosis, may also have significant physical problems. The child with muscular dystrophy steadily loses his ability to control his muscles, becoming more and more handicapped over time. The child with cystic fibrosis requires constant medical monitoring and usually becomes progressively worse through the first two decades of life. In every instance, early diagnosis and treatment are critical—not because the disease can be eliminated but because such early intervention may prolong the child's life or the period of comfort. Early diagnosis and treatment may also help the family to come to terms with the conditions and limitations of the disease.

## SEX DIFFERENCES IN ATYPICAL DEVELOPMENT

One of the most fascinating facts about atypical development is that virtually all forms of disorder are more common in boys than in girls. I've put some of the comparisons in Table 14.5.

How are we to explain differences like this? One possibility is that the female, as I mentioned in Box 14.1, is somehow naturally "buffered" against environmental stresses. Girls are less likely to inherit any recessive disease that is carried on the sex chromosomes. Perhaps the double X chromosome provides some general kind of added protection that the boy does not have.

Hormonal differences may also play a role. For example, excess aggression may have a hormonal basis (see Chapter 11). Sex differences in other areas might result from greater demands being placed on boys, thus creating greater stress for them to deal with.

Whatever the explanation—and none of the existing explanations seems very satisfactory to me—it is nonetheless extremely interesting that girls do seem to be less vulnerable.

## THE IMPACT OF AN ATYPICAL CHILD ON THE FAMILY

Throughout this chapter I have touched on the impact of the child's problem on the family. Of course, in some instances (such as cultural-familial retardation or some kinds of emotional disturbance), deficiencies or inadequacies in the family are part of the *cause* of the child's atypical development. But whether the cause lies (partly or

Table 14.5

**Sex differences in the incidence of atypical development**

| Type of Problem | Approximate Ratio of Males to Females |
|---|---|
| School problems: children testing below grade level in basic subjects (includes children with learning disabilities) | 3 to 2 |
| Physical handicaps | |
| Visual problems | 1 to 1 |
| Hearing problems | 5 to 4 |
| Speech defects | 3 to 2 |
| Emotional problems | |
| Hyperactivity (widely varying estimates) | 3 to 1 |
| Hyperaggressiveness and its equivalent | 5 to 1 |
| Anxiety-withdrawal | 2 or 3 to 1 |
| Severe emotional disorders (autism and others) | 3 to 1 |
| Estimated number of all children with all diagnoses seen in psychiatric clinics | 2 to 1 |

*Sources: Profiles of Children,* 1970; Anthony, 1970; Eme, 1979; Achenbach, 1982.

wholly) in the family or not, once a child does show some form of deviant development, the family is inevitably affected, usually adversely. Even parents of gifted children face remarkably complex problems, as they try to keep up with their child's rapid development and try to find appropriate or even adequate schooling. (Imagine being Michael's parents, for example. Whew!) Most of what I want to focus on here, though, is what happens in a family with a mentally or physically handicapped child.

*Grief* When parents first realize that their child is not normal—whether that realization comes at birth or much later—the natural reaction is a form of grief, almost as if the child had died. (In fact, of course, the fantasy "perfect child" did die or was never born. The parents grieve for the child-that-never-will-be.) As with other forms of grief, denial, depression, and anger are all natural elements. For many parents, there is also some guilt (e.g., "If only I hadn't been drinking while I was pregnant").

In some cases, this process may result in an emotional rejection of the infant, aggravated by the fact that for the atypical infant, it is difficult (or totally impossible) to enter fully into the mutually adaptive process, such as the blind infants I described in Box 14.2. Such rejection seems to be particularly common when the marital relationship is conflicted or when the family lacks adequate social support (Howard, 1978).

*Adaptation by the Family* Once the initial shock and grief are dealt with (to the extent that they can be), the family must work toward an ongoing adaptive system with the atypical child. There are often massive financial burdens; there are problems of finding appropriate schooling (both problems shared by parents of gifted children as well); there are endless daily adjustments to the child's special needs.

There is a very great price to be paid by many parents for this adaptation. Parents of retarded or atypical children are more likely to be chronically depressed, to have lower self-esteem, and to have lower feelings of personal competence (Howard, 1978). Where the marital relationship was poor before the birth of the child, the presence of the handicapped child in the family system seems to increase the likelihood of further discord. However, there is no consistent indication that having an atypical child invariably results in marital disharmony or increased risk of divorce (Howard, 1978; Korn, Chess, & Fernandez, 1978).

The fact that many (even most) parents manage to adapt effectively to the presence of an atypical child is testimony to the devotion and immense effort expended. But there is no evading the fact that rearing such a child is very hard work and that it strains the family system in ways that rearing a normal child does not.

## INTERVENTIONS AND TREATMENTS

For many parents of atypical children, one of the keys to their own ability to adapt effectively is the availability of support from outside the family, in the form of special treatment or intervention programs, parent groups, or institutions to care for the child. Let me touch on just a few of the options.

### Treatment for the Child, Training for the Parents

Probably the most common intervention is some kind of individual therapy or training for the child. Heber's special intervention for potentially retarded children is an example of this. Physical therapy for children with physical handicaps, special Braille training for the blind, and the equivalent are also direct interventions with the child.

In recent years, however, the most common form of intervention has included parents much more fully, either by having them participate in the special program or by training them to deliver the service to the child (Wiegerink et al., 1980; Hanson, 1981). Parents of children with behavior problems may be helped to examine the pattern of their discipline with their children; parents of physically handicapped children may be taught how to stimulate and play with their children; parents of children with learning problems may be taught specific games or projects to undertake at home that are actually part of the children's treatment; parents with low education or living in poverty, whose children are at higher risk for retardation, may be given special training in methods for stimulating their children.

For example, Marci Hanson (1981) has described a special stimulation program for Down's syndrome infants beginning when the infants were a few months old. The parents were taught special stimulation procedures and then implemented them with their own infants at home. Staff members visited the families regularly (weekly or biweekly), and together the parent and staff member planned the program for the next period. Children who had received this treatment showed far less decline in developmental rate than is typical of untreated Down's infants (although their rate was still less than normal).

In general, programs that involve both direct service to the child and participation and training of the parents seem to be particularly effective, although there is not a lot of really good research supporting this conclusion. I suspect that some parents are much less ready, willing, or able than others to undertake major home-based training programs with their handicapped child. Interventions that focus on the parents may thus be useful or effective with only a portion of parents. Still, the shift toward inclusion of parents in intervention plans seems to me to be a very good change.

## Interventions in the Public Schools: Mainstreaming versus Special Classes

Despite newer intervention programs for infants and toddlers, a large portion of the task of responding to the needs of atypical children falls on the public school system. The Federal Education for All Handicapped Children Act (Public Law 94-142), passed in 1975, requires that each state have programs for all school-age and preschool handicapped children. Further, it requires that, wherever possible, the handicapped child be **mainstreamed**—a word that many of you may have heard bandied about.

Mainstreaming does *not* mean that every atypical child must be taught full-time in a regular classroom. It does mean that children must be placed in the "least restrictive environment" consistent with their disability. This has meant that many children who had previously been taught in special, segregated classes are now spending part or all of their school hours in a regular classroom. Educable mentally retarded children, in most instances, are being assigned full-time to regular classes; children with physical handicaps, such as blindness, or those with learning problems are spending part of each day in a regular classroom and part with a special education teacher or in a special classroom.

The alternative to mainstreaming is some sort of special class (see Figure 14.4)—a system that dominated school treatment of the atypical child until recently.

**Figure 14.4** This is a good example of a special class for retarded children carried out within a public school. The class is very small, so there is a great deal of individual instruction. With "mainstreaming" becoming a dominant theme in education for the handicapped, these special classes will become less common but will still exist (all day or part of a day) for those children with severe handicaps or significant retardation.

It would be splendid if I could tell you which of these two alternatives is best for atypical children, but I cannot—at least not with any confidence. There is a great scarcity of decent research (in which children have been assigned randomly to regular or special classes, for example). The evidence we do have does not show a big advantage to regular classroom placement. Borderline retarded children (IQs of 80 or so) seem to do somewhat better academically in regular classrooms (Budoff & Gottlieb, 1976), but retarded children with lower IQs may do better in special classes. This may only be true, though, if the special classes are clearly organized, with maximum expectations for the children's development.

Socially, handicapped children also do not do better in regular classrooms. There was some hope in the beginning that exposure to handicapped children would reduce some of the prejudice against them on the part of "able-bodied" children, but there is little evidence that this has happened (Vandell et al., 1982).

As Edward Zigler has cogently pointed out (Zigler & Muenchow, 1979), whether mainstreaming will ultimately be found to benefit children will depend very heavily on whether regular classroom teachers are adequately trained and given adequate support. "Without adequate support personnel to assist regular-class teachers with the education of handicapped (particularly EMR) [educable mentally retarded] students, mainstreaming is doomed to fail" (p. 994).

What Public Law 94-142 *has* done is to put a significant legal tool in the hands of parents. They are now in a far better position to insist on information and on treatment for their children than they were. But the new law has not magically solved the problem of educating atypical children.

## Residential Treatment

A third type of treatment, recommended primarily for those children with such severe handicaps that they cannot readily be cared for at home, is some form of institutional or residential care. With the increasing emphasis on involvement of parents in the treatment of atypical children, the number of children in institutional care has declined. Still, some children can't be handled at home or in the school, so there remains a need for residential facilities. The most common are institutions for profoundly retarded children and adults. Many children in such institutions also have physical handicaps.

Children with severe emotional problems, such as some autistic or schizophrenic children, are also cared for in institutions. In most cases, the expressed aim of the care is to provide therapy of some kind for the child so that he can be returned to his family. Regrettably, the success of these efforts for the severely disturbed child is not outstanding. Many excellent programs have succeeded in modifying children's behavior sufficiently so that they can live at home, but the beneficial changes often don't last outside the supportive environment of the residential community (Quay, 1979).

## A FINAL POINT

I want to end this chapter, as I began it, by stating strongly that the development of the "atypical" child is really much more like "typical" development than it is unlike it. It is very easy, when dealing with an atypical child, to be overwhelmed by the sense of differentness. But the sameness is there, underneath.

## SUMMARY

1. Approximately 15 to 20 percent of all children will need some form of special assistance because of atypical development.
2. The most common problems are reading difficulties and short-term behavior problems.
3. Children with mental retardation, normally defined as IQ below 70 and significant problems of adaptation, represent approximately 2.5 percent of the population.
4. Retarded children also show slower development and more immature forms of information-processing strategies.
5. The two basic categories of causes of mental retardation are physical problems, such as genetic anomalies or brain damage, and cultural-familial problems. Children with cultural-familial retardation ordinarily come from families in which the parents have low IQs and provide little stimulation for the child.
6. Interventions with cultural-familial retarded children have been successful in raising the children's IQ to the normal range, which demonstrates the important role of the environment in some forms of retardation.
7. Children with specific learning disabilities make up about 1 percent of the school population. Most display their difficulty in some aspect of reading. The problem *may* be caused by undetected minimal brain damage, uneven or slow brain development, or other kinds of physical dysfunction.
8. Emotional problems of children can be divided into two groups, according to the severity or persistence of the problem. Mild or moderate problems include hyperactivity, excessive aggression, anxiety, or depression. These may have genetic or biological origins but are also more common in certain types of families or following stress.
9. Serious emotional problems, including autism and childhood schizophrenia, are much scarcer. Autism develops in the early months of life and includes problems in relating to others and with

language. Schizophrenia develops later and includes immature or bizarre behavior and delusions or hallucinations.

10. The best prognosis for the deaf child occurs when identification is made early, hearing aids are used where possible, and the child is taught signing and lip reading from the earliest years of life. Special schooling is usually required.

11. Blind children, in contrast, can often function in regular school classrooms but may have difficulty with personal relationships because of lack of typical attachment behaviors (e.g., eye contact).

12. Boys show almost all forms of atypical development more often than girls do. This may reflect genetic differences, hormone differences, or differences in cultural expectations.

13. Families with atypical children experience chronically heightened stress and demands for adaptation. This is frequently accompanied by depression or other disturbance in the parents.

14. Interventions with atypical children increasingly involve the parents as well as the child.

15. "Mainstreaming" of atypical children into regular school classrooms wherever possible is now legally mandated. The verdict is still out on the effects of the practice.

16. It is important to remember that the development of atypical children is basically the same as for normal children in many respects.

## KEY TERMS

**Adaptive behavior**  An aspect of a child's functioning often considered in diagnosing mental retardation. Can the child adapt to the tasks of everyday life?

**Autism**  A severe form of emotional/language disorder, appearing in infancy.

**Behavior problem**  The general phrase used to describe mild or moderate forms of emotional difficulty, including aggressiveness, shyness, anxiety, and hyperactivity.

**Brain damage**  Some insult to the brain, either during prenatal development or later, that results in improper functioning of the brain.

**Childhood-onset pervasive developmental disorder**  Term used in DSM-III to describe a pattern of severe emotional disturbance that begins after infancy (and is thus not autism) but does not include the delusions common in schizophrenia.

**DSM-III**  The third edition of the *Diagnostic and Statistical Manual of Mental Disorders* of the American Psychiatric Association,

listing the currently agreed categories of emotional disturbance.

**Dysgraphia**  A form of specific learning disability in which the individual has difficulty with writing.

**Dyslexia**  A form of specific learning disability in which the individual has difficulty with reading.

**Giftedness**  Normally defined in terms of very high IQ (above 135 to 150) but may also be defined in terms of remarkable skill in one or more specific areas, such as mathematics or memory.

**Hearing-impaired**  The phrase currently used in place of "hard of hearing" to describe children or adults with significant hearing loss.

**Hyperactivity**  A pattern of behavior characterized by overactivity, restlessness, distractibility, and short attention span.

**Inborn errors of metabolism**  Any one of several inherited disorders (including PKU) resulting in a lack of certain enzymes needed to digest or metabolize particular foods. Some such disorders are associated with retardation if not treated.

**Mainstreaming**  The word used to describe the placement of atypical children in regular school classrooms whenever possible.

**Mental retardation**  The label used for a pattern of functioning including low IQ, poor adaptive behavior, and poor information-processing skill.

**Schizophrenia**  A severe form of emotional disturbance seen in adults and in some adolescents. The term *childhood schizophrenia* is also sometimes used to describe children with childhood-onset pervasive developmental disorder.

**Specific learning disability (SLD)**  A disorder in understanding or processing language or symbols. Most often shown in reading problems.

## SUGGESTED READINGS

Edgerton, R. B. *Mental retardation.* Cambridge, Mass.: Harvard University Press, 1979.
This is an excellent, brief, readable introduction to the whole topic.

Farnham-Diggory, S. *Learning disabilities.* Cambridge, Mass.: Harvard University Press, 1978.
Another excellent, brief introductory discussion from the same series as the Edgerton book.

Gallagher, J. J. *Teaching the gifted child.* Boston: Allyn & Bacon, 1975.
For those of you who are prospective teachers, this would be an excellent introduction to the topic of giftedness and how to handle gifted children in the school.

Goleman, D. 1,528 little geniuses and how they grew. *Psychology today,* 1980, *13,* 28–43.
A brief and fascinating description of some of the findings from the latest interviews with the gifted individuals first studied by Terman in the 1930s.

Meisels, S. J., & Anastasiow, N. J. The risks of prediction: Relationships between etiology, handicapping conditions, and developmental outcomes. In S. G. Moore & C. R. Cooper (Eds.). *The young child: Reviews of research* (Vol 3). Washington, D.C.: National Association for the Education of Young Children, 1982.
An excellent (and very understandable) discussion of several different theories of the causes or origins of atypical development.

Rutter, M. *Helping troubled children.* New York: Plenum, 1975.
This is not a new book, but I like Michael Rutter's style so much that I recommend it anyway. It is an excellent introduction to the full range of emotional problems in children and their treatment.

# 15.
# *putting it all together: the developing child*

Ann is $2\frac{1}{2}$. She is talking a blue streak now, putting three, four, or even more words together into sentences. Sometimes it seems to her mother that every third sentence has "no" in it: "No milk!" "No more shoes today." "Daddy no coming." She is getting into everything, trying out the knobs on the stove, playing in the toilet bowl, emptying her clothes or the silverware out of drawers. And when her mother tells her no or limits her, Ann is likely to cry or scream—something she didn't do even a few months ago. But Ann is also beginning to share her toys with the little girl next door when they play together, so it is not all negative. They are beginning to show a few signs of "make-believe" play, too, which is also new.

Just recently, Ann started to go to nursery school in the mornings because her mother has gone back to work half-time. Ann now seems more interested in other children, but she is also having trouble eating, which hasn't happened for quite a while. You really have to coax her to get any food into her at all these days. And she wakes up more at night. It is a time of great change, fascinating to watch but frustrating at times to live with.

David is 14, and his body is just beginning to show big changes. There's a little fuzz on his upper lip; he has grown out of all his pants; and his face and jaw are beginning to change, too. The morning shower has also now become a lengthy and intensely private affair! David has just started high school. He's taking a science course and a course in algebra, and he complains a little that they are both very hard. He isn't used to having to do experiments. When he's not in school, he and his group of friends play a bit of pick-up basketball in the gym or "hang out" at one another's houses. David isn't really dating yet, but there's a group of girls who are friends, and the two groups of youngsters go to dances together and sometimes sit together at lunch.

David isn't getting along with his parents quite as well these days as he used to. It seems to him that they nag him a lot about getting home on time and they're too strict about where he goes with his friends. They are also beginning to pressure him (so he thinks) about getting good grades, now that he's in high school. "If you want to go to college, you have to think about what classes you're taking and about working hard." David knows he is going to have to face all that, but he doesn't feel ready yet. In fact, he's a little depressed about the whole thing. High school is harder than he thought it would be. And he's really interested in a girl in the crowd he hangs around with, but he's still too scared to ask her out. Sometimes when it all gets to be too much, he yells at his mother and then spends a few hours in his room with the door locked and the music turned up as loud as he dares.

For David's parents, this is all a little bewildering. Two years ago, the whole family seemed to get along fine. Now they never know what will set David off. He is alternately affectionate and withdrawn. But they're trying to be supportive and realize that "this, too, shall pass."

Both of these children are imaginary, but I think any parent who has had a child go through one of these periods will recognize the description. (I trust my own children will forgive me for borrowing a bit from them, too!) Each of these two vignettes is also intended to raise some points about development that I think are vital but that I haven't been able to emphasize as much as I'd like in the rest of the book.

## SOME BASIC POINTS

### The Interlocking Nature of Development

First, all the different threads of development occur together in a complex weave. I've talked about language, perception, thinking, physical changes, and social development separately in order to give you some sense of the full sweep of changes over time in each "thread" of development. But in the real world, all of these changes happen together and interact with each other in intricate ways. I have tied some of these threads together as I have gone along, but I need to integrate things for you a bit more systematically here.

### Transitions and Consolidations

A second point I hope Ann and David illustrate is that I think development proceeds in a series of phases, with alternating periods of rapid growth accompanied by disruption or disequilibrium, followed by times of relative calm or consolidation. Actually, change is going on all the time, from birth through adolescence (and through adulthood and aging, too). But I am persuaded that there are particular times when the changes pile up, when the child develops a whole range of new skills at once or there are new demands placed on her, such as school or when her body changes rapidly. These "pileups" of change often seem to result in the child's coming "unglued" for a while. The old patterns of relationships, of thinking, and of talking don't work very well anymore; but it takes a while to work out the new patterns. And during the transition, the child may show temporary behavior problems or even lose some skills that she had had before.

*Crisis* is really too strong a word for what happens at these transition points. Erikson sometimes uses the word *crisis*; more often he uses the term *dilemma*. Klaus Riegel (1975) once suggested the lovely phrase *developmental leaps*, which conveys quite nicely the sense of excitement and blooming opportunity that often accompanies these pivotal periods. I'm going to use the more pedestrian term *transition* because it sounds less negative than crisis and less cumbersome than developmental leaps.

After each of these transitions has been weathered, the child settles into a more stable, steady change period that I have come to call *consolidation*. The child is putting together all the new skills, demands, and roles and gradually developing a new equilibrium. The whole period of childhood (and adulthood, for that matter) can thus be seen as a series of alternating transitions and consolidations.

## Development as a System

Even these two basic principles, though, are not enough to understand any child's development. I now think that at least one more ingredient is necessary—namely, an understanding of the *system* in which the child grows. One of the key forces, of course, is the child's own inner "push" along a developmental path, almost like a train with a powerful engine moving along a track. Children grow up willy-nilly. They get bigger, they walk, they talk, they figure out that objects are permanent, that they can be grouped in classes, that relationships are reciprocal. They go through puberty, they become adults. Obviously, some children get "derailed," either by grossly unhelpful environments (like Genie, whom I described in Chapter 8) or by some inborn deficiency or disability. But most children follow a remarkably similar path. Part of that similarity is produced by maturational change; a very large part results from the child's own drive to explore, manipulate, and understand.

This developmental progression is also occurring within an environment—a family, a culture. Parents bring their own particular personalities, particular skills, particular assumptions to the task of child rearing. They create stimulating or less-stimulating environments for the child; they provide consistent or inconsistent control; they are loving or indifferent. And these family qualities have an important impact on the speed with which the train moves along the track. The family may even affect the particular track on which the child's development takes place.

So far, this is pretty straightforward stuff. I haven't said anything very startling. But I am more and more persuaded that development is not just some sort of sum of the child's own maturational or developmental sequences and the richness or adequacy of the family environment. We also have to think about the ways in which the child influences the family and the way the parents' own development or life experiences affect how the family operates.

A 2-year-old like Ann makes quite different demands on parents than does an 8-month-old. All of a sudden, the issue of control moves to center stage. Some parents who may have been perfectly splendid with their infant—loving, caring, responsive—now find themselves having a darn hard time coping with 2-year-oldness. The family equation—the family *system*—changes, not only because the child has changed but because the *match* between the parents' qualities or strengths and the child's needs has changed.

Similarly, parents do not stop changing when they become parents. They go to school, become good at a new job, perhaps face the death of a grandparent or parent, and so on. In a word, many adults grow. Inevitably, such changes in parents alter the developmental system for the child, too. And of course, *having* a child forces the parent to learn, to adapt, and that, too, changes the system.

This way of looking at the child's development is new, and there is little or no research that connects up all these parts of the system. Some of what I will say in this chapter is thus speculation. But I think it is critical to begin to talk about the full context, the full family system, when we talk about a child's development. It is not enough to say that the child is developing *in* a family. The child's development is *part* of the family.

## Four Broad Periods

In the rest of this chapter I want to explore the interlocking threads of development, the family environment, and the complex system of development in four broad periods: infancy, the preschool years, the early school years, and adolescence. The division into these particular "stages" is partially arbitrary; I can think of other divisions that would be reasonable. But these four periods correspond to stages described in several theories, and there do seem to be important transition points in between them.

# INFANCY

## Patterns of Development

Let me begin my attempt at an integrated look at development by exploring the links between the developmental paths I have traced in each chapter. In Figure 15.1, I have laid out some of the key events by age. The chapters of this book have corresponded to the rows of this figure; now we need to think about the columns, or about chains of influences across rows. I have suggested some of the *possible* linkages with arrows, although you should realize that most of these linkages have not been studied directly.

One of the early arrows is between the set of changes in the brain that seems to take place at about 6 to 8 weeks of age and the baby's ability to tell his mother from other people just by looking at her. The chain may go something like this: At birth, many of the baby's actions are governed by quite primitive parts of the brain. But at around 2 months of age, cortical functioning seems to "switch on" more com-

*impulses*

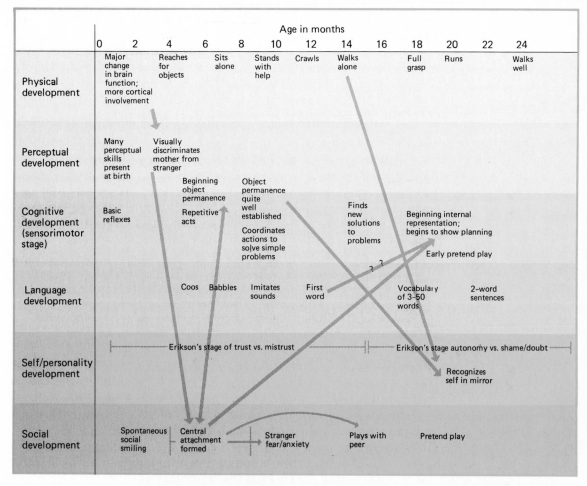

**Figure 15.1** A brief summary chart showing some of the links between parallel sequences or "lines" of development during the first two years of life.

pletely, particularly in vision. It is at this point that the baby begins to look at the insides of figures rather than just their edges; he switches from identifying *where* things are to trying to figure out *what* things are. Now, instead of looking at the edges of people's faces, he looks at the features and within a month can tell mom's (or maybe dad's) face from the face of a stranger.

If you look again at the figure, you'll now see another arrow from "discriminates mom from other faces" to "forms central attachment." We see the first signs of the child's attachment at 3 to 4 months, just as or just after the child is first making the visual discrimination. And then within a month or two, the child has a full-blown central attachment. I am not saying that the visual discrimination *causes* the attachment (after all, blind infants become attached, too). I am saying that these events are linked for most children.

Another arrow points from "beginning object permanence" toward the child's first attachment. Even if a child can tell the difference between mom's face and a stranger's face, it is probably also necessary for her to have at least some beginning grasp of object permanence for real attachment to occur. That is, the child must begin to realize that mom is a permanent person and continues to exist even when out of sight.

Another arrow, suggested by Sibylle Escalona (1981), connects walking and the child's emerging concept of self, especially the sense of having a self that is separate from the mother. Once the child can walk, he can move away from the mother, then close to her, then away, all by his own choice. As Escalona says, walking and related physical changes bring about

> a growing awareness of separateness, of a kind of body self, and hence also lead to lessening and gradual disappearance of taken-for-granted symbiotic unity with mother. There begins to be a sense also of psychological distance, difference from, and degree of independence of the mother. (p. 89)

Probably, as the arrows in the figure show (and as I discussed in Chapter 10), there is also a link between the child's understanding of object permanence and the emergence of a clear sense of a separate self.

Sroufe's research on the consequences of secure versus insecure first attachments, which I talked about in Chapter 11, leads me to put in the arrow between attachment and cognitive development and between attachment and peer relationships. Children with secure attachments explore more freely from the "safe base" of the mother (or other central person). This exploration may lead to more rapid cognitive development (Main, 1983); certainly we know that it is related to more skillful relationships with peers.

The one arrow with a question mark on it is between the child's early language (the first word) and the child's development of internal representation. As you know by now, there is some argument among linguists about whether children use those first words as a basis for internal representation or whether they learn (or invent) words for categories they have already developed nonverbally.

I am quite certain that there are many more connections among these developments than I have sketched or than present theorists have even suggested. Some of these lines of development (the rows) are heavily determined by physical maturation, while others require particular kinds of experience. But the physical changes affect the experience, and the understandings or skills that emerge affect other developmental pathways.

### The Importance of Environment and Experience

I have talked several times about the effect of family environments on the developments shown in Figure 15.1. I do not need to repeat myself here. But there is one broader question I want to raise: Is infancy a *critical period* for certain kinds of experiences, or, alternatively, is development during this period more robust, more fixed than at other ages?

Oddly, I think the answer is "both." In the area of physical and cognitive development, the first 12 to 18 months seem to be strongly influenced by maturation. These developments are, as Sandra Scarr and Robert McCall have said (Scarr-Salapatek, 1976; McCall, 1981b), strongly *canalized.* To use the analogy of the engine pulling the train along the tracks again, motor and mental development are on a strongly fixed track, very difficult to derail. To be sure, the environment makes a difference (perhaps influencing the speed of movement along the track), but a very wide range of environments is adequate to support the basic steps of development.

An exception to this highly canalized pattern is the development of children who come into this world with some handicap—being low birth weight or even being temperamentally very difficult. These infants are more easily "derailed" and thus require a more nurturing, more stimulating environment to develop optimally.

In the case of early social development (particularly attachments), the quality of the early experience seems to make a much bigger difference for children. Children with exceptionally poor early relationships *can* recover later if the environment improves, but the security or insecurity of the first attachment seems, to some extent, to move children onto different developmental "tracks." The different tracks are not going in totally different directions—one to New York and the other to San Francisco. But to use a currently favorite word of developmental psychologists, the developmental *trajectories* of securely attached and insecurely attached children may be different, with repercussions all along the way later on.

Thus, the richness of the early environment and the quality of the child's relationships with his parents both matter in the first two years, but the relationships may be the more critical for the later paths of development. To put it *very* simply: For an infant, love is more important than toys.

### The Child's Transitions and Their Effect on the Family

For parents, the period from their child's birth until her second birthday is not all one undivided stretch. The child's transitions have powerful effects on parents and on the quality of the relationship between the parent and the child. Let me give you two examples.

**Figure 15.2** The physical transition that infants pass through at about 2 months of life generally makes the baby much more responsive, much more social, and easier to care for. It is thus a pleasant change for most parents.

The first big transition, at about 2 months of age, almost always makes life a lot easier for parents. Think about all the things that change in a baby at about that time: She usually begins to sleep five to six hours at night (hallelujah!); she begins to make eye contact regularly and smiles spontaneously; she is awake and alert for longer periods. These are really big changes for parents. The more predictable eye contact and the more frequent smiling make "dancing" with the infant not only *much* easier, they make it a lot more fun. Parents get really hooked on their 2- to 3-month-old babies and will often tell you that the baby finally began to seem "human" at about this age. Having the baby sleep through the night also eases the fatigue of the mother and makes it much easier for the parents to have private time together, including time for a satisfying sexual relationship. (It is very hard to have good sex if you find yourselves constantly stopping in the middle to get up to soothe a crying baby or trying to carry on despite the baby's wails.) The baby's transition thus affects the marital relationship, which in turn, affects the way the parents relate to the infant.

Another transition at 8 to 10 months of age also affects parents' lives. At this age babies are beginning to creep and crawl (and get into more things), and they also frequently show separation anxiety or fear

**Figure 15.3** The child's transition at 8 to 10 months, in contrast to the 2-month changes, often makes parents' lives more difficult. Babies who cry and fuss like this one when being separated from mom make it more difficult to leave the child with a baby-sitter and may upset parents.

of strangers. Suddenly you find that the baby screams at the sight of a baby-sitter or even grandma. This makes it much harder for the parents to spend time together without the infant, and the baby's greater mobility not only means that someone has to keep the infant in sight all the time, it also usually means that the furniture has to be rearranged or treasured objects put out of reach. In other words, after a fairly easy stretch from 2 to 3 months till about 8 months, the parents must now readjust their daily lives again.

### The Family's Transitions and Their Effect on the Child

Significant family changes or parental developments that may affect the child's progress are harder to talk about, since they are much less similar from one family to the next. But two come to mind.

For a first child, parents must go through a major period of adjustment simply to having a child at all. There is a great deal of research that shows that parents typically get *less* satisfied with their marriages after the birth of their first child (Rollins & Galligan, 1978). The family roles change; parents have less private and relaxed time with each other; the child takes center stage. How a parent copes with this rather sudden rise in dissatisfaction will surely affect the interaction he or she develops with the infant.

A second transition in parents' lives that is common (but by no means universal) during the child's infancy is the mother's return to work. Something like 40 percent of women with children under age 3 are now working part-time or full-time, and it is more and more common for mothers to go to work (or return to work) during the child's first year. For the child this means a change in caregiver for part of each day; it also means a change in the parents' relationship with each other (again, less private time for the parents) and in the division of labor at home. Most working mothers continue to do the major share of the child care and housework (Condran & Bode, 1982), which has consequences for children as well. Working mothers are more tired and simply have less time to spend playing with or responding to the baby. There is no indication, by the way, that this has a generally bad effect on infants. But it *changes* the system and requires the development of a new equilibrium in the family.

## THE PRESCHOOL YEARS: FROM 2 TO 6

### Patterns of Development

The preschool years also demand new adaptations within the family as the child moves rapidly through a highly significant series of changes. Again, I have tried to map the parallel developments in a chart, Figure 15.4.

I find it harder to draw arrows across the different rows here than I did with the infancy chart. This *might* mean that preschool children's development is more "disconnected" or unintegrated, but I suspect the problem lies in me (and my fellow psychologists) and not in the child. For all of our studies of preschool children, we have really only very primitive ideas about the ways in which the several threads weave together during this age. Still, let me suggest a few chains or sequences.

One chain connects the child's growing interaction with peers with the child's emerging cognitive skill. As the child moves out from the "safe base" of the central attachment, play with other children becomes more and more interesting and central to the child. Two and 3-year-olds, left alone, play with toys and may show some pretend play. But when children play together, they expand one another's experience with objects, suggest new ways of pretending to one another. Since this play with objects seems to be a key part of the child's growing cognitive skill, we can see that time spent in play with other youngsters is much more than social. Such shared play with objects helps to develop awareness of the ways in which objects are the same and different

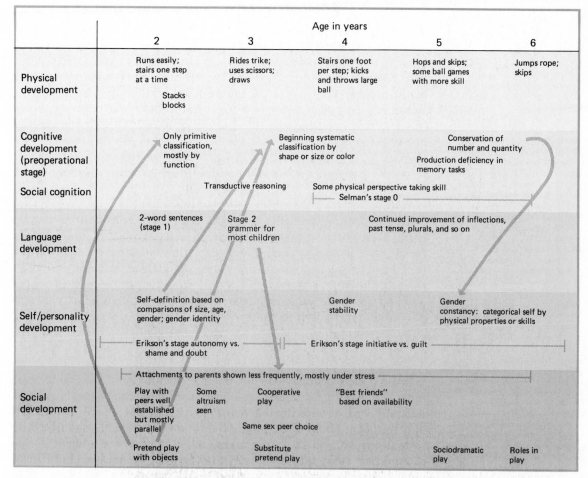

**Figure 15.4** A brief summary of the parallel developments during the preschool years, with a few arrows suggesting some possible linkages between them.

from one another, which is a key to the child's growing ability to classify things.

One of the first areas in which we see the child's classification skill is in gender identity, which begins to be seen at about 2½ or 3. Noticing whether other people are boys or girls and what toys boys and girls play with is itself the first step in the long chain of sex-role learning. So the preschooler's emerging cognitive skill lies at the root of her gender concept as well. In fact, the gender concept and other concepts of constancy or conservation seem to develop in parallel, as the child (toward the end of this period) discovers that objects have characteristics that are not strictly visible—characteristics like quantity or weight or gender.

Since so much of the child's growing cognitive understanding is rooted in play with other children, we can see the essential intertwining of the development of social and intellectual competencies.

It is more difficult to link specific new physical skills to particular changes in a child's social or mental growth. I don't think that children shift to cooperative from parallel play because they now know how to walk up stairs one foot at a time. But the child's increasing skill in movement does have several general effects: She can explore and examine objects in new ways (such as stringing small beads or stacking six or seven blocks), and she can roam farther and farther afield, which increases the range of her experience. The fact that she can also talk more skillfully means, too, that she can range farther from mom and still be able to stay in touch pretty well.

The sense one gets of this period is that the child is making a slow but immensely important shift from dependent baby to independent child. This shift is made possible by physical change, by language, by many and varied play encounters with other children, by new abilities to control impulses. At the same time (and from some of the same causes), the child's thinking is *decentering*, becoming less egocentric and less tied to the outside appearances of things. Pretend play is probably a key ingredient in these changes.

## The Importance of Environment and Experience

For the child's cognitive development, the quality of the family (and school) environment in the preschool years seems to be really critical. Actually, I agree with Burton White (1975) that the crucial period probably begins at about 12 or 14 months, when the child's language starts to really spurt and she can understand so much more of what is said around her. Now, talking to the child, reading to her, playing games, having varied and fascinating toys, allowing the child full range of exploration (consistent with safety, of course) seem to make a very big difference in the eventual "power" of the child's thinking, as measured by something like an IQ test. Children raised in poverty environments, for example, still look pretty much like more advantaged children at 12 months, but by 2 or 3 they have fallen behind.

I do not mean to imply by this that none of these stimulating things is useful with babies in the first year. (At the most basic level, varied stimulation may be critical in furthering the development of the brain and nervous system in the early months.) But the stimulating qualities of the child's world seem to increase markedly in importance in the second, third, and fourth years.

Besides environmental variety and richness, another ingredient that seems to make a big difference at this age is the amount of restriction or punishment that parents use. Two-year-olds can be very trying creatures. Virtually all children—even those with secure attachments and good development—go through a period of ornery opposition, testing limits, saying no. Parents quite naturally find themselves limiting, restricting, saying no in return. But there seems to be a delicate balance here between needed restriction—which helps the child develop impulse control as well as assuring safety (Escalona, 1981)—and excessive restriction. Too much restriction limits the child's ability to explore and play, which has an effect on the whole constellation of cognitive/social changes I've just been describing.

## The Child's Transitions and Their Effect on the Family

From the parents' perspective, the most potent transition the child goes through is precisely the set of changes I have just been talking about, at around 18 to 24 months. Part of what is happening is that the child is beginning that all-important shift from dependence to independence; he has figured out that he is a distinct person and different from mom; he can talk, walk, run. He is trying out his limits. But all these newfound skills and new independence are not accompanied by impulse control. Two-year-olds are pretty good at doing; they are lousy at *not* doing. They see something, they go after it; when they want something, they want it *now*! If frustrated, they wail or scream or shout. (Isn't language wonderful?) A large part of the conflict parents experience with children at this age comes about because the parent *must* limit the child. But as Escalona points out (1981), the child has to have at least some restriction, some opposition from parents in order to learn impulse control.

This is a crucial transition for children; for parents it may be an upheaval. It may help to remember, as you drag young Johnny away from the cat after he has pulled its tail for the thirty-fifth time, that all of this is helping him learn both independence and impulse control. But it doesn't help a lot. There is going to be friction, and it is likely to last for six to seven months. During this time, the rate of positive reinforcements from the child goes way down, which may affect parents' sense of competence or self-esteem. Such a loss of confidence in one role is likely to spill over into other roles as well, so that the marital relationship may also suffer, especially if the parents find themselves disagreeing about the amount of restrictiveness or punitiveness to apply to the child.

Two other apparently more minor transitions in the preschool period have equally large effects on parents: the disappearance of the child's afternoon nap and the child's insistence on getting dressed herself. Nap time is a glorious event for the caregiving parent—the one or two hours of quiet when you can put your feet up and have a cup of coffee or get the housework done. Children give up afternoon naps at widely varying ages, but sometime during the preschool period, this pattern typically fades slowly away, and with it fades the parent's quiet time. Sometime in these same years, most children also begin to insist

**Figure 15.5** The famous "terrible 2s" require a major change in the family system, involving not only new kinds of control and discipline but also reorganization of the house. Parents who may have been able to handle the needs of an infant very well may find themselves adjusting less well to this phase, or the reverse.

on tying their own shoes or putting on their own coats. Independence strikes again! Imagine, though, that you have worked out a wonderful routine for the mornings, getting everyone out of bed, dressed, fed breakfast, and ready for the day. It works splendidly until Emily insists on tying her own shoes, which may take 10 or 15 minutes. You may find yourself getting up a half hour earlier just to accommodate the new timing (and few people get up earlier without some stress), or you may try to squeeze everything into the same time frame and find yourself frustrated with and angry at young Emily.

These may seem like small changes, but they illustrate the continuous need for the parents, the family, the system, to adjust and adapt to the child's changing needs and changing behaviors.

### The Family's Transitions and Their Effect on the Child

The parellel process, of course, is the need for the child to adapt to changes in the parents or in the family. Probably the most common family change in this period is the birth of a new sibling. Children are often spaced two to three years apart, so a firstborn child will fre-

**Figure 15.6** Children in the preschool period continue to demand that they be given a chance to do things themselves. Parents are usually delighted, but sometimes it means leaving extra time for the child to dress himself or tie his own shoes. Patience, they say, is a virtue!

quently find herself coping with a new brother or sister just at the time she is going through the 2-year-old period I've been talking about.

The adjustment of the older child to this huge change in her environment seems to be easier if the spacing between the children is either very close (within a year or so) or fairly wide (three years or more)

(White, 1975; Lewis & Kreitzberg, 1979). Two years apart seems to be especially difficult for both the child and the parents, for reasons you can imagine, given what I have said about the transition the older child is going through at age 2 and the widely differing demands made on the parent by a newborn and a 2-year-old.

Still, despite all the mutual adjustments needed, most children and their families survive the preschool years. In fact, past the major transition at 2 to 3, the consolidation years from 3 to 6 are often very satisfying and exciting ones for both child and parent. New skills, new vistas open up almost daily, and the child's gradually increasing independence slowly frees the parent of the job of constant supervision. By age 5 or 6, the child is ready for the next big change: school.

## THE ELEMENTARY-SCHOOL YEARS: FROM 6 TO 12

### Patterns of Development

The chart showing the parallel lines of development during this period is in Figure 15.7. You may notice, if you compare the three charts so far, that as the child gets older, the range of ages during which some development takes place gets longer. In infancy, we can pinpoint a fairly narrow range of times when something happens, like crawling or walking or the first strong attachment. In contrast, the changes in this chart are spread over several years for any one child and may range over four or five years across different children. What I have given you, then, is the sequence and the average or typical ages.

As it happens, I have talked more in earlier chapters (particularly Chapters 7 and 12) about the possible connections among the developmental sequences at this age than at any other, so most of these ideas are not new. At the beginning of this age period is a whole set of changes in children's thinking and behaving that seem to be connected: (1) Gender constancy develops at about the same time as the early forms of conservation and seems to reflect the beginning of the child's realization that objects and people can stay the same in some way(s), even while they seem to change. More fundamentally, these changes mean that the child is "looking beyond the surface" of things. (2) We see the same "looking beyond the surface" in children's ideas about other people, too, and in their social perspective taking. Children of this age know that other people feel and think differently. (3) Gender constancy, in turn, is related to the child's greater attention to same-sex models, to the intense sex stereotyping that is typical of 6- and 7- and 8-year-olds, and to the almost exclusively same-sex composition of children's groups at these ages.

I am not sure that I want to say that the cognitive change (conservation or gender constancy) *causes* the new pattern of social relationships, because the child's earlier play and interaction with other young-

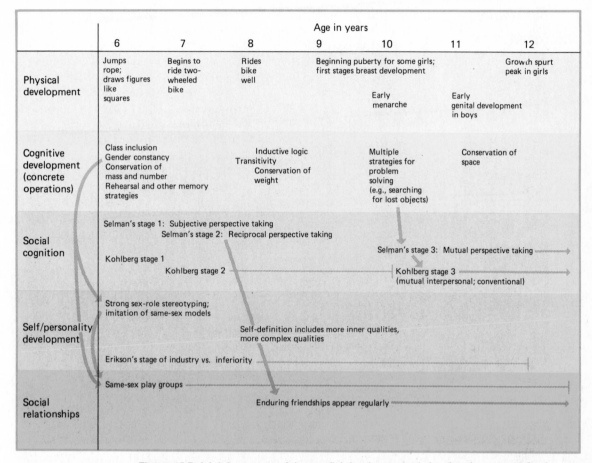

**Figure 15.7** A brief summary of the parallel developments during the elementary-school years (age 6 to 12), with a few arrows suggesting possible linkages between them.

sters is part of the source of the cognitive change. The social and the intellectual lines are linked together, so that first one "leads," then the other.

We see a similar connection between cognitive and social changes in the middle of this period, at about 8, when we begin to see enduring friendships among children at around the same time as they shift into Selman's second stage of interpersonal understanding, called reciprocal perspective taking. Again, I do not know which comes first; it does seem clear that these two changes strengthen each other, since experience in a lasting friendship increases the child's knowledge of another person's feelings and ideas and needs, which makes him more aware of the reciprocity. But the understanding of reciprocity also makes an enduring friendship more possible.

Finally, there is a set of linked events late in this period between

**Figure 15.8** One of the consequences of the child's new gender constancy is a *strong* preference for playmates of the same sex at this age. Most social institutions like Boy Scouts or Girl Scouts in this age range are organized by sex, presumably because of children's strong preferences.

the emerging beginnings of formal operations, the beginning of Selman's level 3 (mutual perspective taking), and Kohlberg's conventional level of moral reasoning. As I described in Chapter 12, these seem to develop in that order, with each step necessary but not sufficient for the one that follows. Some elements of systematic and flexible thinking may thus be necessary for the child to be *able* to grasp the idea of truly mutual relationships or for the later steps of moral reasoning.

Just what role physical change plays in this collection of developments I do not know. Clearly there *are* physical changes going on. Girls, in particular, are going through the first steps of puberty during elementary school. But we simply don't know whether the rate of physical development in these years is connected in any way to the rate of the child's progress through the sequence of cognitive or social understandings. There has been no research that I know of that hooks the first row in Figure 15.7 with any of the other rows, except that bigger, more coordinated, early-developing children are more likely to be popular with peers. Obviously, this is an area in which we need far more knowledge.

## The Importance of Environment and Experience

Just as was true for infancy, my hunch is that the family environment at this age probably has a larger impact on the child's emerging self-concept, personality, or overall competence than on the child's intellectual development. The basic rate (the "trajectory," if you will) of cognitive development that a child shows seems to be pretty well established by school age. Some of this is hereditary difference expressing itself; some is the cumulative effect of the child's early (and persisting) environment; some of it is the child's continuing to follow the groove that she has been in all along (Scarr & McCartney, 1983). Slower-developing children, for example, are likely to choose friends who are at a similar level of skill, and they will choose activities that do not demand complex thinking. By this age, children are shaping their *own* cognitive environments. Family emphasis on academic achievement has some effect, but I think it is harder and harder to change the earlier pattern. Not impossible, just harder.

Socially and emotionally, however, the family environment still has a big impact. The patterns of control, discipline, affection, and communication in the family that I talked about in Chapter 13 all continue to affect the child's self-esteem and his specific behavior with peers. When badly functioning families are given assistance to improve their control and increase their affectionate communication, the child's behavior and attitude usually change dramatically (Patterson, 1980). And when family functioning deteriorates, such as after a divorce, children's behavior with other people deteriorates, too (Hetherington, Cox, & Cox, 1978).

Obviously, the other huge piece of the environment that affects children in this age range is the school they happen to attend. I pointed out in Chapter 13 that differences among schools have a real, measurable effect on children. Even differences in individual teachers can be important. Children's *attitudes* about school and their *motivation to achieve,* as well as their actual achievement, are strongly affected by the expectations and emotional climate of the school they attend. Most of us, when our children reach school age, take whatever comes along in the way of a school or teachers. The research on schools suggests that it is worth your time to investigate your options and to make waves within the school system if necessary.

### The Child's Transitions and Their Effect on the Family

Parents are most likely to notice the transition that marks the beginning of this period. Starting school is a *big event,* even for a child who has been in day care or preschool. It is not just that the child goes away from home for six or seven hours a day; it is also that significant new demands are made on the child that challenge her ability to learn and integrate. Reading and mathematics are fascinating, difficult tasks. In the early days, a child may be hard-pressed. You may see a child who always went to sleep easily and slept like a log now waking up in the middle of the night, needing reassurance of some sort; you may see an increase in colds or other mild illnesses; you may see some "regression" to earlier, clingier forms of attachment behavior. In other words, the parents must not only adjust their daily schedules to get the children ready for school and possibly arrange for after-school care, they also have to cope with a transformation in the child.

Once this transition has been weathered (and it is usually not nearly so difficult as the transition at age 2), the stretch of years from 7 or 8 to 10 or 11 is often fairly peaceful. The family achieves a working system, an emotional equilibrium, that can remain pretty much intact until the child reaches puberty.

One personal note, though. I have a hunch, based entirely on my own experience and observations of other families (for which I have no hard data) that there is another transition, perhaps especially for girls, at about age 9, when the first hormonal changes of puberty begin. The major symptom of this that I have seen is a rather sharp increase in weepiness and crankiness. Just when you thought you had it all together, the system may temporarily fall apart again! I would love to see some decent research on this possibility, linking pubertal age with mood changes in children.

### The Family's Transitions and Their Effect on the Child

There are no *typical* changes in parents or families that I can think of that occur during this age period for most children. Most parents of elementary-school children are in their thirties, with the father intent on work success and the mother most likely working as well. But there are no widely shared family upheavals during these years.

Individual children, though, will be affected by the particular life changes encountered by their own parents. The father or mother may lose a job or be promoted and asked to move across the country. A favorite grandparent may die (as was true for me when I was 10), or the parents may divorce. Children may be affected directly by these changes, such as by a move or by a divorce. They are also affected indirectly, through the changes that take place in the parents. A mother who is returning to school to get training for a new career not only is likely to expect a 9- or 10-year-old to help out around the house more; she is also changing and growing herself, which will both enrich the child's environment and challenge the child's ability to adapt. Psychologists have not yet found good ways to study the effects of many of these changes on children, but it is clear from both theory and observation that they are significant elements in children's lives.

## ADOLESCENCE: FROM 12 TO 20

### Patterns of Development

The summary chart for this period is shown in Figure 15.9. The sequences in each row overlap each other more and more at this point. For each child, the sequences seem to hold, but different children go through the sequences at very different ages and end up at different points. This is especially clear when we look at formal operations, or stages 4 or 5 of moral reasoning, which are not achieved at all by many adolescents or adults.

In some ways the early years of adolescence have a lot in common with the early years of toddlerhood. Toddlers (the now-familiar 2-year-olds) are famous for their negativism and for their constant push for more independence. At the same time they are struggling to learn a vast array of new skills. Teenagers show many of these same qualities, albeit at much more abstract levels. Many of them go through a period of negativism, particularly with parents. And as their bodies become more adultlike and the social pressures on them to behave more like grown-ups increase, their demands for independence become strong and persistent. They want to stay up later, stay out later, come and go when they please, borrow the family car, listen to the music they prefer at maximum volume, wear the clothing and hairstyles that are currently "in" (no matter how unflattering mom and dad may think they are). While this push for independence is going on, they are also facing a whole new set of demands and skills to be learned. High school (or its equivalent) demands more complex thinking; summer jobs demand new levels of responsibility; decisions about college must be made; mature sexuality must be dealt with.

There is, in other words, a major disequilibrium, a transition, that involves every dimension of the young person's development. But while we can see the effects of this disequilibrium very broadly, it is much harder to pin down the causes and connections across the "rows" in the chart.

Some of the possible connections I have already talked about. It seems likely that the changes in the child's thinking from concrete operations to at least beginning formal operations are an important in-

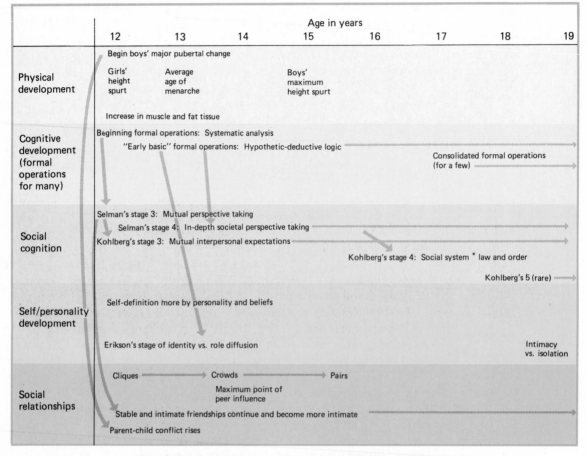

**Figure 15.9** A brief summary of parallel developments during adolescence.

gredient. One of the characteristics of formal operations thinking is the ability to imagine possibilities that you have never experienced and to manipulate ideas in your head. These new skills seem to help foster the broad questioning of old ways, old values, old patterns that are part of adolescence for many teenagers.

There is at least some research evidence to support such a link. As I mentioned in Chapter 12, early formal operations seems to be a necessary but not sufficient condition for the shift to Selman's stage 3 of social perspective taking (intimate mutual relationships) and to stage 3 of Kohlberg's sequence of moral reasoning (the conventional level).

Other researchers have also found some links between early formal reasoning and the process of identity formation (Leadbeater & Dionne, 1981; Rowe & Marcia, 1980). Using Marcia's identity status categories, these investigators have shown that teenagers and young adults who have achieved a clear identity are also much more likely to be reasoning at formal operations than are those who are still in the diffusion or moratorium status. Thus, formal operations thinking seems to *enable* the young person to rethink many aspects of his life, but it does not guarantee that he will do so.

As was true for the elementary-school period, the set of connections about which we know the least are those between the physical changes and the mental/social/personal changes. The physical changes of puberty are massive: large hormone changes, major changes in appearance and size, mature sexuality. It is inconceivable to me that these developments operate independently of all the other sequences of development at the same age. But just what sort of connection might there be?

There could be a direct, causal connection between hormonal and other physical changes and the emergence of new cognitive skills or social behaviors. As J. M. Tanner (1970) says:

> There is clearly no reason to suppose that the link between maturation of [brain] structure and appearance of [cognitive] function suddenly ceases at age 6 or 10 or 13. On the contrary, there is every reason to believe that the higher intellectual abilities also appear only when maturation of certain structures is complete. (p. 123)

There is remarkably little research exploring such possible linkages, but there are recent bits of evidence consistent with such a view. For example, I mentioned in Chapter 6 (in the section on sex differences) that girls who go through puberty later seem to show better spatial ability than do those who go through puberty earlier. Obviously, puberty cannot *cause* formal operations directly, since a great many adolescents never reach formal operations. But the physical changes of puberty may be *necessary* for some aspects of complex thinking.

An indirect effect of physical change is also plausible. When the child's body grows and becomes more like that of an adult, the parents begin to treat the child differently, and the child begins to see himself as a soon-to-be-adult. Both of these changes may trigger some of the searching self-examinations that are part of this period of life. The change in status is also acknowledged socially by a change in schools and by new cognitive demands. Thus, *looking* like an adult, as well as feeling the sexual impulses of an adult, may be the single element that unbalances the system and forces the new accommodations. The fact that family discord increases when a boy starts puberty, regardless of how old he is when that happens, fits with this idea. Hence, the onset of puberty ought to be a better predictor of social and cognitive changes than mere age. In general, that seems to be true, but our fund of knowledge about this is slim.

### The Importance of Environment and Experience

All of what I said about family environment in the last section seems to be true here, too: The family "climate" as well as the teenager's own experiences have an effect on her sense of competence and well-being. The level of cognitive richness in the family, in contrast, is probably much less formative at this stage, while the intellectual climate at school is significant in shaping the young person's attitudes, motivations, and skills.

The particular peer group with which a teenager becomes involved also has a significant impact on the developing adolescent, especially at around age 13 and 14, when conformity to peer pressure is at its height. For example, cigarette smoking or marijuana or hard drug use are more common among teens whose friends also use drugs (Kandel, 1974). As the young person moves into more intimate partner relationships and begins to achieve the more complex understanding that is characteristic of Selman's level 4, the impact of the peer group declines. But lifetime habits or behavior patterns may well have been established during the time of maximum peer influence.

### The Young Person's Transitions and Their Effect on the Family

The adolescent transition may be the one point at which parents most *expect* to have to make big adjustments. Certainly the popular press has prepared all of us to expect difficulties with our children when they hit adolescence. Some of that expectation is well founded. At the very least, there is a *transition,* and a new family equilibrium does have to evolve, just as it did at age 2 or age 6. From the parents' perspective, a number of issues are likely to be important:

- The teenager is demanding power—the power to make decisions for herself, to be given responsibility and trust. Parents have been comfortably wielding that power, and giving it up may be difficult.

- At the same time, the teenager gives off very mixed messages: He demands power but still wants to be nurtured and cared for as well. This can be confusing, to say the least.

- The teenager is going through major sexual changes just at a time when many adults (who may now be in their forties) are feeling some physical decline. For many adults at this point, there is a revival of adolescentlike issues about sexuality, which may be heightened if their own children are going through puberty (and may, in some cases, lead to extramarital sexual experiments).

- To complicate matters, the fact that teenagers typically stay up later at night means that parents may lose the one time during the day when they had some quiet and private time together. This loss of privacy affects the parents' sexual life as well as their nonsexual intimacy. Perhaps as a result, many parents (particularly fathers) report that marital satisfaction is at its lowest ebb during their children's adolescence (Rollins & Galligan, 1978).

- At age $15\frac{1}{2}$ or 16 (at least in the United States), the teenager's demand to learn to drive, and then to be given permission to use the family car, forces another set of adjustments. Independent use of the car is a symbol of responsibility and trust; it also requires rearrangement of family schedules, added cost for insurance, and a lot of staying up late at night worrying about car wrecks (I speak from experience!).

Thus, having teenagers in the house requires the family to alter their traditional style of interacting in fundamental ways. For most families, this adjustment is accompanied by a stressful time at the beginning of adolescence. What is remarkable is that most families manage to move through this adjustment time rather well, and a new equilibrium is formed in the late teen years. Obviously, some families and some teenagers get into serious difficulties. And serious difficulties in these years—such as involvement with drugs or delinquency or early pregnancy or the like—can have major repercussions for the young person's later life. I do not want to minimize the difficulties faced by families whose teenagers have followed such a path. But on the whole I think that for most families a lot of the popular press descriptions about lasting and inevitable disharmony between parents and children during adolescence are exaggerated.

### The Family's Transitions and Their Effect on the Young Person

As was true at earlier ages, major family transitions will affect many of the aspects of the teenager's progress. A divorce at this age causes one to two years of disruption, just as it did in younger children. Moving, having one or both parents change jobs or go back to work, even the birth of a new sibling will change the family system in important ways and affect the adolescent. Of course, not all of the effects are bad. For example, the teenager whose mother goes back to school or to work may be expected to take on a much larger load of housework (the sound of loud complaining can now be heard), but over the long term such responsibility helps to foster independence and competence. In general, adolescents seem to adjust more easily to major family changes than do younger children, presumably because their greater intellectual skill and social perspective-taking ability enables them to see the situation from the parents' perspective a bit more and to understand the reasons for the change.

## A FINAL POINT: THE JOY OF DEVELOPMENT

I want to finish this chapter—and the book—by reminding you of something I said at the very beginning. In the midst of all the "crises" and "transitions" and "readjustments," there is a special *joyous* quality to development. When a child masters a new skill, she is not just pleased, she is delighted and will repeat that new skill at length, quite obviously getting vast satisfaction from it. A 5-year-old I know learned to draw stars and drew them on everything in sight, including paper, walls, clothes, and napkins. It was so much *fun* to draw stars. A 10-year-old

**Figure 15.10** The joy of discovery!

who learns to do cartwheels will delightedly display this new talent to anyone who will watch and will practice endlessly.

The same joyous quality can be part of the family's development as well. Confronting and moving successfully through one of the periodic (and inevitable) upheavals in family life can be immensely pleasing. Watching your child progress, liking your child, enjoying walking or talking together are all deeply satisfying parts of rearing children. When parents cry at their son's or daughter's high school graduation or at their wedding, it is not merely sentiment. It is an expression of that sense of love, pride, and wonderment that they have gotten this far.

To be sure, not all families feel such a sense of pleasure. When a family does *not* manage to weather the various transitions and crises, when a satisfying system is not developed, when there is discord and disharmony and depression, it can be one of the most painful experiences on earth. If you find yourself in such a situation, do not hesitate. Get help. Most communities have low-cost family services or mental health clinics available; school psychologists may be able to make referrals; there are classes for parents through the YMCA or other community organizations. Rearing children is hard work and makes immense demands on your own capacities for growth. Do not be ashamed to get help if you need it. But be prepared, too, for the excitement and the joy involved in your own growth and in watching your child grow as well.

## SUMMARY

1. The several threads of development—physical, intellectual, emotional—are linked together in complex ways, with different patterns of connection at each of several ages.

2. The child's development may be thought of as a series of alternating periods of transition and consolidation. The transitions occur when there are individual major changes or pileups of smaller change that require abandonment of old patterns of behavior and development of new ones.

3. These developments of the child occur within the larger context of a family system. The parents must adjust to the child's transitions; the child must adjust to the family's transitions. Together they create a "climate" in which the child grows.

4. In infancy, there are important links between the different developmental sequences. For example, changes in the brain at 2 months affect the child's discrimination ability, which makes recognition of the mother possible, which helps make specific attachment possible.

5. In the first two years, the general level of stimulation of the family environment is important for the child, but the quality of the par-

ent-infant relationship is probably more critical, since it establishes the emotional base for later growth.

6. Several of the child's transitions demand special adaptations from the parent, including the transition at 2 months and the one at 8 to 12 months, when the child begins crawling and then walking.

7. The child, too, is affected by the parents' adjustment to parenthood and by family changes such as the mother's return to work.

8. During the preschool period, there are several links between the child's cognitive and social development and development of self: play with peers, particularly pretend play, helps to foster cognitive development; development of skillful language enables the child to stray farther from a "safe base"; classification skill relates to the child's emerging categorical self-concept.

9. The degree of cognitive and verbal stimulation provided for the child within the family from age 1 to 5 seems to be especially critical for the rate of the child's cognitive development and may be more important (more formative) at this period than at other times in development.

10. The child's major transition at age 18 to 24 months, including a demand for greater independence, combined with negativism, makes especially difficult demands upon the parents for adaptation.

11. One common change in families during this period is the birth of a new sibling, which has a major impact on the older child's daily life.

12. At school age, we see a set of apparently related changes in cognition that take the child beyond the physical appearances of objects or people to a beginning understanding of underlying rules and properties. Conservation, gender constancy, and subjective perspective taking are part of this change.

13. These linked changes, in turn, affect the child's choice of playmates (same-sex) and adult models (same-sex).

14. Reciprocal perspective taking, emerging in the middle of this age range, is also related to the development of lasting friendships.

15. The quality of family control and communication in this period seems to be particularly important for the child's emerging self-esteem and competence, while the intellectual climate of the school is important for cognitive progress.

16. The child's transition at 6 to 7, when starting school, requires the development of a new family system. The child, too, must adjust to changes in the parents' lives, such as (possibly) divorce.

17. In adolescence, a major disequilibrium takes place, probably triggered both by the physical changes of puberty and by the mental changes of early formal operations. These changes affect identity formation, moral reasoning, and social perspective taking as well as relationships with parents.

18. Parental adjustment to the child's adolescent transition is complex and may involve a fair amount of family disorganization for a short period.
19. Throughout all the transitions and consolidation periods, children and young people experience excitement, joy, and pleasure from successfully mastering developmental tasks. Parents, too, experience delight in watching their children develop and satisfaction in their own accompanying growth.

## SUGGESTED READINGS

Many of the books I have recommended in earlier chapters are relevant here as well. But I also suggest several books that give the flavor of particular ages.

Brazelton, T. B. *Infants and mothers: Differences in development.* New York: Dell, 1969.
This isn't a new book, but it is excellent and still extremely relevant. If you have a newborn child or plan to have a child, I highly recommend this book. Brazelton follows three children through their first year and comments on the changes.

Brazelton, T. B. *Toddlers and parents.* New York: Dell, 1974.
This is the companion to the infancy book; it covers the children through about age 3 and is just as good. Lots of specific examples and lots of very sensitive advice.

Murphy, L. B., & Moriarty, A. E. *Vulnerabilty, coping and growth.* New Haven, Conn.: Yale University Press, 1976.
This isn't a book about a particular age group, but it deals with a set of issues I have come to see as extremely important. It presents many interesting case studies of children followed from infancy through adolescence.

White, B. W. *The first three years of life.* Englewood Cliffs, N.J.: Prentice-Hall, 1975.
A highly readable book, full of useful descriptions of the development of children in the early years, along with specific advice to parents about such things as choosing toys, coping with 2-year-olds, and the like. I do not agree with all of what White says, but there is a great deal of useful information in this book.

# references

Abel, E. L. Behavioral teratology of alcohol. *Psychological bulletin*, 1981, *90*, 564–581.

Achenbach, T. M. *Research in developmental psychology: Concepts, strategies, methods.* New York: Free Press, 1978.

———. *Developmental psychopathology* (2d ed.). New York: Wiley, 1982.

Achenbach, T. M., & Edelbrock, C. S. The classification of child psychopathology: A review and analysis of empirical efforts. *Psychological bulletin*, 1978, *85*, 1275–1301.

———. Behavioral problems and competencies reported by parents of normal and disturbed children aged 4 through 16. *Monographs of the Society for Research in Child Development*, 1981, *46* (1, Whole No. 188).

———. *Manual for the child behavior checklist and child behavior profile.* Burlington, Vt.: Child Psychiatry, University of Vermont, 1982.

Achenbach, T. M., & Weisz, J. R. A longitudinal study of developmental synchrony between conceptual identity, seriation, and transitivity of color, number, and length. *Child development*, 1975, *46*, 840–848.

Acredolo, L. P., & Hake, J. L. Infant perception. In B. B. Wolman (Ed.). *Handbook of developmental psychology.* Englewood Cliffs, N.J.: Prentice-Hall, 1982.

Adler, A. *Studies in analytical psychology.* New York: Norton, 1948.

Ainsworth, M. D. S. Attachment and dependency: A comparison. In J. L. Gewirtz (Ed.). *Attachment and dependency.* Washington, D.C.: V. H. Winston, 1972.

———. Attachment: Retrospect and prospect. In C. M. Parkes & J. Stevenson-Hinde (Eds.). *The place of attachment in human behavior.* New York: Basic Books, 1982.

Ainsworth, M. D. S.; Bell, S. M.; & Stayton, D. J. Individual differences in strange situation behavior of one-year-olds. In H. R. Schaffer (Ed.). *The origins of human social relations.* London: Academic Press, 1971.

Ainsworth, M. D. S.; Blehar, M.; Waters, E.; & Wall, S. *Patterns of attachment.* Hillsdale, N.J.: Erlbaum, 1978.

Ainsworth, M. D. S., & Wittig, B. A. Attachment and exploratory behavior of one-year-olds in a strange situation. In B. M. Foss (Ed.). *Determinants of infant behavior* (Vol. 4). London: Methuen, 1969.

Allik, J., & Valsiner, J. Visual development in ontogenesis: Some reevaluations. In H. W. Reese & L. P. Lipsitt (Eds.). *Advances in child development and behavior.* New York: Academic Press, 1980.

American Psychiatric Association. *Diagnostic and statistical manual of mental disorders* (3d ed.). Washington, D.C.: American Psychiatric Association, 1980.

Amsterdam, B. Mirror image reactions before age two. *Developmental psychobiology*, 1972, *5*, 297–305.

Anastasiow, N. J., & Hanes, M. L. *Language patterns of poverty children.* Springfield, Ill.: Thomas, 1976.

Anderson, C. W.; Nagle, R. J.; Roberts, W. A.; & Smith, J. W. Attachment to substitute caregivers as a function of center quality and caregiver involvement. *Child development*, 1981, *52*, 53–61.

Andrews, S. R.; Blumenthal, J. B.; Johnson, D. L.; Kahn, A. J.; Ferguson, C. J.; Lasater, T. M.; Malone, P. E.; & Wallace, D. B. The skills of mothering: A study of parent-child development centers. *Monographs of the Society for Research in Child Development*, 1982, *47* (6, Whole No. 198).

Angrist, S. S.; Mickelsen, R.; & Penna, A. N. Sex

differences in sex-role conceptions and family orientation of high school students. *Journal of youth and adolescence,* 1977, *6,* 179–186.

Anthony, E. J. The behavior disorders of childhood. In P. H. Mussen (Ed.). *Carmichael's manual of child psychology* (Vol. 2, 3d ed.). New York: Wiley, 1970.

Appel, M. H. The application of Piagetian learning theory to a science curriculum project. In M. H. Appel & L. S. Goldberg (Eds.). *Topics in cognitive development* (Vol. 1). New York: Plenum, 1977.

Archer, J. Sex differences in maturation. In K. J. Connolly & H. F. R. Prechtl (Eds.). *Maturation and development: Biological and psychological perspectives.* Clinics in Developmental Medicine No. 77/78. London: William Heinemann, 1981.

Archer, S. L. The lower age boundaries of identity development. *Child development,* 1982, *53,* 1551–1556.

Arco, C. M. B. Pacing of playful stimulation to young infants: Similarities and differences in maternal and paternal communication. *Infant behavior and development,* 1983, *6,* 223–228.

Arend, R.; Gove, F. L.; & Sroufe, L. A. Continuity of individual adaptation from infancy to kindergarten: A predictive study of ego-resiliency and curiosity in preschoolers. *Child development,* 1979, *50,* 950–959.

Asher, S.; Renshaw, P. D.; & Hymel, S. Peer relations and the development of social skills. In S. G. Moore & C. R. Cooper (Eds.). *The young child: Reviews of research* (Vol. 3). Washington, D.C.: National Association for the Education of Young Children, 1982.

Badger, E. Effects of parent education program on teenage mothers and their offspring. In K. G. Scott, T. Field, & E. Robertson (Eds.). *Teenage parents and their offspring.* New York: Grune & Stratton, 1981.

Baer, D. M. An age-irrelevant concept of development. Paper presented at the annual meeting of the American Psychological Association, New York, 1966.

Baldwin, A. L. Socialization and the parent-child relationship. *Child development,* 1948, *19,* 127–136.

———. The effect of home environment on nursery school behavior. *Child development,* 1949, *20,* 49–62.

Bandura, A. *Aggression: A social learning analysis.* Englewood Cliffs, N.J.: Prentice-Hall, 1973.

———. *Social learning theory.* Englewood Cliffs, N.J.: Prentice-Hall, 1977.

———. Self-efficacy mechanism in human agency. *American psychologist,* 1982, *37,* 122–147.

Bane, M. J., & Jencks, C. Five myths about your IQ. *Harper's,* 1973, *246,* 28–40.

Barenboim, C. The development of person perception in childhood and adolescence: From behavioral comparisons to psychological constructs to psychological comparisons. *Child development,* 1981, *52,* 129–144.

Barnard, K. E.; Bee, H. L.; & Hammond, M. A. Developmental changes in maternal interactions with term and preterm infants. *Infant behavior and development,* 1984. (a)

———. Home environment and mental development in a healthy, low risk sample: The Seattle study. In A. W. Gottfried (Ed.). *Home environment and early mental development.* New York: Academic Press, 1984. (b)

Barnard, K. E., & Eyres, S. J. *Child health assessment. Part 2: The first year of life* (DHEW Publication No. HRA 79-25). Washington, D.C.: U.S. Government Printing Office, 1979.

Barrera, M. E., & Maurer, D. Recognition of the mother's photographed face by the three-month-old infant. *Child development,* 1981, *52,* 714–716.

Barrett, D. E.; Radke-Yarrow, M.; & Klein, R. E. Chronic malnutrition and child behavior: Effects of early caloric supplementation on social and emotional functioning at school age. *Developmental psychology,* 1982, *18,* 541–556.

Bates, E.; Bretherton, I.; Beeghly-Smith, M.; & McNew, S. Social bases of language development: A reassessment. In H. W. Reese & L. P. Lipsitt (Eds.). *Advances in child development and behavior* (Vol. 16). New York: Academic Press, 1982.

Batter, B. S., & Davidson, C. V. Wariness of strangers: Reality or artifact? *Journal of child psychology and psychiatry,* 1979, *20,* 93–109.

Baumrind, D. Child care practices anteceding three patterns of preschool behavior. *Genetic psychology monographs,* 1967, *75,* 43–88.

——. Current patterns of parental authority. *Developmental psychology monograph,* 1971, *4* (1, Part 2).

——. Socialization and instrumental competence in young children. In W. W. Hartup (Ed.). *The young child: Reviews of research* (Vol. 2). Washington, D.C.: National Association for the Education of Young Children, 1972.

——. The development of instrumental competence through socialization. In A. D. Pick (Ed.). *Minnesota symposium on child psychology* (Vol 7). Minneapolis: University of Minnesota Press, 1973.

——. A dialectical materialist's perspective on knowing social reality. In W. Damon (Ed.). *Moral development.* San Francisco: Jossey-Bass, 1978.

——. Rejoinder to Lewis's reinterpretation of parental firm control effects: Are authoritative families really harmonious? *Psychological bulletin,* 1983, *94,* 131–142.

Bayley, N. Comparisons of mental and motor test scores for ages 1–15 months by sex, birth order, race, geographical location, and education of parents. *Child development,* 1965, *36,* 379–411.

——. *Bayley scales of infant development.* New York: Psychological Corporation, 1969.

Bee, H. L.; Barnard, K. E.; Eyres, S. J.; Gray, C. A.; Hammond, M. A.; Spietz, A. L.; Snyder, C.; & Clark, B. Prediction of IQ and language skill from perinatal status, child performance, family characteristics, and mother-infant interaction. *Child development,* 1982, *53,* 1134–1156.

Bell, L. G., & Bell, D. C. Family climate and the role of the female adolescent: Determinants of adolescent functioning. *Family relations,* 1982, *31,* 519–527.

Bell, S. M., & Ainsworth, M. D. S. Infant crying and maternal responsiveness. *Child development,* 1972, *43,* 1171–1190.

Belsky, J. Child maltreatment: An ecological in-

tegration. *American psychologist,* 1980, *35,* 320–335.

Belsky, J., & Steinberg, L. D. The effects of day care: A critical review. *Child development,* 1978, *49,* 929–949.

Bem, S. L. The measurement of psychological androgyny. *Journal of consulting and clinical psychology,* 1974, *42,* 155–162.

Berberian, K. E., & Snyder, S. S. The relationship of temperament and stranger reaction for younger and older infants. *Merrill-Palmer quarterly,* 1982, *28,* 79–94.

Bereiter, C.; Hidi, S.; & Dimitroff, G. Qualitative changes in verbal reasoning during middle and late childhood. *Child development,* 1979, *50,* 142–151.

Berg, J. M. Aetiological aspects of mental subnormality. In A. M. Clarke & A. D. B. Clarke (Eds.). *Mental deficiency: The changing outlook.* New York: Free Press, 1974.

Berndt, T. J. Developmental changes in conformity to peers and parents. *Developmental psychology,* 1979, *15,* 608–616.

——. Age changes and changes over time in prosocial intentions and behavior between friends. *Developmental psychology,* 1981, *17,* 408–416. (a)

——. Effects of friendship on prosocial intentions and behavior. *Child development,* 1981, *52,* 636–643. (b)

——. The features and effects of friendship in early adolescence. *Child development,* 1982, *53,* 1447–1460.

Bernstein, A. C. How children learn about sex and birth. *Psychology today,* 1976, *9,* 31–35.

Bertenthal, B. I., & Fischer, K. W. Development of self-recognition in the infant. *Developmental psychology,* 1978, *14,* 44–50.

Best, D. L.; Williams, J. E.; Cloud, J. M.; Davis, S. W.; Robertson, L. S.; Edwards, J. R.; Giles, H.; & Fowles, J. Development of sex-trait stereotypes among young children in the United States, England, and Ireland. *Child development,* 1977, *48,* 1375–1384.

Biemiller, A. J. The development of the use of graphic and contextual information in children learning to read. *Reading research quarterly,* 1970, *6,* 75–96.

Binet, A., & Simon, T. *The development of intelligence in children.* Baltimore: Williams & Wilkins, 1916.

Birch, H. G., & Lefford, A. Intersensory development in children. *Monographs of the Society for Research in Child Development,* 1963, *28* (Whole No. 89).

Bissell, J. S. Planned variation in Head Start and Follow Through. In J. C. Stanley (Ed.). *Compensatory education for children, ages 2 to 8.* Baltimore: Johns Hopkins University Press, 1973.

Blehar, M. C. Anxious attachment and defensive reactions associated with day care. *Child development,* 1974, *45,* 683–692.

Blehar, M. C.; Leiberman, A. F.; & Ainsworth, M. D. S. Early face-to-face interaction and its relation to later infant-mother attachment. *Child development,* 1977, *48,* 182–194.

Blewitt, P. *Dog* versus *collie:* Vocabulary in speech to young children. *Developmental psychology,* 1983, *19,* 602–609.

Block, J. *Lives through time.* Berkeley, Calif.: Bancroft, 1971.

Bloom, L. *One word at a time.* The Hague: Mouton, 1973.

Bloom, L.; Merkin, S.; & Wootten, J. *Wh*-questions: linguistic factors that contribute to the sequence of acquisition. *Child development,* 1982, *53,* 1084–1092.

Bornstein, M. H.; Kessen, W.; & Weiskopf, S. Color vision and hue categorization in young human infants. *Journal of experimental psychology: Human perception and performance,* 1976, *2,* 115–129.

Bornstein, M. H., & Teller, D. Y. Color vision. In P. Salapatek & L. B. Cohen (Eds.). *Handbook of infant perception.* New York: Academic Press, 1982.

Bottoms, S. F.; Rosen, T. G.; & Sokol, R. J. The increase in the cesarean birth rate. *The New England journal of medicine,* 1980, *302,* 559–563.

Boukydis, C. F. Z., & Burgess, R. L. Adult physiological response to infant cries: Effects of temperament, parental status, and gender. *Child development,* 1982, *53,* 1291–1298.

Bower, T. G. R. The visual world of infants. *Scientific American,* 1966, *215,* 80–92.

———. Infant perception of the third dimension and object concept development. In L. B. Cohen & P. Salapatek (Eds.). *Infant perception: From sensation to cognition.* New York: Academic Press, 1975.

———. *The perceptual world of the child.* Cambridge, Mass.: Harvard University Press, 1977. (a)

———. Blind babies see with their ears. *New scientist,* 1977, *73,* 256–257. (b)

———. Visual development in the blind child. In A. MacFarlane (Ed.). *Clinic in developmental medicine on vision.* London: Spastics International Medical Publication, 1978.

Bowlby, J. *Attachment and loss* (Vol 1), *Attachment.* New York: Basic Books, 1969.

———. *Attachment and loss* (Vol. 2), *Separation, anxiety, and anger.* New York: Basic Books, 1973.

———. *Attachment and loss* (Vol. 3), *Loss, sadness, and depression.* New York: Basic Books, 1980.

Brackbill, Y. Obstetrical medication and infant behavior. In J. D. Osofsky (Ed.). *Handbook of infant development.* New York: Wiley, 1979.

Brackbill, Y., & Nevill, D. D. Parental expectations of achievement as affected by children's height. *Merrill-Palmer quarterly,* 1981, *27,* 429–441.

Bradley, R. H., & Caldwell, B. M. The relation of infants' home environment to mental test performance at fifty-four months: A follow-up study. *Child development,* 1976, *47,* 1172–1174.

———. Home observation for measurement of the environment: A validation study of screening efficiency. *American journal of mental deficiency,* 1977, *81,* 417–420.

———. Screening the environment. *American journal of orthopsychiatry,* 1978, *48,* 114–129.

Braine, M. D. S. The ontogeny of English phrase structure: The first phase. *Language,* 1963, *39,* 1–13.

Brainerd, C. J. Neo-Piagetian training experiments revisited: Is there any support for the cognitive-developmental stage hypothesis? *Cognition,* 1974, *2,* 349–370.

———. Learning research and Piagetian theory. In L. S. Siegel & C. J. Brainerd (Eds.). *Alter-*

natives to Piaget: Critical essays on the theory. New York: Academic Press, 1978.

Brazelton, T. B. *Infants and mothers: Differences in development.* New York: Dell, 1969.

———. *Toddlers and parents.* New York: Dell, 1974.

Brenner, J., & Mueller, E. Shared meaning in boy toddlers' peer relations. *Child development,* 1982, *53,* 380–391.

Brody, E. B., & Brody, N. *Intelligence: Nature, determinants and consequences.* New York: Academic Press, 1976.

Broman, S. H.; Nichols, P. L.; & Kennedy, W. A. *Preschool IQ: Prenatal & early developmental correlates.* Hillsdale, N.J.: Erlbaum, 1975.

Bromwich, R. M. Focus on maternal behavior in infant intervention. *American journal of orthopsychiatry,* 1976, *46,* 439–446.

Bromwich, R. M.; Khoka, E.; Burge, D.; Baxter, E.; Kass, W.; & Fust, S. A parent behavior progression. In B. Weissbound & J. Musick (Eds.). *Infants: Their social environments.* Washington, D.C.: National Association for the Education of Young Children, 1981.

Bronfenbrenner, U. Toward an experimental ecology of human development. *American psychologist,* 1977, *32,* 513–531.

———. *The ecology of human development.* Cambridge, Mass.: Harvard University Press, 1979.

Bronson, G. W. The postnatal growth of visual capacity. *Child development,* 1974, *45,* 873–890.

Brooks-Gunn, J., & Matthews, W. S. *He and she: How children develop their sex role identity.* Englewood Cliffs, N.J.: Prentice-Hall, 1979.

Broverman, I. K.; Broverman, D.; Clarkson, F. E.; Rosenkrantz, P. S.; & Vogel, S. R. Sex-role stereotypes and clinical judgments of mental health. *Journal of consulting and clinical psychology,* 1970, *34,* 1–7.

Brown, A. L.; Bransford, J. D.; Ferrara, R. A.; & Campione, J. C. Learning, remembering, and understanding. In J. H. Flavell & E. M. Markman (Eds.). *Manual of child psychology* (Vol III, 4th ed.). New York: Wiley, 1983.

Brown, J. *Nutrition for your pregnancy: The University of Minnesota guide.* Minneapolis: University of Minnesota Press, 1983.

Brown, R. *Social psychology.* New York: Free Press, 1965.

———. Development of the first language in the human species. *American psychologist,* 1973, *28,* 97–106. (a)

———. *A first language: The early stages.* Cambridge, Mass.: Harvard University Press, 1973. (b)

Brown, R., & Bellugi, U. Three processes in the acquisition of syntax. *Harvard educational review,* 1964, *34,* 133–151.

Brown, R.; Cazden, C.; & Bellugi, U. The child's grammar from I to III. In J. P. Hill (Ed.). *Minnesota symposia on child psychology* (Vol. 2). Minneapolis: University of Minnesota Press, 1969.

Brumback, R. A., & Staton, R. D. Learning disability in childhood depression. *American journal of orthopsychiatry,* 1983, *53,* 269–281.

Budoff, M., & Gottlieb, J. Special-class EMR children mainstreamed: A study of an aptitude (learning potential) treatment interaction. *American journal of mental deficiency,* 1976, *81,* 1–11.

Bullock, M., & Gelman, R. Preschool children's assumptions about cause and effect: Temporal ordering. *Child development,* 1979, *50,* 89–96.

Buss, A. H., & Plomin, R. A. *Temperament theory of personality development.* New York: Wiley, 1975.

Butler, N. R., & Goldstein, H. Smoking in pregnancy and subsequent child development. *British medical journal,* 1973, *4,* 573–575.

Butterfield, E. C.; Siladi, D.; & Belmont, J. M. Validating theories of intelligence. In H. W. Reese & L. P. Lipsitt (Eds.). *Advances in child development and behavior* (Vol. 15). New York: Academic Press, 1980.

Caldwell, B. M., & Bradley, R. H. Manual for the home observation of the environment. Unpublished manuscript. Little Rock, Ark.: University of Arkansas, 1978.

Campbell, S. B. G., & Taylor, P. M. Bonding and attachment: Theoretical issues. In P. M. Taylor (Ed.). *Parent-infant relationships.* New York: Grune & Stratton, 1980.

Campione, J. C.; Brown, A. L.; & Ferrara, R. A. Mental retardation and intelligence. In R. J.

Sternberg (Ed.). *Handbook of human intelligence.* Cambridge, England: Cambridge University Press, 1982.

Campos, J. J.; Langer, A.; & Krowitz, A. Cardiac responses on the visual cliff in prelocomotor human infants. *Science,* 1970, *170,* 196–197.

Carey, W. B. The importance of temperament-environment interaction for child health and development. In M. Lewis & L. A. Rosenblum (Eds.). *The uncommon child.* New York: Plenum, 1981.

Carlsson, S. G.; Fagerberg, H.; Horneman, G.; Hwang, C.; Larsson, K.; Rodholm, M.; Schaller, J.; Danielsson, B.; & Bundewall, C. Effects of various amounts of contact between mother and child on the mother's nursing behavior: A follow-up study. *Infant behavior and development,* 1979, *2,* 209–214.

Caron, A. J., & Caron, R. F. Cognitive development in early infancy. In T. M. Field, A. Huston, H. C. Quay, L. Troll, & G. E. Finley (Eds.). *Review of human development.* New York: Wiley, 1982.

Carr, J. Young children with Down's syndrome: Their development, upbringing and effect on their families. London: Butterworth, 1975.

Carter, D. B., & Patterson, C. J. Sex roles as social conventions: The development of children's conceptions of sex-role stereotypes. *Developmental psychology,* 1982, *18,* 812–824.

Caudill, W., & Frost, N. A comparison of maternal care and infant behavior in Japanese-American, American, and Japanese families. In U. Bronfenbrenner & M. A. Mahoney (Eds.). *Influences on human development.* Hinsdale, Ill.: Dryen Press, 1972.

Chall, J. S. *Learning to read: The great debate.* New York: McGraw-Hill, 1967.

Chase, W. P. Color vision in infants. *Journal of experimental psychology,* 1937, *20,* 203–222.

Chess, S., & Thomas, A. Infant bonding: Mystique and reality. *American journal of orthopsychiatry,* 1982, *52,* 213–222.

Chi, M. T. Knowledge structure and memory development. In R. S. Siegler (Ed.). *Children's thinking: What develops?* Hillsdale, N.J.: Erlbaum, 1978.

Chilman, C. S. Social and psychological research concerning adolescent child-bearing: 1970– 1980. *Journal of marriage and the family,* 1980, *42,* 793–806.

Chomsky, N. *Aspects of a theory of syntax.* Cambridge, Mass.: M.I.T. Press, 1965.

———. *Reflections on language.* New York: Pantheon Books, 1975.

Chukovsky, K. *From two to five.* Berkeley: University of California Press, 1963.

Chumlea, W. C. Physical growth in adolescence. In B. B. Wolman (Ed.). *Handbook of developmental psychology.* Englewood Cliffs, N.J.: Prentice-Hall, 1982.

Clark, E. V. What's in a word? On the child's acquisition of semantics in his first language. In E. Moore (Ed.). *Cognitive development and the acquisition of language.* New York: Academic Press, 1973.

———. Knowledge, context, and strategy in the acquisition of meaning. In D. P. Date (Ed.). *Georgetown University round table on language and linguistics, 1975.* Washington, D.C.: Georgetown University Press, 1975.

———. Strategies and the mapping problem in first language acquisition. In J. Macnamara (Ed.). *Language learning and thought.* New York: Academic Press, 1977.

Clarke-Stewart, K. A. Interactions between mothers and their young children: Characteristics and consequences. *Monographs of the Society for Research in Child Development,* 1973, *38* (Whole No. 153).

Clarke-Stewart, K. A., & Hevey, C. M. Longitudinal relations in repeated observations of mother-child interaction from 1 to 1 $\frac{1}{2}$ years. *Developmental psychology,* 1981, *17,* 127–145.

Clifton, R. K.; Morrongiello, B. A.; Kulig, J. W.; & Dowd, J. M. Newborns' orientation toward sound: Possible implications for cortical development. *Child development,* 1981, *52,* 833–838.

Coates, S. *Preschool embedded figures test.* Palo Alto, Calif.: Consulting Psychologists Press, 1972.

Cochran, M. M., & Brassard, J. A. Child development and personal social networks. *Child development,* 1979, *50,* 601–616.

Cohen, L. Our developing knowledge of infant perception and cognition. *American Psychologist,* 1979, *34* 894–899.

Colby, A.; Kohlberg, L.; Gibbs, J.; & Lieberman, M. A longitudinal study of moral judgment. *Monographs of the Society for Research in Child Development,* 1983, *48* (1–2, Whole No. 200).

Cole, M., & Traupmann, K. Comparative cognitive research: Learning from a learning disabled child. In W. A. Collins (Ed.). *Aspects of the development of competence: The Minnesota symposia on child psychology* (Vol. 14). Hillsdale, N.J.: Erlbaum, 1981.

Colombo, J. The critical period concept: Research, methodology, and theoretical issues. *Psychological bulletin,* 1982, *91,* 260–275.

Comstock, G.; Chaffee, S.; Katzman, N.; McCombs, M.; & Roberts, D. *Television and human behavior.* New York: Columbia University Press, 1978.

Condran, J. G., & Bode, J. G. Rashomon, working wives, and family division of labor: Middletown, 1980. *Journal of marriage and the family,* 1982, *44,* 421–426.

Coopersmith, S. *The antecedents of self-esteem.* San Francisco: Freeman, 1967.

Cowart, B. J. Development of taste perception in humans: Sensitivity and preference throughout the life span. *Psychological bulletin,* 1981, *90,* 43–73.

Crain, W. C. *Theories of development.* Englewood Cliffs, N.J.: Prentice-Hall, 1980.

Crnic, K. A.; Greenberg, M. T.; Ragozin, A. S.; Robinson, N. M.; & Basham, R. B. Effects of stress and social support on mothers and premature and full-term infants. *Child development,* 1983, *54,* 209–217.

Crockenberg, S. B. Infant irritability, mother responsiveness, and social support influences on the security of infant-mother attachment. *Child development,* 1981, *52,* 857–865.

———. Social support and the maternal behavior of adolescent mothers. Paper presented at the biennial meetings of the Society for Research in Child Development, Detroit, 1983.

Czikszentmihalyi, M.; Larson, R.; & Prescott, S. The ecology of adolescent activity and experience. *Journal of youth and adolescence,* 1977, *6,* 281–294.

Dale, P. S. *Language development: Structure and function* (2d ed.). New York: Holt, Rinehart and Winston, 1976.

Damon, W. *The social world of the child.* San Francisco: Jossey-Bass, 1977.

Damon, W., & Hart, D. The development of self-understanding from infancy through adolescence. *Child development,* 1982, *53,* 841–864.

Danner, F. W., & Day, M. C. Eliciting formal operations. *Child development,* 1977, *48,* 1600–1606.

Danner, F. W., & Lonky, E. A cognitive-developmental approach to the effects of rewards on intrinsic motivation. *Child development,* 1981, *52,* 1043–1052.

Davidson, E. S.; Yasuna, A.; & Tower, A. The effect of television cartoons on sex-role stereotyping in young girls. *Child development,* 1979, *50,* 597–600.

DeCasper, A., & Fifer, W. Of human bonding: Newborns prefer their mothers' voices. *Science,* 1980, *208,* 1174–1176.

de Chateau, P. Effects of hospital practices on synchrony in the development of the infant-parent relationship. In P. M. Taylor (Ed.). *Parent-infant relationships.* New York: Grune & Stratton, 1980.

Dempster, F. N. Memory span: Sources of individual and developmental differences. *Psychological bulletin,* 1981, *89,* 63–100.

Dennis, M.; Sugar, J.; & Whitaker, H. A. The acquisition of tag questions. *Child development,* 1982, *53,* 1254–1257.

Dennis, W. Causes of retardation among institutional children: Iran. *Journal of genetic psychology,* 1960, *96,* 47–59.

Detterman, D. K., & Sternberg, R. J. *How and how much can intelligence be raised.* Norwood, N.J.: Ablex, 1982.

DeVoe, M. W. Cooperation as a function of self-concept, sex and race. *Educational research quarterly,* 1977, *2,* 3–8.

DeVries, R. Constancy of generic identity in the years three to six. *Monographs of the Society for Research in Child Development,* 1969, *34* (Whole No. 127).

The Diagram Group. *Child's body.* New York: Paddington, 1977.

Dickerson, J. W. T. Nutrition, brain growth and development. In K. J. Connolly & H. F. R.

Prechtl (Eds.). *Maturation and development: Biological and psychological perspectives.* Clinics in Developmental Medicine No. 77/78. London: Heinemann, 1981.

Dicks-Mireaux, M. J. Mental development of infants with Down's syndrome. *American journal of mental deficiency,* 1972, *77,* 26–32.

Dickson, W. P.; Hess, R. D.; Miyake, N.; & Azuma, H. Referential communication accuracy between mother and child as a predictor of cognitive development in the United States and Japan. *Child development,* 1979, *50,* 43–59.

DiPietro, J. A. Rough and tumble play: A function of gender. *Developmental psychology,* 1981, *17,* 50–58.

DiVitto, B., & Goldberg, S. The effects of newborn medical status on early parent-infant interaction. In T. Field, A. Sostek, S. Goldberg, & H. H. Shuman (Eds.). *Infants born at risk.* New York: Spectrum, 1979.

Dobson, V., & Teller, D. Y. Visual acuity in human infants: A review and comparison of behavioral and electrophysiological studies. *Vision research,* 1978, *18,* 1469–1483.

Dollard, J.; Doob, L. W.; Miller, N. E.; Mowrer, O. H.; & Sears, R. R. *Frustration and aggression.* New Haven, Conn.: Yale University Press, 1939.

Dominick, J. R., & Greenberg, B. S. Attitudes toward violence: The interaction of television exposure, family attitudes, and social class. In G. A. Comstock & E. A. Rubenstein (Eds.). *Television and social behavior* (Vol. 3). Washington, D.C.: U.S. Government Printing Office, 1972.

Doyle, A-B. Friends, acquaintances, and strangers: The influence of familiarity and ethnolinguistic background on social interaction. In K. H. Rubin & H. S. Ross (Eds.). *Peer relationships and social skills in childhood.* New York: Springer-Verlag, 1982.

Dreyer, P. H. Sexuality during adolescence. In B. B. Wolman (Ed.). *Handbook of developmental psychology.* Englewood Cliffs, N.J.: Prentice-Hall, 1982.

Dunn, H. G.; McBurney, A. K.; Ingram, S.; & Hunter, C. M. Maternal cigarette smoking during pregnancy and the child's subsequent development: II. Neurological and intellectual maturation to the age of 6½ years. *Canadian journal of public health,* 1977, *68,* 43–50.

Dunphy, D. C. The social structure of urban adolescent peer groups. *Sociometry,* 1963, *26,* 230–246.

Dunst, C. J.; Brooks, P. H.; & Doxsey, P. A. Characteristics of hiding places and the transition to stage IV performance in object permanence tasks. *Developmental psychology,* 1982, *18,* 671–681.

Eckerman, C. O., & Whatley, J. L. Toys and social interaction between infant peers. *Child development,* 1977, *48,* 1645–1656.

Edgerton, R. B. *Mental retardation.* Cambridge, Mass.: Harvard University Press, 1979.

Edwards, C. P., & Lewis, M. Young children's concepts of social relations: Social functions and social objects. In M. L. Lewis & L. Rosenblum (Eds.). *The child and his family.* New York: Plenum, 1979.

Egeland, B., & Sroufe, L. A. Attachment and maltreatment. *Child development,* 1981, *52,* 44–52. (a)

———. Developmental sequelae of maltreatment in infancy. In R. Rizley & D. Cicchetti (Eds.). *Developmental perspectives on child maltreatment.* San Francisco: Jossey-Bass, 1981. (b)

Ehrhardt, A. A., & Baker, S. W. Fetal androgens, human central nervous system differentiation, and behavior sex differences. In R. C. Friedman, R. M. Richart, & R. L. Vande Wiele (Eds.). *Sex differences in behavior.* New York: Wiley, 1974.

Eichorn, D. H.; Hunt, J. V.; & Honzik, M. P. Experience, personality, and IQ: Adolescence to middle age. In D. H. Eichorn, J. A. Clausen, N. Haan, M. P. Honzik, & P. H. Mussen (Eds.). *Present and past in middle life.* New York: Academic Press, 1981.

Eisenberg-Berg, N., & Hand, M. The relationship of preschoolers' reasoning about prosocial moral conflicts to prosocial behavior. *Child development,* 1979, *50,* 356–363.

Elardo, R.; Bradley, R.; & Caldwell, B. The relation of infants' home environments to mental test performance from six to thirty-six months: A longitudinal analysis. *Child development,* 1975, *46,* 71–76.

Emde, R.; Baensbauer, T.; & Harmon, R. Emotional expression in infancy: A biobehavioral study. *Psychological issues,* 1976, *10* (1, Whole No. 37).

Eme, R. F. Sex differences in childhood psychopathology: A review. *Psychological bulletin,* 1979, *86,* 374–395.

Emmerich, W., & Shepard, K. Development of sex-differentiated preferences during later childhood and adolescence. *Child development,* 1982, *18,* 406–417.

Entwisle, D. R., & Baker, D. P. Gender and young children's expectations for performance in arithmetic. *Developmental psychology,* 1983, *19,* 200–209.

Erikson, E. H. *Childhood and society.* New York: Norton, 1950, 1963.

———. *Identity and the life cycle.* New York: Norton, 1959, 1980.

———. *Insight and responsibility.* New York: Norton, 1964.

———. *Dimensions of a new identity: The 1973 Jefferson lectures in the humanities.* New York: Norton, 1974.

Eron, L. D. Parent-child interaction, television violence, and aggression of children. *American psychologist,* 1982, *37,* 197–211.

Eron, L. D.; Huesmann, L. R.; Brice, P.; Fischer, P.; & Mermelstein, R. Age trends in the development of aggression, sex-typing, and related television habits. *Developmental psychology,* 1983, *19,* 71–77.

Escalona, S. K. The reciprocal role of social and emotional developmental advances and cognitive development during the second and third years of life. In E. K. Shapiro & E. Weber (Eds.). *Cognitive and affective growth: Developmental interaction.* Hillsdale, N.J.: Erlbaum, 1981.

Etaugh, C. Effects of nonmaternal care on children: Research evidence and popular views. *American psychologist,* 1980, *35,* 305–319.

Fagan, J. F. III, & McGrath, S. K. Infant recognition memory and later intelligence. *Intelligence,* 1981, *5,* 121–130.

Fagot, B. I. Sex differences in toddlers' behavior and parental reaction. *Developmental psychology,* 1974, *10,* 544–558.

Fagot, B. I., & Kronsberg, S. J. Sex differences: Biological and social factors influencing the behavior of young boys and girls. In S. G. Moore & C. R. Cooper (Eds.). *The young child: Reviews of research* (Vol. 3). Washington, D.C.: National Association for the Education of Young Children, 1982.

Fantz, R. L. A method for studying early visual development. *Perceptual and motor skills,* 1956, *6,* 13–15.

Fantz, R. L., & Fagan, J. F. III. Visual attention to size and number of pattern details by term and preterm infants during the first six months. *Child development,* 1975, *46,* 3–18.

Fantz, R. L.; Fagan, J. F. III; & Miranda, S. B. Early visual selectivity. In L. B. Cohen & P. Salapatek (Eds.). *Infant perception: From sensation to cognition* (Vol. 1). New York: Academic Press, 1975.

Farber, S. L. *Identical twins reared apart: A reanalysis.* New York: Basic Books, 1981.

Farnham-Diggory, S. *Learning disabilities.* Cambridge, Mass.: Harvard University Press, 1978.

Farran, D. C.; Haskins, R.; & Gallagher, J. J. Poverty and mental retardation: A search for explanatoins. In J. J. Gallagher (Ed.). *Ecology of exceptional children.* San Francisco: Jossey-Bass, 1980.

Fein, G. G. Pretend play in childhood: An integrative review. *Child development,* 1981, *52,* 1095–1118.

Feingold, B. F. *Why your child is hyperactive.* New York: Random House, 1975.

Ferguson, T. J., & Rule, B. G. Effects of inferential set, consequence severity, and basis for responsibility on children's evaluation of aggressive acts. *Developmental psychology,* 1980, *16,* 141–146.

———. Influence of inferential set, outcome intent, and outcome severity on children's moral judgments. *Developmental psychology,* 1982, *18,* 843–851.

Feshbach, S. Aggression. In P. H. Mussen (Ed.). *Carmichael's manual of child psychology* (Vol. 2, 3d ed.). New York: Wiley, 1970.

Field, T. M. Effects of early separation, interactive deficits, and experimental manipulations on infant-mother face-to-face interaction. *Child development,* 1977, *48,* 763–771.

———. Social perception and responsivity in early infancy. In T. M. Field, A. Huston, H.

C. Quay, L. Troll, & G. E. Finley (Eds.). *Review of human development.* New York: Wiley, 1982.

Field, T. M.; De Stefano, L.; & Koewler, J. H. III. Fantasy play of toddlers and preschoolers. *Developmental psychology,* 1982, *18,* 503–508.

Field, T. M., & Widmayer, S. M. Developmental follow-up of infants delivered by cesarean section and general anesthesia. *Infant behavior and development,* 1980, *3,* 253–264.

Fischer, K. W. A theory of cognitive development: The control and construction of hierarchies of skills. *Psychological review,* 1980, *87,* 477–531.

Flavell, J. H. Developmental studies of mediated memory. In H. W. Reese & L. P. Lipsitt (Eds.). *Advances in child development and behavior* (Vol. 5). New York: Academic Press, 1970.

———. *Cognitive development.* Englewood Cliffs, N.J.: Prentice-Hall, 1977.

———. On cognitive development. *Child development,* 1982, *53,* 1–10. (a)

———. Structures, stages, and sequences in cognitive development. In W. A. Collins (Ed.). *The concept of development: The Minnesota symposia on child psychology* (Vol. 15). Hillsdale, N.J.: Erlbaum, 1982. (b)

Flavell, J. H.; Eaverett, B. A.; Croft, K.; & Flavell, E. R. Young children's knowledge about visual perception: Further evidence for the Level 1–Level 2 distinction. *Developmental psychology,* 1981, *17,* 99–103.

Fogel, A. Peer versus mother directed behavior in one- to three-month-old infants. *Infant behavior and development,* 1979, *2,* 215–226.

Forbes, G. B. Growth of the lean body mass in man. *Growth,* 1972, *36,* 325–338.

Ford, M. E. Social cognition and social competence in adolescence. *Developmental psychology,* 1982, *18,* 323–340.

Fraiberg, S. Blind infants and their mothers: An examination of the sign system. In M. Lewis & L. A. Rosenblum (Eds.). *The effect of the infant on its caregiver.* New York: Wiley, 1974.

———. The development of human attachments in infants blind from birth. *Merrill-Palmer quarterly,* 1975, *21,* 35–334.

———. *Insights from the blind.* New York: New American Library (Meridian Books), 1977.

Freedman, D. G. Ethnic differences in babies. *Human Nature,* 1979, *2,* 36–43.

Freeman, J. The intellectually gifted. *New directions for exceptional children,* 1981, *7,* 75–86.

Freud, S. Three contributions to the theory of sex. *The basic writings of Sigmund Freud* (A. A. Brill, trans.). New York: Random House (Modern Library), 1905.

———. *A general introduction of psychoanalysis* (J. Riviere, trans.). New York: Washington Square Press, 1965 (originally published 1920).

Friedman, S. L.; Zahn-Waxler, C.; & Radke-Yarrow, M. Perceptions of cries of full-term and preterm infants. *Infant behavior and development,* 1982, *5,* 161–173.

Frueh, T., & McGhee, P. E. Traditional sex role development and amount of time spent watching television. *Developmental psychology,* 1975, *11,* 109.

Furth, H. *Piaget for teachers.* Englewood Cliffs, N.J.: Prentice-Hall, 1970.

Galbraith, R. C. The confluence model and six divergent data sets: Comments on Zajonc and Bargh. *Intelligence,* 1982, *6,* 305–320.

Gallagher, J. J. *Teaching the gifted child* (2d ed.). Boston: Allyn & Bacon, 1975.

Ganchrow, J. R.; Steiner, J. E.; & Daher, M. Neonatal facial expressions in response to different qualities and intensities of gustatory stimuli. *Infant behavior and development,* 1983, *6,* 189–200.

Garbarino, J. Changing hospital childbirth practices: A developmental perspective on prevention of child maltreatment. *American journal of orthopsychiatry,* 1980, *50,* 588–597.

Garbarino, J., & Sherman, D. High-risk neighborhoods and high-risk families: The human ecology of child maltreatment. *Child development,* 1980, *51,* 188–198.

Garber, H., & Heber, R. Modification of predicted cognitive development in high-risk children through early intervention. In D. K. Detterman & R. J. Sternberg (Eds.). *How and how much can intelligence be increased.* Norwood, N.J.: Ablex, 1982.

Gardner, B. T., & Gardner, R. A. Two comparative psychologists look at language acquisition. In K. Nelson (Ed.). *Children's language* (Vol. 2). New York: Gardner Press, 1980.

Garn, S. M. Continuities and change in maturational timing. In O. G. Brim, Jr., & J. Kagan (Eds.). *Constancy and change in human development.* Cambridge, Mass.: Harvard University Press, 1980.

Garn, S. M.; Clark, D. C.; & Guire, K. E. Growth, body composition, and development of obese and lean children. In M. Winick (Ed.). *Childhood obesity.* New York: Wiley, 1975.

Gelman, R. Logical capacity of very young children: Number invariance rules. *Child development,* 1972, *43,* 75–90.

Gentner, D. Why nouns are learned before verbs: Linguistic relativity versus natural partitioning. In S. A. Kuczaj II (Ed.). *Language development* (Vol. 2), *Language, thought, and culture.* Hillsdale, N.J.: Erlbaum, 1982.

Gerbner, G. Violence in television drama: Trends and symbolic functions. In G. A. Comstock & E. A. Rubenstein (Eds.). *Television and social behavior* (Vol. 1). Washington, D.C.: U.S. Government Printing Office, 1972.

Gerbner, G.; Gross, L.; Morgan, M.; & Signorielli, N. The "mainstreaming" of America: Violence profile no. 11. *Journal of communication,* 1980, *30,* 10–29.

Gerson, R. P., & Damon, W. Moral understanding and children's conduct. In W. Damon (Ed.). *Moral development.* San Francisco: Jossey-Bass, 1978.

Gesell, A. *The mental growth of the preschool child.* New York: Macmillan, 1925.

Gesell, A., & Thompson, H. Learning and growth in identical twins: An experimental study by the method of co-twin control. *Genetic psychology monographs,* 1929, *6,* 1–123.

Gewirtz, J. L., & Boyd, E. F. Does maternal responding imply reduced infant crying? A critique of the 1972 Bell and Ainsworth report. *Child development,* 1977, *48,* 1200–1207.

Gibson, E. J. *Principles of perceptual learning and development.* Englewood Cliffs, N.J.: Prentice-Hall, 1969.

Gibson, E. J., & Levin, H. *The psychology of reading.* Cambridge, Mass.: M.I.T. Press, 1975.

Gibson, E. J., & Walk, R. D. The "visual cliff." *Scientific American,* 1960, *202,* 64–71.

Giele, J. Z. Women's work and family roles. In J. Z. Giele (Ed.). *Women in the middle years.* New York: Wiley, 1982.

Gilligan, C. New maps of development: New visions of maturity. *American journal of orthopsychiatry,* 1982, *52,* 199–212. (a)

———. *In a different voice: Psychological theory and women's development.* Cambridge, Mass.: Harvard University Press, 1982. (b)

Ginsburg, H. J., & Miller, S. M. Sex differences in children's risk-taking behavior. *Child development,* 1982, *53,* 426–428.

Ginsburg, H., & Opper, S. *Piaget's theory of intellectual development.* Englewood Cliffs, N.J.: Prentice-Hall, 1969.

Goldberg, S.; Perlmutter, M.; & Myers, N. Recall of related and unrelated lists by two-year-olds. *Journal of experimental child psychology,* 1974, *18,* 1–8.

Golden, M.; Birns, B.; Gridger, W.; & Moss, A. Social class differentiation in cognitive development among black preschool children. *Child development,* 1971, *42,* 37–46.

Golden, M.; Rosenbluth, L.; Grossi, M.; Policare, H.; Freeman, H.; & Brownlee, E. *The New York City infant day care study.* New York: Medical and Health Research Association of New York City, 1978.

Goldin-Meadow, S.; Seligman, M.; & Gelman, R. Language in the two-year-old. *Cognition,* 1976, *4,* 189–202.

Goldsmith, H. H. Genetic influences on personality from infancy to adulthood. *Child development,* 1983, *54,* 331–355.

Goldsmith, H. H., & Campos, J. J. Toward a theory of infant temperament. In R. N. Emde & R. J. Harmon (Eds.). *The development of attachment and affiliative systems.* New York: Plenum, 1982.

Goldsmith, H. H., & Gottesman, I. I. Origins of variation in behavioral style: A longitudinal study of temperament in young twins. *Child development,* 1981, *52,* 91–103.

Goleman, D. 1,528 little geniuses and how they grew. *Psychology today,* 1980, *13,* 28–43.

Goodenough, F. L. *Measurement of intelligence*

*by drawings.* New York: Harcourt Brace Jovanovich, 1926.

———. *Anger in young children.* Minneapolis: University of Minnesota Press, 1931.

Goren, C. C.; Sart, M.; & Wu, P. K. Visual following and pattern discrimination of face-like stimuli by newborn infants. *Pediatrics,* 1975, *56,* 544–549.

Gottman, J. M., & Parkhurst, J. T. A developmental theory of friendship and acquaintanceship processes. In A. Collins (Ed.). *Minnesota symposia on child psychology* (Vol. 13). Hillsdale, N.J.: Erlbaum, 1980.

Graham, P. Epidemiological studies. In H. C. Quay & J. S. Werry (Eds.). *Psychopathological disorders of childhood* (2d ed.). New York: Wiley, 1979.

Greenberg, J., & Kuczaj, S. A., II. Towards a theory of substantive word-meaning acquisition. In S. A. Kuczaj II (Ed.). *Language development* (Vol. 1): *Syntax and semantics.* Hillsdale, N.J.: Erlbaum, 1982.

Greenberg, M., & Morris, N. Engrossment: The newborn's impact upon the father. *American journal of orthopsychiatry,* 1974, *44,* 520–531.

Grinker, J. A. Behavioral and metabolic factors in childhood obesity. In M. Lewis & L. A. Rosenblum (Eds.). *The uncommon child.* New York: Plenum, 1981.

Grossman, K.; Thane, K.; & Grossmann, K. E. Maternal tactual contact of the newborn after various post-partum conditions of mother-infant contact. *Developmental psychology,* 1981, *17,* 158–169.

Grotevant, H. D., & Thorbecke, W. L. Sex differences in styles of occupational identity formation in late adolescence. *Developmental psychology,* 1982, *18,* 396–405.

Grusec, J. E., & Arnason, L. Consideration for others: Approaches to enhancing altruism. In S. G. Moore & C. R. Cooper (Eds.). *The young child: Reviews of research* (Vol. 3). Washington, D.C.: National Association for the Education of Young Children, 1982.

Grusec, J. E.; Saas-Kortsaak, P.; & Simutis, Z. M. The role of example and moral exhortation in the training of altruism. *Child development,* 1978, *49,* 920–923.

Gurucharri, C., & Selman, R. L. The development of interpersonal understanding during childhood, preadolescence, and adolescence: A longitudinal follow-up study. *Child development,* 1982, *53,* 924–927.

Haith, M. M. *Rules that babies look by.* Hillsdale, N.J.: Erlbaum, 1980.

Hanson, M. J. Down's syndrome children: Characteristics and intervention research. In M. Lewis & L. A. Rosenblum (Eds.). *The uncommon child.* New York: Plenum, 1981.

Hardy-Brown, K.; Plomin, R.; & DeFries, J. C. Genetic and environmental influences on the rate of communicative development in the first year of life. *Developmental psychology,* 1981, *17,* 704–717.

Harley, J. P.; Ray, R. S.; Tomasi, L.; Eichman, P. L.; Matthews, C. G.; Chun, R.; Cleeland, C. S.; & Straisman, E. Hyperkinesis and food additives: Testing the Feingold hypothesis. *Pediatrics,* 1978, *61,* 818–828.

Hartup, W. W. Peer interaction and social organization. In P. H. Mussen (Ed.). *Carmichael's manual of child psychology* (Vol. 2, 3d ed.). New York: Wiley, 1970.

———. Aggression in childhood: Developmental perspectives. *American psychologist,* 1974, *29,* 336–341.

———. The origins of friendships. In M. Lewis & L. A. Rosenblum (Eds.). *Friendship and peer relations.* New York: Wiley, 1975.

———. Perspectives on child and family interaction: Past, present, and future. In R. M. Lerner & G. B. Spanier (Eds.). *Child influences on marital and family interaction.* New York: Academic Press, 1978.

Hay, D. F.; Nash, A.; & Pedersen, J. Interaction between six-month-old peers. *Child development,* 1983, *54,* 557–562.

Hayden, A. H., & Haring, N. G. Early intervention for high risk infants and young children: Programs for Down's syndrome children. In T. J. Tjossem (Ed.). *Intervention strategies for high risk infants and young children.* Baltimore: University Park Press, 1976.

Hayes, L. A., & Watson, J. S. Facial orientation of parents and elicited smiling by infants. *Infant behavior and development,* 1981, *4,* 333–340.

Haynes, H.; White, B. L.; & Held, R. Visual accommodation in human infants. *Science,* 1965, *148,* 528–530.

Hazen, N. L., & Durrett, M. E. Relationship of security of attachment to exploration and cognitive mapping abilities in 2-year-olds. *Developmental psychology,* 1982, *18,* 751–759.

Heber, F. R. Sociocultural mental retardation—a longitudinal study. In D. Forgays (Ed.). *Primary prevention of psychopathology* (Vol. 2). Hanover, N.J.: University Press of New England, 1978.

Hechtman, L., & Weiss, G. Long-term outcome of hyperactive children. *American journal of orthopsychiatry,* 1983, *53,* 532–541.

Helfer, R. Relationship between lack of bonding and child abuse and neglect. In M. H. Klaus, T. Leger, & M. A. Trause (Eds.). *Maternal attachment and mothering disorders: A round table.* Johnson & Johnson Baby Products Co., 1975.

Henley, E. D., & Altman, J. The young adult. In D. W. Smith, E. L. Bierman, & N. M. Robinson (Eds.). *The biologic ages of man.* Philadelphia: Saunders, 1978.

Henneborn, W. J., & Cogan, R. The effect of husband participation on reported pain and the probability of medication during labour and birth. *Journal of psychosomatic research,* 1975, *19,* 215–222.

Hennig, M., & Jardim, A. *The managerial woman.* Garden City, N.Y.: Doubleday, 1976.

Herzog, E. W.; Enright, M.; Luria, O.; & Rubin, J. Z. Do gender labels yield sex differences in performance or is label a fable? *Developmental psychology,* 1982, *18,* 424–430.

Hess, E. H. "Imprinting" in a natural laboratory. *Scientific American,* 1972, *227,* 24–31.

Hess, R. D., & Camara, K. A. Post-divorce relationships as mediating factors in the consequences of divorce for children. *Journal of social issues,* 1979, *35,* 79–96.

Hess, T. M., & Radtke, R. C. Processing and memory factors in children's reading comprehension skill. *Child development,* 1981, *52,* 479–488.

Hetherington, E. M. Divorce: A child's perspective. *American psychologist,* 1979, *34,* 851–858.

Hetherington, E. M.; Cox, M.; & Cox, R. The af-
termath of divorce. In M. H. Stevens, Jr., & M. Mathews (Eds.). *Mother/child, father/child relationships.* Washington, D.C.: National Association for the Education of Young Children, 1978.

Hetherington, E. M., & Martin, B. Family interaction. In H. C. Quay & J. S. Werry (Eds.). *Psychopathological disorders of childhood* (2d ed.). New York: Wiley, 1979.

High/Scope Foundation. Can preschool education make a lasting difference? Bulletin of the High/Scope Foundation, no. 4, Fall 1977.

Hines, M. Prenatal gonadal hormones and sex differences in human behavior. *Psychological bulletin,* 1982, *92,* 56–80.

Hobbs, N. *The futures of children.* San Francisco: Jossey-Bass, 1975.

Hodgson, J. W., & Fischer, J. L. Sex differences in identity and intimacy development in college youth. *Journal of youth and adolescence,* 1979, *8,* 37–50.

Hoffman, M. L. Moral development. In P. H. Mussen (Ed.). *Carmichael's manual of child psychology* (Vol. 2, 3d ed.). New York: Wiley, 1970.

Horn, J. L. Trends in the measurement of intelligence. *Intelligence,* 1979, *3,* 229–240.

Horn, J. M. The Texas adoption project: Adopted children and their intellectual resemblance to biological and adoptive parents. *Child development,* 1983, *54,* 268–275.

Horowitz, F. D. The first two years of life: Factors related to thriving. In S. G. Moore & C. R. Cooper (Eds.). *The young child: Reviews of research* (Vol. 3). Washington, D.C.: National Association for the Education of Young Children, 1982.

Howard, J. The influence of children's developmental dysfunctions on marital quality and family interaction. In R. M. Lerner & G. B. Spanier (Eds.). *Child influences on marital and family interaction: A life-span perspective.* New York: Academic Press, 1978.

Hunt, J. V. Predicting intellectual disorders in childhood for preterm infants with birthweights below 1501 gm. In S. L. Friedman & M. Sigman (Eds.). *Preterm birth and psychological development.* New York: Academic Press, 1981.

Hunter, F. T., & Youniss, J. Changes in functions of three relations during adolescence. *Developmental psychology,* 1982, *18,* 806–811.

Huston-Stein, A., & Higgens-Trenk, A. Development of females from childhood through adulthood: Career and feminine role orientations. In P. B. Baltes (Ed.). *Life-span development and behavior* (Vol. 1). New York: Academic Press, 1978.

Hutt, S. J., & Hutt, C. (Eds.). *Behavior studies in psychiatry.* New York: Pergamon Press, 1970.

Hutt, S. J.; Lenard, H. G.; & Prechtl, H. F. R. Psychophysiological studies in newborn infants. In L. P. Lipsitt & H. W. Reese (Eds.). *Advances in child development and behavior.* New York: Academic Press, 1969.

Ianco-Worrall, A. D. Bilingualism and cognitive development. *Child development,* 1972, *43,* 1390–1400.

Ingram, D. Early patterns of grammatical development. In R. E. Stark (Ed.). *Language behavior in infancy and early childhood.* New York: Elsevier/North-Holland, 1981.

Inhelder, B., & Piaget, J. *The growth of logical thinking from childhood to adolescence.* New York: Basic Books, 1958.

Jacklin, C. N., & Maccoby, E. E. Social behavior at 33 months in same-sex and mixed-sex dyads. *Child development,* 1978, *49,* 557–569.

Jackson, E.; Campos, J. J.; & Fischer, K. W. The question of decalage between object permanence and person permanence. *Developmental psychology,* 1978, *14,* 1–10.

Jacobson, J. L. The role of inanimate objects in early peer interaction. *Child development,* 1981, *52,* 618–626.

Jacobson, J. L.; Boersma, D. C.; Fields, R. B.; & Olson, K. L. Paralinguistic features of adult speech to infants and small children. *Child development,* 1983, *54,* 436–442.

James, W. *Psychology: The briefer course.* New York: Harper & Row, 1961 (originally published in 1892).

Jensen, A. R. *Bias in mental testing.* New York: Free Press, 1979.

———. Obstacles, problems, and pitfalls in differential psychology. In S. Scarr (Ed.). *Race, social class, and individual differences in I.Q.* Hilsdale, N.J.: Erlbaum, 1981.

Jensen, K. Differential reactions to taste and temperature stimuli in newborn infants. *Genetic psychology monographs,* 1932, *12,* 361–479.

Johnston, J. M. Punishment of human behavior. *American psychologist,* 1972, *27,* 1033–1054.

Johnston, L. *Do they ever grow up?* Wazada, Minn.: Meadowbrook Press, 1978.

Jones, K. L.; Smith, D. W.; Ulleland, C. N.; & Streissguth, A. P. Pattern of malformation in offspring of chronic alcoholic mothers. *Lancet,* 1973, *1,* 1267–1271.

Jones, M. C. The later careers of boys who were early- or late-maturing. *Child development,* 1957, *28* 115–128.

———. Psychological correlates of somatic development. *Child development,* 1965, *36,* 899–911.

Josselson, R.; Greenberg, E.; & McConochie, D. Phenomenological aspects of psychosocial maturity in adolescence. Part I: Boys. *Journal of youth and adolescence,* 1977, *6,* 25–56. (a)

———. Phenomenological aspects of psychosocial maturity in adolescence. Part II: Girls. *Journal of youth and adolescence.* 1977, *6,* 127–144. (b)

Joy, L. A.; Kimball, M.; & Zabrack, M. L. Television exposure and children's aggressive behaviour. In T. M. Williams (Chair). *The impact of television: A natural experiment involving three communities.* A symposium presented at the annual meeting of the Canadian Psychological Association, Vancouver, June 1977.

Jung, C. G. *Analytical psychology.* New York: Moffat, Yard, 1916.

———. *The integration of personality.* New York: Holt, Rinehart and Winston, 1939.

Kacerguis, M. A., & Adams, G. R. Erikson stage resolution: The relationship between identity and intimacy. *Journal of youth and adolescence,* 1980, *9,* 117–126.

Kagan, J. Reflection-impulsivity and reading ability in primary grade children. *Child development,* 1965, *36,* 609–628.

———. *Change and continuity in infancy.* New York: Wiley, 1971.

————. Emergent themes in human development. *American scientist,* 1976, *64,* 186–196.

————. Discussion of cognitive development in relation to language. In R. E. Stark (Ed.). *Language behavior in infancy and early childhood.* New York: Elsevier/North-Holland, 1981.

Kagan, J.; Kearsley, R.; & Zelazo, P. *Infancy: Its place in human development.* Cambridge, Mass.: Harvard University Press, 1978.

Kagan, J.; Lapidus, D. R.; & Moore, M. Infant antecedents of cognitive functioning: A longitudinal study. *Child development,* 1978, *49,* 1005–1023.

Kagan, J., & Moss, H. A. *Birth to maturity.* New York: Wiley, 1962.

Kagan, J.; Rosman, B. L.; Day, D.; Albert, J.; & Phillips, W. Information processing in the child: Significance of analytic and reflective attitudes. *Psychological monographs,* 1964, *78* (Whole No. 578).

Kamii, C., & DeVries, R. Piaget for early education. In R. K. Parker (Ed.). *The preschool in action* (2d ed.). Boston: Allyn & Bacon, 1974.

Kamin, L. J. *The science and politics of IQ.* Hillsdale, N.J.: Erlbaum, 1974.

————. Commentary. In S. Scarr (Ed.). *Race, social class, and individual differences in I.Q.* Hillsdale, N.J.: Erlbaum, 1981.

Kandel, D. B. Inter- and intragenerational influences on adolescent marijuana use. *Journal of social issues,* 1974, *30,* 107–135.

Kaplan, E., & Kaplan, G. The prelinguistic child. In J. Elliot (Ed.). *Human development and cognitive processes.* New York: Holt, Rinehart and Winston, 1971.

Kaye, K. *The mental and social life of babies: How parents create persons.* Chicago: University of Chicago Press, 1982.

Kaye, K., & Marcus, J. Infant imitation: The sensori-motor agenda. *Developmental psychology,* 1981, *17,* 258–265.

Keasey, C. B. Implications of cognitive development for moral reasoning. In D. J. DePalma & J. M. Foley (Eds.). *Moral development: Current theory and research.* Hillsdale, N.J.: Erlbaum, 1975.

Keating, D. P. Thinking processes in adolescence. In J. Adelson (Ed.). *Handbook of adolescent psychology.* New York: Wiley, 1980.

Keating, D. P., & Bobbitt, B. L. Individual and developmental differences in cognitive-processing components of mental ability. *Child development,* 1978, *49,* 155–167.

Keating, D. P., & Clark, L. V. Development of physical and social reasoning in adolescence. *Developmental psychology,* 1980, *16,* 23–30.

Keeney, T. J.; Cannizzo, S. R.; & Flavell, J. H. Spontaneous and induced verbal rehearsal in a recall task. *Child development,* 1967, *38,* 935–966.

Keller, A.; Ford, L. H., Jr.; & Meacham, J. A. Dimensions of self-concept in preschool children. *Developmental psychology,* 1978, *14,* 483–489.

Keller, C. A. Epidemiological characteristics of preterm births. In S. L. Friedman & M. Sigman (Eds.). *Preterm birth and psychological development.* New York: Academic Press, 1981.

Kempe, R. S., & Kempe, H. *Child abuse.* Cambridge, Mass.: Harvard University Press, 1978.

Keniston, K. Student activism, moral development, and morality. *American journal of orthopsychiatry,* 1970, *49,* 577–592.

Kennell, J. H.; Jerauld, R.; Wolfe, H.; Chesler, C.; Kreger, N. C.; McAlpine, W.; Steffa, M.; & Klaus, M. H. Maternal behavior one year after early and extended post-partum contact. *Developmental medicine and child neurology,* 1974, *16,* 172–179.

Kessner, D. M. *Infant death: An analysis by maternal risk and health care.* Washington, D.C.: National Academy of Sciences, 1973.

Kitchen, W. H.; Ryan, M. M.; Rickards, A.; McDougall, A. B.; Billson, F. A.; Deir, E. H.; & Naylor, F. D. A longitudinal study of very low-birthweight infants. IV: An overview of performance at eight years of age. *Developmental medicine and child neurology,* 1980, *22,* 172–188.

Klaus, H. M., & Kennell, J. H. *Maternal-infant bonding.* St. Louis: Mosby, 1976.

Klaus, R. A., & Gray, S. W. The early training project for disadvantaged children: A report after five years. *Monographs of the Society for Research in Child Development,* 1968, *33* (Whole No. 120).

Klein, M., & Stern, L. Low birth weight and the battered child syndrome. *American journal of diseases of children,* 1971, *122,* 171–178.

Kohlberg, L. Development of moral character and moral ideology. In M. L. Hoffman & L. W. Hoffman (Eds.). *Review of child development research* (Vol. 1). New York: Russell Sage Foundation, 1964.

———. A cognitive-developmental analysis of children's sex-role concepts and attitudes. In E. E. Maccoby (Ed.). *The development of sex differences.* Stanford, Calif.: Stanford University Press, 1966.

———. Stage and sequence: the cognitive-developmental approach to socialization. In D. Goslin (Ed.). *Handbook of socialization theory and research.* Skokie, Ill.: Rand McNally, 1969.

———. The cognitive-developmental approach to moral education. *Phi Delta Kappan,* June 1975, 670–677.

———. Moral stages and moralization: The cognitive-developmental approach. In T. Lickona (Ed.). *Moral development and behavior: Theory, research, and social issues.* New York: Holt, Rinehart and Winston, 1976.

———. *The meaning and measurement of moral development.* Worcester, Mass.: Clark University Press, 1980.

———. *Essays on moral development* (Vol. 1): *The philosophy of moral development.* New York: Harper & Row, 1981.

Kohlberg, L., & Elfenbein, D. The development of moral judgments concerning capital punishment. *American journal of orthopsychiatry,* 1975, *45,* 614–640.

Kohlberg, L., & Ullian, D. Z. Stages in the development of psychosexual concepts and attitudes. In R. C. Friedman, R. M. Richart, & R. L. Vande Wiele (Eds.). *Sex differences in behavior.* New York: Wiley, 1974.

Kopp, C. B. Perspectives on infant motor system development. In H. M. Bornstein & W. Kessen (Eds.). *Psychological development from infancy: Image to intention.* Hillsdale, N.J.: Erlbaum, 1979.

Kopp, C. B., & McCall, R. B. Predicting later mental performance for normal, at-risk, and handicapped infants. In P. B. Baltes & O. G. Brim, Jr. (Eds.). *Life-span development and*

*behavior* (Vol. 4). New York: Academic Press, 1982.

Kopp, C. B., & Parmelee, A. H. Prenatal and perinatal influences on infant behavior. In J. D. Osofsky (Ed.). *Handbook of infant development.* New York: Wiley, 1979.

Kopp, C. B., & Vaughn, B. E. Sustained attention during exploratory manipulation as a predictor of cognitive competence in preterm infants. *Child development,* 1982, *53,* 174–182.

Korn, S. J.; Chess, S.; & Fernandez, P. The impact of children's physical handicaps on marital quality and family interaction. In R. M. Lerner & G. B. Spanier (Eds.). *Child influences on marital and family interaction: A life-span perspective.* New York: Academic Press, 1978.

Korner, A. F.; Hutchinson, C. A.; Koperski, J. A.; Kraemer, H. C.; & Schneider, P. A. Stability of individual differences of neonatal motor and crying patterns. *Child development,* 1981, *52,* 83–90.

Krebs, D., & Gillmore, J. The relationship among the first stages of cognitive development, role-taking abilities, and moral development. *Child development,* 1982, *53,* 877–886.

Kremenitzer, J. P.; Vaughan, H. G., Jr.; Kurtzberg, D.; & Dowling, K. Smooth-pursuit eye movements in the new-born infant. *Child development,* 1979, *50,* 442–448.

Kreutzer, M. A.; Leonard, C.; & Flavell, J. H. An interview study of children's knowledge about memory. *Monographs of the Society for Research in Child Development,* 1975, *40* (1, Whole No. 159).

Kuczaj, S. A., II. The acquisition of regular and irregular past tense forms. *Journal of verbal learning and verbal behavior,* 1977, *49,* 319–326.

———. Children's judgments of grammatical and ungrammatical irregular past tense verbs. *Child development,* 1978, *49,* 319–326.

———. Evidence for a language learning strategy: On the relative ease of acquisition of prefixes and suffixes. *Child development,* 1979, *50,* 1–13.

———. On the nature of syntactic development. In S. A. Kuczaj II (Ed.). *Language develop-*

*ment* (Vol. 1): *Syntax and semantics*. Hillsdale, N.J.: Erlbaum, 1982.

Kuhn, D.; Nash, S. C.; & Brucken, L. Sex role concepts of two- and three-year-olds. *Child development*, 1978, *49*, 445–451.

Kuhn, T. S. *The structure of scientific revolutions*. Chicago: University of Chicago Press, 1962.

Kurdek, L. A., & Berg, B. Correlates of children's adjustment to their parents' divorces. In L. A. Kurdek (Ed.). Children and divorce. *New directions for child development*, 1983, *19*, 47–60. San Francisco: Jossey-Bass, 1983.

Labov, W. *Language in the inner city: Studies in the black English vernacular*. Philadelphia: University of Pennsylvania Press, 1972.

Ladd, G. W. Effectiveness of a social learning method for enhancing children's social interaction and peer acceptance. *Child development*, 1981, *52*, 171–178.

———. Social networks of popular, average, and rejected children in school settings. *Merrill-Palmer quarterly*, 1983, *29*, 283–307.

Lakin, M. Personality factors in mothers of excessively crying (colicky) infants. *Monographs of the Society for Research in Child Development*, 1957, *22* (Whole No. 64).

Lamb, M. E. The development of father-infant relationships. In M. E. Lamb (Ed.). *The role of the father in child development* (2d ed.). New York: Wiley, 1981.

———. Individual differences in infant sociability: Their origins and implications for cognitive development. In H. W. Reese & L. P. Lipsitt (eds.). *Advances in child development and behavior* (Vol. 16). New York: Academic Press, 1982. (a)

———. Parent-infant interaction, attachment, and socioemotional development in infancy. In R. N. Emde & R. J. Harmon (eds.). *The development of attachment and affiliative systems*. New York: Plenum, 1982. (b)

Lamb, M. E.; Frodi, M.; Hwang, C.; & Frodi, A. M. Effects of paternal involvement on infant preferences for mothers and fathers. *Child development*, 1983, *54*, 450–458.

Lamb, M. E.; Frodi, A. M.; Hwang, C.; Frodi, M.; & Steinberg, J. Mother- and father-infant interaction involving play and holding in traditional and nontraditional Swedish fami-

lies. *Developmental psychology*, 1982, *18*, 215–221.

Lamb, M. E., & Hwang, C. Maternal attachment and mother-neonate bonding: A critical review. In M. E. Lamb & A. L. Brown (Eds.). *Advances in developmental psychology* (Vol. 2). Hillsdale, N.J.: Erlbaum, 1982.

Lamke, L. K. Adjustment and sex-role orientation. *Journal of youth and adolescence*, 1982, *11*, 247–259. (a)

———. The impact of sex-role orientation on self-esteem in early adolescence. *Child development*, 1982, *53*, 1530–1535. (b)

Lane, D. M., & Pearson, D. A. The development of selective attention. *Merrill-Palmer quarterly*, 1982, *28*, 317–337.

Langlois, J. H., & Downs, A. C. Mothers, fathers, and peers as socialization agents of sex-typed play behaviors in young children. *Child development*, 1980, *51*, 1237–1247.

Laosa, L. M., & Brophy, J. E. Effects of sex and birth order on sex-role development and intelligence among kindergarten children. *Developmental psychology*, 1972, *6*, 409–415.

Lavatelli, C. *Piaget's theory applied to an early childhood curriculum*. Boston: American Science and Engineering, 1970.

LaVoie, J. C. Ego identity formation in middle adolescence. *Journal of youth and adolescence*, 1976, *5*, 371–385.

Lawton, J. T., & Hooper, F. H. Piagetian theory and early childhood education: A critical analysis. In L. S. Siegel & C. J. Brainerd (Eds.). *Alternatives to Piaget: Critical essays on the theory*. New York: Academic Press, 1978.

Lazar, I., & Darlington, R. Lasting effects of early education: A report from the consortium for longitudinal studies. *Monographs of the Society for Research in Child Development*, 1982, *47* (Whole No. 195).

Leadbeater, B. J., & Dionne, J. The adolescent's use of formal operational thinking in solving problems related to identity resolution. *Adolescence*, 1981, *16*, 111–121.

Leaf, D. A. Exercise and pregnancy compatible. *The physician and sportsmedicine*, 1982, 9, 22, 24.

Leboyer, F. *Birth without violence*. New York: Knopf, 1975.

Lefkowitz, M. M. Smoking during pregnancy: Long-term effects on offspring. *Developmental psychology,* 1981, *17,* 192–194.

Leonard, L. B.; Chapman, K.; Rowan, L. E.; & Weiss, A. L. Three hypotheses concerning young children's imitations of lexical items. *Developmental psychology,* 1983, *19,* 591–601.

Lepper, M. R. Intrinsic and extrinsic motivation in children: Detrimental effects of superfluous social controls. In W. A. Collins (Ed.). *Minnesota symposia on child psychology* (Vol. 14). Hillsdale, N.J.: Erlbaum, 1980.

Lesser, G. S.; Fifer, G.; & Clark, D. H. Mental abilities of children from different social class and cultural groups. *Monographs of the Society for Research in Child Development,* 1965, *30* (Whole No. 102).

Lewin, R. Starved brains. *Psychology today,* 1975, *9* (4), 29–33.

Lewis, C. C. How adolescents approach decisions: Changes over grades seven to twelve and policy implications. *Child development,* 1981, *52,* 538–544.

Lewis, M. Self-knowledge: A social cognitive perspective on gender identity and sex-role development. In M. E. Lamb & L. R. Sherrod (Eds.). *Infant social cognition: Empirical and theoretical considerations.* Hillsdale, N.J.: Erlbaum, 1981.

Lewis, M., & Brooks, J. Self-knowledge and emotional development. In M. Lewis & L. A. Rosenblum (Eds.). *The development of affect.* New York: Plenum, 1978.

Lewis, M., & Brooks-Gunn, J. *Social cognition and the acquisition of self.* New York: Plenum, 1979.

———. Visual attention at three months as a predictor of cognitive functioning at two years of age. *Intelligence,* 1981, *5,* 131–140.

Lewis, M.; Feiring, C.; & Weinraub, M. The father as a member of the child's social network. In M. E. Lamb (Ed.). *The role of the father in child development* (2d ed.). New York: Wiley, 1981.

Lewis, M., & Kreitzberg, V. S. Effects of birth order and spacing on mother-infant interactions. *Developmental psychology,* 1979, *15,* 617–625.

Lewis, M., & Schaeffer, S. Peer behavior and mother-infant interaction in maltreated children. In M. Lewis & L. A. Rosenblum (Eds.). *The uncommon child.* New York: Plenum, 1981.

Liben, L. S. The development of deaf children: An overview of issues. In L. S. Liben (Ed.). *Deaf children: Developmental perspectives.* New York: Academic Press, 1978.

Liberman, I. Y., & Shankweiler, D. Speech, the alphabet and teaching to read. In L. B. Resnick & P. A. Weaver (eds.). *Theory and practice of early reading.* Hillsdale, N.J.: Erlbaum, 1977.

Liberman, I. Y.; Shankweiler, D.; Liberman, A. M.; Fowler, C.; & Fischer, F. W. Phonetic segmentation and recoding in the beginning reader. In A. S. Reber & D. Scarborough (Eds.). *Reading: Theory and practice.* Hillsdale, N.J.: Erlbaum, 1976.

Lickona, T. Moral development and moral education. In J. M. Gallagher & J. A. Easley, Jr. (Eds.). *Knowledge and development* (Vol. 2), *Piaget and education.* New York: Plenum, 1978.

Liebert, R. M., & Schwartzberg, N. S. Effects of mass media. In M. R. Rosenzweig & L. W. Porter (Eds.). *Annual review of psychology* (Vol. 28). Palo Alto, Calif.: Annual Reviews, 1977.

Light, R. J. Abused and neglected children in America: A study of alternative policies. *Harvard educational review,* 1973, *43,* 556–598.

Linn, S.; Reznick, J. S.; Kagan, J.; & Hans, S. Salience of visual patterns in the human infant. *Developmental psychology,* 1982, *18,* 651–657.

Lipsitt, L. P. Infant learning. In T. M. Field, A. Houston, H. C. Quay, L. Troll, & G. E. Finley (Eds.). *Review of human development.* New York: Wiley, 1982.

Lipsitt, L. P., & Kaye, H. Conditioned sucking in the human newborn. *Psychonomic science,* 1964, *1,* 29–30.

Ljung, B. O.; Bergsten-Brucefors, A.; & Lindgren, G. The secular trend in physical growth in Sweden. *Annals of human biology,* 1974, *1,* 245–256.

Loeber, R. The stability of antisocial and delinquent child behavior: A review. *Child development,* 1982, *53,* 1431–1466.

Loehlin, J. C., & Nichols, R. C. *Heredity, environment and personality.* Austin, Tex.: University of Texas Press, 1976.

Lovaas, O. I. *Language acquisition programs for nonlinguistic children.* New York: Irvington, 1976.

Lytton, H. Do parents create, or respond to, differences in twins? *Developmental psychology,* 1977, *12,* 456–459.

McCabe, A. E.; Siegel, L. S.; Spence, I.; & Wilkinson, A. Class-inclusion reasoning: Patterns of performance from three to eight years. *Child development,* 1982, *53,* 779–785.

McCall, R. B. *Infants: The new knowledge.* Cambridge, Mass.: Harvard University Press, 1979.

———. Early predictors of later IQ: The search continues. *Intelligence,* 1981, *5,* 141–148. (a)

———. Nature-nurture and the two realms of development: A proposed integration with respect to mental development. *Child development,* 1981, *52,* 1–12. (b)

McCall, R. B.; Appelbaum, M. I.; & Hogarty, P. S. Developmental changes in mental performance. *Monographs of the Society for Research in Child Development,* 1973, *38* (Whole No. 150).

Maccoby, E. E. Commentary on G. R. Patterson, "Mothers: The unacknowledged victims." *Monographs of the Society for Research in Child Development,* 1980, *45* (Whole No. 186). (a)

———. *Social development: Psychological growth and the parent-child relationships.* New York: Harcourt Brace Jovanovich, 1980. (b)

Maccoby, E. E.; Doering, C. H.; Jacklin, C. N.; & Kraemer, H. Concentrations of sex hormones in umbilical-cord blood: Their relation to sex and birth order of infants. *Child development,* 1979, *50,* 632–642.

Maccoby, E. E., & Jacklin, C. N. *The psychology of sex differences.* Stanford, Calif.: Stanford University Press, 1974.

———. Sex differences in aggression: A rejoinder and reprise. *Child development,* 1980, *51,* 964–980.

McCord, J. The Cambridge-Sommerville youth study: A sobering lesson on treatment, prevention, and evaluation. In A. J. McSweeny, W. J. Fremouw, & R. P. Hawkins (Eds.). *Practical program evaluation for youth treatment.* Springfield, Ill.: Thomas, 1982.

McCord, W.; McCord, J.; & Zola, I. K. *Origins of crime.* New York: Columbia University Press, 1959.

Macfarlane, A. Olfaction in the development of social preferences in the human neonate. In *Parent-infant interaction.* Amsterdam: CIBA Foundation Symposium 33, new series, ASP, 1975.

———. *The psychology of childbirth.* Cambridge, Mass.: Harvard University Press, 1977.

Macfarlane, J. W.; Allan, L.; & Honzik, M. P. A developmental study of the behavior problems of normal children between twenty-two months and fourteen years. *University of California publications in child development* (Vol. 2). Berkeley, Calif.: University of California Press, 1954.

McGraw, M. D. *Growth: A study of Johnny and Jimmy.* Englewood Cliffs, N.J.: Prentice-Hall, 1935.

McKinney, J. D., & Edgerton, M. Classroom adaptive behavior. Paper presented at the biennial meetings of the Society for Research in Child Development, Detroit, April 1983.

McNeill, D. *The acquisition of language: The study of developmental psycholinguistics.* New York: Harper & Row, 1970.

Magenis, R. E. Parental origin of the extra chromosome in Down's syndrome. *Human genetics,* 1977, *37,* 7–16.

Main, M. Exploration, play, and cognitive functioning related to infant-mother attachment. *Infant behavior and development,* 1983, *6,* 167–174.

Malina, R. M. Motor development in the early years. In S. G. Moore & C. R. Cooper (Eds.). *The young child: Reviews of research* (Vol. 3). Washington, D.C.: National Association for the Education of Young Children, 1982.

Marano, H. Breast-feeding. New evidence: It's far more than nutrition. *Medical world news,* 1979, *20,* 62–78.

Marcia, J. E. Development and validation of ego identity status. *Journal of personality and social psychology,* 1966, *3,* 551–558.

———. *Studies in ego identity.* Burnaby, British Columbia: Simon Fraser University, 1976.

———. Identity in adolescence. In J. Adelson (Ed.). *Handbook of adolescent psychology.* New York: Wiley, 1980.

Marcus, D. E., & Overton, W. F. The development of cognitive gender constancy and sex role preferences. *Child development,* 1978, *49,* 434–444.

Markman, E. M. Empirical versus logical solutions to part-whole comparison problems concerning classes and collections. *Child development,* 1978, *49,* 168–177.

Markman, E. M.; Cox, B.; & Machida, S. The standard object-sorting task as a measure of conceptual organization. *Developmental psychology,* 1981, *17,* 115–117.

Martin, C. L., & Halverson, C. F., Jr. A schematic processing model of sex typing and stereotyping in children. *Child development,* 1981, *52,* 1119–1134.

———. The effects of sex-typing schemas on young children's memory. *Child development,* 1983, *54,* 563–574.

Martorano, S. C. A developmental analysis of performance on Piaget's formal operations tasks. *Developmental psychology,* 1977, *13,* 666–672.

Massad, C. M. Sex role identity and adjustment during adolescence. *Child development,* 1981, *52,* 1290–1298.

Masters, J. C.; Ford, M. E.; Arend, R.; Grotevant, H. D.; & Clark, L. V. Modeling and labeling as integrated determinants of children's sex-typed imitative behavior. *Child development,* 1979, *50,* 364–371.

Matheny, A. P., Jr.; Wilson, R. S.; Dolan, A. B.; & Kranz, J. Z. Behavioral contrasts in twinships: Stability and patterns of differences in childhood. *Child development,* 1981, *52,* 579–588.

Mayer, J. Obesity during childhood. In M. Winick (Ed.). *Childhood obesity.* New York: Wiley, 1975.

Meilman, P. W. Cross-sectional age changes in ego identity status during adolescence. *Developmental psychology,* 1979, *15,* 230–231.

Meisels, S. J., & Anastasiow, N. J. The risks of prediction: Relationships between etiology, handicapping conditions, and developmental outcomes. In S. G. Moore & C. R. Cooper (Eds.). *The young child: Reviews of research* (Vol. 3). Washington, D.C.: National Association for the Education of Young Children, 1982.

Meltzoff, A. N., & Moore, M. K. Newborn infants imitate adult facial gestures. *Child development,* 1983, *54,* 702–709.

Mervis, C. B., & Mervis, C. A. Leopards are kitty-cats: Object labeling by mothers for their thirteen-month-olds. *Child development,* 1982, *53,* 267–273.

Messer, S. B., & Brodzinsky, D. M. The relation of conceptual tempo to aggression and its control. *Child development,* 1979, *50,* 758–766.

Mikkelsen, M., & Stone, J. Genetic counseling in Down's syndrome. *Human heredity,* 1970, *20,* 457–464.

Milavsky, J. R.; Kessler, R. C.; Stipp, H. H.; & Rubens, W. S. *Television and aggression: A panel study.* New York: Academic Press, 1982.

Miller, G. A. The magical number seven, plus or minus two: Some limits on our capacity for processing information. *Psychological review,* 1956, *63,* 81–96.

Minton, C.; Kagan, J.; & Levine, J. A. Maternal control and obedience in the two-year-old. *Child development,* 1971, *52,* 1873–1974.

Mischel, W. A social learning view of sex differences in behavior. In E. E. Maccoby (Ed.). *The development of sex differences.* Stanford, Calif.: Stanford University Press, 1966.

———. Sex typing and socialization. In P. H. Mussen (Ed.). *Carmichael's manual of child psychology* (Vol. 2). New York: Wiley, 1970.

Mitchell, S. K.; Hammond, M. A.; & Bee, H. L. Parents' marital stability and cognitive performance, academic achievement, and behavior problems in school-aged children. Paper presented at the biennial meetings of the Society for Research in Child Development, Detroit, 1983.

Money, J. Ablatiopenis: Normal male infant sex-reassigned as a girl. *Archives of sexual behavior,* 1975, *4,* 56–72.

Monkus, E., & Bancalari, E. Neonatal outcome. In K. G. Scott, T. Field, & E. G. Robertson (Eds.). *Teenage parents and their offspring.* New York: Grune & Stratton, 1981.

Montemayor, R., & Eisen, M. The development of self-conceptions from childhood to adolescence. *Developmental psychology,* 1977, *13,* 314–319.

Montpetit, R. R.; Montoye, H. J.; & Laeding, L. Grip strength of school children, Saginaw, Michigan: 1899–1964. *Research quarterly,* 1967, *38,* 231–240.

Morse, P. A., & Cowan, N. Infant auditory and speech perception. In T. M. Field, A. Houston, H. C. Quay, L. Troll, & G. E. Finley (Eds.). *Review of human development.* New York: Wiley, 1982.

Mosher, F. A., & Hornsby, J. R. On asking questions. In J. S. Bruner, R. R. Olver, & P. M. Greenfield (Eds.). *Studies in cognitive growth.* New York: Wiley, 1966.

Mueller, E., & Brenner, J. The origins of social skills and interaction among playgroup toddlers. *Child development,* 1977, *48,* 854–861.

Munsinger, H., & Douglass, A., II. The syntactic abilities of identical twins, fraternal twins, and their siblings. *Child development,* 1976, *47,* 40–50.

Murphy, L. B., & Moriarty, A. E. *Vulnerability, coping, and growth.* New Haven, Conn.: Yale University Press, 1976.

Murray, A. D.; Dolby, R. M.; Nation, R. L.; & Thomas, D. B. Effects of epidural anesthesia on newborns and their mothers. *Child development,* 1981, *52,* 71–82.

Murray, J. P. *Television & youth. 25 years of research and controversy.* Stanford, Calif.: The Boys Town Center for the Study of Youth Development, 1980.

Mussen, P. H., & Jones, M. C. Self-conceptions, motivations, and interpersonal attitudes of late- and early-maturing boys. *Child development,* 1957, *28,* 243–256.

Naeye, R. L. Relationship of cigarette smoking to congenital anomalies and perinatal death. *American journal of pathology,* 1978, *90,* 289–293.

Nash, S. C. The relationship among sex-role stereotyping, sex-role preference, and the sex difference in spatial visualization. *Sex roles,* 1975, *1,* 15–32.

Neimark, E. D. Longitudinal development of formal operations thought. *Genetic psychology monographs,* 1975, *91,* 171–225.

———. Toward the disembedding of formal operations with confounding with cognitive style. In I. Sigel, D. Brodzinsky, & R. Golinkoff (Eds.). *Piagetian theory and research: New directions and applications.* Hillsdale, N.J.: Erlbaum, 1981.

———. Adolescent thought: Transition to formal operations. In B. B. Wolman (Ed.). *Handbook of developmental psychology.* Englewood Cliffs, N.J.: Prentice-Hall, 1982.

Nelson, Katherine. Structure and strategy in learning to talk. *Monographs of the Society for Research in Child Development,* 1973, *38* (Whole No. 149).

———. Individual differences in language development: Implications for development of language. *Developmental psychology,* 1981, *17,* 170–187.

———. The syntagmatics and paradigmatics of conceptual development. In S. A. Kuczaj II (Ed.). *Language development* (Vol. 2): *Language, thought, and culture.* Hillsdale, N.J.: Erlbaum, 1982.

Nelson, Katherine; Rescorla, L.; Gruendel, J.; & Benedict, H. Early lexicons: What do they mean? Paper presented at the biennial meetings of the Society for Research in Child Development, New Orleans, 1977.

Nelson, Keith. Facilitating children's syntax acquisition. *Developmental psychology,* 1977, *13,* 101–107.

Nelson, N. M.; Enkin, M. W.; Saigal, S.; Bennett, K. J.; Milner, R.; & Sackett, D. L. A randomized clinical trial of the Leboyer approach to childbirth. *The New England journal of medicine,* 1980, *302,* 655–660.

Newberger, C. M., & Cook, S. J. Parental awareness and child abuse: A cognitive-developmental analysis of urban and rural samples. *American journal of orthopsychiatry,* 1983, *53,* 512–524.

Newcombe, N., & Bandura, M. M. Effect of age at puberty on spatial ability in girls: A question of mechanism. *Developmental psychology,* 1983, *19,* 215–224.

Nichols, P. L. Minimal brain dysfunction: Associations with perinatal complications. Paper presented at the biennial meetings of the Society for Research in Child Development, New Orleans, 1977.

Nisan, M., & Kohlberg, L. Universality and variation in moral judgment: A longitudinal and cross-sectional study in Turkey. *Child development,* 1982, *53,* 865–876.

Norman-Jackson, J. Family interactions, language development, and primary reading achievement of black children in families of low income. *Child development,* 1982, *53,* 349–358.

O'Connor, S.; Vietze, P. M.; Sandler, H. M.; Sherrod, K. B.; & Altemeier, W. A. Quality of parenting and the mother-infant relationships following rooming-in. In P. M. Taylor (Ed.). *Parent-infant relationships.* New York: Grune & Stratton, 1980.

Oden, S. Peer relationship development in childhood. In L. G. Katz (Ed.). *Current topics in early childhood education* (Vol. 4). Norwood, N.J.: Ablex, 1982.

O'Donnell, M. *Around the corner.* New York: Harper & Row, 1966.

Oller, D. K. Infant vocalizations: Exploration and reflectivity. In R. E. Stark (Ed.). *Language behavior in infancy and early childhood.* New York: Elsevier/North-Holland, 1981.

Olson, G. M. The recognition of specific persons. In M. E. Lamb & L. R. Sherrod (Eds.). *Infant social cognition.* Hillsdale, N.J.: Erlbaum, 1981.

O'Malley, P. M., & Bachman, J. G. Self-esteem: Change and stability between ages 13 and 23. *Developmental psychology,* 1983, *19,* 257–268.

Overton, W. F., & Reese, H. W. Models of development: Methodological implications. In J. R. Nesselroade & H. W. Reese (Eds.). *Life-span developmental psychology: Methodological issues.* New York: Academic Press, 1973.

Parke, R. D., & Tinsley, B. R. The father's role in infancy: Determinants of involvement in caregiving and play. In M. E. Lamb (Ed.). *The role of the father in child development* (2d ed.). New York: Wiley, 1981.

Parkinson, C. E.; Wallis, S.; & Harvey, D. School achievement and behavior of children who were small-for-date at birth. *Developmental medicine and child neurology,* 1981, *23,* 41–50.

Parmelee, A. H.; Wenner, W. H.; & Schulz, H. R. Infant sleep patterns from birth to 16 weeks of age. *Journal of pediatrics,* 1964, *65,* 576–582.

Parsons, J. E.; Adler, T. F.; & Kaczala, C. M. Socialization of achievement attitudes and beliefs: Parental influences. *Child development,* 1982, *53,* 310–321.

Passman, R. H., & Longeway, K. P. The role of vision in maternal attachment: Giving 2-year-olds a photograph of their mother during separation. *Developmental psychology,* 1982, *18,* 530–533.

Pastor, D. L. The quality of mother-infant attachment and its relationship to toddlers' initial sociability with peers. *Developmental psychology,* 1981, *17,* 326–335.

Patterson, G. R. *Families: Applications of social learning to family life.* Champaign, Ill.: Research Press, 1975.

———. Mothers: The unacknowledged victims. *Monographs of the Society for Research in Child Development,* 1980, *45* (Whole No. 186).

Paulsen, K., & Johnson, M. Sex-role attitudes and mathematical ability in 4th-, 8th-, and 11th-grade students from a high socioeconomic area. *Developmental psychology,* 1983, *19,* 210–214.

Pedersen, F. A.; Zaslow, M. J.; Cain, R. L.; & Anderson, B. J. Cesarean childbirth: Psychological implications for mothers and fathers. *Infant mental health journal,* 1981, *2,* 257–263.

Pederson, E.; Faucher, T. A.; & Eaton, W. W. A new perspective on the effects of first-grade teachers on children's subsequent adult status. *Harvard educational review,* 1978, *48,* 1–31.

Pederson, F. A. Father influences viewed in a family context. In M. E. Lamb (Ed.). *The role of the father in child development* (2d ed.). New York: Wiley, 1981.

Pennington, B. F.; Bender, B.; Puck, M.; Salbenblatt, J.; & Robinson, A. Learning disabilities in children with sex chromosome anomalies. *Child development,* 1982, *53,* 1182–1192.

Perfetti, C. A., & Lesgold, A. M. Coding and comprehension in skilled reading and implications for reading instruction. In L. B. Resnick & P. A. Weaver (Eds.). *Theory and practice of early reading.* Hillsdale, N.J.: Erlbaum, 1977.

Peskin, H. Puberal onset and ego functioning. *Journal of abnormal psychology,* 1967, *72,* 1–15.

Peskin, H. Influence of the developmental schedule of puberty on learning and ego functioning. *Journal of youth and adolescence,* 1973, *2,* 272–290.

Petersen, A. C., & Taylor, B. The biological approach to adolescence. In J. Adelson (Ed.). *Handbook of adolescent psychology.* New York: Wiley, 1980.

Peterson, G. H.; Mehl, L. E.; & Leiderman, P. H. The role of some birth-related variables in father attachment. *American journal of orthopsychiatry,* 1979, *49,* 330–338.

Phillips, J. R. Syntax and vocabulary of mothers' speech to young children: Age and sex comparisons. *Child development,* 1973, *44,* 182–185.

Piaget, J. *The moral judgment of the child.* New York: Macmillan, 1932.

———. *The origins of intelligence in children.* New York: International Universities Press, 1952.

———. *Play, dreams and imitation in childhood.* New York: Norton, 1962.

———. Development and learning. In R. Ripple & V. Rockcastle (Eds.). *Piaget rediscovered.* Ithaca N.Y.: Cornell University Press, 1964.

———. Piaget's theory. In P. H. Mussen (Ed.). *Carmichael's manual of child psychology* (Vol. 1, 3d ed.). New York: Wiley, 1970. (a)

———. *The science of education and the psychology of the child.* New York: Viking Press, 1970. (b)

———. *The development of thought: Equilibration of cognitive structures.* New York: Viking Press, 1975.

Piaget, J., & Inhelder, B. *The psychology of the child.* New York: Basic Books, 1969.

Pines, M. The civilizing of Genie. *Psychology today,* September 1981, *15,* 28–34.

———. Baby, you're incredible. *Psychology today,* 1982, *16* (2), 48–52.

Pitkin, R. M. Nutrition during pregnancy: The clinical approach. In M. Winick (Ed.). *Nutritional disorders of American women.* New York: Wiley, 1977.

Plomin, R. Critique of Scarr and Weinberg's IQ adoption study: Putting the problem in perspective. *Intelligence,* 1978, *2,* 74–79.

Plomin, R., & DeFries, J. C. Genetics and intelligence: Recent data. *Intelligence,* 1980, *4,* 15–24.

———. The Colorado adoption project. *Child development,* 1983, *54,* 276–289.

Plomin, R., & Foch, T. T. Sex differences and individual differences. *Child development,* 1981, *52,* 383–385.

Plomin, R., & Rowe, D. C. Genetic and environmental etiology of social behavior in infancy. *Developmental psychology,* 1979, *15,* 62–72.

Pollitt, E.; Mueller, W.; & Leibel, R. L. The relation of growth to cognition in a well-nourished population. *Child development,* 1982, *53,* 1157–1163.

Powell, B., & Steelman, L. C. Testing an undertested comparison: Maternal effects on sons' and daughters' attitudes toward women in the labor force. *Journal of marriage and the family,* 1982, *44,* 349–355.

Power, C., & Reimer, J. Moral atmosphere: An educational bridge between moral judgment and action. In W. Damon (Ed.). *Moral development.* San Francisco: Jossey-Bass, 1978.

Prader, A.; Tanner, J. M.; & Von Harnack, G. A. Catch-up growth following illness or starvation. *Journal of pediatrics,* 1963, *62,* 646–659.

Prechtl, H. F. R., & Beintema, D. J. The neurological examination of the full-term newborn infant. *Clinics in developmental medicine* (Vol. 12). London: Heinemann, 1964.

*Profiles of children.* 1970 White House Conference on Children. Washington, D.C.: U.S. Government Printing Office, 1970.

Provence, S. Development from six to twelve months. In J. D. Nospitz (Ed.). *Basic handbook of child psychiatry* (Vol. 1). New York: Basic Books, 1979.

Provence, S., & Lipton, R. *Infants in institutions.* New York: International Universities Press, 1961.

Quay, H. C. Residential treatment. In H. C. Quay & J. S. Werry (Eds.). *Psychopathological disorders of childhood* (2d ed.). New York: Wiley, 1979.

Quay, H. C., & Werry, J. S. *Psychopathological disorders of childhood* (2d ed.). New York: Wiley, 1979.

Radin, N. The unique contribution of parents to childrearing: The preschool years. In S. G. Moore & C. R. Cooper (Eds.). *The young child, reviews of research* (Vol. 3). Washington, D.C.: National Association for the Education of Young Children, 1982.

Ramey, C. T. Consequences of infant day care. In B. Weissbound & J. Musick (Eds.). *Infants: Their social environments.* Washington, D.C.: National Association for the Education of Young Children, 1981.

Ramey, C. T.; Farran, D. C.; & Campbell, F. A. Predicting IQ from mother-infant interactions. *Child development,* 1979, *50,* 804–814.

Ramey, C. T., & Haskins, R. The modification of intelligence through early experience. *Intelligence,* 1981, *5,* 5–19. (a)

———. Early education, intellectual development, and school performance: A reply to Arthur Jensen and J. McVicker Junt. *Intelligence,* 1981, *5,* 41–48. (b)

Rank, O. *The trauma of birth.* New York: Harcourt Brace Jovanovich, 1929.

Rappoport, L. *Personality development: The chronology of experience.* Glenview, Ill.: Scott, Foresman, 1972.

Rasch, E.; Swift, H.; Riesen, A. H.; & Chow, K. L. Altered structure and composition of retinal cells in dark-reared mammals. *Experimental cell research,* 1961, *25,* 348–363.

Read, M. S., & Felson, D. *Malnutrition, learning, and behavior.* Bethesda, Md.: National Institute of Child Health and Human Development, 1976 (ERIC Document Reproduction Service No. ED 133–395).

Reed, E. W. Genetic anomalies in development. In F. D. Horowitz (Ed.), *Review of child development research* (Vol. 4). Chicago: University of Chicago Press, 1975.

Reese, H. W., & Overton, W. F. Models of development and theories of development. In L. R. Goulet & P. B. Baltes (Eds.). *Life-span developmental psychology.* New York: Academic Press, 1970.

Reisman, J. M., & Shorr, S. I. Friendship claims and expectations among children and adults. *Child development,* 1978, *49,* 913–916.

Resnick, L. B. The future of IQ testing in education. *Intelligence,* 1979, *3,* 241–254.

Restak, R. M. Newborn knowledge. *Science 82,* 1982, *3,* 58–65.

Reynolds, N. J., & Risley, T. R. The role of social and material reinforcers in increasing talking of a disadvantaged preschool child. *Journal of applied behavior analysis,* 1968, *1,* 253–262.

Rheingold, H. L., & Cook, K. V. The contents of boys' and girls' rooms as an index of parents' behavior. *Child development,* 1975, *46,* 459–463.

Ricciuti, H. N. Developmental consequences of malnutrition in early childhood. In M. Lewis & L. A. Rosenblum (Eds.). *The uncommon child.* New York: Plenum, 1981.

Riegel, K. F. Adult life crises. A dialectic interpretation of development. In N. Datan & L. H. Ginsberg (Eds.). *Lifespan developmental psychology: Normative life crises.* New York: Academic Press, 1975.

Riesen, A. H. The development of visual perception in man and chimpanzee. *Science,* 1947, *106,* 107–108.

Richardson, J. G., & Simpson, C. H. Children, gender, and social structure: An analysis of the contents of letters to Santa Claus. *Child development,* 1982, *53,* 429–436.

Ringler, N. M.; Trause, M. A.; & Klaus, M. H. Mother's speech to her two year old, its effects on speech and language comprehension at 5 years. *Pediatric research,* 1976, *10,* 307.

Rivers, C.; Barnett, R.; & Baruch, G. *Beyond sugar & spice: How women grow, learn, and thrive.* New York: Putnam, 1979.

Roberge, J. J., & Flexer, B. K. Further examination of formal reasoning abilities. *Child development,* 1979, *50,* 478–484.

Roberts, K. Comprehension and production of word order in stage I. *Child development,* 1983, *54,* 443–449.

Robertson, E. G. Adolescence, physiological maturity, and obstetric outcomes. In K. G. Scott, T. Field, & E. Robertson (Eds.). *Teenage parents and their offspring.* New York: Grune & Stratton, 1981.

Robinson, H. B. The uncommonly bright child. In M. Lewis & L. A. Rosenblum (Eds.). *The uncommon child.* New York: Plenum, 1981.

Roche, A. F. Secular trends in stature, weight, and maturation. In A. F. Roche (Ed.). Secular trends in human growth, maturation, and development. *Monographs of the Society for Research in Child Development,* 1979, *44* (Whole No. 179).

————. The adipocyte-number hypothesis. *Child development,* 1981, *52,* 31–43.

Roffwarg, H. P.; Muzio, J. N.; & Dement, W. D. Ontogenetic development of the human sleep-dream cycle. *Science,* 1966, *152,* 604–619.

Rogoff, B. Schooling and the development of cognitive skills. In H. C. Triandis & A. Heron (Eds.). *Handbook of cross-cultural psychology* (Vol. 4), *Developmental psychology.* Boston: Allyn & Bacon, 1981.

Rollins, B. C., & Galligan, R. The developing child and marital satisfaction of parents. In R. M. Lerner & G. M. Spanier (Eds.). *Child influences on marital and family interaction: A life-span perspective.* New York: Academic Press, 1978.

Rosenkrantz, P.; Vogel, S.; Bee, H.; Broverman, I.; & Broverman, D. M. Sex-role stereotypes and self-conceptions of college students. *Journal of consulting and clinical psychology,* 1968, *32,* 287–295.

Rosenthal, D.; Wender, P. H.; Kety, S. S.; Welner, J.; & Schulsinger, F. The adopted-away offspring of schizophrenics. *American journal of psychiatry,* 1971, *128,* 87–91.

Rosett, H. L., & Sander, L. W. Effects of maternal drinking on neonatal morphology and state regulation. In J. D. Osofsky (Ed.). *Handbook of infant development.* New York: Wiley, 1979.

Rosner, B. S., & Doherty, N. E. The response of neonates to intra-uterine sounds. *Developmental medicine and child neurology,* 1979, *21,* 723–729.

Ross, G.; Kagan, J.; Zelazo, P.; & Kotelchuck, M. Separation protest in infants in home and laboratory. *Developmental psychology,* 1975, *11,* 256–257.

Rosso, P. Maternal nutrition, nutrient exchange, and fetal growth. In M. Winick (Ed.). *Nutritional disorders of American women.* New York: Wiley, 1977. (a)

————. Maternal-fetal exchange during protein malnutrition in the rat: Placental transfer of a-amino isobutyric acid. *Journal of nutrition,* 1977, *107,* 2002–2005. (b)

Rothbart, M. K., & Derryberry, D. Development of individual differences in temperament. In M. E. Lamb & A. L. Brown (Eds.). *Advances in developmental psychology* (Vol. 1). Hillsdale, N.J.: Erlbaum, 1981.

Rovet, J., & Netley, C. The triple X chromosome syndrome in childhood: Recent empirical findings. *Child development,* 1983, *54,* 831–845.

Rowe, I., & Marcia, J. E. Ego identity status, formal operations, and moral development. *Journal of youth and adolescence,* 1980, *9,* 87–99.

Rubin, K. H., & Daniels-Beirness, T. Concurrent and predictive correlates of sociometric status in kindergarten and grade 1 children. *Merrill-Palmer quarterly,* 1983, *29,* 337–351.

Rubin, K. H., & Everett, B. Social perspective-taking in young children. In S. G. Moore & C. R. Cooper (Eds.). *The young child: Reviews of research* (Vol. 3). Washington, D.C.: National Association for the Education of Young Children, 1982.

Rubin, Z. *Children's friendships.* Cambridge, Mass.: Harvard University Press, 1980.

Rubinstein, E. A. Television and behavior. Research conclusions of the 1982 NIMH report and their policy implications. *American psychologist,* 1983, *38,* 820–825.

Ruble, D. N.; Balaban, T.; & Cooper, J. Gender constancy and the effects of sex-typed televised toy commercials. *Child development,* 1981, *52,* 667–673.

Ruble, D. N., & Brooks-Gunn, J. The experience of menarche. *Child development,* 1982, *53,* 1557–1566.

Ruopp, R., & Travers, J. Janus faces day care: Perspectives on quality and cost. In E. F. Zigler & E. W. Gordon (Eds.). *Day care: Scien-*

*tific and social policy issues.* Boston: Auburn House, 1982.

Rutter, M. Parent-child separation: Psychological effects on the children. *Journal of child psychology and psychiatry,* 1971, *12,* 233–260.

———. *Helping troubled children.* New York: Plenum, 1975.

———. Family, area and school influences in the genesis of conduct disorders. In L. Hersov, M. Berber, & D. Schaffer (Eds.). *Aggression and antisocial behavior in childhood and adolescence.* Elmsford, N.Y.: Pergamon, 1978. (a)

———. Diagnosis and definition of childhood autism. *Journal of autism and childhood schizophrenia,* 1978, *8,* 139–161. (b)

———. Early sources of security and competence. In J. S. Bruner & A. Garton (Eds.). *Human growth and development.* London: Oxford University Press, 1978. (c)

———. Maternal deprivation, 1972–1978: New findings, new concepts, new approaches. *Child development,* 1979, *50,* 283–305.

———. Social-emotional consequences of day care for preschool children. In E. F. Zigler & E. W. Gordon (Eds.). *Day care: Scientific and social policy issues.* Boston: Auburn House, 1982.

———. School effects on pupil progress: Research findings and policy implications. *Child development,* 1983, *54,* 1–29. (a)

———. Cognitive deficits in the pathogenesis of autism. *Journal of child psychology and psychiatry,* 1983, *24,* 513–531. (b)

Rutter, M.; Yule, B.; Quinton, D.; Rowlands, O.; Yule, W.; & Berger, M. Attainment and adjustment in two geographical areas, III: Some factors accounting for area differences. *British journal of psychiatry,* 1975, *126,* 520–533.

Saario, T. N.; Jacklin, C. N.; & Tittle, C. K. Sex role stereotyping in the public schools. *Harvard educational review,* 1973, *43,* 386–416.

Sacks, E. Intelligence scores as a function of experimentally established social relationships between child and examiner. *Journal of abnormal and social psychology,* 1952, *46,* 354–358.

Saigal, S.; Nelson, N. M.; Bennett, K. J.; & Enkin, M. W. Observations on the behavioral state of newborn infants during the first hour of life. A comparison of infants delivered by the Leboyer and conventional methods. *American journal of obstetrics and gynecology,* 1981, *139,* 715–719.

Salapatek, P. Pattern perception in early infancy. In L. B. Cohen & P. Salapatek (Eds.). *Infant perception: From sensation to cognition* (Vol. 1). New York: Academic Press, 1975.

Salk, L. The effects of the normal heartbeat sound on the behavior of the newborn infant: Implications for mental health. *World mental health,* 1960, *12,* 168–175.

Sameroff, A. J. Development and the dialectic: The need for a systems approach. In W. A. Collins (Ed.). *The Minnesota symposia on child psychology* (Vol. 15). Hillsdale, N.J.: Erlbaum, 1982.

Sameroff, A. J., & Cavanaugh, P. J. Learning in infancy: A developmental perspective. In J. D. Osofsky (Ed.). *Handbook of infant development.* New York: Wiley, 1979.

Sameroff, A. J., & Chandler, J. J. Reproductive risk and the continuum of caretaking casualty. In F. D. Horowitz (Ed.). *Review of child development research* (Vol. 4). Chicago: University of Chicago Press, 1975.

Sameroff, A. J.; Seifer, R.; & Zax, M. Early development of children at risk for emotional disorder. *Monographs of the Society for Research in Child Development,* 1983, *47* (7, Whole No. 199).

Sanders, B.; Soares, M. P.; & D'Aquila, J. M. The sex difference on one test of spatial visualization: A nontrivial difference. *Child development,* 1982, *53,* 1106–1110.

Sattler, J. M. *Assessment of children's intelligence.* Philadelphia: Saunders, 1974.

Savin-Williams, R. C. Dominance hierarchies in groups of early adolescents. *Child development,* 1979, *50,* 923–935.

Scanlon, L. J.; Savage-Rumbaugh, S.; & Rumbaugh, D. M. Apes and language: An emerging perspective. In S. A. Kuczaj II (Ed.). *Language development* (Vol. 2): *Language, thought, and culture.* Hillsdale, N.J.: Erlbaum, 1982.

Scarr, S. From evolution to Larry P., or what

shall we do about IQ tests? *Intelligence,* 1978, *2,* 325–342.

———. (Ed.). *Race, social class, and individual differences in I.Q.* Hillsdale, N.J.: Erlbaum, 1981. (a)

———. A reply to some of professor Jensen's commentary. In S. Scarr (Ed.). *Race, social class, and individual differences in I.Q.* Hillsdale, N.J.: Erlbaum, 1981. (b)

———. Having the last word. In S. Scarr (Ed.). *Race, social class, and individual differences in I.Q.* Hillsdale, N.J.: Erlbaum, 1981. (c)

Scarr, S., & McCartney, K. How people make their own environments: A theory of genotype → environment effects. *Child development,* 1983, *54,* 424–435.

Scarr, S., & Weinberg, R. A. Intellectual similarities within families of both adopted and biological children. *Intelligence,* 1977, *1,* 170–191.

———. The Minnesota adoption studies: Genetic differences and maleability. *Child development,* 1983, *54,* 260–267.

Scarr-Salapatek, S. An evolutionary perspective on infant intelligence: Species patterns and individual variations. In M. Lewis (Ed.). *Origins of intelligence.* New York: Plenum, 1976.

Schachter, F. F., & Strage, A. A. Adults' talk and children's language development. In S. G. Moore & C. R. Cooper (Eds.). *The young child: Reviews of research* (Vol. 3). Washington D.C.: National Association for the Education of Young Children, 1982.

Schlesinger, H. S., & Meadow, K. P. *Sound and sign.* Berkeley, Calif.: University of California Press, 1972.

Scollon, R. *Conversations with a one-year-old.* Honolulu: University of Hawaii Press, 1976.

Scott, K. G. Epidemiologic aspects of teenage pregnancy. In K. G. Scott, T. Field, & E. Robertson (Eds.). *Teenage parents and their offspring.* New York: Wiley, 1979.

Scott, L. H. Measuring intelligence with the Goodenough-Harris drawing test. *Psychological bulletin,* 1981, *89,* 483–505.

Sears, P. S., & Barbee, A. H. Career and life satisfactions among Terman's gifted women. In J. C. Stanley, W. C. George, & C. H. Solano (Eds.). *The gifted and the creative.* Balti-more: Johns Hopkins University Press, 1977.

Sears, R. R. Sources of life satisfactions of the Terman gifted men. *American psychologist,* 1977, *32,* 119–128.

Sears, R. R.; Maccoby, E. E.; & Levin, H. *Patterns of child rearing.* Stanford, Calif.: Stanford University Press, 1977 (originally published in 1957 by Harper & Row).

Segalowitz, N. S. Issues in the cross-cultural study of bilingual development. In H. C. Triandis & A. Heron (Eds.). *Handbook of cross-cultural psychology* (Vol. 4), *Developmental psychology.* Boston: Allyn & Bacon, 1981.

Selman, R. L. Toward a structural-developmental analysis of interpersonal relationship concepts: Research with normal and disturbed preadolescent boys. In A. Pick (Ed.). *Tenth annual Minnesota symposium on child psychology.* Minneapolis: University of Minnesota Press, 1976.

———. *The growth of interpersonal understanding.* New York: Academic Press, 1980.

Selman, R. L., & Damon, W. The necessity (but insufficiency) of social perspective taking for conceptions of justice at three early levels. In D. J. DePalma & J. M. Foley (Eds.). *Moral development: Current theory and research.* Hillsdale, N.J.: Erlbaum, 1975.

Selman, R. L.; Schorin, M. Z.; Stone, C. R.; & Phelps, E. A naturalistic study of children's social understanding. *Developmental psychology,* 1983, *19,* 82–102.

Sharp, D.; Cole, M.; & Lave, C. Education and cognitive development: The evidence from experimental research. *Monographs of the Society for Research in Child Development,* 1979, *44* (1–2, Whole No. 178).

Shatz, M., & Gelman, R. The development of communication skills: Modifications in the speech of young children as a function of the listener. *Monographs of the Society for Research in Child Development,* 1978, *38* (Whole No. 152).

Shields, J. *Monozygotic twins brought up apart and brought up together.* London: Oxford University Press, 1962.

Shigetomi, C. C.; Hartmann, D. P.; & Gelfand, D. M. Sex differences in children's altruistic behavior and reputation for helpfulness. *Developmental psychology,* 1981, *17,* 434–437.

Siegler, R. S., & Richards, D. D. The development of intelligence. In R. J. Sternberg (Ed.). *Handbook of human intelligence.* Cambridge, England: Cambridge University Press, 1982.

Simmons, R. G.; Blyth, D. A.; Carlton-Ford, S.; & Bulcroft, R. A. Differences between boys and girls as they move into adolescence. Paper presented at the biennial meetings of the Society for Research in Child Development, Detroit, 1983.

Singer, D. G. A time to reexamine the role of television in our lives. *American psychologist,* 1983, *38,* 815–816.

Sinnott, J. M.; Pisoni, D. B.; & Aslin, R. N. A comparison of pure auditory thresholds in human infants and adults. *Infant behavior and development,* 1983, *6,* 3–18.

Skinner, B. F. *Verbal behavior.* Englewood Cliffs, N.J.: Prentice-Hall, 1957.

Skodak, M., & Skeels, H. M. A follow-up study of children in adoptive homes. *Journal of genetic psychology,* 1945, *66,* 21–58.

Slaby, R. G., & Frey, K. S. Development of gender constancy and selective attention to same-sex models. *Child development,* 1975, *46,* 849–856.

Slaby, R. G.; Quarfoth, G. R.; & McConnachie, G. A. Television violence and its sponsors. *Journal of communication,* 1976, *26,* 88–96.

Slaughter, D. T. Early intervention and its effects on maternal and child development. *Monographs of the Society for Research in Child Development,* 1983, *48* (Whole No. 202).

Slobin, D. I. A case study of early language awareness. In A. Sinclair, R. J. Jarvella, & W. J. M. Levelt (Eds.). *The child's conception of language.* Berlin: Springer-Verlag, 1978.

———. Crosslinguistic evidence for basic child grammar. Paper presented at the biennial meetings of the Society for Research in Child Development, Detroit, 1983.

Smith, A. N., & Spence, C. M. National day care study: Optimizing the day care environment. *American journal of orthopsychiatry,* 1981, *50,* 718–721.

Smith, D. W. Prenatal life. In D. W. Smith, E. L. Bierman, & N. M. Robinson (Eds.). *The biologic ages of man* (2d ed.). Philadelphia: Saunders, 1978.

Smith, D. W.; Bierman, E. L.; & Robinson, N. M. (Eds.). *The biologic ages of man* (2d ed.). Philadelphia: Saunders, 1978.

Smith, D. W., & Stenchever, M. A. Prenatal life and the pregnant woman. In D. W. Smith, E. L. Bierman, & N. M. Robinson (Eds.). *The biologic ages of man* (2d ed.). Philadelphia: Saunders, 1978.

Snow, C. E., & Ferguson, C. A. (Eds.). *Talking to children.* Cambridge, England: Cambridge University Press, 1977.

Snow, M. E.: Jacklin, C. N.; & Maccoby, E. E. Sex-of-child differences in father-child interaction at one year of age. *Child development,* 1983, *54,* 227–232.

Snyder, L. Communicative and cognitive abilities and disabilities in the sensorimotor period. *Merrill-Palmer quarterly,* 1978, *24,* 161–180.

Solnit, A. J., & Provence. S. Vulnerability and risk in early childhood. In J. D. Osofsky (Ed.). *Handbook of infant development.* New York: Wiley, 1979.

Sostek, A. M.; Scanlon, J. W.; & Abramson, D. C. Postpartum contact and maternal confidence and anxiety: A confirmation of short-term effects. *Infant behavior and development,* 1982, *5,* 323–330.

Spelke, E. S. Exploring audible and visible events in infancy. In A. D. Pick (Ed.). *Perception and its development: A tribute to Eleanor J. Gibson.* Hillsdale, N.J.: Erlbaum, 1979.

Spelke, E. S., & Owsley, C. J. Intermodal exploration and knowledge in infancy. *Infant behavior and development,* 1979, *2,* 13–27.

Spence, J. T., & Helmreich, R. L. *Masculinity and femininity.* Austin, Tex.: University of Texas Press, 1978.

Sroufe, L. A. Wariness of strangers and the study of infant development. *Child development,* 1977, *48,* 731–746.

———. Attachment and the roots of competence. *Human nature,* 1978, *1,* 50–56.

———. The coherence of individual development: Early care, attachment, and subsequent developmental issues. *American psychologist,* 1979, *34,* 834–841.

Stamps, L. E. Temporal conditioning of heart rate responses in newborn infants. *Developmental psychology,* 1977, *13,* 624–629.

Staub, E. A child in distress: The influence of nurturance and modeling on children's attempts to help. *Developmental psychology,* 1971, *5,* 125–132.

————. *Positive social behavior and morality* (Vol. 2), *Socialization and development.* New York: Academic Press, 1979.

Steele, B. F., & Pollock, C. B. A psychiatric study of parents who abuse infants and small children. In R. E. Helfer & C. H. Kempe (Eds.). *The battered child* (2d ed.). Chicago: University of Chicago Press, 1974.

Stein, Z.; Susser, M.; Saenger, G.; & Morolla, F. *Famine and human development: The Dutch hunger winter of 1944–1945.* New York: Oxford University Press, 1974.

Steinberg, L. D. Transformations in family relations at puberty. *Developmental psychology,* 1981, *17,* 833–840.

Steiner, J. E. Human facial expressions in response to taste and smell stimulation. In H. W. Rese & L. P. Lipsitt (Eds.). *Advances in child development and behavior* (Vol. 13). New York: Academic Press, 1979.

Stern, D. *The first relationship: Infant and mother.* Cambridge, Mass.: Harvard University Press, 1977.

Sternberg, R. J. The evolution of theories of intelligence. *Intelligence,* 1981, *5,* 209–230. (a)

————. Novelty-seeking, novelty-finding, and the developmental continuity of intelligence. *Intelligence,* 1981, *5,* 149–155. (b)

————. Reasoning, problem solving, and intelligence. In R. J. Sternberg (Ed.). *Handbook of human intelligence.* Cambridge, England: Cambridge University Press, 1982.

Sternglanz, S. H., & Serbin, L. A. Sex role stereotyping in children's television programs. *Developmental psychology,* 1974, *10,* 710–713.

Steuer, F. B.; Applefield, J. M.; & Smith, R. Televised aggression and the interpersonal aggression of preschool children. *Journal of experimental child psychology,* 1971, *11,* 422–447.

Straughan, R. From moral judgment to moral action. In H. Weinrich-Haste & D. Locke (Eds.). *Morality in the making.* New York: Wiley, 1983.

Strauss, M. S. Abstraction of prototypical information by adults and 10-month-old infants. *Journal of experimental Psychology,* 1979, *5,* 618–631.

Strayer, F. F. Social ecology of the preschool peer group. In A. Collins (Ed.). *Minnesota symposia on child psychology* (Vol. 13). Hillsdale, N.J.: Erlbaum, 1980.

Streissguth, A. P.; Barr, H. M.; Martin, D. C.; & Herman, C. S. Effects of maternal alcohol, nicotine, and caffeine use during pregnancy on infant mental and motor development at eight months. *Alcoholism: Clinical and experimental research,* 1980, *4,* 152–164.

Streissguth, A. P.; Landesman-Dwyer, S.; Martin, J. C.; & Smith, D. W. Teratogentic effects of alcohol in humans and laboratory animals. *Science,* 1980, *209,* 353–361.

Streissguth, A. P.; Martin, D. C.; Martin, J. C.; & Barr, H. M. The Seattle longitudinal prospective study on alcohol and pregnancy. *Neurobehavioral toxicology and teratology,* 1981, *3,* 223–233.

Sullivan, H. S. *The interpersonal theory of psychiatry.* New York: Norton, 1953.

Svejda, M. J.; Campos, J. J.; & Emde, R. N. Mother-infant "bonding": Failure to generalize. *Child development,* 1980, *51,* 775–779.

Svejda, M. J.; Pannabecker, B. J.; & Emde, R. N. Parent-to-infant attachment: A critique of the early "bonding" model. In R. N. Emde & R. J. Harmon (Eds.). *The development of attachment and affiliative systems.* New York: Plenum, 1982.

Szasz, S. *The body language of children.* New York: Norton, 1978.

Taitz, L. S. Modification of weight gain by dietary changes in a population of Sheffield neonates. *Archives of diseases of childhood,* 1975, 50, 476–479.

Tanner, J. M. Physical growth. In P. H. Mussen (Ed.). *Carmichael's manual of child psychology* (Vol. 1, 3d ed.). New York: Wiley, 1970.

————. Growth and endocrinology of the adolescent. In L. J. Gardner (Ed.). *Endocrine and genetic diseases of childhood and adolescence* (2d ed.). Philadelphia, Pa: Saunders, 1975.

———. *Fetus into man: Physical growth from conception to maturity.* Cambridge, Mass.: Harvard University Press, 1978.

Tanner, J. M.; Whitehouse, R. H.; Marshall, W. H.; Healy, M. J. R.; & Goldstein, H. *Assessment of skeletal maturity and prediction of adult height: TW2 method.* New York: Academic Press, 1975.

Terman, L. M. *The measurement of intelligence.* Boston: Houghton Mifflin, 1916.

———. Mental and physical traits of a thousand gifted children. *Genetic studies of genius* (Vol. 1). Stanford, Calif.: Stanford University Press, 1925.

Terman, L., & Merrill, M. A. *Measuring intelligence: A guide to the administration of the new revised Stanford-Binet tests.* Boston: Houghton Mifflin, 1937.

Terman, L., & Oden, M. *Genetic studies of genius* (Vol. 4), *The gifted child grows up.* Stanford, Calif.: Stanford University Press, 1947.

———. *Genetic studies of genius* (Vol. 5), *The gifted group at mid-life.* Stanford, Calif.: Stanford University Press, 1959.

Terrace, H. S. How Nim Chimpsky changed my mind. *Psychology today,* 1979, *13,* 65–76.

Terrace, H. S.; Petitto, L. A.; Sanders, R. J.; & Bever, T. G. On the grammatical capacity of apes. In K. E. Nelson (Ed.). *Children's language* (Vol. 2). New York: Gardner Press, 1980.

Thomas, A., & Chess, S. *Temperament and development.* New York: Brunner/Mazel, 1977.

Thompson, R. A., & Lamb, M. E. Stranger sociability and its relationships to temperament and social experience during the second year. *Infant behavior and development,* 1982, *5,* 227–287.

Thompson, R. A.; Lamb, M. E.; & Estes, D. Stability of infant-mother attachment and its relationship to changing life circumstnaces in an unselected middle-class sample. *Child development,* 1982, *53,* 144–148.

———. Harmonizing discordant notes: A reply to Waters. *Child development,* 1983, *54,* 521–524.

Thompson, S. K. Gender labels and early sex

role development. *Child development,* 1975, *46,* 339–347.

Tieger, T. On the biological basis of sex differences in aggression. *Child development,* 1980, *51,* 943–963.

*Time.* Outcry over "Wuf Tickets." August 20, 1979, p. 61.

Tomlinson-Keasey, C.; Eisert, D. C.; Kahle, L. R.; Hardy-Brown, K.; & Keasey, B. The structure of concrete operational thought. *Child development,* 1978, *50,* 1153–1163.

Trahey, J. Down the tube. *Working women,* 1979, *4,* 30.

Trites, R. L., & Laprade, K. Evidence for an independent syndrome of hyperactivity. *Journal of child psychology and psychiatry,* 1983, *24,* 573–586.

Trotter, R. J. Baby face. *Psychology today,* 1983, *17* (8), 14–22.

Ullian, D. Z. The child's construction of gender: Anatomy as destiny. In E. K. Shapiro & E. Weber (Eds.). *Cognitive and affective growth.* Hillsdale, N.J.: Erlbaum, 1981.

Ungerer, J. A.; Zelazo, P. R.; Kearsley, R. B.; & O'Leary, K. Developmental changes in the representation of objects in symbolic play from 18 to 34 months of age. *Child development,* 1981, *52,* 186–195.

U.S. Department of Health, Education and Welfare. *Smoking and health: A report of the Surgeon General* (DHEW Publication No. PHS 79-50066). Washington, D.C.: U.S. Government Printing Office, 1979.

Uzgiris, I. C. Patterns of cognitive development in infancy. *Merrill-Palmer quarterly,* 1973, *19,* 21–40.

Vandell, D. L.; Anderson, L. D.; Ehrhardt, G.; & Wilson, K. S. Integrating hearing and deaf preschoolers: An attempt to enhance hearing children's interaction with deaf peers. *Child development,* 1982, *53,* 1354–1363.

Vandell, D. L., & Powers, C. P. Day care quality and children's free play activities. *American journal of orthopsychiatry,* 1983, *53,* 493–500.

Vandell, D. L.; Wilson, K. S.; & Whalen, W. T. Birth-order and social-experience differences in infant-peer interaction. *Developmental psychology,* 1981, *17,* 438–445.

van Doorninck, W. J.; Caldwell, B. M.; Wright, C.; & Frankenberg, W. K. The relationship between twelve-month home stimulation and school achievement. *Child development,* 1981, *52,* 1080–1083.

Vaughn, B.; Egeland, B.; Sroufe, L. A.; & Waters, E. Individual differences in infant-mother attachment at twelve and eighteen months: Stability and change in families under stress. *Child development,* 1979, *50,* 971–975.

Vaughn, B. E., & Waters, E. Attention structure, sociometric status, and dominance: Interrelations, behavioral correlates, and relationships to social competence. *Developmental psychology,* 1981, *17,* 275–288.

Vellutino, F. R. Alternative conceptualizations of dyslexia: Evidence in support of a verbal-deficit hypothesis. *Harvard educational review,* 1977, *47,* 334–354.

Vygotsky, L. S. *Thought and language.* New York: Wiley, 1962.

Waber, D. P. Sex differences in mental abilities, hemispheric lateralization, and rate of physical growth at adolescence. *Developmental psychology,* 1977, *13,* 29–38.

Wachs, T. D., & Gruen, G. E. *Early experience and human development.* New York: Plenum, 1982.

Waldron, S.; Shrier, D. K.; Stone, B.; & Tobin, F. School phobia and other childhood neuroses: A systematic study of the children and their families. *American journal of psychiatry,* 1975, *132,* 802–808.

Walker, L. J. Cognitive and perspective-taking prerequisites for moral development. *Child development,* 1980, *51,* 131–139.

Wallerstein, J. S., & Kelly, J. B. *Surviving the breakup: How children and parents cope with divorce.* New York: Basic Books, 1980.

Walters, R. H., & Brown, M. Studies of reinforcement of aggression. III: Transfer of responses to an interpersonal situation. *Child development,* 1963, *34,* 563–571.

Wandersman, L. P., & Unger, D. G. Interaction of infant difficulty and social support in adolescent mothers. Paper presented at the biennial meetings of the Society for Research in Child Development, Detroit, 1983.

Waterman, A. S. Identity development from ad-

olescence to adulthood: An extension of theory and a review of research. *Developmental psychology,* 1982, *18,* 341–358.

Waterman, A. S.; Geary, P. S.; & Waterman, C. K. Longitudinal study of changes in ego identity status from the freshman to the senior year at college. *Developmental psychology,* 1974, *10,* 387–392.

Waters, E. The reliability and stability of individual differences in infant-mother attachment. *Child development,* 1978, *59,* 483–494.

Waters, E.; Vaughn, E. E.; & Egeland, B. R. Individual differences in infant-mother attachment relationships at age one: Antecedents in neonatal behavior in an urban, economically disadvantaged sample. *Child development,* 1980, *51,* 208–216.

Waters, E.; Wippman, J.; & Sroufe, L. A. Attachment, positive affect, and competence in the peer group. *Child development,* 1979, *50,* 821–829.

Watson, J. D., & Crick, F. H. C. Molecular structure of nucleic acids: A structure for deoxyribose nucleic acid. *Nature,* 1958, *171,* 737–738.

Watson, J. S. Smiling, cooing, and "The Game." *Merrill-Palmer quarterly,* 1972, *18,* 323–339.

Wechsler, D. *Wechsler intelligence scale for children.* New York: Psychology Corporation, 1949.

Weikart, D. P. Relationship of curriculum, teaching, and learning in preschool education. In J. C. Stanley (Ed.). *Preschool programs for the disadvantaged.* Baltimore: Johns Hopkins University Press, 1972.

Wellman, H. M. The foundations of knowledge: Concept development in the young child. In S. G. Moore & C. R. Cooper (Eds.). *The young child: Reviews of research* (Vol. 3). Washington, D.C.: National Association for the Education of Young Children, 1982.

Wellman, H. M., & Somerville, S. C. The development of human search ability. In M. E. Lamb & A. L. Brown (Eds.). *Advances in developmental psychology* (Vol. 2). Hillsdale, N.J.: Erlbaum, 1982.

Wellman, H. M.; Somerville, S. C.; & Haake, R. J. Development of search procedures in real-life spatial environments. *Developmental psychology,* 1979, *15,* 530–542.

Werner, E. E.; Bierman, J. M.; & French, F. E. *The children of Kauai.* Honolulu: University of Hawaii Press, 1971.

Werner, E. E.; Simonian K.; Bierman, J. M.; & French, F. E. Cumulative effect of perinatal complications and deprived environment on physical, intellectual, and social development of preschool children. *Pediatrics,* 1967, *39,* 489–505.

Westin-Lindgren, G. Achievement and mental ability of physically late and early maturing school children related to their social background. *Journal of child psychology and psychiatry,* 1982, *23,* 407–420.

Weymouth, F. W. Visual acuity of children. In M. J. Hirsch & R. Wick (Eds.). *Vision of children: An optometric symposium.* Philadelphia: Chilton, 1963.

White, B. L. *The first three years of life.* Englewood Cliffs, N.J.: Prentice-Hall, 1975.

Wiegerink, R.; Hocutt, A.; Posante-Loro, R.; & Bristol, M. Parent involvement in early education programs for handicapped children. *New directions for exceptional children,* 1980, *1,* 67–86.

Williams, J. E.; Bennett, S. M.; & Best, D. L. Awareness and expression of sex stereotypes in young children. *Developmental psychology,* 1975, *11,* 635–642.

Williams, R. L. Black pride, academic relevance and individual achievement. *Counseling Psychologist,* 1970, *2,* 18–22.

Wilson, R. S. Twins and siblings: Concordance for school-age mental development. *Child development,* 1977, *48,* 211–216.

———. Synchronies in mental development: An epigenetic perspective. *Science,* 1978, *202,* 939–948.

———. The Louisville twin study: Developmental synchronies in behavior. *Child development,* 1983, *54,* 298–316.

Winick, M. *Nutrition in health and disease.* New York: Wiley, 1980.

Witkin, H. A.; Dyk, R. B.; Faterson, H. F.; Goodenough, D. R.; & Karp, S. A. *Psychological differentiation.* New York: Wiley, 1962.

Wolff, P. H. Normal variation in human maturation. In K. J. Connolly & H. F. R. Prechtl (Eds.). *Maturation and development: Biological and psychological perspectives. Clinics in developmental medicine* No. 77/78. London: Heinemann, 1981.

Wylie, R. C. *The self concept: Theory and research on selected topics* (Vol. 2, Rev. ed.). Lincoln Neb.: University of Nebraska Press, 1979.

Yeates, K. O.; MacPhee, D.; Campbell, F. A.; & Ramey, C. T. Maternal IQ and home environment as determinants of early childhood intellectual competence: A developmental analysis. *Developmental psychology,* 1983, *19,* 731–739.

Yogman, M. W. Observations on the father-infant relationship. In S. H. Cath, A. R. Burwitt, & J. M. Ross (Eds.). *Father and child: Developmental and clinical perspectives.* Boston: Little, Brown, 1982.

Youniss, J. *Parents and peers in social development: A Sullivan-Piaget perspective.* Chicago: University of Chicago Press, 1980.

Zahn-Waxler, C., & Radke-Yarrow, M. The development of altruism: Alternative research strategies. In N. Eisenberg (Ed.). *The development of prosocial behavior.* New York: Academic Press, 1982.

Zahn-Waxler, C.; Radke-Yarrow, M.; & King, R. A. Child-rearing and children's prosocial initiations toward victims of distress. *Child development,* 1979, *50,* 319–330.

Zajonc, R. B. Birth order and intelligence: Dumber by the dozen. *Psychology today,* 1975, *8* 37–43.

———. Validating the confluence model. *Psychological bulletin,* 1983, *93,* 457–480.

Zajonc, R. B., & Bargh, J. The confluence model: Parameter estimation for six divergent data sets on family factors and intelligence. *Intelligence,* 1980, *4,* 349–362.

Zajonc, R. B., & Marcus, G. B. Birth order and intellectual development. *Psychological review,* 1975, *82,* 74–88.

Zeskind, P. S., & Lester, B. M. Acoustic features and auditory perceptions of the cries of newborns with prenatal and perinatal complications. *Child development,* 1978, *49,* 580–589.

———. Analysis of cry features of newborns with differential fetal growth. *Child development,* 1981, *52,* 207–212.

Zeskind, P. S., & Ramey, C. T. Preventing intellectual and interactional sequelae of fetal malnutrition: A longitudinal, transactional, and synergistic approach to development. *Child development,* 1981, *52,* 213–218.

Zigler, E., & Butterfield, E. G. Motivational aspects of changes in IQ test performance of culturally deprived nursery school children. *Child development,* 1968, *39,* 1–14.

Zigler, E., & Muenchow, S. Mainstreaming: The proof is in the implementation. *American psychologist,* 1979, *34,* 993–996.

# author index

# subject index